SO-AAM-439

CORPORATE OFFICER'S AND DIRECTOR'S DESK BOOK—
WITH
MODEL DOCUMENTS,
AGREEMENTS, AND FORMS

CORPORATE OFFICER'S AND DIRECTOR'S DESK BOOK— WITH MODEL DOCUMENTS, AGREEMENTS, AND FORMS

William E. Read

Prentice-Hall, Inc.   Englewood Cliffs, N.J.

Prentice-Hall International, Inc., *London*
Prentice-Hall of Australia, Pty. Ltd., *Sydney*
Prentice-Hall of Canada, Ltd., *Toronto*
Prentice-Hall of India Private Ltd., *New Delhi*
Prentice-Hall of Japan, Inc., *Tokyo*
Prentice-Hall of Southeast Asia Pte. Ltd., *Singapore*
Whitehall Books, Ltd., *Wellington, New Zealand*

Library of Congress Cataloging in Publication Data

Read, William E
  Corporate officer's and director's desk book—with
model documents, agreements, and forms.

  Includes index.
  1. Directors of corporations—Legal status, laws,
etc.—United States. 2. Corporation law—United
States—Forms. I. Title.
KF1423.R43   346.73'06642   79-28185
0-13-174607-3

To my wife, Dorothy,
and our children,
William, Mary, Nancy, and David.

About the Author

William Read is Professor of Law at the University of Louisville where he teaches courses in corporate law, securities regulation, business planning, and professional ethics.

The author's broad-gauged background includes practical experience in a Wall Street law firm serving mainly corporate clients. He has also been an inside lawyer and corporate secretary for a major corporation.

Among Professor Read's credits are participation in the drafting of the revised Kentucky Corporation Act and service as visiting professor at the University of Leeds. He was educated at Hamilton College and Harvard Law School.

What This Desk Book Will Do for You

As officer or director of a business corporation you have assumed a burden of heavy and many-sided legal and ethical responsibilities. You face choices which become more consequential and more complex as your enterprise expands and prospers. Unfortunately, at the same time your problems are increasing the demands on your time and attention are also multiplying. How do you prepare yourself in advance for crises that you will meet—turning points that may determine your success as a corporate officer or director?

This book does that advance preparation for you and simplifies your reporting and administrative procedures, step-by-step. I have identified the most crucial pressure points in corporate decision-making where you need the most help. These points involve predominantly legal and ethical decisions; you know where to find the business pressure points. I have organized these critical areas so you can find what you need to know, and understand and use what you find, with the help of preparatory warnings, explanations, examples, suggestions, checklists, and model documents. The book is written both to be read and to serve as an on-the-job reference for answers at the fingertips. While the chapters and sections of the text and the Appendix of model documents, agreements, and forms build on one another, most of them make sense if used by themselves.

What I have done is create the kind of desk book that I wish someone had put into my hands when I became a corporate officer. It is a single volume, one-stop resource tool that busy corporate managers can turn to when they see new and unfamiliar problems or decisions appearing on the horizon. When a legal or ethical crisis is in sight, it is usually too late to prepare for it on your own in a systematic way. You do not have time to spend hours in the library reading up on your inherent powers as a corporate officer, or what happens when your board of directors is deadlocked, or how to distinguish between a business opportunity that belongs to your corporation and one that you are free to seize for yourself. And the problems and decisions may be imbedded in such unfamiliar language

9

and legal machinery that you are at a loss to know how to start discussing them with your lawyer.

In this situation, when confronted with making legal and ethical choices about which your mind is less than clear, what you need is a quick, reliable way to find a handle to the problem. To avoid being caught unprepared, you need a way to educate yourself rapidly about what may happen (whether you want it to or not) and about what is available to make happen what you want to happen.

This book is aimed to give you that kind of help. It alerts you to possibilities; it explains terminology and mechanics; it marks danger areas; it arms you with knowledge and understanding and samples of legal instruments that may help you to keep your crises from becoming disasters and perhaps even to turn them into opportunities. The essence of effective defense is to avoid being surprised. This book tries to help keep you from being surprised by the legal and ethical complexities of corporate life.

When I talk about legal and ethical considerations I am referring to those that may put *constraints* on what you can do (and that you may be able to impose on others) in pursuing business objectives. While I will be most directly and systematically concerned with legal constraints, many legal rules in the corporate area have a substantial ethical content. For example, what is legally permissible or not permissible frequently becomes a question of what is "fair" or "unfair." And in some situations you may want to do what is fair whether or not you are legally required to do so. Just as you need to know your business in order to make business decisions of which you will be proud, you similarly need to know your law and ethics in order to make legal and ethical choices that will stand you in good stead.

How does this book try to accomplish these objectives? Its progression is to describe how corporate machinery works and what you can do with it; then to open up what I think are the most basic and typical kinds of situations in which you are likely to find yourself. The first six chapters (Part I) are mainly concerned with corporate structures and functions: getting a corporation started (Chapter 1); the roles of shareholders in its ownership (Chapter 2) and government (Chapter 3), of directors in its management (Chapter 4), and of officers, employees, and agents in its operation (Chapter 5); and special accommodations that can be made for closely held corporations (Chapter 6). The next four chapters (Part II) are about the major developmental problems of a corporation's growth and maturity: pumping money in and out (Chapters 7 and 8); antitrust and unfair competition, problems which accompany success (Chapter 9); and transfers of corporate control (Chapter 10). The final two chapters (Part III) focus on individual rather than corporate concerns: your individual exposure to legal liabilities (Chapter 11); and how you balance the allegiance demanded by your corporate position against the demands of society and of your own conscience (Chapter 12).

Each chapter ends with a checklist of points to watch for. Highlighting and extending answers and guidelines in the chapters, the checklists serve to focus your decision-making and to point you to the instant help available in the *234 model documents, agreements, and forms which this desk book features in a concluding Appendix.* Chapter sections and particular model documents are also matched in a Table of Appendix References.

In eight lettered categories the Appendix collects for you pertinent legal instruments you are most likely to need: (A) articles of incorporation, (B) by-laws, (C) other start-up documents, (D) shareholder materials, (E) instruments to change corporate structures, (F) director resolutions, (G) authorizations to act for the corporation, and (H) agreements. Like the *Desk Book* these legal instruments are keyed to the Model Business Corporation Act and carry a mythical coal mining enterprise, Dighaldoe Corpoation, through its life cycle of getting started, governing itself, dealing with outsiders, staying close, going public, merging, and dissolving. While the coherence and workability of this system of models is my sole responsibility, I was helped in putting it together by the Model Act forms prepared by the ABA Committee on Corporate Laws and by the forms appearing in George Seward's Basic Corporate Practice, published by the American Law Institute.

How should you use the *Desk Book* and its Appendix? Here is a simple example that may be helpful. You want to know what can be done to keep your corporation close by limiting transfers of its shares to outsiders. You turn to Chapter 6 on close corporations where you find that your topic is covered in Section 6.2(b). There you learn that an agreement among shareholders restricting their share transfers is available in Appendix H.2(a) and that for provisions you might want in your articles or by-laws you can consult A.6(e), (f), and (g); and B.14. You could also find your way to these parts of the Appendix through Chapter 6 entries in the Table of Appendix References.

There are limits to what one desk book can do. This one deals with tax and accounting problems only when and to the extent that it seems impossible to avoid them. Similarly, other broad areas that you might expect to find in a book about corporate law and ethics—notably, problems involving your relations with your employees, your professional advisors, those with whom you do business, and the government agencies that regulate you—seem too closely tied to your individual operations to warrant inclusion in detail and are dealt with only as they enter into concerns capable of more general treatment.

In summary, my purpose in writing this *Desk Book* is to present a coherent, useable road map, highlighting signs, signals, and pitfalls to avoid in administration—a program of fingertip answers acquired as a lawyer representing corporations, as a corporate officer, and as a law school teacher. The single strongest lesson that I have learned is: know what you are doing, and when to do it, and be able to document your decisions. In response to that lesson, this book was written for professionals with the demanding and increasingly complex responsibilities of serving our corporations as officers and directors—that they may act with confidence when they make their critical legal and ethical choices.

William E. Read

Acknowledgements

In recognizing those who have helped me in this effort, I can name only a few of my most obvious benefactors. The University of Louisville gave me the support, intellectual and logistical, that enabled me to get it done. Marilyn Peters transformed my yellow legal pads into a typed manuscript. And a host of others have contributed to what is in the book. Former colleagues at Hughes, Hubbard & Reed and at Campbell Soup Company helped to educate me in the ways of corporate law and ethics and of corporate life. Faculty colleagues at the University of Louisville have stimulated and encouraged me to think systematically about these ways. My wife's understanding support of this project from its beginning and her editorial assistance in its final stages helped bring it to fruition. Perhaps most important of all, over the years hundreds of law students have repeatedly challenged me to give them understandable explanations of how and why the corporate system works.

Table of Contents

15

CORPORATE OFFICER'S AND DIRECTOR'S DESK BOOK— WITH MODEL DOCUMENTS, AGREEMENTS, AND FORMS

Table of Appendix References

Section	Document	Appendix
3.1(a)	Director resolution: Place of shareholder meeting	F.2(a)
3.1(a)	By-laws: Place of shareholder meeting	B.2(a)
3.1(b)	By-laws: Calling special meetings	B.2(c)
3.1(c)	By-laws: Notices of meetings	B.2(d)
3.1(c)	Notice: Of annual meeting	D.1(a)
3.2	Proxy: For annual meeting	D.1(b)
3.3(a)	Articles: Quorum for shareholder meetings	A.6(c)
3.3(a)	By-laws: Quorum for shareholder meetings	B.2(e)
3.3(b)	Articles: Action by shareholders	A.6(c)
3.3(b)	By-laws: Action by shareholders	B.2(e)
3.3(b)	Agreement: Voting trust	H.3
3.3(c)	Director resolution: Nominating directors	F.4(a)
3.3(d)	Articles: Cumulative voting	A.6(b)
3.3(f)	Director resolution: Approving plan of merger	E.4(a)
3.3(f)	Director resolution: Submitting plan to shareholders	E.4(b)
3.3(g)	Articles: Voting as a class	A.4(c)
4.1(a)	Articles: Number of directors	A.6(a)
4.1(a)	By-laws: Number of directors	B.3(e)-(g)
4.1(a)	Shareholder resolution: Number of directors	D.4(a)
4.1(a)	Articles: Amendment of by-laws by directors	A.8
4.1(a)	Articles: Amendment of by-laws by shareholders	A.11
4.1(b)	By-laws: Emergency by-laws	B.13
4.1(b)	By-laws: Filling board vacancies	B.3(i)
4.1(b)	Shareholder resolution: Filling board vacancies	D.4(e)
4.1(b)	Director resolution: Filling board vacancies	F.4(b)
4.1(c)	By-laws: Director qualifications	B.3(c),(d)
4.1(c)	By-laws: Duties of president and secretary	B.4(e),(g)
4.1(c)	By-laws: Organizational meeting of directors	B.3(j)
4.2(a)	Director resolution: Regular board meeting	C.2(b)
4.2(a)	By-laws: Regular board meetings	B.3(j)
4.2(a)	By-laws: Calls & notices of special meetings	B.3(k),(1)
4.2(a)	By-laws: Waiver of notice	B.10
4.2(a)	Board minutes: Waiver of notice	C.2(b)
4.2(b)	By-laws: Executive and other committees	B.3(o)
4.2(b)	By-laws: Board action without meeting	B.3(p),(q)
4.2(b)	Director resolution: Executive and other committees	F.5(a)
4.3(a)	Director resolutions: Proposing amendments to articles	E.1
4.3(a)	Director resolution: Approving plan of merger or consolidation	E.4(a)

Section	Document	Appendix
10.1(b)	Director and shareholder resolutions and articles for filing: Dissolution	E.7
10.3(a)	Director Resolution: Filling vacancies on board	F.4(b)
11.3(b)	Shareholder resolution: Ratifying insider transaction	D.5(e)
11.3(c)	Agreement: Release of trade secrets	H.4(h)
11.3(d)	Shareholder resolution: Employee compensation and benefits	D.5(a),(b)
11.3(d)	Director resolution: Compensation committee	F.5(a)
11.5(a)	Shareholder resolution: Ratifying inside transaction	D.5(e)
11.5(b)	Articles: Indemnification	A.9
11.5(b)	By-laws: Indemnification	B.6
11.5(b)	Shareholder resolution: Approving indemnification	D.5(f)-(h)

Part One

CORPORATE

STRUCTURE AND FUNCTION:

Critical Considerations

1

Creating Corporate Structure

29

1

Creating Corporate Structure

While you, as a corporate officer or director, are by definition part of already existing corporate structure, you can better understand the special corporate world you inhabit, and be better prepared for later stages of your own and your corporation's development, if you give some initial thought to the process—a genesis combining invocation of legal magic and the making of practical choices—by which corporate structure is created. With corporations, as with governments, how they are "constituted" sets the stage for how they work. Also, as your enterprise grows and diversifies, you will face the need to form new subsidiaries, affiliates, and divisions. And, looking further ahead, you may someday be creating corporate structure on your own behalf.

When we think about the alternatives to and advantages of doing business as a corporation (Section 1.1)—and how these advantages may be lost through missteps (Section 1.6)—we more fully appreciate why business corporations are among the twentieth century's most significant intellectual achievements and why understanding how they work is worth some effort. And attention to the crucial decision-points in creating corporate structure helps us comprehend what may happen down the road. For example, the legal rules that apply to a corporation are determined by *where* it is incorporated (Section 1.2) and by what is put in its articles of incorporation (Section 1.5); its peace and prosperity may be affected by the name it receives (Section 1.3); and its government, management, and operation depend on who is put in its positions of power (Section 1.4).

Chapter 1, in addition to identifying opportunities and dangers in creating corporate structure, provides corporate officers and directors a good place to start in sharpening their thinking about their legal and ethical choices. With its

31

focus on *how* basic corporate structure is created, it builds a necessary foundation—particularly with its illustrations and its utilization of the Model Business Corporation Act—for dealing with the specifics of structure and function involved in owning, governing, managing, and operating corporations which are detailed in Chapters 2 through 5, and with the more complex corporate and individual concerns which are developed in later chapters.

As indicated in the introduction, a mythical coal mining venture called Dighaldoe Corporation is introduced in this chapter and continued in subsequent chapters to provide concrete settings for some of the discussion and for the model legal instruments in the Appendix, which are matched with chapter sections in the Table of Appendix References. Assistance in finding relevant models in the Appendix is also provided in the checklists of points to watch out for at the end of this and subsequent chapters.

Section 1.1 The Decision to Incorporate

Most of the world's business (and government) is done by "agents," i.e., by individuals who are acting on behalf of someone else, called their "principal." Even individual proprietors usually have employees. The principal-agent relationship—characterized by legal obligations on the principal when the agent acts within the scope of his powers and by the duties of care and loyalty owed by the agent to his principal—is one of our most basic legal relationships and needs to be understood at the outset of any discussion of corporateness. A fundamental variable in this relationship is in kinds of principals: individuals, firms of partners, corporations, or governments. Here the focus is on the choice between partnership and corporation. (A century ago we would have had also to consider joint stock companies and business trusts, which are now largely obsolete.)

(a) Partnerships; Subchapter S corporations

First, we take a quick look at the characteristics of partnerships, the most probable alternative to incorporation. What makes them different from corporations?

A partner is both principal and agent. He is liable, as principal, for partnership obligations; and he has an agent's power to bind and owes an agent's duties of care and loyalty to his firm (and his partners). Partnerships are fragile, because they dissolve when a partner retires or dies. They resemble exclusive clubs, because new partners can be black-balled. A partner's share of firm profits and his participation in management depend on the partnership contract. Most important, each partner is liable for all the partnership's debts, so all his assets are put at risk. However, you can set up limited partnerships with one or more general partners who manage the enterprise, plus limited partners who are liable only to the extent of their investment; the catch is that the limited partner has no voice in the management of the business.

Our federal income tax laws do not recognize the separate existence of partnerships. They tax individual partners directly on their share of partnership income, whether it is distributed to them or not, and no tax is levied on the firm. All the partnership does is file an information return that shows the allocation of profits and losses to the individual partners.

Corporations differ from partnerships largely because the corporation is organized as a separate and distinct legal entity. Unless something unusual happens, none of the individuals—shareholders, directors, officers, or employees—is liable for acts of the corporate agents: only the corporation is. The corporateness of the principal also makes it indestructable: it can last indefinitely. And ownership interests in the corporate entity can be divided into shares and freely transferred, without affecting either the existence or the operations of the corporation. Our tax laws regard the corporation as separate from its owners and corporate income is taxed separately when earned by the corporation and again if it is distributed to shareholders (the so-called "double taxation" of corporate income, that may be a deterrent to incorporation).

When would a partnership make more sense than a corporation? Where concerns about liability, continuity, transferability, raising new capital, and plowing money back into the business are minimal, and where it is difficult to avoid double taxation by distributing profits to shareholders as salaries.

> ▪ An example would be a highly profitable, well established, low risk, family business, which does not need additional capital; the family includes young people who can succeed to management; and the business supports family members who can not participate in its operations. Here a partnership would avoid the complications of introducing shareholders, directors, and officers, and the double taxation on business earnings paid out as dividends. Liability, continuity, transferability, and financing problems do not loom large enough to tip the scales in favor of incorporation. This conclusion might, of course, be altered by changes in the character of the business or in the composition of the family.

It may be possible to have the tax advantages of a partnership and the limited liability and other advantages of a corporation if you can qualify your enterprise as a Subchapter S corporation under Sections 1371-78 of the Internal Revenue Code. The main conditions for making and maintaining an election under Subchapter S are: fifteen or fewer shareholders, all of whom are individuals or estates (though certain trusts can be shareholders); no non-resident alien shareholders; only one class of stock; consent of all shareholders to the election; and a specific portion of receipts from active business rather than passive investments. While these conditions (particularly the limits of 15 shareholders and one class of stock) curb flexibility in corporate planning, in some situations—for example, if the business expects losses, or if shareholders expect to withdraw all corporate earnings as dividends each year—a Subchapter S election can have important tax advantages.

(b) Advantages of corporateness; Section 1244 shares

Since this book is for corporate officers and directors, rather than for partners, the focus is on situations where a corporation does make more sense than a partnership. There are five traditional advantages of corporations over partnerships:

—Only the corporation is ordinarily liable for corporate obligations; partners are individually liable.

—Corporations survive changes in ownership and management; partnerships do not.

—Ownership interests in corporations generally are freely transferable; partners can block entrance of new partners.

—Corporations facilitate aggregating resources in a single owner; partnerships have divided ownership.

—Corporate governmental structure permits centralized control of resources; partnership control is fragmented.

These features have made corporations the main form, under both capitalism and socialism, for organizing the large, complicated enterprises needed to finance and administer twentieth century technology.

To make more specific some of the ways a corporation can help you achieve the results you want, and to illustrate how corporations can help small and medium sized enterprises, we use a hypothetical enterprise, Dighaldoe Corporation, to which we return from time to time.

Assume that three entrepreneurs—Digges, Hall, and Doe—want to join forces in a coal mining business: Digges is to provide $20,000 in cash and services in getting the mining operations started worth $80,000; Hall is to contribute trucks for transporting coal worth $80,000 and services in getting the trucking operations started worth $20,000; Doe is to contribue $100,000 in cash. They want to share ownership and profits equally. They all want to avoid individual liability, and they plan to plow substantial earnings back into the business to expand it. They may need additional financing, but they do not want to share control with outsiders. They want the business to continue even if one of them dies or retires. They want to be able to liquidate their individual interests easily. And they want management of day-to-day operations in the hands of Digges and Hall, but Doe wants a say on policy matters.

A corporation—with Digges and Hall as officers, and Digges, Hall, and Doe as equal shareholders and directors, and with any outside financing through debt or non-voting shares—can accomplish their objectives quite neatly. In contrast, there would be serious difficulties in trying to do business as a partnershp: personal liability; lack of continuity and transferability; difficulty in apportioning management roles among Digges, Hall, Doe, and outside investors; and individual taxes on earnings retained in the business.

For a sample agreement among the three entrepreneurs on forming, naming, financing, and operating their new corporation, see Appendix H.1(a).

In making their plans they should keep in mind the favorable treatment available under §1244 of the Internal Revenue Code for losses on the shares of small business corporations. Section 1244 provides ordinary loss treatment, up to $50,000 on an individual return or $100,000 on a joint return for losses which would otherwise be capital losses on shares that meet the following requirements for "section 1244 stock": that the shares be original issue common stock of a domestic corporation; that on issue of the shares the aggregate of money on other property received by the corporation for all stock (not just §1244 stock) as capital and paid-in surplus does not exceed $1 million; that the shares be issued "for money or other property (other than stocks and securities)"; and that during the five years before the loss the corporation derives more than 50% of its gross receipts from sources other than royalties, rents, dividends, interests, annuities, and sales or exchanges of stocks or securities.

Once you have decided that your business should be incorporated, the next objective is to maximize the benefits of incorporation by the way you set up your corporation. The material that follows does not try to teach you how to form a corporation; rather, it alerts you to some of the policy decisions you will have to make. The mechanics of incorporation vary from state to state, and you should seek the help of a lawyer, and possibly of a corporate service organization, to implement your decisions. My aim is to help you prepare to give your lawyer sensible instructions.

The question here is: How do you achieve the biggest pay-off from your basic decision to incorporate? This question involves you in a series of critical choices along the road to incorporation, including:

—Where should you incorporate and qualify your corporation?
—What name should you give it?
—What people should you designate to fill corporate positions?
—What provisions do you want in your articles of incorporation and by-laws?

You also should give some preliminary thought to what happens if the incorporation is defective.

Section 1.2 Where to Incorporate and Qualify

(a) Your state of incorporation

At the outset you need to choose the state in which you are going to incorporate. While there have been perennial proposals for federal incorporation laws, the chartering of business corporations is still, and will probably continue to be, a state function. Your choice dictates the state corporation law under which your business will operate.

If your enterprise will operate within a single state, or if its anticipated out-of-state activities are limited to sales to customers in other states, there is a strong presumption in favor of incorporation in your home state. It is usually cheaper and easier to incorporate at home. Legal bills are fewer and lower, meetings and filings are simpler, and you are exposed to fewer taxes and other unpleasantness.

The main competitor to your home state is usually Delaware. Incorporation in Delaware may make sense if you anticipate that your business operations will become so spread out that no one state will be appreciably more convenient as a home base than will be several others; or if the laws, taxes, or business climate of your home state are so unfavorable that they offset the normal advantages of home state incorporation. Extreme examples of these two types of situations, where Delaware incorporation would seem to be indicated, would be:

—A market research enterprise that plans to have offices and employees in the top twenty marketing areas in the country, with data processing centers in Philadelphia, Chicago, Atlanta, and Los Angeles.

—An enterprise to mine a rare mineral, available only in State X, where there is a substantial franchise tax on the shares of corporations incorporated in X, where the corporation laws are very restrictive and require many reports, and where the state government has a tradition of being anti-business.

Statutory differences among the states are diminishing, in large part due to adoption by an increasing number of states of the Model Business Corporation Act drafted by the American Bar Association.

> ▪ This Act is referred to as the "Model Act" and is used throughout the book as a "typical" state corporation statute. Section numbers refer to the 1969 publication of the Model Act.

Delaware still has an edge over many states because its corporation laws have received more complete judicial interpretation, and because the attitudes of Delaware legislators, judges, and administrators have generally shown a more sympathetic attitude to business problems than those in most other states. About a third of the corporations with shares listed on the New York Stock Exchange were incorporated in Delaware.

(b) Qualification in other states

Not only do you need to choose your state of incorporation, but also, unless your business is confined to a single state, you need to give thought to the other states in which you may want to qualify your corporation to do business. Qualification is formal permission from a state, other than your state of incorporation, to do business in that state. A condition of qualification is that your corporation accept service of process (to start law suits against it) within the state on a registered agent of your corporation or a state officer. Qualification may also subject your corporation to taxes it might otherwise not have to pay.

> ▪ **When judges and lawyers in State X talk about a "domestic corporation" they mean a corporation organized under the laws of X; to them a "foreign corporation" is usually not a Mexican or Italian corporation (they might call these "alien corporations") but simply a corporation organized under the laws of a state other than X. The Model Act contains a series of provisions relating to qualification of "foreign corporations."**

The rule of thumb on where to qualify, in order to hold down your exposure to service of process, taxes, and house keeping chores, is to qualify only where it is unavoidable. How do you decide? Key considerations are the locations of your plants, warehouses, sales offices, and employees. The legal question is whether you are "doing business" in a particular state. Operating a plant is clearly doing business. Soliciting orders, by itself, with orders being filled by shipment from outside the state, has been held not to be doing business. Filling orders from a warehouse, or maintenance of a sales office or a local sales force probably is doing business.

In doubtful situations you should ask your lawyer: what will happen if I do not qualify? Unless the consequences are quite serious (like a daily fine, or inability to enforce contracts made in the state), you may wish to assume the calculated risk of not qualifying. Also, you should consider whether you can reduce exposure of your main business to a particular state by conducting your operations in that state through a subsidiary.

> ▪ **For example, if you need to purchase vital raw materials in a state where taxes or liability rules are unfavorable, you may be able to re-**

duce your exposure to trouble in that state by doing your purchasing there through a subsidiary. Similarly, you may wish to consider subsidiaries for other special functions, such as sales, transportation, warehousing, research or foreign operations.

To make the separateness of a subsidiary stand up, you should be careful that it is adequately capitalized, is permitted to earn a fair profit, has a legitimate business purpose (not just to save taxes or avoid service), and maintains a separate corporate existence and identity (officers, meetings, records, bank accounts, letterheads, and signs).

Section 1.3 A Name for Your Corporation

Along with deciding on states for incorporation and qualification, you must select a name for your corporation. The selection of a name deserves more care and attention than you might think. While it is not legally difficult to change a corporate name, it can be costly if you invest large sums in trying to build up good will for a name that you later abandon—and the costs are the same whether abandonment is forced upon you or done voluntarily because the name does not accomplish your objectives. Thus, with the choice of a name, it is prudent to be as sure as you can be before you have made your advertising and promotional investment.

(a) Complying with state corporation laws

We start with the relatively easy part of making sure that your proposed name is in compliance with the corporation law of the state you have picked for incorporation. The Model Act requires of your proposed corporate name (§8):

—That it contain the words "corporation," "company," "incorporated," "limited," or an abbreviation of one of these words (this requirement is intended to avoid confusion with partnerships by warning the public of limited liability);

—That it not contain a word or phrase that is misleading about the purposes of your corporation (you can defend against this requirement by stating your corporate purposes very broadly in your articles of incorporation: see Appendix A.1(c) for suggested statement of purposes for Dighaldoe Corporation); and

—That it not be "deceptively similar" to the name of another corporation organized or qualified in the state, or to a name which has been reserved or registered in the state (any person intending to organize or qualify a corporation can "reserve" a corporate name for 120 days (§9), and any American corporation, without qualifying in the state, can "register" its name (§10)).

After you have chosen a corporate name, you should have your lawyer, or a corporate service organization, obtain clearances and make reservations for the name in the proposed state of organization and in all states where you plan to qualify your corporation (see Appendix C.1(a) and (b)). And after your corporation is formed, you should have him see to it that your corporate name is registered in all states having registration provisions.

(b) Choosing the right name

Much trickier than complying with state corporation laws once you have chosen a name are the deliberations that should precede your name selection. Here you should be trying to avoid two big problems, one largely business, the second largely legal. On the business side, you want to make sure that the name you pick will fit your long-term needs (corporate image, marketing, advertising, etc.). Many factors can turn what seems like a good name this year into a handicap a few years later. On the legal side, you want to make sure that the name you pick does not get you into trouble with existing businesses, or with other people or institutions that may claim that your name is likely to cause confusion.

> ▪ **The experiences of Standard Oil Company of New Jersey (now Exxon) offer classic examples of both these problems. Other "Standard Oil" Companies, through legal providings, forced Standard of New Jersey to stop using the names "Standard" and "Esso" in extensive marketing areas. In finding a suitable name for nation-wide marketing, Standard of New Jersey made several tries: Humble, Enco, and now Exxon.**

What are some of the things that you should do to help you avoid these troubles? You should try to project how your name will look if your business or the people in it change, or if public attitudes about what is fashionable change; these projections may slow you down in including technological terms, family names, or current jargon.

> ▪ **A successful corporate name of recent vintage is "Xerox". Its virtue is that it had *no* prior meaning, and its corporate user has thus been free to make its meaning grow with the business. It is probable that similar thinking went into the coining of Exxon.**

And you should find out all you can about possible conflicts with or preemptions of your proposed name. Here a lawyer specializing in trademark work can be helpful. He will know how to cause searches to be made of registered trademarks, federal and state, and how to secure the services of organizations that can do searches for unregistered trade names that may cause you trouble. It is easier and cheaper to clear a name *before* you start using it.

> ▪ **Suppose that our friends Digges, Hall, and Doe want to call their coal mining corporation Dighaldoe Corporation. They have this name searched and it appears clear except for one small blemish: John Dighaldo has operated a one-man, unincorporated, now almost defunct coal mine in another state, where he had registered that he was doing business as Dighaldo Mining Company. Discreet inquiries indicate that for $500 John Dighaldo will assign the good will of his business and agree not to use his name in connection with mining coal. If Digges, Hall, and Doe plan to use the name they have selected, it would probably be wise for them to invest the $500 as insurance against future trouble. For a sample agreement on clearing a corporate name in this situation, see Appendix H.1(b).**

Section 1.4 Filling Corporate Positions

Along with choosing places to incorporate and qualify and selecting a name, you must designate people to fill various corporate positions: incorporators, shareholders, directors, officers, agents for service of process, and other agents.

> ▪ **Note that a corporate service organization can be useful. If you want to preserve anonymity during the early stages, or if your own people do not want to be bothered with preliminary meetings, you can use service organization people as incorporators—and even as temporary shareholders, directors, and officers—to get your corporation started.**
>
> **It is important that legal papers served on your corporation get promptly into the hands of your lawyers to avoid default judgments, etc. Operational people at your offices, plants, and other locations may not be sensitive to this need. Thus, you should consider using a corporate service organization as your registered agent for service of process in all states where you need to register an agent. These organizations can also be helpful in assuring that your corporation makes the necessary filings in various states, and in keeping you up to date on changes in state laws.**

Under the Model Act, you need at least one incorporator, which can be an unqualified corporation (§53); a registered agent, which can be a domestic or a qualified foreign corporation (§12); and at least one shareholder, one director, a president, one or more vice presidents, a secretary, and a treasurer, all of whom can be the same person, except that the president and secretary cannot be the same person if there is more than one shareholder (§§36, 50). Some states still have residence, citizenship, or share ownership requirements for directors and some officers, and not all states permit one-director boards. There seem to be no legal restrictions on who can hold shares in your corporation.

The statutory requirements in filling corporate positions have become so loose that choices are largely dictated by business rather than legal considerations. In addition to determining how you want decision-making power distributed within your corporation, a problem which we consider at length in the following chapters, you need to give thought to mundane matters like the availability of individuals to attend meetings and to sign documents.

> ▪ **For example, if your sales manager will be traveling most of the time, you may not want to count on this executive to conduct, or even to attend, board meetings, or to perform the administrative duties of president, secretary, or treasurer; however, giving your sales manager the office of vice president, assuming you have other vice presidents to act in the president's absence, would seem to present no problems.**

Section 1.5 Articles of Incorporation

Articles of incorporation are filed with the secretary of state of the state where you decide to incorporate (and also in the states where you decide to qualify). Their acceptance by the state of incorporation makes them your "charter" and formally starts your corporation's existence. You do not change your articles lightly, since changes must be approved by your shareholders and filed with your states of incorporation and qualification.

By-laws are your less formal rules for internal corporate government. They can be adopted and changed by your board of directors and state filings are not required.

> ▪ **However, if your corporation is subject to the federal securities laws, you must keep the SEC and any stock exchanges on which your shares are listed informed about what your by-laws provide.**

With both articles and by-laws many of the provisions are fairly standard; your lawyer simply follows the forms. There are, however, some choices that will require your decision. This section outlines some of these choices in preparing your articles. Discussion of by-laws is deferred until we deal with internal corporate government. For suggested articles, by-laws, and other start-up documents, see Appendix A, B, and C.

(a) Par value; authorized shares; classes of shares

Your corporation is owned by shareholders who will purchase their ownership shares by paying the corporation in money, property, or services. These initial payments for shares are carried on the books of the corporation as "capital" or "paid-in surplus" depending on what "par value" is assigned in the articles of incorporation to the shares, and these figures are not affected by subsequent transfers of the shares to new shareholders (the corporation may not even know what is paid). There is a basic cluster of choices that you must make about provisions in your articles relating to how your corporation will be "capitalized."

To understand these choices you need to understand what is meant by "capital," "paid-in surplus," and "par value." The authorized capital of a corporation is the number of shares authorized in the articles times the par value for these shares stated in the articles (see Appendix A.2(a)); the actual capital is the number of shares issued and outstanding times par value. There can be several "classes" of shares with different par values (see Appendix A.2(b) and (c)). Paid-in surplus is the excess over par value paid for shares when they are originally issued.

> ▪ If the articles of Dighaldoe corporation authorize 5000 shares of $10 par common stock, its authorized capital will be $50,000 (5000 × $10). If 3000 shares are issued for consideration valued at $100 per share, its actual capital will be $30,000 (3000 × $10) and its paid-in surplus $270,000 (3000 × ($100-$10)).

Who cares about capital? Mainly creditors and accountants. The capital of a corporation is supposed to provide a fund which will be available to creditors for the payment of a corporate debt. This protection is important because creditors can ordinarily look only to corporate assets for satisfaction of their claims. Creditors may be hurt, and may have claims against individuals, if shares are issued for less than par value ("watered"), or if part of the capital is used to pay dividends or is otherwise used up ("capital impairment").

The choices that you have to make are:

—What will the par value (or values) be?
—How many shares will be authorized?
—How many shares will be issued?
—Will there be more than one class of shares?

It is the usual practice to assign low par values ($1 to $10) in an effort to reduce watered share problems and to make it easier to pay dividends and repurchase shares (see Section 8.1(b)).

▪ For example, where shares are being issued for property, as in our Dighaldoe coal mining illustration where Hall was to contribute trucks worth $80,000, it would be prudent not to assign the full $80,000 to par value (capital). If Hall was slated to receive 800 shares for his trucks, which would mean that he was paying $100 per share at the $80,000 valuation, a $10 par will permit $90 per share to be assigned to paid-in surplus, as in the above illustration. (For these 800 shares, the right hand side of the balance sheet would show $8,000 in capital and $72,000 in paid-in surplus.) This procedure would protect Hall against a claim that, since the trucks were really worth only, say, $40,000, he had not paid the full par value for his shares. And, in many states, the $72,000 assigned to paid-in surplus might be available for the payment of dividends. Of course, if you were a creditor of the coal mining corporation you would not be enthusiastic about this procedure.

It is also the usual practice to authorize more shares in your articles of incorporation than you plan to issue, and to try to maintain a cushion of "authorized but unissued" shares. This cushion is handy if you want to issue more shares to acquire another business or to retain a valued employee. Without such a cushion, you will need to go back to your shareholders for an amendment to your articles increasing the number of authorized shares and you will need to file your amended articles in states where you are organized or qualified. Apart from the expense and bother of the meeting and the filings, the need for a meeting may get in the way of the quick action that may be called for in making an acquisition. Thus, the authorized but unissued shares cushion is a matter of continuing concern. You can save time, money, and possible embarrassment by taking care of any amendments to your articles that may be needed at your annual meetings of shareholders, and thus avoid the need for special meetings.

Whether you wish to authorize more than one class of shares will depend largely on how you plan to finance your enterprise. The two main kinds of shares are "common" and "preferred." Common shares typically have voting rights, but no fixed dividend rates (when we talk about shareholders, we usually mean holders of common shares); preferred shares typically do not have voting rights, but their dividend rates are fixed, and they come in ahead of common shares on dividends and liquidation. Preferred shares are useful when you want to raise additional money but you do not want to dilute your voting control or your prospects for increased earnings.

▪ Recall that where Digges, Hall, and Doe need additional financing, but do not want to share control with outsiders, we suggest they might use debt or non-voting shares. It should be remembered, however, that more than one class of stock will disqualify their corporation for Subchapter S treatment. Digges, Hall, and Doe will probably not want to be

taxed under Subchapter S, because they plan to plow back earnings. If they did want to preserve the Subchapter S option, they should try to do their outside financing with debt.

(b) Purposes and powers; ultra vires

A corporation owes its existence to a governmental act. Early corporations were individually chartered (by the crown in Great Britain, and by state legislatures after we gained our independence) for limited purposes and with limited powers. Fortunately for the development of corporations, there arose a doctrine of "implied powers" to do things necessary for performance of stated purposes. However, until quite recently, a large segment of corporation law was devoted to claims that corporations had acted "ultra vires": beyond their powers. This claim could be used both by the corporation and by outsiders to try to get out of unfavorable deals. These claims have become rare, because purposes can be stated very broadly (see Appendix A.1(c)), which will yield almost unlimited implied powers; and because very broad powers are now conferred on corporations by state laws. There are, however, still some points that you need to watch on the purposes and powers clauses in your articles.

Your articles should not confuse purposes (objectives) and powers (capabilities for achieving objectives). If what you want to be a purpose is drafted so that it can be mistaken for a power, you may unintentionally limit your purposes.

> ▪ **If the articles of Dighaldoe Corporation state mining coal as a purpose, and if they also refer to acquiring shares of other corporations in such a way that the latter could be construed as a power, Dighaldoe might be held to be empowered to acquire shares only in the furtherance of coal mining; whereas, if acquiring shares is clearly made a separate purpose, Dighaldoe would be empowered to make acquisitions unrelated to coal mining—and could thus become a "conglomerate" if it wished.**

You want a broad statement of purposes, but there is still some danger that if the statement is completely unspecific it will be held a nullity. The safest practice would seem to be an extensive list that sets out all the specific purposes you and your lawyer can think of followed by a general clause stating your purpose to engage in any activity that is lawful.

The current trend is away from detailed recitals of powers. As indicated above, state statutes now grant broad general powers which need not be individually enumerated in the articles. Some lawyers think that it is enough to state your purposes broadly and that powers need not be mentioned in the articles; others recommend that you include a catch-all recital of all powers conferred by the laws of the state of incorporation; others would go still further, as does Appendix A.1(c), and include a clause that all objects and purposes shall be construed also as powers, but that such enumeration of specific powers shall not limit powers granted by law. Since out-of-state third parties (such as financial institutions) to whom the articles may be presented may expect to find detailed powers clauses, it may save trouble to recite your powers both broadly and in detail.

There are three areas where ultra vires claims are still sometimes made: charitable contributions, guarantees of debts of others, and corporate participation in partnerships. The problem with the first two is the difficulty in finding a business purpose when the corporation is just being kind and using corporate resources for objectives that may not directly help the corporation. As to the third, the problem is more conceptual: whether an artificial legal person can be a partner. The Model Act tries to lay all these issues to rest, more or less, with the following provisions:

> *Each corporation shall have power ... to lend money and use its credit to assist its employees; ... to make contracts and guarantees; ... to make donations for the public welfare or for charitable, scientific or educational purpose; ... to be a promoter, partner, member, associate, or manager of any partnership, joint venture, trust or other enterprise (§4).*

The Model Act also provides that an act or transfer by a corporation shall not be invalid for lack of corporate capacity, except that such lack of capacity may be asserted in proceedings:

—by a shareholder against the corporation to enjoin the act or transfer;
—by or for the corporation against its officers or directors; and
—by the attorney general to dissolve the corporation.

This provision would seem to eliminate the assertion of ultra vires by the corporation or by the other party when the transaction is with an outsider.

(c) Preemptive rights; cumulative voting; indemnification

In preparing your articles of incorporation you will be asked to make other decisions, less basic than those about capital structure and corporate purposes, but still with important consequences on how your corporation will function. Do you want your shareholders to be entitled to participate in new issues of shares? Do you want to allow them to cumulate their votes for director candidates? Do you want to protect individuals who act for the corporation from liabilities because of their corporate positions?

The ownership and voting rights of shareholders, which are discussed in Chapters 2 and 3, can be substantially changed by issuing additional shares, particularly in corporations that are small and closely held.

> ▪ **If the three founders of Dighaldoe Corporation—Digges, Hall, and Doe—each held 1000 voting shares, and if Digges and Hall were able to cause Dighaldoe to issue 1000 new shares to each of their wives, Doe's position would change from a one-third to a one-fifth share of the ownership, control, and earnings of Dighaldoe.**
>
> **Compare a large, widely held corporation, with two million shareholders, that issues 100,000 new shares to raise additional funds. The effect on individual shareholders will be minimal.**

The rights of existing shareholders to pro rata shares of new issues are called "preemptive rights." In most states you can provide in your articles whether or not shareholders are to have these rights (see Appendix A.5(a), (b), and (c)), although state laws vary as to what happens if your articles are silent on this subject. If your corporation is to be publicly held, preemptive rights probably do not make much sense. As the illustration indicates, shareholders do not need them, and they may be a nuisance when the corporation wants to issue new shares to raise money, for an acquisition, or under a plan to encourage share ownership by employees. But if your corporation is small and closely held, preemptive rights can be an important protection for minority shareholders.

Whether directors are elected on a seat-by-seat basis by a majority or plurality vote of the shares or under a system of proportional representation (called "cumulative voting" in corporate usage) can (like preemptive rights) make a difference to minority shareholders of close corporations, but is of less concern to shareholders of public corporations.

> ▪ **If Digges, Hall, and Doe each want a say in the management of Dighaldoe, cumulative voting would be a way of assuring each a seat on its board if, as we have been assuming, voting shares were divided equally among them. But with seat-by-seat voting any two of them could combine to exclude the third from the board.**
>
> **Again, compare a public corporation where no one shareholder controls more than one or two per cent of the vote. Cumulative voting would have little impact.**

The mechanics and policy considerations of cumulative voting (and the related topic of dividing the board into classes) are discussed in Chapter 3. Here we alert you that these are among the matters that you will have to decide when you are preparing your articles to get your corporation started (see Appendix A.6(b)).

Officers, directors, employees, and agents of your corporation may find themselves parties to civil, criminal, administrative, and investigative proceedings because of their positions; these proceedings may involve expenses, fines, and settlements which should be borne by the corporation. To assure that the corporation has the power to indemnify them for these costs, and to maintain liability insurance for them, you should consider including specific grants of these powers in your articles (see Appendix A.9). We will return to indemnification and insurance in Chapter 11 when we focus on your own exposure to liability.

Section 1.6 Defects in Your Corporateness

Since incorporation is a bundle of privileges (limited liability, continuity, etc.) made available to you by the law, the law can place conditions on your enjoyment of these privileges. It can deny them to you if your incorporation is "defective," and it can take them away from you if you abuse them. Thus, a necessary condition to maximizing the benefits of incorporation is to make sure that you do not make the wrong moves which may jeopardize getting or keeping your corporateness. What are these wrong moves; what are their consequences; how can you avoid them?

(a) Defective incorporation

The critical step of the incorporation process is the filing of the articles of incorporation, signed by the incorporators, with the secretary of state. If that office finds the articles in order and that all fees and taxes have been paid, it issues a "certificate of incorporation" and corporate existence begins. Possible defects that may creep in before issuance of the certificate include: improper corporate name; omission of essential clauses from the articles; improper signature of the articles by the incorporators; and failure to pay a filing fee. Under the Model Act, pre-issuance defects can not be raised to attack the incorporation except by the state in a proceeding to revoke the certificate or to compel dissolution of the corporation (§56). Defects that may occur after issuance of the certificate include: failure to make required filings (some states require filing in the county where the corporation's registered office is situated); payment of inadequate considerations for shares; and failure to elect directors or officers. While post-issuance lapses may cause you trouble, it would seem that they can not undo your corporate existence. Thus, once your certificate is issued it becomes difficult for people with whom you deal on behalf of the corporation to hold you individually liable; your main threat of trouble is from the state. Of course, if you do not secure issuance of the certificate, your corporation does not come into existence and you may have to go back and start over.

The best defense against the delays and inconveniences caused by incorporation defects is the choice of a careful, conscientious lawyer, who will make sure that you have touched and continue to touch all bases. You can help insure this kind of legal service if you, yourself, take seriously the corporate formalities of filings, fees, meetings, minutes, etc., and do not lead your lawyer to suppose that you do not mind if he cuts a few corners or that you are impatient with legal niceties. Lawyers are more likely to extend themselves for clients who appear to want and appreciate careful, ethical craftsmanship. And it is prudent to remember that irregularities that seem picayune when your corporation is small may rise up to haunt you when your business has grown and you want to go public or sell out.

(b) Abuse of corporateness

Ethical considerations are also important in predicting the kind of conduct that may lead a judge to conclude that, even though your corporation was properly formed, it has been used so unfairly to other people (including tax officials) that its corporateness should be temporarily disregarded and individual liability imposed on the real people behind the corporation (called "piercing the corporate veil" and "disregarding the corporate fiction"). Examples are unitary businesses that have been fragmented into many corporations (say, the owner of 100 taxicabs who forms 50 corporations to operate them) and businesses that have not been provided with enough capital to pay claims against the corporation (say, a swimming pool corporation that is without liability insurance or other funds to pay claims). Here it will be your conscience, as much as your lawyer's, that will have to decide how far you are going to go. We return to this problem in Chapter 11. For now it suffices that you be alerted that limited liability, which is your main reason for incorporation, may prove illusory if you try to push too far the advantages of doing business in the corporate form.

CHECKLIST OF POINTS TO WATCH OUT FOR IN GETTING YOUR CORPORATION STARTED

(References after headings are to Sections of Chapter 1.)

1. Subchapter S corporations and Section 1244 shares (Section 1.1)

Have you explored taking advantage of these federal tax law options?
Subchapter S permits certain closely held corporations with a single class of shares to enjoy the limited liability of corporations while retaining the tax status of partnerships. This option is, of course, unattractive for growth enter-

prises like Dighaldoe that plan to plow back income into the business, but it should be explored where income is expected to be distributed each year to shareholders.

In contrast, Section 1244, which permits capital losses on qualified shares to be treated as ordinary losses, provides an unalloyed tax benefit that should be grasped wherever possible. The main requirements are that the shares be original issue common shares paid for by money or other property, and that the corporation have capital and paid-in surplus of $1 million or less and derive over 50% of its gross receipts from operations, rather than investments or royalties.

2. State of incorporation (Section 1.2(a))

Can you justify incorporating elsewhere than in your home state?

While Delaware is favored as a place to incorporate because of permissive and well-developed corporation laws and a pro-business climate, for predominantly local businesses Delaware incorporation usually costs more than it is worth, especially if your home state has the Model Act. Lack of a clearly defined home state or a very unfavorable home state are considerations which may overcome the presumption in favor of home state incorporation.

3. Qualification in other states (Section 1.2 (b))

Are you keeping your qualifications at a minimum?

A corporation is supposed to "qualify" in states, other than its state of incorporation, where it "does business." Tests for doing business are unclear; and, in doubtful cases, the disadvantages of qualification (exposure to fees, taxes, and being sued) usually outweigh the advantages (availability of local courts and avoidance of penalities). Hence, the rule of thumb is: Do not qualify except where you are clearly doing business or where you may be held to be doing business and the penalties for unauthorized business are very severe.

Keep in mind that you may be able to reduce the exposure of your parent corporation by use of subsidiaries.

For an authorization at the first meeting of a board of directors of qualifications in specified other states, see Appendix C.2(b).

4. Choosing a corporate name (Section 1.3)

Is the name you have chosen available and suitable?

Naming a corporation involves satisfying state regulations, avoiding conflicts with existing names, and selecting a name that will be good for the long pull: a combination of problems calling for joint help from your legal and marketing advisors. Since missteps can entail costly litigation and advertising outlays, careful and expert planning is essential.

For the provision in the articles of incorporation fixing the corporate name and information about the words it must contain, see Appendix A.1(a). For an agreement clearing the name of Dighaldoe Corporation from a possible conflict, see Appendix H.1(b).

5. Protecting a corporate name (Section 1.3)

Have you utilized available reservation and registration procedures?

Once you have chosen the right name for your corporation you will want to start protecting it from others. Under the Model Act (§9) you can reserve for 120 days the right to use a name in states where you plan to incorporate and qualify. This can be done in the name of your lawyer or other nominee, who can transfer the reservations to you when appropriate. For the application for reservation and the notice of transfer, see Appendix C.1(a) and (b).

Post-incorporation protection can be provided by registering your corporate name in those states which permit registration of non-qualified foreign corporations. For general discussion of resisting unfair business tactics, see Section 9.2.

6. Corporate service organizations (Section 1.4)

Can they help you?

Assistance from corporate specialists is available for many of the details connected with getting a corporation started and keeping its house in order: checking on availability of corporate names, filing papers with state offices, providing incorporators and temporary directors and officers, holding initial meetings, and providing registered officers and agents in various states. These services enable you to proceed anonymously, to keep current on state laws, and to be assured that filings will be made on time and that you will promptly receive papers served on you. Urge your lawyer to investigate whether these services should be used.

7. Authorized shares (Section 1.5(a))

Have you a sufficient cushion of authorized but unissued shares?

A function of the articles of incorporation, filing of which brings your corporation into being, is to state the number of shares it is authorized to issue. It is usually a good idea to provide a larger authorization than you plan to issue in order to have authorized but unissued shares available for contingencies, such as attracting a sought-after employee or acquiring another business. A cushion of authorized but unissued shares enables you to proceed with what you want to do without the delays and expenses of shareholders' meetings and state filings to amend your articles. See Section 10.1 for discussion of a hypothetical acquisition by Dighaldoe Corporation using authorized but unissued shares.

For statements of authorized shares in the articles, see Appendix A.2(a),(b), and (c).

8. Corporate purposes and powers (Section 1.5(b))

Have you stated your corporation's purposes and powers broadly enough?

Articles of incorporation define a corporation's purposes and powers. To forestall claims that your corporation is departing from its purposes or exceeding its powers, your articles should take full advantage of the all-inclusive statements permitted by most modern corporation laws.

For a clause in the articles that makes a statement of purposes and powers that is both very detailed (for the benefit of those looking for something specific) and of maximum breadth and generality (just in case something has been omitted), see Appendix A.1(c).

9. Preemptive rights and cumulative voting (Section 1.5(c))

Do you want these protections for minority shareholders?

Articles of incorporation may grant or withhold shareholders' rights to participate, proportionately to their share holdings, in new issues of shares (preemptive rights) and in being represented on the board of directors (cumulative voting). For discussions of these protections, which are generally more appropriate for close than for public corporations, see Section 6.2(a) on preemptive rights as one means of controlling ownership of close corporations, and Section 3.3(d) on the mechanics of and policy considerations for and against cumulative voting.

Make sure that your lawyer has drafted your articles to achieve the results that you want.

For clauses in the articles that make, respectively, denials and grants, unrestricted and restricted, of preemptive rights, see Appendix A.5(a), (b), and (c). For an article providing for cumulative voting, see Appendix A.6(b).

10. Assuring your corporate status (Section 1.6)

Have you guarded adequately against your corporation being found to be defective or sham?

Judges can choose to disregard a corporation when prescribed legal steps for its formation are omitted or when the corporate form of doing business is being abused. Your best protection is an informed and conscientious lawyer who will keep you from cutting corners in the incorporation process and from using your corporateness for unfair advantages. While findings of defective or sham incorporation are rare, when they happen they can be expensive because they result in individual liability for the shareholders. For discussion of corporateness and individual liabilities, see Section 2.1(a) on the nature and separateness of corporations, Section 11.1(b) on defective incorporation, and Section 11.2 on disregard of corporateness.

2

Owning Your Corporation

2

Owning Your Corporation

Along with the creation of your corporation, you need to be thinking about how it will be "owned," and about what ownership in the corporate context means. Property rights, individual and institutional, are basic to any legal system, and part of the magic of corporations is what they enable you to do with property rights through the interposition of separate, artificial, legal persons between flesh and blood owners and things to be owned.

At the outset, it is essential to distinquish between two kinds of objects of ownership: interests *in* the corporation (shares); and assets *of* the corporation (which can be almost anything: money, land, buildings, goods, patents, copyrights, contractual rights, good will, securities of other corporations, etc.)

> ▪ **Can a corporation own shares in itself? While it can buy its own shares with its own money, once acquired by the corporation, the shares cease to be shares in the full sense. Called "treasury shares"— because they are held in the corporate treasury—reacquired shares are like authorized but unissued shares: they do not receive dividends, participate in liquidation, nor vote. But, again like authorized but unissued shares, treasury shares can be transferred to outsiders, whereupon they regain their full status as ownership shares, entitled to dividends, liquidation participation, and votes.**

Thus, we start with the very basic notion that shareholders are owners, not of their corporation's assets, but of shares in the corporation itself.

The ability of a corporation either to bring together or to keep apart ownership rights in all sorts of assets has many uses. A corporation can be utilized to gather together the resources, human and material, needed for transportation, communication, and energy systems; for extracting minerals; and for

55

assembling complex products and selling them to broad markets. In the opposite direction, a corporation can be used to segregate ownership of particular assets— as when a "holding company" is formed to hold shares of another corporation, or when separate corporations are formed to carry on particular parts of a business, or to operate in particular geographical areas, or to own a particular piece of property. Corporate ownership is a box into which you can put what you want. You may have many different reasons for putting a particular thing in a particular corporate box: to minimize taxes or exposure to liability; to comply with local legal requirements; to preserve a trademark; or to facilitate sale of interests in the thing to others.

In this chapter, as its title implies, we are mainly interested in ownership of corporate shares, rather than ownership of corporate assets. As to corporate assets, the same general rules of property law that apply to natural persons apply to corporations. In later chapters we examine what you, as a corporate officer and director, can and can not do with corporate property. Now we are concerned with the puzzle, peculiar to corporateness, of how a corporation itself is owned: in short, this chapter is about the rights and functions of shareholders as owners of a corporation. It examines what it is that shareholders are supposed to own; how their ownership rights are represented, transferred, and identified; their rights to participate in corporate assets through dividends and liquidation; and their ability to seek, on behalf of the corporation, court intervention in its management. Chapters 3 and 6 deal with shareholders as the voting constituency of corporate government and with ownership controls for close corporations.

Section 2.1 Corporate Shares: What Are They?

While a substantial part of the property holdings of the American middle and upper classes is represented by corporate shares, there is pervasive lack of understanding among the many millions of shareholders as to just what they own. Since shareholding in public corporations requires little diligence and even less skill, it has been a convenient way to transfer wealth from husband to wife and from one generation to another. Shareholding in close corporations may be somewhat less well suited for transfers of wealth, but such shareholding is the way that a large part of the medium and small-sized businesses in this country are owned. In this section we examine briefly the nature and separateness of the thing owned: the corporation; then we consider the kinds of securities that are used to share corporate ownership. We return to the uses of corporate securities in financing the corporation in Chapter 7.

(a) Nature and separateness of corporations

Three major theories have been developed to explain the nature of the corporate entity. The "organic" approach treats corporations as social organizations with real existence independent of the recognition accorded them by law; it argues that while the law recognizes corporations, it does not really create them. The "legal fiction" approach treats corporations as purely legal creations, without existence but for the law. The "functional" approach ignores whether and how corporations exist and treats them as useful short-hand ways to describe a bundle of events and predictable consequences. These three theories roughly parallel the three major schools of legal philosophy: natural law that claims that legal concepts, like "corporations," do not depend on legislatures and judges for their existence; legal positivism that claims that law is a system of rules made and enforced by political authorities; and legal realism that claims that it does not matter what law is: what matters is how people doing law work function.

In this book we fortunately do not have to choose among these theories; each can contribute to our understanding of corporations. While it seems true, in a sense, that the law can make corporations appear and disappear, it also seems true that some corporations constitute parts of our social fabric that transcend their purely legal status. And most people who work with corporations are less interested in whether they are working with real animals (like horses and mules) or with fictional beasts (like unicorns and centaurs) than they are in predicting what will happen if they make certain legal and business moves. No one of the three theories about corporations seems adequate in itself to explain corporations as we experience them; we seem to need all three concepts—social organism, legal fiction, and bundle of events and consequences—to fill out our picture of corporateness.

On a less philosophical level, the existence or non-existence of a corporation as a separate entity becomes of practical interest to its shareholders when someone, most likely a tax collector or other corporate creditor, seeks to lift or to pierce the corporate veil in order to get at the shareholders; or when a shareholder is himself a creditor of the corporation in competition with outside creditors for satisfaction of claims from corporate assets. In both of these situations shareholders will be urging that the separateness of the corporation should be respected; that the law should be consistent in the way it treats the legal personality of corporations. Creditors, on the other hand, will be urging that what the law has granted (corporateness) the law can take away in the interest of justice. The law in these situations seems to be developing in the direction of the functional approach. For some purposes—as where the corporation seems to have been created largely to avoid taxes, or where a shareholder-creditor is in competition with outside creditors, or where the corporation is under-capitalized—corporate separateness will not be given its full effect. But for other, more ordinary, purposes—like holding property, or making contracts, or committing torts—the corporation will remain a separate legal person. For further discussion of when corporate separateness may be disregarded with resultant individual liability, see Section 11.1(b).

In the balance of this chapter we assume that the separate entity of the corporation will be respected to the extent that shareholders can be said to own undivided shares in something distinct from the corporate assets or even from the corporate business. Our concern is to convey a notion of what it means to share in the ownership of a corporation.

(b) Kinds of corporate securities

In considering how a corporation is owned it is necessary to distinguish ownership from debt. Corporations have two main methods of raising money: (1) selling shares or (2) borrowing, either by long-term loans (bonds and debentures) or short-term loans (notes). The legal consequences of these two methods are quite different. A sale of shares, or "equity financing," does not create a new corporate obligation; rather, the ownership of the corporation is further subdivided. Borrowing, or "debt financing," on the other hand, creates a new corporate obligation, but leaves the ownership of the corporation unchanged. Even when a loan is secured by a lien or a mortgage, such security interest is usually in property of the corporation and does not represent a further subdivision of the ownership of the corporation itself.

> ▪ And there is no further subdivision of ownership of the corporation even when a shareholder pledges his shares in the corporation to secure a corporate debt. The shareholder will have parted with a portion of his own ownership interest in the corporation, but no new shares in the corporation will have been created. So far as ownership of the corporation is concerned, the situation is indistinguishable from a shareholder pledging his shares as security for a personal loan.

We consider in Chapter 7 the relative tax and other advantages of equity and debt financing. Here our point is a very simple one: shareholders are owners of the corporation, while bondholders and noteholders are among its creditors.

> ▪ You can, of course, make things more complicated by giving creditors a right to convert their debt interest into an equity interest.

Within the category of owners we also need to distinguish among "classes" of shareholders. The Model Act provides that "shares may be divided into one or more classes ... with such designations, preferences, limitations, and relative rights as may be stated in the articles of incorporation" (§15). The most significant differences among shareholders relate to voting rights and preferences for payment of dividends and in distributing corporate assets on liquidation. As we have noted, when we talk about shareholders we usually mean those with common shares: shares with voting rights, but without preferences on dividends or liquidation. Preferred shares, typically shares without voting rights but with preferences on receipt of dividends and participation in liquidation, are ownership interests with many of the functional characteristics of bonds: fixed income, fixed liquidation rights, and no participation in control or growth.

> ▪ Note that preferred shares fulfill some of the functions of limited partnerships.

Section 2.2 Representation and Transfer of Corporate Shares; Identification of Shareholders

(a) Certificates representing shares

The physical manifestation of shares are "certificates." For a certificate representing common shares, see Appendix C.3(a) and (b). Status as a shareholder, however, is not legally dependent upon having a certificate. The main functions of certificates are to provide evidence of ownership and something tangible that can be delivered when shares are transferred. With the increase in the volume of share trading and the attendant paper work, there are predictions that we will see the elimination of share certificates except where they are specifically requested. Most large corporations are maintaining their share transfer records electronically which makes the physical handling of certificates largely surplusage. And brokers are encouraging customers to leave shares in the brokers' custody, thereby enabling brokers to reduce the number of certificates and transfers on the records of the corporation by registering customers' shares with the issuers in composite accounts in the names of the brokers or their nominees.

For listed shares, we need to consult both stock exchange rules and state corporation laws for requirements as to what share certificates must contain. Stock exchange rules, aimed at preventing counterfeiting, call for steel engraving of portions of the certificates (borders and "vignettes": pictures, frequently with lightly draped classical figures).

> ▪ These requirements have tended to concentrate the printing of share certificates with a few companies which also specialize in printing currency for some foreign countries.

Both stock exchange and state law requirements for share certificates have become less demanding in recent years. For example, it is no longer necessary that charter provisions about preferred shares be set forth on the certificate. The Model Act (§23) has reduced the requirements for share certificates to the elementary facts needed to identify

—the corporation: its name and state of incorporation;
—the shareholder: his, her, or its name; and
—the shares: number, class, series, and par value;

plus, if more than one class of shares is authorized, a statement that the corporation will furnish to a shareholder, upon request and without charge, a full statement of the rights of each class. Also, each certificate usually bears an identifying number.

Legal requirements remain strict for certificates for shares subject to transfer restrictions. Under the Uniform Commercial Code any restriction on transfer of the shares imposed by the corporation unless "noted conspicuously" on the certificate "even though otherwise lawful is ineffective except against a person with actual knowledge of it" (§8-204). The Delaware corporation act contains a similar provision (§202).

The Model Act (§23) requires that certificates bear signatures of the president or a vice president and the secretary or an assistant secretary. These signatures may be facsimiles if the certificate is manually signed on behalf of a transfer agent or registrar, other than the corporation itself or an employee of the corporation. Certificates bearing facsimile signatures of former officers may continue to be issued. The Model Act forbids issuance of a certificate until it is fully paid; however, Delaware permits issuance of certificates for partly paid shares subject to call for the unpaid part, but the certificate must show the total amount to be paid and the amount actually paid (§156).

Lost, destroyed, or stolen share certificates present problems for both the corporation and the shareholder. The usual practice is for the corporation to issue a replacement certificate on the condition that the shareholder furnish the corporation an affidavit describing what has happened to the old certificate and an indemnity bond from a surety company protecting the corporation from any liability that it may incur upon the old certificate. Since indemnity bonds are expensive, a few corporations, in the interests of shareholder relations, have made it a practice to replace certificates in some situations without the indemnity bond, relying on the affidavit and an individual undertaking of the shareholder to hold the corporation harmless. For by-laws authorizing directors to set terms for certificate replacement, see Appendix B.7(c).

▪ **Because of the nuisance and expense of certificate replacement, it is suggested that you urge your shareholders to keep their certificates in safe deposit boxes.**

(b) Fractional shares

In most states corporations may issue certificates for fractional shares, and such shares will be entitled proportionately to dividend, liquidation, and voting rights of full shares. The most common occasion for fractional share interests are share dividends that, as applied to particular shareholdings, do not produce even numbers of shares.

▪ **If a corporation declares a share dividend of one share for each 100 shares outstanding, all shareholders with holdings not in even multiples of 100 will receive fractional shares. If the dividend is five shares for each 100 shares outstanding, only those with holdings in even multiples of 20 will not receive fractional shares.**

Fractional shares may also result from stock splits, reverse splits, recapitalizations, mergers, and consolidations.

▪ **A stock split may produce fractional shares if the second figure of the split formula is more than one: e.g., if the split is 3 for 2 any shareholder with an odd number of shares will receive a ½ share. The result is the same in the case of a reverse split (say, 1 for 2), or of an exchange on a recapitalization, merger or consolidation where the shares being turned in are more than one: e.g., an exchange of two or more X shares for one Y share.**

Two methods of avoiding the issuance of fractional share certificates, both sanctioned by the Model Act (§24) and the Delaware Corporation Act (§155), have developed in recent years. One method involves the use of "scrip." Not unlike trading stamps, scrip entitles the holder to receive a full share certificate upon surrender of enough scrip before a stated date, but does not give the holder dividend, liquidation, or voting rights. To protect scrip holders against forfeitures, it is frequently provided that scrip outstanding on a stated date may be sold by a trust company and the proceeds held for the benefit of the scrip holders. The second method avoids the need for issuing either certificates or scrip by authorizing the corporation to pay in cash those entitled to fractional shares "the fair value of fractions of a share determined as of the time when those entitled to receive such fractions are determined" (Model Act §24). When the shares are traded, fair value is usually determined by the corporation selling the composite total of fractional shares. Corporations sometimes give shareholders a choice of having their fractional shares sold for them or of buying an additional fraction to give the holder a full share.

> ▪ **You will want to avoid the nuisance of carrying fractional shares on your books—probably using the second, fair value method. For a director resolution authorizing purchase of fractional shares, see Appendix F.1(e).**

(c) Transfer of shares

Ownership of shares is ordinarily transferred from one shareholder to another by the shareholder in whose name the shares are registered executing a document called a "stock power," so called because it grants a power of attorney to someone to transfer the shares on the books of the corporation. These are separate from the certificates, though the certificates themselves usually carry on the back an assignment form (See Appendix C.3(b)).

> ▪ **A situation where the separate assignment is recommended is where the transferred shares are to be mailed. If the certificate and the assignment form are mailed in separate envelopes the shares will remain unnegotiable until the two parts are put together. This precaution is particularly essential when, as is frequently the case, the stock power is "in blank": i.e., does not designate the transferee or the person authorized to make the transfer.**

It is customary for transfer agents to require that the signature of the transferring shareholder be guaranteed by a bank or broker.

A corporation is required to keep at its registered office or principal place of business, or at the office of its transfer agent or registrar, a record of its shareholders, giving their names and addresses, and the number and class of shares held; this record may be "in written form or in any other form capable of being converted into written form within a reasonable time" (Model Act §52).

> ▪ **This provision authorizes the practice, referred to above, of putting shareholder records on computers. To comply with most state corporation laws it will be necessary to convert the record "into written form" at the time of the corporation's annual meeting of shareholders. See Model Act §31.**

Corporations do not ordinarily need outside transfer agents and registrars until they become publicly owned with their shares listed on stock exchanges. Stock exchange rules specify requirements for transfer agents and registrars.

Transfer agents do most of the work in processing transfers and it has been predicted that registrars, like share certificates, will cease to be required.

Detailed legal rules governing the issue and transfer of "investment securities" (which include shares and debt securities) as negotiable instruments, including rules formerly contained in the Uniform Stock Transfer Act, are set forth in Article 8 of the Uniform Commercial Code, which has been adopted in most states. It covers securities in both registered and bearer forms. Shares are always in registered form; bonds are usually, but not always, in bearer form.

(d) Identification of shareholders

A variety of events in corporate life makes it necessary for the officers and directors of a corporation to be able to say with precision (or have said on their behalf) who are its shareholders at a given time and how many shares of what class each of them hold. Recurring events calling for shareholder identification are dividend payments and shareholder meetings; occasional events include rights offerings, splits, mergers, consolidations, and liquidation. Since shares in many corporations are more or less constantly being transferred, the shareholder list is more like a movie than a still picture. Thus, the identification required for a dividend, meeting or other event calls for a mechanism for stopping the film at a single frame or, in the alternative, for letting the film run on but identifying a particular frame as representing "the picture" of the shareholder list. For a by-law authorizing use of either method, see Appendix B.7(e).

The law provides for procedures closely analogous to these alternatives. The board of directors may order that the share transfer books be closed on a given day for a period up to fifty days: that the film be stopped and the dividend be paid to the shareholders of record that appear in that frame. However, since the audience and the management usually want the film to go on, this procedure is seldom used. Alternatively, the Model Act provides that the board of directors "may fix in advance a date as the record date for any such determination of shareholders, such date in any case to be not more than fifty days and, in the case of a meeting of shareholders, not less than ten days prior to the date on which the particular action, requiring the determination of shareholders, is taken" (§30). The fixing of a record date (usually "at the close of business on") identifies the crucial frame and allows the show to go on. For a board of directors resolution fixing a record date, see Appendix F.3(a).

In identifying shareholders entitled to receive dividends or to vote, the corporation is not required to go behind its own records. The person whose name appears on the books of the corporation on the record date gets the dividend or the vote, even though he may be a trustee, a nominee, or even a thief. Where the record owner is holding the shares for a beneficial owner, it is up to the record owner to pass on the dividend to or to secure voting instructions from the beneficial owner.

> ▪ **We see later that the corporation sometimes assists record owners in securing voting instructions from beneficial owners.**

Section 2.3 Shareholder Participation in Corporate Assets Through Dividends and Liquidation

Thus far in this chapter we are concerned with defining the nature of corporate shares and with outlining procedures used in dealing with them. Now we come to the substantive part of share ownership (a subject to which we return in greater detail in Chapter 8): participation in interim distributions of corporate assets through dividends and in their final distribution on liquidation. The shareholders break through the corporate shell and get their hands on shares of the corporate property. How do we reconcile this break-through with the notion that shareholders own the corporation but not its property? Much of this section is an effort to respond to this question.

(a) Dividends

People buy shares in a corporation in order to share in its profits, growth, and control. Shareholders participate in corporate profits through dividends.

> ▪ **Of course, shareholders also "participate" in profits that are plowed back into the business if their shares thereby become more valuable.**

Dividends are usually paid in cash, although they can also be distributions of the corporation's own shares ("share dividends") or of corporate property (most commonly shares of another corporation, although dividends in whiskey and other tangible property are not unknown).

> ▪ **Note that share dividends do not distribute corporate assets, even if made from treasury shares, but simply increase the number of pieces (shares) into which ownership of the corporation is divided.**

Dividends are "declared" from time to time by the board of directors. For a board resolution declaring a dividend out of earned surplus, see Appendix F.3(b). With public corporations the usual practice is to declare and pay dividends on a quarterly basis. The declaration recites the per share amount of the dividend and the payment date and identifies shareholders entitled to receive it by use of a record date: "shareholders of record at the close of business on _____." There is usually a two or three week spread between the record date and the payment date. With public corporations it is essential that information concerning director dividend action be made public immediately to avoid any suspicion that there has been unfair trading on the basis of the information by insiders or their "tippees" (see Section 11.4).

> ▪ To assure prompt dissemination of dividend information it is a common practice for someone, frequently the secretary, to leave the board meeting when the dividend resolution is adopted and give instructions for the release of information concerning the directors' action to the wire services and principal newspapers. This practice is the outgrowth of cases where corporations, and corporate insiders and their tippees, have found themselves in legal difficulties when dividend information was not promptly disseminated.

Legal problems involving dividends mainly concern the sources out of which they can be declared and paid, although occasionally controversy arises over when directors can be compelled to declare (or not to declare) dividends. In some states, which follow the "balance sheet" test, dividends can be paid out of any "surplus," earned or unearned, that shows on the corporation's balance sheet. An increasing number of states are, however, following the Model Act (§45) in requiring that dividends be paid out of earned surplus. Under the "earned surplus" test, dividends may not be paid directly out of surplus generated by adopting a par value substantially less than the consideration actually paid to the corporation for the shares, or by unrealized appreciation in value of assets of the corporation.

> ▪ In examples in Chapter 1 we assume that 3,000 Dighaldoe shares, $10 par, were issued for $120,000 in cash, $80,000 in property, and services valued at $100,000. The actual consideration was $100 per share; the $90 per share that actual consideration exceeded par value would be called paid-in surplus. Thus, the Dighaldoe balance sheet would show:

Assets		Liabilities	
Cash	$120,000	Capital	$30,000
Property	80,000	Paid-in	
Services	100,000	surplus	270,000
	$300,000		$300,000

> I suggested that the $270,000 paid-in surplus might be available for the payment of dividends. It is now necessary to qualify that suggestion in several respects.
>
> The paid-in surplus would be available for dividends only in a state which uses the balance sheet test. And, since the corporation has only $120,000 in cash, there are obvious practical limits on what can be paid out in dividends.

While under the earned surplus test Dighaldoe has to await some earnings before declaring dividends, the low par is not without dividend significance. The paid-in surplus can not be used directly as a source of dividends, but it can be used indirectly: to reduce or eliminate an earned surplus deficit, and thus make possible the payment of dividends when earnings are earned. The writing off of negative earned surplus against unearned surplus is called a "quasi-reorganization." If Dighaldoe loses $20,000 in its first fiscal year, but anticipates earnings in its second year, a quasi-reorganization would change the right hand side of its balance sheet by reducing paid-in surplus from $270,000 to $250,000 and eliminating the negative earned surplus, making it possible to create an earned surplus in the second year from which dividends could be paid.

The Model Act offers an alternative provision, called "nimble dividends," which permits the payment of dividends, even when there is no earned surplus, out of "net earnings of the current fiscal year and the next preceding fiscal year taken as a single period" (§45(a)). For a board resolution declaring a nimble dividend out of current earnings, see Appendix F.3(c). They are called nimble dividends because directors (like Jack jumping over the candle stick) must be nimble and quick in declaring dividends when they have current earnings.

▪ Suppose again that Dighaldoe losses $20,000 in its first fiscal year; earns $13,000 in its second year; and loses $7,000 in its third year. At this point it would have an earned surplus deficit of $14,000 ($27,000—$13,000). It would, however, have $6,000 ($13,000 - $7,000) available for nimble dividends under the Model Act alternative if the dividend declaration is made before the close of its third fiscal year or within a reasonable time thereafter. Note that a nimble dividend could *not* be declared at the close of the second fiscal year, because Dighaldoe did not have net earnings for the first and second years "taken as a single period"; rather, it had a net loss of $7,000.

When might a shareholder seek to compel the directors to declare a dividend? This situation is most likely to arise in a close corporation with some of the shareholders receiving substantial salaries from the corporation and others relying on dividends for their income from the business. The salaried group will be more inclined to plow earnings back into the business in hopes of future growth; the non-salaried group will be more interested in receiving distributions of earnings. Since judges do not like to interfere in business judgments, and since the declaration of dividends is supposed to be a management decision for the directors to make, it will take a very strong showing of unfairness to individual shareholders to persuade a judge to order a board of directors to declare a dividend. Factors that might incline a judge in this direction include: exorbitant salaries; unreasonably large accumulation of earned surplus (i.e., a succession of profitable years with little or no dividends); and evidence that withholding of dividends was part of a scheme to force certain shareholders to sell out their interests.

> ▪ **Our hypothetical Dighaldoe Corporation would have the makings of a dividend-withholding controversy if Digges and Hall are officers and Doe is not. However, if Doe is a director and if unanimous voting for director action is required (as will be suggested in Chapter 6), Doe could retaliate to dividend withholding by refusing to approve salaries for Digges and Hall.**

It is conceivable that a shareholder might also seek judicial intervention to compel the directors *not* to declare a dividend on the grounds that it would be against the best interests of the corporation, or that it would unfairly favor one group of shareholders over another.

> ▪ **For example, preferred shareholders might attack a "nimble" dividend to common shareholders on the grounds that, by diverting current earnings from being used to repair an earned surplus deficit, the nimble dividend imperiled the continued ability of the corporation to pay preferred dividends in the future.**

As with suits to compel dividends, a strong case would be needed to convince a judge that he should interfere with a board decision.

Suits by shareholders to compel or to stop dividends are special cases of shareholder participation in corporate management through shareholder suits, the subject of Section 2.4, below.

(b) Liquidation

How do you put a corporation to rest? The Model Act provides that, after filing the statement of intent to dissolve with the secretary of state of the state of incorporation:

> *the corporation shall proceed to collect its assets, convey and dispose of such of its property as are not to be distributed in kind to its shareholders, pay, satisfy and discharge its liabilities and obligations and do all other acts required to liquidate its business and affairs, and, after paying or adequately providing for the payment of all its obligations, distribute the remainder of its assets, either in cash or kind, among its shareholders according to their respective rights and interests (§87).*

To determine the "respective" rights and interests of shareholders to participate in liquidation of the corporation you look to the provisions of the articles of incorporation. Where there is only one class of shares (common), there will be no "respective" rights and the articles will usually be silent on liquidation rights: each shareholder will simply be entitled to share pro rata in whatever is left after the corporation's debts have been paid. But where the corporation has more than one class of shares (usually common and preferred), the articles will set out any differences in their liquidation rights (see Appendix A.3(d)). Preferred shareholders are usually entitled to receive the face amount of their shares after payment of debts and before any payment to common shareholders, who divide what is left.

> ▪ **The position of common shareholders on liquidation is like that of residuary legatees under a will: they are last in line, but there is no limit on what they may get.**

As with dividends, shareholders can seek judicial assistance either in trying to bring on or to halt the dissolution and liquidation of their corporations. We return to this subject in Chapter 6 when we deal with dissolution and liquidation as a way of dealing with conflict and deadlock within a close corporation.

Section 2.4 Shareholder Participation in Corporate Management Through Shareholder Suits

We now move from looking at how, as an owner of his corporation, a shareholder may participate in its assets to how, still as an owner, he may participate in its management (a function normally entrusted, as we see in Chapters 4 and 5, to directors and officers) through three kinds of shareholder suits: individual, class, and derivative. Since majority shareholders can ordinarily work their will, if they have one, through their voting power (as we see in Chapter 3) and thus do not need to ask the courts for help, this section will be mainly about how minority shareholders can seek a piece of the action by going to court. We examine the varieties of shareholder suits, special procedural requirements for class and derivative suits, and some of the substantive functions that shareholders suits perform. We return to shareholder suits again in Chapter 11 when we focus on how officers and directors cope with their individual liabilities.

(a) Kinds of shareholder suits

As suggested above, shareholders may ask for judicial help in three different capacities. They may sue on their own behalf, as individual shareholders, when they claim that some corporate action will affect them unfairly.

▪ In Chapter 1 we use the illustration of Digges and Hall causing Dighaldoe Corporation to issue 1,000 new shares to each of their wives. If Doe had no protective rights within the corporation (like preemptive rights, or unanimous voting requirements), or if Digges and Hall ignored his protective rights, Doe might go to court on his own behalf to try to block these new share issues which would reduce from one-third to one-fifth his own share of the ownership, control, and earnings of Dighaldoe.

Shareholders may also ask for judicial help in a "class action" on behalf of themselves and other shareholders similarly situated. Here the shareholder is suing as the "representative" of a larger group of shareholders.

▪ If X Corporation has two classes of shareholders, preferred and common, and if P, a preferred shareholder, has reason to believe that X is failing to abide by the provisions in its articles of incorporation concerning the rights of preferred shareholders, P might bring a class action against X and its directors and officers on behalf of all preferred shareholders.

The objection of preferred shareholders to nimble dividends, used as an illustration in the preceding section, would be another instance of a shareholder class action.

These illustrations should not leave the impression, however, that the word "class" has the same meaning in the terms "class action" and "class of shares." For example, all common shareholders with fractional shares would not constitute a separate class of shares but might constitute a separate class for the purpose of bringing a class action.

Finally, shareholders may bring a "derivative action" on behalf of the corporation itself to enforce a corporate right that the corporation has failed to enforce for itself.

▪ If D, a director of X Corporation, has made a large profit in a transaction with X without disclosure of his interest to his fellow directors, and if the officers and directors of X are unwilling to proceed against D, then P, a shareholder of X at the time of the transaction, may be able to bring a derivative action against D on X's behalf.

The differences between these three kinds of law suits turn upon the nature of the interest being asserted: is it an individual interest of the shareholders suing; or is it a common interest of a class of shareholders; or is it an interest of the whole corporation? It is not always possible to answer these questions with assurance, particularly where the allegedly wrongful action is by a person or group with substantial shareholdings and the injury to the shareholders bringing the suit is a consequence of something that was done to the corporation. In such a situation the suing shareholders, to be on the safe side, may join claims of all three kinds in a single legal proceeding (as the plaintiffs did in *Birnbaum* v. *Newport Steel Corp.,* 193 F. (2d) 461 (2d Cir. 1952), to which we return in Section 10.3(c)). The judge, however, will have to sort out what sort of claim is before him in order to hear and decide the case. As we will see, procedures are different in individual, class, and derivative suits. Also the effects of judgments are different. Any relief granted in an individual suit will go to the individual shareholders who are the plaintiffs; in a class suit the results will be shared by all the members of the class (except those who have requested that they be excluded from the class); in a derivative suit the recipient is the corporation. Conversely, a judgment on the merits denying relief will be effective to cut off any future assertion of claims by, as the case may be, the individual plaintiffs, any non-excluded members of the class, or the corporation.

Defendants in shareholder suits can be the corporation, its officers and directors, and outsiders. In derivative suits, where the interest asserted belongs to the corporation, the position of the corporation is complicated. Derivative suits developed as an "equitable" way for a corporation to assert a claim when the officers, directors, and majority shareholders who could authorize its "legal" assertion refused to act. Equity judges permitted shareholders to bring a proceeding against the corporation saying, in effect: either assert the claim against the person who injured you or we will do it for you. If the "corporation" continued to refuse to act and if it failed to justify its inaction, the judge would hear the claim. Thus, a derivative suit was originally two law suits: the shareholder against the corporation to compel action; then the corporation against the alleged wrongdoer. Under modern practice the two steps have been largely merged, but considerable uncertainty remains as to whether the corporation should be treated as a plaintiff or a defendant (which may become important in determining whether there is "diversity of citizenship" between plaintiffs and defendants to provide a basis for trying the case in a federal court), and as to whether the corporation can be represented in the law suit by the lawyer representing the "real" defendants, who frequently are officers and directors of the corporation. The trend seems to be to treat the corporation as a defendant but to require that it be separately represented.

(b) Special controls for class and derivative suits.

Procedural controls, beyond those needed for suits where plaintiffs are suing for themselves alone, are needed for class and derivative suits where shareholder-plaintiffs are suing as representatives or "champions" of other persons: other shareholders or the corporation. Controls are needed to protect defendants, usually corporate officers and directors, from being harassed by nuisance suits and to protect the absent persons, mainly other shareholders who may be affected by the suit, from having their interests inadequately or unfairly represented. These special procedural controls relate to the institution, conduct, and disposition of class and derivative suits.

The most important requirements for starting class suits are that the class be sufficiently numerous that joining all the members of the class as parties in the suit is impracticable; that there be questions of law or fact common to the entire class; and that the plaintiff be able adequately and fairly to represent the class. In addition to these necessary conditions, there also must be an affirmative reason for a class suit, such as risk that individual suits will result in inconsistent judgments or judgments adversely affecting the rights of non-parties (as when shareholders are attacking a corporate reorganization), or conduct by the defendant based on the "classness" of the class (as when a corporation refuses to allow alien shareholders to vote, or where a municipal corporation refuses to allow minority residents to use a public park). During the suit the judge may make protective orders to guard the rights of absent class members. Except when there are reasons for making the judgment apply to the whole class, individual members of the class will be given a chance to "opt out" of the class and proceed on their own, and the judge is supposed to make a reasonable effort to notify class members of this option. Finally and significantly, the suit may not be settled without the judge's approval and with notice to the whole class. Judicial control of settlements affords protection against plaintiffs permitting themselves to be bought off to the detriment of the class.

> ▪ **Note that the class size requirement will usually preclude shareholders of close corporations from bringing class actions: joinder of all shareholders in the class will ordinarily be practicable. While there is no clear line, classes numbering 40 or 50 members would approach the limits of practicable joinder.**

Class action rules, stated for federal courts in Rule 23 of the Federal Rules of Civil Procedure (which have been adopted in substance in many states), give judges broad discretionary powers in hearing and managing class actions, and attitudes of individual judges toward class actions vary considerably. This type of suit has been the subject of controversy and litigation in recent years because it has been made the vehicle for various kinds of "public interest" causes, among them consumer, environment, welfare, minority rights, and civil liberties.

Special controls for derivative suits differ from those for class actions mainly by being more concerned with erecting road blocks to bringing suit and less concerned with controlling the suit once it is brought. There are no problems about the size of the class or absent class members, since the suit is brought on behalf of the corporation.

Two quite different approaches to controlling derivative suits have developed. The approach of the Federal Rules (Rule 23.1), which has been adopted by many states, emphasizes protecting the interests of the corporation by requiring that the plaintiff-shareholder exhaust his remedies within the corporation before bringing suit and that the judge approve any settlement of the suit (as with class actions). On the other hand, the approach of the Model Act (§49), which has been adopted by some important states (probably a minority), emphasizes protecting the defendants. Reflecting the fear that derivative suits will be used as "strike suits" against officers and directors, the Model Act tries to discourage derivative suits by making shareholders who bring them individually liable to the defendants for the expenses of defending the suit, including attorneys' fees, if suit was brought "without reasonable cause," and by requiring the suing shareholder to give security for such expenses if their shares are worth less than $25,000, or represent less than five per cent of the shares. Both Federal Rule 23.1 and Model Act §49 require that the plaintiff be a shareholder "at the time of the transaction of which he complains"—in order to preclude the purchase of a grievance. The Model Act does not require judicial approval of settlements.

A practical consideration, not mentioned in most of the formal rules on derivative suits, is the matter of the plaintiff's attorney's fees if the suit is successful. These fees must be approved by the court and are usually paid by the corporation, since it is the beneficiary of the successful suit; they are likely to run from 20 to 40 per cent of the total recovery. The incentive that causes most derivative suits to be undertaken is the prospect of a substantial fee (often in the tens, sometimes in the hundreds, of thousands of dollars) for the plaintiff's lawyer.

(c) Substantive functions of shareholder suits

The functions of individual and class suits by shareholders are like those of similar suits by other people: to secure judicial help in asserting rights, interests, and grievances. Suits by shareholders are functionally unique only in being based on ownership interests in corporations and in usually being directed against a corporation or its officers, directors, or other shareholders. Plaintiffs assert complaints arising from their rights, as shareholders, in their shares and in the assets and governance of the corporation. For example, shareholders may allege that the corporation has refused to recognize them as shareholders; or that they should participate in a new issue of shares; or that a plan of corporate reorganization is unfair; or that they have been denied the right to vote; or that a corporate decision should have been submitted to shareholder vote; or that the corporation should (or should not) be dissolved and liquidated. Note that these claims generally involve things done (or not done) *by* and not *to* the corporation.

The functions of derivative suits, on the other hand, are quite different from those of ordinary law suits because plaintiffs are asserting rights, not of their own or of others like them, but of the corporation, a separate legal person.

▪ **Derivative suits differ from suits by fiduciaries, like trustees, on behalf of their beneficiaries because shareholders are not under a duty to protect corporate interests. They seem most to resemble suits by taxpayers or citizens to try to compel public officials to perform their duties.**

Derivative suits function for corporate management as an extra conscience (akin to auditors and ombudsmen) which prods, with the prospect of judicial sanctions, corporate officers and directors to do the right thing for their corporations. It is thought that, since neither the SEC nor state officials can effectively police the care and loyalty with which corporations are managed, those persons who arguably have the most to lose from bad management—the owners—should have a limited and controlled right to participate in management to the extent of having a chance to convince a judge that the corporation has been mismanaged. As we will see, allegations of incompetent or unfaithful management can take many forms. Some of the major categories include neglecting responsibilities, failing to enforce corporate rights, self-dealing, appropriating corporate opportunities, trading on inside information, and unfairly preferring one group of shareholders over another.

In summary, it seems that when we call shareholders "owners" of the corporation we are saying something different than what we mean when we speak of people owning "things"; and it is also different than what we mean when we speak of individuals and partners owning a "business." The uniqueness of shareholder ownership results from the interposition between the shareholders and the things and the business of something we call the corporate personality, with its own structure of government, management, and operation. In the chapters that follow we will be examining this structure.

CHECKLIST OF POINTS TO WATCH OUT FOR
IN OWNING YOUR CORPORATION

(References after heading are to Sections of Chapter 2.)

1. The magic of corporate separateness (Section 2.1 (a))

Are you using it to fullest advantage?

Corporations rank with the wheel and the internal combustion engine as devices that help us do what we want to do. Corporations enable resources to be instantly aggregated, separated, and transferred, and risk to be precisely limited. To use corporate separateness to fullest advantage, one must combine respect for its limitations (as we saw at the close of Chapter 1) with imaginative appreciation of its potentialities. This means thinking through what you want to achieve and then hiring the best legal talent available to fashion the appropriate corporate machinery.

2. Choices for corporate investment (Section 2.1 (b))

What will influence your choices between debt and equity and between common and preferred shares?

If you expect your enterprise to be very profitable you will want to finance it to the extent possible by borrowing so you will not have to share profits with other shareholders. And you will want your own shares to be common shares so there will be no limit on your dividends or capital gains (and perhaps also to take advantage of §1244). At the other extreme, if you are mainly interested in protecting your capital and getting an assured return on it, common shares will be less attractive to you than debt securities or preferred shares. The main factors to be balanced in making these decisions are: How much risk are you willing to take? Is current income more important than long-term gain? Do you want to participate in control? And how important is §1244 treatment?

3. Share certificates and their transfers (Section 2.2 (a)-(c))

How can you minimize housekeeping problems relating to lost certificates, fractional shares, and share transfers?

For a certificate representing common shares, see Appendix C.3 (a), and for an assignment of shares represented thereby, appearing on the reverse side of the certificate, see Appendix C.3 (b).

The complications of replacing lost, destroyed, or stolen certificates can be reduced if shareholders are urged to keep them in safe deposit boxes. For by-laws on replacement of certificates, see Appendix B.7 (c).

To avoid the nuisance of issuing fractional shares, take advantage of the authorization in the Model Act (§24) that a corporation may pay those entitled to fractional shares the "fair value" thereof. For a director resolution authorizing purchase of fractional shares, see Appendix F.1 (2).

Risk of mailing negotiable securities can be avoided by using a separate "stock power" instead of the assignment forms on the reverse side of the certificate, and mailing the certificate and stock power in separate envelopes.

4. Identification of shareholders (Section 2.2 (d))

How are shareholder lists fixed for participation in dividends, meetings, and other events?

Alternative ways of determining shareholders entitled to participate in a dividend, meeting, or other event are: (1) to close the corporation's transfer books for a period before the event, or (2) to select a "record date" in advance of the event and to declare that shareholders of record at the close of business on that date are entitled to participate. For a by-law empowering the directors to use either of these procedures, see Appendix B.7 (e).

Since the period before the event may be as long as 50 days, and since closing the corporation's transfer books for this long may create problems, the record date method is ordinarily used. For a director resolution fixing a record date, see Appendix F.3 (a).

5. Declaring dividends (Section 2.3 (a))

What are the major legal constraints on how and when your corporation declares dividends?

You will need a procedure for promptly making public information about dividend action by your directors to guard against charges of trading upon inside information. For further discussion of this problem, see Section 11.4.

You will need to know whether your state of incorporation limits dividends to earned surplus and whether it permits "nimble dividends" from current earnings. For director resolutions declaring dividends from earned surplus and from current earnings, see Appendix F.3 (b) and (c), respectively. And for a resolution declaring a dividend in the corporation's own treasury shares (for which neither surplus nor earnings is needed since no "assets" are distributed), see Appendix F.3 (e).

Law suits to compel your corporation to declare dividends are most likely if your corporation is closely held with some shareholders not participating in management.

For general discussion of the legal constraints upon and the tax consequences of distribution of your corporation's assets to its shareholders, see Chapter 8.

6. Corporate dissolution and liquidation (Section 2.4 (a))

How do you end your corporation and distribute its property?

Dissolution is the legal death of a corporation. Liquidation is the distribution of its estate.

The usual method of dissolution is corporate suicide: voluntary dissolution by act of the corporation. For the needed documents—director resolution recommending dissolution, shareholder resolution to dissolve, statement of intent to dissolve, and articles of dissolution—see Appendix E.7 (a)-(d), respectively. For an agreement among shareholders to consent to voluntary dissolution, see Appendix H.2 (e).

After dissolution and payment of the corporation's debts it is liquidated by distributing its assets among its shareholders. If there is only one class of common shares, each will take pro rata. If there is more than one class of shares, their respective rights are established by the articles of incorporation. Hence, preferred shareholders should take a lively interest in the drafting of the articles. For articles establishing liquidation rights of preferred shares, see Appendix A.3 (d).

For discussion of dissolution and liquidation of a deadlocked close corporation, see Section 6.4 (d).

7. Shareholder suits in general (Section 2.4 (a))

How can minority shareholders challenge corporate management decisions through shareholder suits?

In making your management decisions as corporate officer or director it may be dangerous to ignore their effect on minority shareholders. While such shareholders lack voting power to proceed against you within the corporation, they have an array of legal weapons in the various kinds of lawsuits they can bring—individual, class, and derivative—against you, the corporation, and others. For discussion of how to cope with your individual liability in such suits, see Chapter 11, particularly Section 11.5.

8. Procedural controls on shareholder suits (Section 2.4 (b))

How can you combat such suits at the procedural level?

The law, recognizing that shareholder suits, particularly class and derivative suits, are often brought for their nuisance value, has sought to control their institution, conduct, and disposition. State procedures are generally more favorable to defendants than federal procedures. It will be considerably to your advantage if the forum is a state with the provisions of Model Act §49, which makes plaintiffs liable for expenses of defending suits brought "without reasonable cause" and requires plaintiffs to give security for such expenses where their stakes in the corporation are small.

9. Substantive responses to shareholder suits (Section 2.4 (c))

How can you minimize your individual liabilities?

The best defense to attacks on your management decisions is, of course, to make decisions that are legally correct and ethically justified: to avoid corner-cutting and unfairness. But accusations can be made about even the most careful and honorable managers. Hence, you will also want to take advantage of protections offered by indemnification and insurance which are discussed in Section 11.5 (b). For articles authorizing indemnification and insurance, see Appendix A.9.

3

Governing Your Corporation

3

Governing Your Corporation

In Chapters 1 and 2 we tried to convey the magic by which a new corporate person is created and the unique problems surrounding how that person is "owned." We now begin to examine the structure and functioning of the corporate person, starting with the same people who are our concern in Chapter 2, the shareholders. But now our focus shifts from shareholders as owners of the corporation itself to shareholders as the voting constituency of corporate government: from their legal-proprietary rights to their political-governmental functions. Also, our focus shifts from shareholders as persons to shares as units of voting power, because votes adhere to shares rather than to shareholders. In the chapters that follow we will continue our examination of how corporations are structured and of how they function into the more concrete and particular levels of corporate management and operations, and then we will look at how this complex system of structure and function can be fitted to the special needs of close corporations.

In barest outline, an American corporation, whether it involves one natural person or several million, functions through a three-tiered structure: at the base (or at the top, if you prefer) are the shareholder-electors who vote, mainly to elect directors, but also to pass on other proposals; in the middle are the director-managers, who meet to elect officers and to make policy decisions; and at the operational level are the officer-executives who execute policy and carry on the business of the corporation aided by its employees and agents.

> ▪ Note that shareholders, directors, and officers are institutional components of the corporate structure in a sense that employees and agents are not. They are part of the family, not just hired help. Their ties to the corporation are organic, not just contractual. These ties are not

81

unlike those that bind electors and officials (as distinguished from employees and agents) to civil government. Governments and corporations can exist—legally, at least—without employees, but they cannot exist without electors and officials.

Shareholders, as owners of the corporation, can command directly neither the obedience nor the loyalty of corporate officers and directors, because it is to the corporation, not to the shareholders, that obedience and loyalty are owed. It is through their voting power in the corporation that shareholders can make their wishes felt. This chapter will examine the mechanics of convening shareholder meetings, annual and special; how shareholders vote by proxy; the conduct and business of shareholder meetings; and some of the things officers and directors can do to keep their shareholder constituencies happy.

Keep in mind that ordinarily only the common shareholders are entitled to vote, although in exceptional circumstances preferred shareholders can be given the right.

> **• For example, the articles of incorporation may provide that, if preferred dividends are unpaid for a stated time, preferred shareholders are entitled to vote. Also they would be able to vote on a change in the articles affecting their rights.**

The general rule is one share, one vote, and normally shareholder voting can take place only at meetings. However, the Model Act (§145) and the Delaware Act (§228) provide that, if *all* shareholders consent in writing to a proposal, action may be taken without a meeting. In effect, voting at a meeting can be dispensed with upon unanimous consent: a meaningful option only for close corporations.

Section 3.1 Convening Shareholder Meetings

(a) Times and places of annual meetings

The by-laws of the corporation (see Appendix B.2(b)) usually provide that the annual meeting of shareholders will be held at a designated hour on a designated day of the year (say at 2:00 p.m. on the third Wednesday of October if the corporation is on a fiscal year ending June 30).

> **• For public corporations an interval of approximately 3½ months is usually allowed between the end of the fiscal year and the date of the annual meeting to provide time for preparing year-end financial statements, for writing and printing the annual report, and for preparing and clearing proxy soliciting material (2 to 2½ months); and for then distributing the annual report and proxy materials, and securing the**

return and tabulation of proxies (4 to 6 weeks). You will want to work out a detailed time-table for the events leading up to your annual meeting.

While technical "calls" (see below) are not required for annual meetings, someone, usually the board of directors or the president, must take the initiative to set the machinery in motion to convene the meeting. By-laws will usually be interpreted to permit the board to make limited postponements of annual meetings, but the Model Act provides that, if the annual meeting is not held within any 13 month period, a shareholder may apply to a court for an order that a meeting be held (§28). It is probably not within the power of the board to accelerate the time of the annual meeting, since to do so would reduce the term of office of individual directors.

Turning from time to place, the corporation act and the by-laws usually empower the board to designate (see Appendix F.2(a)) where the annual meeting will be held, although the corporation act or the by-laws may designate (see Appendix B.2(a)) a place (frequently the registered office of the corporation) if no other place is designated. Most states now permit meetings to be held outside of the state of incorporation. The Model Act provides:

> *Meetings of shareholders may be held at such places within or without this State as may be stated in or fixed in accordance with the by-laws. If no other place is stated or so fixed, meetings shall be held at the registered office of the corporation. (§28)*

Public corporations frequently move their annual meetings from place to place to give more shareholders a chance to attend. Also because of the limitation of size, it is often impractical to hold these meetings at a corporate office, so hotels, convention centers, armories, and the like are used.

(b) Calls of special meetings

Directors and officers are under a legal obligation to hold annual meetings on certain dates. Special meetings, on the other hand, are held only when "called." The call of a special meeting should specify its time, place, and purposes. The Model Act provides:

> *Special meetings of the shareholders may be called by the board of directors, the holders of not less than one-tenth of all the shares entitled to vote at the meeting, or such other persons as may be authorized in the articles of incorporation or the by-laws (§28).*

Calls are usually made by the board, although by-laws frequently authorize calls by the chairman of the board, the president, or a designated number of directors (see Appendix B.2 (c)). The power of the holders of one-tenth of the shares entitled to vote to call meetings is more significant for a close than for a public corporation because of the expense in enlisting a large number of widely scattered shareholders.

> ■ Note that in Dighaldoe Corporation, where Digges, Hall, and Doe each hold one-third of the voting shares, any one of them could call a special meeting. Compare this situation with a public corporation with 1,000,000 widely distributed shares, where a shareholder call might require thousands of supporters.

The legal power to call special meetings may be an important tactical weapon in struggles between opposing corporate factions. For example, if a faction which controls the board is opposed by a faction which includes the president, the president may be able to call a special shareholders' meeting in the hope of upsetting his rivals' majority by removals from or additions to the board.

> ■ A similar problem can arise in attempted transfers of corporate control. Suppose group A, which has been controlling the board of X corporation with less than a majority of X's voting shares (we will explore later how this is possible), agrees to sell its X shares and its control of X's board to group B. If P, president of X, has the power to call a shareholders' meeting and if P is not a party to the transfer, group B should insist that group A amend X's by-laws to eliminate P's calling power as a prior condition to the purchase. Otherwise, there is the danger that P will upset the transfer of control to group B by calling a special meeting of shareholders that will put a majority of P's own adherents on the board.

(c) Notices, adjournments, and record dates

While annual meetings do not require calls, it is necessary that the shareholders entitled to vote at both annual and special meetings be given, in the words of the Model Act: "Written notice stating the place, day and hour of the meeting and, in case of a special meeting, the purpose or purposes for which the meeting is called," which must be mailed not less than ten nor more than fifty days before the meeting date (§29) (see Appendix B.2(d)). Notwithstanding this provision, annual meeting notices usually do recite purposes. And both annual and special meeting notices, after setting forth specific purposes, usually conclude with a catch-all purpose: "to transact such other business as may properly come before the meeting or any adjournment or adjournments thereof" (see Appendix D.1(a)). We will be considering what this recital means.

Assuming that the by-laws do not otherwise require, a fresh notice for an adjourned meeting is not required if the time and place of the adjourned meeting is announced at the meeting at which the adjournment is taken; however, if the adjournment is for an extended period or if a new record date is fixed for the adjourned meeting, a new notice should be given. Any business that could be transacted at the original meeting can be done at the adjourned meeting.

Our examination of dividends in Chapter 2 included the fixing of "record dates," by which the specific shareholders entitled to vote or to receive dividends are determined. Under the Model Act, the record date (like the notice) must be not less than ten nor more than fifty days before the meeting (§30). Holders "of record" (according to the records of the corporation) on the record date of shares with voting rights will be entitled to vote at the meeting, even though the ownership of the shares may change between the record date and the meeting, and even though the "beneficial" owner on the record date is someone other than the record owner.

Section 3.2 Proxy Voting by Shareholders

In the absence of a provision in the articles of incorporation requiring that shareholders vote at meetings in person, it is the general rule that shareholders may vote in person or "by proxy." This section explores how proxies are granted and voted, areas governed by the laws of the state where the corporation is incorporated; how proxies are solicited from shareholders, an area which, as to public corporations, has been made subject to extensive federal regulation; and the special problems, also subject to federal regulation as to public corporations, of proxy contests (where rival factions are soliciting proxies for the election of directors), and of shareholder proposals (where directors may be required to make the proxy machinery available for voting on proposals that they oppose).

Note that the word "proxy" can be used to convey three different meanings: to refer to a *person* authorized to act for another ("P made A his proxy to vote P's shares"); to refer to the *authority* of a person authorized to act for another ("P gave A his proxy to vote P's shares"); and to refer to the *document* granting the authority ("P signed a proxy authorizing A to vote P's shares").

The typical proxy document is likely to use the word in all three of these senses (as we will be doing in this book). The document itself will be designated "Proxy" and "Proxy No. ____." It will recite that the signer hereby appoints A, B, and C "the proxies of the signer" and will describe how "this proxy will be voted" (see Appendix D.1(b)).

For public corporations the proxy document is usually a punch card, for use in data processing equipment, punched with the number of shares held by the shareholder whose name and address is imprinted on the card. Some corporations also imprint the number of shares on the card. However, this practice increases postage costs in mailing proxy material: under U.S. Postal Service mail-classification regulations imprinting the number of shares "personalizes" the proxy card, making it necessary that the material be sent by first class mail; without the number of shares the material can be sent by third class mail.

The proxy persons are usually officers or directors of the corporation (say, the chairman of the board, the president, and the secretary) who are most likely to be at the meeting. As a hedge against emergencies, they will be named as follows: "A, B, and C, and each of them, with power of substitution." This language empowers any one of A, B, or C, or anyone designated by A, B, or C, to vote the shares.

(a) Granting and voting of proxies

Proxy voting involves an agency relationship with the shareholder as the principal and with the person authorized to vote the shareholder's shares at a designated meeting as the agent.

> ▪ **Proxy voting resembles proxy marriage with the shareholder in the position of the absent bride or groom and the proxy in the position of her or his stand-in at the ceremony. However, the corporate proxy, who is typically granted all the powers the shareholder would possess if personally present, would seem to have broader delegated powers than the marital stand-in.**

The proxy relationship differs from the usual principal-agent relationship in how it happens. Usually the principal takes the initiative to find and empower the agent. With proxies, the agent typically seeks out the principal and asks to be empowered. It is this "solicitation" process that has become the subject of federal regulation.

Other aspects of the granting and voting of corporate proxies continue to be governed by the agency and corporation law of the state of incorporation. Questions most likely to arise concern the signing and revocation of proxies. The general rule on signing is that the shareholder of record should sign as his name appears on the corporate record, subject to the following qualifications:

—If shares are held jointly, any one of the joint owners may sign.

—If shares are held by an executor, administrator, trustee, guardian or other fiduciary, the fiduciary may sign, indicating the capacity in which he is signing.

—If shares are held by a corporation, the signature should be the full corporate name, by a duly authorized officer.

Proxies are ordinarily revocable until they are voted. If, as sometimes happens in a proxy contest, a shareholder grants successive proxies to different agents, all but the last proxy are considered revoked. Thus, it is important that shareholders date their proxies. The granting of a proxy, or a series of proxies, does not prevent the shareholder from attending the meeting, revoking the proxy, and voting in person; however, mere attendance does not of itself revoke the proxy.

The usual management proxy card does not list director-candidates. The shareholder can authorize that his shares be voted in the election of directors as set forth in the proxy statement, or he can withhold authority to vote in the election of directors. The card does not provide means for him to direct that his shares be voted for some of the candidates named in the proxy statement, nor to direct that some but not all of his shares be voted for the named candidates. As to proposals for shareholder action, however, whether proposed by the directors or by individual shareholders, the proxy card provides boxes for the shareholder to direct his vote "for" or "against," with an indication of which way the directors recommend. The management card usually states that, unless the shareholder otherwise specifies, his proxy will be voted for management nominees for directorships and as recommended by the directors with regard to proposals.

As proxy cards are received by the corporation or its transfer agents during the four to six week period between the mailing of proxy material and the meeting, running totals are maintained of numbers of shares to be voted for director-nominees and for and against proposals. At the meeting final totals are determined, taking into account proxies and revocations delivered at the meeting, and these final share totals are included in ballots signed by the individual proxies and cast for the various items of business to be acted upon at the meeting. Frequently the proxy ballots will be virtually the only ballots cast at the meeting.

(b) Solicitation of proxies; federal regulation

While technical rules about granting and voting proxies remain subject to state law, for public corporations the more discretionary area of disclosure requirements for proxy solicitations has been largely taken over by federal regulation under SEC supervision. Failures by corporate managements to make adequate disclosures to their shareholders when they asked them for their prox-ies, combined with the unwillingness of state legislatures to impose stricter rules, led to inclusion in the Securities Exchange Act of 1934 of Section 14. This statute empowers the SEC to regulate the solicitation of proxies for listed corpo-rations and for those with assets over $1,000,000 and 500 or more shareholders.

The SEC has exercised its delegated powers under Section 14 largely through regulations which specify what must appear in the "proxy statement," the document which accompanies the proxy card and the notice of the meeting (sometimes there is also an informal letter from the chairman or the president). This collection of documents comprise the "proxy soliciting material" which is mailed to shareholders (frequently with the annual report) 4 to 6 weeks before the meeting. The suggested 2 to 2½ months interval between the end of the fiscal year and mailing of the annual report and proxy soliciting material is needed in part because proxy soliciting material of regulated corporations must be cleared with the SEC in advance of mailing to shareholders.

SEC regulations call for disclosure in management proxy statements of detailed information about the following when directors are to be elected:

(1) Director nominees:
   (a) their names, principal occupations or employment and other busi-ness affiliations (these should include directorships and part-nerships in other business organizations, but need not include charitable and education affiliations, such as memberships on hos-pital and university boards),
   (b) length of service as directors
   (c) number of the corporation's shares beneficially owned, (nominees usually "disclaim" beneficial ownership of shares held by other members of their families, and by trusts under which they are income beneficiaries),
   (d) service on committees of the board of directors, and
   (e) whether directors are elected by a majority or plurality of the votes cast or by cumulative voting.

(2) Remuneration and retirement benefits for top management:
   (a) aggregate direct remuneration paid or accrued to each of the corpo-ration's five most highly paid executive officers or directors whose total remuneration exceeds $50,000, and to all directors or officers during the fiscal year, and
   (b) the aggregate of contingent forms of remuneration, which includes, though it is not limited to, the following: pension or retirement plans; employment contracts; deferred compensation plans; an-

nuities; stock options and stock appreciation rights; stock purchase, profit-sharing, and thrift plans.

When other matters, in addition to or other than the election of directors, are to be acted upon at the shareholders' meeting at the request of the directors—such as mergers, consolidations, acquisitions, employee benefit plans, and charter amendments—the management proxy statement is required to set forth detailed information concerning such matters.

> ▪ As suggested in Chapter 1, shareholder action on acquisitions may be avoided if the corporation has a sufficient cushion of authorized but unissued shares that amendment of the articles is unnecessary to authorize issue of the shares needed for the acquisition. And if the parent owns 90% of the shares of the acquired company, it can be merged into the parent company by a "short form" merger which will not require approval of the shareholders of either company (see Model Act §75).

It has become customary for management proxy statements to seek authority to vote for a resolution by shareholders ratifying action of the board appointing a named accounting firm independent public accountants for the current fiscal year.

> ▪ Shareholder ratification of appointment of independent public accountants, while not legally required, is a useful way of emphasizing the independence from management of the outside auditors. Ratification, by a majority of the votes cast, seems preferable to appointment by the shareholders: shareholders of a public corporation are seldom in a position to make an informed selection of outside auditors; and since the shareholders meeting is usually not held until 3 or 4 months into the current fiscal year, it does not seem right to leave the corporation without outside auditors during this period. As a precaution, the proxy statement should state that if the resolution is rejected, or if the named firm declines to act or becomes incapable of acting, or if their employment is discontinued, the directors will appoint other public accountants whose continued employment after the following annual meeting of shareholders shall be subject to ratification by the shareholders.

After setting forth any shareholder proposals (see subsection (d), below), management proxy statements usually conclude with a brief catch-all section dealing with matters not mentioned in the proxy statements, how the proxy solicitation will be financed and conducted, and revocation of proxies, along the following lines:

—Other matters: Management knows of no other matters to be presented at the meeting. If other matters come before the meeting, it is the intention of management proxies to vote on such matters in accordance with their best judgment.

▪ **In practice, proposals of substance not mentioned in the proxy statement are seldom voted upon at the meeting. The chairman will rule out of order proposals that management does not want voted upon. If management wants a shareholder vote, the chairman will adjourn the meeting until a new proxy solicitation can be made securing specific authorization for proxies to vote shares for or against the new proposal.**

—Costs and methods of solicitation: The corporation will bear the cost of the management solicitation. Copies of proxy soliciting material will be mailed to shareholders, and employees of the corporation may communicate with shareholders to solicit their proxies. Brokers and others holding shares in their names, or in the names of nominees, may request and forward copies of the material to beneficial owners and seek authority for execution of proxies, and the corporation will reimburse them for their expenses at rates approved by the New York Stock Exchange.

▪ **If the corporation plans to hire professional proxy solicitors, or to use advertising or follow-up mailings, appropriate disclosure should be made.**

—Proxy revocation: A shareholder giving a proxy may revoke it by notifying the secretary in writing any time before it is voted.

(c) Proxy contests

When only a management slate of director-candidates is in the field, shareholders' only choices are to grant or withhold authority to vote their shares for the management candidates. These choices increase when a "proxy contest" is precipitated. A proxy contest can be called a corporate rebellion: an effort to transfer corporate power by soliciting proxies from shareholders to elect or to remove directors against the wishes of a majority of the incumbent directors.

The insurgents in a proxy contest may be a faction of the existing management. As we will see, factions are more likely to develop if the directors are elected by cumulative voting. And in some situations it may be hard to tell which side is the "management" entitled to use corporate resources in waging the contest.

▪ **Suppose the board of X corporation becomes divided into two factions: one supporting A, the president; the other supporting B, who**

wants to be president. B convinces a majority of the directors that A should be removed from office, but before the board has acted A calls a special shareholders' meeting to remove B and his supporters as directors and to replace them with A's nominees. Is the president or the majority of the board the "management" of X corporation? More to the point, which side can use corporate resources for their solicitation? While it is clear that both sides would be entitled to the corporation's shareholder list (because even an outsider would be so entitled), the cases leave it unclear whether both sides could use corporate funds and employees.

The more common proxy contest involves not an internal uprising but rather an attack by an outside group, where there is no question about who is management and where the effort is to replace all or substantially all of the incumbent directors. Here, as noted above, the outside group could secure the shareholder list (which is available for any "proper corporate purpose," which has been held to include a proxy contest) but would be required, at least initially, to finance their proxy solicitation themselves. If they win the fight and install a friendly board, it is predictable that the new board will authorize that they be reimbursed for their expenses. In such situations the cases support the corporation paying all of the battle costs: those of the defeated incumbents because they were the management when the battle began; those of the victorious insurgents because they are now the management. Unsuccessful insurgents must bear their own costs.

> ■ **This result is in line with the general principles of political struggle: a regime is legitimate until it is replaced; and the only legitimate revolutions are those that succeed.**

Proxy contests can be very expensive. For some of the larger contests, the costs on each side have run into hundreds of thousands of dollars. The normal costs of a proxy solicitation—legal fees for preparing soliciting materials and clearing them with the SEC; costs of printing and mailing the materials to shareholders; and costs of tabulating the returns—for most listed corporations run into tens of thousands of dollars. The costs rise if professional proxy solicitors are used to "get out the vote." In a hard fought contest there are usually professional solicitors on both sides and there are other additional costs, such as multiple mailings to answer charges made by the other side, advertisements, telephone calls, entertainment, and other campaign expenditures.

In recent years the expense of proxy contests combined with depressed stock market prices has caused some groups interested in securing control of a corporation to substitute tender offers for proxy contests. With a tender offer, the outsider uses his money to buy the shares themselves instead of spending it for campaign expenses to secure only proxies. We return to tender offers in Chapter 10.

SEC regulation of proxy contests has increased substantially in the last two decades to require more complete disclosure of the parties behind attempts of opposition group to elect their own director-candidates through the solicitation of proxies. These regulations have been motivated in part by fear that proxy contests were being launched by "raiders" as parts of schemes to "loot" corporate assets. Corporations considered prime targets for raids are those with book values in excess of market values, poor earnings and dividend records, and large numbers of disgruntled shareholders.

(d) Shareholder proposals

A virtually cost-free, but not highly effectual, way for individual shareholders to seek support from their fellow shareholders for proposals, generally not approved by their directors and officers, concerning corporate government, management, and operations, is provided by the use of the proxy machinery for "shareholder proposals." SEC regulations require, subject to several important conditions, that managements include in their proxy soliciting material descriptions of and opportunities to vote for or against proposals properly submitted by individual shareholders. Note that, unlike proxy contests—where contestants must make their own solicitations naming their own proxies—proponents of shareholder proposals get a free ride on the management solicitation and management proxies are required to vote on shareholder proposals as instructed by the shareholders executing the proxies, even though they may thereby be voting against the recommendations of the directors.

As might be expected, shareholder proposals are but rarely adopted by a majority of the shareholders of a corporation. They do, however, serve significant functions, and their use seems to be increasing. They provide a simple, inexpensive method of bringing minority positions to the attention of thousands, and sometimes millions, of shareholders—to the extent, of course, that shareholders bother to read proxy soliciting material at all. Furthermore, they require officers and directors to come up with plausible reasons why they are recommending that shareholders vote against such proposals.

> ▪ **There have even been a few shareholder proposals that have been adopted by managements. The following practices, now quite general, have been the subjects of shareholder proposals: shareholder action to approve independent public accountants, holding annual meetings at locations where more shareholders can attend, and distributing to shareholders post-meeting reports summarizing what happened at shareholder meetings.**

In order for directors and officers to be required to include specific shareholder proposals in the management proxy soliciting materials, the proposals must meet conditions relating to the procedures followed in asserting them, their subject matter, and the frequency with which they can be repeated.

A proposal for annual meetings must be submitted by a shareholder of record to the corporation at least 70 days before the date on which proxy materials were mailed to shareholders the year before. It must contain the resolution proposed for adoption by the shareholders and a statement, of not more than 200 words, of reasons in support of the resolution.

Directors and officers are not required to include in their proxy materials shareholder proposals on the following:

—Personal claims or grievances of the shareholder.

—Requests for action concerning a matter, including a general economic, political, racial, religious, social or similar cause, that is not significantly related to the corporation's business or within its control. Abolition by a bus company of racially segregated seating was held to be within this exemption.

—Matters relating to the conduct of the ordinary business operations of the corporation, such as prices, wages, and choice of suppliers.

> ▪ **Some managements with confidence that shareholders will follow their recommendations have adopted a policy of avoiding arguments with the SEC about doubtful shareholder proposals by including them in the proxy materials in the expectation that they will be voted down.**

Kinds of shareholder proposals that are typically accepted for submission to shareholder vote include: adoption of cumulative voting for election of directors; dollar limits on pensions paid to retired employees; periodic resubmission to shareholders of employee benefit plans; elimination or modification of stock option plans; limitations on charitable giving by the corporation; reports to shareholders on minority employment; replacement of the firm of independent public accountants who act as auditors.

In addition to procedural and subject-matter requirements, managements' obligations to include shareholder proposals in their proxy materials are further limited by SEC rules on the frequency with which proposals need to be re-submitted. To minimize repeated voting on the same proposals, in order to harass managements or to publicize individual shareholders or their fringe causes, a management's obligation to re-submit a proposal is made contingent upon when the proposal was last submitted and the percentage of the shareholder vote which it then received. The SEC formula for resubmissions is as follows:

If substantially the same proposal has been submitted to shareholders within the past 5 calendar years, it may be omitted from the management's proxy material for a meeting held within 3 calendar years after the last previous submission; provided that

(i) If the proposal was submitted at only one meeting, it received less than 3 per cent of the votes; or

(ii) If the proposal was submitted to only two meetings, it received on its second submission less than 6 per cent of the votes; or

(iii) If the proposal was submitted at three or more meetings, it received on its latest submission less than 10 per cent of the votes. (See SEC Rule 14a-8)

▪ **Thus, if a proposal receives less than 3% of the vote, it may be omitted for the next three meetings. If a proposal gets over 3%, it may be repeated once, within the five year period, but to be repeated again within this period it must get over 6%. If a proposal gets over 3% the first try and over 6% the second try, it may be repeated a third time during the five year period, but to be repeated a fourth time, it must get over 10% on the third try. Thus, if a proposal gets 3.1% in 19X5, 6.1% in 19X6 and 10.1% in 19X7, management would have to include it in 19X8. However, if it received only 9.9% in 19X8, it could be omitted in 19X9.**

Section 3.3 Conducting Shareholder Meetings

In this chapter we have been examining how shareholder meetings are convened and how shareholders can empower others to vote their shares by proxy. Now, with these preliminaries behind us, we proceed to the main course: the actual conduct and business of shareholder meetings. A fundamental point to keep in mind is that shareholder meetings differ from most other kinds of meetings in that the operational units that are counted are not persons but shares. With the help of the proxy system, thousands and even millions of shareholders may be physically absent while their shares are legally present and voting.

This section considers how many shares must be present to hold a meeting and how the voting is done in general; then it looks at shareholder voting on some specific questions: election of directors (without and with cumulative voting and classes of directors), removal of directors, and extraordinary proposals; finally, it examines voting by classes of shares.

(a) Quorum requirements

For a meeting to be a legal meeting there must be a legal quorum: a minimum percentage, fixed by law, of the shares outstanding and entitled to vote on the record date for the meeting must be present at the meeting in person or represented by proxy. Absent a quorum, there can be no legal meeting, and any efforts on behalf of the shares present to transact business is without legal effect.

▪ The statutes and cases are in conflict as to whether once a quorum is present it can be broken by some of the shares withdrawing from the meeting. The better rule seems to be that a quorum must be present when any item of business is to be acted upon.

Particularly in close corporations, as we will see in Chapter 6, quorum requirements may provide a way for shareholders to veto shareholder action that they oppose by staying away from the meeting and preventing a vote. Thus, the percentage of shares required for a quorum is a matter worthy of careful attention.

The minimum (and in a few states a maximum) percentages of shares entitled to vote for shareholder meeting quorums are fixed by state corporations acts and by the articles of incorporation and by-laws of individual corporations (see Appendix A.6(c) and B.2(e)). Most state acts provide that in the absence of some other provisions, a majority of the shares entitled to vote constitute a quorum. Under the Model Act (§32) a greater or lesser quorum than a majority can be required, in the articles or by-laws, except that the quorum may not be less than one-third of the shares entitled to vote at the meeting. Treasury shares and shares held by a subsidiary cannot be counted in determining the presence of a quorum. Under the Delaware Act (§216) a quorum seems to be whatever is provided in the certificate of incorporation or by-laws.

Public corporations generally do not vary the majority quorum requirement. Close corporations may try to tailor quorum provisions to meet their special needs.

—A high quorum protects minority shareholders from the majority, but makes it more difficult to hold meetings and increases the danger of deadlock. With a 75% quorum requirement, 26% of the shares can prevent a meeting.

—A low quorum makes it easy to hold meetings and makes deadlocks unlikely, but permits a minority to act without majority participation. With a 40% quorum requirement, as few as 21% of the shares may be able to elect directors or to take other shareholder action.

(b) General voting requirements

Quorum requirements are stated as percentages of the total shares entitled to vote at the meeting. While a few basic corporate changes may require the affirmative vote of a percentage of such total shares, voting requirements for most shareholder actions are stated as percentages of the shares represented at the meeting.

▪ Note that, in addition to shares entitled to vote and shares represented at the meeting, there is a third possible denominator for the fraction: shares actually voting. And under some state laws, directors can be elected by a plurality of the votes cast.

As with quorums, percentages required for voting are fixed by state incorporation acts and by articles and by-laws (see Appendix A.6(c) and B.2(e)). The usual requirement is that the affirmative vote of a majority of the shares represented at the meeting are needed for a director-candidate to be elected or for a proposition to carry. Under the Model Act (§32) a greater than majority vote can be required in the articles or by-laws. Again as with quorums, public corporations generally do not vary the majority voting requirement, while close corporations may set higher-than-majority requirements to protect minority shareholders.

▪ Why are high voting requirements needed if the corporation already has high quorum requirements? A minority shareholder might not want to prevent a meeting from being held at all; he might only want to be able to block specific proposals.
      Conversely, why are high quorum requirements needed if there are high voting requirements? A minority shareholder might not want to have to attend the meeting in order to exercise his veto powers.

As we have noted, it is the person in whose name shares are registered at the close of business on the record date for the meeting who is entitled to vote these shares. The corporation need not concern itself with any fiduciary or other restrictions (such as voting trusts (see Appendix H.3) or voting agreements) that may limit the registered owner's freedom of action as to how he votes his shares. And only shares that are issued and outstanding on the record date can be voted (or be counted in determining a quorum). Thus, authorized but unissued shares, issued shares that have been reacquired by the corporation (called "treasury shares," because they are said to be held in the corporate treasury), and shares held by majority-owned subsidiaries of the corporation (and thus essentially treasury shares) are not included in shares entitled to vote.

(c) Election of directors:
seat-by-seat voting for full board

The principal governmental act performed by shareholders is to vote their shares for the election of directors. It is through their power to elect the board of directors that shareholders participate in corporate government.

The "normal" election procedure is to fill all of the seats on the board each year at the corporation's annual meeting by some form of majority or plurality voting, with each voting share carrying the right to cast one vote for one candidate for each seat. (A shareholder may vote for a candidate or may refrain from voting; he cannot just vote "against" a candidate.) In effect, each seat is filled in a separate election. As we will explore in sub-section (d), quite drastic departures from this election procedure may be introduced through use of cumulative voting and classes of directors.

Within the normal, seat-by-seat procedure for electing directors several variations are possible as to the vote required to elect directors. Is a plurality (the largest number of votes of any of the candidates) sufficient, or is a majority (more than half) required? And if a majority is needed, a majority of what: of the shares outstanding and entitled to vote, of the shares represented at the meeting and entitled to vote, or of the votes cast? To answer these questions your lawyer will need to examine the wording of your corporation act and of your articles and by-laws.

> ▪ **To illustrate the different possible results, suppose that a corporation has 1,000 shares entitled to vote, of which 600 are represented at the meeting and 500 are voted in an election to fill a seat for which there are three candidates—A, B, and C—who receive, respectively, 300, 100, and 100 votes. A would have both a plurality and majority of the votes cast; however, he would not have the affirmative vote of either a majority of the shares represented at the meeting (301) or a majority of the shares outstanding (501).**

While the Model Act and the Delaware Act are in agreement in requiring the larger majority based on outstanding shares for shareholder approval of extraordinary proposals—such as, amendments to the articles of incorporation, mergers and consolidations, and dissolution—the two Acts are quite different on ordinary shareholder voting, including election of directors.

—The Delaware Act provides: "the certificate of incorporation or by-laws of any corporation may specify the number of shares ... the holders of which shall be present or represented by proxy at any meeting in order to constitute a quorum for, and the votes that shall be necessary for, the transaction of any business" (§216). Thus, a Delaware corporation may provide for election of directors by a majority or a plurality of the votes cast at the meeting.

> ▪ **For maximum flexibility and as a precaution against elections being deadlocked when there are more than two candidates, a Delaware public corporation will probably want to provide for election by a plurality of the votes cast.**

—The Model Act provides: "If a quorum is present, the affirmative vote of the majority of shares represented at the meeting and entitled to vote on the subject matter shall be the act of the shareholders, unless the vote of a greater number or voting by classes is required by this Act or the articles of incorporation or by-laws" (§32). Thus, a Model Act corporation may not provide for election of directors by a majority or plurality of the votes cast.

> ▪ **Note that shareholders (whose shares are represented at the meeting for quorum purposes and for purposes of determining the majority needed for election) who do not vote at all, vote against a candidate as effectively as they would if they had voted for someone else.**

How are director-candidates nominated? The usual procedure is for the existing board of directors to designate (see Appendix F.4(a)), well in advance of the meeting (three or four months for public corporations, because of the time required for preparation and clearance of proxy materials and solicitation of proxies), a slate of candidates whose names and data will be set forth in the management's proxy statement. As we saw in Section 3.2(c) on proxy contests, if dissident directors or shareholders wish to offer opposition candidates to some or all of the management's candidates, the dissidents must make their own proxy solicitation. Then shareholders will have a choice between rival candidates.

Absent a proxy contest, the options of a shareholder of a public corporation are to vote for or not to vote for the management candidates. If he signs and returns his proxy, his shares will be represented at the meeting for quorum and majority purposes and will be voted for the management candidates. If he throws his proxy in the waste basket, his shares will not be represented at the meeting for quorum or majority purposes. If he signs and returns his proxy with instructions that it not be voted for management candidates, his shares will be represented at the meeting for quorum and majority purposes but will not be voted in the election of directors.

> ▪ **Under the Model Act, this latter course seems to be the most negative response a shareholder can make since it makes election of the management candidate more difficult. But for a Delaware corporation with a majority or plurality of the votes cast provision, this course seems to have no consequences.**

If he wants to take the trouble of making the necessary changes in the proxy form (which public corporations do not ordinarily make easy for him to do), he can also sign and return his proxy with instructions that it not be voted for *some* of the management candidates. Then his shares will be represented at the meeting for quorum and majority purposes for election to each seat but will be voted only as he has instructed.

Under seat-by-seat voting each seat is filled separately without regard to the size of the board; any votes cast for losing candidates have no effect. Consequently, the group that controls enough shares to elect one candidate ordinarily can elect the whole board. Under the most stringent conditions for majority voting, those who control 50% plus one share of the shares outstanding and entitled to vote are assured of being able to name all of the directors, no matter the size of the board. This all-or-nothing elective power generally makes sense for public corporations because it reduces the danger of the board being divided into factions that distrust one another; however, it also leads to self-perpetuating boards, particularly with corporations with widely distributed shares, because the chances are minimal that an opposition group will be able to muster the votes needed to oust the incumbents.

(d) Election of directors: cumulative voting and classes of directors

In Chapter 1 we saw that cumulative voting is an alternative to seat-by-seat voting that you may want to write into your articles of incorporation (see Appendix A.6(b)) especially, as we see in Chapter 6, if yours is a close corporation. We now need to examine the mechanics of and the policy considerations for and against cumulative voting. We also examine the device of electing directors by classes, which has been mainly used to offset the effects of cumulative voting.

Cumulative voting is a way of providing minority representation on a board of directors. It developed, most strongly in the Middle West and South, in the late nineteenth century as part of the populist opposition to big business. In some states it has been made mandatory; more generally, it is optional.

Under cumulative voting each shareholder entitled to vote in the election may cast votes, equal to the number of shares he holds times the number of directors to be elected, and may cumulate his votes for one or more candidates as he chooses: each seat is *not* regarded as a separate election.

> ▪ If a shareholder holds 100 shares in a corporation for which three directors are to be elected, under cumulative voting he may cast 300 votes for one candidate or divide his 300 votes among the candidates. In contrast, under seat-by-seat voting, he may cast 100 votes for each seat; while he may split his votes among candidates for the same seat, he may not transfer votes from one seat to another.

Like proportional representation, cumulative voting makes possible what is not possible under seat-by-seat voting: shareholders or groups of shareholders controlling less than half the shares may be able to elect some of the directors. And the larger the total number of directors to be elected, the smaller the minority needed to elect a director. Since it takes one more candidate than there are seats to be filled to create a contest, by dividing the total number of shares entitled to vote by the number of seats to be filled *plus one* and then adding one share to the resulting number of shares, we can determine the number of shares needed to assure representation on the board in a given situation. It is important that officers, directors, and shareholders of close corporations understand the mathematics of cumulative voting, particularly the consequences of changing the number of directors to be elected.

> **▪ Suppose there are 1,000 shares entitled to vote with shareholders A, B, and C holding 648, 251, and 101 shares, respectively. Under seat-by-seat voting A would have a clear majority for each seat, no matter how many seats were being filled, and could name all of the directors. Under cumulative voting, however, A can be assured of this result only if a single director is being elected. If two directors are being elected B and C can join forces and elect one of the directors: together they have 352 shares and the best A can do when two seats are filled is to vote 324 shares for each seat.**
>
> **If we increase the number of directors to be elected to three, A's position improves. He now can fill two seats, voting 324 shares for each seat, because even if B and C join forces against him the best they can muster for *two* seats is 176 shares each. B's position also improves when the seats to be filled are increased from two to three: now he has enough votes to elect a director without C's help, because he has just over one-fourth of the shares (the vote would probably be 324 shares each for A's two candidates; 251 shares for B's candidate). C's 101 shares have become, in effect, disenfranchised.**
>
> **If we increase the number of directors to be elected to nine, A's position remains essentially the same because he can fill six seats, which means that he can still choose two-thirds of the board. But there is a power shift between B and C, because now C's 101 shares are no longer disenfranchised: they can elect one director if nine seats are being filled, with B's 251 shares electing the other two (the vote would probably be 108 shares each for A's six candidates, 126 and 125 for B's two candidates, and 101 shares for C's candidate). B's control power would diminish from one-third to two-ninths, and, to maintain his position as against A, B must now make an alliance with C.**

The number of directors that are elected each year can be changed, not only by changing the size of the board, but also by dividing the board into classes so that (like the United States Senate) only a portion of the board stands for election each year. In states where cumulative voting is mandatory (and sometimes where it is optional), corporations wishing to keep fairly large boards but also wishing to reduce the impact of cumulative voting have resorted to election of directors by classes. In a few states this device has been disallowed as contrary to the purposes of cumulative voting. At the other extreme, at least one court permitted the division of a three seat board into three classes which effectively transformed cumulative voting into seat-by-seat voting. The Model Act has taken the middle position of permitting provision in the articles of incorporation for classification of directors (with or without cumulative voting) but only when the board of directors shall consist of nine or more members, and the number of classes are limited to two or three, making three directors the minimum class (§37).

> • In our illustration, B would favor dividing a nine member board into three classes; it would restore his undivided control of one-third of the board, because he could name one of the three directors elected each year. C, on the other hand, would oppose classification since he stands to lose his assured seat.
>
> A has interests in both directions. With nine seats being filled each year, the seats he does not control are split between B and C, which might be to A's advantage. But if A should want to control all the seats by acquiring more shares, he can achieve this end more readily with classification. With nine seats being filled each year, he needs 801 shares to assure eight seats and 901 to assure nine; with three seats being filled, he can assure all nine seats with 751 shares (with which he can elect three directors each year by voting his shares 251, 250, 250— leaving the outstanding 249 shares powerless.

(e) Removal of directors

Like the impeachment power of legislatures and the power of universities to dismiss tenured faculty, the power of shareholders to remove directors is rarely used because of its very potency. Removal is such a raw exercise of power that it usually requires in practice an extreme case of misconduct. Also, shareholders as a body, particularly if they are numerous, are an awkward tribunal before which to try allegations of misconduct. If there are ways to work around removal proceedings—such as requesting resignations, waiting for terms to expire, or increasing the size of the board and voting down the offending directors—they will usually be used.

Removal raises several legal questions that need examination: whether your state corporation law requires a showing of cause for removal; whether the vote required for removal is integrated with cumulative voting and classes of directors; and how removal is to be handled when shares of particular classes are entitled to elect directors.

Partly because of the difficulties, both procedural and substantive, in proving the existence of cause, the trend of the law is to eliminate the cause requirement and to make removal or non-removal simply a matter for shareholder vote.

■ The problem is illustrated by the difficulties experienced in the impeachment proceedings against President Nixon in formulating the grounds for impeachment.

The Model Act has adopted the approach of allowing removal to be either "with or without cause," providing:

> *At a meeting of shareholders called expressly for that purpose, directors may be removed in the manner provided in this section. Any director or the entire board of directors may be removed, with or without cause, by a vote of the holders of a majority of the shares then entitled to vote at an election of directors. (§39)*

Under the Model Act, if the proposition before the shareholders is the removal of the entire board, removal can be accomplished by a majority vote, without regard to whether directors were elected by cumulative voting. This procedure seems fair, because cumulative voting can be used in electing the new board, and any removed directors who still have the allegiance of enough shareholders to elect them by cumulative voting can be put back on the board. The Model Act goes on to provide for selective removal of less than the entire board as follows:

> *In the case of a corporation having cumulative voting, if less than the entire board is to be removed, no one director may be removed if the votes cast against his removal would be sufficient to elect him if then cumulatively voted at an election of the entire board, or, if there be classes of directors, at an election of the class of directors of which he is a part (§39).*

■ Suppose, in our illustration of 1000 shares divided 648 in A, 251 in B, and 101 in C, with a three member board of which A has elected two members and B and C the third, A causes a shareholders meeting to be called to remove directors. A, with a majority of the shares, can remove the entire board. But he cannot by himself remove the director elected by B and C. They can cast their 1056 votes (352 x 3 = 1056) against their director's removal, and these votes "would be sufficient to elect him if then cumulatively voted at an election of the entire board." In other words, A's 1944 cumulative voting votes (648 x 3 = 1944) would be insufficient to remove a single director if B and C cast their 1056 votes against removal, because 751 votes would be sufficient to elect a single director to a board of three: the best other candidates could do would be 750, 750, and 749.

Note that in this illustration we have transposed shares into votes in order to fit the language of the Model Act. Note also that, by providing that a director may not be removed if the votes against his

removal would elect him at an election of the *entire* board, the Model Act guards against cumulative voting being under-cut by dividing the board into classes and then removing.

To cover situations where shares of particular classes are entitled to elect directors, the Model Act provides:

Whenever the holders of the shares of any class are entitled to elect one or more directors by the provisions of the articles of incorporation, the provisions of this section shall apply, in respect to the removal of a director or directors so elected, to the vote of the holders of the outstanding shares of that class and not to the vote of the outstanding shares as a whole (§39).

▪ If class A shareholders are entitled to elect three out of nine directors, a majority of class A shares can remove all of the Class A directors. For removal of less than all the class A directors, the above requirements about votes sufficient to elect if voted cumulatively shall apply.

(f) Extraordinary proposals for shareholder vote

State corporation acts have usually prescribed more rigorous procedures for securing shareholder approval of extraordinary proposals that, if adopted, would change the corporation's basic structure, its separateness, or even its very existence, than those prescribed for shareholder voting on the ordinary, recurring items of business—such as, election of directors, designation of independent public accountants, and adoption or amendment of employee benefit plans. These extraordinary proposals fall into three general categories:

—Amendments to the articles of incorporation and reductions of stated capital: changes in the corporation's internal structure which do not involve outsiders;

—Mergers and consolidations with other corporations and sales or exchanges of all or substantially all of the corporation's assets other than in the ordinary course of business: situations where dissenting shareholders have specified rights; and

—Dissolution of the corporation and revocation of dissolution proceedings.

For these extraordinary proposals, the directors are required to adopt resolutions setting forth the proposed action and directing that it be submitted to a vote at a meeting of shareholders (see Appendix E.4(a) and (b)), which may be either the annual or a special meeting. Shareholders shall be informed of the proposal in the notice of the meeting. Model Act provisions concerning the shareholders to be given notice vary, depending on the category of the proposal as follows:

—For internal amendments, notice must be given to "each shareholder of record entitled to vote thereon" (Model Act §§59, 69).

—For mergers, etc., notice must be given to "each shareholder of record, whether or not entitled to vote at such meeting" (Model Act §§73, 79).

—For dissolutions, notice must be given to "each shareholder of record entitled to vote at such meeting" (Model Act §§84, 89).

As to shareholder voting, there are special requirements concerning both the number of affirmative votes needed for the approval of extraordinary proposals and (as we will see in sub-section (g)) whether approval by classes of shares is needed. Formerly, state corporation acts characteristically required greater-than-majority votes (two-thirds and, sometimes, three-quarters) for approval of extraordinary proposals. Neither the Model Act nor the Delaware Act any longer require greater-than-majority votes. Now the difference between the vote required for ordinary and extraordinary proposals has narrowed to a question of how a "majority" is determined. For ordinary proposals, "the affirmative vote of the majority of the shares represented at the meeting and entitled to vote on the subject matter" suffices (Model Act §32). For extraordinary proposals, "the affirmative vote of the holders of a majority of the shares entitled to vote thereon" is required (Model Act §§59, 69, 73, 79, 84, 89). The difference, of course, is whether shares not represented at the meeting will be counted in fixing a "majority."

> ▪ Recall the illustration in sub-section (c) of the corporation with 600 shares represented at the meeting out of 1,000 shares entitled to vote. The affirmative vote of 301 shares would be needed for an ordinary proposal and 501 shares for an extraordinary proposal.

(g) Voting by classes of shares

The Model Act provides that the shares of a corporation may be divided into classes "with such designations, preferences, limitations, and relative rights as shall be stated in the articles of incorporation"; the articles "may limit or deny the voting rights of or provide special voting rights for the shares of any class to the extent not inconsistent with the provisions of this Act" (§15).

When there are classes of shares, the question arises whether a proposal requires for adoption, not only a majority of the total shares, but also a majority of each class. The answer depends on whether any class of shares is entitled to vote upon the proposal *as a class;* if so, approval by a majority of that class as well as by a majority of the total shares is required. For ordinary proposals the Model Act provides:

If a quorum is present the affirmative vote of the majority of shares represented at the meeting and entitled to vote on the subject matter shall be the act of the shareholders, unless the vote of a greater number or voting by classes is required by this Act or the articles of incorporation or by-laws (§32).

▪ While the Act is not specific on this point, it would appear that when voting by classes is required on an ordinary proposal, for the proposal to be adopted requires the affirmative vote of a majority of both the shares of each class of shares *represented at the meeting* and entitled to vote thereon and of the total shares *represented at the meeting* and entitled to vote thereon.

   As to extraordinary proposals, the Model Act is specific (in most cases) in providing that, if any class of shares is entitled to vote on the proposal as a class, the proposal shall be adopted upon receiving "the affirmative vote of a majority of the shares of each class entitled to vote thereon as a class and of the total shares entitled to vote thereon" (§§59, 73, 79, 84).

In general, the articles of incorporation and by-laws will control whether classes of shares are entitled to vote as a class (see Appendix A.4(c)). However, the Model Act (§60) grants what might be called an entrenched power to holders of classes of shares to vote as a class upon a proposed amendment to the articles of incorporation, whether or not entitled to vote thereon by the provisions of the articles, if the amendment would:

—Change the number of authorized shares, par value, or rights (including preemptive rights, and rights to accrued but undeclared dividends) of the shares of the class;

—Effect an exchange, reclassification, or cancellation of the shares of the class, or an exchange of shares of another class into the shares of the class;

—Put another class ahead of the shares of the class as to rights and preferences; or

—Divide the class of shares into series.

And a class of shares is also entitled to vote as a class upon a plan of merger or consolidation with another corporation which contains a provision which, if contained in a proposed amendment to the articles, would entitle the class of shares to vote as a class (Model Act §73).

Section 3.4 Shareholder Relations

We now turn briefly, at the close of this chapter on corporate government, from technicalities of shareholder voting to practicalities of keeping on good terms with your shareholder-constituents. Officers and directors of close corporations seldom need to make a special project of maintaining good relations with their shareholders. Frequently they *are* the shareholders; and, if not, shareholder relations usually are simply a part of business, family, and personal relations.

With public corporations the situation is quite different. Shareholders are an anonymous, shifting, widespread mass of strangers: a mailing list. It is mainly through the mail that officers and directors communicate with these shareholders. Annual and interim financial reports, proxy statements, dividend mailings, reports of meetings, special mailings, welcoming (and occasionally farewell) letters are the customary channels of communication from officers and directors to their public shareholders. The annual report, with pictures, charts, and carefully worded narratives about the year's accomplishments and problems, is the document which usually receives the most attention. Considerable effort also goes into planning and staging annual meetings; some corporations move them about the country from year to year to expose them to different groups of shareholders.

From a public relations point of view, shareholder relations are like institutional advertising. The objective is to project a positive image of good business, good management, and good citizenship. You try to make your shareholders feel that their money is well invested. More immediately, you want them to support you with their proxies, and to hold and perhaps increase their ownership of your shares. Defensively, you do not want them to use their proxies against you, nor to support shareholder proposals that you think are misguided, nor to sell out their shares in response to a tender offer.

Practices differ as to where responsibility for shareholder relations is assigned within public corporations: to the lawyers, the accountants, the public relations people, or the marketing people. The corporate secretary frequently finds himself doing most of the work, often because the chief executive and the board want to keep close watch over what goes out to shareholders and the corporate secretary is on hand for them to supervise.

Here are a few suggestions that may be helpful to officers and directors who find themselves involved in shareholder relations:

—Allow yourself plenty of lead time (six to nine months) in starting your planning for your annual report and your annual meeting.
—Keep your shareholder relations program so that it looks simple and inexpensive. Shareholders seldom like to think their money is being used for lavish efforts to woo them.

—Keep down mailing costs by combining annual reports and proxy materials; post-meeting reports and dividend mailings also may be able to be combined by careful scheduling; arrange to mail as much as possible by third class mail.

—Solicit the cooperation of all parts of your corporation in coming up with fresh, interesting, positive things to tell your shareholders. Some examples: successful new products, new plant locations, acquisitions of new businesses, personnel changes, research developments, community services, awards, government contracts, overseas developments, new trademarks and trade names, etc.

—When you have bad news for shareholders, give it to them promptly and straightforwardly; try to accompany the bad news with positive information about what you are doing to improve the situation.

CHECKLIST OF POINTS TO WATCH OUT FOR IN GOVERNING YOUR CORPORATION

(References after headings are to Sections of Chapter 3.)

1. Planning for annual meetings of shareholders (Section 3.1 (a) and (c))

Why do you need a detailed time-table?

Particularly for public corporations, each year's shareholder meeting is the culmination of a series of inter-locking events spread over approximately $3\frac{1}{2}$ months: the end of the corporation's fiscal year and preparation of its financial statements; nomination of a slate of directors; fixing a record date and preparation and clearance with the SEC of proxy materials (which may include shareholder proposals); preparation of the annual report; mailing to shareholders of the annual report, notice of meeting, and proxy materials; and tabulating proxies. It calls for carefully orchestrated contributions by officers and directors and their lawyers, accountants, transfer agents, and public relations staff.

2. Calling special meetings of shareholders (Section 3.1 (b))

Should the president be empowered to call special meetings?

To minimize formalities and to provide for emergencies, by-laws originally should empower the corporation's president along with its board and one-tenth of its shareholders to call special meetings of shareholders. For such a by-law, see Appendix B.2 (c). However, there have been cases where a president has used this power to thwart a board majority by calling a meeting of shareholders and persuading them to replace a majority of the board with the president's nominees. To guard against such a move, a board majority should amend the by-laws to revoke the president's calling power as soon as he appears to be taking a position adverse to them.

3. Proxy solicitations, in general (Section 3.2 (a))

How do you get out the vote at minimum cost?

Devices for getting out the proxy vote include: pleas for return of proxies on the mailing envelope; allowing time for follow-up mailings; special handling of large share holdings, including calls by corporate employees and agents; efforts to secure the cooperation of brokers, banks, and nominees; and use of professional proxy solicitors. The latter are expensive and are more likely to be used for proxy contests than in uncontested solicitations. The aim is to build up the habit among your shareholders of returning their proxies.

Costs can be reduced by mailing proxy materials "piggy-back" with your annual reports, and by *not* imprinting proxy cards with the number of shares held. Such imprinting "personalizes" the card, requiring that the mailing be by first-class instead of third-class mail.

For a form of proxy card, see Appendix 2.1 (b).

4. Disclosures about officers and directors in proxy statements (Section 3.2 (b))

How much will your privacy be invaded?

If your corporation has assets of over $1 million and 500 or more share-holders, the SEC requires that its proxy statements disclose the business affiliations and share holdings in the corporation of nominees for directorships and the remuneration for the past year and stock option transactions for the past five years of its five most highly paid executive officers or directors whose remuneration exceeded $50,000.

5. Proxy contests (Section 3.2 (c))

Who pays for them?

Proxy contests usually end up being financed by the corporation except for expenses of unsuccessful outside challengers. Successful challengers become insiders, who then can vote themselves reimbursement. Inside defenders can assure that they are reimbursed whether they win or lose. The cost of unsuccessful proxy contests has helped make tender offers more popular (see Section 10.2): a challenger at least ends up with a block of shares which frequently can be sold at a profit.

6. Shareholder proposals (Section 3.2 (d))

How should you respond to them?

A timely shareholder request for inclusion of a proposal in your proxy materials poses the choice of acquiescing or refusing. If you refuse, the shareholder will probably seek to involve the SEC. Unless the proposal is clearly one that you need not include under SEC rules—an ordinary business decision, a personal grievance of the shareholder, or a broad social cause outside your control and unrelated to your business—you will probably include the proposal, being confident it will be voted down, rather than get into a public controversy with the shareholder and possibly the SEC. However, if the proposal's legal status is doubtful, and if its inclusion would have strongly negative public relations consequences, you may decide to fight out whether the law requires that you include it. In any event, legal resistance will probably delay the time when you will be required to put the proposal before your shareholders, thereby possibly blunting its public relations impact.

7. Quorum and voting requirements at shareholder meetings (Section 3.3 (a) and (b))

What are the pros and cons of high and low requirements?

Normal requirements are majorities for quorums and voting, but these may be varied upward as to voting and either upward or downward (to one-third of the shares entitled to vote) as to quorums. Public corporations usually stick to majorities, but close corporations may have reasons for variations. A high quorum requirement protects minority shareholders from unwanted meetings, and a high voting requirement enables them to block individual actions, but both may cause deadlocks. A low quorum requirement facilitates holding of meetings, but it also permits action by minorities.

For articles making 90% of the shares a quorum and requiring a 90% vote, see Appendix A.6 (c). For by-laws providing alternative language for majority or greater-than-majority voting, see Appendix B.2 (e).

8. Election and removal of directors (Section 3.3 (c)-(e))

What do you need to know about normal and cumulative voting?

With normal, non-cumulative voting, each board seat is filled or emptied by a separate election, giving a majority of the shares power to elect and to remove all of the directors. You will need to know whether in your corporation this action can be taken by a majority, or perhaps just by a plurality, of shares *voted* at the meeting (as is possible in Delaware), or whether a majority of shares *represented* at the meeting is required (as is the case under the Model Act).

With cumulative voting, each seat is not regarded as a separate election; shareholders are entitled to votes equal to their shares times the number of seats to be filled and may cumulate these votes for candidates as they choose. Thus, cumulative voting makes possible some minority representation if two or more directors are being elected; and, the more directors being elected, the smaller the minority needed for representation. In cases of removal of less than a full board, a director is protected from removal if the votes against his removal would suffice to elect him in an election of the full board. But a full board can be removed by a majority vote, since a new full board will then be elected by cumulative voting. You will need to know how to calculate optimum distributions of votes under cumulative voting, a process that will be influenced by the number of directors to be elected. Note that this number can be reduced by dividing the board into classes of three or more directors.

For articles requiring cumulative voting for election of directors, see Appendix A.6 (b).

9. Shareholder approval of basic corporate changes (Section 3.3 (f) and (g))

What extra is required?

Ordinarily shareholder action is by affirmative vote of a majority of shares represented at the meeting. But basic corporate changes—amendments to articles, merger, and dissolution—require a majority of shares entitled to vote, whether or not they are represented at the meeting. And when shares are divided into classes such basic changes require approval by separate majorities by classes of shares entitled to vote, as well as an overall majority of all shares entitled to vote. These considerations are important in determining what is needed for voting control in particular situations.

10. Shareholder relations (Section 3.4)

Should keeping shareholders happy be treated as a legal, financial, or public relations function?

Since maintenance of good relations between officers and directors and their shareholders transcends the particular concerns of lawyers and of financial and public relations specialists, responsibility for these relations should be assumed by top management. Marks of a good shareholder relations program include careful planning; the appearance of simplicity, frugality, and candor; and imaginative efforts to involve all levels of the corporation in keeping shareholders interested in what it is doing.

4

Managing Your Corporation

CONTENTS

111

4

Managing Your Corporation

Chapter 3 begins our examination of the structure and functioning of corporations at the governmental level of shareholder voting power. While voting by shares is a notion peculiar to corporations, voting itself is an accepted way for institutions to make basic decisions. As we move on to how a corporation is "managed," our general experience provides fewer models to guide us. This middle area of corporate decision-making creates puzzles about both the function of managing and the structure that is supposed to perform this function: the board of directors. And the board of directors is the feature of corporateness that is usually the most unfamiliar and bothersome to those making the transition to a corporation from a partnership or an individual proprietorship. An objective of this chapter is to give meaning to the cryptic statement, found in most state corporation acts, that the business and affairs of a corporation shall be managed by a board of directors. We will try to dispel some of the fog that surrounds the notions "board of directors" and "manage."

▪ I suspect that many of you who *are* directors are less than completely clear about what is expected of a director.

While many states now permit one person corporations, the historical purpose of corporations has been to enable several people who want to do something together to form a single, separate, additional person.

▪ One way of illustrating the point that a corporation is an *additional* person has been to point out: if, before incorporation, *n* persons were involved in an enterprise, after incorporation the number of persons has become *n* + 1.

113

As ownership of a corporate person is shared by its shareholders, similarly, its management is supposed to be shared by its directors. And, like shareholders, directors must ordinarily act together in duly constituted meetings.

> ▪ In fact, directors are even more meeting-bound than are shareholders. Most ownership powers of shareholders accompany them outside of meetings, but there is very little that directors of American corporations can do except in meetings.

The idea of collective management by a board of directors seems to come harder than the idea of collective ownership by shareholders. Perhaps this difference is due to the different ways we think about ownership and management. We see ownership as passive, amenable to occasional attention; but we see management as active, needing continuous attention. How can people who meet only once a month manage a business?

> ▪ Managers I have known have felt unable to take vacations of more than two or three weeks at a time for fear that they would "lose touch" with the business.

In this chapter we look first at structure: how a board of directors is put together and how it holds meetings; then we look at its functions: the management decisions that a board is supposed to make; and finally, we look at its functioning: how a board goes about doing its job. We save for later chapters special director problems of close corporations (Chapter 6) and directors' liabilities and conflicts of interest (Chapter 11).

Section 4.1 Constituting Your Board of Directors

In Chapter 3 we saw how directors are elected by shareholders. In this section we are concerned with how a board of directors is put together in the structural sense: its size and terms of office; how vacancies are filled; how directors are "qualified" and how a board is "organized."

(a) The number of directors and their terms of office

The Model Act provides (§ 36):

The board of directors of a corporation shall consist of one or more members. The number shall be fixed by, or in the manner provided in, the articles of incorporation or the by-laws, except as to the number constituting the initial board, which number shall be fixed by the articles of incorporation.

Thus, you can arrange to have the number of directors fixed by the articles (see Appendix A.6(a)), by the by-laws (see Appendix B.3 (e) and (f)) or by shareholder or director resolution (see Appendix B.3(g) and D.4(a)).

While the Model Act permits you to select any number of directors you desire, some state corporation acts specify a minimum number, most commonly three. For close corporations the size of the board is usually dictated by the number of participants who want to take part in policy making.

> ▪ **In our Dighaldoe example all three of the participants would probably want to be directors.**

For public corporations board size is more a matter of choice; the optimum number of directors is generally considered to be between nine and fifteen, although there are major companies with boards numbering in the 20s and 30s.

In addition to deciding about the size of your board, you also need to pay attention to how you want the number of directors to be increased and decreased. In line with its provision on number of directors, the Model Act permits changes to be "by amendment to, or in the manner provided in, the articles of incorporation or by-laws" (§36). If, as is usually the case, the articles provide that the by-laws may be amended by the directors (see Appendix A.8; but compare Appendix A.11), the effective choice will be between specifying the number of directors in the articles, or in a shareholder resolution, either of which will require shareholder approval of changes; and setting up a procedure permitting changes by directors through by-law amendments or resolutions of the board of directors. As we will see, if your corporation is closely held, you may want to require shareholder approval of changes in board size.

> ▪ **Note that having the number of directors set by shareholder resolution may be the optimum method for a close corporation because it retains shareholder control but avoids the filings required for amendments to the articles.**

However, with most public corporations it is desirable to have the flexibility of enabling the board to change its own size.

> ▪ **For example, if directors of a public corporation learn that a sought-after person is willing to join them, it is useful for them to be able to create a vacancy for him themselves without having to go to the shareholders.**
>
> **Most public corporations fix the number of directors in their by-laws. While by-law amendments of listed corporations are filed with the SEC and the stock exchange, state filings are not required.**

A limitation upon the power of both shareholders and directors to change the size of the board is that "no decrease shall have the effect of shortening the term of any incumbent director" (Model Act §36). Thus if you want to eliminate both a director and his seat, you must either remove the incumbent before decreasing the number of directors, or wait for his term to expire. You cannot "remove" a director simply by abolishing his seat.

The term of a director is "until the next succeeding annual meeting, except in the case of classification of directors" (Model Act §36). However, if the annual meeting is not held, or if a successor is not elected or is unable to qualify, the incumbent "shall hold office ... until his successor shall have been elected and qualified" (Model Act §36; see sub-section (c) for discussion of qualification).

> ▪ **Recall that the Model Act provides (§28) that, if an annual meeting is not held within any 13-month period, a shareholder may apply to a court for an order that a meeting be held.**

It follows that a "vacancy" does not occur when the term for which a director is elected expires but a successor is not elected or does not qualify: in this situation the incumbent continues to hold office (although it would seem that his seat can now be abolished, since abolition would not "have the effect of shortening [his] term" (Model Act §36)).

(b) Filling vacancies on the board

A board seat may be vacated between annual meetings of shareholders by the death, resignation, disqualification, or removal of an incumbent director; vacancies may also be created by increasing the size of the board. The Model Act provides (§38):

> *Any vacancy occuring in the board of directors may be filled by the affirmative vote of a majority of the remaining directors though less than a quorum of the board of directors.*

Directors so elected to fill vacancies serve out unexpired terms of their predecessors; but where a vacancy results from an increase in the number of directors (where there would, of course, be no predecessor) and is filled by the board, the new director's term shall continue "only until the next election of directors by the shareholders" (Model Act §38).

This section of the Model Act permits "reconstituting" a board that is reduced to less than a quorum by deaths, resignations, disqualifications, or removals. This power may be useful if something happens to eliminate a majority of the board. If *all* of the seats are vacated, normal procedures would seem to require that the board be reconstituted by the shareholders at a special meeting called for that purpose. However, the Model Act authorizes "emergency by-laws" (see

Appendix B.13) which may provide that the board may approve a list of "officers or other persons" who shall, during an emergency and in a designated order of priority, "to the extent required to provide a quorum at any meeting of the board of directors, be deemed directors for such meeting" (§27A).

Where control of a board is to be transferred from one shareholder or group of shareholders to another, a frequently used method of putting a new board of directors in office is for the old board to resign, one by one, with the remaining directors electing a new director to fill each vacancy as it occurs.

> ▪ For example, suppose A, B, and C are to be replaced as directors by X, Y, and Z. First, A resigns and B and C elect X to fill the vacancy; then, B resigns and C and X elect Y; finally, C resigns and X and Y elect Z. Of course, under the Model Act provision (§38) that less than a quorum can fill vacancies, the first two steps can be combined by having A *and* B resign, and C alone then elect X and Y.

For discussion of federal disclosure requirements and possible questions concerning the legality of these so-called "seriatim" resignations followed by election by "cooptation," see Sections 10.2(a) and 10.3.

(c) Qualification of directors; organizing the board

We saw that directors hold office until their successors are "elected and qualified" (Model Act §36), which assumes that it may be possible for elected directors not to be "qualified." In the past, state corporation acts have imposed qualifications such as share ownership, residency in the state, citizenship, and age. The trend is toward making such qualifications optional rather than mandatory. The Model Act provides (§35):

> *Directors need not be residents of this State or shareholders of the corporation unless the articles of incorporation or by-laws so require. The articles of incorporation or by-laws may prescribe other qualifications for directors.*

Where share ownership is a qualification for being a director—whether by the state corporation act, articles, or by-laws—this requirement can be used as a simplified way of removing directors of close corporations by securing assignments of their qualifying shares which will be held for the day when those in control want to get them out (as when officials are required by their superior to put resignations on file which can be used when the superior wishes).

> ▪ Suppose that X corporation has subsidiaries Y and Z. The management of X wants A, B, and C, employees of X, to serve as directors of Y

and Z, but also wants to be able to remove them from these director-ships whenever the X management wishes. To accomplish this objec-tive have the articles or by-laws (see Appendix B.3 (d)) of Y and Z require that directors be shareholders and have X transfer qualifying shares in Y and Z to A, B, and C on the condition that they each execute assignments of these shares back to X. By recording these assign-ments on the books of Y and Z, X will be able to disqualify A, B, or C. This procedure provides a quicker, cleaner way of getting directors out of office than removal proceedings.

From here on we assume that your corporation has a duly elected and qualified board of directors and that it is ready to hold meetings. In the next section we examine the structure of board meetings. But first we need to mention the "organizational meeting" that a newly elected board customarily holds imme-diately after the annual meeting of shareholders.

To hold meetings, a board needs a chairman to preside and a secretary to take minutes. The by-laws usually provide that the president or, if there is one, the chairman of the board, shall serve as chairman at board meetings, and that the secretary of the corporation shall keep the minutes of board meetings (see Appendix B.4(e) and (g)). With these provisions, it is not necessary for each board to designate a chairman and secretary for its meetings separately from its desig-nation of corporate officers. Thus, the principal business at the organizational meeting is the election and appointment of officers of the corporation and the appointment of any committees of the board. The by-laws usually provide that no notice is needed for the organizational meeting (see Appendix B.3(j)), which does not exactly fit either the regular or special category.

Section 4.2 Holding Meetings of Your Board of Directors

As with shareholders, a director's ultimate power is exercised by voting at meetings. But director voting differs from shareholder voting. For a director, the rule is one person, one vote, without regard to his share holdings; and a director must vote in person—there is no proxy voting by directors. Because each director vote is cast in person and counts the same, the consultation that precedes voting becomes more important. Particularly with public corporations, the board of directors is more of an interacting group (like a court or a jury) than are the shareholders (who frequently resemble a political electorate or participants in a public opinion poll).

In this section we are concerned first with mechanics of board meetings—times, places, calls, notices, quorums, voting, and minutes—and then with permitted departures from formal meeting procedures. These are housekeeping details that we need to get before us before going on to more substantive inquiries about the director's job and how it is done.

(a) Mechanics of board meetings

A board of directors usually fixes by its own resolution the time and place for its regular meetings (see Appendix C.2(b)). No law sets their frequency, but most boards meet monthly. A typical general resolution will provide that regular meetings will be held at the corporation's general offices at, say, 2:00 p.m. on the third Wednesday of each month. The place and time for particular meetings may be varied by special resolution.

> ▪ Some corporations make it a practice to hold occasional board meetings at plant locations. Such meetings enable directors to observe plant operations and to get acquainted with plant executives on their home ground, and plant employees are encouraged to feel that the directors are interested in what they are doing.

Regular board meetings do not require calls or notices (see Appendix B.3(j)), although the secretary ordinarily sends the directors informal reminders of regular meetings with the proposed agendas of business to be transacted. Procedures for calls and notices for special meetings are usually set out in the by-laws (see Appendix B.3(k) and (l)). Typically, the chairman (or president) or any two directors may call a special meeting. Then the secretary is supposed to give formal notice of the place, time, and purpose of the meeting to each director. The Model Act is quite relaxed about the formalities of notice, providing (§43):

> *Attendance by a director shall constitute waiver of notice of such meeting, except where a director attends a meeting for the express purpose of objecting to the transaction of any business because the meeting is not lawfully called or convened. Neither the business to be transacted at, nor the purpose of, any regular or special meeting of the board of directors need be specified in the notice or waiver of notice of such meeting unless required by the by-laws.*

> ▪ As a simply accomplished precaution against quibbles about the legality of special meetings, it is recommended that the secretary make it a practice at all such meetings to secure the signatures on a waiver of notice of all directors, whether in attendance or not.

Under the Model Act (§40), a majority of the full board (including vacancies) constitutes a quorum for transacting business, unless a greater number is required by the articles of incorporation or by-laws.

▪ For example, if the articles or by-laws call for a board of eight and there are two vacancies, five out of the six directors will be needed for a quorum, because vacancies do not reduce the number needed for a quorum. Note that under the Model Act the majority quorum provision may be varied on the up but not on the down side. However, Delaware also permits variation on the down side.

And the act of a majority of the directors present at a meeting where a quorum is present shall be the act of the board, unless the act of a greater number is required by the articles or by-laws.

▪ In the above illustration, concurrence of four directors will be needed if six are present and of three if five are present, because vacancies and absences do reduce the number needed to carry a vote. Again, note that under the Model Act the majority voting provision may be varied on the up but not on the down side. However, as this illustration shows, it is possible for a minority of the full board to act for the corporation.

If six directors attend the meeting and one leaves, there will still be enough for a quorum and three will be enough to carry a vote. But if five attend and one leaves, there will no longer be a quorum present, and even though all four of the remaining directors vote in favor of a proposal, it will not be the act of the board. Thus, if one or two of those in attendance are opposed to a pending proposal and sense that the vote is likely to go against them, they can block the proposal by leaving the meeting and breaking the quorum.

The secretary is ordinarily responsible for the writing and custody of board minutes. He will circulate them to directors for suggested corrections, frequently with the notification about the next meeting. The form of the minutes is largely a matter of taste. Recommended practice favors spare minutes that say no more than is necessary, omitting discussion, names of movers and seconders, and how individual directors voted and confining minutes largely to texts of resolutions adopted and bare recitals of other action taken.

(b) Permitted departures from formal meeting requirements

In recognition that traditional requirements that boards of directors may act only at legally convened meetings are sometimes unduly restrictive, the Model Act, while not going so far as to permit that boards of directors be dispensed with altogether, has liberalized traditional rules in several important ways:

—The articles of incorporation may provide that designated powers and duties conferred or imposed on the board of directors shall be exercised or performed by other designated persons (§35). This broad provision would seem to authorize, among other things, election of officers directly by shareholders.

—An executive committee of directors may exercise all the authority of the board except amending the articles and by-laws, and making recommendations to shareholders on mergers, consolidations, sales of assets, and dissolutions (§42).

—Action required to be taken at a board or committee meeting may be taken without a meeting upon the written consent of *all* the directors or committee members (§44).

—For situations where a catastrophe makes it impossible to convene a quorum of the board or a committee, emergency by-laws may be adopted (§27A).

However, the norm is that directors perform their functions only at legal meetings. Now we are in a position to examine these functions.

Section 4.3 Responsibilities and Powers of Your Board of Directors

As we have already noted, directors have only collective management powers. They are not corporate agents because they do not have the power as individuals to bind the corporation in transactions with outsiders.

> ▪ **For example, a deed signed individually by each of the directors of a corporation would not be effective to convey corporate real estate to an outsider.**

And, with a few exceptions—such as calling a meeting, signing a waiver of notice, and consenting to action without a meeting—their acts as directors outside of meetings are without legal effect.

If directors are not agents of the corporation, what are they? In a sense, they are the corporation itself, not something separate from the corporation. Like shareholders and officers, directors are part of the corporation's organic structure. They are neither the owners of the corporation (like shareholders) nor the doers of its business (like officers); rather, they are the link between the owners and the doers. They are elected by the owners, and they, in turn, elect or appoint the principal doers, the officers. But they are supposed to be managers as well as electors. Most of this section will be about what the law means when it assigns management of the business and affairs of a corporation to its board of directors. Stated more directly, our question here is: what kinds of decisions should you, as a corporate officer, take to your board of directors? The question seems to have a two-part answer: an easy legal part, that you take to your board decisions assigned to the board by your state corporation law, and by your articles of incorporation and by-laws; and a much harder business part, that you take to your board decisions that transcend the usual and regular course of your corporation's business.

> ■ Recall that in Section 3.3 we were concerned with the kinds of decisions that the directors should take to the shareholders. Now we have a similar, and more complex, problem at the officer-director level. And we will return to this subject in Chapter 5 when we focus on officers' powers.

(a) Responsibilities expressly assigned to your board of directors

Most of the legally assigned responsibilities relate to internal corporate affairs rather than to dealings with outsiders, although a few outside transactions are expressly assigned to directors. Outside transactions expressly requiring board action include authorizing mortgages and liens on corporate property, guarantees by the corporation of obligations of others, and dispositions of unessential corporate assets.

In the area of internal corporate affairs, we can start by saying that decisions that require shareholder approval generally need to be formulated by the board of directors into a recommendation that the shareholders can accept or reject. Decisions of this kind include the following:

—Amendments to the articles of incorporation (see Appendix E.1);

—Plans of merger or consolidation (however, 90% owned subsidiaries may be merged into the parent without shareholder approval of either corporation) (see Appendix E.4(a) and E.5(a));

—Dispositions of substantially all the corporate assets other than in the regular course of business (dispositions in the regular course of business, and mortgages and pledges, whether or not in the regular course of business, can be authorized by the board without shareholder action) (see Appendix E.6(a));

—Recommendations that the corporation be dissolved (see Appendix E.7(a));

—Approvals of issues of stock rights or options to corporate directors, officers, or employees, and not to shareholders generally (rights or options can be issued to shareholders generally by the board without shareholder action, if done in accordance with the articles of incorporation) (see Appendix F.6(b)).

In addition to these basic corporate decisions where board of directors action is a necessary preliminary to shareholder action, there is also a substantial group of slightly less basic decisions that are usually assigned to directors by state corporation laws and by articles of incorporation and by-laws. These include:

—Making, altering, amending, and repealing by-laws (see Appendix C.2(b) and E.3) (traditionally this power was vested in the shareholders; the modern trend has been to give it to the directors exclusively, unless it is reserved to the shareholders by the articles; however, it can be argued that shareholders have an inherent power to take the by-laws into their own hands);

—Election or appointment and removal of officers (president, secretary, and treasurer are to be elected; other officers and assistant officers and agents are to be elected or appointed by the board or as prescribed by the by-laws (Model Act §50) (see Appendix F.4(c));

—Declaration of dividends and making distributions to shareholders from capital surplus (dividends may be in cash, property, or the corporation's own shares) (see Appendix F.3(b)-(g));

—Designating, from among the board members, executive and other committees (for example, finance, audit, and compensation committees, the need for which we will discuss) (see Appendix F.5);

—Filling vacancies on the board (see Appendix F.4(b));

—Calling special meetings of shareholders (see Appendix F.2(a));

—Fixing record dates for corporate actions (meetings, dividends, stock rights and options, etc.) (see Appendix F.3(a));

—Approving loans by the corporation to employees and directors (see Appendix F.6(c) and (d));

—Authorizing and fixing the consideration for new issues of shares and of stock rights and options (see Appendix C.2(b), (d), and (e));

—Creating and abolishing reserves;

—Providing for regular meetings of the board (see Appendix C.2(b));

—Approving the form of share certificates and procedures for their replacement (see Appendix C.2(b)); and

—Designating transfer agents and registrars.

(b) General management powers of your board of directors

The law gives us only general and indirect guidance in drawing a dividing line between those business decisions that should be submitted to the board of directors and those that corporate officers or their subordinates can make on their own. Our problem here is the reverse image of the problem in the next chapter, on officers' inherent powers: if a given power inheres in a particular office, it would seem to follow that that power is *not* a necessary part of the board's management responsibilities.

Is this just a lawyers' quibble, or are some real interests affected by whether particular business judgments are made by the board or by one or more officers or agents? What difference does it make how you define the management powers of your board of directors? To outsiders dealing with what they think is the corporation, it may make a difference as to whether they have a corporate obligation or something else. The officer or agent who signs the contract on behalf of the corporation is also interested in whether the corporation is bound, because if it is not he may be bound personally (see Sections 5.2 and 11.1). And the corporate secretary who attests the signature of the officer or agent as the duly authorized act of the corporation has an interest in his own integrity, and in the liability he may incur for a false attestation. Finally, the corporation and its shareholders have an interest in corporate decisions being made by the people who are supposed to make them. Presumably, director scrutiny provides greater assurance that requisite standards of care and loyalty have been observed by the people purporting to act for the corporation. Thus, there is no lack of people who have real interest in who has power to decide for the corporation.

The kinds of decisions we are talking about as needing director action are those that pertain to the corporation's operations, but which may have lasting consequences, such as: buying and selling real estate; making long-term contract commitments; and granting continuing authorizations to act for the corporation. But whether particular decisions should be called "management" or "policy" decisions on which the board should have a say, or should be called day-to-day operations in the regular course of business that officers and their subordinates should be free to do on their own, will depend in part on factors extraneous to the kinds of decisions they happen to be. These factors include the size and nature of the corporation's business, the history of relations between the corporation's board and its officers and agents, and the kinds of authorizations outsiders dealing with the corporation expect (or even demand).

We get down to sort of a rule of reason: under these circumstances is it reasonable to refer this particular decision to the board? Suppose you are an officer of a medium-sized, close manufacturing corporation that needs to build a new plant that will cost several million dollars, and which will be the corporation's largest single capital expenditure. The plant can be financed largely with retained earnings, but some short-term borrowing will be needed. Your officers are not in the habit of taking many decisions to your board, in part because your board is mostly composed of officers; but you anticipate that the contractors you will be dealing with will be quite fussy about authorizations. Which of the whole series of business judgments involved in this project would you refer to your board?

In applying a rule of reason, a division along the following lines seems to make sense:

—Decisions for the board: authorization of a lump sum expenditure for a new plant with authority to the president and his delegates to make contracts needed to carry out the project; authorization to purchase specific real estate needed for the plant; authorization to borrow specific amounts needed to finance plant construction.

—Decisions (among others) not for the board: choice of specific contractors and details of construction; arrangements for transportation, power, water, ingredients, employees, etc., for the new plant; securing the needed government permits and clearances.

Because of the basic authorization to the president and his delegates, you could assure your contractors that contracts were being signed with board authority, but you would be following your practice of not bothering the board with the details of your business. Real estate is treated with more formality and deserves a separate resolution. Since the short-term borrowing is out of the ordinary, it also calls for specific authorization. The decisions of whether and where to build this plant, how much to spend, and how to raise the money, appear to be management decisions for the board. But all the subordinate decisions of how to implement these basic decisions seem best left to the officers. For the documents for an authorizations system, see Appendix G.

Section 4.4 How Your Board of Directors Does Its Job

We now turn from the functions of your board of directors, in the sense of its legally assigned (both expressly and by reasonable implication) responsibilities and powers, to its functioning, in the sense of how it actually fulfills its responsibilities and exercises its powers—from what is expected of your directors to what they do. In this section we focus on some of the variables that may influence how your board operates, including: who is on it; how it is viewed by your shareholders and officers, particularly your chief executive officer; how committees can help it do its job; and what resources are made available to it. We also look briefly at some alternative models for boards suggested by practices of European corporations.

(a) Composition of your board of directors

The basic classifications of kinds of boards of directors of American corporations can be called "inside," "outside," and "mixed." All of the members of a purely inside board depend upon the corporation as their primary source of income, either as shareholders or employees. In contrast, all members of an outside board except the chief executive officer (and perhaps his next-in-command) do not depend upon the corporation as their primary source of income but have other careers (such as lawyers, bankers, executives (active or retired) of other corporations, accountants, educators, foundation executives, or newspaper editors). Mixed boards, of course, contain a blend of insiders and outsiders.

How does a board's composition affect its functioning?

Insiders are usually better informed about the corporation's business than are outsiders and are less dependent upon the chief executive for their information. While wearing their officers' hats, insiders are likely to see little point in taking decisions to the board. Directors will have already had their in-put as officers and employees, and director review of officers' decisions may seem to have little meaning if officers are reviewing themselves. Another characteristic of inside employee-directors is that they are probably dependent upon the president for their jobs and are unlikely to be critical of his decisions.

Outside directors have the advantages of independence and broader outlook and the disadvantages of lack of information about or real involvement in the business of the corporation. Studies of outside boards have revealed that they are probably of little help to the chief executive in establishing policies, and that they seldom ask probing questions. On the other hand, they are of considerable help to him as advisors and counselors; they provide a useful discipline by causing him to justify his decisions more carefully than he otherwise would; and in times of crisis, when the chief executive must be replaced, they provide continuity and a tribunal for designating his successor. For large, publicly held corporations, these considerations would seem to tip the scales in favor of preponderantly outside boards. Thus, as your corporation grows larger and less closely held, the advantages of outside directors increase.

> ▪ For example, in our coal mining hypothetical, where Digges, Hall, and Doe want to keep control of the business among themselves, it would not make much sense to put outsiders on the board. However, if they

need to raise a lot of outside money, an investment banker or a lawyer on the board might be useful.

Another factor is the shortage of good outside directors. It may be difficult for the scrambling smaller corporation to attract the kind of outside director talent that will really be of help. Rather than settling for outside people who would accept directorships mainly in the hopes of furthering their own interests, the struggling corporation may do better to stick with its own people (recognizing, however, that you can sometimes find a young lawyer or banker who will grow with your business and will, over the years, prove to be a valuable director).

(b) Shareholder and officer attitudes toward your board of directors

With public corporations, shareholder attitudes toward boards of directors have little impact on their selection or functioning. Of course, directors like to have happy, contented shareholders, and the board of a corporation that is doing poorly is more in danger of being ousted in a proxy contest or takeover bid. But generally, shareholders either go along with self-perpetuating management slates of directors or sell their shares.

The situation is quite different with close corporations, because here the shareholders actually pick their directors. When you are asked to be a director of a close corporation, quite likely it will be made clear what is expected of you: whether your role is to be an active manager or a passive functionary. This message will be conveyed whether you are an insider or an outsider, and in either case you will probably adapt yourself to these expectations. If you accept a directorship, you will want to please your shareholders, and you are likely to be more responsive to their wishes than to any conceptions you may have about the legal and ethical duties of directors. However, you can get into an ethical bind if the wishes of the shareholders who picked you seem to be at odds with the interests of the corporation as a whole, or if your own interests conflict with corporate interests. We return to this quandary in chapters 11 and 12.

For both public and close corporations, how the directors do their jobs is pervasively influenced by how the corporate officers, particularly the chief executive officer, view the role of the board. What a board does depends in large part on what it is *given* to do. A board ordinarily cannot generate its own work; it can merely respond to what the officers put before it.

▪ **In this dependence upon others to generate their business, boards of directors resemble courts.**

A spectrum of possible attitudes by presidents toward their boards is suggested in the following sketches of the mind-sets of three hypothetical corporate presidents:

—President A: The directors are my superiors in the corporate hierarchy. I owe them my job; I am answerable to them on how well I do my job; they can replace me at any time. They are the legal managers and policy makers of the corporation; I am the one who executes their policies. I will submit to them each decision that involves a policy question.

—President B: The directors are a useful group of elder statesmen. They provide a backboard off which I can bounce ideas. My desire to explain things clearly to them and to persuade them to go along with my proposals helps to sharpen my thinking. And if I should be run over by a truck they might help prevent a war of succession within the corporation. I will submit major policy questions to them, but I will expect them to follow my recommendations.

—President C: The directors are a nuisance. They are a collection of kibitzers that I must humor, but they have no real role in running the business. I could do better without them. They have no real power; I am the real manager and policy-maker of the corporation. Just let them try and replace me. And I don't care what happens after I die or resign (then people will realize who has been holding this business together). I will only submit matters to them when my lawyers tell me I have no other choice, and I will not tolerate any obstruction from them.

President A is the legal model: he probably exists only rarely, if at all, in real life. President C is the power model: he probably exists all too often. President B, obviously somewhere in between, can be called the pragmatic model: the "good" president talking about a "good" board. But note that while B's tone is respectful, in substance he is closer to the power model than to the legal model. He acknowledges that the board has some utilitarian value (mainly for him), but he (like C) sees himself as the real decision-maker and (unlike C) the board as his "helpers." Neither B nor C expect their boards to do more than endorse what they, the presidents, have already decided. The nearer a president is to A, the more complete information he would be likely to furnish his board to assist it in making a decision. However, the nearer a man comes to A in his thinking, the less likely it is that he will make it to the presidency. Perhaps all we should hope for are enlightened, decent B's.

(c) Board committees

Since boards frequently have fifteen or more members, they may be able to handle some matters more effectively by dividing into committees. Here we consider briefly four kinds of committees: executive, finance, audit, and compensation (see Appendix B.3 (o), F.5(a)).

We have already noted that the Model Act permits a board of directors to delegate most of its powers to an executive committee (§42). Executive committees are used to make decisions on behalf of the board between board meetings, to sift out the more important items for full board attention, and to formulate recommendations on matters being submitted to the board. They probably permit some director review of more items than would otherwise be possible, and, in theory, they permit the full board to focus on only the most important decisions. The strongest argument against an executive committee is that it tends to divide the board into first and second class citizens: board members who are not on the executive committee get the impression that decisions have already been made before they reach the full board, and a corollary of this argument usually is that matters that are important enough to go to the directors at all are important enough to go to the full board. This argument is quite persuasive if you have a board that works well together as a group with more or less general participation. However, if your board is already factionalized, or is given to long-winded discussions, an executive committee cannot do much harm and might do some good.

Finance committees are used where the corporation is engaged in frequent and complicated financial moves to raise capital (through short-term borrowing, lease-back arrangements, long-term debt, sale of equity shares, etc.) which require board action. Here the committee can do a specialized sifting and reviewing job and spare the full board unnecessary immersion in financial details.

Audit committees have a similar, but even more basic function: to consult, independently of the officers, with the corporation's auditors, both inside and outside, and to assure the full board that the financial statements accurately reflect the condition of the corporation and that material information is not being withheld from the directors, or the shareholders. This committee, like the compensation committee, should be composed of directors who are not employees.

▪ **Another argument for having outside directors is to have people to serve on your audit and compensation committees.**

Compensation committees have the important function of passing on the compensation of top management. By assigning outside directors to this task, embarrassing conflicts of interests may be avoided. This committee can be useful in awarding stock options, bonuses, deferred compensation, and other special benefits for officers and senior executives (see Section 11.3(d)(iii)).

These specialized board committees, particularly audit and compensation, are not subject to the divisiveness argument used against executive committees:

they function only occasionally during the year; they carry little prestige; and frequently it is possible to give each of the outside directors assignments on at least one of these committees. I would recommend that every corporation with outside directors should seriously consider having audit and compensation committees.

(d) Resources available to your board

Probably the greatest impediments to the effectiveness of directors are caused by their lack of information, staff, and time to make reasoned decisions, or by their lack of independence to make their own decisions. It is difficult for outside directors to "manage" an enterprise when they know so much less about it than do those they are supposed to direct; and it is difficult for inside directors to direct their own superiors. It is rare that a board of directors has any full-time staff assigned to it; thus, any staff work that is done for it is done under the supervision of inside management.

Possible correctives for this situation include a full-time inside board, not dependent on the president for their positions, whose main job is long-range planning and policy making; an active, assertive, independent corporate secretary who will take it upon himself to be "special counsel" for the board in trying to keep it informed; or assignment of an assistant secretary to the board with the full-time job of preparing data for it. Each of these correctives has its limitations. Few corporations have the depth in management talent to take its best people off the firing line and put them to directing. Few corporate secretaries can or will take a responsibility for the board independent of the president. And it will be difficult for anyone in inside management, short of the president, to have the clout and the background needed to extract and get out to the directors the information that they need. The best hope for board effectiveness probably is in the hands of corporation presidents. If, like our hypothetical president, B, they see the usefulness of a well-informed board, they may be willing to make available the information and staff to put it together. And for information to be of much use to directors, it needs to be sent out to them well in advance of the board meeting so they will have time to think about it.

> ▪ **It is suggested that when a president knows that tough policy decisions are looming, he send out preliminary data to directors several months in advance so that directors have more of a chance to get up to speed with the officers.**

Traditionally directors have worked for the honor and a modest stipend for attending meetings. The trend in recent years has been to increase director compensation in several ways. Meeting fees have increased several-fold, and are being supplemented by annual retainers which are paid without regard to meeting attendance. Also directors have been made eligible for corporation group health plans; this has helped make directorships attractive to retired people.

> ▪ **The Model Act (§35) authorizes the board to fix its own compensation "unless otherwise provided in the articles of incorporation."**

(e) European board practices

In Great Britain, and to a lesser extent on the European continent, corporations have been able to draw on a group of professional directors, who sit on as many as 30 or 40 boards and who, presumably, have become expert in directing. Although a few lawyers and investment bankers have aspired to this role in the United States, the idea has never really caught on. Until recently we have not paid our directors enough for one to be able to make a career of directing; and our business leaders have been unconvinced that directing should be a recognized profession.

German corporations have a practice of two-tiered boards of directors which may be worth studying for what it might do for American corporations. The German practice, which will probably become more common throughout Europe as the Common Market develops, emphasizes the distinction between policy-making and operational responsibilities of top management of a corporation. The policy-making board is made up largely of outsiders (many bankers) and meets less frequently than does the operational board. The latter includes representatives of employees, as well as the top operating managers. Roughly, the policy-making board operates somewhat like the finance committee of an American board.

It is to be hoped that we will develop in the United States an increasingly deep pool of knowledgeable, public-spirited men and women who are available (and called upon) to serve as outside directors of our business corporations, both large and small, and who will bring to these assignments the courage and the know-how to get involved in their management responsibilities, the forbearance to leave operations to their executives, the wisdom to know the difference between management and operations, and the integrity to fulfill their fiduciary responsibilities of care and loyalty.

CHECKLIST OF POINTS TO WATCH OUT FOR
IN MANAGING YOUR CORPORATION

(References after headings are to Sections of Chapter 4.)

1. Changing the number of directors (Section 4.1 (a))

Why may you choose to reserve this power to shareholders if your corporation is close but grant it to directors if it is public?

To avoid having your control position in a close corporation weakened through changes in the number of directors, you may wish to reserve this power to the shareholders (see Section 6.3 (b)). This can be done by having the number of directors set by shareholder resolution or by fixing the number of directors in the by-laws and requiring shareholder action to change the by-laws. The number of directors may also be fixed in the articles, but then any changes would require state filings.

Requiring shareholder action for changes in the size of the board is inappropriate for most public corporations, since directors are not ordinarily chosen to represent specific shareholders, and since there are pluses in a board being able to create vacancies for desirable new directors.

For articles fixing the number of directors, see Appendix A.6(a). For alternative by-laws on number of directors, see Appendix B.3(e) (fixed in by-laws and changed by amendment thereto), B.3(f) (fixed in by-laws and changed by director resolution), and B.3(g) (fixed in by-laws and changed by shareholder resolution). For a shareholder resolution fixing the number of directors, see Appendix D.4(a). For a director resolution amending by-laws on number of directors, see Appendix E.3(b).

2. Filling vacancies on the board (Section 4.1 (b))

How do you put a new board in power following an emergency or a transfer in share control?

Vacancies may be filled by a majority of remaining directors though less than a quorum (Model Act §38). Successive resignations and elections can be used to effect a change-over of board membership. For federal requirements concerning information that must be furnished shareholders when directors are replaced without shareholder vote, and possible questions about the legality of such replacement, see Sections 10.2 (a) and 10.3.

For by-laws, a shareholder resolution, and a director resolution on filling vacancies on a board, see Appendix B.3 (i), D.4 (e), and F.4 (b), respectively.

3. Qualification of directors (Section 4.1 (e))

How can share ownership for director qualification be used as a simple way to remove directors?

Where share ownership is made a qualification for becoming or remaining a director, the tenure of directors of a close corporation can be controlled by securing assignments in blank of their qualifying shares which can be used to disqualify them. This procedure is used by public corporations as to those serving as directors of subsidiaries. Like a resignation kept on file, it avoids the bother of removal proceedings.

For by-laws on director qualifications, see Appendix B.3(c) and (d).

4. Waivers of notice of special board meetings (Section 4.2 (a))

Why are they a good idea?

As a precaution against the sufficiency of notice for special board meetings being questioned, your corporate secretary should make it a practice to have each director, whether in attendance or not, sign a waiver of notice of the meeting.

For a by-law on waiver of notice, see Appendix B.10. For reference to waiver of notice in the minutes of a board meeting, see Appendix C.2 (b).

5. Quorums for board meetings (Section 4.2 (a))

How can individual directors use quorum requirements to thwart unwelcome board action?

Under the Model Act (§40) a minimum quorum for board action is a majority of the full board. Particularly where seats are vacant or directors unable to attend, minorities sometimes can block action by not attending or by leaving meetings.

6. Board action without meetings (Section 4.2 (b))

What devices are available to avoid board meetings?

Except for amending articles or by-laws or recommending mergers, consolidations, sales of assets, or dissolutions, an executive committee may be empowered to act for the board between meetings. And by-laws may provide for board action without a meeting by written consent of all directors.

For by-laws authorizing executive and other committees, see Appendix B.3(o). For by-laws concerning action without a meeting, see Appendix B.3 (p) and (q). For a director resolution establishing executive and other committees, see Appendix F.5 (a). For further discussion of board committees, see Point 11.

7. Matters requiring board action (Section 4.3 (a) and (b))

What kinds of decisions should officers take to the board of directors?

It is obviously impractical for corporate officers to submit all of their business decisions to the board of directors. In addition to decisions expressly assigned to the board—by state corporation law, articles, or by-laws—board approval should be secured of transactions outside the corporation's "usual" business. However, even with such approval it is still possible that the purported corporate action may be invalid and there may be individual liability by corporate officers. This is another area, like guarding against your corporate status being defective or sham, where you need the best legal advice you can get. The text introduces you to this difficult subject and helps you formulate the right questions for your lawyers.

8. Composition of the board of directors
(Section 4.4 (a))

What are the strengths and weaknesses of inside and outside directors?

Inside directors are better informed about and more involved in the corporation's affairs, but they may be unable to be objective. Outside directors can have broader and more independent perspectives, but they may lack information and involvement. As your corporation grows, the strengths of outside directors become more important. However, good outside directors are hard to find.

9. Shareholder attitudes toward your board
(Section 4.4 (b))

Why are they more important when your corporation is close?

Shareholders in public corporations ordinarily go along with management or sell their shares. But with close corporations shareholders actually pick the directors, who are likely to be responsive to what shareholders want if they wish to remain directors. Thus, directors of close corporations are more vulnerable to the individual liability and allegiance problems discussed in Chapters 11 and 12.

10. Attitudes of the president toward your board
(Section 4.4 (b))

Why are they important, whether your corporation is close or public?

It is difficult for a board to initiate action; generally it is confined to responding to proposals of the president. While some presidents may regard themselves as answerable to their boards, they are more likely to see themselves as really managing the corporation—with, at the most, advisory assistance from the board. Whatever these attitudes, it is important that presidents and their aides keep in mind that—notwithstanding business and personal realities—the board has a formal legal role that it is dangerous to ignore. And an able, adequately informed board can be an asset rather than just a nuisance. For discussion of how a board's effectiveness can be enhanced, see Point 12.

11. Board committees (Section 4.4 (c))

Can they help you?

Dividing a board into committees can promote efficiency at the possible expense of "togetherness." An executive committee empowered to act for the board between meetings (see Point 6) adds flexibility but carries the danger of creating a caste system among directors. This danger is less with specialized committees—finance, audit, and compensation—which are probably a good idea if your board is large and independent enough to provide qualified people to staff them.

For by-laws authorizing committees of and created by the board, see Appendix B.3 (o). Note that it authorizes creation of committees with non-board members. For director resolutions on committees, see the following in Appendix F.5: (a) determining committees of the board; (b) designating directors to serve on a committee; (c) creating a committee not confined to directors; (d) authorizing committees to establish meeting procedures; (e) removing a committee member; and (f) filling a committee vacancy.

12. Effectiveness of your board (Section 4.4 (d))

How can you improve it?

Effective boards need able, dedicated people who have the information, time, and independence to fulfill their management responsibilities. Their effectiveness can be enhanced if they have some staff within the corporation who are able to combine access to information with loyalty to the board: matters largely in the hands of the president.

5

Operating Your Corporation

―――――――――――――――― CONTENTS ――――――――――――――――

5

Operating Your Corporation

In this and the two preceding chapters we sort out governing, managing, and operating a corporation. We have seen that governing is election of managers and approval of basic corporate changes by shareholders, and that managing is election of officers and setting corporate policies by directors. Now we get to operating, which we can call administering a corporation's internal organization and executing its policies by officers and their subordinates. At each of these three levels--shareholders, directors, and officers—we are also separating structures, functions, and functioning. Structures are largely institutions and their procedural rules; functions are akin to roles: what particular participants are supposed to do under substantive rules; and functioning is how corporate players actually play their roles.

It is true that viewed as functioning enterprises corporations seldom fit neatly into the compartments fashioned for them by legal theory. For example, shareholders of close corporations often do most of their own managing and operating. And, in a corporation with groups of shareholders, the directors may represent a particular group or coalition of groups and may be the real power center, with the officers actually serving as agents of the directors rather than of the corporation. And, in a widely held corporation, real power frequently gravitates to the officers, who are able to use the proxy machinery to elect whom they wish to the board of directors. But notwithstanding these blurrings of the lines, there remain real and important differences between day-to-day operations, which are our concern in this chapter, and corporate government and management, which we have been examining. The requirement that shareholders and directors act at meetings assumes that their problems can be resolved by yes or no votes, an obviously impracticable way of resolving operating problems that call for continuity, autonomy, and discretion.

It also should be noted that thus far we have been mainly concerned with people who act organically *as* the corporation: shareholders who act as its owners and its electorate, and directors who act as its management. Now we are ready to concentrate on people who act vicariously *for* the corporation: officers, employees, and agents.

▪ **Note, however, that officers act *as*, as well as *for*, their corporations, since they are both corporate officials and corporate agents.**

In this chapter we look first at corporate officers. Since this book is addressed to corporate officers, we go into considerable detail about their selection, duties, and powers. Then we look at subordinate employees and agents: how they are appointed and empowered, and their powers, liabilities, and rights. Finally, we examine some of the ways of keeping track of who can act for your corporation. The diversity of potential operational problems precludes an attempt in this book to treat corporate operations exhaustively. Instead, we focus on a few basic facets of operational structure and function that are likely to be pertinent to most corporate enterprises.

Section 5.1 Corporate Officers: Their Selection, Duties, and Powers

At the outset, we need to pay attention to the difference between officers' duties and their powers. Duties relate mainly to internal administration; powers relate to executing policy and usually involve creation of corporate obligations to outsiders. Duties include presiding at and recording meetings, reporting to shareholders and directors, maintaining custody of the corporate seal and of corporate funds. Powers include appointing subordinate officers, employees, and agents and making and authorizing contracts and transfers of property. Presidents and vice presidents have both duties and powers (i.e., they are both administrators and executives); whereas, secretaries and assistant secretaries and treasurers and assistant treasurers have mainly duties (i.e., they are mainly administrators). Generally, powers can involve more legal complications than can duties. Powers can have unexpected legal consequences even when properly used; but there are seldom other than routine legal consequences when duties are performed.

Powers of officers can be either expressly spelled out (in a statute, by-law, resolution, or delegation), or implied from a course of conduct. Also (a slightly different distinction), powers can be either inherent in an office or delegated to an officer by a superior. When exercising an inherent power, an officer is acting as part of the corporate principal; when exercising a delegated power he is acting as a corporate agent. This distinction becomes important when a third party deals with an officer in a transaction which the law calls a part of his inherent power (or not a part of this power) and as to which there has been no delegation of authority.

In this section we examine some of the legal rules on how officers are selected, qualified, compensated, and removed; how corporate officers go about ascertaining their duties and powers from corporate documents; and the perplexing legal puzzle: what are the inherent powers of corporate officers, especially the president?

(a) Selection, qualification, compensation, and removal of officers

Most state corporation acts require that designated officers (usually a president, a secretary, and a treasurer) be elected by the board of directors and permit other officers to be elected or appointed as the by-laws may provide.

Statutory officers—i.e., those required by statute—are to be elected by the board of directors "at such times and in such manner as may be prescribed by the by-laws" (Model Act §50). As noted in Section 4.1(c), officers are usually elected and appointed at the board's organizational meeting, which is its first meeting after the annual meeting of shareholders (see Appendix C.2(b)). There must, of course, be a quorum of directors present, and the affirmative votes of a majority of the directors present are needed to elect each officer. Terms of office are usually until the next organizational meeting of the board and until their successors are elected and have qualified.

> ▪ As with the usual terms for directors, these terms for officers prevent gaps in case successors are not elected or qualified.

Non-statutory officers are usually elected or appointed by the board at the same time and for the same terms as statutory officers, although by-laws sometimes authorize a president to appoint some of the non-statutory officers. A chairman of the board and any vice presidents are usually elected by the board; assistant secretaries, assistant treasurers, a general counsel, and a comptroller are frequently appointed by the board, and sometimes by the president.

As for qualifications for officers, by-laws sometimes require that one or more of the officers—usually the chairman of the board, and the president, and, more rarely, the executive vice president—be chosen from the board of directors (see Appendix B.4(a)).

▪ Certainly the officer, chairman of the board or president, who presides at board meetings should be a director. However, sometimes the "chairman of the board" is not an officer of the corporation but merely the director designated by the directors to be their chairman.

The Model Act provides (§50): "any two or more offices may be held by the same person, except the offices of president and secretary." A reason for this exception is to provide a separate person to attest to the president's authority to sign documents.

▪ Note that this exception, which has not been followed in several states, precludes a completely one-person corporation, where one person is the sole shareholder and director and fills all the offices. If you want to form a one-person corporation you should have your lawyer check the law of your state on this point.

Compensation of officers elected or appointed by the board is usually fixed by the board, and that of officers appointed by the president, subject to approval of the board (see Appendix B.4(j)).

The board of directors has the power to remove, without having to show cause, any officer or agent of the corporation, and any officer or agent of the corporation may resign at any time. However, a removal requires an honest judgment by the board that it will serve the best interest of the corporation, and a removal or a resignation may subject the corporation or the officer or agent to liability for breach of contract (See Appendix B.4(c).) The Model Act provides (§51):

Any officer or agent may be removed whenever in [the board's] judgment the best interest of the corporation will be served thereby, but such removal shall be without prejudice to the contract rights, if any, of the person so removed. Election or appointment of an officer or agent shall not of itself create contract rights.

▪ Suppose C Corporation contracts with P that P will serve as president of C for five years at an annual salary of $100,000. After P has been elected president of C and been in office for six months, the board of C votes to remove P from office. P thereupon ceases to be president of C. However, if the five-year contract is upheld (as it probably would be), C may continue to be liable to P for his salary for the balance of the contract period (subject to P's duty to "mitigate damages" by seeking other employment).

If P had resigned after six months he would cease to be president of C; C would not be liable to P for future salary and C might have a claim against P for damages suffered by C because of P's breach of their contract.

(b) Express duties and powers of corporate officers

State corporation acts generally refer you to your by-laws and board resolutions for the express duties and powers of your officers. Typically, by-laws provide:

—The president shall preside at shareholder and director meetings; be the corporation's chief executive and administrative officer (we will return to what this statement means); have power to appoint such officers, agents, and employees as in his judgment may be needed to transact the corporation's business; and report periodically to the board on the corporation's operations and financial condition (see Appendix B.4(e)).

—Vice presidents shall perform duties and have powers assigned by the board or the president (see Appendix B.4(f)).

—The secretary (or an assistant secretary) shall record proceedings of shareholder and director meetings; have custody of the corporate seal and affix it and countersign documents on the order of the board, the president, or a vice president; and perform other duties assigned by the board, the president, or a designated vice president (see Appendix B.4(g) and (i)).

—The treasurer and assistant treasurers shall have custody of the corporation's funds and securities; disburse and administer such funds and securities as directed by the board, the president, or a designated vice president; and perform other duties assigned by the board, the president, or a designated vice president (see Appendix B.4(h) and (i)).

These by-laws provisions are, of course, just a beginning of an effort to ascertain the express duties and powers of your officers. Duties and powers of vice presidents depend entirely on what is assigned to them, and secretaries and treasurers can be assigned additional duties. Thus, beyond the by-laws, you need to know what assignments of duties and powers have been made by board resolutions and by delegations (see Appendix B.5 and G). We explore this question further in Section 5.3.

(c) Inherent duties and powers of corporate officers

While some duties can be called "inherent" (in the sense that officers should do them whether or not they are spelled out), this adjective is more often coupled with powers than with duties. As we have noted, powers involve more potentiality for legal entanglements with outsiders than do duties; legal disputes frequently turn on whether a transaction is within an officer's "inherent powers," but a judge will seldom be asked to decide whether an officer has failed to perform an "inherent duty." We will, therefore, limit this subsection to inherent powers not expressed in statutes, by-laws, resolutions, or other corporate documents.

The kind of situation we are concerned with here is when someone outside the corporation has what he thinks is a contract with, or a conveyance of property from, the corporation, by virtue of a document signed by a corporate officer on behalf of the corporation, but there is no express grant of authority to the officer to sign such a document and no express representation by the corporation to the outsider that the officer has such authority. Thus, the issue is squarely presented whether the officer has power to bind the corporation because of the very nature of the officer's office. We deal first with inherent powers of a president, and then with inherent powers of other officers.

(i) Inherent powers of a president

Most of the cases involve presidents, because they are supposed to be the most powerful of officers, and because by-laws tend to be cryptic about their powers, often simply describing the president as "the executive officer" or "the chief executive officer" (compare Appendix B.4(e)). There are so many different views in the decided cases about the inherent powers of a president that it is important that you consult your lawyer about how the cases in your state seem to go.

While these cases generally arise in a context of third party claims, it should be kept in mind that the board of directors has an interest in how these cases are resolved. As we suggested in Section 4.3(b), the problems of the general management responsibilities of the board and of officers' inherent powers are counterparts of the same problem: officers' powers are broadened only at the expense of director prerogatives.

The view that is most protective of director prerogatives is that found in some of the older cases (though also in some not so old) that a president, as such, has no greater power to bind the corporation than any other director. He is just another director. And we have seen that individual directors have no power to act for the corporation outside of board meetings. The consequence of this approach is that any power a president purports to exercise must be traceable to an express grant of authority by the board. This view has been rejected in most states because it is felt that it obstructs the flow of business by requiring excessive caution about whether contracts and conveyances are properly authorized and that it unduly involves the board in the day-to-day business of the corporation. It is, however, consistent with corporate theory that directors manage and officers execute. If you discover that you are in a state that follows this approach, you may be able to soften its rigours by having your board pass very broad delegations of authority to your president to sign contracts and conveyances and to authorize other officers, employees, and agents to sign such documents (see Appendix G.2(a), G.3(b), and G.5(a)).

In contrast, the view that is least protective of directors' prerogatives is at the other extreme: that a president, as the corporation's executive officer, has inherent power to make any contract or conveyance that the board of directors could authorize. While this approach may speed the doing of business by eliminating the need for caution about authorizations, and while it may be consistent with the expectations that most people have about the powers of a president, it is an approach that is difficult to reconcile with the management powers that are supposed to be reserved to the board. The law is tilting in the direction of this view, but few states have gone all the way in adopting it. If you find that the law in your state is following this trend, you may be able to preserve some management role for your board of directors by having the board adopt by-laws or pass resolutions which expressly limit the contracting and conveying powers of your president to dimensions appropriate for your business. You will also want to take steps to make these limits known to outsiders.

The approach that you are most likely to find in your state is between these two extremes: that a president has inherent powers beyond those of other directors, but these powers do not extend to all transactions that the board could authorize. The ritual language for stating the dividing line is "ordinary course of business." A president may, without specific board authorization, make contracts and conveyances in the ordinary course of business, but no transactions that are unusual or extraordinary. The distinctions that we tried to make and illustrate in Section 4.3, between policy decisions that should be referred to the directors and day-to-day operating decisions that officers should be free to make on their own, are applicable here, even though we have now moved from internal allocation of functions to the issue of corporate liability to outsiders.

▪ **To put our problem firmly in its present context, assume that your corporation is the outsider dealing with the president of another corporation. You are not much interested in how the president and the directors divide their internal administration, but you are very interested in what assurances of the president's authority you should ask for from the other side. This determination involves a prediction as to whether a judge (or perhaps a jury) would characterize the transaction as ordinary or extraordinary. The safe thing to do, of course, is to ask for evidence of board authorization if the transaction could possibly be called anything other than routine. At the same time, you will want to avoid losing a deal or alienating a customer or supplier by asking for what may seem to be unreasonable assurances. It is delicate judgments like this that you are paid to make. Here I am trying to give you the legal background so you can make these judgments with an awareness of their possible consequences.**

Bringing suit and hiring employees have generally been held to be within a president's inherent powers, although hiring may become extraordinary if it purports to be permanent or for long terms (say, more than five years). Settling claims of the corporation, and transactions involving real estate (unless the corporation is in the business of buying and selling real estate) are among those that are more likely to be characterized as extraordinary. The additional title of "general manager" may broaden the inherent management powers of a president (or of a vice-president).

(ii) Inherent powers of other officers

To assess the inherent powers of vice presidents we must first ask whether a particular transaction is within the inherent power of the president. If it is not, we can ordinarily assume that it is not within a vice president's power. But if it is something a president could do without express authorization, we must go on and ask whether it is reasonable to assume that it is a power that he shares with this vice president. Factors that may help in answering this question include:

—The vice presidents title: titles like executive vice president, or senior vice president, or vice president-general manager, indicate substantial sharing of general powers with the president; in contrast, a vice president-personnel would seem to have power to hire, but not power to buy and sell real estate.

—The size of the corporation: the larger the corporation the greater the apparent need for the president to share powers with vice presidents.

—The volume and recurrence of the transactions: for example, where a publishing company routinely executes contracts with authors, an author is probably justified in not requiring proof that a vice president who signs his contract has authority to do so.

Non-officer executives, with titles such as "director" or "manager" may have agency powers to act for the corporation comparable to those of vice presidents. There is a conceptual difficulty in calling their powers "inherent" because they do not have a corporate office in which a power can inhere. However, particularly in very large corporations, the distinction between executives who are corporate officers and those who are not ceases to be very meaningful.

Secretaries and treasurers have quite limited inherent powers. Unlike many vice presidents, they are not in the general management chain of command; rather they are assigned by law specialized administrative duties which are not susceptible to much expansion into the area of inherent powers. A secretary does, however, probably have power to certify to outsiders what the board of directors has done, and the corporation will be bound by such certifications.

▪ **For example, assume that S, the secretary of C corporation, certifies to a third person, T, that the board of C has authorized P, C's president, to convey Blackacre to T, and that in reliance on S's certification T accepts a deed for Blackacre signed by P on behalf of C. Actually, the board of C has expressly directed P not to convey Blackacre to anybody. If T had no reason to doubt P's authority or S's certification, it would seem that C will be bound by S's representation of P's authority.**

A treasurer's inherent powers are limited to those needed for the care and custody of corporate funds and securities. These powers might include opening bank accounts, renting safe deposit boxes, and perhaps even investing surplus funds.

▪ **An exception to this general rule exists in Massachusetts where, by a business custom that has been incorporated into law, treasurers are accorded quite broad general management powers.**

The inherent powers of assistant secretaries and assistant treasurers cannot, of course, exceed those of secretaries and treasurers, and may be even more limited.

Section 5.2 Corporate Employees and Agents: Their Appointment, Powers, Liabilities, and Rights

We now move from corporate officers, who are parts of the corporate structure, to corporate employees and agents, whose relationships with the corporation are contractual rather than organic. Since you generally have an option whether you enter into a contract, employment and agency relationships can be said to be voluntarily entered into by the corporation. The law insists that someone (albeit a single person) play the corporate roles of shareholder, director, president, secretary, and treasurer; but employees and agents are optional. Legal questions with employees and agents generally involve contract and agency law rather than the law of corporations. Not being parts of the corporate structure, corporate employees and agents do not have corporate duties to perform in the same sense that officers do. They may, however, have significant powers to obligate or impose liabilities upon their corporations, and their employments or agencies may include performance of administrative duties, and they may have liabilities and rights vis à vis the corporation and third persons. In this section we look first at how they are appointed and empowered, and then at the individual liabilities and rights of agents of corporations.

(a) How corporate employees and agents are appointed and empowered

By-laws and board of director resolutions frequently authorize the president to appoint such non-elective officers, employees, and agents as he judges necessary and proper for the transaction of the business of the corporation (see Appendix B.4(e)). This power carries with it power to delegate the president's appointing power to vice presidents and others down the chain of command and to write, and to delegate authority to write, job descriptions defining the duties of, and delegations of specific powers to, appointees. A president also is frequently given power to remove any person he has power to appoint (see Appendix B.4(c)) (and the Model Act (§51) gives the board power to remove any "officer or agent"), but a president might not delegate downward his removal power quite as freely as he might his appointing power.

> ▪ **For example, a president who delegates to the vice president-sales selection of regional and district sales managers might reserve to himself power to remove them. By allowing autonomy of choice but keeping the more potent removal power, he would be retaining the ultimate control he should have as president.**

In summary, power to appoint and empower employees and agents resides in the president as chief executive officer. As a corporation gets larger and more complicated, more and more of this power is delegated to subordinates. This diffusion of power happens without much regard to whether the corporation is closely or publicly held.

We now need to sort out three kinds of people who are used in operating a corporation: employees, agents, and independent contractors. Employees work for the corporation on a regular basis; they may or may not be its agents, depending on whether they are empowered to represent the corporation in dealings with outsiders.

> ▪ **Officers are usually, but not always, employees and are sometimes agents (a lawyer who serves as secretary would be an example of a non-employee officer; he would probably be an agent as lawyer but not as secretary). Directors, purely as directors, are neither employees nor agents.**

Persons who are not employees can be empowered to act as agents for the corporation. Independent contractors are neither employees nor agents: they are persons doing work for the corporation under special contracts. The ways that these three kinds of people can obligate the corporation to third persons can be summarized:

—Corporate employees can create liability by the corporation for wrongful acts in the course of their employment.

—Corporate agents can, depending upon their authority and powers, bind the corporation to contracts and property transfers; the corporation is not, however, ordinarily liable for their wrongful acts.

—Independent contractors cannot obligate the corporation either by their wrongful acts or their contracts and property transfers.

• Suppose that X corporation employees A as a lathe operator and B as a purchasing agent, retains C as a lawyer, and contracts with D for plumbing work. A is an employee but not an agent of X. B is both an employee and an agent. C is an agent but not an employee. D is neither an employee nor an agent. X will be liable for the wrongful acts done while on X's business of employees A and B, and for authorized contracts made in X's name by agents B and C, but for neither the wrongful acts nor contracts of independent contractor D.

The employment of corporate employees is a familiar and uncomplicated event. The empowering of corporate agents is less familiar and more complicated. There are at least four different ways that an agent, either employee or non-employee, can be endowed with power to obligate the corporation to outsiders.

The agent may be informed that he has authority to bind the corporation in a designated way by a representative of the corporation (usually his superior in the corporate hierarchy if he is an employee) who has authority to make such representations. The agent is then said to have "actual authority." He may be informed by being expressly told in so many words ("express actual authority"), or by implication, as where he does something on behalf of the corporation and the corporate representatives do not object, making it reasonable for him to believe that he has authority ("implied actual authority"). With actual authority, whether express or implied, the representations flow from the corporate representative to the agent. It is immaterial whether outsiders know about the representations.

Secondly, an outsider may be led to believe by the corporate representative that the agent has authority that he does not actually have. The agent is then said to have "apparent authority." We only get to this situation when the agent does not have actual authority. Like actual authority, apparent authority can be express or implied. The outsider may be expressly (but erroneously) told in so many words by the corporate representative that the agent has authority ("express apparent authority"); or the outsider may be informed by implication, as where the outsider knows that the agent has done something for the corporation before and corporate representatives have not objected, making it reasonable for the outsider to believe that the agent has authority ("implied apparent authority"). With apparent authority, whether express or implied, the representations flow from the corporate representative to the outsider. It is immaterial whether the agent knows about the representations.

A third method of empowering agents comes into play when an agent with neither actual nor apparent authority has purported to act for the corporation and, before the outsider changes his position on the basis of the invalidity of the transaction, the corporation elects to accept the benefits and obligations of the transaction and communicates this election to the outsider. The corporation is said to have "ratified" the unauthorized transaction. Since the effectiveness of the ratification dates back to the original transaction, the transaction must be one that the corporation could make at that time.

> ▪ Hence the difficulty, discussed in sub-section (b) below, in allowing a new corporation to "ratify" contracts made on its behalf by promoters before the corporation was formed.

Even where an agent has neither actual nor apparent authority and the corporation does not ratify, the corporation may still be bound if the agent has "inherent agency power" by virtue of his position in the corporation. The inherent powers of corporate officers, discussed in Section 5.1, are a special case of this general principle. It seems to be based on the notion that when the corporation gives someone a title like "general manager" or "general agent" (or "president"), the law should give the title-holder powers to bind the corporation which are not dependent upon proof of representations to the agent or to outsiders. Persons dealing with agents with these titles should be able to assume, with no duty of inquiry, that the agents are empowered to act for the corporation. It would slow down business too much if outsiders had to check up on their authority.

> ▪ While you cannot avoid having a president, you can avoid such titles as "general manager" and "general agent."

(b) Individual liabilities, duties, and rights of agents of corporations

In Chapter 11 we deal with the individual legal positions of corporate shareholders, directors, and officers. Corporate employment by itself does not involve special liabilities and rights. Thus, in this subsection we focus upon corporate agents as agents, without regard to whether they are also shareholders, directors, officers, or employees. This endeavor takes us into some agency doctrine about the three-cornered relationships among the corporate principal (P), an agent of the corporation (A), and an outside third party (T). We look first at A's liabilities to T; then at his duties to P; and finally at his rights against T and P.

Before making this examination we need to note the basic proposition that when A has authority, actual or apparent, or inherent power to do what he does on behalf of P, and when T knows that he is dealing with an agent for P, then A will *not* be liable to either P or T. So far as P is concerned, A has done what P told A to do or what P told T that A could do or what A is empowered by his position to do; so far as T is concerned, he got what he bargained for: a deal with P. A can rest easily.

(i) A's liabilities to T

Departures from this normal situation which may make A liable to T can occur in at least three ways:

—When A exceeds his authority or power and P does not ratify;

—When A does not disclose to T that he is acting as an agent; and

—In a context peculiar to corporations, when A is acting on behalf of a corporation that has not yet been formed.

If A purports to bind P in a way that he is not actually authorized to do and there is no basis for a claim of apparent authority, and if P is not bound because P has ratified or because A has inherent agency power, T will not have received what he bargained for: a deal with P. T has been misled by A as to A's power to bind P. Thus, T will be able to sue A for the damages he has suffered due to A's breach of an "implied warranty of authority." In the words of the Restatement of the Law of Agency (§329):

> *A person who purports to make a contract, conveyance or representation on behalf of another who has full capacity [i.e., is competent and of legal age] but who has no power to bind, thereby becomes subject to liability to the other party thereto upon an implied warranty of authority, unless he has manifested that he does not make such warranty or the other party knows that the agent is not so authorized.*

If A purports to bind himself to T when he actually is acting as an agent for P, T will have the obligations of both P and A. A is said to be an agent of an "undisclosed principal." Here T gets more than he bargained for: the obligation of P, in addition to that of A. T cannot be deprived of his deal with A against his will, because the obligation of A, with whom he thought he was dealing as a principal, is what T bargained for; but, unknown to T, he was also getting the obligation of P.

> ▪ **Suppose P Corporation wants to acquire a tract of land, Blackacre, for a new plant, but fears that if T, the owner of Blackacre, knows of P's interest the asking price will soar. P authorizes A, a lawyer who knows T, to promise T $500 for a 90 day option to buy Blackacre for $100,000 without disclosing to T that A is acting as an agent for P. If the option agreement is entered into it will be between T and A, and only A will be able to exercise the option, unless T consents to assignment of A's rights to P; but A holds the option on behalf of P, and both A and P are bound by the promise to pay T $500 for the option.**

In this situation T has a choice whether he will hold A to his deal or take advantage of his unexpected claim against P. The choice becomes easy if either A or P is insolvent or has left the jurisdiction or there is some other impediment to assertion of a claim against him.

> ▪ **If A promises T that if T will run for public office A will contribute $50,000 to T's campaign, and if A is acting for an undisclosed principal, P Corporation, which cannot legally make political contributions, it would seem that if T has any claim it would have to be against A alone.**

A contract made by a corporate promoter (A) with a third party (T) on behalf of a projected but yet unformed corporation (P) has presented a conceptual puzzle, because the principal does not exist when the contract is made. An English judge said that A could no more bind an unformed corporation than he could bind his horse by making a contract on the horse's behalf. But before the incorporation process became quick and inexpensive, pre-incorporation contracts were needed to line up the resources required for a new venture. What the parties usually intended was that the promoter would be liable until the corporation was formed (because they wanted a binding deal, and the promoter was the only one that could be bound), and then the corporation would take over the obligation. But the traditional legal rule has been that, since ratification relates back to the time of the original contract, P must be in existence at that time to be able to ratify. To get around this impasse, American judges evolved a new legal doctrine called "adoption," which created a new contract between T and P when P was formed. However, the adoption doctrine left it unclear whether A continued to be liable to T on the original contract. Of course, if T consented to substituting P's obligation for A's, then there would be what the law calls a "novation" and A would be off the hook.

While the law is still murky about promoters' liability on pre-incorporation contracts, there is now a practical way around the problem under modern corporation acts which permit quick, easy, and cheap incorporation: form the corporation before making contracts with outsiders.

(ii) A's duties to P

Turning from A's possible liabilities to T to A's duties to his principal, P, they can be summarized as follows: an agent should represent his principal with care and loyalty. A's duty to exercise reasonable care when acting for P can be subsumed under the obligation we are all under not to injure another by our negligence.

> ▪ **If A happens to be a lawyer representing a client, P, a violation of A's duty of care to P would be called "malpractice."**

A's duty of loyalty to P is more complicated and more peculiar to the agency relationship. The general principle of an agent's duty of loyalty is, in the words of the Restatement of the Law of Agency (§387): "to act solely for the benefit of the principal in all matters connected with his agency." The Restatement goes on to make its admonition more specific by spelling out the following duties which an A, with a possible conflict of interest, owes to a P who does not know about A's interest in transactions within A's agency (§§388-96):

—To give P any profit which A makes;

—To refrain from dealing with P *as* or *for* an adverse party;

—When acting on his own account with P's knowledge, and when acting for two P's with their knowledge in a transaction between them, to deal fairly with his principal or principals and to disclose all facts that A knows or should know would affect their judgment in dealing with A or in permitting his dual agency;

—To refrain from competing with P and from acting for persons whose interest conflicts with P's;

—To refrain from using or communicating information confidentially given A by P in violation of A's duties, in competition with or to the injury of P, on his own behalf or on behalf of another, although the information does not relate to the transaction in which he is employed, unless the information is a matter of general knowledge; and

—After termination of the agency:

—to refrain from using or disclosing to third persons, on his own account or on account of others, in competition with P or to his injury, trade secrets, written lists of names, or other similar confidential matters given him only for P's use or acquired by A in violation of duty;

—to account for profits from the sale or use of trade secrets and other confidential information, whether or not in competition with P; and

—to refrain from taking advantage of a still subsisting confidential relation created during the prior agency relationship.

▪ **Suppose again that P Corporation wants Blackacre for a plant site and retains A, a lawyer, to act for P. If A receives a referral fee from another lawyer whom he employs to make a title search on Blackacre, A should give the fee to P. If A himself secretly owns Whiteacre, another tract that may also be suitable for P's plant, he should not sell Whiteacre to P without disclosing his interest and any facts about Whiteacre that may affect P's decision. If T asks A to represent T in the sale of Blackacre, A should not do so without full disclosure to both P and T. It would be wrong for A, after he has been retained by P, to secure an option on his own behalf for Blackacre, or to offer to T to help him sell Blackacre. If A**

learns confidentially from P that P also wants Greenacre for another project, it would be wrong for A to secure an option on his own behalf for Greenacre or to disclose P's interest in acquiring Greenacre to anyone else. If A learns confidentially from P that after Blackacre is acquired and the plant built, P plans to buy large quantities of a byproduct of a chemical plant near Blackacre owned by X, it would be wrong, even after termination of A's agency for P, for A to contract with X on A's own behalf for X's output of the by-product or to disclose P's interest in the by-product to anyone else.

We return to the problems of the duty of loyalty and conflicts of interest in Chapter 11.

(iii) A's rights against T and P

If A is personally obligated to T on a contract or conveyance, T will, on his side of the deal, normally be obligated to A. And T is under the usual duties not to injure A by T's wrongful acts. But A has no special rights against T arising out of A's agency relationship with P.

As against P, A does have special rights flowing from what is called P's "duty to indemnify" A. The Restatement of the Law of Agency (§§438-40) describes P's duty to make A whole for any loss or expense suffered or incurred by A in reasonably executing P's affairs as including the following, unless otherwise agreed between P and A:

—authorized payments made by A on behalf of P;

—payments on contracts upon which A is authorized to make himself liable, and upon obligations arising from the possession or ownership of things which he is authorized to hold for P;

—payments of damages to T which A is required to make because of the authorized performance of an act which constitutes a tort or a breach of contract;

—expenses defending unfounded but good faith actions by T arising from A's authorized conduct; and

—payments benefiting P made by A under such circumstances that it would be inequitable for indemnity not to be made.

Unless otherwise agreed, P is not subject to a duty to indemnify A:

—for loss or harm not benefiting P arising from unauthorized acts or resulting solely from A's negligence or other fault; or

—if P has otherwise performed his duties to A, for physical harm caused by authorized acts, for harm suffered as the result of torts, other than the tortious institution of suits, committed on A because of his employment, or for harm suffered by the refusal of T to deal with A; or —if A's loss resulted from an enterprise which he knew to be illegal.

> ▪ Suppose once again that P Corporation wants Blackacre for a plant site and retains A, a lawyer, to act for P. If A pays T $500 for an option on Blackacre; or if A pays $10,000 as a down payment under a contract with T to buy Blackacre; or if A takes title to Blackacre for P and pays taxes thereon; or if P backs out of the contract to buy Blackacre from T and A becomes liable to T for damages for breach of contract; or if A takes title to Blackacre for P and is sued by a plaintiff who is injured on Blackacre and mistakenly believes that A has been negligent; or if A uses his own funds for necessary maintenance of Blackacre: in each of these situations, A would seem to have a right to be indemnified by P unless P and A have otherwise agreed. However, if A, having taken title to Blackacre for P, negligently injures thereon a third person to whom A is required to pay damages; or if A, in carrying on his negotiations with T for the purchase of Blackacre, suffers physical harm from T or some other third person; or if A, having taken title to Blackacre for P, pays a bribe to a public official to secure a zoning variance that will permit erection of a plant on Blackacre: in each of these situations, A would not seem to have a right to be indemnified by P unless P and A have otherwise agreed.

Section 5.3 Deciding and Keeping Track of Who Can Act as and for Your Corporation

We are examining how officers, employees, and agents operate a corporation by performing their administrative duties and exercising their executive powers. Before leaving this topic we need to focus briefly on how you, as a corporate officer or director, keep track of who does what in acting as and for your corporation. Since corporations by their nature cannot act themselves, they must have "vicars" to personify and represent them. In this section we will first look at how duties are assigned and powers granted, and then at some techniques that you (and your corporate secretary) can use to help the functioning of your system of vicarious corporate action. In the preceding sections we have been concerened with the legal basis for operational duties and powers; here we assume the legal basis and move on to the more practical challenge of how to designate and control your corporation's organs and agents.

> ▪ When you play tennis, your hand is a part of you (an organ) and what your hand does, you do; your racquet, in contrast, is not a part of you, but legally is under your control (resembling an agent), and you are as "responsible" for what it does as you are for what your hand does. To the law, it does not matter whether you hit me with your hand or your racquet.

(a) Assigning duties and granting powers

As we have seen, duties relate to internal administration and powers relate to executing policy. By electing, appointing, and naming people to corporate positions we assign them the duties of these positions. Duties are usually more closely tied to titles than are powers, although some titles do carry inherent powers, and powers can be granted by titles rather than by names. Duties are assigned to offices and positions in by-laws, resolutions, tables of organizations, operating procedures, job descriptions, organization charts, and other documents which set up the "infra-structure" of a corporation. With a small corporation this structure is likely to be rudimentary; with a large corporation these combinations of positions, duties, and people can become very complex.

The process of granting powers to act for a corporation in dealings with outsiders usually starts with board resolutions authorizing the president to do designated things, to designate other officers, employees and agents who shall share some or all of his authority, and possibly also to delegate to subordinates the power to designate those who shall share the authority. Then there follows a series of designations and delegations and sub-delegations of authority to people or positions down the chain of command. Note that the board may authorize three things: to act for the corporation; to authorize others to act for the corporation; and to authorize others to authorize still others to act for the corporation.

> **▪ For example, the board may authorize the president to open, and to authorize the treasurer to open, a bank account with X Bank, and to authorize the treasurer to designate those authorized to make deposits into and withdrawals from such bank account.**

There are two main types of authorizations: one-shot and continuing. Examples of one-shot authorizations include purchase of a particular piece of real estate for not more than a designated price (see Appendix G.1(a)); hiring a particular person (see Appendix G.3(a)); opening a particular bank account (see Appendix G.4(a)); building a specified plant at not more than a designated cost (see Appendix G.6(a)). Most of these authorizations involve management decisions on which the board of directors should act. From some of them may flow other authorizations to enable these basic decisions to be implemented.

> **▪ For instance, an authorization to build a plant will entail many diverse individual transactions spread over months or years and requiring more specific authorizations. However, with the basic authorization from the board it will not be necessary to go back to the board for the implementing authorizations: these can be made by officers and their subordinates (see Appendix G.6(b) and (c)).)**

Examples of continuing authorizations include those for purchasing supplies needed in the regular operations of your corporation (usually not exceeding a designated dollar amount per purchase and limited to a particular type or types of supplies) (see Appendix G.2); making deposits in and withdrawals from designated bank accounts (usually not exceeding a designated dollar amount per withdrawal, and frequently limiting the source of deposits to, say, transfer checks from other designated accounts (see Appendix G.4(b)-(i)); and hiring salaried and hourly-paid employees for the regular operations of the corporation (usually not exceeding designated rates of compensation, and without authority to promise lengths of tenure) (see Appendix G.3(b)-(e)).

In formulating board resolutions and designations, delegations, and subdelegations, there are rewards from precise wording. Your objective can be said to be *controlled flexibility*: to grant only the authority needed to carry out the responsibility that your board wants to entrust to particular corporate officers, employees, and agents; but, at the same time, to allow enough leeway so that your operating people are not constantly needing to refer decisions to higher authority.

Control is achieved by clarity in defining limits. These limits can take many forms. They can be expressed in terms of the time when the authority can be exercised; of dollar amounts as to which the corporation can be committed, per transaction and per time period; of locations (plants or geographical areas) for or in which commitments can be made; of the specific items that can be the subject of transactions (such as land, kinds of supplies and products, or services); of the kinds of transactions that can be entered into (such as purchases, sales, leases, mortgages, or contracts); and of the third persons (by name or category) with whom the agent can deal.

On the other side, flexibility is achieved by making your limits realistic and workable, with designating and delegating authority sufficiently decentralized that your board and president do not need to be involved in the fine-tuning of your authorizations system. To this end, your authorizations should be under more or less continuous review to adjust dollar limits to inflation and to keep all limits compatible with the growth in experience and responsibility of your authority-holders.

(b) Compiling and disseminating information about duties and powers

Not only do the substantive components of your corporation's system of duties and powers need careful and continuing attention for effective functioning, but you also need a well thought-out procedure for keeping informed those among your people who need to know who in your organization is responsible for and authorized to do what in operating your corporation. Both of these tasks, the drafting of the documents that assign duties and grant powers, and the compiling and dissemination of information about them, frequently end up on the desk of the corporate secretary. And this result seems appropriate, because he is the officer responsible for recording shareholder and board action, for keeping and applying the corporate seal, and for vouching for what are proper corporate acts (see Appendix B.4(g)). To perform his own duties he must know who can do what and he must share this knowledge with those who are doing the doing. Thus, our question in this sub-section is: how can a corporate secretary best function as a clearing house or information system for data about corporate duties and powers?

Try this effective technique: Maintain a book or "data bank" which puts together and keeps up to date a composite picture—made up of duties, positions, incumbents, authorizations, designations, delegations, and sub-delegations—which enables one to ascertain through whom the corporation operates in specific situations.

> **■ These books are sometimes called "Continuing Authorizations Books," because authorizations (as distinguished from duties and powers) of the continuing variety (as distinguished from one-shot authorizatons) have most needed this kind of attention. Ideally, however, the secretary's book would serve to inform generally about who does what as and for the corporation below the shareholder and director level—i.e., in operating the corporation, as this function is conceived in this chapter.**

Among the sources the secretary will utilize in putting together this composite picture of the corporation's human operating parts and agents are:

—state corporation acts and court decisions, for the general duties and inherent powers of a corporation's officers and agents;

—the corporation's articles of incorporation and by-laws, for more specific assignments of duties and grants of powers;

—shareholder and director resolutions, for still more specific assignments and grants;

—acts by officers and those under them delegating authority and making designations pursuant to delegations of authority;

—acts by shareholders, directors, officers, and those under them electing and appointing people to offices and positions.

Each corporate secretary will need to fashion his own approach to his clearing house function. Here are a few suggestions that may be helpful:

—Use articles, by-laws, resolutions and delegations tailor-made for your corporation. While suggested forms may give you some ideas, use your own ingenuity and your knowledge of your special situation. In particular, resist efforts by banks to impose upon your corporation their forms for your bank account management.

—Wherever possible, grant authorities by titles rather than by names. You thereby reduce the need to change your authorizations each time people change jobs.

—Use broad categories, multiple signers, and powers to delegate and to authorize sub-delegation. All of these devices help keep your system flexible, and minimize your need to tinker with details and to go back to your board or your president for minor adjustments.

—Work out procedures with your personnel department that will insure that you get prompt information about personnel changes.

—Try to educate your president and his operating subordinates about the benefits of clear, understandable lines of duties and powers.

—Keep your book up to date and in the hands of all your people who need to know who can do what. You may want to maintain your book like a looseleaf service. If your corporation is large, the clerical work in keeping your book current can be a full-time assignment for a subordinate. If your corporation is very large, you may literally need a data bank utilizing electronic equipment. But, however, you maintain your data, keep in mind that its accuracy is your individual responsibility as corporate secretary.

CHECKLIST OF POINTS TO WATCH OUT FOR IN OPERATING YOUR CORPORATION

(References after headings are to Sections of Chapter 5.)

1. One-person corporations (Section 5.1 (a))

Do you know where they are permitted?

If you want a completely one-person corporation, you will be limited in the states where you can incorporate. While some states permit this procedure, many follow the Model Act (§50) in requiring separate persons for president and secretary, and others have even more troublesome requirements, such as at least three persons on the board of directors.

**2. Express duties and powers of corporate officers and agents
(Section 5.1 (b))**

Where do you find them?

You start with your corporation's by-laws and then look at its director resolutions and delegations. As suggested in Point 10, your corporate secretary should put together this information for you.

For by-laws on duties and powers of corporate officers and agents, see Appendix B.4(e)-(i) and B.5. For director resolutions and officer delegations concerning authority to act for the corporation in transactions with others, see Appendix G, which is discussed in Point 9.

**3. Inherent powers of corporate officers to act
for your corporation (Section 5.1 (c))**

Why do you need to pay attention to legal rules on such powers?

If your state of incorporation is one of the few that limit a president's inherent powers—i.e., those that flow from his office and need not be expressly stated—to those of other individual directors, your board will want to delegate to your president broader powers. Conversely, if your state goes to the other extreme and gives a president powers to take any action the board could authorize, your board should consider expressly limiting these powers in your by-laws or by resolution to dimensions appropriate to your business; and those with whom your corporation does business should be notified of these limitations. If, as is more likely, your state gives a president inherent powers to act for his corporation in the "ordinary course" of its business, then your board's task, rather than to expand or limit inherent powers, will be to clarify them with more specific statements of express powers, as is done in the Appendix at B.4 (e)-(i), B.5 and G.

**4. Authority of those acting for other corporations
with which you deal (Section 5.1 (c))**

How can you protect yourself?

Where appropriate you can ask for certified copies of the by-law, resolution, or delegation authorizing the representative of the other corporation to act for it in the transaction under consideration. The certification would be by the secretary of the other corporation.

You can rely on this certification (and others with whom your corporation deals can rely on certifications by your corporate secretary) because the secretary of a corporation has inherent power to bind his corporation when he certifies that other officers and agents are authorized to act for the corporation, even when they are not in fact so authorized. Hence, the need for the corporate secretary to keep informed about who can act for the corporation, as discussed in Point 10.

5. Power of president to appoint and remove corporate agents (Section 5.2 (a))

Why might a president delegate power to appoint agents but retain power to remove them?

A president may wish to retain ultimate control over those who represent the corporation in its operations by keeping removal power in his own hands even when he delegates appointing power to subordinates. Power to remove, since removal checkmates appointments, is more potent then power to appoint. Note that the Model Act (§51) gives the board of directors power to remove any officer or agent. For appointees to know that they can be removed only by the president or the board may concentrate their loyalties.

6. Inherent powers of corporate agents (Section 5.2 (a))

Why may you want to avoid titles like "general manager" and "general agent"?

The authority, actual or apparent, of corporate agents can be limited by the representations the corporation makes to them and to outsiders; but the "inherent agency power" of some agents by virtue of their positions in the corporation, like the inherent power of the president, is less subject to the corporation's control. While a corporation cannot avoid having a president (and thus must deal with presidential powers as suggested in Point 3), a simple protection against unwanted obligations from the acts of agents is to avoid titles, like "general manager" and "general agent", which have the aura of general power to bind the corporation akin to that of a president.

7. Individual liabilities of corporate agents to outsiders (Section 5.2 (b))

What protections are available against such liabilities?

Corporate agents may be individually liable to outsiders, not only when they exceed their authority or power and the corporation declines to ratify the transaction made on its behalf, but also when they do not disclose their status as agents, and when they act for a corporation that is not yet in existence.

If non-disclosure of the agency is in the interest of the corporation, as when an agent secures options in his own name on property in which the corporation is interested, the agent is protected by the corporation's duty to indemnify him for loss or expense incurred in acting for the corporation. Note that in this situation the outsider gets an unexpected benefit: the obligation of the corporation as well as of the agent.

For the problem of agents who act for corporations not yet in existence a simple solution has been furnished by modern corporation acts which enable quick, inexpensive incorporation: form the corporation before closing any deals.

8. Individual liabilities of corporate agents to the corporation (Section 5.2 (b))

How can these liabilities be avoided?

A short answer is that a corporate agent may protect himself by acting within his authority and with care and loyalty. He will know and respect the limits of his authority; and he will not make profits for himself, or act secretly for more than one principal, or make unauthorized use or disclosure of confidential information. A longer answer is set forth in Chapter 11.

9. Deciding who can act when for your corporation (Section 5.3 (a))

How can top management keep control but delegate routine?

As your corporation grows, more transactions with outsiders will be delegated to subordinates. Appendix G provides a framework of resolutions, delegations of authority to act, and sub-delegations of authority to act—for various transactions, one-shot and continuing: purchasing and selling particular property (G.1), purchasing for regular operations (G.2), hiring (G.3), operating bank accounts (G.4), borrowing (G.5), and building a new facility (G.6).

The objectives are control and flexibility. Control is achieved by clearly defined limits on authorities: by dollar amounts, transactions, time periods, locations, items, and outsiders. Flexibility is achieved by using realistic limits, broad categories, multiple signers, authorities by titles rather than names (so that they are not made obsolete by personnel shuffles), and tailor-made authorizations which permit maximum recourse to delegations and sub-delegations.

10. Keeping track of who can act when for your corporation (Section 5.3 (b))

Who should provide a clearing house for this information?

A carefully crafted scheme of authorizations, delegations, and sub-delegations is of little use unless reliable information is readily available to those who need to know who is authorized to do what. Whatever the size and complexity of your enterprise, your corporate secretary is the logical officer to be responsible for maintenance of this information system. The secretary takes part in generation of authorizations by the board and by officers and their delegates; and , as indicated in Appendix B.4 (g) and discussed in Point 3 above, duties and powers of the secretary include certifying that documents executed on behalf of the corporaton are duly authorized.

6

Accommodating Your Corporation To the Special Needs of Closeness

165

6

Accommodating Your Corporation To the Special Needs of Closeness

The corporate form is available to an industrial complex, like General Motors, and to a single person (whether natural or legal). While all corporations, no matter their size or ownership, are each separate legal persons, their factual characteristics and needs can vary enormously. Our objective in this chapter is to look at some of the things that you can do to make the corporate machinery, which has been our concern in the preceding chapters, accommodate your special needs if your corporation is close. These needs can be broadly summarized: to stay close, to get away from majority voting (i.e., to protect minorities), and to be able to break deadlocks. This chapter will deal first with the legal recognition accorded close corporations in state corporation acts, and then with what you can do under these laws to fashion for a close corporation suitable ownership controls, forms of governance, and ways of handling internal dissension.

Section 6.1 Statutory Recognition and Definition of Close Corporations

Corporation laws in Europe and Canada have long had separate provisions for what have been called " incorporated partnerships" or "private companies." Corporations of the latter sort are restricted as to the right to transfer shares, the number of shareholders, and invitations to the public to subscribe

167

to shares. In the United States, however, until recently the states each have had one corporation act that applied to all corporations. And owners of close corporations have frequently had legal difficulties, despite the ingenuity of their lawyers, in fitting their business needs into the Procrustean beds of statutory norms.

This problem has eased considerably in recent years because of two developments in our state corporation laws. Delaware and a few other states have tried to define a "close corporation" and have enacted special provisions for this category of corporations. The Model Act, on the other hand, has backed away from this definitional problem, because of the difficulty in drawing a line between a corporation that is close and one that is not, and instead tries to provide enough flexibility that its provisions can be adapted to the needs of corporations of various degrees of closeness but without establishing a category of "close corporations." The Delaware approach eases some drafting problems by earmarking close corporation provisions. However, the Model Act provides substantive equivalents without the need for putting a label on your corporation, which is helpful in borderline cases.

The Delaware Act, following the European and Canadian approach, defines a close corporation as one having a certificate of incorporation which does the following: limits shareholders of record to a specified number, not exceeding 30; provides for transfer restrictions on shares; and provides that the corporation shall make no "public offering" of its shares within the meaning of federal securities laws (§342 (a)). In counting shareholders, where husband and wife or other groups of persons hold shares together, the group shall be counted as one shareholder (§342 (c)).

Upon a two-thirds vote of shareholders of record of each class of outstanding shares, an existing regular corporation can elect to become a close corporation (§344); and, upon a similar vote, a close corporation can elect to cease to be a close corporation, unless its certificate of incorporation requires a greater than two-thirds vote (which provision cannot itself be changed by a vote less than that required to terminate close corporation status) (§346). A close corporation can lose its close corporation status involuntarily by breaching any of the qualifying conditions in its certificate.

▪ **Suppose the certificate of close corporation X specifies not more than 10 shareholders. When there are nine shareholders, shareholder A dies leaving his shares in equal parts to his three children, B, C, and D. Since there will now be 11 shareholders, X stands to lose its close corporation status. Thus, it might have been prudent for the organizers of X to have set the specified number of shareholders higher (perhaps at the statutory maximum of 30) if they had wanted close corporation status to survive passage of shares to the next generation.**

Section 6.2 Ownership Controls for Close Corporations

Whatever the difficulties in drawing a line, the essence of closeness in a corporation is a limited and limitable number of owners. Closeness is threatened by new owners, whether they are introduced by issuance of additional shares or by transfers of shares already issued. Additional shares have the further consequence of diluting the existing owner's shares unless the existing owners participate proportionately in the new issue. In this section we will look at protections for the preservation of closeness that the law makes available: against new issues of shares; and against unrestricted transfers of outstanding shares.

(a) Protections against new issues

Preemptive rights, which entitle existing shareholders to pro rata parts of new share issues, provide some protection against the diluting effects of increasing the number of shares and should be made mandatory in the articles of close corporations (see Appendix A.5(b) and (c)). These rights, which operate independently of any status as a close corporation, are available in all states. They do not, however, completely protect a minority shareholder. If his resources are limited, he can be "swamped" by a new issue so large that he cannot afford to buy his pro rata share. Judges have recognized an equitable right of minority shareholders to be protected against such maneuvers if the minority shareholder himself has not been guilty of unethical conduct.

> ▪ **For example, if A, a 20% shareholder in X Corporation, used his resources to set up a competing business employing trade secrets he had learned from X, a court might not intervene if X took action to issue additional shares which gave A the choice of investing an additional $200,000 in X or seeing his 20% interest drop to 1%. However, a court probably would intervene if A were the innocent widow of a former "partner" in X whom the survivors were trying to "freeze out."**

Also, preemptive rights do not prevent the issue and public distribution of new shares; they simply give existing shareholders a right of first refusal. A shareholder has no assurance that other shareholders will not decline to exercise their rights, making their shares available for sale to newcomers.

What more effective safeguards than preemptive rights are available to the original shareholders of a close corporation? The strongest protection would seem to lie in carefully drawn provisions in the articles of incorporation relating to the number of authorized shares and the vote required for amendment of the articles. If the authorized shares are limited to the number scheduled to be issued to the original shareholders (see Appendix A.2(a)), and if the vote required for amendment of the articles is large enough to require assent from all original shareholders (see Appendix A.6(c)), each owner will be able to veto any proposed new issue. Of course, this arrangement also carries the danger that needed outside equity financing will be blocked by a recalcitrant shareholder.

> ▪ **For example, if Digges, Hall, and Doe are each to be issued 1,000 shares in Dighaldoe Corporation, the articles can provide for only 3,000 authorized shares and require a vote of 75% or more of the outstanding shares to amend the articles. Then any of the three owners can block any increase in the authorized shares (including the maneuver suggested in Chapter 1 of Digges and Hall diluting Doe's interest by issuing shares to their wives).**

If the original shareholders want to assure that their respective shares in voting control and growth prospects remain the same, but are willing to have newcomers share in ownership and a fixed percentage of the profits, the articles can be drawn to entrench the number of voting shares, as suggested above, but to permit authorization of preferred shares by a smaller vote that would not require unanimity.

> ▪ **For example, if Dighaldoe articles can be amended to authorize preferred shares with approval of two-thirds of the voting shares, none of the three partners can alone block the sale of preferred shares to raise outside money.**

Since, even without special voting provisions, a majority of the original shares can prevent new issues, this threat to closeness is more easily contained than are transfers of outstanding shares.

(b) Protections against transfers

An important part of ownership is freedom to transfer what you own to others. The law has a bias in favor of protecting this freedom. And the corporate norm is for shares to be freely transferable. But free transferability imperils closeness. The problem is to reconcile these individual and group interests.

The devices of preemptive rights and limitations on the number of authorized shares are of no assistance in protecting the original shareholders against transfers. While transfers to new people, unlike new issues, do not subtract from the ownership, control, or profit sharing rights of the remaining shareholders, they can materially change the nature of the enterprise by altering or adding to the ownership group.

▪ **For example, transfers can destroy the corporation's status as a Subchapter S corporation for federal income tax purposes or its status as a "close corporation" under the Delaware corporation act.**

The main protective measures against share transfers are agreements among the original shareholders (see Appendix H.2(a)), frequently supplemented by provisions in the articles or by-laws (see Appendix A.6(e)-(g) and B.14), placing restrictions on their rights to transfer their shares. In the past, the principal legal question with such restrictions was whether they operated as "unreasonable restraints on alienation," with much attention to whether the new shareholder acquired the shares with notice of the restrictions. While this question still has some vitality, the emphasis has shifted to putting together provisions that are agreeable and fair to the parties and that will be workable when needed.

What kinds of restrictions are available? The Model Act is quite cryptic on this subject, saying simply that the articles may include "any provisions restricting the transfer of shares" (§54 (h)). The Delaware Act is much more explicit. Its special provisions on close corporations permit articles establishing "the qualifications of stockholders, either by specifying classes of persons who shall be entitled to be holders of record of stock of any class, or by specifying classes of persons who shall not be entitled to be holders of stock of any class or both" (§342 (b)). In a general provision (§202), not confined to close corporations, the Delaware Act provides that transfer restrictions may:

—be enforced against the holder or any successor or transferee of the holder "including an executor, administrator, trustee, guardian, or other fiduciary";

—obligate the holder to offer the restricted shares to the corporation or to other holders and the corporation or other holders to purchase such shares;

—require the corporation or other holders to consent to transfer of the restricted shares; and

—prohibit transfer of the restricted shares to designated persons or classes of persons if the classification is "not manifestly unreasonable" (and transfer restriction to maintain Subchapter S status is "conclusively presumed to be for a reasonable purpose").

But even if a Delaware transfer restriction is held not to be authorized by these general provisions, a corporation which is a close corporation shall nevertheless have an option to acquire the restricted shares at a fair price before they can be transferred elsewhere (§349).

The Delaware Act would not appear to permit blanket prohibitions of transfers, but in such cases would allow a close corporation to acquire the illegally restricted shares. Limited prohibitions can be imposed whether or not the corporation is a close corporation. The Act appears to authorize a right-of-first-refusal in the corporation or other holders, and the granting of options which obligate the holder to offer his shares or obligate the corporation and other holders to purchase them, or both. Restrictions can be made applicable to involuntary transfers in the event of death, disability or bankruptcy of the original holder.

Events that may bring a transfer restriction into play, besides death, disability, or bankruptcy, include a desire or need on the part of the shareholder to sell his restricted shares, and a deadlock between factions in the corporation. Different price and time formulas may be appropriate for different events.

In order for transfer restrictions to be effective against outsiders, the share certificates should make specific reference to them (see §8-204 of the Uniform Commercial Code).

The most difficult problem with transfer restrictions is how to fix the price that the corporation or the other shareholders will pay for the restricted shares. Here the interest of the selling shareholder (or of his estate) in receiving a price that fairly reflects what he is selling must be balanced against the interest of the remaining shareholders that the enterprise continue to be financially viable. The fact that the drafting of these provisions almost of necessity takes place behind a veil of ignorance as to who will survive, helps make them fair. There are several alternative methods for setting a price; these include agreements, outside offers, market value, and book value. In the section of the Delaware Act giving the corporation an option to purchase where a transfer restriction is declared invalid, the price is that agreed upon by the parties or if they cannot agree, the court may appoint an appraiser. An agreed price is clearly the most satisfactory, but may be difficult to set in advance when values are changing. However, the effects of change can be mitigated by providing in the basic agreement for annual agreement upon the value of the shares.

> ▪ Assume that Digges, Hall, and Doe, the equal owners of Dighaldoe Corporation, have an agreement that upon the death or disability of any of them, his executor or guardian will sell and the corporation will buy his shares at the price most recently agreed upon by the parties, and that the price will be renegotiated at the close of each fiscal year (see Appendix H.2(a)). Doe is older than Digges and Hall and in poor health. The business is growing more profitable and expanding. Doe should insist that the price renegotiations take place on schedule to assure a price that is as current as possible. Digges and Hall have an ethical, and perhaps a legal, duty to renegotiate the price on schedule and in good faith.

For a right-of-first-refusal restriction, there may be an outside offer which can be treated as the market value which the buyers should meet, assuming it can be shown that the offer is not collusively aimed at forcing a purchase at an unreasonable price. For close corporations there is almost never a market value in the sense that shares of public corporations have a market value. Cost of shares, book value, and liquidating value are seldom reliable indications of true value because they do not reflect intangible going value nor the effects of inflation. Thus, in the absence of a recent agreed price, or a bona fide outside offer, the use of an outside appraiser seems the best solution, although this method is frequently slow and expensive, and care should be used in spelling out how the appraiser will be selected.

In agreements whereby shareholders each grant options on their shares on the happening of designated events, the preferred practice is to give the first option to the corporation, so that other shareholders will not be faced with the alternative of increasing their investments in the business or seeing their shares of it shrink. A corporate purchase increases the ownership shares of the remaining shareholders at the expense of funds on which they have a claim in exact proportion to their original stakes in the business.

> **■ If Dighaldoe Corporation buys Doe's shares, Digges and Hall will each increase their ownership by one-sixth (from one-third to one-half) at a "cost" to each of them of one-sixth of the corporate assets (assuming a fair price is paid for Doe's shares), because they now each own one-half of a corporation that has one-third less assets than it had before the buy-out.**

However, corporate purchase of the shares is in effect a partial liquidation of the business. Thus, to provide for situations where the corporation does not have liquid funds to buy out the departing shareholder, it is prudent to provide a second option to the remaining shareholders to take over, pro rata, the departing shareholder's interest in the business.

> **■ Then Digges and Hall would each own one-half of an undiminished business but at a direct cost to them of one-sixth of its total value, again assuming that a fair price is paid for Doe's shares.**

Section 6.3 Governance of Close Corporations

A close corporation typically needs to stay close, not only in the number of its owners (in the sense of "closely held"), but also in the ways that it makes and executes its decisions (in the sense of "closely knit").

> **■ Thus, since closeness is not solely a matter of ownership, it seems more appropriate to refer to the kind of corporation that is the subject of this chapter as "close corporations," rather than "closely held corporations."**

In this section we look at some of the special governance problems of close corporations and at some of the ways of dealing with them at shareholder and director levels.

> ▪ **Use of the word "governance" is meant to emphasize functions and functioning rather than structures and to encompass what both shareholders and directors do (called "governing" and "managing," respectively, in Chapters 3 and 4) but not the "operating" of close corporations by officers, employees, and agents. Differences between public and close corporations seem to fade at the operating level.**

Ideal conditions for smooth, close corporate functioning are informality, participation, and unanimity. Unfortunately, these are not conditions that are compatible with hierarchical corporate patterns. A small group of people—who are each simultaneously shareholders, directors, officers, employees, and agents—may find it difficult and frustrating to try to observe the niceties of the divisions of corporate responsibilities and powers that we have discussed in earlier chapters. They may not want to hold formal meetings, with chairmen and secretaries and minutes; nor to decide issues among themselves by majority votes; nor to keep separate their roles as owners, managers, and executives; nor to observe a designated chain for the flow of information and commands. In short, they may not want to do the things needed to preserve order and coherence in a large organization. On the contrary, they may want to function more like a family: to argue among themselves informally until they have achieved consensus and then to act promptly upon what they have decided; and, if some of their number remain unconvinced, they may want to be able to defer action until they are all in agreement.

It will be seen that the tendency in the governance of close corporations is to enhance the role and powers of the shareholders (the owners) and to diminish those of the boards of directors (the elected managers).

(a) Shareholders

Under the Model Act (§145), if all shareholders consent to proposed action in writing they can act without a formal meeting. This procedure is useful where shareholders are scattered and a meeting would be inconvenient. While this provision is not limited to close corporations, it would be difficult for widely held corporations to use it.

The Model Act also provides that the articles of incorporation may require more than a majority of the shares present at a meeting for passage of a proposal (§32) (see Appendix A.6(c)). By setting high quorum and voting requirements, minority shareholders can be protected against their wishes being overridden.

However, such requirements also increase the possibilities of deadlocks. A close corporation might set high voting requirements for all shareholder votes, whereas a public corporation would be likely to use more than majority votes only for basic changes, like mergers and consolidations.

Another Model Act clause aimed mainly at close corporations is a very broad provision that (§34): "Agreements among shareholders regarding the voting of their shares shall be valid and enforceable in accordance with their terms." Thus, so-called "pooling agreements," whereby a group of shareholders agree to pool their shares and vote together, will be upheld.

> ▪ **For example, Digges and Hall could agree that they would vote together as shareholders at all times and if they could not agree they would vote as a named "arbitrator" might decide. The framing of such agreements among some but not all of the owners raises ethical problems for a lawyer who is supposed to be representing all the owners. Should counsel for Dighaldoe Corporation draw up such an agreement? Does he have a duty to tell Doe that the other two owners are forming a coalition within the corporation to which he will not be a party?**

A more formal way of aggregating shareholder votes is through a "voting trust," under which shareholders assign record ownership of their shares to a trustee who votes the shares but passes on dividends to the beneficial owners (see Appendix H.3). Voting trusts are in most states limited to ten years in duration and can not be kept secret from non-participating shareholders. Voting trusts are used for shares in public as well as close corporations, frequently in connection with a loan where shares are pledged as security, or where a corporation has had financial difficulties and the creditors, as a condition of extending long term credit, want some control over management until the loan is repaid.

Under both the Model Act and the Delaware Act it is possible for shareholders to take over many of the directors' functions. In fact, in Delaware shareholders of a close corporation may completely replace the board of directors to the extent that no directors need be elected (§351). In a less all-or-nothing fashion, the Model Act and the general Delaware provision (not limited to close corporations) permit the powers and duties of the board to be "exercised or performed to such extent and by such person or persons" as shall be provided in the articles of incorporation (Model Act §35; Delaware Act §141). Under this language, it would appear that shareholders can retain the power to elect officers, but leave the other "powers and duties" of the board unchanged.

There may be some dangers in completely merging the powers and duties of shareholders and directors, because directors have legal inhibitions against agreeing on how they will vote and against voting in their own interest that do not apply to shareholders. Since shareholders who function as directors also assume the liabilities of directors, a complete merger of these roles may subject shareholders to liabilities that they would not otherwise have if they are unable to clearly establish whether a particular action is taken as shareholders or as directors.

> ▪ **For example, assume that Dighaldoe is a close Delaware corporation with charter provisions that its business is to be managed by the shareholders rather than by a board of directors; and that all action is to be by unanimous vote of the shareholders. Assume further that Digges and Hall have agreed that they will vote together, with an arbitrator deciding when they are in disagreement; and that a vote on whether the corporation will give Digges a five-year employment contract is taken, with Digges and Doe voting for the proposal, and Hall voting against. Can Digges compel Hall to vote as the arbitrator directs? Can Digges' vote be counted? Both questions seem to turn on whether they were voting as shareholders (arbitration provision applies and Digges' vote counts) or as directors (arbitration provision would not apply and Digges' vote would not count). It would seem that it might be easier to earmark clearly in what capacity they were acting if the corporation had a legally separate board of directors.**

Delaware has, in addition to its provision for management of a close corporation without a board of directors, a provision (§350) that a "written agreement among the stockholders of a close corporation holding a majority of the outstanding stock entitled to vote" is not invalid, as between the parties, "on the ground that it so relates to the conduct of the business and affairs of the corporation as to restrict or interfere with the discretion or powers of the board of directors. The effect of any such agreement shall be to relieve the directors and impose upon the stockholders who are parties to the agreement the liability for managerial acts or omissions which is imposed on directors to the extent and so long as the discretion or powers of the board in its management of corporate affairs is controlled by such agreement." This provision seems to say that if majority shareholders agree how a close corporation shall be managed the agreement is enforceable between them and they shall be liable, in place of the directors, for any managerial misconduct brought on by the agreement.

> ▪ **It appears that this provision would validate application of the Digges-Hall voting agreement to their voting on the employment contract, and would impose on Hall an obligation to follow the directions of the arbitrator. Any liability for the employment contract then would, under the statute, fall on Digges and Hall as shareholders, not as directors. Any liability on Doe for the employment contract would fall on him as a director, since he was not a party to the voting agreement, but the statute seems to relieve the directors of liability. However, there is some doubt that management is "controlled" by the agreement, since Doe's vote is needed for any management decision.**

(b) Directors

Our discussion in Chapter 4 of directors as managers included cursory references to close corporations: the likelihood that boards of close corporations will be mainly inside boards, with an occasional lawyer or banker from outside the corporation; and the importance of shareholder attitudes to the functions and functioning of a close corporation's board of directors. And we have seen that, unlike the anonymous, passive, transient owners of public corporations, who have no choice but to elect boards of directors to act as managers, owners of close corporations typically are able and eager to do their own managing.

Assuming that a close corporation has a board of directors (as most do), the main problem is how to limit the powers of the board and to reserve as many powers as possible to the shareholders, with particular attention to protecting minority shareholders. Shareholders of public corporations are all more or less minority, and they have the way out of selling their shares. Minority shareholders of close corporations, however, are much more vulnerable because they seldom can sell out for lack of a market for their shares; also, they may be hobbled by share transfer restrictions. Since the directors are usually the alter egos of the majority shareholders, protecting minority shareholders frequently means curbing the directors.

What are some of the protective devices relating to directors that you can put into your articles of incorporation? Cumulative voting for election of directors, as we have seen, helps provide minority shareholder representation on the board (see Appendix A.6(b)). You may want to consider combining with cumulative voting a specification in your articles (instead of in your by-laws) of the number of your directors so that the size of your board can be changed only by shareholder vote (see Appendix A.6(a)). If the directors can reduce the size of the board by amendment to the by-laws, they can undercut the effectiveness of cumulative voting.

> ▪ **For a five-person board, a shareholder with 17% of the voting shares is assured one seat; for a three-person board, this percentage goes up to 26%.**

Even more fundamentally, you may want to provide in your articles that shareholder action is needed to amend your by-laws (see Appendix A.11). Note that you will need specifically to reserve this power in your articles. The Model Act provides (§27):

> *The power to alter, amend or repeal the by-laws or adopt new by-laws, subject to repeal or change by action of the shareholders, shall be vested in the board of directors unless reserved to the shareholders by the articles of incorporation.*

In fact, reservation of by-law amendment to the shareholders is probably a better way of handling the number-of-directors question, since leaving the number of directors in the by-laws, instead of putting this provision in the articles, but allowing only the shareholders to change the by-laws, gives the shareholders the desired control without necessitating a filing with the state whenever the shareholders want to change the size of the board.

Perhaps a still more effective way to protect a minority owner with enough shares to elect one director is to set the quorum and voting requirements sufficiently high that the board will not be able to act without the presence and affirmative vote of that director (see Appendix A.6(d)). Both protections, quorum and voting, seem essential. Without a high quorum requirement, the majority could meet at a time when the minority representative was unable to be present and pass what they wanted. Without a high voting requirement, the only way the minority director could protect himself would be to stay away from all meetings, which would bring the board of directors to a standstill, many times unnecessarily because the minority director may have only one piece of business that he wants to block.

To protect a minority shareholder who does not have enough votes to elect a director, it will be necessary to reserve as many powers as possible to the shareholders and then place high enough quorum and voting requirements on shareholder action that they cannot act without the minority shareholder. This protection is less satisfactory than at the director level because shareholders do not ordinarily have before them many "management" decisions. Thus, to assure unanimity on policy decisions in running the business, you will want to assure through cumulative voting and the size of the board that each owner is represented on the board and that each director has the power to block a meeting or an affirmative vote.

Section 6.4 Dealing With Conflict Within Close Corporations

In planning a close corporation the desirability of restrictions on share transfers to protect against strangers coming in and of quorum, voting and other devices to protect against non-unanimous action may seem self-evident. However, if we shift our viewpoint further along in the life of a close corporation, to maturity and middle age, we discover that these protective measures may themselves produce trouble. The owners, unable to sell their shares to outsiders, are locked in an intimate business relationship; and each owner can block business decisions by staying away from meetings or by voting against majority proposals. We have the makings of intense conflicts within the corporation. And, even aside from minority veto power, the owners may become evenly split on how the business should be run. These dissensions are not confined to matters of high policy. They can arise from personality conflicts and from accumulations of petty differences. And some of the most bitter conflicts are not only intracorporate but also intrafamily.

What can be done when a close corporation finds itself in this sort of impasse? Ways of dealing with corporate dissension include: finding a way to continue the business in spite of personal distrust and animosity; submission of the dispute to a third party; a split-up where one side to the dispute sells its shares and the business continues; dissolution of the corporation. These approaches roughly resemble the alternatives—coexistence, counseling, separation, and divorce—for dealing with unhappy marriages.

(a) Carrying on despite conflict

Social groups without conflict exist, if at all, only in heaven. This is true whether the group is a family, a church congregation, a political party, a university faculty, a social club, a labor union, a governmental agency, or a business enterprise. Thus, the most common and sensible way to deal with conflict within a close corporation is for the antagonists to learn to live with their conflict.

Many businesses have continued to be profitably operated despite great mutual ill will among their owners. If the owners can confine their bickering to peripheral matters that will not immobilize the business, the painful route of coexistence is usually the best one. Just as husbands and wives who would rather be apart stay together "for the sake of the children," so also do owners of close corporations who would rather not be associated with one another stay together "for the sake of the business." This level of dissension, annoying but tolerable, sometimes happens when some or all of the original owners die or become disabled and their successors have trouble getting along with the survivors or with one another.

Where a corporation is producing profits for its owners and providing employment for people in the community, and where part of the owners want to continue the business, a judge will be reluctant to order dissolution of the corporation. Instead, he will urge the shareholders to try to work out their differences and to carry on.

But suppose things are so bad that they can not or will not carry on. What happens then?

(b) Submission of disputes to third parties

One of the contributions of law to social relations has been to provide alternatives to duels, family feuds, vigilantism, and various other kinds of self-help when people disagree, in the form of third parties that can step between the antagonists and try to resolve for them what they seem unable to resolve for themselves. Arbitration and the use of neutral and "provisional" directors have been the principal ways for close corporations to provide third-party referees for situations where contending factions are unable either to work out or to live with their conflicts. All of these kinds of referees have their limitations and problems.

For shareholders of a close corporation who are considering making some use of arbitration to help them resolve thier internal disputes, here are some of the questions they should ask themselves:

—Do they want to bind themselves in advance to submit all questions on which they are in disagreement to arbitration, or only to consider on a case by case basis the use of arbitration as disagreements arise?

—Do they want to name an arbitrator now? If not, how will he be selected? Do they want to use the facilities for selecting arbitrators of the American Arbitration Association?

Before opting for arbitration you should ask your lawyer the status of arbitration agreements in your state. Note that anything you do on arbitration will be by agreement rather than by provisions in your articles or by-laws. Also bear in mind the negative attitude of judges in many states about arbitration. Traditionally, agreements to arbitrate future disputes could be revoked by either party at any time before a dispute was submitted for arbitration, and until an award was made either party could terminate the arbitrator's power to act. Furthermore, if a party to an arbitration agreement went to court despite the agreement, breach of the arbitration agreement could not be raised as a defense. However, New York and many other states have liberalized their laws on arbitration: their courts will now enforce an agreement to arbitrate future disputes, and they no longer require that the dispute be "justiciable"—i.e., one that a court could decide—for it to be arbitrable. But even in New York judges have been reluctant to permit corporations to turn over to arbitrators recurring management decisions, or decisions that seem inappropriate for arbitrators, such as whether a director should be removed; they will, however, permit arbitration of some matters that involve business judgment if they involve one-shot rather than recurring decisions.

Aside from the legal problems of how an arbitration agreement will fare in court, there are serious practical limitations on the usefulness of arbitrators. Unless you have a "permanent" arbitrator named in advance, the process of selecting an arbitrator can be very slow and painful. And arbitration proceedings are expensive, since there are the fees of the arbitrator (or arbitrators) and the lawyers on both sides. Also, it will be difficult to find an arbitrator who is impartial yet who knows enough about your business to make informed decisions on such questions as selecting management personnel, investing in new plant or equipment, or entering new markets.

Use of a neutral director avoids some of the drawbacks of arbitration. He is named in advance; he will have a chance to become familiar with your business; and the cost should be much lower than for arbitration because lawyers should not be needed to present the cases of the contending factions. But the neutral director has some drawbacks of his own. It may be difficult for him to remain neutral, since he will be on the scene and subject to the emotional interplay between the factions. And where will you find this Solomon-like person who will have the thankless job of trying to keep peace and who may subject himself to possible personal liability if he makes what a court later decides was a wrong decision?

Under the Delaware Act (§353) there is a procedure whereby a court, upon application of a designated number of directors or shareholders of a close corporation, may appoint "an impartial person who is neither a stockholder nor a creditor of the corporation" as a "provisional director" of the corporation "if the directors are so divided respecting the management of the corporation's business and affairs that the votes required for action by the board of directors cannot be obtained with the consequence that the business and affairs of the corporation can no longer be conducted to the advantage of the stockholders generally." A "provisional director" might be useful where deadlock on the board can be broken by one more vote—as where the board is evenly divided, or where a proposal requiring the affirmative vote of three-fourths of those voting has failed by a vote of two for and one against—but it would seem to be of no use where a unanimous vote is required.

> ▪ From the minority shareholder's point of view, this provision presents a possible reason for not being satisfied with a greater than majority vote (or quorum) requirement short of unanimity.

In fact, the whole idea of conflict resolution by a third party—whether he be arbitrator, neutral director, or provisional director—is inconsistent with the principle of unanimity and should be opposed by a shareholder who thinks he may find himself in a minority position and does not want to be forced into action he does not approve.

> ▪ Can you imagine the United States, or the Soviet Union, or any of the "great powers" possessing the veto on the United Nations Security Council agreeing to any kind of third party resolution of disputes which might result in their vetos being overridden?

(c) Resolving conflict by one side selling its shares

A time honored way to achieve peace has been for one of the contestants to yield and to retire from the field. Where owners of a close corporation conclude that their conflicts are such that they cannot live with them or resolve them, even with the help of third parties, their next best course is for one of the contending factions to sell its shares. A preexisting buy-sell agreement—permitting any shareholder to state the price at which he will either buy or sell, and leaving to other shareholders to decide which way the deal will go (see Appendix H.2(d))—is useful for the rare case where a shareholder is able to arrive at a price so fair that he is willing to be on either side of the deal. However, ordinarily the deadlocked shareholders are faced with the questions of who sells to whom and at what price.

In identifying who will be the seller, there is not usually much doubt when impasse results from a minority owner or group using a unanimity requirement to block corporate action. But if the contending factions are more or less evenly divided—so that it is not a recalcitrant minority against the organization—neither side may be in a position to demand that the other leave, and each may see itself as the legitimate management of the corporation and thus entitled to remain. In this situation there may be protracted jockeying for position and it may not be possible even to get to the question of price. Sometimes a faction that is really willing to sell will be slow to acknowledge its willingness in order to exact a better price.

Assuming it is determined who is going to sell, there can be several possible sorts of purchasers: the corporation; all of the remaining shareholders (on a pro rata basis or otherwise); less than all of the remaining shareholders; or one or more outsiders. Factors to be considered in selecting the purchaser include who has funds available for the purchase, how the remaining shareholders want ownership to be divided after the purchase, and the effect of any restrictions on transfers of shares on the purposed sale. A purchase by the corporation or by the remaining shareholders on a pro-rata basis will leave their shares unchanged as among themselves. A purchase by the corporation will amount to a partial liquidation of the corporation; both working capital (excess of current assets over current liabilities: a measure of liquidity) and, if the purchased shares are retired, stated capital (par value times shares: a cushion for protection of creditors) will be reduced. A sale to the remaining shareholders requires them to increase their investment in the corporation, which may be a hardship for some of them. A sale to outsiders introduces new owners into the picture. Whether the non-selling shareholders can prevent such a sale will depend on whether the shares being sold are subject to restrictions on transfers in the articles or by-laws or by agreement (see Appendix A.6(e)-(g), B.14, and H.2(a)). There may be similar questions if the purchase is by existing shareholders on other than a pro rata basis. And if the corporation has a first option on the shares, it may be necessary to go through the formality of offering the shares to the corporation before selling them to someone else.

■ As we will see in Section 8.2, if the primary obligation to repurchase is on the remaining shareholders, and if the corporation actually makes the purchase, there is a danger of a constructive dividend to the remaining shareholders.

The price question is subject to the difficulties that we discussed in Section 6.2(b) in connection with drafting transfer restrictions, with the difference that instead of planning for the future (when the parties may be inclined to be objective, not knowing which side of the deal they will be on), the parties are faced with an actual purchase and sale after the battle lines have been drawn. If the corporation already has a price determination procedure as a part of its share transfer restrictions with provisions for annual negotiation of value or for an outside appraisal, it would seem that the same procedure should be used in case of a sale of shares to resolve an impasse. In the absence of such a procedure, price becomes an issue for negotiation. There is some danger that a recalcitrant minority shareholder will try to exploit the nuisance value of his shares to exact a premium price. Also even a substantial shareholder, once he has decided to sell out, may cease to have much interest in the continued well-being of the enterprise and may push for all he can get. On the other hand, those in control of the corporation frequently can exert pressure on the dissidents by increasing their own salaries and paying only meager dividends. Courts of equity will sometimes intervene, at the request of one side or the other, and try to compel the parties to negotiate in good faith.

A few states (South Carolina, Connecticut, and Montana) have adopted an English practice of authorizing a court-ordered buyout of a dissenting shareholder when dissolution might be appropriate but would prejudice one or more shareholder groups. The court may order purchase of the shares by other shareholders or by the corporation at a fair price fixed by the court. The English practice (adopted in full only in South Carolina) also permits the court to go beyond the compulsory buyout of shares and make any changes it deems necessary in the corporation's articles for regulating its affairs in the future.

(d) Dissolution and liquidation

If all else fails, the business can be terminated. A corporation is "dissolved" when its legal existence ceases. The assets and business of a corporation are "liquidated" when assets are sold, debts paid, and the residue distributed to the shareholders. Under the Model Act a corporation may be dissolved, without court action, by written consent of all of its shareholders (§83), and by "the act of the corporation," which consists of a board of directors resolution recommending dissolution to the shareholders (see Appendix E.7(a)) and adoption of the recommendation by a majority of the shareholders entitled to vote (see Appendix E.7(b)) (§84). The corporation then, after making the required filings with the secretary of state (see Appendix E.7(c) and (d)), shall proceed "to liquidate its business and affairs" (§87).

For an agreement among shareholders to consent to voluntary dissolution under Section 83 of the Model Act, if a majority favors dissolution and if the majority and minority are unable to agree upon a price or an appraiser for a sale of shares, see Appendix H.2(e). Such an agreement would prevent a minority from blocking dissolution under a greater-than-majority voting requirement for shareholder action (see Appendix A.6(c)).

American courts have generally considered that they are without authority to dissolve or liquidate a corporation without specific statutory authority. The Model Act (§97) gives courts power "to liquidate the business and affairs of the corporation" in an action by a shareholder when it can be established:

> *That the directors are deadlocked in the management of the corporate affairs and the shareholders are unable to break the deadlock, and that irreparable injury to the corporation is being suffered or is threatened by reason thereof; or ... That the shareholders are deadlocked in voting power, and have failed, for a period which includes at least two consecutive annual meeting dates, to elect successors to directors whose terms have expired or would have expired upon the election of their successors.*

Courts have been reluctant to exercise this power when the corporation was functioning profitably and usefully—i.e., when they thought liquidation would sacrifice going value to the harm of shareholders, or harm the community by eliminating employment.

A Delaware provision (§226), not limited to close corporations, empowers a court, upon application of a shareholder, to appoint a "custodian" for the corporation where:

> *(1) At any meeting held for the election of directors the stockholders are so divided that they have failed to elect successors to directors whose terms have expired or would have expired upon qualification of their successors; or*
> *(2) The business of the corporation is suffering or is threatened with irreparable injury because the directors are so divided respecting the management of the affairs of the corporation that the required vote for action by the board cannot be obtained and the stockholders are unable to terminate this division.*

The authority of the custodian "is to continue the business of the corporation and not to liquidate its affairs and distribute its assets except when the court shall otherwise order."

In addition, Delaware has a special provision on appointment of a custodian for a close corporation when the certificate provides for management by the stockholders "and they are so divided that the business of the corporation is suffering or is threatened with irreparable injury and any remedy with respect to such deadlock provided in the certificate of incorporation or by-laws or in any written agreement of the stockholders has failed"; or when a stockholder has a right to dissolution (§352). A stockholder has such a right when the certificate of a close corporation grants to any stockholder or to any specified number or percentage of stockholders "an option to have the corporation dissolved at will or upon the occurence of any specified event or occurence" (§355).

The Delaware Act appears to permit organizers of corporations to go further than does the Model Act in assuring that shareholders may obtain dissolution if they want it. Whether this is a good thing is another question. Some commentators have applauded the courts that have been reluctant to order winding up under the Model Act. The intermediate Delaware provision of a custodian that does not liquidate may provide a useful way of allowing deadlocked corporations to carry on.

If you are an officer or director of a deadlocked but functioning close corporation, you are more likely to be against dissolution than for it, because dissolution will eliminate your corporate position and you may be quite willing to continue indefinitely without having "successors" elected. In other words, if the deadlock only affects elections and not operating decisions, you, as an incumbent, will probably be prepared to live with it, since you presumably believe the business to be in good hands. However, if the deadlock is also immobilizing crucial operational decisions and endangering your own investment in the business, or if you think that you and your group will probably be able to buy the business when it is put up for auction in the liquidation proceedings, your ownership interests, present and prospective, will outweigh your interests as an incumbent officer or director and you will see dissolution as the best way out.

CHECKLIST OF POINTS TO WATCH OUT FOR
IN ACCOMMODATING YOUR CORPORATION TO
THE SPECIAL NEEDS OF CLOSENESS

(References after headings are to Sections of Chapter 6.)

1. Choice of statutes (Section 6.1)

Delaware or the Model Act?

Delaware and a few other states provide a separate category of close corporations, following the practice in Europe and Canada. This approach simplifies drafting of articles and by-laws but can cause problems in borderline situations. For example, in Delaware a close corporation loses its status if the number of shareholders exceed the number specified in its articles, which cannot be more than 30. Some protection against sudden increases in numbers of shareholders—say from shares passing to a large number of heirs—can be provided by leeway (perhaps all the way to the maximum of 30) in the number of shares specified in the articles.

The Model Act, instead of creating two kinds of corporations, has very flexible general provisions. Each corporation can write its own ticket with carefully drafted articles and by-laws. While this approach is more cumbersome and puts more of a premium on legal skill, there are fewer dangers of surprises.

2. Protection against new issues (Section 6.2 (a))

Why are both preemptive rights and limits on authorized shares needed?

Preemptive rights, in the unrestricted form suggested in Appendix A.5(b), of shareholders to participate pro rata in new share issues are necessary but not sufficient protections of closeness. To avoid new issues in which some shareholders cannot afford to participate, preemptive rights should be supplemented by articles which do not authorize more shares than those already outstanding and which can be amended only with assent of all shareholders. For articles setting the number of authorized shares, see Appendix A.2 (a); for articles setting high voting requirements for shareholder action, see Appendix A.6 (c). To reduce the danger that such provisions will block needed equity financing, articles can be made more easily amendable for issuance of non-voting preferred shares.

3. Protection against share transfers (Section 6.2 (b))

How can transfers be controlled?

A share transfer may be triggered by the death, disability, bankruptcy, or cessation of corporate employment of a shareholder; or just by his desire or need to sell; or by deadlock among the shareholders. Transfers can be controlled by agreements among original shareholders, as suggested in Appendix H.2 (a), requiring that the shares first be offered to the corporation and then to other shareholders, with the offering price fixed by annual agreement, and by provisions in the articles or by-laws. For articles giving the corporations and other shareholders successive options at fair market value when shares are offered or when the holder dies or leaves the corporation's employ, and establishing how to determine fair market value, see Appendix A.6 (e)-(g). To allow these provisions to be changed without state filings, they can be put in the by-laws, as indicated in Appendix B.14.

4. Protection against unfair prices (Section 6.2 (b))

Why will senior shareholders want up-to-date valuations?

Ways of valuing shares for purchase by the corporation or other shareholders include outside offers, which, if bona fide, provide perhaps the fairest indicia of value; an agreed price that is revised annually by the shareholders; and, as last resort, an independent appraisal. Since outside offers may not be available when shareholders die, or are disabled or ready to retire from active employment, and since outside appraisals are slow, expensive, and often unreliable, senior shareholders should insist upon annual updating of agreed prices to take into account growth and inflation.

5. Identity of the transferees (Section 6.2 (b))

How should the alternatives be ordered?

Under the agreement in Appendix H.2 (a) and the articles in A.6 (e) and (f)—covering shareholders who desire to transfer or who die or cease to be employees—first options to purchase their shares are given to the corporation and second options to the remaining shareholders; to the extent that neither take up their options, shares may be sold to outsiders. This ordering seems reasonable. If the corporation is the transferee, the interests of remaining shareholders are protected without shareholders having to invest new money in the corporation. However, purchase by the corporation reduces its assets and may be against its interests or unfair to its creditors. In these situations remaining shareholders should be given a chance to be the transferees. And if neither corporation nor shareholders choose to buy, transfer of the shares should cease to be restricted.

6. Governance of close corporations at the shareholder level (Section 6.3 (a))

What changes are appropriate in shareholder voting?

While shareholders normally act at meetings with majority quorums and votes, it is possible for shareholders to act without meetings by unanimous written consent or to require high quorums and votes at meetings. Also, shareholders (unlike directors) may agree to vote together and may combine their votes more formally in voting trusts.

For articles requiring high quorums and votes, see Appendix A.6 (c). For a voting trust agreement, see Appendix H.3.

7. Combining the roles of shareholders and directors (Section 6.3 (a))

What are the advantages of a legally separate board of directors?

The tendency in close corporations is to move power and functions from directors to shareholders, even to the extent possible in Delaware of eliminating directors. However, directors (unlike shareholders) are not supposed to agree in advance how they will vote, nor to vote as directors to further their own interests. Combining the roles of shareholders and directors may create ambiguity about the capacity in which the shareholder-directors are acting and cast doubt on the legality of action—taken pursuant to agreement, or in which the actors are interested—that would be clearly legal if taken by shareholders, but illegal if taken as directors. It is easier to keep these lines clear if the corporation has a legally separate board of directors.

8. Protecting minority shareholders from the directors (Section 6.3 (b))

What legal devices are available?

Among the legal protections for minority shareholders that should be considered in writing the articles are: election of directors by cumulative voting (Appendix A.6 (b)) so that minorities can be represented; specification of the size of the board (Appendix A.6 (a)) so that cumulative voting can not be under-cut by the board reducing its size; requiring shareholder action to change by-laws (Appendix A.11); and quorum and voting requirements at the board level (Appendix A.6 (d)) sufficiently high to give veto power to directors elected by the minority.

9. Arbitration agreements (Section 6.4 (b))

Will you want one as a way of handling internal conflict?

Keeping a corporation close and erecting protections for minorities increase the likelihood of disputes and deadlocks. Should you plan ahead for these unhappy situations by having an arbitration agreement among the owners of your close corporation? Negative factors are the expense and delay of arbitration proceedings; difficulty in finding competent and neutral arbitrators; and possible unenforceability of arbitration agreements. You will need to decide whether you think that these factors are outweighed by the imperfect insurance against crippling impasses that an arbitration agreement offers.

10. Sellouts (Section 6.4 (c))

What are the problems in resolving conflicts by one side sellings its shares?

A quick, inexpensive and lasting solution to conflict is for one side to retire from the corporation. Problems include, in ascending order of seriousness:

who sells; to whom; at what price? The seller is usually the minority or less active interest. The purchaser is usually the corporation or the remaining owners. And there are several ways of fixing a price. As with transfer restrictions, price problems are eased by recently agreed upon valuations and by bona fide outside offers. And, on the chance that one side can hit upon a price at which it would *either* buy or sell, a buy-sell agreement like the one suggested in Appendix H.2 (d) is a worthwhile precaution. But often the only way to arrive at a price is by good faith negotiation: this means that the minority avoids claims for nuisance value and that the majority (which probably controls salaries and dividends) avoids starvation tactics. Where parties cannot agree on a price they may be able to agree on an appraiser to fix a price.

11. Dissolution (Section 6.4 (d))

How can dissolution at the option of the majority be assured?

When all else fails, dissolution of the corporation may be the only solution. The Model Act provides three routes to dissolution: (1) by court action when directors or shareholders are deadlocked, upon application of a shareholder (§97); (2) by act of the corporation, which requires a shareholder vote but not court action (§84) (the normal route); and (3) by written consent of all shareholders (§83), which requires neither shareholder vote nor court action. But the first two of these routes may be blocked: a court may decline to dissolve a deadlocked corporation, especially if it is profitable and providing employment; and, in a corporation with greater-than-majority voting requirements, minority shareholders can prevent dissolution by act of the corporation. However, shareholders can agree in advance, as suggested in Appendix H.2 (e), that if the majority determine that the corporation should be dissolved and if they cannot agree with the minority on a sellout price or on an appraiser to fix such a price, then all shareholders will execute a written consent that the corporation be voluntarily dissolved, paving the way for dissolution under Model Act §83.

Part Two

COPING WITH GROWTH, SUCCESS, AND CHANGE

7

Financing Your Corporation

―――――――――――――――― CONTENTS ――――――――――――――――

193

7

Financing Your Corporation

In an important sense corporations are, as emphasized in the preceding chapters, organizations of people, governed by rules and roles. But in perhaps an even more important sense corporations are also organizations of wealth: *the* organizations of wealth, as we noted in Chapter 1, which seem to have been best suited for financing twentieth century technology. Recall that the rule for shareholder voting is not one shareholder one vote, but rather one share one vote; and since there is ordinarily no limit on concentrations of share holdings, corporate power rests not on a head count but on a dollar count. When Marx talked about administration of persons through legal coercion being replaced by "administration of things," he was calling attention to this distinction between the legal unit of the person and the economic unit of the dollar.

Now we have reached the point where we need to investigate the ways that dollars may be pumped into and out of your corporation. Whether it is large or small, public or close, your corporation will be receiving and distributing wealth, usually in the form of money. And whatever the form of the wealth coming in or going out, your corporation will need to account for these transactions on its books and in its tax returns in terms of dollars.

Borrowing, selling shares in itself, and plowing back its own earnings are ways new money flows into a corporation. In turn, money flows out as debt payments (including salaries), cash dividends, share repurchases (redemptions), and capital distributions (liquidations). When wealth is "at rest" in the corporation, it is shown on the left side of the balance sheet as assets (cash, securities, accounts receivable, inventories, plant and equipment) and on the right side as liabilities (debts, capital stock, surplus).

In Chapters 1 and 2 we sketched some distinctions between debt and equity financing and mentioned how preferred shares provide a form of equity

195

financing with some of the characteristics of debt: fixed return and liquidation preference (see Sections 1.5 (a) and 2.1 (b)). We now need to combine this theory with some of the practices of the money markets. We will assume that your business can not generate and retain enough earnings to avoid the need to bring in new money from outside. You can still avoid going very far afield if you can find the necessary financing among your own resources or those of your family or friends (as we assume below in Section 7.1). The next closest money sources are your local banks, commercial and savings. Other, more remote sources of private capital, requiring more sophistication in how you approach them, include insurance companies, investment companies, mutual funds, pension and other trust funds, and endowment and other charitable foundations. In the public or quasi-public sector, usually involving time and red tape, are the companies established under the Small Business Investment Company Act and specialized federal and state lending agencies, such as local Industrial Development Commissions. Finally, there is the general investing public which may be reached through a public offering of securities.

How a corporation goes about raising money is influenced by its size, maturity, and capital needs. In this chapter we examine three hypothetical situations, characteristic of different, but not necessarily successive, stages in a corporation's development and needs. First, we assume that a business which you have operated as a proprietorship is about to be expanded and incorporated by bringing in an already identified new source of capital. Then, we assume that you and others want to start a new enterprise requiring substantial outside capital, which you cannot obtain from banks or other institutional lenders, but that you want to avoid a full-scale public distribution. Finally, we look at a situation where you have decided to take the plunge and go to the general investing public. In Chapter 8 we turn to the out-flow of corporate funds in the form of distributions to shareholders.*

Section 7.1 Incorporating an Expanding Proprietorship (or Partnership)

For the purposes of this section, assume the following:

A has been engaged for several years as a sole proprietor in a modest business of manufacturing and selling a consumer product with the help of a few employees. He sees opportunities to expand his business into new

---

*Much of Chapters 7 and 8 has grown out of teaching seminars in Business Planning using the excellent collections of materials and problems assembled by David R. Herwitz (Foundation Press, 1966) and by William H. Painter (West Publishing Co., 1975).

lines and new market areas if he had more capital—say about $50,000. B, the father of C, one of A's ablest employees, is willing to invest $50,000 in A's business if B is assured $4,000 per year in income from his investment and if C, who has only $2,000 to invest, is given participation equal to A's in the management and growth of the expanded business. A's books show that his original investment plus earnings retained in the business less depreciation come to about $40,000 (which is A's basis for tax purposes). It would cost A about $70,000 to replace the assets of the business (mainly inventory and equipment) but if he had to liquidate his buisness he probably could only realize about $30,000. Income of A's business before taxes, after allowance for reasonable salaries, was $12,500 for the last fiscal year. A estimates that the planned expansion will enable this income to be at least doubled.

This section explores some of the decisions that A, B, and C will need to make in setting up a corporation, ABC Inc., to implement what they want to do. We concentrate on: how to value A's existing business; how to structure their individual participations in ABC; and how to minimize their federal income taxes.

(a) Putting a value on a going business

In order to set up ABC's books of account, a dollar amount must be assigned to the business that A is exchanging for his ABC shares. If A were simply incorporating his business by himself he could be quite arbitrary in assigning this value. But, because A is bringing in B and C to participate in the new corporation, this valuation becomes crucial in the allocation of interests among A, B, and C. A is concerned that the value be high enough to give him a fair share in the ownership of the business he has built up; B and C, on the other hand, are concerned that the value be low enough to protect the new money that they are contributing. How should A, B, and C go about making this valuation?

> ▪ Other situations calling for valuation of a going business include a purchase offer by someone interested in acquiring it, and the imposition of estate or gift taxes when the business is transferred by death or gift. The discussion that follows is based in part on a widely used publication of the Small Business Administration, SBA Management Aid No. 166, 1964, available in W. Painter, Business Planning (1975) 13.

A corporation with actively traded shares is being continuously evaluated by the "invisible hand" of the market. While market quotations are usually accepted as establishing values of individual shares (witness the rule in merger statutes (e.g., Model Act §80) that dissenting holders of listed shares are not entitled to appraisal rights, since they can simply sell their shares on the exchange), market transactions are not always reliable guides to values of whole enterprises or of large blocks of shares, particularly if the shares carry with them power to control the corporation.

> ▪ Corporate theorists have long debated whether the "control premium" added to ordinary share value belongs only to the fortunate holder or holders of the control shares or whether it is a corporate asset to be shared with other shareholders. While a few notable cases have required sharing, the prevailing judicial response has been to treat control as the private property of the controllers. We will explore this question further in Chapter 10 on transfers of control.

Closely held businesses are not, of course, susceptible to this kind of market evaluation, and about the only times a business such as A's can be said to have an ascertainable market value are when recent, bona fide offers have been made to purchase it. Thus, in our situation it is necessary to look for other evaluation methods.

We can try to value A's business by a piece-by-piece evaluation of its assets (asset value); we can seek an overall enterprise value by projecting how much would be invested to secure what it can earn (capitalized earnings); and we can combine these approaches. A significant difference between them is that no account is ordinarily taken or self-developed goodwill or other intangibles in totaling asset values (although purchased goodwill might be treated as an asset), whereas capitalized earnings will reflect going concern value, since a business that has developed goodwill will ordinarily produce more earnings and be a less risky investment than a new, untried business.

(i) Asset valuation

A keeps books of account in which dollar amounts are assigned to the assets and debts of his business. The "book value" or "net worth" of his business is the excess of its assets over its debts. This amount, which we are assuming is about $40,000, is probably the only clear-cut measure of value which A has of his business. Individual assets are carried on his books at original cost less depreciation. In a period of inflation original cost usually understates current value, and the understatement is increased if the last-in, first-out (LIFO) method of inventory valuation and the rapid depreciation of plant and equipment desirable for tax purposes are used. But book values can also err on the high side if earnings are low and if assets are unproductive and include unsaleable items, such as obsolete plant, specialized equipment, and slow-moving inventory. For plant and equipment valuation, the alternatives to book value are replacement cost and liquidation value ($70,000 and $30,000, respectively, in our illustration): what you could buy the assets for if you had to replace them, and what you could sell them for if you had to liquidate your business.

Replacement cost takes account of inflation by reflecting current price levels, but it is likely to overstate value, especially if the business has been going on very long ("several years" in our illustration). In starting a new business it is improbable that you would reproduce all the assets of the old business. But replacement cost, with allowance for depreciation, may be useful as a ceiling figure for asset valuation, because no reasonable buyer would pay more for A's plant and equipment than the cost of buying comparable assets from other sources. Replacement cost is usually the work of an appraiser rather than an accountant, and an appraiser's allowance for depreciation is likely to be lower than an accountant's because it will be based more on the physical condition of the property and less on the spreading of its cost over its estimated service life. Thus, if a professional appraiser puts going-concern values on A's physical assets, they are likely to be on the high side (which helps to explain our $70,000 figure).

In contrast with going-concern valuation, liquidation or salvage valuation assumes that A is going out of business and is forced to sell his physical assets for whatever they will bring. Time is an important factor, because what you can get for property frequently depends on how long you can wait for an eager buyer. Liquidation value is ordinarily assumed to be immediate sale value. It provides a floor figure for enterprise valuation: no reasonable seller would sell his business for less than he could salvage by going out of business and selling off his assets.

(ii) Capitalized earnings

While piece-by-piece asset valuation has been the dominant way to value small businesses with inquiry frequently limited to balance sheet figures, in recent years there has been growing recognition that in small business valuations, as in large ones, attention needs to be paid to enterprise earning powers.

> ▪ **For example, since 1959 the Internal Revenue Service has favored valuing shares of closely held corporations that sell products or services to the public primarily on the basis of earnings.**

After examing how the earnings approach works, we will look at some of the special problems in applying it to a small business.

The essential ingredients for a capitalization of earnings calculation are an annual earnings figure, based on past experience and future probabilities, and a "multiplier" to convert the earnings amount into the capital amount that would, in light of the risks involved, be invested to secure these earnings.

$$\text{Earnings} \times \text{Multiplier} = \text{Capitalized Earnings}$$

We need to determine what annual return can be expected from A's business and then how much a reasonably prudent investor would risk to buy a chance of getting that return. These calculations are not unlike those made by reasonably prudent poker players and horse players in deciding whether to stay in a hand and to bet on a horse: How much may I win and what is my chance of winning? How much am I willing to pay to buy that chance?

We start with the past earnings record of the business. Our hypothetical, where we stipulated that for the last fiscal year A's earnings were $12,500, does not tell us all we need to know. A five-year history of earnings would help to show trends. Adjustments would be required for things like non-recurring items of income or expense, unusually large bad debts, inventory write-offs, too high or too low salaries, and any nonbusiness ventures of the enterprise. Accounting procedure variations, such as whether equipment is charged as an expense item the year it is bought or amortized over several years, could also decrease or increase earnings.

In our case future earnings projection might seem to be further complicated because A's business will change with infusion of B's capital and restructuring of management to include C, causing a double valuation problem: the old business and the new. However, since A and B are buying into the new business, A with his old business and B with cash, we can say the start-up value of the new business (which is what we are seeking) will equal the value of A's old business plus B's $50,000. Thus, it would seem that we can confine our valuation efforts to the old business. And we will assume that $12,500 fairly represents its earning power.

Our next task is to choose the multiplier (also called "capitalization rate," "value-earnings ratio," and "price-earnings ratio"), that should be used to convert A's earnings into enterprise value. The size of the multiplier varies inversely with risk: the greater the risk of generating the expected earnings (if they depend, for example, on the expertise of a single individual), the smaller the multiplier.

> ▪ Suppose two businesses, X and Y, both are earning $100,000. X is established and has a record of growth and very favorable future prospects. Y has not established itself and is in a highly competitive field where the prospects are cloudy. A prudent investor in X might be satisfied with an 8% return on his investment—which means he is willing to capitalize X at 12½ times earnings ($1,250,000). But before an equally prudent investor would invest in Y he might require a much higher return—say 20%, which would capitalize Y at five times earnings ($500,000).

In determining a multiplier to apply to A's earnings we would want to assess not only the financial and managerial strengths and weaknesses of A's business and its position in its industry, but also such external influences as the position of the industry in the general economy and the state of the economy, regional and national (and, perhaps, international).

· If a corporation (Z) were considering acquisition of A's business for Z shares, Z's own multiplier would be used to test whether Z's earnings would be diluted by the acquisition. For example, if Z shares are selling at 10 times Z's earnings, Z could pay A, in return for A's business, Z shares worth up to $125,000 (10 times A's earnings) without diluting Z's earnings, assuming that A's business could continue to earn $12,500. But keep in mind that $12,500 is before taxes.

The most widely-used work on multipliers, Dewing, *Financial Policy of Corporations* (5th ed. 1953), suggests multipliers of only four or five for small, scantily capitalized businesses like A's. While the Dewing multipliers are thought by some to be unrealistically low for large enterprises (the top of the Dewing multiplier scale is ten), in the lower ranges of the scale there is little evidence that value-earnings ratios have similarly increased. Thus, using a multiplier of five and earnings of $12,500, the capitalized earnings value of A's business would be $62,500, compared with replacement cost of $70,000, book value of $40,000, and liquidation value of $30,000.

What are the problems in trying to apply the capitalization of earnings approach to small enterprises like A's? One difficulty is that entrepreneurs often fail to isolate compensation for their own services from the earnings of the business, making it necessary to deduct reasonable compensation before multiplying earnings. Note that we stipulated that A's income figure made allowance for reasonable salaries.

A more complex difficulty is whether in measuring A's contribution to the proposed new corporation allowance should be made for income taxes that the corporation will have to pay on the income A is contributing. A's income figure was given as $12,500 before taxes in line with the practice of not deducting individual income taxes in valuing a proprietorship or partnership. However, in valuing a corporation estimated corporate income taxes normally are deducted. And the value of the enterprise should not depend on whether it is incorporated. Thus, to make allowance for the expectation that the earnings A is contributing will be taxable to the corporation (at the 17% rate applicable the corporation's first $25,000 of income), we should reduce our mulitplier by one-fifth, from five to four, reducing the capitalized value of A's business to $50,000.

If A had long-term debt we would be faced with a further complication. Large enterprises often treat such debt as part of ownership and do not deduct interest thereon from the earnings to be capitalized. Then, to isolate the value of the equity interest, the face amount of the debt would be subtracted from the total enterprise value. However, this approach understates equity value for a small enterprise with a multiplier that is low in relation to the multiplier inherent in any normal interest rate on the debt. An alternative approach, more suitable for a small enterprise, is to value the equity interest directly by capitalizing only the post-interest income and then to use a somewhat lower multiplier (because the excluded interest represents the least risky part of total earnings, since it must be paid "off the top"). To illustrate the difference between these two approaches, assume in our case that B were to take $50,000 face amount of long-term 8% bonds or notes and that the new corporation, which is now earning $20,000 after taxes, is being evaluated. The effect of the disparity between the multiplier of 12.5 inherent in the 8% interest rate on the debt and the much lower multiplier (five) appropriate for overall evaluation of the enterprise, combined with deduction of the face amount of the debt can be seen from the following comparison:

—If the equity were valued by multiplying total earnings ($20,000) by a multiplier of five and then subtracting the face amount of the debt ($50,000), the remaining equity value would be $50,000.

—But if the equity were valued directly by multiplying post-interest earnings ($16,000) by the smaller multiple of four, equity value would be $64,000.

Stated another way, the former method assumes that multipliers and interest rates will be compatible and does not recognize the "leverage" secured when an enterprise that is presumed to be earning 20% on its capital borrows at 8%.

In our situation, if A's business is valued at $50,000, A and B would be making equal contributions. Both are making some trade-offs. A is relinquishing sole ownership and control of a business he built up himself in return for some much needed capital on more favorable basis than he would be able to get it from another source. On the other hand, B is risking new money at a rate considerably below the rate inherent in the multiplier appropriate for A's business in return for his son getting a share in control and participation in growth. The equities would seem to balance off.

(b) Structuring participations in an expanded business

Once A, B, and C have settled on a value that will be assigned to A's existing business and will thereby quantify A's contribution to the new corporation, they can proceed to consider how they will structure their individual participations in ABC. Let us assume that their investments will total $104,000: $52,000 by A ($50,000 in the form of his business and $2,000 in cash); $50,000 by B (cash); and $2,000 by C (cash). Also recall that B's investment is conditioned on an assured return of $4,000 year (8% on $50,000) and C's equal participation with A in the management and growth of the expanded business.

▪ **While B's passive role seems adaptable to that of a limited partner, with A and C functioning as equal general partners, A and C would then be exposed to unlimited personal liability—a situation that would**

be particulary unacceptable to A because of C's limited assets and contribution to the business. Also, if they expect to plow earnings back into the business, a partnerhsip would have tax disadvantages.

Since ABC will be a close corporation, most of Chapter 6 on accommodating a corporation to the special needs of closeness will be relevant in setting up ABC, including the following:

—Protections against new issues of shares (preemptive rights and limits on authorized shares) and against transfers of existing shares (restrictions by agreements and by charter and by-law provisions) (see Section 6.2);

—Requirements for greater-than-majority quorums and votes by shareholders and directors (see Section 6.3); and

—Conflict-resolution devices, such as arbitration, buy-sell agreements, and dissolution (see Section 6.4).

As we will see, it should be possible to provide for equal sharing of control between A and C through a board with an even number of members who are elected by cumulative voting. A probable initial board would be four members, comprised of the three parties and a person designated by A. But before they get to the board the parties need to agree upon a design for the capital structure of ABC. The challenge is to reconcile equal shares for A and C in voting control and growth participation with their widely disparate capital contributions ($52,000 by A and only $2,000 by C). Three possible capital structures are: use of only common shares for all three participants; use of two types of investment, with A and C taking common shares, and B taking some kind of senior securities (preferred shares or debt); and use of three types of investment, with A dividing the common shares with C for part of A's investment, and A and B each receiving a different kind of senior security.

Why not have ABC simply issue 104,000 common shares at $1 per share (or 10,400 shares at $10, or 1,040 at $100, or 104 at $1,000), with 52,000 shares going to A, 50,000 to B, and 2,000 to C? This arrangement would divide voting control evenly between A, on one hand, and B and C, on the other. A would probably not object, because he would have the one-half interest he expects in voting control and profit participation. B and C, however, would be less happy. B would not have any priority ahead of A and C for income or distribution on liquidation: he would have to take his chances with the others and would not have the assured return on his investment that he wants. And C would not have the equal participation with A that his father is bargaining to get for him in the future control and growth of ABC, because he would be dependent on his father's shares for equal control with A, and he would be entitled in his own right to less than a 2% participation in future growth and profits. Furthermore, C cannot be sure that B's shares will not pass to someone else. Thus, B and C would reject an all-common-shares structure.

Since B wants assured income and security, and is not interested in the control and growth which A and C want to divide, why cannot everyone be accomodated by giving B senior securities and dividing the common shares between A and C? Now the shoe is on the other foot. B and C would be delighted with this arrangement because all of their objectives would be met: protection for B and independent equality for C. But observe the plight of A. He would in effect be making a transfer to C of an undivided one-half interest in the business that he is putting into the new corporation. C would be entitled to one-half of net income and one-half of net assets upon liquidation of a business capitalized at $104,000 to which he has contributed only $2,000.

To meet A's legitimate objections to C's windfall under the two-tier approach a third tier is needed for the bulk of A's investment. The shares issued to A and C can be divided into two classes: a class of voting, participating common shares to be divided equally between A and C which would represent their cash contributions of $2,000 each; and a class of non-voting, non-participating (in earnings above a designated amount) preferred shares to be issued only to A which would represent A's contribution of his $50,000 business. This arrangement avoids the windfall to C by giving A a prior claim for income and upon liquidation for his $50,000 contribution, but retains C's equal share in control and growth as represented by increased earnings and assets. Since it would also seem that A's preferred shares should be junior to B's investment, as spelled out below, we have arrived at a three-tiered structure.

But why do we need a third tier? Why not give A the same kind of senior security that is planned for B? Apart from tax considerations, there are other reasons for giving B a more senior position—a result that can be achieved by giving B super preferred shares or debt securities (bonds or notes). One who supplies fresh cash to an under-capitalized buisness is entitled to seniority because of his superior bargaining position. There are more enterprises like A's seeking capital than there are people willing to invest in them.

> ▪ **Why should anyone invest in A's business at 8% when he can get a comparable return from an established utility or large industrial corporation?**

Furthermore, when a going enterprise is incorporated it is hard to justify debt treatment for contribution of assets, like A's, that are already committed to the business and are presumedly needed for its operations. "Real" creditors could object to A's "lending" his old business to ABC and require that A's "debt" be subordinated to the claims of other creditors (see Section 11.1 (b) (ii), below).

In summary, on the basis of the character and size of their investments, B, the contributor of fresh cash, is entitled to a position senior to A and C; and A, the contributor of a going business, to a position senior to C, who brings only nominal cash and the promise of future services. But, while C is the most junior party in terms of tangible investment, he is investing himself and can stake a claim to be fairly compensated for his services. He can secure effective seniority over A as a shareholder by becoming a creditor of ABC through a long-term employment agreement (say five years) specifying his compensation. Then C's contractual claims will have priority over dividend payments.

(c) Tax planning for the new corporation and its investors

In setting up their new corporation it is important for A, B, and C to be aware of possible federal income tax consequences to both ABC as an entity and to themselves as individual taxpayers. While corporate and individual consequences become intertwined, particularly in a corporation as intimate as ABC, we focus first on some of the more distinctly corporate tax questions, relating to both ordinary income and capital gains, before turning to the tax impacts on the individual investors.

(i) Corporate tax planning

As to the taxes which ABC will have to pay on its operating income, we have already noted that, in valuing A's existing business by capitalizing its projected earnings, allowance should be made for the fact that these earnings ($12,500, before taxes) will be taxable to ABC at the 17% rate applicable to its first $25,000 of income. We made this allowance by reducing our multiplier from five to four, thus reducing our capitalized earnings valuation from $62,500 to $50,000.

> ▪ **We could, of course, have reached the same result by keeping the multiplier at five and reducing the projected earnings by one-fifth, from $12,500 to $10,000.)**

One of the reasons for structuring part of the investment in ABC as debt is that ABC then can, to the advantage of all of its investors, increase its after-tax income by deducting interest payments from its taxable income. In contrast, dividend distributions to equity investors are not deductible. The structure on which we settled gives A an equity investment of $52,000 ($2,000 common and $50,000 preferred), B a debt investment of $50,000, and C an equity investment of $2,000 common. But why not double the interest deduction by giving A debt instead of preferred shares for his business? When we made this suggestion earlier we noted that for ABC to be so thinly capitalized would be unfair to creditors: their cushion of permanent equity investment would be reduced to $4,000. On similar grounds, the Internal Revenue Service would probably disallow deduction of interest payments to A, although it would probably go along with interest payments to B. A and B would be regarded differently because, while it is hard to justify debt treatment of contribution of assets such as A's which were already committed to the business, it is much easier to justify debt treatment of contribution of new funds by B, an outsider.

> ▪ **If A rather than B were contributing the cash, we would have new but not outside money. In considering whether to allow deduction of interest payments to A, the IRS would examine more closely than in the case of B's contribution whether ABC was too "thin"—i.e., whether the new money should be treated as part of the permanent capital needed to operate the business.**

Tax detriments, to the disadvantage of all of ABC's investors, are in store for ABC because it will probably receive A's assets at their old basis in A's hands ($40,000), even though ABC will be "paying" A (in preferred shares) $50,000 for these assets. Thus, the assets will have less than full value to ABC for tax purposes because of the effects of their low basis on their depreciation and sale.

> ▪ **ABC's ordinary income taxes will be increased because depreciation allowances will be reduced; and if the assets are sold before they are fully depreciated, ABC's capital gains tax will be increased.**

As we will see shortly, the unchanged basis will be a consequence of qualifying incorporation of ABC as tax-free under IRC §351, which A will want to do in order to avoid capital gains tax on the $10,000 increment *now*. The shift of the tax burden for the increment from A to the corporation provides an additional reason for subordinating A's position relative to B's in the structure of ABC.

The structure proposed for ABC with two classes of shares will disqualify it for partnership tax treatment as a Subchapter S corporation. However, since A and C will probably want to plow earnings back into the business for several years and to compensate themselves with deductible salaries rather than non-deductible dividends, Subchapter S treatment will not be to their advantage (see Section 1.1(a)).

The common shares planned for A and C will qualify as §1244 stock, thereby permitting losses (of up to $50,000 on an individual return, or $100,000 on a joint return) on sale, exchange, redemption, or worthlessness of such shares to be treated as ordinary rather than capital losses (see Section 1.1(b)). Since §1244 treatment can only operate to the advantage of A and C, they should take advantage of it. The requirements for §1244 treatment can be summarized as follows:

—Section 1244 stock must be original issue common shares. Thus, neither A's preferred shares nor B's debt securities qualify for §1244 treatment.

—Section 1244 stock can be issued for money or other property, but not for services or for stock or other securities. Thus, the discussion below about the consideration for ABC's common shares is relevant to their §1244 qualification.

—Section 1244 stock must be shares of a "small business corporation," a category limited by the amount of money and other property received by the corporation as capital or paid-in surplus, which cannot exceed $1 million. In contrast with Subchapter S, the number of shareholders and classes of shares are irrelevant.

(ii) Individual tax planning

We now move from the tax precautions needed at the corporate level to some of the more specific concerns of the individual investors. The situation of B, the provider of $50,000 in cash in return for debt securities in this amount, is relatively simple because we have not introduced possible complications, like a discount from the face amount of the debt and how interest and discount are accounted for in the payment of installment obligations. B will simply have ordinary income from interest payments and there will be no tax consequences to him when his principal is repaid. The situations of A and C, however, even under our simple fact assumptions, are more complex.

> ▪ We will return briefly to B with regard to a possible gift to C and its effect on the basis of B's debt securities.

We have already alluded to A's problem arising from the appreciation of the value of his business from $40,000 (his basis) to $50,000 (the amount for which he is "selling" it to ABC). Can he avoid paying capital gains tax on what looks like a "realization" of this appreciation? As for C, his main problem arises from the circumstances that for an investment of only $2,000 he is receiving a one-half interest in the control and the growth prospects of a $104,000 business. Can he avoid paying ordinary income tax on the difference between $2,000 and the "real" value of what he is getting? And we will see that A shares this problem with C in two ways: if $2,000 is less than full payment for C's common shares then $2,000 would seem to be also inadequate consideration for A's shares; and if C's shares are partially for services rather than wholly for cash, then the tax-free status of the incorporation under §351 is in jeopardy.

Our analysis of these sticky problems starts with IRC §1032 which provides that neither gain nor loss is recognized by a corporation when it issues its shares, whether original issue shares or treasury shares, in exchange for money or property. But when shares are issued for services, the corporation takes a deduction for their value as a business expense, and the person performing the services receives ordinary income in the amount of the fair market value of the shares. And, while "bargain purchases" of shares at less than fair market value are not ordinarily taxable events, when they are made by corporate employees of their employer's shares they are treated as compensation income to the extent of the bargain. The fact that A and C will not have begun work for ABC when they receive their shares will be immaterial because their employment by ABC is an essential part of the business plan. Thus, one prong of our problem is the sufficiency of the cash consideration for the common shares.

The other prong relates to the consideration for A's preferred shares. While a simple *purchase* of shares for cash does not ordinarily result in a tax to the purchaser, and his basis in the shares is the price paid, when shares are acquired in an *exchange* for property (as A's preferred shares will be), *prima facie* there is a taxable exchange and the transferor (A) would be subject to capital gains tax to the extent that the fair market value of the shares ($50,000) exceeds his basis in the property ($40,000). However, an important exception to the general rule requiring recognition of gain or loss upon an exchange, is made available by §351 which provides for non-recognition of gain or loss in connection with a transfer of cash or property, but not of services, to a corporation in exchange for its shares or securities under carefully limited circumstances.

Section 351 provides for a tax-free incorporation if the transferors receive only stock or securities, including debt obligations—i.e., if they do not receive any "boot" in addition to the stock or securities—and if, after the transfer, the transferors' stock ownership enables them to be "in control" of the corporation. Control is defined in §368 (c) to mean ownership of 80% of the corporation's total voting shares and 80% of all other classes of shares. Since to secure the 80% of voting shares to qualify for §351 treatment requires that the common shares of both A and C be for cash or property and not for services, it appears that both prongs of our tax problem (compensation income on the common and capital gains on the preferred) turn on the sufficiency of the cash consideration for the common shares.

In response to the assertion that $4,000 is insufficient consideration for the common, A and C have the choice of trying to find ways of augmenting the consideration, other than by services, or of meeting the assertion head-on and trying to establish that $4,000 is sufficient. As I will try to show in the balance of this sub-section, the latter seems the better course.

In confession and avoidance, A might claim that whatever the separate value of the common, he is paying in full for one-half share in a $104,000 business by bringing in a $50,000 business and $2,000 in cash. In other words, any excess over $2,000 in the value of his common must be counter-balanced by a deficiency in the value of his preferred. C, in turn, might claim that any short-fall in what he is paying for his common in relation to its real value must be considered a gift from his father who is making an investment in an untried company that he would not otherwise make. Between father and son, they are matching A's $52,000 investment. These not implausible arguments do seem to meet the compensation income and §351 problems, by providng non-service explanations for the common stock purchases. However, they would probably have the unhappy results of reducing the bases of A and B in their $50,000 investments by whatever amounts were assigned to the common. Also, these explanations seem at variance with the actual business purposes and expectations of the parties.

> ▪ **If the business succeeds, first B's debt and then A's preferred shares are likely to be retired. Thus, the lower bases for these investments will have foreseeable adverse tax results which are not compensated for by the higher bases which A and C will have in their common, since it is anticipated that A and C will continue to hold these shares.**

A better choice for the parties would seem to be to try to establish that the common shares being issued to A and C are worth no more than is being paid for them, $4,000: that on the basis of current asset valuation that is all that they are worth. If ABC were liquidated immediately, it is unlikely that there would be anything left for the common shares after providing for B's debt and A's preferred shares. In fact, using the assumed $30,000 liquidation value of A's business, there would not be enough to satisfy A's liquidation preference.

A counter argument would be to ask: how about ABC's expectations of future profits and the power of the common shares to control the business and to share its growth? Even if profits of the expanded business do not exceed the $10,000 after-tax earnings of the present business, there would still be, after providing $8,000 for an 8% return on the $100,000 face amount of the senior securities, $2,000 for the common. And if A's estimate that the planned expansion will double earnings comes true, the residual income for the common shares goes up to $12,000 ($20,000—$8,000). Furthermore, it is doubtful that the parties would sell ABC common to outsiders at the price it is being sold to A and C.

In response to this rosy picture of the ABC common, the following points can be made:

—In valuing a business as small and untried as ABC more reliance should be put on current asset value than on estimated earnings, and any assignment of value for control of such a closely held enterprise is inappropriate and speculative.

—Allowance has already been made for estimated earnings in arriving at the value of the part of ABC represented by A's business, and this asset value is reliable because it has been negotiated out between A and B, whose interests are adverse on the question of the value of A's business.

—Even if earnings expectations are realized, there is small likelihood for dividends on the common shares for many years since retained earnings will be needed for working capital, expansion, and retirement of B's debt (and possibly A's preferred).

—For a cash basis taxpayer to receive an unsecured right to secure future payments of unascertainable amounts does not ordinarily constitute a taxable event. If ABC succeeds, then the Treasury will have its proper chance to take its tax bite. To try now to tax the expectations of A and C would not only be unfair but would also have a chilling effect on small business enterprises struggling to raise new capital.

Section 7.2 Raising Outside Capital, While Avoiding Registration and Minimizing Taxes

This section focuses on an enterprise that differs from ABC in several ways. It is a new project trying to get started, rather than a going business trying to expand; it needs to raise considerably more outside money than ABC did; and, perhaps most significantly, it has not yet found the sources of that outside money. Of course, in raising these funds, it wants to minimize its entanglements with federal and state securities regulations and its exposure to federal taxes. Our hypothetical situation in this section is as follows:

M, N, and O are computer programmers, until recently employed by P Corporation, who want to set up their own business. Their plan is to do programming on a contract basis for universities, hospitals, foundations, local governments, and other non-profit organizations. They investigated the potentialities of this field for P, but their superiors rejected their recommendation that P enter this business. They estimate that they will need about $300,000 to finance their enterprise, which they want to incorporate under the name "Unidata, Inc." They each have about $20,000 to invest. They have been turned down for loans by local banks and lending agencies, but they believe they can raise upwards of $100,000 among their friends and acquaintances; and Q, a stockbroker friend, believes that he can bring in at least an equal amount from his customers and others. In return for this effort, Q wants to be able to buy Unidata shares at the same price as M, N, and O. R, a lawyer, and S, an accountant, are willing to provide their services in return for Unidata shares.

The participants agree upon a tentative capital structure for Unidata consisting of 50,000 Class A common shares, to be offered to outside investors at $5 per share, and 69,000 Class B common shares, to be issued at $1 per share as follows: 20,000 shares each to M, N, and O for cash; 5,000 shares to Q for cash; and 2,000 shares each to R and S for services.

If all 119,000 shares are sold, Unidata will start business with assets of $315,000 in cash and $4,000 in services, and each share will have a book value of about $2.67 ($319,000 ÷ 119,000); Q's "compensation" will be $8,350 (5,000 x ($2.67 − $1.00), and that of R and S, $5,340 each (2,000 x $2.67).

(a) Preliminary problems

(i) Relations with a former employer

In addition to routine concerns involved in starting a new corporation discussed in Chapter 1, including making sure that the name "Unidata" will be available for their business, M, N, and O have a special threshold concern, tangentially related to raising money, because they plan to exploit what was originally a "corporate opportunity" of their former employer, P Corporation (see Section 11.1 (a) (iii)). They learned of a need and investigated the potentialities of exploiting it as part of their work for P: on P's time and using P's resources. If P had wanted to seize the opportunity for itself, P would have been entitled to do so. If the programmers had implemented their plan to exploit the opportunity themselves while still employees of P, or even if they had waited to do so until after leaving P but without disclosing it to P, they would be in violation of their fiduciary duties to P, and P could impose a "constructive trust" on their new business and its profits.

Does rejection by their superiors at P of their recommendation that P enter this business clear the way for them to proceed on their own? Or should they try to secure a more definite release from P? There are risks either way. If they go ahead without more and the business prospers, P, perhaps with new managers, may try to claim the business, arguing that the decision by their superiors not to follow their recommendation did not amount to a disclaimer by P of the business. On the other hand, approaching P now for a more definite disclaimer may just stir matters up and cast doubt on what they already have rather than improving their position. While it is not an easy decision, the balance would seem to tip in favor of their trying to get something more definite from P before proceeding. If P is not willing to release to them now any business plans or trade secrets which they developed relating to their proposed business while employed by P (see Appendix H.4(h)), there is substantial danger that P will make trouble for them later. Also, if they do not get a clear release from P and if they do not disclose to outside investors the possibility of P asserting claims against Unidata, they risk, not only losing their investments in Unidata, but also incurring personal liability to outside investors if claims by P diminsh the value of Unidata shares.

(ii) Securing underwriting or selling assistance

From here on we assume our programmers are able to clear the name "Unidata" and secure a satisfactory release from P. But before plunging into their securities and tax law problems, we need to take a brief look at the marketing aspects of selling securities which may explain their willingness to let their friend Q, the stockbroker, in on the ground floor with them.

When large, established corporations sell their securities to the public, the offering is usually "underwritten" by an investment banker, or by a syndicate of investment bankers, who agree to purchase the whole offering and assume the risk of being able to sell it to the public. A "firm-commitment" underwriting in this full sense is probably out of the question for a small, untried venture like Unidata. What it might be able to find is an investment firm willing to do a "best-efforts" underwriting: the firm would agree to use, for a commission of 15% to 20%, its best efforts to sell the Unidata shares, with no guarantee to buy what it cannot sell. To raise $200,000 under such an arrangement, public sales of as much as $250,000 may well be needed.

In our hypothetical situation Q is, in effect, offering to use his best efforts to raise $100,000 in return for being allowed to buy 5,000 shares at $1 per share. As we have noted, Q's "compensation" for these efforts will be at the most $8,350, or about $8\frac{1}{3}\%$. His dollar compensation will be less if all Class A shares are not sold, and his percentage compensation may be more or less, depending on total sales and the portion thereof he is responsible for. That Q will be trying to sell only part of the Class A shares and will profit from sales he does not make (and conceivably could profit without making any sales) seems to be more than offset by the fact that he is being compensated for his efforts in shares rather than in cash.

(b) Federal regulation of the sale of securities

(i) Reasons for avoiding registration

The Securities Act of 1933 requires that public offerings in interstate commerce of securities over designated dollar amounts be "registered" with the Securities and Exchange Commission. For several reasons Unidata will want to try to avoid registration. The most compelling reasons are cost and time. Whether it is underwritten or not, a registered public offering would involve legal, accounting, printing, and insurance expenses of $30,000 to $50,000, and would consume several months. Thus, a successful $250,000 registered offering with a 20% selling commission might net the issuer only $150,000.

Additional reasons why Unidata will strive to avoid an SEC registration include the following:

—Registration may require more disclosure about what M, N, and O have discovered and about their business plans than they wish to make. Part of the attractiveness of their project is that they have come upon what appears to be an unmet need. If they are forced to say too much about it, other organizations—perhaps better connected and with stronger staffing and financing—may be motivated to exploit their findings.

—Registration would increase potential personal liabilities of all of the insiders for any misleading statements or omissions in the disclosures required for registration.

▪ For example, the problems discussed about about what they say concerning their relations with P will be intensified if they have to register.

And all of the insiders seem to be covered under § 11 of the Securities Act of 1933 imposing civil liabilities for false registration statements: M, N, and O as directors; Q as an underwriter (as defined in §2 (ii)); R as an expert; and S as an accountant.

—S could not be compensated in Unidata shares if he is to certify the financial statements required for registration; the certifying accountant must be "independent," and under SEC rules "any direct financial interest" in the corporation destroys independence. While registration would not preclude R, the lawyer, from receiving shares as compensation, nor Q, the stockbroker, from being permitted to buy "cheap shares," registration may complicate these plans, as will be noted below.

(ii) Ways of avoiding registration

The legal challenge is to find a way that Unidata shares can be sold as the parties want to sell them without registering the offering with the SEC. The emphases in the statutory registration requirement—on the identity of the offerees ("public offering") and on the geographical scope ("in interstate commerce") and dollar magnitude of the offering—suggest three possible exemption routes for Unidata: as a private offering, as an intrastate offering, or as a small issue.

Can their plan—for M, N, and O to solicit friends and acquaintances in an effort to raise $100,000 or more, and for Q to do the same with his customers and others—be made to qualify for exemption as a private offering by careful tailoring of their invitation lists? Suppose they decide that they will quietly approach a total of not more than 35 financially sophisticated prospects who can each afford to risk $10,000 (2,000 shares) on Unidata, in the hopes that 20 to 25 of them will be forthcoming. Such an offering satisfies many of the criteria of a private offering: the number of offerees is limited; there is to be no advertising; the offerees are capable of evaluating the merits and risks of the investment and able to bear its economic risks; and the offerors can take reasonable care to assure that purchasers are not buying for resale by requiring that they sign "investment letters" affirming their investment intentions (see Appendix H.6(b)). However, a crucial ingredient of a private offering is missing. The offerees do not have access— because of employment, family relationship, or economic bargaining power—to the kind of information about Unidata that registration would provide. Availability of the private offering exemption turns, not on the number nor on the sophistication of offerees, but on whether they need the protection of registration because of their lack of access to information. The SEC has indicated that a transaction tends to become public when the promoters begin to bring in a diverse group of uninformed friends, neighbors, and associates; and that "sophistication" is not a substitute for access to information: even a person who knows his or her way around can lack ways of knowing about a particular enterprise.

Our next inquiry is whether the proposed offering can qualify for the intrastate exemption. Here the statute requires that the issue be offered and sold only to persons resident within a single state and that the issuer be incorporated by and doing business within that state. The exemption is not dependent upon the non-use of the mails or instruments of interstate commerce in the distribution. The intention is to exempt local financing by local industries, carried out through local investment. The local industry part would not create problems in our case. The corporation need not be doing business *only* within the state of incorporation, but there must be substantial operational activities in that state for which proceeds of the offering are "primarily" intended; minor use of proceeds (for, say, sales activities) in other states is permissible. The constraints on where the offerees and purchasers may reside, on the other hand, will probably cause more difficulties, since not enough prospects able to invest $10,000 in Unidata are likely to be found in its home state. And these difficulties are intensified by the strict interpretation given by the SEC to the residence requirement. An offer to a single non-resident, or a resale by a resident to a non-resident, kills the exemption for the whole issue; and to be a resident an offeree must have a subjective intent to remain in the state, which may be difficult for the offeror to ascertain. Thus, it appears that Unidata should not plan to rely on the exemption for local offerings.

Our last resort for avoiding registration is the partial exemption for small issues. It would seem that the $250,000 Class A offering can qualify for treatment under the SEC's Regulation A, promulgated pursuant to §3 (b) of the Securities Act. That Act authorizes the Commission to create exemptions "where the aggregate amount at which such issue is offered to the public" does not exceed $2 million; the SEC has exempted issues up to $1.5 million.

Under Regulation A Unidata must file with the appropriate SEC regional office (rather than in Washington) a "notification" (the counterpart of a registration statement) disclosing the terms of the offering of its Class A shares, names of directors and officers, the method of selling the securities, and planned use of the proceeds. Since the issue exceeds $50,000 and Unidata is a "promotional company" (i.e., it has not had income from its planned operations in either of the last two years), it must also make available to offerees an "offering circular" (the counterpart of a prospectus) disclosing data about its insider-held Class B shares, including names and addresses of holders, their positions in Unidata, their share holdings, their percentage of ownership before and after the Class A offering, and the amounts paid for their shares. Also, a statement along the following lines will be required:

> *Before the offering contemplated hereby, the book value of the holdings of officers, directors, and promoters in Class B shares was approximately $1 per share. If the offering of Class A shares is successful, the book value of Class B shares will be increased at no cost to the holders to approximately $2.67 per share. Accordingly, an investment of $5 per share in Class A shares will be reduced to a book equity of $2.67 per share.*
>
> *Assuming that all of the 50,000 Class A shares offered hereunder shall be issued, the existing officers, directors, and promoters as a group will hold 58% of the total outstanding shares at the cost of $69,000, and the public will hold 42% of the total outstanding shares at a cost of $250,000.*

■ These figures assume that Q, R, and S will be included among the officers, directors, and promoters.

Unidata's status as a promotional company means that, in applying the $1.5 million maximum under Regulation A, it must aggregate the $250,000 Class A shares and the already issued $69,000 Class B shares, unless the Class B shares are kept off the market for a year by, say, escrowing them with someone who is neither a director nor shareholder. While this precaution obviously is not needed in order to stay under $1.5 million, compliance with Regulation A is only half the battle. It is also necessary to have established a basis for exemption, other than under Regulation A, for the Class B shares. If all of the insiders reside in the state where Unidata is to be incorporated and do business, the intrastate exemption will be available. If they do not, the private offering exemption will be available, since all of them will have the requisite access to information about Unidata, provided that none of them are acquiring their shares for resale. (Of course, Q, the stockbroker, would be the most suspect.) Thus, even though escrowing the Class B shares will not be needed to protect the small issue exemption for the Class A, escrowing may still be a good idea to protect the private offering exemption for the Class B (see Appendix H.6(c)).

(iii) Issuing shares for professional services

Does issue of shares to a stockbroker, a lawyer, and an accountant to secure their professional services create special SEC problems? Is it of significance that their shares will be of a different class (but identical except for selling price) than shares being offered to outsiders?

Q's shares will add to the disclosure required for offering Class A shares and, as suggested above, may complicate a private offering exemption for the Class B issue. An offering circular must include information about the nature and amount of commissions and discounts for underwriting and selling agents. This requirement would seem to cover Q's arrangement to buy "cheap" Class B shares along with M, N, and O prior to the Class A offering to outsiders. And inclusion of Q's shares in the Class B issue will defeat the private offering exemption for that issue if he cannot satisfactorily establish the necessary investment intention. Since a stockbroker is in the business of selling stock, the SEC may suspect that he is buying for resale rather than for investment. To fortify this point, in addition to the escrow arrangement mentioned above, a written investment commitment should be secured from Q.

Are the situations of R and S, who are paying for their Class B shares only with their professional services, significantly different from that of Q, who is paying cash for his shares at the same rate as M, N, and O? Since R and S will not be underwriting nor selling agents, their transactions will not require the same sort of disclosure in the offering circular as will Q's. But, like Q, they will need to take their shares with investment intention to preserve the private offering status for the Class B; and, while they will be less suspect than Q, it seems a wise precaution to get investment letters from them (and from M, N. and O). In another sense,their positions are more complicated than Q's, because receipt of shares may conflict with their professional responsibilities.

Since no shares are being registered, R, the lawyer, will not need to give a formal opinion as an expert that Unidata shares will be legally issued, fully paid, and non-assessable. While he could give this opinion for a registration and still hold shares of the issuer, this conclusion would be less clear if he were to receive shares for his services from the very issue upon the legality of which he is passing, because then he would be certifying that his services are worth the value of the shares being paid for them. And even where he is receiving shares from a different issue, and where a formal opinion is not required, some lawyers would have ethical qualms, particularly with a corporation as closely held as Unidata will be, about potentially conflicting demands on their loyalties if they are both a shareholder and legal advisor to the corporation as a whole.

The dangers in the position of S, the accountant, can be stated more definitely. While he can be paid for his services with shares because financial statements for an offering circular do not need to be certified, his share holdings will prevent him from serving as the independent public accountant who certifies the corporation's financial statements for a later registered offering. However, he may be disqualified from this role even without the shares, because the SEC takes the view that an accountant who is closely associated with the promoters of an enterprise and who plays a significant role in its formative business decisions lacks the necessary "independence" to certify its financials for registration.

(iv) Use of senior securities for outside investors

Before leaving federal regulation, we should briefly examine the possibility of offering to outside investors, instead of common shares, some sort of senior securities, such as convertible preferred shares or convertible debentures. The main argument for senior securities is their increased saleability: buyers would get both assured income and a chance to convert to common and thereby share in growth if the business thrives. Arguments against senior securities include possible legal complications under the Trust Indenture Act of 1939 and the private offering exemption, and the burden of fixed charges. The legal points have little impact in our situation. The expense of preparing a trust indenture can be avoided because the offering does not exceed $250,000.

> ■ **The demanding requirements of the Trust Indenture Act apply unless the issue is exempt under the private offering or intrastate exemptions, or unless it is for $250,000 or less.**

And we do not plan to use the private offering exception for securities sold to outsiders.

> ■ **If we were so planning, convertibility might cause problems because the underlying common shares obtainable upon conversion might be more widely distributed than the primary senior securities.**

But the business argument against senior securities is quite persuasive. The burden of fixed charges that preferred shares or debentures would put on a struggling, capital-shy enterprise like Unidata during its early years would seem to make their use unwise.

(c) State regulation of the sale of securities

In reaction to stock swindles of the late 19th and early 20th centuries, most states enacted "blue sky" laws. These laws were so called because they were said to be efforts to protect buyers "from speculative schemes which have no more basis than so many feet of 'blue sky'" (Hall v. Geiger-Jones Co., 242 U.S. 539, 550 (1917)). Federal securities legislation of the 1930's was a consequence of inadequacies of this state regulation; but federal laws supplemented rather than displaced state laws, leaving security sales subject to both state and federal controls.

Blue sky laws vary widely from state to state. Most states declare "fraud" in security sales a crime and require securities dealers to register. Registration of individual security issues, as under federal law, is less generally required. While not nearly as expensive and time-consuming as federal registrations, state registrations of individual issues are still experiences to be avoided whenever possible. We concentrate on two blue sky questions, one substantive, the other procedural, using the Uniform Securities Act for our legal guidelines: Will Unidata's "promotional" nature cause blue sky problems? How can Unidata minimize its state registrations? The geographical incidence of both these questions is, of course, quite narrow, since Unidata need be concerned only with states where selling efforts will be made.

(i) Reasonability of insider participation

Section 306 (a) of the Uniform Securities Act outlaws "unreasonable" promoter participation in the corporation whose securities are being sold: that is, the difference between what the promoters are paying for their shares ($1 per share in our case) and what the public will pay ($5 per share) should not be unreasonable.

> ▪ **Note that here the state laws are more ambitious than the federal laws, which concentrate on disclosure and avoid substantive judgments on prices.**

In comparison with what other companies have done without blue sky trouble, the participation of the Unidata promoters does not seem unreasonable. The few states (California, Florida, Mississippi, New Mexico, and Texas) that have rule-of-thumb percentage tests governing promoters' participations are the most likely to cause trouble. But even under the more stringent of these, Unidata would seem to be able to qualify. For example:

—Florida requires money or property (not services) investment by promoters of at least 25% of the dollar amount of securities offered to the public. 25% of $250,000 is $62,500. By including Q among the Unidata promoters, their investment will be $65,000. Since R and S are contributing services, their investments can not be counted.

—Texas requires that 10% of the proposed capital stock be paid for by promoters. 10% of $319,000 is $31,900, well under the amount being invested by the Unidata promoters.

If Unidata were nearer the line of unreasonableness it would want to consider measures—like the ones we have considered in connection with federal regulation of escrowing the promoters' shares or of offering outsiders senior securities—to strengthen the relative position of the outsiders.

> ▪ **As we have noted, escrowing would be the preferable measure because of the business arguments against senior securities.**

(ii) Minimizing state registrations

Section 402 (b)(9) of the Uniform Securities Act exempts from state registration offers to not more than ten persons in the state if the seller reasonably believes that all buyers in the state are buying for investment and if no remuneration is paid "directly or indirectly for soliciting any prospective buyer in this state." This provision warns us that care is in order about where Q solicits, since he is being paid remuneration for soliciting; and about getting investment letters from some purchasers. The following ground rules are suggested:

—That Q should limit solicitation to Unidata's home state and to states where there would be independent reasons for blue sky compliance or where compliance problems are minimal;

—That while Q may accept unsolicited orders from other states, he should refer inquiries from other states to M, N, and 0 (since the exemption turns on soliciting not selling); and

—That investment letters should be secured from all buyers—whether from Q or from M, N, or O—in states where the issue is not registered.

(d) Tax aspects of the sale of securities

The most serious federal tax problem in Unidata's proposed financing derives from the same source as the substantive problem under state securities regulations: the difference between the prices paid for Unidata shares by inside and outside investors. And the tax problem itself is akin to that in the preceding section of C, who was obtaining for only $2,000 one-half the common shares of a $104,000 business: possible "bargain purchase" of shares which may be compensation income when the purchaser performs services for the corporation.

Among Unidata's other tax problems perhaps the most significant is the question, also discussed in the preceding section, of qualification of shares under § 1244.

*(i) Effects of different share prices to
insiders and outsiders*

As we have noted, if all 50,000 shares of Unidata Class A common are sold to outsiders at $5 per share, the insiders who have bought Class B common for $1 per share will end up with shares having a book value of $2.67. Will the $1.67 per share increment—or possibly even the $4 per share spread between insiders and outsiders—be taxable as compensation income for the insiders?

> **• With the $1.67 increment, possible additional taxable income amounts to $33,400 each for M, N, and O (20,000 x $1.67), $8,350 for Q (5,000 x $1.67), and $3,340 for R and S (2,000 x $1.67). R and S will have compensation income of $2,000 each apart from the "bargain purchase."**

The compensation income problem of Unidata insiders can be approached as simply a matter of share valuation, with focus on the shares rather than the shareholders, or the approach can be whether particular shareholders have received income that should be called compensation.

Some guidance as to how the share valuation approach may work is provided by the following two Tax Court decisions from the early 1960's:

> —*Berckmans* v. *Commissioner,* ¶61,100 P-H Memo TC (1961), held that an insider's purchase of shares at $1 on April 15, 1955, followed by an underwritten and registered public offering at $8.50 on May 31, 1955, did not constitute a bargain purchase resulting in compensation income because the uncertainties surrounding the underwriting, the registration, and the success of the public offering made the shares worth only $1 on April 15.
>
> —*Dees* v. *Commissioner,* ¶62,153 P-H Memo TC (1962), reached a different result where the insider purchased shares at $1 and $1.50 *after* there had been sales to the public at $16. The court found compensation income in the amount of $4.50 per share, distinguishing Berckmans on the ground that in Dees the indications were that the public offering would succeed.

These two cases teach us that the insiders should complete their purchases of Unidata Class B shares well in advance of the offering of the Class A shares. Even with a comparable six week interval, however, Berckmans and Unidata may be distinguishable because underwriting and registration involve a greater number of technical "contingencies" than does Unidata's less formal plan for selling its shares; although, in terms of actual expectations, Unidata's offering would seem beset with more dangers that it will not succeed than was the offering in Berckmans.

Under the share valuation approach distinctions between different groups of insiders must be largely confined to the stages in the unfolding of the project at which they buy their shares. M, N, and O, the principals in Unidata, might buy their shares first, when the rest of the project is formally unfixed. At this point they could quite plausibly argue as follows: Whatever the value of our shares may later become, right now they can not possibly be worth more than $1 per share, because Unidata's only assets are our own $1 per share contributions. Then, somewhat later, when Q, R, and S acquire their shares, they too might argue (but considerably less forcibly) that the value is still only $1 per share because the public offering is still in the future and the only new assets are Q's $5,000 and the services of R and S, all of which came to Unidata at $1 per share. However, this argument by Q, R, and S becomes difficult because the only reason for the issue of their shares is the projected public offering and significant parts of the actual consideration for their shares (and the "ground floor" opportunity they provide) are the services that they will perform in raising outside money for Unidata.

By introducing the idea of selling shares in stages we begin to shift our focus from shares and their values to purchasers of shares and their roles in the financing. Professor Herwitz suggests that we distinguish between two kinds of insiders: "promoters" and "enterpreneurs." Promoters expect compensations for their services in helping put the deal together, services that are ordinarily completed with the financing and which do not influence the long-term success of the enterprise. Entrepreneurs, on the other hand, are the principals who have launched the business with all the risks that accompany a new venture, and who expect to be part of it for the long pull; they can influence its success or failure because they will be part of its management. From this distinction, Herwitz concludes that, when entrepreneurs take shares for less than what outsiders pay, the spread represents "a kind of 'entrepreneurial increment' rather than compensation income" and that "the premium paid by outsiders may be regarded as the cost of being permitted to share in the entrepreneur's venture rather than as compensation income for the entrepreneur's future services"; and he points out that "a large amount of compensation income in advance should not be lightly inferred." (D. Herwitz, *Business Planning* (1966) 275-76)

This distinction between entrepreneurs and promoters widens the difference in roles between M, N, and O and Q, R, and S that was emerging when we looked at share values in relation to times of purchase. It is true that Q, R, and S can claim that they too are entrepreneurs because they are venturing their time and talent for Unidata with no assurance of being paid and that it is unfair to tax them now on "income" they may never receive. However, they are not commiting themselves to Unidata as the principals are, and they will be performing services that soon will be substantially completed in return for their shares. In a sense, they too are outsiders being permitted to join in the entrepreneurs' venture, but at a reduced price in return for their help.

Since, as we will see, there are separate §1244 reasons for having the insiders purchase in stages, it would seem that overall tax liabilities will be minimized by M, N, O buying their shares before Q, R, and S buy theirs. Both groups can make the Berckmans argument for $1 being the true value and the Herwitz "entrepreneurial increment" argument for the spread not being compensation income; however, it must be recognized that the chances of Q, R, and S succeeding with either argument are doubtful.

(ii) Qualification of shares under §1244

As suggested in Sections 1.1 (b) and 7.1 (c) (i), qualifying shares under §1244 is one of those rare tax opportunities to make a move that may help you but cannot hurt you. Holders of qualified shares may treat any loss on the shares up to $50,000 ($100,000 on joint returns) as ordinary losses that can be used to reduce ordinary income; without qualification such losses could be used only to reduce capital gains. We also detailed requirements for §1244 qualification, which can be summarized: issuance of original issue common shares for money or property (other than stock or securities) by a "small business corporation" with capital and paid-in surplus not exceeding $1 million and which derives more than 50% of its income from operations, rather than investments or royalties.

All Class A and Class B shares will be original issue common; and Unidata will qualify as a small business corporation, since its capital and paid-in surplus will be well under $1 million. But the requirement that §1244 shares be issued only for money or property, and not for services, introduces some complexities for Unidata. While the Class A shares for outsiders and the Class B shares for the principals (M, N, and O) meet this test, the Class B shares destined for the lawyer (R) and the accountant (S) clearly do not; and, as is apparent from our discussion above, the Class B shares for the stockbroker (Q) are questionable. Q is paying the same money consideration as are M, N, and O, but he is also performing stock-selling services for his right to buy at the principals' price.

The failure of all Unidata shares to qualify under §1244 makes it advisable that Unidata shares be issued in four separate offerings: 60,000 Class B shares to M, N, and O; 5,000 Class B shares to Q; 4,000 Class B shares to R and S; 50,000 Class A shares to outsiders. All of the offerings except those to R and S should try for 1244 treatment, although Q may have trouble establishing that his shares are issued "for money or other property."

Section 7.3 Raising Outside Capital by Offering Securities to the Public

Thus far in this chapter we have dealt with seekers of capital with quite modest needs that could be met from a limited number of identifiable sources. Now we examine a more ambitious enterprise that is poised to take the plunge of "going public" by offering a new issue of its securities to the general investing public. We are mainly concerned with the accompanying complications of underwriting and SEC registration and some of the long-term consequences of being publicly held. In this section we do not try to cover state blue sky problems nor listing on a securities exchange, and there will be little about tax planning.

At the outset we need to recapitulate briefly some of the arguments, con and pro, as they affect both the corporation and its controlling shareholders, for transforming the status of a corporation from close to public. Negative entailments of going public are numerous.

—The corporation will lose the special corporate flexibilities and tax saving opportunities that are available to close corporations. It will incur the expense, in money and in executive time and attention, involved in a public offering. And it will be subjected to more extensive disclosure about its business and to ongoing reporting and clearance chores.

—For the shareholders, there will be increased exposure to personal liabilities, possible tax disadvantages, and perils to their control positions.

> ▪ **The disadvantages of being public, combined with depressed share prices, have caused some public corporations to "go private" by reacquiring the holdings of public shareholders.**

On the plus side, however, there are substantial incidental benefits, corporate and individual, from going public, in addition to the main objective of raising money.

—For the corporation, a successful public offering is a mark of its business maturity which enhances its financial position. When its shares are publicly traded they are more readily useable for acquiring other businesses. And if it sells consumer goods, broad share ownership may be a source of consumer loyalty.

—For individual shareholders, public ownership, by providing a market for their shares, may bring several benefits: they can diversify their investments by selling some of their shares; if they want to hold their shares, public trading may increase their value; and a market value for their shares will be established for estate tax purposes.

Our vehicle in this section is the mythical coal mining venture, Dighaldoe Corporation, that we introduced in Chapter 1. Recall that in setting up their business, Digges, Hall, and Doe anticipated that they might need additional capital, but they also wanted to keep control among themselves. We now assume that several years have passed and that their venture has prospered. While they have been able to meet some of their capital needs by reinvesting earnings and by short-term borrowing, they have now reached the point where they need about $2.8 million in fresh money to provide adequate working capital and to take the next steps in their development. Also their investment advisers and estate planners are urging that they diversify their holdings and that they establish a market value for their Dighaldoe shares. After being told about all of the problems of going public, they still want to go ahead. We further assume that Doe is able to interest First Appalachia, a reputable investment banking firm, in helping them with a public offering.

(a) Preliminary legal and financial questions

Before entering the procedural thicket of underwriting and registration, we need to examine two questions, one legal and the other financial, that First Appalachia will want resolved before it undertakes an underwriting for Dighaldoe. The legal question is: Are Dighaldoe's existing shares "duly issued, fully paid and non-assessable"? The considerably more complex financial question is: What kind and quantity of securities should be offered to the public and how should the new issue be fitted into Dighaldoe's financial structure?

(i) Status of Dighaldoe's existing shares

A public offering calls for a legal opinion that Dighaldoe's existing shares are duly issued, fully paid, and non-assessable under the law of the state where it is incorporated. The lawyer giving this opinion must examine Dighaldoe's articles of incorporation and how its shares were issued to satisfy himself that the shares are authorized and not "watered." We are assuming, as suggested in Chapter 1, that Dighaldoe's charter authorized 5,000 shares of $10 par common stock and that each of the three participants received 1,000 shares which were valued on Dighaldoe's books at $100 per share ($10 capital + $90 paid-in surplus). All of these shares are clearly authorized and Doe's shares, for which he paid the full

$100,000 in cash, are clearly fully paid. But the payment situation is less tidy as to the shares that went to Digges, which were issued partly for mining services, and as to those that went to Hall, who paid no cash but contributed only trucks and trucking services. Since both the mining and trucking services were to be performed in connection with getting Dighaldoe's operations started, they were "future" services at the time the shares were issued. And as to both services and trucks we have the question of whether they were worth the values assigned.

In dealing with these problems, Dighaldoe's lawyers can get substantial help from the Model Act (§ 19), which provides:

> *The consideration for the issuance of shares may be paid, in whole or in part, in money, in other property, tangible or intangible, or in labor or services actually performed for the corporation. When payment of the consideration for which shares are to be issued shall have been received by the corporation, such shares shall be deemed to be fully paid and non-assessable. . . . In the absence of fraud in the transaction, the judgment of the board of directors or the shareholders, as the case may be, as to the value of the consideration received for shares shall be conclusive.*

This provision seems applicable to the shares issued to Digges and Hall in two respects. Shares issued for future services appear to become fully paid and non-assessable when the services are "actually performed", or, stated more broadly, payment of the consideration for shares—whether money, property, or services—can validate their earlier issuance. And, in the absence of fraud, the directors or shareholders of the corporation can resolve the valuation question, both as to property and services, by exercising their "judgment."

To bring the Dighaldoe shares clearly under the Model Act provision it appears advisable for the directors and shareholders to adopt resolutions prior to the public offering, if they have not already done so, acknowledging that the promised services have been duly performed by Digges and Hall, and adjudging that the values of the property and services received as consideration for their shares were correctly stated on Dighaldoe's books (see Appendix C.2(b)-(e)).

> ▪ While action by both directors and shareholders is not required, it can do no harm, and it may provide some insurance against trouble. And hindsight now shows us that it would have been neater for Dighaldoe to have adopted resolutions of this sort when it received Hall's trucks and when the start-up services of Digges and Hall were completed.

(ii) Structuring Dighaldoe's new issue of securities

Now we turn from the past to the future. How many of what kind or kinds of new securities should Dighaldoe issue to raise the $2.8 million that it needs? In answering these questions, First Appalachia's views about marketability of the new issue and about Dighaldoe's long-term financial health should be given weight. Advice in structuring an offering can be an important part of an underwriter's services.

Fundamental to the structure of the new issue are decisions on what the relative positions—as to control, income participation, and liquidation—of the old and the new investors should be. This problem is, in part, similar to the one we faced in Section 7.1 where we needed to put a value on a going business that was about to incorporate and expand. In a sense, Digges, Hall, and Doe are "buying into" an expanded business by contributing their old business. Thus, we need to look at Dighaldoe's net worth and its earnings, and to consider what capitalization rate (multiplier) should be used to convert its earnings into value. Let us suppose that its net worth is now $600,000 (up $300,000 by virtue of retained earnings from the original $300,000), that its earnings (after taxes and reasonable salaries) are running at a rate of about $100,000 per year, and that a prudent investor in Dighaldoe would be satisfied with an $8\frac{1}{3}\%$ return—which means that he would be willing to capitalize Dighaldoe at 12 times earnings, i.e., at $1.2 million. If this capitalized earnings figure is used to value Dighaldoe's existing business, and if $2.8 million new money is added, Dighaldoe will grow to a $4 million business, of which Digges, Hall, and Doe should together receive a 30% interest (their $1.2 million contribution ÷ the $4 million total).

> ▪ Of course, if Dighaldoe had already gone public, we would not need to "construct" its market value in this fashion: there would be real, rather than hypothetical, prudent investors.

After the broad outlines of participations in the expanded business have been agreed upon, the planners can turn to its details. What changes are needed in Dighaldoe's articles of incorporation and by-laws? Should the new securities be equity or debt? If equity, should the new shares have the same rights as those held by Digges, Hall, and Doe, or should they carry different voting, income, or liquidation rights? If debt, should the new bonds or debentures be convertible to common shares? Here are some of the considerations that influence how these questions are answered:

Digges, Hall, and Doe have two major objectives that are somewhat at cross purposes. They want to establish a market for their own shares, which dictates that at least a part of the new issue be in common shares like their own. But they also want to keep control of their business and if all of the $2.8 million new issue is in common shares their holdings will, as we have noted, drop to 30% of the total. They might reconcile their objectives of creating a market and protecting their control position by splitting the new issue, roughly $1.2 million in common shares and $1.6 million in some sort of non-voting senior securities, debt or preferred shares. And this course has other attractions: since Dighaldoe is now earning $16\frac{2}{3}\%$ on its net worth ($100,000 earnings $\div$ $600,000 net worth), fixed yield (say $8\frac{1}{3}\%$) senior securities will provide considerable leverage; and if the senior securities are debt, Dighaldoe can deduct interest from taxable income. On the other hand, a senior security issue of $1.6 million at $8\frac{1}{3}\%$ will saddle Dighaldoe with fixed charges of $133,333, considerably more than its present income. If the expanded business is not able to maintain the present earning rate, or if the coal business slumps, Dighaldoe will be in more serious trouble than if it had financed its expansion with common shares.

First Appalachia is likely to add its voice in favor of an all common issue in order to provide the maximum market in Dighaldoe shares. In addition to its probable views about the incompatibility of fixed charges and the vicissitudes of the coal business, First Appalachia wants the new issue to be sellable to a broad spectrum of customers and to be freely tradeable in the "after market" (the buying and selling of shares following the initial sale). And it may be influenced by the reluctance of some investors to become part of what looks like a permanent minority. Thus, First Appalachia will probably urge Digges, Hall, and Doe to relinquish their majority position and to rely on their control of the proxy machinery to maintain their control of Dighaldoe's board of directors.

We now assume that First Appalachia has agreed that, for purposes of planning the new issue, the existing Dighaldoe business will be valued at $1.2 million; we also assume that Digges, Hall, and Doe have agreed that the new $2.8 million issue will be in common shares with the same rights as their own holdings. This result can be achieved by amending Dighaldoe's articles of incorporation to increase the authorized common to 150,000 shares (from 5,000 shares), to reduce their par value to $1 (from $10), and to split the existing 3,000 shares 10 for 1, giving Digges, Hall, and Doe each 10,000 new shares (see Appendix E.1(a) and E.2). Dighaldoe's articles and by-laws should also be amended to eliminate shareholders' preemptive rights and other provisions which were recommended in Chapters 1 and 6 for protection of shareholders of close corporations which are unsuitable for a public corporation (see Appendix E.1(b)-(g), E.2, and E.3). Then Dighaldoe will be in a position to sell 70,000 of the new shares to the underwriters at $40 per share and will receive therefore the desired $2.8 million. There will remain a cushion of 50,000 authorized but unissued shares as recommended in Section 1.5. After these transactions, the right hand side of Dighaldoe's balance sheet will show:

Capital stock (100,000 shares, $1 par)	$ 100,000
Paid-in surplus	3,000,000
Earned surplus	300,000
	$3,400,000

- **Of the paid-in surplus, $2,730,000 ($39 ($40 - $1 par) x 70,000 shares) is from the new issue and the remaining $270,000 is from Digges, Hall, and Doe when Dighaldoe was organized.**

(b) Selling securities through an underwriting

Now we turn from the structure of Dighaldoe's public offering to some of the mechanics involved in getting it done. There being no legal requirement that Dighaldoe sell its shares through a middle man, why not dispense with First Appalachia and sell the shares directly to the public? By describing the underwriter's role in planning a new issue we have begun our answer. And its selling role is even more crucial. Selling securities, like selling other things, is a special capability, requiring quite unique experience and organization. In short, if Dighaldoe tried itself to market $2.8 million of its shares it would probably fail.

- **Public offerings directly from company to investor are most common in blue chip companies; they generally take the form of offerings of rights to existing shareholders to purchase additional shares.**

As we noted in Section 7.2 (a) (ii), investment firms like First Appalachia can provide two basic kinds of assistance in selling securities to the public: firm-commitment underwriting and best-efforts underwriting. With the former, the issuing corporation (or selling shareholder) sells the securities to a group of investment bankers, usually with a single firm acting as manager of this "underwriting group," who in turn sell them to a larger "selling group" of securities dealers, who sell them to the public. With the latter, the underwriters do not buy the securities but rather act as agents for the issuer in selling the securities to the public through sub-agents.

More practically significant than the legal distinction between buyer and agent are its economic consequences. Firm-commitment underwriters assume the market risk and, like wholesalers and retailers of goods generally, the underwriters and the selling group are compensated by the spreads between their buying and selling prices. Best-efforts underwriters, on the other hand, assume no market risk and, like brokers and sales agents, are compensated in the form of commissions which may be shared with sub-agents. Unless an issuer is so well established that the market risk is negligible—which, of course, is not the case with Dighaldoe—it will obviously prefer a firm-commitment underwriting, even though it will be more costly, because it enables the issuer to know in advance how much money will be forthcoming and when. We assume that First Appalachia is willing to organize a group to do a firm-commitment underwriting for Dighaldoe.

The formal underwriting agreement between Dighaldoe and the underwriters is not to be signed until just before the registration statement becomes effective and not until after Dighaldoe has incurred most of the expenses of registration, which will probably total about $50,000, exclusive of insurance. This seemingly unbusinesslike timing is dictated in part by the underwriters' insistence upon warranties from Dighaldoe as to the accuracy and completeness of the registration statement. However, at the outset of the underwriting and registration process the basic terms of the underwriting are arrived at informally, and perhaps embodied in a "letter of intent"; furthermore, Dighaldoe can rely on the customs of the investment banking community and First Appalachia's concern for its reputation to assure performance of its informal commitments.

What can Dighaldoe expect to find in the underwriting agreement? Apart from provisions fixing the price that the underwriters agree to pay Dighaldoe for its shares and the time and place of the closing (probably seven to ten days after signing the agreement at the office of Dighaldoe's transfer agent), and provisions concerning the consequences of default by members of the underwriting group, Dighaldoe will discover that the agreement is largely designed for the protection of the underwriters. In addition to providing warranties about the accuracy and completeness of the registration statement, Dighaldoe is expected to agree to qualify the shares being offered under the blue sky laws of States designated by the underwriters, to provide an adequate supply of copies of the prospectuses, to file any post-effective amendments to the registration statement that may be needed, to furnish subsequent financial reports to underwriters and shareholders, to pay the expenses of registration, and to indemnify the underwriters against liability from false statements in the registration statement. Finally, the agreement sets out a list of conditions to which the underwriters' obligation to buy Dighaldoe's shares at the closing is subject, including:

—Effectiveness of the registration statement;
—Opinions of lawyers representing Dighaldoe and the underwriters as to the validity of proceedings;
—Certification by Dighaldoe's officers that its warranties are accurate as of the closing date;
—Letter of assurance by Dighaldoe's independent auditors of no adverse material changes in its financial condition; and
—Nonoccurence of designated events between the agreement and the closing that might adversely affect the securities market (the "market out" clause).

We have assumed that preliminary negotiations result in a price to the underwriters of $40 per share for 70,000 shares, providing Dighaldoe a total of $2.8 million. We now further assume that the underwriters plan to offer these shares to the public at $45 per share, which will yield them $3,150,000, providing a discount of $350,000 to compensate them for their expenses in organizing the sale, the risk that they may be unable to sell the shares, and interest on the $2.8 million which will be tied up for an indeterminate period. This $5 per share spread, equal to about 11% ($5 ÷ $45) of the price to public investors, also must provide any profit for the underwriters.

(c) Registering securities with the SEC under the 1933 Act

Dighaldoe's decision to go public involves it in negotiations on two fronts: with underwriters in order to sell its shares, and with the SEC in order to "register" them. The latter chore is imposed by the Securities Act of 1933 which seeks to protect investors by requiring sellers of securities to disclose material facts about what they are offering and by preventing misrepresentations in connection with such sales. The act empowers the SEC to supervise disclosure and to police misrepresentation; it does not, however, empower the Commission to pass upon the merits of securities nor upon the fairness of offering prices. The Act hinges on its §5, which makes it unlawful to sell a non-exempt security unless a "registration statement" is in effect and unless the sale is accompanied or preceded by a "prospectus": a document summarizing the more important information in the registration statement, of which it is a part, which is to be made available to prospective investors.

(i) Filing the registration statement with the SEC

In this section we are assuming that the sale of Dighaldoe's new shares does not qualify as an exempt offering—local, private, or small—under any of the exemptions detailed in Section 7.2. For Dighaldoe the registration process will involve filing with the SEC in Washington a full scale registration statement, following Form S-1, disclosing:

- —the names of those participating in Dighaldoe's direction, management, or control;
- —their security holdings in and rumuneration from Dighaldoe, including any option, bonus, or profit-sharing privileges;
- —Dighaldoe's capital structure, history, and earnings;
- —its financial statements, certified by independent accountants;
- —payments to promoters made within the past two years or intended to be made;
- —acquisitions of property not in the ordinary course of business, and interests in such acquisitions of directors, officers, and principal shareholders;
- —pending or threatened legal proceedings; and
- —the purposes to which proceeds of the offering are to be applied.

The registration statement will need to include information about the relative holdings of insiders and the public, similar to the information required about Unidata in the preceding section, substantially as follows:

Before the offering contemplated hereby, the book value of the holdings of officers and directors in Dighaldoe shares was $20 per share [$600,000 ÷ 30,000 shares]. If the offering is successful, the book value will be increased at no cost to the holders to $34 per share [$3,400,000 ÷ 100,000 shares]. Accordingly, an investment of $45 per share in Dighaldoe shares will be reduced to a book equity of $34 per share.

Assuming that all of the 70,000 shares offered hereunder shall be issued, the existing officers and directors as a group will hold 30% of the total outstanding shares at the cost of $600,000, and the public will hold 70% of the total outstanding shares at a cost of $3,150,000 [$45 x 70,000 shares].

After the registration statement is filed it is examined by the staff of the SEC's Division of Corporate Finance for compliance with the Commission's standards of disclosure and Dighaldoe is advised by an informal letter (sometimes called the "deficiency letter") of any material non-compliance. Arrangements should be made for an agent to pick up this letter in Washington and to read it over the telephone to a stenographer to avoid delay in mailing. The staff looks for errors of both omission and inclusion. For example, it might ask for more information about:

—insiders' participations in Dighaldoe's securities, if the disclosures outlined above are not made; or

—how proceeds of the issue will be used (it does not suffice just to say that they will be added to Dighaldoe's general funds); or

—potential liabilities under employee pension plans; or

—whether Dighaldoe's properties are owned or leased and whether any are in the exploratory stage as to the quantity and quality of coal reserves; or

—special characteristics of coal mining that affect prices and earnings, such as seasonal fluctuations in production and demand, labor (including safety) and transportation costs, the incidence of strikes, and availability of other energy sources.

In the other direction, the SEC asks for elimination of statements (most likely favorable) about Dighaldoe's business or its shares that the staff considers "irrelevant" or "predictive" (the SEC takes a similarly negative attitude toward predictions in proxy soliciting materials), on the ground that an issuer should confine itself to relevant "facts" and let investors draw their own conclusions. The registration statement is also examined closely in light of the Commission's accounting rules (Regulation S-X) which set standards for the financial statements and for the "independence" of the accountant certifying them. As we have noted, an accountant lacks independence if he has a financial interest in the issuer or has served it as a promoter, underwriter, voting trustee, director, officer, or employee.

A registration statement becomes "effective" 20 days after filing, but the 20 day period starts anew after each amendment. To prevent its statement becoming effective before deficiencies are worked out, Dighaldoe files a formal "delaying amendment" within 20 days of its original filing and then, when it files a substantive amendment to correct deficiencies (which Dighaldoe's lawyers have resolved in telephone or personal conferences with the SEC staff), it asks that the effective date, which otherwise would be 20 days after the last amendment, be "accelerated" to the date planned for signing the underwriting agreement. On, or very shortly before, the effective date a final amendment is filed fixing the price ($45) at which Dighaldoe's shares will be offered to the public.

> ▪ **Fixing the price to the public is deferred until just before effectiveness to give the underwriters maximum maneuverability in light of market conditions. Of course, the selling dealers need to be able, during the period between filing and effectiveness, to tell investors with substantial precision what the price is likely to be.**

(ii) Distributing prospectuses, preliminary and final, to investors

The disclosure which the Securities Act was enacted to achieve is supposed to be made to the SEC in the registration statement as a prelude to getting investment information to prospective investors in the prospectus; and the 20 day waiting period between filing and effectiveness was envisaged as a hiatus in the distribution process for investors to study the prospectus. This expectation has been largely frustrated.

For most of the waiting period a complete, definitive prospectus is not available; a final prospectus is not required to be, and ordinarily is not, sent to investors until after they have committed themselves to buy the security. As we have noted, corrective amendments responsive to SEC comments and the price amendment are not filed until near the end of the waiting period; and pressures of the way underwritings actually work forced the SEC to permit acceleration of effectiveness to almost immediately after these filings. All that is available for investors during the waiting period is the preliminary "red herring" prospectus: so-called because warnings about its status must be printed in red across its cover.

There have been impediments, legal and practical, to relying on the preliminary prospectus to get information to investors before the effective date. At this point the securities are not yet "registered" and cannot be legally sold under § 5. At first the SEC tried to meet this legal difficulty with a fiction (a time-honored official response to troublesome laws) that a preliminary prospectus was not an "offer." This expedient did not work because sellers of securities were still afraid that distribution of a preliminary prospectus might be combined with other communications to investors to support a finding of illegal offers. In 1954 the Act was amended to permit written offers to sell (but not sales or contracts of sale) between filing and effectiveness; in addition, offers to sell before filing were expressly made illegal. While preliminary negotiations or agreements between an issuer and underwriters and among underwriters are permitted before filing (under § 2 (3)), offers to dealers and investors must await filing.

After the 1954 amendments, although caution to avoid "offers" was still indicated in communicating with dealers and investors before filing, there were no legal inhibitions on giving them a preliminary prospectus before effectiveness. But the more intractable practical problem remained as to how the SEC could compel such distributions. To this end the SEC has announced that it will refuse acceleration of effectiveness unless the registrant has provided underwriters and dealers with enough copies of the preliminary prospectus for adequate distribution to investors. But this measure does not assure that copies will reach investors. As a further effort in this direction, an SEC rule declares it a "deceptive practice" to fail to deliver a preliminary prospectus to a purchaser a reasonable time before the sale.

(d) Coordinating the steps of a public offering

With this background about some of the parts of the underwriting and registration processes, we are now ready to put these parts together in a time schedule which will coordinate Dighaldoe's public offering. A key date in our schedule is when we can expect to have Dighaldoe's financial statements, which are the heart of the registration statement. Thus our planning involves consultation with the independent accountant chosen to certify the statements as well as with the underwriters. First Appalachia, the managing underwriter, will probably insist upon certified statements as of a date not more than 90 days prior to filing with the SEC, even though certified statements as of a less recent date would satisfy SEC requirements. We will assume that Dighaldoe has adopted a fiscal year that ends on June 30 (see Appendix B.11) and that its independent accountant says that his audit for the last fiscal year will be completed by September 10. Thus, if the registration statement can be filed by September 28, the year-end financials will be not more than 90 days old when filed.

> ▪ It is obviously preferable, in order to avoid the expense of a special audit, to time a registration so that the regular year-end audit can be utilized.

Before September 10 Dighaldoe's officers and lawyers need to be doing several things so that on September 10 they are ready to send to the printer, along with the financials, the rest of the registration statement. They should, of course, reach tentative agreement with First Appalachia on the terms of the offering which may, as we have suggested, be embodied in a letter of intent. This agreement should be reached at least a month before the audit is expected to be completed—i.e., by about August 10, to enable the following steps to be taken during the period August 10-25:

—Send questionnaires to Dighaldoe's officers, directors, and 10% shareholders about their shareholdings, remuneration for services, and interests in material transactions with Dighaldoe.

—Gather Dighaldoe corporate documents for review and reproduction as exhibits where required.

—Interview Dighaldoe's officers and prepare memoranda on its history and operations.

This schedule leaves about two weeks (August 25—September 10) for the lawyers representing Dighaldoe and First Appalachia to put together the prospectus and other parts of the registration statement, exclusive of financials. First Appalachia lawyers are also doing preliminary work for any state blue sky filings that are contemplated (see Section 7.2(c)).

For several days after September 10, the date that the financials and the rest of the registration statement go to the printer, the Dighaldoe and First Appalachia lawyers are in close contact with the printer, receiving daily page proofs, making revisions, and securing revised page proofs. A Dighaldoe directors' meeting is set for about September 18. At this meeting there are presented printed copies of the registration statement, in as final form as possible, and signature pages for signing by Dighaldoe's officers and directors and by its lawyer and independent accountant. If all goes well, the registration statement is ready for filing with the SEC in Washington on about September 21, a week before the September 28 deadline.

After the filing comes a period of relative calm for Dighaldoe, during which

—First Appalachia lines up its selling group of dealers;

—the preliminary prospectus is distributed to underwriters, dealers, and investors; and

—the SEC staff combs the registration statement for deficiences.

Since three to six weeks are likely to go by before the SEC produces its deficiency letter, Dighaldoe's lawyer files a delaying amendment on about October 9 (18 days after the filing on September 21). He should also, as we have suggested, arrange to pick up the deficiency letter when it is ready: which we will assume happens on October 20. This event triggers another hectic period for Dighaldoe and First Appalachia lawyers as they try to resolve the deficiencies among themselves and with the SEC staff and then work with the printer in preparing the first amendent to the registration statement. From October 20 on the events march quickly; we assume the following sequence:

October 20-25	—Preparation and printing of first amendment.
October 23	—"Due Diligence" meeting, attended by Dighaldoe officers and representatives of First Appalachia, to acquaint underwriters and dealers with Dighaldoe and the offering.
October 26	—Filing with SEC by Dighaldoe's lawyer of first amendment and letter requesting acceleration of effective date to October 30.
October 30	—Signing of agreement among underwriters and of underwriting agreement; filing of price amendment with SEC; and registration declared effective by SEC.
November 7	—Closing at which Dighaldoe delivers 70,000 shares and First Appalachia delivers a check for $2.8 million in payment therefor.

With, or perhaps even before, the tentative agreement of August 10, First Appalachia has begun lining up other underwriters. As we have noted, organization of the selling group of dealers on the basis of firm offers is supposed to await filing of the registration statement on September 21, and actual sales of securities are supposed to await its effectiveness on October 30. If the offering is very successful, the whole issue may be sold on the effective date. If the offering is very unsuccessful, First Appalachia and the other underwriters may have to put substantial numbers of Dighaldoe shares "on the shelf" to be sold when and at what price they can be. More likely, the results will be somewhere between these extremes, with the shares being sold over a fairly short period after the effective date. While Digges, Hall, and Doe would, of course, prefer that the new Dighaldoe shares be snapped up by the public at the $45 price—for what it will mean as to the market value of their own shares and as to prospects for future offerings—the direct market risk for the success of this offering is on the underwriters.

(e) Continuing 1934 Act consequences of going public

The Securities Act of 1933 focuses quite narrowly on the disclosure required in connection with a specific event: a public offering of securities. The

Securities Exchange Act of 1934 extends "investor protection by disclosure" to a much broader range of events, including selling and buying "used" securities (as distinguished from new issues), operation of securities exchanges, and activities of broker-dealers. Parts of the 1934 Act that most affect corporate officers and directors are anti-fraud provisions in § 10, which we save for Chapter 11 since their application is not confined to public corporations; proxy rules under § 14—regulating solicitation of proxies from shareholders, conduct of proxy contests, and handling of shareholder proposals—which we discuss in Section 3.2; and registration and reporting requirements in § § 12 and 13 and regulation of insider reporting and trading in § 16, the long-term consequences of which are our concern in this subsection.

While § § 12, 13, 14, and 16 originally applied only to corporations with securities listed on a national exchange, amendments to the Act in 1964 broadened their application to all corporations with assets over $1 million and 500 or more shareholders. Investors in corporations with securities traded over-the-counter which meet these quite modest "size" tests of being publicly held are now accorded the same disclosure protections as investors in listed corporations. We will assume that after its public offering Dighaldoe meets the size tests. Thus, the fact that its shares are not listed but are traded over-the-counter does not affect the consequences discussed here.

> **▪ Securities of the thousands of corporations whose shares are unlisted—usually because numbers of shares outstanding, number of shareholders, and size of earnings do not justify listing—as well as U.S. Government and muncipal bonds, are traded in the "over-the-counter" market. This market is made up of securities dealers who may or may not be members of an exchange; their trading is done mainly by telephone, acting either as principals or as brokers for customers.**

(i) Registration and reporting: § § 12 and 13

Under § 12 of the 1934 Act Dighaldoe is required to file with the SEC a registration application supplying information about:

—its organization, financial structure, and nature of its business;
—the securities outstanding;
—its directors, officers, underwriters, and principal shareholders;
—their remuneration and material contracts with Dighaldoe;
—bonus and profit-sharing arrangements;
—management and service contracts;
—options with respect to securities;
—material contracts; and
—all important financial statements duly certified.

This 1934 Act registration is to be distinguished from the registration of the new issue of Dighaldoe's shares under the 1933 Act discussed in subsection (c) above. The 1934 Act registration, designed to provide a continuing bank of data about Dighaldoe, calls for information similar to, but less detailed than, information required for the 1933 Act registration, designed to provide the basis of an investment decision. But the most striking difference between the two filings is less in their contents than in the ways they are handled, both by corporations and by the Commission. 1933 Act filings are meticulously prepared by experienced lawyers and accountants and then carefully examined by the SEC staff. In contrast, 1934 Act registration applications are usually the product of corporate employees, except to the extent that financial reports must be certified, and the SEC is not staffed to police the avalanche of 1934 Act material that it receives the same way it does 1933 Act filings. Contributing to this different handling are differences in the consequences of inadequate information: the threat of individual and corporate liabilities is much less serious with 1934 Act registration; and, perhaps more significantly, since there is no public offering at stake the sanction of a stop order is not available.

Section 13 of the 1934 Act supplements § 12 by requiring periodic and special reports from corporations registered under § 12 in order to keep information in their registration applications current. The periodic reports are annual reports on Form 10-K, containing certified financial statements, to be filed within 120 days after the end of each fiscal year (Dighaldoe's 10-Ks are due each year henceforth on or before October 28); and quarterly reports on Form 10-Q giving operating results for each of the first three quarters of its fiscal year, to be filed within 45 days after the end of each of those quarters (none is needed for the fourth quarter). Special reports on Form 8-K are supposed to be filed within 15 days after the occurrence of any of certain major events (like amendments to its articles of incorporation or by-laws and changes in its officers and directors). Assuring timely filing of these reports will probably be a duty of Dighaldoe's corporate secretary.

(ii) Insider reporting and trading: § 16

Because of Congressional concern about the unfairness of trading in a corporation's shares by insiders on the basis of information not available to others, § 16 of the 1934 Act (a) requires directors, officers, and principal shareholders (beneficial owners of more than 10% of any class of shares) to report changes in their share ownership and (b) makes them liable to the corporation for any profits from "short-swing" transactions (purchases and sales or sales and purchases within six months).

The reporting requirement in § 16 (a) requires a Dighaldoe insider to file with the SEC, when Dighaldoe registers under § 12, or within 10 days after he becomes a director, officer, or 10% shareholder, a statement (using Form 3) of the Dighaldoe securities of which he is the "beneficial owner"; within 10 days after the close of each calendar month thereafter during which there is any change in such beneficial ownership he must report (using Form 4) the change. In addition to shares held in trust for him or for his account, an insider is ordinarily considered to be the beneficial owner of shares held by his relatives who share his home.

> ▪ **Thus, Digges is the beneficial owner under § 16 of shares held by his wife or children if they share his home but not of a son or daughter living away from his home.**

The SEC publishes a monthly summary of reports filed under § 16 (a).

In enforcing the short-swing liability provisions in § 16 (b) the federal courts have generally imposed a strict, objective test which does not inquire into an insider's actual knowledge or intentions. Liability has been almost automatic if any two transactions within a six month period can be matched to show a profit. And they do not need to involve the same shares.

> ▪ **For example, suppose that Digges starts with 10,000 Dighaldoe shares. Then, within a six month period, he buys 1,000 shares at $45, sells 1,000 shares at $44, buys 1,000 shares at $43, and sells 1,000 shares at $42. After these transactions he is back where he started with 10,000 shares and has actually lost $2,000. However, under the prevailing interpretation of § 16 (b) he is liable to Dighaldoe for $1,000: his "profit" derived by matching his sale at $44 and his purchase at $43.**

Because of this strict liability, insiders are usually advised to wait six months plus a few days between all of their transactions in their corporation's securities.

> ▪ **The few extra days are recommended to allow for possible disputes about the dates of transactions. For example, if Digges placed his sell order at $44 on July 1 and his buy order at $43 on the following January 2, he still might be liable for his $1000 profit if the sell order was not executed until July 3 and the buy order was executed on the date it was given.**

Enforcement of § 16 (b), which is largely through court action rather than by the SEC, depends upon the diligence of lawyers who make it a practice to examine the reports of insider transactions filed with the SEC under § 16 (a). A § 16 (b) suit is brought by a shareholder as a derivative suit on behalf of the corporation in a federal court (jurisdiction of § 16 (b) suits, like other 1934 Act suits, is exclusively federal). Any recovery from the suit goes to the corporation. However, as with other derivative suits (see Section 2.4), the incentive for bringing the suit is the prospect of a fee for the plaintiff's lawyer from the amount recovered by the corporation from the insiders.

Section 16 (b) has generated a tangle of legal problems about such questions as what is a "purchase" or a "sale," who is a "beneficial owner," when is a profit "realized," and when the SEC can grant exemptions. It has also generated lively debate about the ethical implications of lawyers using § 16 (b) to "stir up" litigation (an unsavory practice known as "champerty") as weighed against the social value of having a corps of "private attorneys general" who are motivated to help the federal government enforce its laws. Where one stands in this debate is likely to depend upon whether one thinks it is a good idea for the federal government to be trying to discourage insider trading.

CHECKLIST OF POINTS TO WATCH OUT FOR IN FINANCING YOUR CORPORATION

(References after headings are to Sections of Chapter 7.)

1. Valuation of a business about to be expanded (Section 7.1 (a))

Why and how is a business valued when it is to be incorporated and expanded with new money?

Small but growing businesses need fresh capital, which often may be secured only if proprietors will share participation with new investors. Incorporation is usually the best way to carry on the expanded enterprise. A preliminary step to incorporation and expansion is fixing relative participations of proprietor and investor: a difficult exercise because it requires putting a value on the going business that is being contributed by the proprietor. Alternative approaches are piece-by-piece appraisal of its tangible assets, and arriving at an overall enterprise value by capitalizing its earnings. Asset appraisals ignore the intangible value of a going concern, and require choice among the original cost, replacement cost, and liquidation value of individual assets. While a value based on capitalized earnings takes into account going concern values and avoids choosing a theory for asset appraisal, its soundness depends on a reliable quantification of earnings and selection of an appropriate multiplier to use in capitalizing them.

Since small businesses are seldom valued at more than four or five times their annual earnings, which assumes a 20 to 25 percent return on investments, they are seldom able to borrow money at a reasonable interest rate without special incentives for the lender, such as a share in the control and future growth of the business.

2. Sharing an expanded business (Section 7.1 (b))

How can the corporate form be used to structure participations in a business being expanded with new money?

After the pre-expansion value of a business has been determined, the corporate form of doing business lends itself to tailoring an expanded enterprise to fit the needs and desires of participants, old and new. Common shares apportion control and participation in future growth. Preferred shares provide ownership interests that carry some protection against loss of income or principal but that do not share in control or future growth. Debt securities provide no ownership interests, but they carry maximum protection against loss of income or principal. As indicated in Point 5, preferred shares and debt are not eligible for § 1244 treatment.

In the situation assumed in Section 7.1 all three kinds of participation might be utilized. A, the proprietor, is willing to share control and growth in return for new investment, and B, the investor, is willing to invest new money equal to the value of A's business if he can allocate the control and growth opportunity to his son, C. To achieve these ends A and C can divide a small issue of common shares; the balance of A's ownership interest can be in preferred shares; and B, by taking debt securities, can have maximum protection for his investment of new money. B will lend money to this enterprise at a reasonable interest rate because his son will have one-half of its control and growth.

3. The "thin" corporation (Section 7.1 (b) and (c))

When may debt participation in a business be treated as equity by its other creditors and by the IRS?

There are dangers that excessive use of debt in structuring corporate investment, leaving insufficient capital for operations, will cause the corporation to be adjudged "thin" and debt investments to be treated as equity, with the results that other creditors receive priority over holders of the debt securities and that the IRS disallows deductions by the corporation for interest payments on these securities. The thinness danger is substantial if the proprietor of the original business receives debt securities in the expanded enterprise, but not if such securities are issued to one who invests new money. Thus, the thinness danger supports the decision to give A, the proprietor, preferred shares instead of debt.

4. Tax-free incorporation (Section 7.1 (c))

Why will the proprietor of the business want its incorporation to qualify as tax-free under IRS § 351, and what problems will he have?

The proprietor will want the incorporation to qualify as tax-free so he will not have to pay a tax on any increase in the value of his business, thus shifting the tax burden for the increment to the corporation. The assets of the business go to the corporation at their old basis, with the result that the corporation's depreciation allowances thereon are reduced, and, if the assets are sold before they are fully depreciated, its capital gains taxes are increased.

For a tax-free incorporation those transferring cash or property—but *not* services—to the corporation must hold at least 80% of its voting shares and 80% of its total shares. The holders of common shares are paying only nominal amounts for their shares. To meet a claim that services are part of the consideration for the common shares, it can be argued that the shares are not worth more than the amounts being paid because of: the senior debt and preferred shares that soak up the rest of the value of the expanded business; the prior discounting of profit expectations in the use of capitalized earnings to value the business being contributed; and the general rule that receipt of a mere chance for future profits is not a taxable event.

5. Investments eligible for § 1244 treatment (Section 7.1 (c))

What investments in the incorporated business will be eligible for §1244 treatment?

Under § 1244 of the IRC, in the case of an individual (not including a trust or estate), a loss on "section 1244 stock" issued to an individual or partnership which would otherwise be treated as a capital loss may be treated as an ordinary loss of up to $50,000 on an individual return or $100,000 on a joint return. To be "section 1244 stock", shares must be original issue common shares; issued for money or other property (other than stock or securities); the capital and paid-in surplus of the corporation at the time of issue must not exceed $1 million; and the corporation, during the five years before the loss, must have derived more than 50% of its gross income from sources other than royalties, rents, dividends, interests, annuities, and sales or exchanges of stocks or securities.

Since only common shares qualify for § 1244 treatment, any investment in a newly incorporated business in preferred shares or debt will not have this tax advantage. Also, since only common shares issued for money or other property qualify, to the extent that shares are issued for services, § 1244 treatment will not be available.

For other discussions of § 1244, see Section 1.1 (b), Section 7.2 (d), and Point 11.

6. Starting a new business using ideas developed for and rejected by a former employer (Section 7.2 (a))

Will a release from the employer be needed?

Ideas developed by employees in the course of their employment normally belong to the employer, whether the ideas are put into use or not. For protection against possible claims by the employer and by outsiders who may invest in the new business without knowledge of the employer's claims, the entrepreneurs should secure a release from the employer. For a release by a corporation to an employee of inventions, discoveries, and trade secrets, see appendix H.4 (h).

**7. Professional assistance in selling shares in a new
   business (Section 7.2 (a) and (b))**

Why might entrepreneurs welcome assistance of a stockbroker willing to sell shares in return for being able to buy "cheap shares" and of a lawyer and accountant willing to be paid in shares?

Selling shares is a special skill, calling for experience and contacts—plus substantial capital when firm-commitment underwriting is used. And underwriters are seldom interested in offerings of small, untried ventures, like the one assumed in Section 7.2, except on a "best efforts" basis at high commissions. Thus, if the entrepreneurs have a stockbroker friend with a customer list who is willing to use his best efforts to sell their securities in return for "being let in on the ground floor" with shares at the same price as the entrepreneurs, they should consider taking advantage of his offer.

And to minimize out-of-pocket expenses in selling shares, it would probably be prudent for the entrepreneurs to accept offers of legal and accounting services in return for shares.

8. Federal registration of share offerings (Section 7.2 (b))

Why and how should it be avoided?

SEC registration is costly in money, time, and executive attention; it requires continuing disclosure of business details and increases exposure of officers and directors to personal liabilities; it forecloses use of an accountant paid in shares and may create problems for a lawyer in this position. In short, it should be avoided like the plague.

Registration of the offering proposed in Section 7.2 probably cannot be avoided on the grounds that it is private or that it is intrastate. Some offerees will not have access to information about the new business that registration would provide, and it is unlikely that the offeree group can be confined to residents of a single state. However, because of the offering's modest size, full scale registration can be avoided under the partial exemption provided by Regulation A. And, apart from requiring some additional disclosures in the "offering circular" and preventing the accountant from certifying financial statements for later registrations, issuing shares for professional services will not create federal problems.

A basis for exemption, other than Regulation A, is needed for shares issued to insiders, both entrepreneurs and professionals. If they are all in the state where the new venture is to be incorporated and conduct most of its operations, the intrastate exemption may be used. If more than one state is involved, the private offering exemption may be used provided none of the insiders are acquiring shares for resale. For protection on this point, the insiders should execute investment letters, as set forth in Appendix H.6 (b), and their shares should be escrowed, as set forth in Appendix H.6 (c). An escrow period of at least two years is suggested to conform to the holding period specified in SEC Rule 144.

9. State "blue sky" laws (Section 7.2 (c))

How can blue sky problems be minimized?

While state regulations on selling securities are less onerous than federal regulations, they should be avoided when possible. The problem is limited because only states where selling efforts are contemplated need be considered. A few states—notably California, Florida, and Texas—have limits on promoters' participations that may be troublesome. General rules-of-thumb to limit blue sky exposure include the following: get investment letters from purchasers in states where the offering is not registered; limit the stockbroker's solicitation to states where the offering is registered, and instruct him to refer unsolicited orders from other states to the entrepreneurs.

10. Possible tax on "compensation income" to insiders (Section 7.2 (d))

Can entrepreneurs and professionals avoid tax on compensation income from bargain purchases?

Insiders will pay less then outsiders and less than book value of shares after sales to outsiders. To minimize chances of being taxed on some or all of these differentials, entrepreneurs and professionals should complete their share purchases well before any shares are offered to outsiders, and entrepreneurs should buy before professionals. Entrepreneurs' chances of avoiding tax on compensation income from bargain purchases are good. They can argue that their "bargains" are not for services but because outsiders are willing to pay a premium to share in their venture; and that, in any event, at the early stage of their purchases they were not bargains because their shares were worth only what they were putting into the corporation. Professionals, however, are performing services for a venture not their own. Consequently, they must argue that their purchases, while later than those of the entrepreneurs, are at an earlier and chancier stage than those of outsiders.

11. Again, investments eligible for § 1244 treatment (Section 7.2 (d))

Who among the entrepreneurs, professionals, and outsiders investing in a new corporation will be eligible for § 1244 treatment?

The effect of and requirements for § 1244 tax treatment are set forth in Point 5.

So long as shares are original issue common (and there may be more than one class of common) stock, issued by a corporation with capital and paid-in surplus not exceeding $1 million and deriving more than half its income from operations, all such shares issued to investors, inside or outside, who pay for them in money or property will be eligible for §1244 treatment. Shares issued to lawyers, accountants, or others for their services will not be eligible. Shares issued to professionals who are allowed to buy "cheap shares" because of their services are questionable.

12. The decision to go public (Section 7.3 (a) and (b))

When may the step from close to public corporation be justified?

Need for large amounts of additional capital or benefits to shareholders and the corporation from having its shares publicly traded may outweigh the negatives—expense, exposure to liability, and long-term reporting require-ments—of going public. A market for a corporation's shares eases estate planning and diversification for shareholders and often enhances share values and corpo-rate prestige.

A prerequisite for a public offering is a legal opinion that existing shares are fully paid; hence the need for care when a corporation is organized. For shareholder and director resolutions at initial meetings establishing that shares are fully paid, see Appendix C.2 (b)-(e).

13. Structural planning for a public offering (Section 7.3 (a))

What kind of shares should be offered and what changes are needed in articles and by-laws?

The public offering obviously needs to be of the same kind of shares as existing shares, which are ordinarily common shares, to provide the desired marketability of insiders' shares. Also, since securities with inferior voting or participation rights may be hard to sell, underwriters usually urge that the public offering be in common shares, with insiders relying on proxies to maintain control if the offering will reduce their holdings to less than a majority.

Articles and by-laws will probably need amendment in preparation for a public offering: often to increase authorized shares and reduce par values; and usually to reallocate powers from shareholders to directors, and to eliminate provisions—such as requirements for preemptive rights, cumulative voting, and high quorums and votes—unsuitable for public corporations. For a collection of 13 sample documents that Dighaldoe Corporation might use in preparation for the public offering described in Section 7.3—including board resolutions proposing and shareholder resolutions approving amendments to articles, articles of amendment for delivery to the secretary of state, and director (or shareholder) resolutions amending by-laws—see Appendix E.1-E.3.

14. Executing a public offering: dealings with
underwriters and the SEC (Section 7.3 (b)-(d))

How long does a public offering take and what are key points along the way that affect who does what?

Minimum time from preliminary agreement between issuer and underwriter to receipt by issuer of its money is about three months. Key points along the way are filing the registration statement with the SEC, and its effectiveness.

During the pre-filing period (about six weeks), lawyers and accountants do most of their work preparing the registration statement. The underwriting group is organized, but no selling efforts with dealers or investors can be legally made.

During the "waiting" period, between filing and effectiveness, when a preliminary prospectus is available, the selling group of dealers is organized, and offers to sell (but not completed sales) can be made. The SEC largely controls the length of this period by how long it takes to write a deficiency letter.

Finally, in the post-effective period—usually short and sweet for the issuer—a definitive prospective is available and actual selling to investors can be done.

Economies are possible through use of year-end audits and financial statements and their availability is a key factor in planning when to file with the SEC. Once the SEC produces its deficiency letter (which should not be entrusted to the mail), effectiveness and closing can usually be brought along quite quickly. Then the issuer has its money, leaving sale of the shares in the hands of underwriters and dealers.

**15. Continuing consequences of going public
(Section 7.3) (e))**

How does public status complicate corporate life?

In addition to new practical concerns—with annual and other reports to shareholders, solicitation of proxies for and conduct of shareholder meetings, and maintenance of healthy "shareholder relations"—public status subjects corporate officers and directors to new legal chores and liabilities under federal security regulations. 1934 Act registration, reporting, proxy, and insider trading rules apply to any corporation with assets over $1 million and 500 or more shareholders, whether or not its shares are listed on an exchange. These requirements add to corporate paper work. More significantly for corporate officers and directors, § 16 of the 1934 Act imposes individual reporting obligations concerning transactions in their corporation's shares and individual liabilities to the corporation for profits from "short swing" transactions within six months of one another. As a rule of thumb, a corporate officer or director should wait six months plus a few days between transactions in his corporation's shares.

8

Distributing
Your Corporation's Assets
To Its Shareholders

CONTENTS

8

Distributing
Your Corporation's Assets
To Its Shareholders

In Chapter 7 we examined several situations where corporate officers and directors want to raise new money for their corporations. Now we examine situations where they want to direct the flow of assets in the other direction: from the corporation back to its shareholders. While a corporation's creditors may be endangered by distributions of its assets, unless the corporation is rendered insolvent or its capital impaired, creditors are seldom in a position to do much about distributions. And the receiving shareholders seldom object. Thus, our problems in this chapter do not revolve about negotiations with outsiders to arrange terms of distributions, as do our financing problems in Chapter 7; rather, emphasis is on more internal, self-induced complications that arise when a corporate entity distributes its wealth to its owners. Debt payments, which also involve outflow of corporate assets but not because of share ownership, are considered only incidentally.

Our two main questions in this chapter are: What are the legal constraints—corporate, accounting, and fiduciary—on a corporation distributing its assets to its shareholders? And what are the tax consequences—to the receiving shareholders, other shareholders, and the corporation—of such distributions?

Section 8.1 Legal Constraints on Corporate Distributions

We have already taken a preliminary look at corporate distributions from the shareholders' side. In Chapter 2, when we were filling out the ownership

249

rights of shareholders, we included in Section 2.3 a description of their rights to share in corporate assets through dividends and liquidations. The mechanics of dividend declaration and legal and accounting problems about what corporate funds can be used for dividend payments were sketched. We saw that some states look mainly at the balance sheet and permit dividends to be paid so long as capital is not invaded and the corporation not rendered insolvent—i.e., out of surplus; that a growing number of states, encouraged by the Model Act, are looking mainly at income statements and limit dividends to accumulated net earnings—i.e., out of earned surplus; and that some states in both groups permit "nimble dividends" from current earnings, notwithstanding the status of the balance sheet or the historical earnings record. We saw that policy decisions about when dividends will be paid are usually left by the courts to the corporation's directors. We also briefly outlined the mechanics of liquidation and the order in which assets are paid out when a corporation is dissolved (and we returned to liquidation in Chapter 6 as a way of dealing with conflict and deadlock in a close corporation). We now take a closer look at the various methods of distribution, relevant accounting concepts, and legal rules on sources of distributions; at the pervasive problem of how to handle asset value; at some special problems introduced when shares are repurchased in installments; and at fiduciary and anti-manipulatory limitations on repurchases. Then we turn to some of the federal income tax consequences of corporate distributions.

(a) Methods of distribution; accounting concepts; sources of distributions

Dividends, distributions from capital surplus, and liquidations involve pro rata distribution to all shareholders of the same class. Another form of distribution, but one that can select its recipients and thus is not necessarily pro rata, is repurchase by a corporation of its own shares.

> ▪ In corporate usage "redemption" is sometimes used interchangeably with "repurchase" and sometimes to refer to a special kind of repurchase where the corporation has an option to buy back ("redeem") its shares, usually preferred shares, under specified conditions. In tax usage, however, as we will see in Section 8.2, "redemption" is used as a more *general* term than "repurchase" to include transactions that the Internal Revenue Code treats as pro rata distributions rather than as purchases.

The legal constraints on funds that can be used for share purchases are usually similar to those on funds that can be used for pro rata distributions. (In contrast, the tax consequences of distributions are profoundly affected by whether or not they are pro rata—i.e., whether or not they are "essentially equivalent to a dividend.")

At the outset we should get before us the following corporate accounting definitions furnished by the Model Act (§2) that will help provide a vocabulary for discussing asset distribution:

—net assets: excess of total assets over total debts;
—stated capital: par value of all issued shares, plus consideration not allocated to capital surplus for no-par issued shares, plus amounts transferred to stated capital, minus reductions of stated capital;
—surplus: excess of net assets over stated capital;
—earned surplus: portion of surplus equal to balance of net profits, gains and losses, minus distributions to shareholders [including share repurchases] and transfers to stated capital and capital surplus from earned surplus;
—capital surplus: surplus other than earned surplus; and
—insolvent: unable to pay its debts as they become due in the ordinary course of business.

■ **Note that the Model Act uses the so-called "equity" definition of solvency which looks only at current assets and liabilities, in contrast with the "bankruptcy" definition which balances total assets against total liabilities.**

The first five of these definitions interlock. The basic concepts are "net assets," a figure which calls for a valuation, usually at cost less depreciation; "stated capital," a figure which is arbitrarily determined by the articles of incorporation and by the issuance of shares; and "earned surplus," a figure which is historically determined, largely from the income statements and the record of distributions. "Surplus" and "capital surplus" are figures that are derived mathematically from the basic concepts as follows:

surplus = net assets minus stated capital;
capital surplus = surplus minus earned surplus.

The Model Act makes earned surplus what might be called the "normal" fund out of which dividends are to be declared (§45) (see Appendix F.3(b)) and shares purchased (§6) (see Appendix F.3 (h)). But it also permits "distributions from capital surplus" (§46) and share purchases from capital surplus under the conditions that the action be authorized by the articles of incorporation (see Appendix E.1 (d) and (e)) or by the affirmative vote of a majority of the shareholders entitled to vote (see Appendix D.3(a) and (b)), and that it not be done at a time when the corporation is insolvent or when the action would render it insolvent. Distributions on final liquidation involve fewer niceties: first all debts are paid and then anything that is left is divided among shareholders according to any priorities set forth in the articles of incorporation (see Appendix A.3(d)).

A director who votes for or assents to any distribution to shareholders in excess of these limitations becomes personally liable to the corporation for the excesses, but he is entitled to contribution from other directors and from shareholders who receive assets knowing that the distribution is illegal (see Section 11.1(a)). Also, under the Model Act (§48), director liability does not apply if the director relies in good faith on the corporation's financial statements, or if, in determining the amount available for distribution, he considers the corporation's assets "to be of their book value."

(b) The valuation problem (again)

This reference to "book value," the single mention of asset valuation in the Model Act, introduces us to an area of uncertainty and controversy. Book values seldom state actual values. Inflation, growth prospects, and development of good will make book value understate actual value; obsolescence and deteriorating market conditions work in the opposite direction. Our question here is: what effect should "actual" value have on measuring the funds available for corporate distributions? In other words, should unrealized appreciation and depreciation operate to increase and decrease "surplus" and "earned surplus"?

To illustrate this problem let us return to Dighaldoe Corporation and now assume that instead of going public, as described in Section 7.3, its story takes a different turn. Doe, who provided most of the original financing, is not receiving a salary from Dighaldoe and needs more current income. He asks the corporation to repurchase his 1,000 shares which represent a one-third ownership of the business. Recall that Dighaldoe has stated capital of $30,000 (3,000 shares, $10 par), capital surplus of $270,000, and earned surplus of $300,000, giving it a book value of $600,000 or $200 per share; and that it is earning $100,000 per year after paying its taxes and reasonable salaries to Digges and Hall. In putting a value on his 1,000 shares Doe would make the same argument that was made on behalf of Dighaldoe in planning the public offering: Dighaldoe shares are worth more than their book value of $200; they should be valued on a capitalized earnings basis using a multiple of 12, which yields an actual value of $400 ($1,200,000 ÷ 3,000 shares). While Digges and Hall might have to acknowledge the fairness of Doe's argument, they can point out that to repurchase Doe's shares for $400,000 Dighaldoe would have to use up all its earned surplus and $100,000 of its capital surplus; furthermore, Dighaldoe is short of working capital and can not come up with the $400,000 in cash. Doe can respond to these objections that with shareholder approval (see Appendix D.3 (b)) the capital surplus can be invaded and that the working capital bind can be met by spreading the repurchase over a period, say 10 years, with Dighaldoe paying him $40,000 per year plus a modest interest, say 5%, on the unpaid balance (see Appendix H.6 (d)).

One of the few court decisions on the issue presented here is *Mountain States Steel Foundries, Inc.* v. *Commissioner,* 284 F. 2d 737 (4th Cir. 1960). There the legal problem was more acute because, unless assets could be revalued, the installment share repurchase would have used up all of the surplus and part of the stated capital, and under the controlling West Virginia statute impairment of capital would have invalidated the repurchase. One of the issues was deductibility for tax purposes of interest paid by the corporation on obligations incurred in an installment repurchase, and this issue was thought to turn on the validity of the repurchase transaction under West Virginia law. In upholding validity the court permitted asset revaluation, saying that the West Virginia statute "did not require a blind acceptance of book values as real" and that "actual values are critical to the inquiry."

While there is some support, both on common sense grounds (such as those articulated by Judge Haynsworth in *Mountain States*) and on a technical reading on the Model Act, for recognizing and recording unrealized appreciation in a corporation's net assets, the traditional view of the accounting profession and the SEC that plant and equipment and other property should not be written up to reflect appraisal, market, or current values which are above cost continues to be dominant.

> ▪ **The traditional view does not, of course, object to writing down (or off) assets which are "over valued" on a corporation's books. Write-downs are charged against earned surplus to the extent that it is available, and then against capital surplus to the extent that it is available, and then against stated capital.**

The traditional view seems likely to continue, at least with regard to corporate distributions, because to permit distributions from unrealized appreciation in asset values unrealistically assumes a liquidity of assets that seldom exists for industrial enterprises. Appreciation is usually in real estate, plant and equipment, inventory, patents and processes, or good will: all assets that are needed for continuing operations, and distributable only if the business is liquidated.

If Digges and Hall decide to permit Dighaldoe to repurchase Doe's shares for $400,000 they should proceed under §6 of the Model Act to authorize by shareholder vote that the purchase be made in part from capital surplus.

> ▪ **Section 6 of the Model Act provides: "To the extent that earned surplus or capital surplus is used as the measure of the corporation's right to purchase its own shares, such surplus shall be restricted [i.e., not available for dividends or other distributions] so long as such shares are held as treasury shares, and upon the disposition or cancellation of any such shares the restriction shall be removed pro tanto." Does this provision mean that directors can, by cancelling repurchased shares, use the same earned surplus for further repurchases? Section 6 seems**

to permit this construction, but it appears inconsistent with the general rule in §70 that the "surplus, if any, created by or arising out of a reduction of the stated capital of a corporation shall be capital surplus." The more sensible interpretation appears to be that the capital surplus resulting from the reduction of stated capital upon the cancellation of repurchased treasury shares survives, but not any surplus (earned or capital) used for the repurchase; and further repurchase of treasury shares from this reduction capital surplus is subject to the requirements of §6 for using capital surplus for share repurchases. Thus, when Dighaldoe repurchases Doe's shares for $400,000, Dighaldoe is left with net worth of $200,000: $30,000 stated capital plus $170,000 capital surplus. Cancellation of Doe's shares moves $10,000 from stated capital to capital surplus, but it does not change net worth.

(c) Installment repurchases

The *Mountain States* case opens up another interesting avenue of speculation: Is an installment repurchase transaction treated as if each installment constitutes a separate repurchase to be tested separately under insolvency and surplus tests? If the corporation becomes insolvent before all installments are paid, does the selling shareholder share with "regular" creditors in the corporation's assets? In other words, does the "insolvency cut-off" of share purchases apply only once, at the original transaction, or does it apply installment-by-installment? And if the insolvency cut-off can operate in midstream, will the selling shareholder get back shares for which he has not been paid? Usually the courts in effect apply the insolvency cut-off in midstream by refusing to allow repurchase obligations parity with claims of general creditors. And the question of returning shares seldom arises, because shares of an insolvent corporation seldom have any value.

If the solvency test is to be applied installment-by-installment, should availability of surplus to support repurchase be similarly determined? For the following reasons it makes more sense to apply the surplus test to the total repurchase obligation at the outset rather than to follow the installment-by-installment approach used for insolvency:

—For protection of creditors: Under the equity definition, the insolvency test looks only to current liabilities and should be reapplied at the time of each installment. But, since the surplus test compares total assets and total liabilities, there is less danger to creditors in applying it to the total face amount of the obligation only at the outset. Also, payment of an installment that impairs capital is a less serious threat to creditors than putting former shareholders on a parity with them in an insolvency liquidation.

—For protection of selling shareholders: A midstream surplus bar hurts selling shareholders, who have parted with their shares but not yet been paid for them, more than does a midstream insolvency bar, because shares of a corporation with impaired capital, which may carry on indefinitely, often still have substantial value.

—For protection of remaining shareholders: If the total obligation is never subjected to the surplus test, as would be the case with installment-by-installment application, there may be unfairness to the remaining shareholders if the corporation has to be liquidated and the selling shareholders are given priority for the full amounts of their claims.

—For clarity of the corporation's accounts: Under a midstream surplus bar, the corporation has the following accounting questions: When is surplus to be restricted? How is cancellation of treasury shares to be accounted for—can all reacquired shares be cancelled or only those for which payment has been made? Must interest as well as principal payments pass the test?

The Model Act (§6) seems to support application of the surplus test only at the time of "purchase" and the insolvency test at the times a corporation makes "purchase of or payment for its own shares."*

(d) Fiduciary and anti-manipulatory constraints

Assuming that a corporation is solvent and has ample surplus, a distribution or repurchase may still be subject to legal constraints if it can be shown to favor insiders unfairly or to be part of a scheme to "manipulate" the market for the corporation's shares. The fiduciary constraint has generated considerably more cases than has the anti-manipulatory constraint. Here we are mainly concerned with share repurchases.

(i) Purchases to benefit insiders

Insiders can use share repurchases in several ways that may violate their fiduciary duties to the corporation and to other shareholders. The price paid for shares purchased from insiders may be unfairly high; or the price paid to outsiders for their shares may be unfairly low. There may be inadequate disclosure to outside sellers about material facts, which brings SEC Rule 10b-5 into play (see Section 11.4(b)). The purpose of the transaction may be calculated to benefit insiders to the detriment of the corporation as a whole.

---

*This discussion of installment purchase transactions is largely derived from Herwitz, "Installment Repurchase of Stock: Surplus Limitations," 79 *Harv. L. Rev.* 303 (1965).

A prime example of situations where purpose becomes crucial is the utilization of corporate purchases of its shares to keep a particular management group in control of the corporation. A series of Delaware cases from the early 1960's illustrate judicial reaction to purchases of this sort in a jurisdiction generally sympathetic to the problems of insiders.

—In *Kors* v. *Carey*, 158 A. 2d 136 (Del. 1960), the management of Lehn and Fink, a manufacturer of drugs and cosmetics, decided that United Whelan, a national drug store chain and a customer of Lehn and Fink with a reputation for waging proxy fights and for business practices repugnant to the Lehn and Fink management, should be eliminated as a shareholder of Lehn and Fink and caused United Whelan's Lehn and Fink shares to be purchased on behalf of Lehn and Fink by a broker. In denying relief in a derivative suit against the Lehn and Fink directors for making purchases for other than a proper corporate purpose, the court held that the directors exercised their honest business judgment in dealing with what they saw to be a threat to the corporation and that price and brokerage commissions were reasonable.

—In *Bennett* v. *Propp*, 187 A. 2d 405 (Del. 1962), the chairman of the board and 11% shareholder of Noma, seller of decorative lighting equipment, upon learning that Textron, a large conglomerate, was trying to acquire more than 50% of Noma's shares, purchased on Noma's behalf large numbers of its shares. Again a derivative suit was brought. This time liability was found, the court holding that the chairman made these purchases "to preserve the control of the corporation in himself and his fellow directors" and that "the elimination of a dissentient faction for genuine business reasons, as in the Kors case, is quite a different thing from the purchase of stock for control purposes before any threat to corporate policy has occurred."

—In *Cheff* v. *Mathes*, 199 A.2d 548 (Del. 1964), officers and directors of Holland Furnace caused the corporation to purchase Holland shares from Maremont, a muffler manufacturer with a reputation for buying companies for liquidation, who was threatening to gain control of Holland. The court denied relief in a derivative suit against the Holland directors, holding that the purchases fit the "business judgment" rule of *Kors* v. *Carey* rather than the "improper desire to maintain control" rule of *Bennett* v. *Propp*.

The lesson of these cases is that corporate officers and directors who are contemplating using corporate funds to get rid of unwelcome shareholders should find business reasons to justify the purchases which are arguably of more general benefit to the corporation than just perpetuating their own control. We return to this subject in Chapter 10.

(ii) Purchases to manipulate prices

Some corporations make a practice of repurchasing their shares on the market in small quantities on a fairly regular basis to provide them with treasury shares to use for such purposes as employee stock option and share purchase plans. Also, a corporation may buy its own shares because management believes that their market price does not reflect their real value, making them a good investment of corporate funds. And share purchases by the corporation will increase earnings per share by reducing the number of shares outstanding. In making these purchases officers and directors sometimes also have the idea that their regular buy orders will have a buoying effect on the market price. This notion involves some dangers because of the anti-manipulatory provisions of the 1934 Act and SEC rules. For example, §9 (a) (2) of the 1934 Act makes it unlawful for any person to effect transactions in a listed security "for the purpose of inducing the purchase or sale of such security by others." However, there have been very few cases brought under these provisions, and it has been generally considered that if the volume of corporate purchases is kept at modest amount in relation to total trading in the corporation's shares there is little danger of being accused of manipulatory practices.

Section 8.2 Tax Aspects of Corporate Distributions

Federal income tax treatment of corporate distributions to shareholders is very complicated. Contributing to this complexity are the several categories of taxpayers who may be affected (shareholders participating in the distribution, other shareholders, and the corporation itself) and the ways that the Internal Revenue Code classifies various kinds of distributions, such as dividends, redemptions, exchanges, and liquidations. And some tax results depend on who, besides the record owner, is treated as owning a corporation's shares, which leads us into a thicket of rules about "attributing" share ownership for tax purposes. This section gives you some starting points and general guides for a rough sort of understanding of some of the basics of this topic.* We first look at consequences to recipient shareholders and then at consequences to other shareholders and the corporation.

---

*Much of this section is based upon discussions in D. Herwitz, *Business Planning* (Mineola, NY: Foundation Press, Inc., 1966) and D. Kahn, *Basic Corporate Taxation* (Ann Arbor, MI: Institute of Continuing Legal Education, 1973).

(a) Impact on shareholders receiving distributions

(i) Dividend and non-dividend distributions

The best entry point for what happens under the IRC to shareholders receiving corporate distributions is §301, which covers all such distributions except distributions of shares in the corporation and distributions in redemption of shares under certain circumstances, including partial and complete liquidation. As to a distribution covered by §301, a distinction is made between one which is a dividend in the tax sense, within the meaning of §316, and one which is not. A distribution which is a dividend must be included in the recipient's gross income; a distribution which is not a dividend reduces the recipient's basis for his shares and is taxable as a capital gain to the extent that it exceeds his basis. Under §316, a distribution is a dividend if it is out of the corporation's "earnings and profits" accumulated after the date of enactment of the first constitutional federal income tax act (February 28, 1913), or of the current year (computed as of the close of the year, regardless of when the distribution is made). Whenever there are earnings and profits, a distribution is deemed to be made therefrom, rather than from another source, and from the most recent earnings and profits.

Individuals receiving taxable dividends may exclude the first $100 of dividends received. A husband and wife are each entitled to a $100 exclusion, but it may only be applied against dividends received by the particular spouse or on jointly owned shares. Corporations receiving taxable dividends may deduct 85% of dividends received; and members of an "affiliated group" of corporations which file separate returns may elect to obtain a 100% dividends received deduction.

Section 302 excepts distributions in redemption of shares from § 301, but only if the redemption distribution is not "essentially equivalent to a dividend," in which case it is treated as "in exchange" for the shares, resulting in a capital gain (or loss) rather than income. And Section 331 similarly excepts distributions in a complete or partial liquidation of the corporation from §301, causing them to be treated as exchanges. Section 346 defines a partial liquidation, like the definition of a non-dividend redemption in §302, in terms of not being essentially equivalent to a dividend. In summary, IRC usage of basic terms seems to fit together as follows:

—Distribution: a general term for a transfer of assets from corporation to a shareholder, as shareholder; can be dividend or non-dividend, pro rata or non-pro rata; includes redemptions.

—Redemption: a kind of distribution where a shareholder surrenders shares to corporation; can be dividend or non-dividend, pro rata or non-pro rata; includes liquidations.

—Liquidation: a kind of redemption which is an exchange and not a dividend; can be complete or partial.

Distributions by a corporation of its own shares to its shareholders are outside this structure because they do not involve distribution of the corporation's assets. Under § § 305, 306, and 307 they are expressly made non-taxable, but under certain circumstances the receiving shareholder may have ordinary income rather than capital gain when he disposes of the shares distributed to him.

The theory of the federal tax law is that ordinary income (dividends) will result to shareholders if (a) corporate earnings and profits are distributed to them (b) on a pro rata basis. As we elaborate below, distributions which are not dividends, either because they are not earnings and profits or because they are not pro rata, may result in capital gains to the recipient shareholders. Undistributed earnings and profits, by themselves, have no tax consequences to a shareholder, even though they may increase the value of his shares. If he sells his shares, he will pay capital gains tax on the difference between his basis and the sales price. To encourage corporations to distribute their earnings and profits, however, §531 imposes a special additional tax on a corporation which accumulates earnings and profits for the purpose of avoiding income tax to its shareholders.

Even though the whole scheme of taxing distributions is based on "earnings and profits," the Internal Revenue Code fails to define this term. It cannot be equated with "taxable income" and comes closer to "increase in earned surplus."

(ii) Redemption transactions

IRC § 302 (d) provides that, absent applicability of one of the exemptions in §302 (b), a corporation's "redemption" of its shares will be treated as a §301 distribution to the shareholder rather than as a purchase of his shares; as we have noted, a §301 distribution will be taxed as a dividend to the extent that it is from earnings and profits.

> **▪ As suggested earlier, it appears that the IRC uses "redemption" as a more general term than "repurchase" thereby avoiding characterization of the transaction as a purchase and sale and leaving open the possibility that it is a §301 distribution treatable as a dividend.**

In the event of dividend treatment, the shareholder's basis for redeemed shares is allocated to any other shares he may hold in the corporation or, if all his shares are redeemed, to any shares "attributed" to him under §318.

These §318 attribution rules, which also become important in applying the §302 (b) exemptions, provide for two main types of situations where one person's shares are attributed to another: situations involving family relationships, and situations involving relationships between individuals and legal entities. Section 318 attribution rules may be summarized as follows:

—Family attribution: an individual is deemed to own shares owned by his spouse, children, grandchildren, and parents.

—Entity attribution, from entities to their owners and beneficiaries, and vice versa: shares owned by a partnership, estate, or trust are deemed owned by the partners or beneficiaries (but trust income is taxable to the grantor to the extent that trust income is attributable to him); conversely, shares owned by a partner, 50% or more shareholder of another corporation, or beneficiary of an estate or trust, are deemed owned by their respective entities.

▪ **Note that where the entity is another corporation attribution operates only one way: from the shareholder to the corporation, and not from the corporation to the shareholder. If A owns 100 shares in X Corporation and 50% or more of the shares of Y Corporation, in considering ownership of X for tax purposes both A and Y would be treated as owning 100 X shares. But if Y owns 100 X shares, A would not be treated as owning these shares.**

In addition, the holder of an option to buy shares is deemed to own the optioned shares. Attributed shares are re-attributed under the §318 rules to someone else except in two situations:

—Shares constructively owned by an individual because of family attribution are not re-attributed to another family member.

▪ **If A, A's wife, and A's wife's father each own 100 X shares, A is treated as owning 200 shares (his own and his wife's), A's wife as owning 300 shares (her own, A's, and her father's), and her father as owning 200 shares (his own and his daughter's). A and his father-in-law are not treated as owning each other's shares by re-attribution through A's wife.**

—Shares constructively owned by an entity are not re-attributed to another owner or beneficiary.

▪ **If A and B are beneficiaries of an estate and 100 X shares owned by A are attributed to the estate, these shares are not re-attributed through the estate to B. However, if the shares are owned by the estate, they are attributed to A and B and then may be re-attributed to members of their families and to other entities of which they are owners and beneficiaries.**

In sorting out which redemptions are treated as purchases and which are treated as § 301 distributions, we can start by distinguishing standards set at the shareholder level and at the corporation level. At the shareholder level, §302 defines three exemptions where a shareholder's position with relation to other shareholders is so changed by a redemption of his shares that the transaction is treated as a purchase.

The first §302 exemption is the linguistically circular test of §302 (b) (1), which was the only test prior to 1954, that the redemption be "not essentially equivalent to a dividend." Before 1970 the courts were split about the meaning of this phrase. One line of cases looked only at "strict net effect": whether the results of the redemption are significantly different than the results of a dividend; a pro rata or nearly pro rata distribution can not qualify, and in determining disproportionateness the attribution rules of §318 apply. A second line of cases used a more relaxed "business purpose" approach: whether the redemption, apart from disproportionateness, served a legitimate, non-tax objective of the corporation of its shareholders. In *United States* v. *Davis,* 397 U.S. 301 (1970), the Supreme Court opted for the "strict net effect" approach and held that the purpose for a redemption is not relevant. The Court also held that redemption of shares of a sole shareholder, after application of attribution rules, cannot qualify as a purchase under §302 (b) (1) because it cannot be other than pro rata.

The second and third §302 exemptions are the so-called "safe harbors" provided for redemptions in the 1954 Code: the "substantially disproportionate" test of §302 (b) (2) and the "complete termination" test of §302 (b) (3).

The substantially disproportionate exemption sets up mathematical tests to identify redemptions that are so far from being proportionate that they will be treated as purchases. To qualify, a shareholder must show, subject to the attribution rules of §318, that immediately after the redemption:

—he owns less than 50% of the total voting shares, and
—his voting shares are less than 80% of his voting shares before the redemption.

▪ **If, before Dighaldoe's public offering, when Digges, Hall, and Doe each held 1,000 shares, Dighaldoe had redeemed 200 of Doe's shares, the transaction would meet the 50% test because Doe would hold 800 to 2800 shares, or about 28%; it would not meet the 80% test because Doe's remaining 800 shares would not be *less* than 80% of his pre-redemption shares. The parties could have changed the tax consequences to Doe by redeeming one more share.**

A redemption that completely terminates a shareholder's interest in the corporation is quite clearly an extreme case of disproportionateness entitled to be treated as a purchase. The main problems under this exemption turn on whether the attribution rules prevent it from operating. Under §302 (c) the family attribution rules do not apply to a redemption of all of a shareholder's shares in a corporation if:

—immediately after the redemption he has no interest in the corporation other than as a creditor ("interest" includes acting as a corporate officer, director, or employee, or performing any service for the corporation, whether or not compensated);

—he does not acquire any such interest, other than shares acquired by bequest or inheritance, within 10 years after the redemption; and

—he files an agreement with his tax return for the year of the redemption promising to notify the IRS within 30 days after acquistion of any interest he may acquire in the corporation within the 10 year period.

If he acquires an interest in the corporation during the 10 year period §302 (c) will not apply and a tax deficiency may be assessed for the year of the redemption. Also, §302 (c) will not apply if within 10 years *before* the redemption the shareholder acquired redeemed shares from or disposed of unredeemed shares to one whose shares are attributable to him under family attribution, unless such acquisition or disposition did not have federal income tax avoidance as one of its principal purposes.

Now we need to examine standards set at the corporate level for distinguishing redemptions treated as purchases and exchanges from those treated as §301 distributions. As we have noted, liquidation is a kind of redemption, but §331 takes complete and partial liquidations out of the category of §301 distributions. Our main problem here is with the §346 definition of partial liquidation. Under §346 a distribution is made in partial liquidation of a corporation if

—it is one of a series made pursuant to a plan of complete liquidation which is effected, *or*

—it is "not essentially equivalent to a dividend" and is in redemption of a part of the corporation's shares pursuant to a plan and occurs during the taxable year of the plan's adoption or the following taxable year.

Under §346 (b) standards are provided for identifying a distribution which will qualify as a partial liquidation because it is caused by the corporation ceasing to conduct a trade or business. While failure to meet those standards creates no inference that the distribution is not a partial liquidation, the cases indicate that some sort of genuine corporate contraction is an essential part of a partial liquidation. The objective is to distinguish such real contraction from covert efforts to distribute corporate earnings and profits.

In *McCarthy* v. *Conley,* 341 F. 2d 948 (2d Cir. 1965), the court said:

The transaction in question was clearly not a vertical liquidation which chopped off part of the productive resources of the enterprise. That portion of corporate capital remained intact. It was a horizon-

tal slice off the top of the nest egg of securities accumulated from past earnings and profits which did not in any degree impair the business activities as they had been carried on.

Examples of qualifying situations include distributions following termination of an unprofitable division, and from insurance proceeds of a part of a business destroyed by fire where it decided not to rebuild. Non-qualifying distributions include those from a reserve set aside for expansion plans which were abandoned, and from assets of a discontinued part of a business that the court concluded to have been only a temporary resting place for corporate earnings and profits. The difference between the two groups of cases can be high-lighted by asking: Was the corporation's hand forced by events, or was it structuring the transaction to achieve favorable tax results for its shareholders?

The dividend equivalence test in §346 differs from the similarly worded test in §302 in being from the corporation's rather than the shareholder's point of view. Since the words have different meanings in the two sections, a distribution may qualify for non-dividend treatment under §346 and not under §302, and vice versa. Section 302 turns on "proportionateness" to the shareholder; §346 turns on "contraction" of the corporation.

(b) Impact on remaining shareholders and on the corporation

In Section 8.1 (b) we returned to Dighaldoe and assumed that instead of going public the corporation redeems Doe's 1,000 shares, and we discussed whether his shares should be valued at book value or actual value. In this subsection we make a similar assumption, leaving open for the time being the price being paid for Doe's shares. Recall that we have learned that §302 gives Doe a "safe harbor" from dividend treatment because the redemption completely terminates his interest in Dighaldoe. Our concerns now are: Can the redemption be a constructive dividend to Digges and Hall? What are the tax effects of the redemption on Dighaldoe?

(i) Remaining shareholders

Dighaldoe's redemption of Doe's shares will increase percentage ownership in Dighaldoe of Digges and Hall from 33 ⅓% to 50% each. A line of cases holds that if the corporation's payment for shares being redeemed is made "on behalf" of the remaining shareholders it will be considered a dividend to them. Thus, in planning for a redemption, care should be taken that the remaining shareholders have themselves no "primary and unconditional" obligation to purchase the shares which the corporation plans to redeem. If they have such an obligation the redemption may be construed as a payment by the corporation in satisfaction of the remaining shareholders' debts, and the payment constitute a constructive dividend to them.

> **▪ If Digges and Hall had agreed with Doe that they would purchase his shares when he wanted to retire and then had caused Dighaldoe to make the purchase, they would be held to have received a constructive dividend. But if the agreement was that Dighaldoe would purchase Doe's shares, with Digges and Hall to make the purchase if Dighaldoe failed to do so (see Appendix H.2(a)), purchase by Dighaldoe would not be a constructive dividend to Digges and Hall, because they were only secondarily liable under the agreement.**

In Section 6.4, in dealing with conflict within a close corporation, we suggested that a way of resolving conflict is for one side to sell its shares and mentioned some of the factors to be considered in deciding who would make the purchase. We now have an additional reason for putting the primary obligation for the purchase on the corporation.

Now we need to pay attention to the price that Dighaldoe pays for Doe's 1,000 shares and its relation to fair market value. The IRS takes the position that when a shareholder surrenders shares to the corporation for less than fair market value the remaining shareholders may have received a gift or compensation, and that conversely if more than fair market value is paid the retiring shareholder may have received compensation from the corporation or a gift from the remaining shareholders (Revenue Ruling 58-614). Thus, if Doe is paid book value ($200 per share) and if it can be shown that his shares are really worth more—say $400, the figure assigned for the sale of shares to underwriters in Section 7.3, or even $450, the sales price to the public in Section 7.3—the IRS may claim that Digges and Hall have increased their percentage interests in Dighaldoe at a bargain price, which should be taxable to them as a gift or as compensation. To minimize the possibility of the IRS making this claim it is suggested that the parties stipulate that whatever price they agree upon for the redemption represents "fair market" value for the redeemed shares (see Appendix H.2(a)).

(ii) The corporation: recognition of income

Generally, under IRC §311, distributions to shareholders as shareholders with respect to or in redemption of their shares do not cause recognition of income to the distributing corporation. This general rule applies to all distributions in cash, but there are exceptions when distributions are made in kind. A corporation may realize gain when it distributes.

—installment obligations,
—inventory carried on a "last-in, first-out" basis,

—property subject to a liability in excess of its adjusted basis in the corporation's hands or to investment credit or depreciation recapture provisions, and

—in some situations, since 1969, property which has appreciated in value.

The rationale of these exceptions to nonrecognition is that they all represent property which if retained by the corporation might eventually result in tax liability to the corporation.

If, instead of making a distribution to shareholders, the corporation receives its own shares as consideration for the sale of property by it, or in satisfaction of indebtedness to it, the gain or loss will be recognized.

Assume that Digges, Hall, and Doe agree that the fair market value of Doe's 1,000 shares is $400,000 and that Dighaldoe will redeem them by transferring to him Blackacre, undeveloped land which is also worth $400,000 but on which Dighaldoe's basis is $100,000. Under the general rule before 1969, Dighaldoe could avoid recognizing any gain on the theory that the transaction was a "distribution" rather than a "sale." And it was possible that Dighaldoe could secure a stepped-up basis on Blackacre by buying it back from Doe for $400,000, without Dighaldoe having paid any tax on the appreciation in value and with Dighaldoe and Doe being in the same position as if Dighaldoe had made a distribution in cash to Doe in the first place. While the Tax Reform Act of 1969 added §311 (d), requiring the corporation to recognize gain on distribution of appreciated property as if it had been sold, it excepted from this requirement complete redemption of all shares of a shareholder who has owned for 12 months or more at least 10% in value of the outstanding shares. Since it appears that the Doe redemption would qualify for this exemption, it appears that the above maneuver is still possible unless the distribution and sale are regarded as sham.

If Doe agrees at the outset to resell Blackacre to Dighaldoe the whole arrangement is likely to be held a sham. Absent such an agreement, the presence of a business purpose for the form of the transaction—e.g., if Doe's shares were to be redeemed on an installment basis and if Doe desired to reduce the risk of surplus or insolvency cut-off by having a redemption in kind and following it by resale to the corporation on the same installment terms—might induce recognition of the transaction as not sham if Blackacre is sufficiently separable from Dighaldoe's other assets and from its operations that there is a sufficient interruption of ownership to produce a new basis.

▪ **The possibility of this argument appears to have been recognized in _United States_ v. _General Geophysical Co.,_ 296 F. 2d 85 (5th Cir. 1961), a case where the court found insufficient interruption in the corporation's ownership of the property transferred to create a stepped-up basis. If the 1969 amendment applies the corporation will have to re-**

cognize gain, but in cases of transfer of depreciable property it will end up in a better position than under General Geophysical because the gain will be taxed at capital gain rates while the increase in basis is deductible by depreciation against ordinary income. See D. Herwitz, *Business Planning 1975 Supplement* (1975) 282. Of course, this analysis would not apply to Blackacre, which is undeveloped land, and thus not depreciable.

(iii) The corporation: its earnings and profits

We are assuming that Digges, Hall, and Doe each contribute $100,000 ($100 per share) to Dighaldoe, that Dighaldoe accumulates earnings and profits of $300,000 ($100 per share), that the fair market value of Dighaldoe is $1,200,000 ($400 per share), and that Dighaldoe redeems Doe's 1,000 shares for $400,000. To what extent does this distribution reduce Dighaldoe's earnings and profits? As large a reduction as possible is, of course, to the interest of Digges and Hall, in order to reduce taxability of future distributions.

If a distribution is essentially equivalent to a dividend (which Doe's is not, under §302, because it completely terminates his interest in Dighaldoe), it reduces the corporation's earnings and profits in the same way as any other dividend: if in cash, by the full amount of the money distributed (but not below zero); if in property, by its adjusted basis. Thus, a $400,000 "dividend" to Doe would eliminate Dighaldoe's $300,000 earnings and profits. But, if a distribution is not essentially equivalent to a dividend, IRC §312 (e) provides that "the part of such distribution which is properly chargeable to capital account shall not be treated as a distribution of earnings and profits."

While there seems to be agreement that "capital account" includes capital surplus as well as stated capital, there has been disagreement about how to determine the "part" of a distribution that does not reduce the corporation's earnings and profits. Two lines of authority, each deriving from cases decided in the early 1940's, have developed:

—*Helvering* v. *Jarvis*, 123 F. 2d 742 (4th Cir. 1941), held that the redemption distribution would have to be allocated to capital (and thus not be available to reduce earnings and profits) only to the extent of the capital (including capital surplus) standing behind the redeemed shares. This approach does not have the effect of treating unrealized appreciation as a part of capital. It looks at the distributee's share of capital and treats the balance of what he receives as coming from earnings and profits.

—*Woodward Investment Co* v. *Commissioner*, 46 BTA 648 (1942), held that the redemption distribution could be allocated to earnings and profits only to the extent of that part of earnings and profits as was being distributed. This approach has the effect of treating unrealized appreciation as a part of capital. It looks at the distributee's share of the earnings and profits and limits the earnings and profits that he receives to this share, treating any overage that he receives because of unrealized appreciation as "properly chargeable to capital account."

The different results that these two approaches can lead to is illustrated by applying them to Dighaldoe's redemption of Doe's 1,000 shares for $400,000:

—Under *Jarvis*, since Doe's shares have only $100,000 in "capital" standing behind them, the remaining $300,000 of the redemption reduces Dighaldoe's earnings and profits from $300,000 to zero.

—Under *Woodward*, since the share of Doe's shares in the $300,000 earnings and profits is only $100,000, earnings and profits of $200,000 remain after the redemption.

These widely varying consequences are the result of different treatment of the unrealized $600,000 increase in the fair market value of Dighaldoe's business. Under *Jarvis*, Doe is considered to have received $100,000 in return of his capital, $100,000 in "actual" earnings and profits, and $200,000 in appreciation of value which is also treated as earnings and profits. Under *Woodward*, the $200,000 appreciation is, in effect, included in capital, so that Doe is considered to have received only $100,000 in earnings and profits.

Since any earnings and profits included in a non-dividend distribution are not taxable as ordinary income to the distributee, it is generally to the interest of the IRS to follow the Woodward approach and thereby reduce the effect of distributions on the corporation's earnings and profits available for future taxation. The Service has taken this position in Revenue Ruling 70-731. However, the Tax Court has since followed the *Jarvis* approach in *Herbert Enoch*, 57 T.C. 781 (1972), holding that only paid-in capital (which includes stated capital and capital surplus) is included in a corporation's capital account, and that a redemption reduces its earnings and profits by the amount paid minus the redeemed shares' pro rata share of the capital account (exclusive of unrealized appreciation surplus or depreciation deficit). Further litigation can be expected on this issue.

It seems likely that the *Woodward* approach will eventually prevail because it is hard to justify permitting a corporation's earnings and profits to be eliminated by a distribution which itself escapes ordinary income taxation (under §302), leaving remaining shareholders able to receive tax-free distributions because there are no longer any earnings and profits. And the *Jarvis* approach can also operate unfairly in the other direction if payment to the retiring shareholder is less than capital represented by retired shares, leaving remaining shareholders with an unduly large portion of the corporation's earnings and profits.

- **Redemption at fair market value but below "capital" would not, of course, be possible if we were using "capital" to refer only to stated capital, because then capital would be impaired and the surplus cut-off would operate. As noted above, the IRC uses "capital account" more broadly to include capital surplus.**

Suppose that Dighaldoe's fair market value declines to $270,000 ($30,000 less than its "capital account"), that it has earnings and profits of $60,000, and that it redeems Doe's shares for $90,000 (their fair market value). *Jarvis* would charge the full $90,000 to capital, leaving Digges and Hall to contend with the full $60,000 in earnings and profits. *Woodward,* on the other hand, would reduce earnings and profits to $40,000: a fairer result. In fact, there is some unfairness under *Jarvis,* one way or the other, with any distribution that is either more or less than the exact point where *Jarvis* and *Woodward* coincide: a distribution that equals the distributee's share of capital plus his share of earnings and profits.

CHECKLIST OF POINTS TO WATCH OUT FOR IN DISTRIBUTING YOUR CORPORATION'S ASSETS TO ITS SHAREHOLDERS

(References after headings are to Sections of Chapter 8.)

1. Sources of distributions (Sections 8.1 (a))

Why are directors concerned with where assets being distributed come from?

Dividends and share repurchases are the most common forms of distributions of corporate assets to shareholders. While their tax treatment is quite different, both are subject to legal requirements that they do not render the corporation unable to meet its obligations to creditors (the insolvency test) nor impair its capital (the surplus test). Most states also require that distributions be made from earned surplus, and permit use of capital surplus only if specifically authorized by the articles or by shareholder resolution.

Directors have a large stake in compliance with these legal requirements because they may be individually liable to the corporation for illegal distributions (see Section 11.1 (a)).

For director resolutions authorizing dividends and share repurchases from earned surplus, see Appendix F.3 (b) and F.3 (h). For articles empowering directors to authorize such distributions from capital surplus, see Appendix E.1

(d) and (e); for shareholder resolutions so empowering directors, see Appendix D.3 (a) and (b).

2. Valuation of assets (Section 8.1 (b))

Is unrealized appreciation in asset values available for distribution to shareholders?

Appreciated assets are usually needed for continuation of a corporation's operations and the traditional view has been that, while write-downs of asset values can and should occur, write-ups to create "appraisal surplus" available for distribution to shareholders are illegal. While a contrary view finds support in judicial decisions and in a technical reading of the Model Act, the traditional view still prevails. Thus, in a situation like the proposed repurchase of Doe's shares by Dighaldoe Corporation described in Chapter 8—where the value of a business has grown, and a distribution is desired which would deplete earned but not capital surplus—rather than to attempt to create an appraisal surplus by a write-up of asset values, it would be safer for the directors to secure shareholder authorization for a repurchase from surplus, earned or capital, as suggested in Appendix D.3 (b).

The flexibility provided by having capital surplus available for such uses is one of the reasons for a par value substantially below per share consideration on original issue. Dighaldoe shares were assigned a par of $10 per share in its articles (see Appendix A.2 (a)), and consideration of $100 per share was fixed for the original issue by directors at their first meeting (see Appendix C.2 (b)), creating capital surplus of $90 per share.

3. Installment repurchases (Section 8.1 (c))

Why are they useful and how do they work?

Repurchasing a shareholder's shares in installments provides a way to avoid depleting the corporation's working capital. Typically, the shares are all surrendered but the corporation's obligation to pay for them is spread over several years, turning the shareholder into a creditor. But the shareholder's claims for installment payments are generally subordinated to the claims of outside creditors, which means that the insolvency test is applied separately to each installment. In contrast, the surplus test is more likely to be applied only at the beginning when the shares are transferred; there must then be enough surplus for the whole repurchase, but the repurchase will not be barred before all installments are paid if the surplus subsequently becomes insufficient.

For an agreement on installment repurchase of shares, see Appendix H.6 (d).

4. Purpose of repurchase (Section 8.1 (d))

When may the purpose of repurchase affect its legality?

Repurchases made to benefit officers, directors, or other shareholders are suspect when the price is unfairly high or low, or when one party to the transaction lacks material information, or, especially with public corporations, when the objective is to keep a particular management group in office. However, repurchases to eliminate a "dissentient faction" or a shareholder reputedly a "raider" have been upheld as legitimate exercises of "business judgment." Officers and directors of public corporations authorizing share repurchases should look for business reasons apart from keeping themselves in office. Such reasons include, in addition to getting rid of undesirable shareholders, liquidity of the corporations assets, favorable market prices for repurchases, and ability of the corporation to earn at a high rate in comparison to other available uses of its funds. And care should be taken that the volume and timing of repurchases do not open the corporation and its managers to charges of market manipulation.

5. Tax consequences of distributions to recipient shareholders (Section 8.2 (a))

How are dividends and non-dividends distinguished?

A distribution which is a dividend must be included in recipient's gross income; a non-dividend distribution need not be so included, but it reduces recipient's basis. A distribution from the corporation's earnings and profits (increases in earned surplus) is a dividend unless it is a redemption in exchange for shares and is so disproportionate to the recipient's share holdings that it is not "essentially equivalent to a dividend." Two "safe harbors" of disproportionate distributions established by the IRS are "complete termination" of the interest of one of several shareholders; and a formula for what will be considered "substantially disproportionate": immediately after redemption the shareholder owns less than 50% of total voting shares, and his voting shares are less than 80% of his voting shares before redemption.

Both of these safe harbors are subject to rules under which shares not legally owned by a shareholder are "attributed" to him because of family relations or connections with legal entities. Shares owned by an individuals' spouse, children, grandchildren, and parents are attributed to him. Shares owned by a partnership, estate, or trust are attributed to partners or beneficiaries and to the grantor of a trust to the extent that trust income is taxable to him. Shares owned by a partner, 50% or more shareholder of another corporation, or beneficiary of an estate or trust are attributed to the entity. Optioned shares are attributed to the option holder. Attributed shares are re-attributed to another owner or beneficiary.

Non-dividend redemptions also include complete and partial liquidations. To qualify as a partial liquidation, a redemption must result from a genuine, largely involuntary corporate contraction—examples are distributions from proceeds of sale of an unprofitable division, or of insurance on damaged facilities where there is a decision not to rebuild—as distinguished from a tax-motivated transaction to provide a temporary resting place for corporate earnings and profits before they are distributed to shareholders.

6. Tax consequences of distributions to remaining shareholders (Section 8.2 (b))

When may redemption be a constructive dividend or a gift or compensation to other shareholders?

Redemption may be a constructive dividend to remaining shareholders when it discharges an obligation on them to purchase the redeemed shares themselves. Redemption may be a gift or compensation to them when the redemption price is less than fair market value. (And redemption may be a gift or compensation to recipient shareholders if the price is *more* than fair market value.)

These possibilities underscore the desirability, in an agreement restricting transfer of shares of a close corporation, of provisions which give the corporation the first option to purchase shares of a shareholder who wishes to sell and which specify a procedure for determining fair market value of his shares. For an agreement containing these provisions, see Appendix H.2(a).

7. Tax consequences of distributions to the corporation (Section 8.2 (b))

When will income or gain be recognized and how will earnings and profits be affected?

Distributions to shareholders do not cause recognition of income to the corporation unless they are in property which may eventually result in tax liability to the corporation, such as property that has appreciated in value. But even as to such property, no gain is recognized when it is used to redeem all the shares of one who has held 10% or more of the corporation's shares for at least 12 months, unless the transaction is regarded as sham; as is likely where the shareholder agrees at the outset to sell the property back to the corporation in order to create a stepped-up basis. If the resale comes later, and if it has an independent business purpose, and if there is sufficient interruption of the corporation's ownership, the stepped-up basis may be allowed.

As to the corporation's accumulated earnings and profits, the remaining shareholders want redemptions to reduce them as much as possible to minimize taxability of future distributions. Redemptions that are treated as dividends reduce earnings and profits by their full amount.

There is disagreement about the effect of non-dividend redemptions where the redemption price is greater or less than the distributee's share of capital and capital surplus plus his share of earnings and profits; a situation most likely to arise when the redemption price includes unrealized appreciation in the value of the business, which has not yet become a part of earnings and profits. One theory argues that earnings and profits are reduced the full amount of the redemption price less capital and capital surplus standing behind the redeemed shares, which will cause a disproportionate reduction of earnings and profits because of inclusion of unrealized appreciation in the redemption price. Under this theory a redemption can wipe out earnings and profits, enabling remaining shareholders to receive tax-free distributions. The other theory, favored by the IRS and likely to prevail, argues that earnings and profits are reduced only by that part of earnings and profits which is attributable to the redeemed shares.

9

Problems of Success: Antitrust and Unfair Competition

9

Problems of Success:
Antitrust and Unfair Competition

In the first six chapters we assemble the parts of the corporate structure and describe how they function together. In Chapters 7 and 8 we describe what might be called *the* corporate function: aggregating and distributing wealth. We now have before us the main organic and financial components and processes of business corporations. There remains to be explored in this and the following chapter some of the non-financial problems that arise as corporations mature: problems of success created by the antitrust laws and by unfair competition, and problems of change created by transfers of corporate control.

Section 9.1 Avoiding Antitrust Problems

Antitrust is an appropriate opener for a chapter on problems of corporate success, because when your enterprise is small and struggling it is more likely to be cast as a victim than as a perpetrator of practices constrained by the federal antitrust laws. As your enterprise succeeds and grows—and as it gains power vis-à-vis competitors, suppliers, and customers—your potentialities for antitrust troubles increase apace. Many business people view antitrust, along with taxes, as black arts best left to lawyer-exorcists. This attitude is unfortunate, because you can reduce both your antitrust troubles and your legal bills by understanding the basics of our antitrust laws—at least enough that you can recognize antitrust troubles when they are developing and can separate questions which you can handle from those needing professional attention. Many antitrust questions are especially suited for handling by insiders because they turn on business factors (e.g., what is the relevant market?) about which your lawyers can have only second hand information. And, fortunately for my thesis that antitrust is too important to be left to specialists, the basics of antitrust law are considerably less complicated than tax law. This section deals first with antitrust theory and then with antitrust practice.

(a) Understanding the antitrust laws

(i) Historical development

Antitrust is a largely American concept, the product of our libertarian bias that puts freedom before order. There are a few old English cases refusing to enforce agreements adjudged to be in restraint of trade: for example, by a business firm to stay out of a line of business, or by an individual not to practice a trade or profession. And other industrial countries, particularly those in the European common market, are beginning to adopt legislation with mild antitrust objectives. But generally the kind of anti-competitive activity that can get you into trouble in the United States has been accepted and even encouraged elsewhere, where "cartels" (combinations of producers) have been taken for granted. And there is lack of agreement among economists whether industrial development in the United States has thrived because of, in spite of, or independently of, our antitrust laws. In any event, these laws have not prevented the formation of large and powerful holdings under centralized control.

Like many names, "antitrust" is an historical accident which is now a misnomer, because business "trusts" have long been virtually extinct. Our basic antitrust statute, the Sherman Act of 1890 outlawing monopolies and combinations in restraint of trade, was enacted by Congress in an effort to curb the power of "combines" that sought to control supplies of and prices for basic products—like oil, steel, paper, sugar, and tobacco—by eliminating competitors. The most nortorious of these combinations, Mr. Rockefeller's Standard Oil, was first organized as a trade association in 1874 and then converted into a trust in 1882, which it remained until 1892. "Trust" became a code word for overpowerful business combinations of all sorts.

The Sherman Act caused organizers of business empires to switch from trade associations and trusts to holding companies: corporations which control other corporations through share ownership. Much of our "modern" corporation law is the product of legal ingenuity, aided by legislative compliance at the state level, aimed at providing ways around the Sherman Act. New Jersey led the way (before it was supplanted by Delaware) in making its laws fit the needs of holding companies by allowing New Jersey corporations to hold shares in other corporations and to do all their business in other states. By 1904 the seven largest "trusts" were all New Jersey corporations. Standard Oil's switch in 1892 from trust to holding company format did not save it from being broken up; but the Supreme Court said that a holding company which acquires competing subsidiaries does not necessarily violate the Sherman Act absent a history, like Standard Oil's, of market dominance and price-fixing. *Standard Oil Co.* v. *United States* 221 U.S. 1, 75 (1911).

To foreclose continued use of the holding company route to reduced competition, the Clayton Act in 1914 outlawed acquisition of shares of other corporations where the effect "may be to substantially lessen competition" (the split infinitive was cleaned up in 1950). The Clayton Act did little to slow industrial combinations, however, because combiners and their lawyers again found a legal alternative. The Clayton Act could be side-stepped by acquiring the assets instead of the shares of a competing corporation. This period of antitrust history is nicely illustrated by the putting together of General Motors. Buick and Cadillac were acquired in 1908 and 1909, before the Clayton Act, by buying the shares of the Buick and Cadillac corporations; but when it acquired Chevrolet in 1916, after the Clayton Act, it was by purchase of the assets of the Chevrolet corporation. Not until 1950 did Congress get around to plugging this loop-hole by amending the Clayton Act to outlaw purchase of shares *or* assets that might impair competition.

Since 1950 the way to industrial empire has shifted from combinations of competitors to "conglomerates": combinations of corporations in different lines. This trend has been encouraged by the tax laws, which make a tax loss a thing of value even in a different line of business, and by the business wisdom of diversification, particularly by corporations in lines with dubious futures (e.g., tobacco, movies, textiles, and coal).

The 1950 legislation and the wave of conglomerate mergers and diversification moves that has ensued have focussed attention on the legal meaning of language in the Clayton Act forbidding combinations which lessen competition "in any line of commerce in any section of the country." What is a "line of commerce" and how big is a "section of the country"

> ▪ For example, can A, a Wisconsin beer maker, lawfully acquire B, a New York wine maker? Are beer and wine in different lines? Are Wisconsin and New York in different sections? To legitimatize the acquisition A would, of course, emphasize these differences and argue for several "relevant markets" —divided both by products and geographically. However, if A were accused of having a monopoly in the middle west beer market, A might take the opposite position and argue for a single national market that encompasses wine and beer.

We will return to corporate combinations and the antitrust laws in Chapter 10.

Another part of the 1914 legislation created the Federal Trade Commission and gave it antitrust enforcement responsibilities, including the policing of a new provision outlawing "unfair methods of competition." This was a measure aimed more at deceptive advertising and selling practices than at activities that lessen competition: more at the quality than at the quantity of competition. A further addition to the antitrust statutes was made in 1937 by the Robinson-Patman Act which outlawed unjustifiable price differentials. Again the objective was less to protect the freedom to compete than it was to outlaw a practice regarded as unfair (giving favored customers special prices).

(ii) Substantive meaning

The basic prohibitions of the federal antitrust statutes can be quickly summarized. The Sherman Act makes it unlawful to create a monopoly or to enter into any contract, combination, or conspiracy in restraint of trade. The 1914 and 1937 additions make it unlawful to use unfair methods of competition or price discriminations. These federal laws apply to acts in or affecting interstate commerce. Here we are mainly concerned with the Sherman Act, especially the second part on restraints of trade. Quite early in the Act's history the Supreme Court limited its application to "unreasonable" restraints of trade: a qualification thought necessary because any binding business contract can be said to "restrain trade" by taking its parties out of the market for the trade covered by the contract. In short, the Sherman Act outlaws joint actions which unreasonably restrict freedom to compete. It attempts to create a legally protected commercial freedom to buy and sell comparable to the personal freedoms guaranteed in the Bill of Rights.

The unilateral monopoly part of the Sherman Act is invoked much less frequently than the multilateral restraint of trade part. The distinction between reasonable and unreasonable restraints is paralleled by a comparable, but less clearly articulated, distinction between lawful and unlawful monopolies. There are, of course, legally sanctioned monopolies, such as patent grants, public utilities, radio and television broadcasters, and other enterprises with government franchises. But the distinction that comes out of the monopoly cases deals with a less clearcut kind of legal monopoly. It would not make sense to outlaw being the first producer in a new field; nor would it make sense to prohibit the first comer from trying to keep (and keeping) others out of his field by his own efficient operations, low prices, and satisfied customers. It is this line of argument that has saved benign industrial giants with effective monopoly power, like General Motors, from the antitrust chopping block. Thus far the idea has prevailed that bigness *by itself* is not illegal. It can become illegal if you achieve or maintain bigness by buying out competitors or by eliminating them by means other than your own "fair" competition, or if you use your bigness to dictate prices or to cut off customers or suppliers from other producers; however, price "leadership" by a dominant producer is not illegal.

The concept of monopolies can be stated quite objectively in terms of market control. In contrast, the concept of unreasonable combinations in restraint of trade is more complex and illusive, combining elements of joint action, impairment of freedom, economic damages, and rationality. Unlike a monopoly, which need involve only one person, a combination in restraint of trade needs several persons. There must be at least two persons (A and B) who contract, combine, or conspire together. Somebody must be restrained—ordinarily A or B or both, but A and B might conspire to restrain C (say by threats of economic reprisals) from trading with D—and usually somebody (D in the above illustration) will be hurt by the restraint. And the restraining combination must be unreasonable.

To help explore the reasonableness test, assume this uncomplicated situation: A and B are parties to an agreement that restrains them both; leave open whether any one is hurt by the restraint. How A and B are related is significant. If they are related horizontally as competitors there is a strong presumption that the restraint is unreasonable, because competitors do not need to restrain one another in the ordinary course of business. Also, their customers are likely to suffer from such a restraint (although we can think of a reasonable contract between competitors: A and B might agree to share the cost of hiring someone to lobby against proposed legislation unfavorable to them both). On the other hand, if A and B are related vertically as seller and buyer, the presumption of unreasonability changes, because ordinary business does require that they both surrender some of their freedom. Here the question is whether the surrender of freedom goes beyond the ordinary needs of their business relationship. Such would be the case if A, a seller to B, promises that he will not sell to C or that he will not buy from D; or if B, a buyer from A, promises that he will not buy from E or that he will not resell to F. For these restraints to be unreasonable it is probably not necessary that the persons at whom they are aimed be competitors of the contracting parties. A restraint which is part of an otherwise lawful transaction would seem to become unreasonable if its effect is to take out of the free market some otherwise lawful transaction when such removal from the free market is not a necessary part of the main transaction between the contracting parties. And economic injury to third persons (C, D, E, and F in the above illustration) is the usual consequence of an unreasonable restraint.

The courts have created a category of restraints that they call "per se" violations of the Sherman Act: restraints that by themselves, without further proof of anti-competitive motives or consequences, are presumed to be illegal. The classic per se violation is a price-fixing arrangement among competitors. Suppose that A, B, and C are the only producers of a rare drug helpful to elderly people and, wanting to make it widely available, they agree to sell it at a designated price below cost. Notwithstanding humanitarian intentions and results that appear beneficial, they are violating the Sherman Act because they have surrendered an essential part of their economic freedom to their competitors. Almost any agreement among competitors as to terms of sale, customers, or territories will be similarly classified as per se violations. While contracts between noncompetitors are less likely to be put in the per se category, they are not immune from this treatment. Examples of vertical per se violations include limitations on a buyer's freedom to resell—as to price, territory, or customers—, and "tying" arrangements that extend the patent monopoly by conditioning availability of a patented product or process on purchase or use of unpatented items.

> ▪ **An example of a tying arrangement that is a per se Sherman Act violation: A sells B patented salt processing machinery on the condition that B use therewith only unpatented salt purchased from A.**

How do we reconcile Sherman Act requirements with the generally assumed freedom to select with whom we deal? Suppose A hates B and does not want to do business with him. It would appear that A can unilaterally refuse to deal with B, but he cannot agree with C that A will not deal with B, nor can he condition his dealing with C upon C not dealing with B, although he can make it a practice not to deal with C so long as C deals with B, and perhaps he can publicy announce his practice. A Sherman Act restraint of trade generally requires joint action and does not include unilateral action, but it is not always easy to say when action is unilateral. A's announcement that he does not deal with those dealing with B can change from a unilateral statement of fact to a threat of economic reprisals, which arguably ceases to be unilateral when others are controlled by it. Another kind of difficulty in making the unilateral-multilateral distinction arises when a group of already affiliated corporations make agreements among themselves which would clearly be illegal if made with outsiders. While these so-called "bathtub" conspiracies have been seldom challenged, the Supreme Court has on occasion treated corporate separateness literally and held that common ownership or control does not provide immunity from antitrust laws. For example, in finding that an American corporation had illegally conspired with its partly-owned British and French subsidiaries to fix prices and allocate markets for roller bearings, Mr. Justice Black said:

> *Nor do we find any support in reason or authority for the proposition that agreements between legally separate persons and companies to suppress competition among themselves and others can be justified by labeling the project a "joint venture." Perhaps every agreement and combination to restrain trade could be so labeled.*
> Timken Roller Bearing Co. v. United States, 341 U.S. 593 (1951)

The antitrust statutes supplementary to the Sherman Act have not really entered the mainstream of antitrust law. The 1937 Robinson-Patman Act prohibiting price discrimination may even work against the Sherman Act since it seems to work against market freedom by trying to prevent buyers and sellers from using their relative market power to make the best bargains they can. In a free market a powerful buyer, like a large manufacturer or retailer, is naturally able to negotiate lower prices than other buyers. In any event, the Robinson-Patman Act has had but minor impact becuase there are numerous ways that price differentials can be made legal.

The 1914 prohibition of unfair methods of competition has stayed out of the antitrust mainstream for different reasons relating more to its method of its enforcement than to its content. The FTC's record of implementation of this statute has not been impressive. It has tended to focus on practices of doubtful economic significance, such as using lotteries to sell candy to children, using mock-ups in television commercials, and making unfounded claims about patent medicines. Unlike the meaning of the Sherman Act, which the courts have been able to generalize with relative clarity, the meaning of "unfair methods of competition" seems to be knowable only on a case-by-case basis. Use of unfair methods of competition resembles obscenity: judges admit they cannot define it, but claim they know it when they see it. The cases frequently require drawing a line between the "puffing" traditionally permitted of sellers—exaggerated but innocent enthusiasm about the virtues of what they are selling—and the kind of deceptive practices which should be called unfair methods of competition. This is an area where demands for more rigorous legal and ethical standards can be expected.

(b) Experiencing the antitrust laws

We have been trying to convey what the words of the antitrust statutes mean: what Congress is saying when it tells you that your freedom to do business does not include freedom to limit the free working of the competitive system. Now we need to look at what you can expect from the enforcers of these statutes, and then at how you, helped by your lawyers, can balance your respect for these laws, both in the sense of being law-abiding and of being prudent, with your own business objectives.

(i) How antitrust laws are enforced

Laws on the books and laws in action usually differ, because laws are seldom self-executing: they need the energy and dedication of people whose job it is, or in whose interest it is, to enforce them. For the antitrust laws these people are the lawyers, economists, and investigators in the Antitrust Division of the

Department of Justice and in the Federal Trade Commission, who are charged with enforcing the antitrust laws, plus the business people, aided (and prodded) by their lawyers, who are hurt by antitrust violations.

The Antitrust Division and the FTC maintain continuing surveillance of mergers, acquisitions, patent licensing, and marketing practices of the larger corporations. You can consult with these agencies about the legality of proposed business moves, but there is a reluctance to use this service because to do so calls attention to your plans and raises questions about their legality. It is generally considered wiser to get the best private legal advice you can and then proceed without consulting the government. Of course, if you have already gotten into antitrust trouble you may have no choice but to consult with the government about proposed business moves with possible antitrust consequences. And, depending on the size of the corporations involved, the FTC must be advised in advance of some combinations.

Antitrust enforcement seldom hits you out of the blue. Legal actions are usually preceded by investigations, involving many interviews and extensive file searches that can last for months or years. The cost to your corporation in executives' and lawyers' time in being investigated is a significant part of your potential antitrust troubles, even if the government eventually decides not to bring action against you. Thus, your protective measures should include trying to avoid the appearance of antitrust violations.

Your troubles multiply sharply if the government's decision is to proceed with legal action against you. At this point the Antitrust Division has several choices: whether to bring a criminal prosecution, a civil proceeding, or both; whether to include individuals as well as corporations among the defendants; and whether to name other corporations and individuals as co-conspirators who are not formal parties to the action.

Criminal prosecutions are relatively rare, generally being reserved for willful violations with substantial economic consequences. They require a preliminary presentation of evidence before a grand jury hands down an indictment. Convictions can result in fines upon corporations and individuals and prison sentences for individuals; but very few individuals have gone to prison for antitrust violations. Pleas of nolo contender(no contest), acceptance of which is discretionary with the judge, are used when defendants and the government are able to agree upon changes in defendants' practices that will bring them within the law. Such pleas allow defendants to get off the hook with reduced loss of dignity; they are not formal admissions of "guilt," but the government will require defendants to acknowledge that they have violated the law.

While criminal prosecutions damage corporate and individual reputations more than do the more common civil proceedings, the latter can have severe business consequences. They are brought on behalf of the United States for injunctive relief and money damages. If the court finds an antitrust violation, it can issue far-reaching orders—including divestiture of acquired businesses, dissolution of illegal combinations, and compulsory licensing of patents—which can greatly disrupt a corporation's business. Here the way of settling with the government is through a "consent decree" in which defendants agree to do things that the government considers necessary to redress the situation.

Litigating a case, criminal or civil, carries the chance of winning as well as losing. But if you do not rate your chances of winning as good, a negotiated settlement, by nolo contendere or consent decree, has two substantial advantages: you avoid the cost of litigation, and you can play a larger role in formulating the new, more precise antitrust ground rules under which you will be doing business. But it will be worth a great deal to you to be able to avoid having such ground rules imposed upon you, whether by a contested court order or by settlement, because they are likely to reduce substantially (and sometimes permanently) your freedom to make your own business decisions. For example, an antitrust order has kept meat packing firms out of the business of selling grocery products for over 50 years.

Another important source of antitrust enforcement is the right of individuals and corporations who claim injury from antitrust violations to bring civil actions for "treble damages" (three times actual damages) against alleged antitrust violators, corporate and individual. These suits for "punitive" damages, going beyond compensation in order to punish the wrongdoer, are designed (like §16(b) of the Securities Exchange Act) to provide a host of private attorney generals who will help to deter antitrust violations. Private suits commonly follow government proceedings which have established these violations. These private plaintiffs have what is usually the hardest part of their cases already proven for them and to recover need prove only their own damage and that it was caused by defendants' unlawful acts. An extreme example of private fall-out from successful government antitrust enforcement is presented by the electrical equipment cases, where private damage payments exceeded $400,000,000.

In addition to court proceedings by the Department of Justice and private damage actions, the Federal Trade Commission can bring administrative proceedings and issue orders directing defendants to "cease and desist" from illegal practices. The Commission has its own investigatory and legal staff. Its proceedings result both from its own studies and from complaints submitted to it. Compared with the Antitrust Division, the FTC seems to look less for directly anticompetitive practices and more for practices that indirectly hurt competition by misleading consumers. Frequently its target will be whole industries rather than individual concerns. For example, it has investigated allegedly deceptive practices that seem to have been widely followed in the business of selling funeral services. The FTC approach is to try to make the business more competitive by inducing fuller disclosure to consumers.

(ii) Minimizing antitrust risks

In deciding whether or not to do something which may involve antitrust risks you will need to consider:

—what the law says,
—the likelihood of legal proceedings being brought against you,
—how much risk you are willing to incur to accomplish your business objectives, and
—how you will use your lawyers in reaching a decision.

If the law clearly prohibits what you want to do, and if you want to obey the law, you will abandon or modify your project without needing to balance antitrust risks against business gains. If the law permits more than one interpretation, you may interpret it in your favor, but this requires you to weigh risks and gains. At both stages you may need legal help.

You are the one who must decide what risks you want to take; and you are the one who best knows the importance of your business objectives and the factual context of possible antitrust risks. Thus, it is essential that you do not abdicate too much of the final decision-making to your lawyers. On the other hand, your lawyers are in a better position to say what the law says and to appraise the likelihood that it will be enforced. Antitrust risks are real risks that can hurt you as badly as a fire or a recession. Thus, you should not exclude your lawyers from, nor even keep them at the fringes of, your planning. However, as to isolated transactions, particularly if your corporation because of its modest economic power has not become a prime target for antitrust enforcers, you should consider whether antitrust risks justify the delays and expenses of involving lawyers.

The delays and expenses of legal assistance can be held down by using inside lawyers—i.e., full-time corporate employees rather than outside practitioners. If you have no inside lawyers, the choice becomes whether you go outside or rely on your own judgement: which behooves you to understand what the antitrust laws require and how they are enforced. If you have inside lawyers, you may let them decide whether they will seek outside help, or you may decide on your own to go outside. In general, matters not putting a high premium on objectivity and calling for familiarity with your business and easy working relationships with your people—such as passing on procurement and sales contracts, patent and trademark licensing agreements, advertising, and sales promotion plans—are best handled by inside lawyers (provided, of course, that their position in the corporate pecking order enables them to tell the executives involved what they cannot do). Matters generally suitable for handling by outside lawyers include those that require antitrust expertise, objectivity, high level decisions, protracted attention, extensive manpower, or relations with outsides. Examples include long-range planning, acquisitions, enforcement investigations, litigation, and negotiations with government agencies and private claimants.

Ideally your directors, senior executives, house counsel, and outside counsel will work together to provide guidelines for your front line people routinely exposed to operational antitrust entanglements (mainly your sales and advertising managers, your representatives on trade and industry associations, and those handling your patent and trademark licensing), and to form a council of advisors for higher level corporate decisions with antitrust implications (such as acquisitions, long-term purchase and sales contracts, integration of operations, and changes in your corporate structure). At both operating and planning levels you have alternative ways of doing things with differing antitrust entailments.

At the operating level, the following practical suggestions are offered:

—Price discrimination problems are minimized if you can justify price differentials by the *functions* of purchasers: distributors, wholesalers, retailers, industrial users, and consumers. These classifications should be relatable to your distribution costs and be consistently applied. You should have a cost-related reason for charging A less than B.

—If you want to refuse to deal with someone, the less you say about your reasons or the conditions upon which you would be willing to deal the better. Keep your refusal as "unilateral" as possible.

—Advertising extolling intangibles such as beauty, satisfaction, flavor, coolness, and lightness are easier to justify as "mere puffing" than are more specific claims about safety, therapy, and nutrition. Make your advertising more like poetry and less like a prescription.

—Keep your people in charge of patent licensing separate from your people in charge of sales. In the world of antitrust it is often wise not to let your right hand know what your left hand is doing.

At the planning level, factors to consider include the following:

—In choosing between acquiring a competitor or a supplier or customer, keep in mind that the former entails more antitrust risks. While acquiring a supplier or customer takes business off the market, it is business you could preempt by performing the function yourselve. If you are already in a dominant position and if acquisition of a supplier or customer will hurt your competitors, it will be safer to create new facilities to perform the operation yourself. As you get stronger the more prudent it becomes to choose the route with the least direct impact on existing markets.

—If your position in your industry is already so strong that it will permit only one or two acquisitions without inviting antitrust trouble, husband these opportunities carefully. One approach is to develop a short list of companies that you would most like to acquire and then to wait until one of these becomes available.

—A combination or conspiracy is harder to find if the transaction occurs within a single corporation. If parts of an affiliated enterprise are going to ostensibly "compete" with one another, or if they are going make agreements about prices or territories, it may be preferable for purely antitrust reasons for the parts to be divisions of a single corporation rather than separate corporations. This recommendation is a variation of the suggestion above about staying as "unilateral" as possible.

Section 9.2 Resisting Unfair Business Tactics

As your corporation grows and succeeds it becomes a target for snipers from many sides. These include, in addition to antitrust enforcers, those who seek to interfere with what you have achieved in building public confidence and developing useful information. As to this group, instead of defending yourself against charges of being an outlaw, you will be trying to align the law on your side. This task is not easy because not all seemingly unfair tactics are unlawful, or even unethical. Everyone since Adam has taken advantage of the path-breaking of his predecessors. To reap where we do not sow is a common and not always illegitimate or unworthy aspiration. Thus, a central problem in dealing with business tactics that seem unfair is that you are in a legal and ethical gray area. As a consequence, you should understand as clearly as possible the protections the law provides against tactics to which you may be subjected; at the same time you should plan your affairs to minimize the chances of these inroads being attempted and to be ready to deal with them if they happen, combining recourse to legal remedies with strategems of self-help. In other words, this section is organized on a theory-practice division not unlike the organization of the antitrust section. First the concern is with describing unfair business tactics and their legal status; then with how you may protect yourself against them.

We have already brushed against several parts of our present topic. Section 1.3 recommends that you select a corporate name that can effectively symbolize good will that you hope to build up. Chapter 7 discusses putting a value on the good will you have established when you sell securities to others. Section 9.1 deals with the FTC's role in preventing unfair methods of competition.

Among tactics that we do not try to cover are infringement of patents and copyrights. While patents and copyrights both involve filing applications with federal agencies for grants of limited monopolies, the substance of these grants is quite different. Patents are granted to inventors to encourage disclosure of their inventions—i.e., to discourage keeping them hidden as trade secrets. A patentable invention must be novel and useful and must evidence a spark of discovery; its subject may be a device, a process, or a design. Copyrights, on the other hand, are granted to creators or owners of literary or artistic works to protect the works from exploitation by others. While a copyrighted work is supposed to be original it need not evidence invention, novelty, discovery, nor usefulness. The laws and practices relating to patents and copyrights are too specialized and complicated for explication in this book except as we consider patent protection as an alternative to trade secret protection. Also, it can be argued that patents and copyrights do not belong in this section because infringing them is illegal, not on the ground of intrinsic unfairness, but rather on the ground that it violates limited franchises granted to their owners by the federal government. As we will discover, unfair competition problems *can* arise when someone copies something that is *not* covered by a patent or copyright.

(a) Kinds of unfair business tactics and their legal status

One approach to unfair business tactics is to sort out interests of your corporation that may be affected by such tactics. These interests seem to be of two general kinds: external reputation and internal expertise. As your corporation succeeds it acquires a following with its public—those with whom it deals and who use its products or services—that we call good will. This interest in your corporation's reputation can be affected by a variety of tactics; and those which the law prohibits are given such names as unfair competition and trademark infringement.

> ▪ "Trade libel," a related tactic which we do not treat, involves disparaging statements about a producer or its products. For example, if an automobile buyer who is dissatisfied with what he has bought paints lemons on his automobile and drives it about, may the manufacturer call upon the law to make him either remove the lemons or keep his car off the streets?

A successful corporation also acquires a body of internal information and know-how—relating to procurement, production, personnel, transportation, marketing, etc.—which outsiders may try to discover and exploit. The terms "trade secret" and "proprietary information" are sometimes used for this kind of information. While encroachments upon both external and internal interests are sometimes called "unfair competition," the term is more often confined to unlawful trading on someone else's reputation.

Another approach to our topic is to ask whether the law should focus on the intensity of your corporation's interests, external or internal, *for* which you are seeking protection, or whether its focus should be on the character of the conduct of outsiders *against* which you are seeking protection. Focus on interests leads us to see the problem as primarily a matter of preserving "property rights," and the term "industrial property" has been coined to encompass a variety of legally protected intangible assets, including good will and trade secrets as well as the more clearly defined rights in patents and copyrights.

> ▪ **In Chapter 7 when we put values on whole enterprises we recognized that intangibles are property in the sense that a going business may be worth more (or less) than the sum of its tangible assets; but there we were not called upon to put values on particular intangibles.**

A shift of focus to conduct of outsiders leads us to see the problem as primarily a matter of punishing "torts" (legal civil wrongs), and the term "business torts" has been coined to encompass a variety of unlawful acts. But it becomes apparent with both of these legalistic ways of defining unfair competition—property or tort—that we soon begin to reason in circles when we try to apply them to determine the particular situations where the law will intervene. We find ourselves reasoning:

—The law protects property rights. A has a property right in the interest on which B is encroaching. Therefore, the law will protect A's interest. But what are property rights? They are interests which the law protects. Thus, by calling A's interest a property right, we have assumed our conclusion.

—The law punishes torts. B has competed unfairly with A and unfair competition is a tort. Therefore, the law will punish B. But what are torts? They are conduct the law will punish. Thus, by calling B's conduct a tort, we have again assumed our conclusion.

To escape from this circularity we need to go behind the question-begging notions of A's "property" and B's "tort" and look at A's acutal business situation and at B's actual conduct. We need to recognize that cases are not decided by neatly applying labels but by hard choices between competing claims for the law to intervene in or to stay out of business quarrels.

While the discussion that follows is organized in terms of legal categories—unfair competition, trademarks, and trade secrets—we try to keep in mind that finding the right legal pigeon-hole is only the beginning in predicting how the law will treat particular instances of arguably unfair business tactics.

(b) Unfair competition

In Section 9.1 we noted that the FTC's efforts to fulfill its charge to prevent "unfair methods of competition" have been largely confined to allegedly deceptive advertising and sales practices that appear to violate the public interest. While the unfair competition that is our present concern sometimes involves confusing the public, the public interest component is but a part of a broader inquiry which includes weighing private rights and wrongs.

Unfair competition is an inclusive common law concept that has evolved from many cases, British and American, between private litigants spread over several hundred years. A sampling of these cases, arranged in roughly chronological order, may help to convey a feel for the kinds of situations which may involve unfair competition; these cases will also provide a framework for our analysis of when the law will intervene. In each of the following slightly adapted real cases the issue is whether a court will award A damages from B and restrain B from continuing to do what he is doing:

—Schoolmaster's case: A is the master of a private school. B starts a competing school and lures away some of A's scholars.

—Duck pond case: A earns his livelihood netting wild ducks that alight on his pond. B, without trespassing on A's land, frightens ducks away from A's pond with a cannon because he dislikes A. (This case arose before there was any recognized public interest in the preservation of wild ducks.)

—Barber's case: A is a barber in a town large enough to support but one barber. B, a banker who dislikes A, induces C to open a competing barber shop in A's town by offering to subsidize C until he can put A out of business.

—News services case: A and B operate competing news services. A has more foreign correspondents than B. B sells foreign news stories that B has secured from A's stories in east coast papers in competition with A on the west coast, a practice made possible by the time difference between the coasts. Because B is using the substance but not the form of A's stories, A has no claim to copyright infringement.

—Jeweler's case: A is a jeweler with a national reputation for quality and elegance. B opens a movie theater using A's surname and advertises it as "a gem of a theater."

Note that only in the schoolmaster's and news services cases are A and B competing with one another. Thus, it appears that unfair competition includes tactics which affect but do not necessarily involve competition.

Discussion of these cases with law students reveals a pattern of opinions which are not dissimilar from the actual judicial decisions. There is wide agreement that the law should not intervene in the schoolmaster's case and that it should intervene in the duck pond case and wide disagreement about legal intervention in the remaining three cases. In trying to rationalize these largely instinctive reactions we will use the following five factors which seem relevant in deciding whether the law will intervene:

(1) A's injury: How seriously is A being injured by B's conduct?

(2) Public confusion: How much is the public being confused by B's conduct?

(3) B's gain: How much is B gaining from his conduct?

(4) B's motives: What is B's motivation for his conduct?

(5) Public interest in B's freedom: Is there a public interest in B remaining free to continue his conduct?

Since all five questions involve B's conduct, it is apparent that we are adopting a predominantly tort analysis that is oriented to B's wrongs rather than to A's rights.

Why do opposite conclusions seem to be indicated for the first two cases (neither of which involved public confusion)? If the law were to look only at B's economic gain it would seem that the conclusions should be reversed, because the schoolmaster profits from his conduct, whereas the gain of the duck frightener is purely emotional—as is the banker's in the barber's case. The duck pond case stands out from the rest in that A is not hurt on the market place but in the production phase of his business. These two points—B's solely emotional gain and A suffering sabotage rather than competition—combine with the duck frightener's unattractive motivation and the seeming absence of any public interest in what he is doing to arouse a feeling that this is a stronger case for legal intervention than any of the rest. This B is acting solely out of malice with no regard for his economic gain. In contrast, we feel that the new schoolmaster should be left alone, even though he is intentionally hurting the old schoolmaster, because there is a strong public interest for people to be free to act for their own economic gain and we recognize that other people inevitably get hurt in the process. But we also feel that B in the duck pond case should not be left alone, because there is an even stronger public interest against people being free to hurt other people maliciously, where there is no justification of economic gain. Here B's very lack of profit from his cannon blasts turns the law against him and makes his conduct fit an ancient legal wrong called "malicious mischief."

Does a decision that the law should intervene against the duck frightener dictate a similar decision against the banker who drives a barber out of business?

Some would say it does, arguing that there is no difference in their motivations. But there are aspects of the barbers case that may make it distinguishable. Banker B is not interfering with barber A in his barber shop but in the market place where A can expect interference. What the banker did *looks* more like business as usual than malicious mischief. Judges examine less willingly into motives of bankers than of people who fire cannons over duck ponds. There are reasons for this difference other than class bias: a banker could in his normal business lend money to a new barber in town; if judges begin to probe motives for doing business doubt will be cast on too many transactions; and there is a public interest in people remaining free to use their money as they please. On the other hand, it is not clear that this freedom should include satisfaction of grudges, nor that commerce will be hurt significantly if business people are subject to legal restraints in the rare cases where they can be shown to be acting from malice. It seems probable that a modern court would intervene against the banker if A can prove B's malicious motivation.

In the news services case A's injury and B's gain therefrom are apparent. But there is no significant public confusion, and B's motives are more like the new schoolmaster than the duck firghtener or the banker, because he is moved by business opportunism rather than malice: his conduct will hurt A, but his objective is to make money for himself. Furthermore, there is a possible public interest in preserving B's freedom to do what he is doing. In deciding whether to intervene judges use the following different approaches emphasizing respectively A's rights, B's conduct, and B's freedom:

—The law should intervene because A has a property interest in news that he has gathered. It is the product of his efforts and unless the law protects it he will have no incentive to continue his efforts.

—The law should intervene because it is unfair to permit B to undersell A by using news he has not had the expense of gathering.

—The law should not intervene because to do so will extend the copyright monopoly beyond the limits set on it by Congress. When A publishes his stories the news passes into the public domain for the use of everyone, including B.

After seeming to adopt the first view, the Supreme Court appeared to switch its support to the third view, finding an overriding public interest in everyone, B included, being free to use information that "belongs" to everyone, and arguing that to do otherwise would stifle intellectual freedom. However, the Supreme Court has refused to apply this reasoning to prevent protection of trade secrets.

In the jeweler's case public confusion becomes crucial and trade names become involved—topics that we consider in connection with trademarks. A's injury, limited to possible "dilution" or cheapening of the significance of his name is less clear than in the other four cases. B's gain, the "rub-off" he hopes to get from A's reputation for elegance, is more clear than B's gains in the duck pond and barber's cases but less clear than such gains in the schoolmaster's and news services cases. B's motivation, while economic rather than malicious, is not one that it is in the public interest to foster. His business opportunism is less injurious to A or profitable to himself than was B's in the news services case, but it is calculated to bring him trade by suggesting to the public that they should connect his theater with A's jewelry business, thereby putting A's reputation in jeopardy. The public interest favors freedom to compete but not freedom to confuse. And note that the victims of public confusion will include not only A but also B's competitors and the public. However, since A and B are not competitors, and since B would not ordinarily be precluded from using a name for a theater because it is already being used by a jeweler, if B had not referred to "gem" in his advertising, it is doubtful that a judge would intervene on A's behalf. Without this reference, it would become much more difficult for A to prove B's intention to trade on A's good will.

The most significant question to ask in predicting how unfair competition cases will be decided appears to be: How far does B's conduct depart from ordinary competition? In answering you will need to consider B's motivation, the public interest in his freedom, and the nature of A's injury and B's gain. The schoolmaster's and news services cases are close enough to ordinary competition to make legal intervention unlikely. The other three cases have elements of malice or creation of confusion which make B's conduct different enough from ordinary competition to make legal intervention probable.

(c) Trademarks

Perhaps the most common kind of unfair competition is that exemplified by the jeweler case: A's trademark is misused by B. Now we need to look more closely at what we mean when we say that A has a trademark and that B is misusing it. After noting what trademarks are, we examine how trademark meanings are created and lost and how your trademarks may be misused by others.

(i) Meaning, development, and registration of trademarks

A trademark is a symbol used by A on or in connection with a product or service to indicate its commercial origin. The consequence of a symbol being A's trademark is that the law will assist A in preventing B and others from using it in ways likely to confuse the public. While most commonly a word or words, trademarks can be made up of letters, numbers, pictures, shapes, colors, and combinations of these. The commercial origin indicated by a trademark is typically the manufacturer, but a mark can also point to the designer, processor, maker of a component, assembler, or seller. The trademarked object is usually a product but it can be a service. And B, the outsider misusing the symbol, is usually, but not always, a competitor of A.

Trademarks have developed from marks put on goods to show the craftsman or guild that made them. They still serve as a means for fixing responsibility for quality and workmanship; but as marks move from the back to the "front" of the object with increasingly sophisticated marketing techniques, their principal role becomes enhancement and preservation of the distinctiveness and recognizability of a commercial origin built up by advertising and promotion.

Like patents and copyrights, trademarks may be "registered" by filing documents in a federal office: the Trademark Division of the Patent Office; and state registration of trademarks is also available. Unlike patents and copyrights, trademark registration merely records (like the recording of a deed) and does not create substantive rights, although it does create useful procedural rights such as presumptions of validity and, with federal registrations, the right to bring infringement actions in federal courts. And trademark rights are more illusive than patent and copyright rights, since they do not depend solely on government grant but partly on "meaning," a complex mental and emotional process not subject to legal fiat. Thus, trademarks are created by and depend for their continued existence upon both legal action and factual circumstances.

(ii) Creation of trademarks

To create a trademark you first compose a new symbol and then, by using it as a trademark, educate the public to receive its message. The process is akin to adding a new word to the language: taking existing materials (words, letters, shapes, colors, etc.) and composing them in a novel way, and then trying to breathe new meaning into the composition. Whether you succeed or fail depends on many factors, including whether your composition is actually novel—i.e., does not already mean something else—and whether you succeed in giving it your meaning. For example, National Broadcasting Company adopted a symbol featuring the letter "N" in a fanciful way as a "house mark" for its television offerings, but then discovered that Nebraska educational television was already using substantially the same symbol. To clear the way for the continued use of its mark, NBC paid Nebraska a substantial amount to change its symbol.

The NBC-Nebraska episode teaches the importance of finding and resolving conflicts with other peoples' marks *before* you become committed to a new mark (see discussion in Section 1.3 on choosing a corporate name, and Appendix H.1(b) for an agreement clearing a proposed corporate name). It also illustrates how difficult it is, even for one with the communications resources of NBC, to give trademark meaning to a symbol that already means something else. This difficulty is not confined to symbols already in trademark use by others, but also arises with symbols, usually words, that already have common meanings which get in the way of a desired new trademark meaning. Generic names for things, descriptive words or phrases, family names, and geographical designations are all in this category.

Common sense tells us that soap maker A should not be able to turn the word "soap" into a trademark, because B and other makers of soap need the word to identify their products. Less obviously, but still quite clearly, A should not be able to turn the word "gentle" into a trademark, because others need this word to describe their products. But the need argument cannot be raised at all if A coins a new word (like "Lux"), and the argument becomes weaker if the word is suggestive rather than descriptive of soap (like "Dial," "Dove," "Ivory," "Sweetheart," etc.). Thus, it appears that there is the least legal difficulty in starting with a word that is meaningless apart from its trademark meaning, such as a made-up word (Kodak, Zerox, Exxon) or an existing word without meaning when applied to the product (Camel cigarettes and Alligator shirts).

Arguments by B asserting the unfairness of permitting commercial pre-emption by A of common words of speech apply also to family names and geographical designations when B can claim truthful use of such words. If B's name really is Ford, why cannot B manufacture and sell Ford automobiles? Or if B really makes fried chicken in Kentucy, why cannot B manufacture and sell Kentucky fried chicken? Should Henry Ford and Colonel Sanders be able to deny the words "Ford" and "Kentucky" to the rest of the world? The answer seems to be that B may truthfully use "Ford" or "Kentucky" but not as a trademark.

To explain this answer we need to refer to the notion of "secondary meaning" and the difference between trademark and non-trademark usage. The process by which a descriptive word, family name, or geographical designation can become a trademark is called acquiring a secondary meaning: a word that already has a primary, non-trademark meaning acquires through use and public re-education a secondary, trademark meaning. Secondary meaning can become very firmly established: how many people know that Buick and Chevrolet started as family names? But even if a descriptive word, family name, or geographical designation becomes A's trademark through secondary meaning, B still can use the word, name or designation in non-trademark senses. For example, even if a judge holds that "Lite" has become a trademark for A's beer, it would appear that B can call his product "light beer" if that is a truthful description and if B does nothing, other than to make descriptive use of the word "light," likely to cause consumer confusion. B will need to spell "light" correctly. In the automobile situation, B will need to avoid use of his name in the script style used by Ford Motor Company and probably accompany use of his name with a disclaimer of any connection with that company. In the fried chicken situation, B will need to avoid capitalizing "fried chicken" in referring to his Kentucky fried chicken and he might also be required to rearrange these words and to take other measures to avoid confusion.

Another example of non-trademark usage of a word is in a "trade name": a corporate, divisional, or product name. Trade names can become trademarks, and the same word often appears in trade names and trademarks (corporate names frequently include the corporation's most basic trademark); but names and marks are quite different things. A trade name is a label put on an organization or thing to identify it. A trademark is a more complex expression of relationship, which says: each time you see this symbol you know that the product or service with which it is used comes from a *common* source. It is not necessary that receivers of this message know the *identity* of the source. Many people do not know that the source of products marked "Hot Point" is General Electric.

(iii) Loss of trademark meaning

Meaning is unstable. A word or other symbol that has taken on trademark meaning—whether as a coined, suggestive, or secondary meaning mark—can lose its meaning as an indication of origin and become instead the generic name for a kind of product or service. This change from trademark to generic meaning can happen slowly or quickly. A mark can be used by A, its owner, in A's advertising and by buyer and sellers and by the public in ways that it comes to identify a kind of product rather than to point to a common source, with the result that the mark enters the language as an ordinary word. Former trademarks which now appear uncapitalized in dictionaries include aluminum, cellophane, cola, and linoleum. Failure of A to stop competitors from using his mark on their products or services can also contribute to this gradual change of meaning, sometimes called "going generic" or "falling into the public domain."

Rapid change of meaning can take place if A licenses others to use his mark without retaining control over the nature and quality of the goods or services in connection with which the mark is used. Also a mark used in connection with new or patented products may have no other name when other producers enter the market to produce it. There was a period after the Singer sewing machine patents expired that any producer of a Singer-type sewing machine could use the name "Singer." The word "aspirin" was originally a trademark but has entered the language because there was no other handy name under which it could be sold at retail. Now developers of new drugs and other products often give their discoveries three appelations: a technical generic name (usually unintelligible to consumers), a simplified generic name, and their own "proprietary" trade mark. The simplified generic name gives the public a rememberable generic handle, thereby lessening the need to use the trademark for this purpose.

(iv) Misuse of trademarks by others

Assuming that a word or symbol achieves and maintains a trademark meaning for A, there are several ways that B may use and possibly misuse it. B's use may be competitive or non-competitive; trademark or non-trademark; and B may or may not have justification for his use. For the law to intervene on A's behalf against B, B's use of A's mark must create some likelihood of public confusion; but confusion alone does not justify legal intervention.

The most obvious case for intervention is when B, a competitor of A, uses A's mark as a trademark. Since this kind of use makes a false representation about origin, danger of confusion is assumed without further proof. At the other extreme, the law is unlikely to intervene where A and B are in different fields and B makes non-trademark use of A's mark for which B can assert some justification (say because it is his own name), even if B's use may cause some confusion.

> ■ **If A is Ford Motor Company and B, whose name is Henry Ford, operates a bicycle repair business which he calls "Henry Ford's Bicycle Shop," even if A can find some people who think that B's business has some connection with A, the law is unlikely to intervene.**

As to situations between these extremes, a judge is more likely to intervene because B is using A's mark in a trademark sense and without justification than because A and B are competitors. Competitor B may lawfully make non-confusing, non-trademark use of competitor A's mark in B's advertising. And competitor B may be permitted to use his own name in a trademark sense, even when such use may create some confusion.

> ■ **In Philadelphia there have long been two "Bookbinder's" restaurants: restaurant A bases its use of the name on its line of succession from the original Bookbinder's; restaurant B bases its use on rights of members of the Bookbinder family to use their own name.**

But where B's use of A's mark is as a trademark and lacks justification, even though A and B are in different lines, the law may intervene if A can show danger of confusion. This situation is similar to B's use for a theater of the name A uses for his jewelry business. As we noted, A is not hurt so much by loss of trade as by "dilution" of the meaning of his mark; and A's chances for legal intervention increase if B does anything, beyond using A's mark, to foster confusion which will contribute to such dilution. And in the long run, cheapening of A's name will lead to loss of trade.

(d) Trade secrets

We now move from tactics that jeopardize your corporation's external reputation to those that jeopardize its internal security. Compared with unfair competition and trademarks, trade secret decisions are scarce, making the drawing of legal lines more difficult. The basic legal question with trade secrets is whether the law will intervene to help A when information (X) that A claims gets into the hands of B or C. As with unfair competition, analysis of trade secret protection can be in terms of property, tort, and public interest. We can focus on A and ask whether X is protectable; we can focus on B and ask whether he has acted wrongfully; or we can balance the public interest in A's security and B's freedom. In this subsection we first examine what A can claim as a trade secret; then, in light of some sample situations, what B can and cannot do with X when it comes to him in various ways; and finally, how corporate privacy and the public interest inter-relate.

(i) What can be a trade secret

For information to be protectable it clearly need not be so novel as to be patentable. But it cannot be something already known to the public or that A is under an obligation to make public; and it is probably enough to destroy a secret for it to become known to someone who is under no obligation to maintain its secrecy (thus, trade secrets are considerably more fragile than trademarks). Between these clear cases of patentable secret information and matters of public knowledge there is a broad spectrum of information of varying novelty and secrecy. Most likely to be given affirmative legal protection as trade secrets are the kinds of novel information that most resemble patents: formulas, recipes, and production processes. For items like business plans, lists of customers and suppliers, and data on profit margins and market percentages (sometimes called "proprietary information"), which do not at all resemble patents (because of their lack of novelty) but disclosure of which would aid A's competitors, protection is sometimes limited to exemption from forced disclosure, with A being left to his own devices to keep them confidential. Isolated discoveries—as in the copper discovery case below—are more likely to be affirmatively protected than are the more routine kinds of proprietary information.

Corporate managements tend to take the position that all information they do not choose, or are not legally required, to disclose should be affirmatively protected as trade secrets. Public interest advocates, on the other hand, argue that corporations should have no secrets from their shareholders—which for public corporations means having no secrets—beyond clean-cut situations where disclosure will force the corporation to forfeit a legitimate competitive advantage. In practice the difference between these two positions seems to reduce itself to whether disclosure or non-disclosure has the burden of justification.

(ii) How a secret gets out

Among our sampling of five cases in the unfair competition subsection—involving scholars, ducks, haircuts, news, and prestige—the one that comes the closest to our present problem is the news services case, where news service A had developed news which news service B used for its own profit. A was arguing in effect that its news was still a trade secret on the west coast even though it had been published on the east coast. To give us a wider range of escaping trade secret situations here are three more cases, again based on real cases with which considerable poetic license has been taken:

—Copper discovery case: A is a large mining company. Its geologists discover in Canada what appears to be a huge vein exceptionally rich in copper which extends into land (Blackacre) owned by T. Before A secures an option on Blackacre, B, a land speculator, deduces from a conversation among A's geologists overheard in a Canadian bar that they may have made a discovery involving Blackacre, and buys an option on Blackacre from T for himself. Will the law let B retain his profit?

—Wonder drug case: A is a large pharmaceutical company which has, after spending several million dollars on research and testing, developed X, a new wonder drug. B, an accountant employed by A, makes an unauthorized copy of the formula for X, leaves A's employ, and sells his copy of the X formula to C, a foreign drug manufacturer, for $1,000,000. C then sells X in the United States and elsewhere at prices lower than A's prices, which are calculated to recapture A's costs in developing X. Will the law grant A relief against B and C?

—Space suit case: A is a large rubber company with a federal contract to develop space suits for astronauts. B is an engineer employed by A in charge of the space suit project. C, a smaller rubber company, also secures a space suit development contract and persuades B to come to work for C at a big increase in salary. Will the law grant A relief against B and C?

These cases illustrate some of the many ways secrets can escape: unintentional leaks, industrial espionage, and B's own expertise.

In the copper discovery case A's information about the profit potentialities of Blackacre does not resemble a patentable invention and thus may not be within the narrow meaning of trade secrets. But even if we, not unreasonably, give trade secrets a broader meaning to include this important geological find, the case for legal intervention remains weak because it is hard to find any legally wrongful conduct by B. Eavesdropping is impolite but not illegal. B's opportunism may be morally wrong, but A's own moral position is vulnerable because A was planning to buy Blackacre from T without disclosing A's discovery, although A can argue that A's moral position is better than B's because A invested in the geological studies. A's geologists acted imprudently, but they were not intentionally disloyal to A and B did not corrupt them. As in the news services case, B picked up or found news that had "belonged" to A while it was still secret but that is now fair game for B to exploit. In both cases B is reaping where he did not sow but it is doubtful that the law will interfere. The news services and copper discovery cases teach us that the nature of the information and the amount of A's loss and B's gain are less significant than how B comes by the information and whether it is then still secret. In the copper discovery case the disclosure is very limited (only to B), and the same incident changes information from secret to non-secret and reveals it to B. B is not, as in the news services case, coming upon already public information. The copper discovery case seems to indicate that the tort analysis fits better with common sense than does the property analysis: if A's information were really property and if B found it, as he did here, he would have to give it back to A. But this kind of altruism seems more than the law can demand of B.

In the wonder drug case the X formula appears to be a trade secret even under its narrow meaning; there is substantial economic loss to A and gain to B and C, and B and C are anything but innocent: B appears to be a thief and C a buyer of stolen goods. At the least, B has violated his fiduciary duties to A, and C knew or should have known that B could not rightfully sell him the X formula. Since B was under an obligation to maintain the secrecy of X, his unauthorized copying does not destroy its secret status. For this kind of "industrial espionage," American courts will provide civil remedies (A's damages, an accounting to A of B's and C's profits, and injunctive relief against C's use or further disclosure of the formula) and criminal penalties, to the extent that jurisdiction over B and C can be obtained. Assuming that A's price to the public for the wonder drug is not unreasonable, A's moral position seems unassailable and much stronger than A's in the copper discovery case: instead of being deprived of an expected, and arguably unconscionable gain at the expense of a third party, this A is the innocent victim of the wrongdoings of B and C.

The space suit case is more difficult to decide than either of the other two cases. Rather than a specific item of information, like the copper find or the wonder drug formula, here the escaping data is B's general familiarity with and expertise in A's efforts to design space suits, and it leaves A in the mind of B. Whether this sort of knowledge in B's mind can even be called a trade secret belonging to A seems doubtful, not only because it lacks specificity, but also because it does not seem right for a person's thought processes to become the property of another. (Here B's mind is more than just a receptacle for information, as would be the situation in the wonder drug case if B had memorized X and then gone to work for C.) At this point it is not evident whether A actually will be hurt or C benefited by B's change of jobs, although B does have his higher salary. But most significantly, it is not clear that B or C have acted wrongfully. The case presents in perplexing ambivalence the question of how loyal the law should require an employee to be to his employer:

—On the one hand, it seems unfair to A to permit B to take to C, A's competitor, substantially all the information that has been developed at A's expense about space suit design.

—On the other hand, it seems unfair to B to confine him to using his skills and knowledge only as an employee of A, and unfair to preclude C from hiring people with prior experience.

An Ohio court tried to compromise these interests by permitting B to keep his job with C but subject to an order restraining him from revealing or using space suit information he had learned while employed by A. *B.F. Goodrich Co.* v. *Wohlgemuth*, 192 N.E. 2d 99 (Ohio 1963). The feasibility of such intellectual compartmentalization seems dubious.

(iii) Corporate privacy and the public interest

Apart from law suits about trade secrets, other government action—federal, state, and local—can affect corporate privacy, both negatively and positively. Governments have sharply limited the secret areas of corporate life by numerous reporting and regulatory statutes. We have seen the disclosure required under the federal securities statutes in registration statements, proxy statements, and annual reports. But government action also serves to protect privacy in several ways. Some government filings are treated as confidential—notably tax returns, patent applications, and some informational filings with the Commerce Department and the FTC.

> ▪ **Patent applications remain confidential if a patent is denied but become public if a patent is granted, when the patentee will be protected by his patent monopoly. As we will see, it is not always easy to decide whether to go the patent or the trade secret route.**

Corporate privacy is aided by "in camera" (private) court proceedings and executive sessions of legislative and administrative bodies. And the law contributes to the maintenance of corporate internal security in several important ways: outsiders can be required by contract to accord confidential treatment to corporate data; insiders are under fiduciary duties not to make disclosures which will injure the corporation; and the corporation itself can assert the attorney-client privilege to protect disclosure in court actions of communications with its lawyers, although in a suit between shareholders and the corporation the privilege is not absolute. *Garner* v. *Wolfinbarger*, 430 F. 2d 1093 (5th Cir. 1970), cert. denied, 401 U.S. 974 (1971). But if the movement for "sunshine" laws requiring openness in public business progresses, as it seems to be doing, into the private sector, we can expect shrinkage rather than expansion of what a corporation can keep private.

Needed research and planning is encouraged if corporations can look to the law to help them protect, rather than to force them to share, data and plans useful to their competitors. Affirmative protection is likely to be developed judicially in cases like those discussed above, while forced disclosure will come mainly from legislative and administrative action. In all of these arenas—courts, Congress, and agencies—we can look for continuing tension between those who urge that coporations should be left alone, with the law confining itself to providing protection against wrong-doers, and those who urge that since much of business is no longer private the public needs to know what is going on in business as well as in government. The problem is to learn how to separate information which should remain private for legitimate business reasons from that which should be disclosed in the public interest. And there will probably remain a sizeable third body of information—not secret or private enough to warrant trade secret protection by the courts, but not so affected with the public interest as to warrant forced disclosure—that will be left to the protection of each corporation's own security system.

(e) Protecting yourself against unfair business tactics

This section has been trying to heighten your awareness of threats to your corporation's reputation and privacy, and to give you the basics of relevant law, on the assumption that to deal effectively with a problem it helps to understand it. Now we move on to practical aspects of your resistance to unfair tactics, looking first at how you may utilize available legal machinery and then at self-help measures: an organization based on how you respond to situations rather than on their subject matter. The legal machinery to which you can resort for help in protecting your corporation against unfair business tactics includes court actions, registration of trademarks, and patenting of trade secrets.

(i) Court actions

The most all-purpose kind of available legal help is a court action on behalf of your corporation (A) charging your adversary (B) with unfair competition, trademark infringement, or misappropriation of trade secrets. Before deciding whether to sue, you may try to persuade B to stop what he is doing, usually by having your lawyer write him a stern letter. If this does not work you are faced with the choice of starting suit or seeming to acquiesce in B's conduct. Your decision whether to sue weighs expenses in money, time, and attention that go with litigation and the chances and consequences of it failing, against the importance of your imperiled interests. A's trademarks and trade secrets may be its most valuable assets, representing investments over many years. As we have seen, these intangible assets are fragile because they depend on exclusivity for their very existence; when they are shared with others they cease to be trademarks and trade secrets.

Comparison of the eight sample unfair competition and trade secret cases brings out some of the factors in deciding whether or not to sue. In the duck pond, jeweler, and wonder drug cases, prompt legal action by A seems indicated because of the need for legal relief and the high chances of getting it. But in the schoolmaster's, news services, and copper discovery cases, chances of success seem too small to justify law suits. In the barber's and space suit cases, while law suits may not succeed they seem worth trying, particularly in the space suit case where A may want to impress upon other employees that they cannot take A's trade secrets to its competitors without having to face expensive law suits.

If you decide that A will sue, you are then faced with a series of subordinate decisions in getting under way, beginning with the question of what lawyer A should use. While you probably have had legal help in the pre-decision stages, a different lawyer may be indicated for the actual suit. There are usually reasons for not using A's inside lawyers for litigation, the time demands of which may interfere with their regular work. And A's regular lawyer, inside or outside, may not have the necessary expertise or the local contacts. Thus, you may wish to hire for A a lawyer or firm that specializes in unfair competition and trademark work in the locality where you plan to sue.

You will need to decide in what state or states to bring suit and whether to use state or federal courts. While federal law controls registration and protection of federally registered trademarks, most unfair competition and trade secret issues are controlled by state laws, whether suit is in state or federal court. Different states and federal circuits have varying attitudes about these suits. If a federally registered trademark is involved, or if A and B are citizens of different states (a corporation is a "citizen" of any state where it is incorporated and of the state where it has its principal place of business), A will have the option of suing in a federal court and B will have the option of "removing" the case to a federal court if A sues in a state court. You may want to start several suits if the unfair tactics are being carried on by several Bs in different parts of the country.

Decisions that you will need to work out with your lawyer also include the kinds of temporary or preliminary relief you will seek from the judge. If B's conduct threatens immediate and irreparable harm to A's business, you will seek a "temporary restraining order" until B can appear and defend. Since such orders are handled "ex parte" (i.e., the judge hears only A's side), A will be required to post a bond to compensate B if A's claim is groundless. Whether or not you ask for a temporary restraining order, you probably will seek—in addition to a permanent injunction, damages, and an accounting of B's profits—a preliminary injunction to restrain B while the case is pending. Here the judge hears both sides and does not ordinarily require A to post a bond. The chances of restraining B, both temporarily and preliminarily, from disclosing A's secrets in the wonder drug and space suit cases are better, because of the immediacy of the threatened harm, than are the chances in the jeweler case of restraining B from continuing to use A's name.

(ii) Registering trademarks and patenting trade secrets

In addition to bringing law suits against B's unfair tactics as they happen, A can stake out claims in advance of trouble through registering trademarks and patenting trade secrets. While the alternative to each is reliance on common law rights to bring the kinds of law suits we have been discussing, as we have noted, these steps provide different protections and different considerations control whether you will want to take them. Since registration merely records A's common law trademark rights, whereas successful patent application replaces A's common law trade secret rights with something quite different, patenting a trade secret is a more serious matter than registering a trademark.

Trademark registration.—There are three levels of trademark registrations: federal, state, and foreign; but when we talk about registration we usually mean federal registration. Such a registration puts others on notice of A's claim of trademark rights in the registered symbol, increases the burden of anyone contesting A's claim, and assures A access to federal courts in protecting its rights. State trademark registration may act as an additional deterrent to poachers in a local market and might be of some help when A is suing in the courts of that state. Foreign registrations raise special problems which we will discuss separately. About the only argument against trademark registration—federal, state, or foreign—is cost: in filing fees and legal services, and in time and attention devoted to securing and maintaining registrations. Federal registration seems worth this cost as to any mark for which you have serious commercial intentions. State registration, on the other hand, seems justified only in special situations.

It is important to remember that in the United States and in most other English-speaking countries registration must follow, not precede, use and that use, not registration, creates trademark rights. Thus, when you decide on federal registration for A of a mark that is already in use, you will need to reconstruct the date of its first use in interstate commerce. And if the mark is new you will need to arrange for it to be used in interstate commerce. In either case, you should try to document A's first use, because its rights begin from this date and someone will need to swear to it in A's application for registration. To provide an early date of first use for a new mark, you may wish to arrange for a sale in interstate commerce before cartons and labels are in final form using a specially prepared label displaying the mark as you wish it registered. You will, of course, omit the registration notice ("Reg. U.S. Pat. Off." or the letter "R" in a circle) from this "first use" label. A's application will consist, in the main, of a professionally prepared drawing showing the mark as A has used it, and a sworn statement about when and with what goods or services A used the mark.

If A's mark is likely to be used in foreign countries, you will want to secure its registration in those countries. If possible, try to keep these registrations in the name of your parent American corporation rather than in the names of foreign subsidiaries or affiliates. There are American law firms that specialize in foreign trademark work with agents or correspondents in most of the countries where you are likely to want protection. The foreign situation is complicated, because some countries base ownership of a trademark on registration rather than use and permit marks to be registered before they are used. Thus, you will want to secure all the foreign protection you can to avoid trouble with unscrupulous people who may try to register your mark in foreign countries for themselves. An American serviceman stationed in Asia during World War II used some of his spare time to register in his own name several famous American trademarks and then demanded large sums from their owners to ransom their rights. The owners were able to get most of his registrations canceled but only after expensive and time-consuming legal proceedings.

Legal and administrative work connected with securing and maintaining trademark registrations is well suited for handling by or under the supervision of an inside lawyer. It is recurring, requires coordination with your marketing people, and calls for a trustworthy system of record keeping and calendars of renewal dates. Questions of trademark licensing are more likely to require specialized outside legal assistance; improper licensing can destroy your trademark by making it no longer point to a single guarantor of quality. Trademark licensing involves a delicate balance between exercising enough control over licensees to preserve trademark meaning but not so much that you run afoul of the antitrust laws. This problem becomes central to your business if it includes "franchising" others to operate stores, restaurants, hotels, services, etc., using your trademarks.

Patenting trade secrets.—The decision whether to patent a trade secret is usually made at the highest levels of A's management. As we have noted, it is more serious than a decision to register a trademark, because patenting a trade secret materially alters A's substantive rights. A patent gives A a government-sanctioned monopoly, independent of A's security maintenance but precisely limited both as to time and coverage; a trade secret, on the other hand, lasts only so long as it is kept secret, but it has no time or coverage boundaries. Where A's information consists of a discovery with many potential uses (e.g., an aerosol spray), or is a part of a complicated technology (e.g., chemicals or electronics), or has great potentiality for human welfare (e.g., penicillin or cortisone), then the disclosure and consequent opportunity for widespread use, on A's terms, that go with a patent make sense. But where A's information relates to its particular way of making a product of common use (e.g., recipes and formulas for foods, drinks, and proprietary medicines), or to business techniques for procurement, packaging, transportation, or marketing, then A is unlikely to be able to get a patent and, in any event, the more open-ended trade secret protection which you can control yourself will serve A better. To avoid having to separate the patentable from the non-patentable and to avoid being subjected to the time and coverage limitations of patents and the antitrust dangers of patent abuse, some corporations have chosen largely to eschew patents and to rely on their own security systems. If you decide to seek patent protection for A you will need the help of a patent lawyer to prepare and prosecute A's application, and if it succeeds you will also want legal help in licensing A's patent.

(iii) Self-help measures

In addition to law suits and government filings, there are things you can do on your own to protect A's good will and secrets. These self-help measures usually supplement rather than replace legal protections, and even though you rely mainly on your own vigilance to guard A's intangibles, you are backstopped by availability of legal sanctions against poachers.

Protecting trademarks.—We have discussed what you should consider in selecting a trademark for A. The more distinctive or fanciful and the less generic or descriptive the symbol to which you are trying to give trademark meaning, the easier is your task of creating and preserving this meaning. But whatever the mark may be, there are basic protective measures you should follow. Be sure your own people understand trademark meaning so that they can avoid using A's marks—in its advertising, sales promotions, labels, or sales literature—in ways inconsistent with their trademark status. For example, the owner of the trademark "Scotch" for cellophane tape would be ill-advised to claim that it sells "the original Scotch tape," because it would be implying that there are other, unoriginal Scotch tapes. Compare this generic use of "Scotch" to refer to a kind of product with the careful trademark way this mark is acutally used by its owners. Product is labeled "Scotch brand cellophane tape" with "Scotch" in distinctive lettering accompanied by "R" in a circle and by the statement: "Scotch is a registered trademark of 3M Co."

You also should be on the lookout for improper use—infringing, generic, or descriptive—of A's marks by its competitors and others. Infringing use by competitors is the most dangerous. Failure of A to stop competitor B from using A's mark in connection with B's products may cause the symbol to lose its trademark meaning, and competitors C, D, E, etc., can claim that what B can do they can do also. If A owns the mark "Scotch" and allows B to call his product "Scotch Tape," the symbol no longer points to A as the source, but rather to A or B.

Generic use by competitors also works, albeit somewhat more slowly than infringing use, to erode trademark meaning. If A allows B to refer to his product as "B brand Scotch tape" the symbol will come to mean a kind of tape that anyone can make and sell. And generic use by the public can have similar consequences. If A allows "Scotch tape" to enter the language and be listed in dictionaries as ordinary words—as former trademarks aluminum, cellophane, cola, and linoleum are listed— "Scotch" will similarly lose its trademark meaning. Dangers also arise if other people make descriptive use of A's mark. If A successfully establishes "Lite" as its trademark for beer (being careful to say "Lite beer from A" and not "A's Lite beer"), while B probably can still call its beer "B's light beer," A should take legal action if B calls its product "B's Lite beer," because B is using A's mark descriptively when he should be using the regular word "light" for this purpose.

Someone in your organization should be assigned the task of reviewing uses of A's trademarks by your own people, by competitors, and by the public, and of seeing that A responds to improper uses. Appropriate responses would seem to be:

—for your own people: firm admonitions combined with on-going educational efforts about trademark meaning,

—for competitors: stern warnings followed, if necessary, by legal action, and

—for the public: polite but insistent objections and requests that future improper uses be avoided.

It would be inappropriate for A to sue a magazine or newspaper that misuses its mark in a story or cartoon, but you should not let such incidents go by without objecting. If A has important marks that the public is prone to misuse (sometimes because the effectiveness of A's advertising has made A's mark a "household word"), you are likely to develop a series of form letters appropriate for various circumstances. And if public misuse becomes epidemic you may try to combat it with an advertising campaign designed to set the public straight. Printed mailing pieces that graphically make the point that A's symbol is a trademark, and should only be used as such, can also be helpful, particularly as enclosures to letters of protest to publications and the public.

Protecting trade secrets.—Trade secret protection concentrates on maintenance of internal security among your own people, because there is little that you can do about what outsiders do. Corporate security problems resemble those of other organizations with potential enemies—military establishments, foreign offices, law enforcement agencies, political parties, criminal groups, etc.—where effective security depends on clear perception at the top of what information needs to be protected combined with genuine group loyalty down through the ranks. While these conditions are characteristic of small business enterprises, they become harder to achieve as your organization gets bigger.

Most medium-sized and large corporations find it necessary to exercise some kind of structured control over their most sensitive information. Perhaps the most widely used approach is a rough sort of "need to know" standard: people are only given access to corporate information that they need to know in order to do their jobs. This generally sensible approach is not without problems. Withholding *all* unneeded information from people can make them feel that they are not trusted and can stultify otherwise loyal respect for justified withholding of information. Also, agreement is not always possible on exactly what people need to know to do their jobs, and people who feel they are denied needed information are likely to use this grievance to justify inadequate performance.

Here are a few very general suggestions for protecting your corporation's trade secrets:

—Try to make meaningful separations between sensitive and non-sensitive information, and then be very careful with the truly sensitive.

—When sensitive data has to be disclosed at middle and lower echelons of your organization, reduce risks by compartmentalizing disclosure on the basis of need to know.

—Avoid proliferation of copies of sensitive documents through numbered copies and "eyes only" rules against further copying.

—Discourage gossip and rumor-mongering by your people about corporate affairs both inside and outside the corporation (remember the copper discovery hypothetical).

CHECKLIST OF POINTS TO WATCH OUT FOR ABOUT ANTITRUST AND UNFAIR COMPETITION

(References after headings are to Sections of Chapter 9.)

1. Antitrust and unfair competition as growth problems (Section 9.1 and 9.2)

Why do your attitudes about avoiding antitrust entanglements and resisting unfair business tactics change as your business grows?

When your business is struggling and small, or even medium-sized, legal rules about antitrust and unfair competition seem largely irrelevant. To the extent they interest you, antitrust laws appear as possible sources of help against, and unfair competition rules as part of the structure that favors, the "establishment" of larger competitors, suppliers, and customers that are making you struggle. But the time comes when you are a part of that establishment and your attitudes change. Antitrust entanglements take their place among your hazards of doing business, and now you are a target for those who would misappropriate the reputations and trade secrets of others.

2. Advantages of understanding antitrust laws
   (Section 9.1 (a))

Why not leave antitrust to your lawyers?

Leaving antitrust to your lawyers is costly and inefficient. Since all antitrust problems do not equally require professional attention, you can save legal fees by knowing enough to know when you need help. And most antitrust problems are more economic than legal; handling of them calls for the kind of familiarity with details and nuances of your business and of markets where you buy and sell that can be acquired only by being there.

3. Objectives and enforcement of antitrust laws
   (Sections 9.1 (a) and (b))

What do antitrust laws seek to accomplish and who enforces them?

Antitrust laws seek to protect the freedom of sellers and buyers to bargain against the threats to such freedom of monopoly power and of contractual combinations. They assume that traders should be free to buy and sell in markets where terms are set by bargaining between seller and buyer rather than by a single powerfull seller or buyer (a monopoly) or by an agreement among sellers or buyers (a combination in restraint of trade).

Enforcement of antitrust laws is entrusted to the Antitrust Division of the Department of Justice, the Federal Trade Commission, and to those injured by violations, including consumers. The usual enforcement pattern is a government proceeding to establish a violation, followed by private claims for damages.

4. Using your lawyers
   (Section 9.1 (b))

How can you get optimum antitrust legal assistance?

While, as suggested in Point 2, lawyers need not and should not participate in every antitrust decision, how adroitly you use your lawyers in situations where they are needed largely determines your success in handling antitrust risks. For example, when you consider an important step entailing some antitrust risk, such as an acquisition of or a joint venture with another firm, you should go to your own lawyers, rather than ask advice from a government agency: a step that draws attention to your plans, highlights legal doubts, and probably forces a choice between being over-conservative and not following official advice.

For counsel on such major, non-recurring problems, requiring special expertise and objectivity, you will probably use outside lawyers. And you will generally go outside for jobs that require extensive man power over long periods, such as investigations and law suits. But for routine, recurring antitrust counseling, calling for familiarity with your operations and day-to-day contacts with your people, inside lawyers make more sense.

Things that lawyers, inside or outside, can do for you include: telling you what the legal rules are and how they have been applied to prior fact situations; marshaling relevant operating and market data in your situation and predicting probable applications of legal rules to these facts; and predicting whether antitrust enforcers are likely to be moved by your situation to take enforcement action. Since key variables affecting these predictions are your particular situation and its meaning in the light of legal rules, lawyers cannot serve you effectively if material facts are withheld from them.

In short, pick the right tasks for the right lawyers and give them the information they need.

5. Business protections against antitrust troubles
(Section 9.1 (b))

How can you plan and operate your business to minimize antitrust risks?

Although created in part by market forces beyond your control, the antitrust fact situations likely to confront you and your lawyers are largely of your own making. Some ways of doing business, at both planning and operational levels, generate more antitrust risks than others.

Planning choices by top management with antitrust implications include whether to grow by building new facilities or by acquiring other companies; if the decision is to acquire, what candidates to consider; whether to use divisions or subsidiaries when parts of your business compete with other parts; and what goals to set as to market shares for particular products, recognizing that too much success in occupying a market has its dangers.

At the operating level of buying and selling, practices likely to entail antitrust risks include: consulting with competitors about prices; charging different customers different prices without cost or function justifications; refusing to buy from or to sell to someone because of his dealings with others; making overly specific advertising claims; and mingling sales and patent licensing responsibilities.

6. Responses to charges of antitrust violations
　(Section 9.1 (b))

If charged with violating the antitrust laws, should you resist or negotiate, or do both?

Notwithstanding expert, adroitly used legal counsel and management sensitivity at all levels to antitrust dangers, you and your corporation may still be faced with charges, government or private, of antitrust violations. You will then need a plan of response which is likely to combine resistance and negotiation.

You will probably first explore the seriousness—legal, economic, and psychological—of the charges, the terms upon which they may be settled, and the relative costs of various gradations from hard-line resistance to softer-line negotiation. You will then work out a plan of response, utilizing legal predictions and cost estimates, combined with economic analyses and business judgments about what you can live with. Factors against protracted resistance are the legal fees, file searches, and demands on executive time and attention that are likely to spread over several years, plus the unhappy prospect of ending with a result less favorable than you could have had earlier by negotiation. Factors against early capitulation are loss of dignity, the business advantage in deferring the time when you have to operate under the constraints of a consent decree, and, most important, the possibility that continued resistance will yield a more favorable resolution of the controversy. While early settlements are usually unwise, eventual resolution by settlement frequently makes sense, in part because it increases your control over the publicity given to the case.

7. Legal protections against unfair business tactics
　(Section 9.2 (a))

Why do you need to know about them?

While you are interested in the law of unfair business tactics, as you are in antitrust law, to avoid running afoul of it, you are even more interested in what this body of law can do *for* you: how it can protect the reputation and secrets of your business from unfair use by others. You are a more effective officer or director if you can connect the specifics of your business with the generalities of rules about unfair competition, trademarks, and trade secrets. Like antitrust, this is a part of law that cannot prudently be left to lawyers, because its meaning and application turn on practical judgments, calling for first-hand business knowledge, as to what is "fair" in specific business contexts.

8. Unfair competition
   (Section 9.2 (b))

Why is defendant's conduct more significant than plaintiff's injury?

As the schoolmaster's case demonstrates, Anglo-American law starts with an assumption that all are free to compete in the usual ways with lower prices and better products, even when others get hurt thereby. But a long line of unfair competition cases have limited this freedom in special situations: when defendant hurts plaintiff by doing something that departs from ordinary business practice and in which there is no strong public interest. Examples include interference with plaintiff's production facilities, as in the duck pond case; motivation by malice rather than profit, as in the duck pond and barbers cases; and appropriation of information or goodwill belonging to plaintiff, as in the news services and jeweler cases, respectively. Thus, while your corporation, as plaintiff, will need to show some likelihood of injury to its business from defendant's tactics, its main concern will be to show that these tactics are not a necessary or desirable part of defendant's ordinary business.

9. Choosing trademarks
   (Section 9.2 (c))

How is trademark meaning created and preserved?

Trademark rights are illusive and fragile because they depend on the meaning of symbols. Trademark meaning, indicating that a product has a particular commercial origin, is difficult to give to a symbol that already has another meaning, especially if it already points to another origin, and also if it already has a meaning in ordinary usage: as descriptive term, geographical designation, or family name. And trademark meaning can be lost by a symbol acquiring some other meaning, most commonly by it becoming a generic name for a product.

In choosing a trademark, probably the most serious and costly mistake is to select and invest in a symbol that is "confusingly similar" to someone else's trademark. Then the choice becomes buying out the prior user or sacrificing your investment in the mark and perhaps being liable for damages and profits. Less serious, but also potentially costly and unsatisfactory, is selection of a descriptive, geographical, or family name mark. To convert such a symbol into a trademark takes time and money and never fully succeeds because others may still use the symbol truthfully in its non-trademark (descriptive, geographical, or family name) senses. Symbols with *no* previous meanings (Exxon, Kodak, Zerox) are easiest to turn into trademarks, but even made-up symbols can lose trademark meaning by becoming ordinary words pointing to a product rather than an origin (aspirin, cellophane, linoleum). See Point 12 on protecting trademarks.

10. Trade secrets
(Section 9.2 (d))

When will the law intervene to protect your corporation's private information?

As illustrated by the cases in the text, legal protection of a corporation's private information from disclosure to or use by others depends more on the way information is obtained or used than on the nature of the information, the corporation's proprietary interest in it, or its injury from disclosure or use. An employee who steals and sells a secret formula and a competitor who buys and uses it are both clearly acting wrongfully, and the law will intervene (wonder drug case); and the result would probably be the same whatever the information subjected to this kind of industrial espionage. However, an outsider who simply uses information he overhears (copper discovery case) has done nothing wrong; nor can a competitor who uses information already released (new services case) be charged with wrongdoing in obtaining the information, although the Supreme Court once held wrongful the competitor's manner of use. In the intermediate situation of one with unique technical knowledge gained from employer A going to work for employer B, a competitor, at a higher salary (space suit case), whether the law will intervene becomes unclear, because, although the results resemble industrial espionage, changing jobs is not wrong and ordinarily one can sell his own expertise to the highest bidder.

The fact that the space suit case was litigated shows that the nature of the information makes *some* difference: disclosure of technical information that resembles patentable data is more likely to be cause for legal intervention than disclosure of business or marketing information. While the government may protect such sensitive but non-technical information to the extent of not forcing a corporation to disclose it without safeguards for confidential treatment, corporate employees quite routinely take some such information with them in their heads when they change jobs, and the law generally leaves corporations to do their own policing (see Point 12).

11. Using the law to guard against unfair business tactics
(Section 9.2 (e))

How do you decide whether to bring lawsuits, register trademarks, and apply for patents?

Factors influencing a decision to bring a lawsuit include need for immediate help, chances of getting it, willingness to incur litigation costs, and possible psychological gains. If you decide to sue, you can improve your chances of success by hiring the right lawyers and suing the right defendants in the right courts for the right kinds of relief. The duck pond and wonder drug cases, and to lesser degree the jeweler case, are examples of pressing need for judicial help and probable success in getting it, and the space suit case of psychological incentives (deterrence of other employees) that might outweigh dim chances of success. In the schoolmaster's, news services', and copper discovery cases success seems too unlikely to justify lawsuits; and in the barbers case cost might be an important factor.

Cost, initial and continuing, is the main consideration in deciding whether to register trademarks, because cost is the only reason not to register. Advantages of federal and foreign registrations can be substantial and outweigh maintenance cost as to all marks about which you are serious. The meager advantages of state registrations, however, do not ordinarily justify their expense.

A decision to patent a trade secret effects a more major change in substantive rights and is made at higher management levels than a decision to register a trademark; cost seldom enters the discussion. The choice is whether to give up the formally unlimited but practically fragile rights in a trade secret in exchange for a government-sanctioned monopoly of limited time and coverage. Patents make sense for discoveries that are major and probably will have to be shared some day, that are in areas of complicated technology, or that will be difficult to keep secret. Reliance on trade secret rights makes sense when information is of doubtful patentability, when you want to keep it indefinitely under your sole control, and when you are confident that your security system will keep it secret.

12. Self-help measures against unfair business tactics
   (Section 9.2 (e))

How can you supplement legal protections with your own business practices?

Defenses against poachers of goodwill and trade secrets are not confined to special legal steps. They are part of regular business practices.

To protect your trademarks, your own employees, agents, and distributors need to understand trademark meaning (see Point 9) so they can avoid undermining your marks by misusing them. You should be on the lookout for and react promptly to any uses, internal or external, of your marks in ways inconsistent with their status as your trademarks. Someone in your organization should be assigned responsibility for policing usage of your trademarks and planning how you will react to misuses of them by your own people, by competitors, and by the public.

Trade secret protection is essentially an internal security problem. While the system for information protection within your corporation should be tailored to your own needs, good security systems are characterized by meaningful classifications as to the sensitivity of information, methods for containing truly sensitive data, and avoidance of the deadening and demoralizing effects of secrecy for its own sake.

A corporation's trademarks and trade secrets may also be protected by agreements with employees and outsiders. For an agreement obligating an employee to assign to the corporation and to keep confidential inventions, discoveries, and trade secrets, and to refrain from using the corporation's trademarks, see Appendix H.4 (g) For an agreement with outsiders for confidential treatment of a corporation's trade secrets, see Appendix H.5 (a).

10

Problems of Change: Transfers of Corporate Control

10

Problems of Change: Transfers of Corporate Control

Antitrust and unfair competition problems happen to your corporation largely on the market place; they involve external trade relations, and they can happen to individuals and partnerships as well as to corporations. We now turn to some problems, more internal to your corporation, that flow from its very corporateness: transactions involving transfers of control of the corporation itself.

Corporate control is not a new topic in this book. Examples of previous outcroppings about control include the following:

—In Chapter 3 we note that while proxy contests are one way of seeking corporate control, in recent years tender offers, where the control seeker buys shares instead of compaigning for votes, have become popular.

—In Chapter 4 we describe how control of a board of directors may be transferred without waiting for a shareholders' meeting by seriatim (successive) resignations and filling of vacancies by the other board members (a process sometimes called "cooptation").

—In Chapter 5 we note that, while shareholders usually maintain direct control of close corporations, as shares become more widely-held, with increased proxy voting, control tends to pass to officers and directors who control the proxy machinery.

—In Chapter 6 our concern is with ways to help shareholders of close corporations maintain their control powers.

—And in Chapter 7, where we are interested in putting values on shares, we mention the debate over who should benefit from the "control premium" which attaches to shares that carry with them power to control the corporation.

317

But we have not yet looked at control for its own sake—control as the sought-after objective for which structures are changed, contests waged, and prices bargained. There can, of course, be control struggles and transfers among existing owners and managers within a single corporation. Our focus in this chapter, however, is on control transfers that happen when two or more corporations combine or "merge." Before examining three specific control situations, we briefly outline the historical, economic, and legal background of corporate combinations.

Periods when corporate combinations become popular seem to coincide with periods of general prosperity and rising stock markets. We have had waves of combinations at the beginning of the 20th century, in the late 1920s, and through much of the period since World War II. Disparities between corporations in their price-earnings ratios, characteristic of bull markets, make acquisitions attractive to corporations with shares selling at high multiples of their per share earnings when they can find "target" corporations with higher earnings in relation to market prices of their shares.

> ■ **For example, if shares of corporation A sell at 30 times earnings and shares of corporation B at 10 times earnings, A can increase its rate of return simply by acquiring B at, or even well above, B's market price; the combination is attractive to A, apart from any actual economies that it produces, if earnings from B's operations can be maintained.**

More typically, the motive of the acquiring corporation is that it has built up a surplus which it would rather re-invest than pay out in dividends, and it sees a combination as the best way to achieve plant expansion, vertical integration, or diversification. Acquired or target corporations have a wider variety of motives for wanting to be acquired, including such considerations as inadequate capital, unprofitable operations, lure of capital gains, and aging of their founders or key executives. Combination may provide answers to anticipated estate administration needs both as to liquidity and as to valuation of the acquired corporation's shares. (Recall our struggles in Chapter 7 with valuing close corporation shares.) The 1960s saw increased resort to involuntary combinations through tender offers—where the acquiring corporation goes directly to the shareholders of the target corporation, rather than negotiating with its management—due to the liquid position of many large corporations, making cash offers possible, and apparent scarcity of willing combination partners.

We note in Section 9.1 how corporate combinations have been affected by antitrust laws, particularly by the 1950 amendment to the Clayton Act which prohibits acquisition of shares or assets of another corporation "where in any line of commerce in any section of the country, the effect of such acquisition may be substantially to lessen competition, or to tend to create a monopoly" (Clayton Act§7, 15 U.S.C. §18). A series of Supreme Court decisions in the 1960s narrowed the limits of permissible horizontal, vertical, and conglomerate combinations.

Horizontal combinations between competitors, even when their percentages of the market are small, have become suspect, with the Court adopting flexible definitions of geographical and product markets which recognize that local as well as national competition needs protection and, as to product markets, take account of sub-markets resulting from technology or business practices.

> ▪ Section 9.1 poses a hypothetical acquisition by a Wisconsin beer maker of a New York wine maker and asks whether they are in different geographical and product markets. Growing wine consumption in the United States combined with increasingly national distribution of beer and wine make it easier to argue that this acquisition will have substantial competitive effect.

Vertical combinations with suppliers or customers that foreclose competitors from a substantial portion of a market (say more than 5 per cent) are suspect unless they can be justified as necessary to improve the position of a company that is much weaker than its competitors.

> ▪ For example, it would be easier for American Motors than for General Motors to justify a vertical combination with a steel or rubber producer.

Since conglomerate combinations do not inevitably eliminate some competition, as do horizontal and vertical combinations, they have been outlawed only when the acquired firm was a potential competitor of the acquiring firm, or when the acquisition creates opportunities for anti-competitive reciprocal dealings or market advantages (like volume advertising discounts) or raises significant barriers to new entries into a market.

This chapter, like Chapter 7, is built around three hypothetical illustrations of kinds of control transfer problems. Each uses Dighaldoe Corporation, the coal mining venture that has made several appearances. First we assume that Dighaldoe wants to acquire control of a smaller coal producer, Pigmy Coal Company. Then we assume that Digges, Hall and Doe, the Dighaldoe founders, are faced with an attempt by Octopus, Inc., a conglomerate on the lookout for "special situations," to secure control of Dighaldoe. Finally, we assume that Babylon Corporation, a large coal user that wants a "captive" coal source, approaches Digges, Hall, and Doe with an attractive offer to buy control of Dighaldoe. In the Pigmy situation Dighaldoe is the acquiring corporation and Pigmy is a willing target; in the Octopus and Babylon situations Dighaldoe is the target—unwilling vis-à-vis Octopus, willing vis-à-vis Babylon. Our point of view generally is that of Digges, Hall and Doe, as they successively seek the best ways: to acquire control of another business; to fight off an attempt to take control of their own business; and to sell their control position to an outsider on their own terms.

Section 10.1 Acquiring Control of Another Corporation

"Acquisition" is a general, non-legal term that encompasses any securing of control of a business by an outside interest. Our focus is on acquisitions involving two corporations: an acquirer and a target. For this section we assume that Dighaldoe Corporation, after successfully making the public offering of its shares described in Section 7.3, decides to acquire the business of Pigmy Coal Company, which is incorporated in the same state as Dighaldoe.

Recall that in preparation for its public offering Dighaldoe increased its authorized shares to 150,000. Of these shares 30,000 are held by Digges, Hall, and Doe, 70,000 have been sold to the public for $45 per share, and 50,000 remain authorized but unissued. Assume that Dighaldoe's annual earnings are now running about $4 per share ($400,000); its shares are being traded over-the-counter at about $50 per share; their book value has increased from $34 to $40, representing an increase in earned surplus from $300,000 to $900,000; and Dighaldoe has invested most of its retained earnings and proceeds of the public offering in expanding operations and has no excess working capital. As to Pigmy, assume that its book value is about $300,000, but its market value is unknown because its shares have not been traded; its annual earnings are running about $50,000; and its 1,000 shares are equally owned by Messrs. Pig and My, political refugees from east Asia, who have offered to sell their business to Dighaldoe for $500,000.

We look first at some of the alternative methods and their legal contexts available to Dighaldoe in acquiring control of the Pigmy coal mining business and then at some of the considerations that might influence Dighaldoe in deciding how it should proceed.

(a) Available acquisition methods

The parties have several options as to how they arrange Dighaldoe's acquisition of Pigmy:

—Dighaldoe can acquire Pigmy's assets or its shares;

—Pigmy or its shareholders can receive cash, Dighaldoe shares, or some other consideration; and

—they can proceed with or without corporate changes to either corporation.

Corporate changes are unnecessary if Dighaldoe buys Pigmy's assets or a majority of its shares. If an asset purchase is for cash, Dighaldoe ceases to be interested in Pigmy, which is now a holding company for proceeds of the sale; Pig and My can dissolve Pigmy and divide the proceeds or have Pigmy re-invest the proceeds.

If an asset purchase is for Dighaldoe shares, Dighaldoe will be interested in Pigmy as a substantial Dighaldoe shareholder; Pigmy again becomes a holding company, now of Dighaldoe shares, and Pig and My again have the option of dissolving Pigmy, with the resultant distribution giving each direct ownership of Dighaldoe shares. But if Dighaldoe buys Pigmy shares—whether for cash, Dighaldoe shares, or other consideration—Dighaldoe must exercise the control it has bargained for through Pigmy's corporate processes. Dighaldoe might, of course, choose to use this control to merge Pigmy into Dighaldoe, or to dissolve Pigmy and receive distribution of its assets.

To plan factual changes in corporate control you need to know something about legal rules concerning changes in corporate structure, shareholder voting and appraisal rights, and de facto mergers.

Structural changes.—In non-technical usage the term "merger" refers broadly to the many ways of combining control of two corporations. Its narrower legal meaning is limited to a process, set out in state corporation acts, involving two corporations (A, the surviving corporation, and B, the merging corporation), whereby B vanishes into A. A related process called "consolidation" occurs when two pre-existing corporations, A and B, vanish into a third new corporation, C. With merger, A plus B results in A; with consolidation, A plus B results in C; with both, the population of corporations is reduced by one: merger makes an existing corporation disappear, and consolidation makes two existing corporations disappear and a new corporation come into being.

A "sale of assets" occurs when corporation B sells all or substantially all of its assets to corporation A. In theory, a sale of assets is not a change in corporate structure because A and B remain structurally intact. However, in practice sales of assets can have consequences equivalent to mergers and consolidations and so get some of the same legal protections.

Charter amendments and dissolution are structural changes that may accompany transfers of control but do not themselves transfer control.

Shareholder approval.—Many of the technical legal problems raised by structural changes involve rights of shareholders of combining corporations to vote on changes and the "appraisal" rights of shareholders who dissent from changes to have their shares purchased at "fair value." Most state statutes require in cases of merger or consolidation that shareholders of both A and B approve the action; however "short mergers" between parent and subsidiary corporations are permitted without shareholder approval under provisions like the following in the Model Act:

> *Any corporation owning at least ninety percent of the outstanding shares of each class of another corporation may merge such other corporation into itself without approval by a vote of the shareholders of either corporation (§75).*

While some states require that shareholder approval be by two-thirds of the shares of each class (California) or two-thirds of outstanding shares (Illinois), the trend is toward approval by simple majorities. The Model Act requires approval by a majority of shares of each class for mergers, consolidations, sales of assets, charter amendments, and dissolutions. Delaware requires approval by a majority of shares of each class for charter amendments, but simply a majority of outstanding shares for mergers, consolidations, sales of assets, and dissolutions.

Delaware goes further with mergers and dispenses with approval by the surviving corporation's shareholders if its charter is not amended, its shares retain identical rights before and after the merger, and its shares are not increased by more than 20 percent ($251(f)). The 20 percent provision fits a New York Stock Exchange rule requiring shareholder approval in such situations irrespective of state law. An "upside down" merger—where A, a relatively small corporation, absorbs B, a larger corporation—will, of course, call for issuance by A of so many additional shares as to make qualification under the 20 percent rule impossible.

A non-statutory maneuver to avoid surviving corporation shareholder approval is the so-called "triangular" or "three party" merger which routes shares of A, the surviving corporation, to shareholders of B, the to-be-merged corporation, through C, A's wholly-owned subsidiary, with which B can merge without involving A's shareholders, and which then can be, if desired, merged into A through a short merger. The procedure works as follows: A organizes a subsidiary, C, and transfers to it enough A shares to accomplish the agreed A-B combination; B then merges into C, with B shareholders receiving the A shares held by C as part of the merger and C taking over B's assets and liabilities. If there is some reason for keeping B in existence—as where it has contract or franchise rights of doubtful transferability—a "reverse" triangular merger can be employed: instead of B merging into C, C would merge into B, with C's shareholder, A, receiving all of B's shares as part of the merger, and B's former shareholders receiving C's assets, which consist of its holding of A shares. However, shareholders of A may induce a court to look through a triangular maneuver and grant them voting and appraisal rights under the "de facto merger" doctrine discussed below.

Appraisal rights.—The Model Act ($$80 and 81) gives appraisal rights to shareholders of both surviving and merging corporations to a merger, of both parties to a consolidation, and of the selling corporation in a sale of assets, provided that shareholders seeking appraisal

        —file written objection to the proposed action before the shareholders meeting,

        —do not vote in favor of the action, and

        —within 10 days after the vote make written demand on the surviving corporation for payment of the fair value of their shares.

However, appraisal rights are not available to shareholders of a surviving corporation if

—a vote of its shareholders is not needed to authorize the action (thus eliminating appraisal rights in short mergers and perhaps justifying triangular mergers), or

—their shares are registered on a national securities exchange (on the assumption that it's easy enough for holders of listed shares to secure their fair value by selling them).

Delaware does not grant appraisal rights in cases of sales of assets nor in cases of mergers and consolidations where shares are listed on a national exchange or held of record by more than 2,000 shareholders (§262 (k)) on the assumption that such widely distributed shares can be sold at fair value over-the-counter. Against these assumptions it can be argued that fair value does not always coincide with market value, an argument that receives support from judicial consideration in appraisal cases of such non-market factors as asset value, reproduction cost, capitalized earnings, and history of dividend payments.

De facto mergers.—The de facto merger doctrine is a judicial response in the equity tradition to moves not technically requiring shareholder voting or appraisal rights but which seem to a judge to be equivalent in result to moves carrying these rights. Under the Model Act the de facto merger argument might be raised by shareholders of either corporation where the exchange of shares technique is used, by shareholders of the purchasing corporation in a combination by sale of assets, or by shareholders of the surviving corporation in a triangular merger: all situations where there is no statutory right of appraisal. And in Delaware and other states that do not provide appraisal on either side of an assets acquisition, the argument might also be raised by shareholders of the corporation selling its assets. The de facto doctrine has been held to apply, where, for example, corporation A buys the assets of corporation B, using A shares for the purchase in such quantity that B shareholders secure control of A. See *Farris v. Glen Alden Corp.*, 143 A.2d 25 (Pa. 1958).

As might be expected, the de facto doctrine has not made much headway in Delaware, where courts are unwilling to extend appraisal rights beyond statutory limits. However, in most states, including Delaware, a shareholder who demonstrates that a transaction treats him with manifest unfairness is usually granted relief.

(b) Acquisition planning considerations

From the assumed facts and examination of acquisition options and relevant legal constraints, two preliminary judgments emerge about how Dighaldoe wants to fashion its acquisition of Pigmy:

—Because Dighaldoe is short of cash, it wants to pay for Pigmy with its own shares.

—Because Dighaldoe has public shareholders, it seeks an acquisition procedure that does not require their approval nor give them appraisal rights.

We assume that the parties are able to agree that the price for Pigmy will be 10,000 Dighaldoe shares, leaving open for now whether Dighaldoe gets Pigmy's shares or its assets, and whether Pigmy remains a corporation, is merged into Dighaldoe, or is dissolved. The 10,000 share price represents the $500,000 asking price of Pig and My converted into shares at $50 per share, the current market value. On a capitalized earnings basis, a $500,000 valuation of Pigmy assumes a multiplier of 10 ($500,000 ÷ $50,000), compared with Dighaldoe's multiplier of 12.5 ($5,000,000 ÷ $400,000). On these terms the acquisition increases Dighaldoe's per share earnings from $4 to $4.09 ($450,000 ÷ 110,000 shares) and decreases its per share book value from $40 to $39 ($4,300,000 ÷ 110,000 shares).

> ▪ **The $4,300,000 figure for Dighaldoe's consolidated after-acquisition book value assumes that Pigmy's assets enter Dighaldoe's books at their $300,000 book value on Pigmy's books, rather than at $500,000 or $400,000—the market and book values, respectively, of the consideration, i.e., 10,000 Dighaldoe shares. In accounting terms, using Pigmy's book value would treat the acquisition as a "pooling of interests" rather than a "purchase."**

In this subsection we examine some tax, corporate, and business considerations that have a bearing on how the Dighaldoe-Pigmy acquisition is planned.

(i) Tax considerations: tax-free reorganization

While exchanges of property ordinarily are taxable events, the Internal Revenue Code makes an exception for corporate "reorganizations." Qualification as a tax-free reorganization has two important tax consequences: non-recognition of gain and carryover of basis. Where two corporations combine, as in our Dighaldoe-Pigmy hypothetical, tax-free reorganization status means that no gain is recognized to Dighaldoe or Pigmy or to their shareholders. But it also means that Dighaldoe takes the Pigmy business with its $300,000 existing basis, and that the tax burden for Pigmy's $200,000 appreciation in value prior to the acquisition shifts to Dighaldoe. As noted about a comparable situation in Section 7.1, the low basis can increase Dighaldoe's future taxes on ordinary income by reducing depreciation allowances; for former Pigmy assets sold by Dighaldoe before they are fully depreciated, the low basis will increase Dighaldoe's capital gains taxes.

> ■ In Section 7.1 A's individual proprietorship is incorporated with new investors, B and C, under circumstances that qualify the transaction as a tax-free incorporation under IRC §351, presaging tax detriments for the new corporation, ABC, because it takes A's business at A's basis even though A is being "payed" more than this amount in ABC shares.

Dighaldoe's incentive to structure the transaction as tax-free is also diminished because it appears that Pigmy does not bring with it net operating losses which tax-free status would enable Dighaldoe to utilize.

> ■ Impact of combination transactions on operating loss carryovers is beyond the aspirations of this book. The basic rule is that a net operating loss can be carried back three years and forward seven years, being "used up" against income of these years in chronological order. Following certain tax-free reorganizations, the acquiring corporation succeeds to certain tax attributes of the acquired corporation, including its net operating loss carryover privileges.

To qualify for tax-free treatment, an acquisition must fall within one of the definitions of "reorganizations" in clause (A), (B), and (C) of IRC §368 (a)(1):

—Type A: "a statutory merger or consolidation."

—Type B: "the acquisition by one corporation, in exchange solely for all or a part of its voting stock, of stock of another corporation if, immediately after the acquisition, the acquiring corporation has control of such other corporation (whether or not such acquiring corporation had control immediately before the acquisition)." "Control" in this context "means the ownership of stock possessing at least 80 percent of the total combined voting power of all classes of stock entitled to vote and at least 80 percent of the total number of shares of all other classes of stock of the corporation."

—Type C: "the acquisition by one corporation in exchange solely for all or part of its voting stock (or in exchange solely for all or a part of the voting stock of a corporation which is in the control of the acquiring corporation), of substantially all of the properties of another corporation, but in determining whether the exchange is solely for stock the assumption by the acquiring corporation of a liability of the other, or the fact that property acquired is subject to a liability, shall be disregarded."

These definitions establish three kinds of tax-free reorganizations: (A) formal merger or consolidation under applicable state law, the acquired corporation vanishing into the acquiring corporation or with the acquiring corporation into a new corporation; (B) shares-for-shares exchange, the acquired corporation becoming a subsidiary at least 80 percent owned by the acquiring corporation; and (C) shares-for-assets exchange, the acquired corporation transferring substantially all of its assets to the acquiring corporation. The justification for making these types of transactions tax-free is that acquired corporation shareholders are not "selling out" but are continuing as co-owners of their enterprises, albeit a much augmented enterprise with many other co-owners.

In light of these definitions, if Dighaldoe buys Pigmy's shares or assets for cash or for any consideration other than "solely" for Dighaldoe shares, Pig and My will each have to pay capital gains tax on $100,000. We thus assume that they will sell for $500,000 worth of Dighaldoe shares only on a tax-free basis; and we further assume that Dighaldoe's desire to acquire Pigmy without cash expenditure outweighs the disadvantages of carryover of Pigmy's basis. But note that whether the reorganization is type A, B, or C is being left open.

Transactions which literally fit one of the §368 definitions of tax-free reorganizations may nevertheless be denied tax-free treatment because they are at odds with the spirit of the exemption under one or more of the following judicially created doctrines:

— "Business purpose": As in other areas of tax law, an acquisition must have an independent business purpose and not be designed solely to reduce taxes.

— "Step transaction": Purportedly separate transactions will be treated as one if they are steps in a larger transaction.

— "Continuity of proprietary interest": Shareholders of the acquired corporation must receive a proprietary interest (shares) in the acquiring corporation as a substantial part of the consideration for what is transferred; however, for the purposes of this doctrine proprietary interest need not be common shares, nor need it go to all of the shareholders of the acquired corporation

— "Continuity of business enterprise": The acquiring corporation must conduct some business, although it need not be the same business as that conducted by the acquired corporation.

Type A mergers, while requiring more complicated corporate procedures, avoid definitional entanglements built into types B and C share exchanges and asset acquisitions by the phrases "in exchange *solely* ... voting stock" and "*substantially* all of the properties." Type B exchanges are particularly in danger of being "tainted" by extraneous consideration: for example, previous acquisitions of the acquired corporation's shares for cash may be combined with the share exchange under the step transaction doctrine. While type C asset acquisitions are less vulnerable to taint by extraneous consideration, problems arise about the meaning of "substantially" if less than all of the assets of the acquired corporation are transferred.

Under a type A merger Dighaldoe can issue Pig and My non-voting securities, which it cannot do under types B and C. However, even under types B and C, Dighaldoe can issue shares to finance the Pigmy acquisition with different voting rights than Dighaldoe's other shares.

In summary, it appears that tax considerations confirm the preference on practical grounds for making Dighaldoe shares the consideration to be paid for the Pigmy business but leave unresolved the question of whether the acquisition should proceed by merger, share exchange, or asset acquisition.

(ii) Corporate considerations

In planning how Dighaldoe should acquire Pigmy, Digges, Hall, and Doe will be trying to avoid:

—the need for a shareholder vote to approve the transaction;

—the possibility that dissenting shareholders will assert appraisal rights; and

—any undue and unavoidable jeopardy to their own control of Dighaldoe.

Shareholder vote.—A shareholder vote is not needed to provide authorized but unissued shares for the Pigmy acquisition, because before its public offering Dighaldoe amended its charter to increase its authorized shares to 150,000 (see Appendix E.1(a)), of which 100,000 are issued and outstanding. However, if Dighaldoe wants to issue some different kind of shares for the Pigmy acquisition, a charter amendment approved by shareholders is needed, although such amendment by itself would not involve appraisal rights. While a shareholder vote is needed to merge Pigmy into Dighaldoe before Dighaldoe acquires the Pigmy shares, once these shares are acquired, making Pigmy a wholly-owned subsidiary of Dighaldoe, Pigmy can then be merged into Dighaldoe without shareholder approval (or appraisal rights) because of the short merger provision (see Appendix E.4 and E.5).

Appraisal.—Shareholder appraisal rights vary for the three tax-free acquisition methods: statutory merger, share exchange, and asset acquisition. As we have noted, practically all state statutes give dissenting shareholders of both corporations appraisal rights in connection with statutory mergers, while no state statute requires appraisal when the share exchange method is used, and states which grant appraisal rights in asset acquisitions generally limit them to shareholders of the corporation selling its assets. Thus, it appears that Dighaldoe can avoid appraisals by using either a shares-for-shares or a shares-for-assets acquisition of Pigmy, provided that it does not get into a de facto merger situation or open itself to a claim by public shareholders that they are being treated unfairly. Neither of these possibilities seems substantial: the Pigmy acquisition will not shift control of Dighaldoe; and, while the transaction will reduce book value of Dighaldoe shares slightly (from \$40 to \$39), this reduction seems much too small to support an argument of unfair treatment, particularly because the acquisition will also increase Dighaldoe's per share earnings (from \$4 to \$4.09).

Control.—Issues of 10,000 shares to Pig and My will reduce the combined voting strength of Digges, Hall, and Doe from 30 percent to 27 percent. This reduction in itself should not shake their control position, but introduction of two new large shareholders creates a power base for future proxy contests. Protective measures that might to taken against Pig and My using their voting power in Dighaldoe to threaten the incumbents' control position include a voting trust (see Appendix H.3) and use of different classes of voting shares. A voting trust could be used in connection with any of the three types of tax-free reorganizations, because the IRS looks through the voting trust and considers the voting shares requirement satisfied if underlying shares may vote without regard to who actually does the voting. However, under most state laws voting trusts are limited to durations of ten years. Classification of shares to reduce voting power of Pig and My would provide a more permanent solution, but would require a charter amendment and a shareholder vote. In any event, Pig and My probably will balk at either device because they will not want "second class" shares with reduced market value because of their reduced voting powers. Thus, Digges, Hall, and Doe need to consider whether they are willing that Pig or My or both of them join the Dighaldoe board and become a part of Dighaldoe management, thereby increasing the voting strength of the management coalition from 30 to 36 percent (110,000 shares $\div$ 40,000 shares). If they are not willing to have this happen, they should have serious reservations about proceeding with the transaction.

In summary, corporate considerations, emphasizing the expenses of a shareholder vote and of appraisal rights for dissenting shareholders in connection with a statutory merger, appear to narrow the options to a shares-for-shares or a shares-for-assets acquisition of Pigmy.

(iii) Business considerations

With tax and corporate considerations seeming to leave Dighaldoe with the alternatives of issuing 10,000 shares for Pigmy's shares or its assets, we turn to some business consideration that may help Dighaldoe decide. The choice is between acquiring the whole of the Pigmy business by making Pigmy a subsidiary of Dighaldoe—a neat, uncomplicated, but possibly risky procedure—against a less tidy, more complicated, but possibly safer procedure involving multiple deeds, assignments, and assumptions of liability to convey the assets and liabilities of Pigmy that Dighaldoe wants to take over.

▪ **We noted the tax danger that if less than all of Pigmy's assets are taken the transaction's tax-free status might be in question under the "substantially all" language.**

We will examine some factors that Dighaldoe should consider in making this choice.*

If Pigmy holds valuable franchises, leases, mineral rights, or contracts which are not assignable without consent, share acquisition has an advantage over asset acquisition because the need for obtaining consents is avoided. Similar considerations apply if Pigmy has loan indentures or other agreements which restrict its participation in mergers, consolidations, or transfers of assets. Other considerations that may favor share acquisition, which allows continuation of separate corporate identities, include: the possibility of bringing a union or a different union into the picture; problems of reconciling and meshing different employee benefit plans of the two corporations; and possible business reasons for preserving Pigmy's corporate charter.

In the other direction, if Pigmy is a party to undesirable leases or contracts, including burdensome patent license agreements, share acquisition becomes less attractive. Perhaps most significantly, if Dighaldoe is concerned about possible undisclosed liabilities of Pigmy, a clean-cut purchase of the assets of Pigmy that Dighaldoe wants, leaving Pigmy with all responsibility for its own liabilities, has strong appeal. However, even with a share acquisition, Dighaldoe can secure some protection against contingent and unknown liabilities by including in the deal an agreement that part of the Dighaldoe shares to be issued to Pigmy or its shareholders will be withheld or placed in escrow for a specified period (see Appendix H.6(c)), to be sold at market or to be cancelled at an agreed value, to offset any undisclosed liabilities that arise during that period.

As a rough generalization, the larger the corporations involved the more likely they are to proceed by share rather than by asset acquisition. The acquiring corporation wants to be sure of getting everything and frequently wants to preserve the corporate identity of the acquired corporation; and it is willing to rely on the undertakings of the sellers that there are no substantial hidden liabilities. With smaller, more marginal firms, the acquisition is more typically aimed at specific assets of an unsuccessful operation; and the acquiring side's respect for the reliability of the acquired side is likely to be low.

If Dighaldoe acquires Pigmy's assets there is no question of later merging Pigmy into Dighaldoe, because the Pigmy corporation remains owned by Pig and My, who may decide to leave the Dighaldoe shares in Pigmy or to dissolve Pigmy and distribute the Dighaldoe shares to themselves.

---

*Many of these factors are suggested in Darrell, "The Use of Reorganization Techniques in Corporate Acquisitions," 70 *Harv. L. Rev.* 1183 (1957).

▪ **In a type C reorganization through acquisition of assets, the parties can, without upsetting tax-free status, arrange to have the Dighaldoe shares issued directly to the Pigmy shareholders.**

If Dighaldoe acquires Pigmy shares it will have many choices about how it proceeds further. It can retain and operate Pigmy as a subsidiary. It can transfer Pigmy's assets to Dighaldoe and keep the corporate shell, perhaps for name-holding purposes. It can merge Pigmy into Dighaldoe through a short merger (see Appendix E.5). Or it can dissolve Pigmy and distribute its assets to Dighaldoe (see Appendix E.7). Unless there is some reason for maintaining Pigmy's corporate existence or identity, the decision will probably be to merge it into Dighaldoe. Thus, the final choice between a type B or a type C acquisition of Pigmy by Dighaldoe becomes a business decision.

Section 10.2 Keeping Control of Your Own Corporation

This section is about attempts by outsiders to gain control of your publicly-held corporation and how you, as an incumbent manager of the target corporation, can resist. There are three general ways that outsider A—who may be an individual, corporation or group—can seek control of target corporation B:

—A can wage a proxy contest for votes of B shareholders to elect A's nominees to B's board of directors (see Section 3.2(c)). As we have learned, proxy contests are expensive, difficult to win, and closely regulated by the SEC; and while victory yields control, ownership must be shared with others.

—A can make an exchange offer to B shareholders, asking them to exchange their B shares for A shares or for securities of a corporation controlled by A. Since B shareholders are being solicited to "buy" securities, A's offer will require 1933 Act registration (see Section 7.3).

—Instead of seeking B shareholders' votes or asking them to exchange their B shares, A can try to buy their shares for cash. Prior to 1968 an effort of this sort was virtually free of federal regulation unless A resorted to a "deceptive practice" that might bring the purchase under the SEC's antifraud Rule 10 b-5, which covers both purchases and sales of securities.

Let's now look at the third method involving purchases for cash. A can acquire B shares through open market purchases or through a general offer, called a "tender offer," to all B shareholders indicating that A will buy a designated number of B shares at a designated price. The offer is called a tender offer because B shareholders are being asked to "tender" their shares for purchase by

A. "Takeover"—a general, non-legal term referring to any taking over of control of a corporation by someone not previously in control—is sometimes used in the term "takeover bid" to refer to a tender offer, often when the user wishes to give the offer a sinister or disreputable tinge.

Suppose Dighaldoe becomes the target corporation for a takeover bid. Its officers and directors are in this defensive position because things are not going well. We assume that for some reason their attempt to acquire Pigmy aborts, so that Dighaldoe still has 100,000 shares outstanding: 30,000 held by its managers and 70,000 quite widely distributed as the result of the public offering described in Section 7.3. While its book value has increased to $5,000,000, or $50 per share, it is currently earning only $3.75 per share and its over-the-counter trading price has declined to around $30—i.e., 60 percent of book value and about eight times earnings. On the brighter side, it has recently discovered, but not made public, the probability that its coal reserves may be much more valuable than anticipated.

Now comes Octopus, Inc., a conglomerate with money to invest that seeks out and tries to secure control of businesses with valuable assets that are having operational problems. After capturing control of a concern Octopus may put in a new management and try to improve its operations, sometimes with a view to later selling its control position at a profit; but Octopus may also decide that it can maximize its profits by dismantling the business and liquidating its assets. Dighaldoe has come to the attention of Octopus both because of its falling earnings and low market value in relation to book value and also because Octopus has heard rumors about Dighaldoe's coal reserves. Dighaldoe is advised by the president of Octopus that Octopus has acquired 6,000 Dighaldoe shares by open market purchases and that it plans to make a cash tender offer for the remaining 94,000 shares at $40 per share. If Digges, Hall, and Doe decide to refuse this offer, how can they defend themselves against the takeover bid of Octopus? Before looking at the defense tactics available to them, let's sketch the development of federal regulation in this area.

(a) Federal regulation of takeovers

Genesis of the Williams Act.—Takeover bids through cash tender offers for control of corporations listed on the New York and American Stock Exchanges increased from eight in 1960 to 44 in 1965. The SEC argued that such offers face shareholders with "investment decisions"; that it does not make sense to leave these offers unregulated when proxy contests and share exchanges are regulated; and that therefore legislation was needed to assure that shareholders are informed about the identity and plans of those seeking to buy their shares. In response, opponents argued that the proposed legislation was really to protect incumbent managements rather than shareholders; that some managements deserve to be replaced; that shareholders who are considering selling have no concern with the identity or plans of buyers; and that corporate control should be bargained for competitively like other valuable commodities. The SEC view prevailed and in 1968 Congress adopted the Williams Act amending §13 (the reporting section) and §14 (the proxy section) of the Securities Exchange Act of 1934 by adding §§13 (d) and (e) and 14 (d), (e), and (f).

Open market acquisitions.—Section 13 (d) applies to any "person"—including a "group" who act for the purpose of acquiring, holding, or disposing of securities of a corporation—who, after acquiring shares of a class registered pursuant to §12 of the 1934 Act, is directly or indirectly the beneficial owner of more than 5 percent (originally 10 per cent) of such class. Within 10 days after acquisition the covered person must send to the issuer, to each exchange where the shares are traded, and to the SEC a statement disclosing

—the background and identity of those by whom or for whom the purchases have been or are to be effected;

—the source and amount of funds to be used in making the purchases;

—if the purpose of the purchasers or prospective purchasers is to acquire control of the business of the issuer, any "plans or proposals" which they may have to liquidate the issuer, to sell its assets to or merge it with any other persons, or to make any other major change in its business or its corporate structure;

—the number of such shares beneficially owned, directly or indirectly by the person and by each of his associates; and

—information as to any contracts, arrangements, or undertakings with any person with respect to any securities of the issuer, including transfers, joint ventures, loan or option arrangements, puts or calls, guarantees of loans, guarantees against loss or of profits, division of profits or loss, or giving or withholding of proxies.

Tender offers.—Section 14 (d) makes it unlawful for any person "to make a tender offer" (without defining "tender offer") for any class of shares registered under the 1934 Act if, after consummation of the offer, the person would directly or indirectly be the beneficial owner of more than 5 per cent of such class, unless at the time the offer is made to shareholders the offeror has filed with the SEC the above described statement. Subsections 14 (d)(5)-(7) regulate terms of a tender offer itself. Shares deposited by shareholders in response to a tender offer may be withdrawn during the first seven days of the offer and after the offer has lasted for 60 days. Where more shares are deposited than the offeror is willing to purchase, shares must be taken up as nearly as possible pro rata according to the number of shares deposited by each depositor. When the offeror increases the offering price, the higher price shall be paid to each shareholder whose shares are taken up whether or not they are taken up before the price increase. Under Rule 10b-13, applying also to share exchange offers, once a tender offer has been made, the offeror may not during the term of the offer purchase shares of the target corporation except pursuant to the offer.

Disclosure of "plans or proposals."—There are several difficulties with the requirement that an offeror disclose its plans or proposals to liquidate, sell the assets of, merge, or to change the business or corporate structure of the target corporation (§13 (d)(1)(C)). How is this requirement reconciled with the SEC principle that projections and predictions should be avoided in prospectuses and proxy statements (see Section 7.3 (c) of the text)? With how much detail must an offeror describe its plans? And how definite must plans be to call for disclosure: suppose the offeror is considering several alternatives? It appears that offerors' lawyers will be called upon to devise disclosure language which will simultaneously satisfy the SEC, be sufficiently general to cover possible eventualities without being premature, and avoid undue business disadvantage to the offeror by tipping its hand.

Formation of a "syndicate or group."—The provision in §13 (d)(3) that when two or more persons act together "for the purpose of acquiring, holding, or disposing of" shares of the target corporation their shares shall be combined under the 5 percent test extends coverage of the act beyond outsiders seeking control and beyond situations involving actual or contemplated purchase of shares. Mere formation of a coalition of existing shareholders holding more than 5 percent of a class of shares amounts to an "acquisition" by the group sufficient to trigger filing requirements. *GAF Corp.* v. *Milstein.* 453 F.2d 709 (2d Cir. 1971), cert. denied, 406 U.S. 910 (1972). However, the SEC is authorized to exempt acquisitions not for the purpose of seeking control (§13 (d)(6)(D)). Problems under the §13 (d)(3) include difficulty in ascertaining just when a group is formed and uncertainty whether the filing requirement applies to management groups which pool their interest to fight a takeover; also whether it continues to apply to an insurgent group which has made a filing and then succeeded in its takeover attempt.

Civil liability.—Perhaps the most important provision of the Williams Act is §14 (e) making it "unlawful" to make misstatements or misleading omissions of material facts, "or to engage in any fradulent, deceptive, or manipulative acts or practices in connection with any tender offer." This provision appears to provide an open-ended source of civil fraud liability for tender offers comparable to what Rule 10b-5 does for purchases and sales of securities; and §14 (e) has largely superseded that Rule in cases involving tender offers. Like 10b-5, 14 (e) is not limited to shares registered under the 1934 Act. It appears to authorize civil actions by target corporations and their shareholders, whether or not they have tendered shares; however, the Supreme Court has held that it does not authorize actions by unsuccessful offeror corporations and their shareholders. *Piper* v. *Chris-Craft Industries, Inc.*, 430 U.S. 1 (1977).

Replacement of directors without shareholder vote.—As §14 (e) extends the civil fraud liability of Rule 10b-5 to tender offers, §14 (f) extends the disclosure requirements and injunction potential of the proxy rules to replacement of boards of directors when they are made as part of control transfers following share purchases. Section 14 (f) requires that information about new directors like that required in proxy statements be filed with the SEC and sent to shareholders if a majority of a board are replaced without shareholder vote "pursuant to any arrangement or understanding with the person or persons acquiring securities in a transaction" subject to §§13 (d) or 14 (d). This provision was added at the urging of the SEC to cover seriatim resignations and replacements of directors, which are possible without shareholder approval under most state corporation acts (see Section 4.1 (b) of the text), and to aid shareholders in seeking injunctive relief where information requirements are not met. While §14 (f) introduces a new complication in control transfers, note that it applies only to target corporations already subject to the proxy rules and it does not reach situations where transfer of effective control is achieved by a change of less than a majority of the board or by acquisition of less than 5 percent of the outstanding shares.

With this background we are ready to examine what officers and directors of Dighaldoe should do when confronted with the bid of Octopus for control of Dighaldoe. Their first decision, of course, is whether to oppose the bid, to go along with it, or to seek some compromise for sharing their control with Octopus. While addition of Octopus nominees constituting less than a majority of the Dighaldoe board will not require notification of shareholders under §14 (f) of the Williams Act, the provision does foreclose unannounced transfer of a majority of the board seats to Octopus.

We will assume that the Dighaldoe managers are convinced that their business has a good future under their own management, that in spite of recent reverses they can by a strong effort keep the allegiance of enough of the public shareholders to maintain themselves in control, and that a takeover by Octopus would not be in the best interests of Dighaldoe or its shareholders because of the danger that Octopus would seek a quick profit by selling its coal reserves. Holding these convictions and having decided not to capitulate to nor to negotiate with Octopus, how should Digges, Hall, and Doe proceed? They need to know what is required of Octopus under the Williams Act and, if necessary, seek the assistance of the SEC in holding Octopus to compliance. At the same time, they should be aware of any constraints on their own actions and those of Dighaldoe under federal or state law concerning both their opposition to the Octopus tender offer and any purchases they make of Dighaldoe shares. And they should consider a variety of other defense tactics that might help them.

(b) Legal constraints on the purchaser

The Williams Act applies to Dighaldoe shares because distribution of its shares to 500 or more shareholders in the public offering described in the text at Section 7.3 made it necessary to register Dighaldoe shares pursuant to §12 of the 1934 Act.

> ▪ **This 1934 Act registration is not to be confused with the 1933 Act registration for the public offering itself: see the text at Section 7.3 (e)(ii).**

Because Octopus has bought 6,000 of Dighaldoe's 100,000 outstanding shares, it appears that the provisions of §13 (d) on open market purchases are already applicable, Octopus having acquired more than 5 percent of the Dighaldoe shares. Within 10 days after Octopus makes the acquisition that puts its holdings over 5,000 shares it is required to send to Dighaldoe at its principal executive office by registered or certified mail and to file with the SEC a statement complying with §13 (d). Dighaldoe should find when the Octopus holdings passed 5,000 shares. If Octopus has not made timely compliance with §13 (d) Dighaldoe should report this failure to the SEC. When Dighaldoe receives the information from Octopus required by §13 (d), Dighaldoe will be in a better position to plan its defensive campaign because it will know who is involved in the attempted takeover, where they are getting their money, what their plans are for Dighaldoe (including whether they plan to liquidate it), how many Dighaldoe shares they hold, and any arrangements they may have with other Dighaldoe shareholders about giving or withholding proxies. Also, under §13 (d)(2), Octopus is obligated to keep Dighaldoe and the SEC informed of material changes in these facts.

The president of Octopus says that his corporation plans to make a cash tender offer for the remaining 94,000 Dighaldoe shares. Such an offer will bring §14 (d) into play and it will be unlawful for Octopus to make its offer unless, when it is first made to Dighaldoe shareholders, it files with the SEC a statement containing the information required under §13 (d). This must also be sent to Dighaldoe not later than the date it is sent to shareholders. If Octopus fails to comply with §14 (d), Dighaldoe can ask a federal court to bar Octopus from proceeding with its offer and can ask the SEC to use its powers to halt the offer.

Rule 10b-5, which seems to impose very broad disclosure duties in connection with purchases and sales of securities, arguably can be used by Dighaldoe shareholders who have already sold shares to Octopus as the basis for actions for rescission or an accounting, on the ground that Octopus failed to make disclosure about its information concerning Dighaldoe's coal reserves. However, there has been judicial reluctance "to read Rule 10b-5 as placing an affirmative duty of disclosure on persons who in contrast to 'insiders' or broker-dealers did not occupy a special relationship to a seller or buyer of securities" (Judge Friendly in *SEC* v. *Great American Industries*, 407 F.2d 453 (2d Cir. 1968)). Octopus has no special relation to Dighaldoe shareholders. In fact, it was probably because under Rule 10b-5 there was apparently no duty for those seeking control to make disclosure of their plans or information that the Williams Act was thought to be needed. And those who opposed the Williams Act argued that in the absence of special relationships people should not be forced to disclose what they plan or know when they buy shares.

In disclosing its "plans and proposals" for Dighaldoe under §§13 (d) and 14 (d), will Octopus need to disclose the rumors it has picked up about Dighaldoe's coal reserves? These rumors seem to relate more to its motives than to its plans, and since they are not within the knowledge of nor are they verifiable by Octopus, it would seem that they need not be disclosed. However, §14 (e) has a counterpart to Rule 10b-5 making unlawful "fraudulent, deceptive, or manipulative acts or practices, in connection with any tender offer." While this provision does not seem to reach the open market purchases by Octopus, it may prevent Octopus from lawfully withholding in its tender offer disclosure of whatever information it has about Dighaldoe's coal reserves.

(c) Legal constraints upon the target corporation and its incumbent managers

The two most obvious ways to defend against a takeover attempt are for the target corporation or its incumbent managers to urge outside shareholders not to sell their shares or for them to buy shares themselves. And obviously, these two ways call for the creation of different images about the corporation's prospects. The former way is controlled mainly by federal law; the latter is subject to both federal and state law.

Urging rejection of the tender offer.—Section 14 (d)(4) provides that any solicitation or recommendation to accept or reject a tender offer shall be made in accordance with SEC rules. The SEC has adopted Rule 14d-4 which requires Dighaldoe to file with the SEC specified information. Some of this information must also be sent to shareholders with the written solicitation or recommendation, for example, the identity of the maker of the tender offer and the reasons for accepting or rejecting it, and any arrangements or understandings in regard to the solicitation between Dighaldoe or its management and Octopus. Information required by the SEC (but that does not have to be sent to shareholders) includes information as to all transactions in Dighaldoe shares effected during the past 60 days by Dighaldoe and its officers and directors.

Section 14 (e) prohibits deceptive practices in connection with tender offers. It covers "any solicitation of security holders in opposition to or in favor of any such offer." In opposing the tender offer of Octopus, the Dighaldoe managers will probably want to say all that they can truthfully say about the probable value of its coal reserves. Their chief risk, under §14 (e), would seem to lie in their painting an over-optimistic, rather than an over-pessimistic, picture of Dighaldoe's prospects.

Purchasing of shares.—Legal constraints on share purchases by Dighaldoe and it managers include those imposed by the Williams Act, Rule 10b-5, and state rules about corporate and insider share purchases.

While §§13 (d) and 14 (d) of the Williams Act do not apply to share purchases by Dighaldoe, they may apply to share purchases by its officers and directors. If Digges, Hall, or Doe purchase additional shares to maintain their control they will probably have to file a Williams Act statement. And, as we have indicated, they may be under an obligation to file this statement, even without new purchases, if they form a "group" to oppose the Octopus takeover attempt.

Section 13 (e) makes it unlawful for Dighaldoe to purchase its shares in contravention of SEC rules, which require an issuer-purchaser to provide its shareholders with designated information. After Dighaldoe receives notice of the Octopus tender offer, SEC Rule 13e-1 makes it unlawful for it to purchase its own shares unless it discloses to its shareholders, among other things, the purpose of the purchase and the source of the funds used therefor, including a description of any funds it borrowed for that purpose. Under §13 (e) (2), purchase by or for a person controlling Dighaldoe, which would probably include Digges, Hall, and Doe, would be deemed a purchase by Dighaldoe.

Purchases of Dighaldoe shares by Dighaldoe or its managers without disclosing to sellers Dighaldoe's discovery about the probable value of its coal reserves could well be a deceptive practice under both §14 (e) and Rule 10b-5. Thus, if Dighaldoe and its management are buying shares rather than soliciting shareholders in opposition to the Octopus tender offer, the danger becomes pessimism rather than optimism. Both the corporate repurchase of shares at excessive prices, and the issuance of new shares at insufficient prices, if done to avoid transfers of control, have given rise to causes of action under Rule 10b-5.

Under state laws, in addition to disclosure problems based on considerations of fairness to selling shareholders, Dighaldoe managers can face a charge of possible misuse of corporate funds for private ends if they have Dighaldoe buy shares to protect their control positions. In Section 8.1 (d) concerning fiduciary and anti-manipulative factors that constrain corporations purchasing their own shares, we examined a series of Delaware cases involving corporate purchases made to preserve control positions of incumbent managers. These cases teach us that if Dighaldoe managers want to use Dighaldoe funds to ward off the Octopus threat they should be able to show corporate purposes beyond mere preservation of their own positions. They should try to make the purchases a matter of business judgment to protect the welfare of the whole corporation: for example, against the threat of liquidation to secure a quick profit. Of course, this problem does not arise if Digges, Hall, or Doe purchase Dighaldoe shares for themselves with their own funds.

Other defense tactics.—Besides trying to persuade Dighaldoe shareholders not to sell to Octopus or to sell to Dighaldoe or its managers, a variety of other moves can help thwart the Octopus offensive by making it more expensive and more difficult. Most common would be a law suit claiming Williams Act violations by Octopus. Other moves aimed at confronting Octopus with the purchase of more or higher priced Dighaldoe shares can include the following:

—Issue more shares: Dighaldoe directors might authorize issuance of additional shares, to themselves or to employees or other persons they can count on for support. As with corporate purchases of shares, it helps to have a corporate purpose to justify the additional shares, beyond preserving their own control. And, as noted above, the corporation's sale of new shares to friends of management should be at an adequate price, to avoid problems under Rule 10b-5.

—Defensive merger: To give Octopus a larger fish to swallow Dighaldoe might try to arrange a merger with a third corporation.

—Dividend increase and share split: By increasing the dividend rate and by splitting the shares to make them more marketable, Dighaldoe may be able to increase their market price.

Other moves calculated to put legal road blocks in the way of the Octopus takeover of Dighaldoe include the following:

—Create antitrust problems: Dighaldoe might seek out a defensive merger with a third corporation which is a competitor of Octopus thereby creating antitrust problems for Octopus if it tries to take over the merged business.

—Reincorporate: An increasing number of states have corporation statutes that make takeovers difficult. Dighaldoe could reincorporate in one of these states.

—Charter amendments: Takeover can be made more difficult by amending Dighaldoe's charter to require high votes for charter amendments, mergers, and sales of assets; to increase the number of and classify the directors and to prohibit their removal except for cause; or to create a class of preferred shares for sale to friendly buyers with veto powers over mergers and sales of assets.

—Contract amendments: It may be possible for Dighaldoe to amend its loan agreements or labor agreements to provide that the loan will be defaulted or that wages will increase if there is a change in Dighaldoe's management.

Section 10.3 Selling Control of Your Own Corporation

We come now to a cluster of questions about legal constraints on you as one of those exercising control of a corporation, as to how you transfer control to someone else. (In the next chapter we will consider constraints on how you *exercise* your control.) In Chapter 5 we noted how actual corporate control is exercised by different groups, depending largely on the dispersal of the corporation's shares: by shareholders directly, when shares are closely-held; by directors, when shares are too dispersed for direct shareholder control but not so dispersed as to prevent formation of coalitions to elect representatives to the board; and by officers, when shares are distributed so widely that effective control power depends on control of the proxy machinery. Following its public offering described in Section 7.3, Dighaldoe has been between the second and third of these three stages: its managers represent a coalition of large shareholders, but they must also depend on proxies of outside shareholders because they directly control less than a majority of the shares. Digges, Hall, and Doe are controlling but not majority shareholders. Their control is a consequence not only of their share ownership but also of their corporate offices. They have what is sometimes called "working control."

In this section we will assume that the Pigmy acquisition attempt described in Section 10.1 aborts and that the Octopus takeover bid described in Section 10.2 is successfully resisted, without the Dighaldoe share ownership or structure being changed (i.e., we are assuming that Octopus disposes of its Dighaldoe holdings on the market). Thus, Dighaldoe still has 100,000 shares outstanding: 70,000 widely distributed, and 30,000 held by Digges, Hall, and Doe. We assume that its book value remains as it was in Section 10.2—$5,000,000 or $50 per share; that the favorable information about its coal reserves is publicly known; and that its current annual earnings and market price have risen to $5 and $60 per share, respectively.

Babylon Corporation, a joint venture of several large coal users formed to acquire assured "captive" sources of coal, is attracted to Dighaldoe by its coal reserves. Because of its own working capital problems, Babylon wants to acquire control of Dighaldoe for the least possible cash outlay. If Babylon buys all outstanding Dighaldoe shares at their present market price (which is probably impossible), the cost is $6,000,000. In an effort to secure control of Dighaldoe for $3,000,000, the president of Babylon offers to buy the 30,000 shares of Digges, Hall, and Doe—who constitute the Dighaldoe board of directors—for $100 per share if they will turn over their Dighaldoe directorships to persons named by Babylon. Digges, Hall, and Doe are in agreement that they want to accept the Babylon offer, which will make each of them a millionaire. (We will not try to deal with their tax problems nor with whether they would prefer to receive cash or some other consideration for their Dighaldoe shares.)

This section concentrates on legal and ethical problems, because Dighaldoe managers and Babylon are in agreement about the business terms of their transaction. They now want to know: Is the transaction legal and ethical? Doubts arise largely from what may happen to Dighaldoe public shareholders, owners of 70 percent of the Dighaldoe shares, who are not participants in the transaction. We first examine the position of this sizeable group of de facto minority shareholders in terms of corporate government and their rights to be notified of and perhaps to participate in the passing of control of their corporation from the Dighaldoe people to the Babylonians. We then turn to their ownership rights and the rights, if any, of the corporation as a whole to claim the "control premium" that Dighaldoe managers are to receive for their shares. Finally, we consider whether, apart from procedural rights in corporate government and derivative rights in corporate property, fiduciary rights of public shareholders to be treated with loyalty and fairness by their officers and directors are being violated.

(a) Corporate government

As we have learned in earlier chapters, while shareholders are supposed to elect directors, vacancies on the board occurring between shareholders' meetings may be filled by a majority of the remaining directors (Model Act §38; see Appendix F.4(b)). This provision would appear to enable Digges, Hall, and Doe to relinquish their Dighaldoe directorships to Babylon's nominees (X, Y, and Z) without shareholder action by proceeding as follows: Digges resigns and Hall and Doe elect X to fill the vacancy; Hall then resigns and X and Doe elect Y to fill the vacancy; and finally Doe resigns and X and Y elect Z to fill the vacancy (see Section 4.1 (b)). Working against this scheme, however, are the rules that directors—unlike shareholders who can agree in advance how they will vote—are supposed to keep themselves free to act for "the best interest of the corporation" (Model Act §35), and that it is illegal to buy and sell corporate offices.

Purchase of corporate office.—The leading case on this issue involved facts not unlike ours. D, who owned 28.3 percent of the voting shares of C corporation and controlled its board, agreed to sell his shares to P and to turn over his control of the C board to P. D refused to perform this contract on the ground that it was illegal. A federal court, applying New York law, said the agreement was not illegal on its face and that it should be enforced unless it could be shown that it was not "a practical certainty" that a majority of shareholders would go along with the transfer of control. However, Judge Friendly considered this test unworkable and said that if he were sitting on the New York Court of Appeals he would hold the agreement "violative of public policy save when it is entirely plain that a new election would be a mere formality—i.e., when the seller owned more than 50% of the stock." *Essex Universal Corp.* v. *Yates*, 305 F.2d 572 (2d Cir. 1962). In a subsequent case, where D's share ownership in C was only 3 percent, a New York court held the elections of new directors illegal, saying:

> *The underlying principle is that the management of a corporation is not the subject of trade and cannot be bought apart from actual stock control. . . . Where there has been a transfer of a majority of the stock, or even such a percentage as gives working control, a change of directors by resignation and filling of vacancies is proper. . . . Here no claim is made that the stock interest which changed hands even approximated the percentage necessary to validate the substitution. In re* Caplan's Petition, 246 N.Y.S. 2d 913 (1964), aff'd 249 N.Y.S. 2d 877 (1964).

Williams Act disclosure requirements.—Apparently §14 (f) which was, as we noted in Section 10.2, added to the Securities Exchange Act of 1934 by the Williams Act in 1968 will apply to the Dighaldoe-Babylon situation. Because there is an "arrangement or understanding" with Babylon that new Dighaldoe directors are to be elected "otherwise than at a meeting of security holders," §14 (f) requires that, before the new directors take office, Dighaldoe file with the SEC and transmit to all shareholders of record who would be entitled to vote at a meeting for election of directors information about the new directors substantially equivalent to that required for a proxy statement if they were nominees for election as directors at a shareholders' meeting. Section 14 (f) was inserted at the urging of the SEC to provide timely disclosure to shareholders of any imminent transfers of control so that any shareholders who object to such transfers can seek injunctive relief. It would also seem that upon acquiring the 30,000 Dighaldoe shares Babylon will have to comply with § 13 (d) by sending a statement to Dighaldoe and to the SEC; its plan to transform Dighaldoe into a captive coal producer is certainly a "major" change that requires disclosure. While § 13 (d) does not require that this statement be sent to shareholders, an energetic shareholder who receives the § 14 (f) disclosure could then obtain the § 13(d) statement from the SEC and use it as the basis for seeking for an injunction or other relief. Judge Friendly noted in the *Essex* case: "A special meeting of stockholders to replace a board may always be called, and there could be no objection to making the closing of a purchase contingent on the results of such an election" (305 F. 2d at 581).

In summary, while the Dighaldoe-Babylon agreement for sale of control of Dighaldoe is not necessarily invalid as a matter of state law relating to corporate government, federal disclosure requirements prevent it being performed without notice to shareholders and the SEC and thereby increase the possibility of legal attacks on the transaction. These attacks will probably combine corporate government arguments relating to the sale of corporate offices and directors' duties to act in the corporate interest with other arguments. We now turn to some of these other arguments.

(b) Control as a corporate or a private asset

We move from shareholders' governmental rights to their ownership rights. Here we are concerned not so much with the legality of a control transfer arrangement as with who profits from it. In the preceding subsection no account was taken of the $100 per share price, $50 over book value and $40 over market price, that Babylon is offering Digges, Hall, and Doe for their control shares. Our question now is whether they may keep this "control premium" (which we will assume is $40 per share, or $1,200,000 for 30,000 shares) all for themselves or whether they may have to share it with other shareholders.

Control premiums.—Our starting point is a statement made in 1932 in Berle and Means, *The Modern Corporation and Private Property*:

> [The power to control] is an asset which belongs only to the corporation; and ... payment for that power if it goes anywhere, must go into the corporate treasury.

To put this statement into actual business contexts, we consider two cases from Minnesota and California, neither of which involved control transfers outside the corporations, but which dealt with how power to control can be converted into money.

—The Minnesota case involved a recapitalization of a corporation in order to disperse voting power, which had been concentrated in 44 out of about 430,000 shares, among all shareholders. In return, rights of the 44 old voting shares to participate in the corporation's earnings and assets were increased on a 1000 to 1 ratio. Their voting rights declined from 100% to 9.3%, and their participation rights increased from .0093% to 9.3%. The court refused to interfere with this arrangement, apparently because it had been approved by over 90% of the shareholders and because the old voting shares had a much higher market value than the non-voting shares. *Honigman* v. *Green Giant Co.*, 208 F. Supp. 754 (D. Minn. 1961), aff'd, 309 F. 2d 667 (8th Cir. 1962), cert. denied, 372 U.S. 941 (1963). Note that in the Dighaldoe-Babylon situation we have neither shareholder approval nor difference in market price, because there has been no previous trading in the control shares.

—The California case involved an operating corporation (O) with shares that had book value of over $4,000 per share; these shares had never been split and no effort had been made to make them marketable. A group holding about 85% of O's shares formed a new holding corporation (H) and exchanged their O shares for H shares at a ratio of 100 H shares for one O share, and through publicity and listing on a national exchange created a market for H shares which were soon being traded at $50 per share. The O majority refused to allow the O minority to exchange its O shares for H shares. The court ordered that the minority be given equal treatment. *Jones* v. *H.F. Ahmanson and Co.*, 460 P.2d 464 (Cal. 1969).

From these cases it appears that it is more enlightening to inquire what is being done with control than to try to establish who "owns" it. In the *Honigman* case "minority" shareholders were not being excluded from something in which many of them wanted to share; in the *Jones* case, the exclusion element was strong.

While Adolf Berle's argument that control is a corporate asset is supported by the way corporations are supposed to be governed and by the questionable rightness of allowing power over other peoples' money to be bought and sold, the social morality of the business community accepts the buying and selling of control, and judges have generally been unwilling to interfere with this moral judgment. The general legal (and ethical) rule seems to be that control is a thing of value for those that exercise it and that Digges, Hall, and Doe have no legal duty to other Dighaldoe shareholders to arrange with or exact from Babylon an offer that it also buy their shares at the same price or at any price.

Opportunity theories.—In recent years those who are concerned about private profits in control transfers, instead of arguing that control is a corporate asset—which, as we can gather from the *Honigman* case, may be too rigid a contention to stand up in all situations—have talked about "opportunity" in two ways: whether all shareholders should have equal opportunity to participate in the economic fruits of control (which the *Jones* case seems to affirm); and whether the premium was being paid not just for control but also to exploit a business opportunity that belonged to the corporation. The argument for equal opportunity to sell is that when a control seeker buys on the open market all shareholders have an equal right to sell, so the same right should apply when Babylon quietly approaches the managers of Dighaldoe. See Andrews, "Stockholders' Right to Equal Opportunity in the Sale of Shares," 78 *Harv. L. Rev.* 505 (1965).

Both equality of opportunity to sell and corporate opportunity may help to explain the different results in the *Honigman* and *Jones* cases. In the *Honigman* case the "premium" derived solely from a surrender of voting power: from 100 percent to less than 10 percent. The corporation itself was not involved in the transaction, which was an internal trade-off of "goods" (voting power and asset rights) among its shareholders, most of whom thought they were being treated equally. In contrast, the *Jones* case involved creation of a market for the corporation's shares through a device that excluded 15 percent of its shareholders. It can be argued that they were being denied equal access to an opportunity which was not really a function of control but was there to be exploited by the whole corporation. It is one thing to "sell" control for a profit, and it is something else to "use" control for individual profit rather than for the corporate good.

To summarize where we stand, it appears that it is not unlawful or unethical on its face for Digges, Hall, and Doe—as 30 percent shareholders in control of Dighaldoe—to transfer control to a new board of directors named by Babylon without a Dighaldoe shareholders' meeting (although Dighaldoe shareholders will have to be informed), nor for them to keep for themselves the $1,200,000 control premium which they are receiving. We now need to examine whether there may be special fact aspects of this transfer that (1) may persuade a judge that he should intervene, or (2) lead Digges, Hall, and Doe to conclude that they should not accept Babylon's offer.

(c) Breach of fiduciary duties

Our discussions of director voting and of corporate opportunity have been largely cast in terms of shareholder and corporate rights. We also need to consider our problem in terms of the fiduciary duties of officers, directors, and controlling shareholders to be careful and loyal in protecting the interests of those whose property they are managing. To analyse these duties we need to go beyond the technicalities of how vacancies are filled and beyond abstract questions of who "owns" control. We now need to look at the whole transaction between Dighaldoe and Babylon and its likely consequences to Dighaldoe's public shareholders.

Looting cases.—An important exception to the right of those in control to sell their control at the best price they can get has been developed in the so-called "looting" cases. Many of these cases involve investment companies which are lootable because their assets can be liquidated quickly and quietly. Suppose that Group A is in control of corporation C. Group B offers to buy control of C under circumstances that should warn A that B's intentions may be dishonorable, but A makes no effective inquiry. B gets control of C, appropriates its assets and disappears. Courts have quite uniformly held that S, a shareholder of C who did not participate in the transfer and who is damaged by the looting, may recover from A, who had a duty to make reasonably sure of the buyer's intentions. Sometimes the size of the premium being offered to A for control of C is enough to put A on inquiry about what B is up to.

Newport Steel case.—While Babylon is not a looter in the traditional sense, because it does not plan to liquidate Dighaldoe, it does plan to use Dighaldoe for its own purposes to supply coal to the coal users who have joined to form Babylon. This part of our hypothetical is based on a much litigated transaction involving Newport Steel Corporation. Feldman, who was the president and chairman of the board of Newport, held about 37 percent of its shares and controlled selection of its board; the remaining shares were publicly held. In 1950 Feldman sold his Newport shares to Wilport Corporation for $20 per share, even though their over-the-counter market price was about $12 and their book value about $17. Immediately following the sale Feldman and his associates resigned their Newport directorships and were replaced by Wilport's nominees. Wilport was a syndicate of end-users of steel who wanted an assured source of supply in a market becoming tighter because of the Korean War. Public shareholders of Newport claimed that the failure to disclose to them the selling price or that Newport was to become a captive subsidiary of Wilport was a fraud upon them that violated SEC Rule 10b-5. Their claim failed because the court held that Rule 10b-5 applies only to fraud upon "purchasers" or "sellers" of securities and these plaintiffs were neither. *Birnbaum* v. *Newport Steel Corp.*, 193 F. 2d 461 (2d Cir. 1952), cert. denied, 343 U.S. 956 (1952), to which we refer in Section 2.4 (a).

In a subsequent suit public shareholders of Newport claimed that Feldman had violated his fiduciary duties because part of the consideration for his shares was for power to control allocation of corporate products in a period of short supply. Although there was no claim of fraud, misuse of confidential information, nor outright looting, the court ordered that Feldman share his profits with other Newport shareholders because it found misappropriation of corporate opportunities "in siphoning off for personal gain corporate advantages to be derived from a favorable market situation." *Perlman* v. *Feldman*, 219 F. 2d 173 (2d Cir. 1955). Judge Swan dissented because he saw no fiduciary duty on Feldman as a shareholder not to sell his control shares at a premium, and because there was no convincing evidence that the price paid Feldman included a payment for voting as a director to elect new directors, nor that Wilport would use its control power to hurt Newport.

What do we learn from the looting and Newport Steel cases that will help Digges, Hall, and Doe respond to the Babylon offer? The $100 price is enough above market and book value to put them under some obligation to satisfy themselves that Babylon does not plan to misuse Dighaldoe by paying it less than market prices for coal. It would seem that they should insist upon an undertaking by Babylon on this point. It would help if there were some way, such as by other offers, to show that $100 is a reasonable price for control shares. Babylon's apparent unwillingness to open the offer at this price to other shareholders is disquieting and faces the Dighaldoe managers with some difficult choices. If they urge Babylon to give all shareholders opportunity to deal on an equal basis, as their instincts for fairness may prompt them, Babylon will probably either refuse or reduce its offering price—saying that if it had wanted to proceed this way it would buy shares on the market and then try to oust Dighaldoe management in a proxy fight—and an express refusal by Babylon adds to the danger signals that are already flying about entrusting the corporation to Babylon. But if they do not even try to get equal treatment for all, this omission may be the basis for an accusation against them of lack of care and loyalty. The latter seems the less serious difficulty. Thus, if Digges, Hall, and Doe are convinced that Babylon will lay out only $3 million and if they succeed in obtaining an assurance from Babylon that it will pay fair prices for Dighaldoe coal, they probably should not raise the question of equal opportunity.

In planning the transaction care should be taken that all of the consideration is being paid for the shares and none of it for what Digges, Hall, and Doe are going to do as directors. Here again it will help if it can be shown that $100 per share is a reasonable price for the control block of Dighaldoe shares then trading at $60.

A final thought: There is the possibility that Digges, Hall, and Doe will have moral scruples about selling control of their corporation to someone who is not willing to treat all shareholders on an equal basis. And these scruples may be encouraged by knowledge that the SEC and all the shareholders will be informed of what they are doing and that shareholders will have access through the SEC to the price they are receiving, which may mean that they will have to defend their bargain in court.

CHECKLIST OF POINTS TO WATCH OUT FOR
CONCERNING TRANSFERS OF CORPORATE CONTROL

(References after headings are to Sections of Chapter 10.)

1. Keeping acquisitions tax-free (Section 10.1(b))

How may shareholders of a target corporation be spared being taxed?

Owners of a target corporation will ordinarily consent to an acquisition only if it qualifies as a tax-free reorganization, meaning that it must be (A) a statutory merger or consolidation, (B) a shares-for-shares exchange, the target becoming at least 80% owned by the acquirer, or (C) a shares-for-assets exchange, the target transferring "substantially all" of its assets to the acquirer; all three being situations where target shareholders continue their ownership interest in their enterprise. Each alternative requires payment for the target business in the acquirer's shares.

2. Keeping acquisitions uncomplicated (Section 10.1(b))

How may shareholder votes and appraisal rights be avoided?

An acquisition by a public acquirer becomes more complicated and expensive if shareholders must approve it and if dissenters may insist on being bought out at a "fair value." If the acquisition involves a merger or a change in acquirer's articles, a shareholder vote is unavoidable; and a merger also entails appraisal rights unless the acquirer's shares are listed on a national exchange. Acquisition by exchange can be accomplished without a shareholder vote by having in the articles an available cushion of authorized but unissued shares, as suggested in Section 1.5(a). Hence, considerations of simplicity and economy favor an exchange, either shares-for-shares or shares-for-assets, in preference to a merger.

3. Balancing shares-for-shares and shares-for-assets exchanges (Section 10.1(b))

Why is the choice mainly a business judgment?

A shares-for-shares exchange gives the acquirer control of the whole enterprise, without need for separate conveyances but with the danger of hidden liabilities. A shares-for-assets exchange is more cumbersome but safer. If the acquirer trusts the target's managers to disclose liabilities, and if the acquirer has reasons for wanting the target corporation, as distinguished from its property, it should go the shares-for-shares route, perhaps protecting itself by escrowing the acquirer's shares being transferred to target shareholders for long enough for liabilities to turn up. For an escrow agreement, see Appendix H.6(c). If acquirer does not trust target's managers, or if only identifiable assets (but which may be "substantially all" of target's assets) are wanted, the shares-for-assets route may make more sense.

4. Control of acquirer after an acquisition (Section 10.1(b))

How can those in control of the acquirer protect their position when using shares for an acquisition?

Any sort of tax-free reorganization introduces new shareholders into the acquirer corporation. How they may affect its control depends on the size and cohesiveness of their holdings and their willingness to cooperate with those who control the acquirer. Protective measures include a voting trust, generally limited by law to 10 years duration, and different classes of shares, which have no time limit but require amendment of acquirer's articles and may be unacceptable to target shareholders who may not want to come in as "second class" shareholders, of the acquirer. Relevant questions include: Can those in control live with the new shareholders? Are they willing to have them represented on the acquirer's board? For a voting trust agreement, see Appendix H.3.

5. Disclosure by those attempting a takeover (Section 10.2(a) and (b))

What disclosure does the Williams Act require of an offeror making a tender offer for shares of a target corporation?

Within ten days after acquiring more than 5% of a target corporation's shares, the offeror must inform the target corporation, exchanges where the shares are traded, and the SEC of the offeror's identity and background, the source of his funds, and any "plans or purposes" to liquidate the target corporation, to sell its assets or merge it, or to make major changes in its business or structure. A tender offer for more than 5% of the target's shares is unlawful unless the offeror has filed such a statement. And where, without a shareholder vote, a majority of the board is replaced (the likely consequence of a successful takeover), information similar to that required in a proxy statement must be filed with the SEC and sent to shareholders.

6. Disclosure by those resisting a takeover (Section 10.2(c))

What disclosure does the Williams Act require of a target corporation urging rejection of a tender offer?

If a target corporation solicits its sharesholders to accept or reject a tender offer, it must file with the SEC information similar to that required of the offeror, including information as to transactions in target shares by its officers and directors during the past 60 days; and the solicitation to shareholders must describe any arrangements or understandings between the offeror and the target or its management.

A major concern for the target corporation and its officers in soliciting shareholders to accept or reject a tender offer is that they may misstate or fail to disclose material facts, thereby opening themselves to claims of deceptive practices in violation of §14(e), the tender offer counterpart to Rule 10b-5. For example, in the Dighaldoe-Octopus illustration in Section 10.2, if Dighaldoe solicits its shareholders to reject the Octopus tender offer, care should be taken to avoid overly optimistic statements to shareholders about the probable value of the Dighaldoe coal reserves.

7. Purchasing shares to resist a takeover (Section 10.2(c))

Should the target corporation or individual insiders do the purchasing?

Shares purchases by a target corporation to resist a takeover have the advantage of leaving unchanged the relative positions of the remaining shareholders. However, in the Dighaldoe-Octopus context, Dighaldoe's poor earnings indicate a probable shortage of working capital. Corporate purchases may be hard to justify as prudent uses of corporate funds, unless individual insiders are unable to raise the purchase money and unless the Octopus penchant for quick profits can be construed as a major threat to the whole corporation, not just the insiders. Keep in mind that, whoever makes the purchases, the source of the funds will have to be disclosed to the SEC and the public shareholders.

Individual purchases by Digges, Hall, and Doe carry the danger of claims by sellers that these insider buyers had insufficiently disclosed the value of the coal reserves. Now the problem becomes understatement, rather than overstatement, as it would be if shareholders were being urged not to sell to Octopus, and might make the purchasers liable under Rule 10b-5 as well as under §14(e). And these antifraud rules remain a problem even when the purchasing is done by the corporation, but with less danger of individual liability to Digges, Hall, and Doe.

Another, perhaps decisive, factor is that shares purchased by Dighaldoe become treasury shares which do not vote, while shares purchased by Digges, Hall, or Doe will add to their existing 30% voting strength. This means that a purchase campaign to keep Octopus from acquiring a voting majority would be approximately twice as expensive if waged with corporate purchases. Insiders, who already hold 30,000 shares, can secure a majority of the 100,000 shares outstanding by buying 20,001 shares. But Dighaldoe must buy 40,001 shares to reduce the pool of 70,000 publicly held shares from which Octopus can buy to below 30,000 shares.

8. Other defensive tactics against a takeover (Section 10.2(c))

What can defenders do to make a takeover more costly or more difficult?

Besides urging shareholders not to sell to the tender offeror or to sell to the target or its insiders, a favorite defensive tactic is to start a law suit claiming Williams Act violations. Other moves that make a takeover more expensive include issuing more shares, merging with another larger corporation, and increasing the market price of the shares through a dividend increase or a share split. And a takeover can be made more legally difficult by creating antitrust problems through merger with a competitor of the offeror, by reincorporating in one of the states that make takeovers difficult, or by amending articles or contracts with creditors or labor unions to create various kinds of roadblocks to a takeover.

9. Mechanics of selling corporate control (Section 10.3(a))

How does one control group transfer control to another?

While corporate offices are not supposed to be bought and sold, state law generally upholds the installation of a new board by successive resignations and elections (see Section 4.1(b)) without shareholder vote when the selling group holds shares sufficient for "working control" (28% is enough; 3% is not). However, the Williams Act imposes requirements for disclosure to the SEC and to shareholders in this situation which increase the possibility of legal attacks. These problems can be headed off by calling a special meeting of shareholders to replace the board. Once the new board is in place it can proceed to replace the officers.

10. Control as a corporate or private asset (Section 10.3(b))

May a group selling control keep for themselves the "control premium" they receive for their shares?

Notwithstanding arguments that control is an asset belonging to the whole corporation, the prevailing legal and ethical view is that it is a private asset of those who own the shares that give them working control. While, as we see in Chapter 11, there are limits on how those in control may use their power, the cases generally allow them to sell their control position for their own profit, subject to the fiduciary duties discussed in Point 11.

11. Fiduciary duties of sellers of control (Section 10.3(c))

When may the selling group be liable for a control transfer?

Shareholders ordinarily need be neither careful nor loyal when they sell (or vote) their shares. But controlling shareholders, along with officers and directors, owe fiduciary duties to the corporation not to participate in a transfer of control that is likely to injure the corporation. And an offer to controlling shareholders of an excessively high price for their shares is a danger signal.

In the Dighaldoe-Babylon context assumed in Section 10.3—where Babylon is offering Digges, Hall, and Doe a price substantially above book and market values, where Babylon is disinterested in buying the publicly held shares, and where Babylon is seeking "captive" coal production facilities for its own use—the question becomes whether Babylon is likely to operate Dighaldoe in a way that would injure the public shareholders. As a minimum, Digges, Hall, and Doe should get a promise from Babylon that it will pay fair prices to Dighaldoe for its coal. And they may have ethical qualms about selling control in this situation and these qualms might lead them to wait for a sell-out opportunity with less jeopardy to public shareholders.

Part Three

RECOGNIZING
INDIVIDUAL CONCERNS

11

Problems of Your Individual Liabilities

——————————— CONTENTS ———————————

11

Problems of Your Individual Liabilities

Thus far we have been dealing with corporate structures and corporate problems; our concerns have revolved about your corporation. Now it is time to look in a systematic way at your own problems. In a sense the first ten chapters are a long prologue to this chapter. To understand what may happen to you individually, you need first to have thought about how your corporation functions and how you function as a part of it. With this background more or less filled in, we can proceed to what probably interests you most: as one who is a corporate shareholder, director, officer, employee, or agent, what can happen to you personally?

We have tried to keep before us the difference between you and your corporation. We also need to emphasize a more subtle difference between you as a part of your corporation and you as an independent legal person. It is you in the latter persona that we now address, whereas in earlier chapters the "you" that we address is usually a corporate officer or director. In Chapter 12 we will examine more fully how you handle this duality of self and role.

The granting of limited liability to those doing business as corporations was a policy decision made in the 19th century in Europe and America largely to relieve inactive partners who could find themselves in debtors' prison for debts of their firms. (Sir Walter Scott worked for years writing novels to clear debts of a publishing firm in which he had been a partner.) Limited liability, originally a privilege intended for those associated in large corporations, came to be extended to all corporations. But it is a privilege of such potency that it has needed checks and balances. With early corporations these were provided by the difficulty and

355

expense of incorporation and by restrictions upon what a corporation could do. Now, when a corporation can be easily and cheaply formed to do almost anything, checking and balancing of limited liability must be done by limiting the limitation—i.e., by multiplying situations where corporate participants may be personally liable. Another consequence of the laxity of corporation laws has been that characteristic individual liability situations have shifted from failures to observe formal requirements to alleged misuses of power.

In this chapter the kinds of potential grounds for individual liability are arranged to move from formal and "bright line" aberrations towards alleged misdeeds that call for exercise of discretion. This spectrum of grounds for individual liability includes failure to follow specific legal requirements, abuse of corporate separateness, violation of fiduciary duties of care and loyalty, and improper transactions in your corporation's shares. Following these sections on your substantive liabilities, the chapter concludes with a procedural section on coping with legal actions against you.

Section 11.1 Specific Legal Requirements

Because corporations are creatures of law observance of legally prescribed procedures in their creation and functioning can be crucial. What the law gives the law can withhold. While, as we have noted, formalities have become less onerous, failure to observe them can still cause trouble. And not all specific legal requirements are formalities. This section examines several kinds of quite specific personal liabilities on shareholders, directors, and officers, including those arising from express provisions in corporation statutes, defective incorporation, unauthorized acts, and criminal, administrative, and civil liabilities generally.

(a) Express statutory liabilities

Perhaps most clear-cut of grounds for personal liability are those specified in your state's corporation act. The tendency has been for these to shrink as other states have competed with Delaware in being "liberal." Scrutiny of the Model Act yields only the following express liabilities:

—Payment for shares: A shareholder is liable for failure to pay subscription for shares (§17), and such payment may not be made with promissory notes or future services (§19); except for such payment a holder of or subscriber to shares is under no obligation with respect to shares to the corporation or its creditors (§25).

—Distribution of assets: A director who votes for or assents to the following is liable to the corporation jointly or severally with other directors who similarly vote or assent:

> —declaration of a dividend or other distribution of assets to shareholders contrary to the Act or to the articles of incorporation, for the amount of the distribution;
>
> —purchase of the corporation's own shares contrary to the Act, for the consideration paid over what could have been lawfully paid.

A director who is held liable is entitled to contribution from shareholders who knowingly receive unlawful distributions and from other directors who also vote for or assent to the distribution. A director who relies in good faith on financial statements of the corporation represented to be correct by the president or officer in charge of the corporation's books of account or its independent auditors, or who, in good faith, in determining the amount available for distribution, considers assets to be of their book value is not liable. (§48)

—Examination of books and records: An officer or agent who refuses to allow a shareholder, or a shareholder's agent or attorney, to examine and make extracts from the corporation's books and records of account, minutes, and records of shareholders, for any proper purpose, is liable to the shareholders in a penalty of ten percent of the value of the shareholder's shares in addition to any other damages or remedy afforded by law, unless the shareholder

> —has within two years sold or offered for sale or assisted in the procuring of a shareholder list for this or another corporation; or
>
> —has improperly used information secured by examination of the books or records of this or another corporation; or
>
> —was not acting in good faith or for a proper purpose in making the demand. (§52)

> ▪ **Requesting a shareholder list for a proxy contest or for a shareholders' derivative suit are considered proper purposes.**

Some state corporation acts impose other express liabilities. For example, New York makes the ten largest shareholders liable for payment of wage claims (N.Y. Bus. Corp. L. §630).

> ▪ **New York makes an exception for publicly traded corporations; this enables lawyers in public offerings to give their opinions that the shares offered are "legally issued, fully paid, and non-assessable." See Section 7.2(b)(iii) of the text.**

Some states require certain minimum amounts of stated capital to be paid in before business is done and make shareholders and directors personally liable for corporate debts if this condition is not met. Ohio makes incorporators and directors liable for the amount of the deficiency if the capital stated in the articles is not paid in (Ohio Code §1701.12).

(b) Defective incorporation

Since corporations can be created only by following the law, it has seemed inescapable to some judges that if the law is not followed there can be no corporation and that those who do business in its name must be either partners or agents for non-existent principals, with the result that they are individually liable for obligations of the business. While this result is logical it frequently also is harsh, and other judges have sought ways to soften it. For example, if the legal defect is merely a formal one, like the omission of a seal or signature, they find the omitted step to be "directory" but not "mandatory."

> **▪ An Illinois court used this formula to legitimatize over 4,300 Illinois corporations formed without seals during a period when Illinois law required seals. *People* v. *Ford,* 128 N.E. 479 (Ill. 1920)**

Where an enterprise is carried on in good faith belief in its validity as a corporation, judges sometimes allow its principals to escape individual liability by calling the enterprise a "de facto corporation," the legal existence of which can be attacked only by the state. Some but not all of the states which recognize the de facto doctrine apply it only when articles of incorporation have been filed but some other defect prevents de jure (legal) incorporation. In these states, if no articles have been filed before the liability is incurred, some other formula is needed; and some judges have used the principle that outsiders who deal with a business as a corporation are "estopped" from claiming that there is no corporation, apparently on the theory that the principals have relied on the outsider's treatment of the business as a corporation to enter transactions which they would not have entered as individuals.

> **▪ Shareholder S invests in and is elected president of what he thinks is corporation C. C's attorney fails to file its articles until several months after C starts to do business, and during this period third party T sells eight electric typewriters to C. C was apparently unable to pay for them so T sued S. A Maryland court held that T, having dealt with C as if it were a corporation and having relied on the credit of C rather than that of S, is estopped to assert that C was not incorporated when the typewriters were purchased. *Cranson* v. *International Business Machines Corp.,* 200 A.2d 33 (Md. 1964). While S's personal liability would be an**

unexpected windfall for T, the court's decision seems difficult to justify because S was in a better position than T to know about the defect and seems the less "innocent" of the two. Estoppel ordinarily involves a preventable misrepresentation by the party being estopped. This decision may reflect a desire to protect an individual against a large corporation; however, its effect could be to persuade large corporations that they should insist on personal guarantees from people like S before they extend credit to businesses like C.

The Model Act has two provisions which, read together, appear to codify the results of the de facto doctrine in its limited form—i.e., confined to situations where articles are filed—and to eliminate corporations by estoppel. Corporate existence begins upon issuance of a certificate of incorporation and the certificate is "conclusive evidence" of effective incorporation except as against the state in a proceeding to cancel the certificate or for involuntary dissolution of the corporation (§56). On the other hand, all who "assume to act as a corporation without authority to do so shall be jointly and severally liable for all debts and liabilities incurred or arising as a result thereof" (§146). It would seem that §146 can be interpreted to include unknowingly acting as a corporation without authority of a certificate, thereby eliminating the uncertainties of the de facto and estoppel doctrines by making issuance of the certificate the crucial event.

(c) Unauthorized acts

Since shareholders and directors, as such, lack agency powers to act *for* a corporation in dealing with outsiders—their roles being to act *as* the corporation's government and management by discussing and voting in meetings—they will not be subjected to personal liabilities for "unauthorized" acts unless they "assume to act as a corporation without authority so to do" and thereby incur personal liability under Model Act §146. In contrast with this position of shareholders and directors, Chapter 5 shows that corporate agents—without regard to whether they are also shareholders, directors, officers, or employees—can be individually liable to third persons. This liability is for "breach of implied warranty of authority" if the agent exceeds his authority or powers and the corporation does not ratify what he has done; and the agent may be liable as a principal if he does not disclose to the third party that he is acting as an agent, or if he acts for a corporation that has not yet been formed. Chapter 5 also shows that corporate agents are individually liable to their corporations if they violate their fiduciary duties of care and loyalty, and we will shortly be considering these duties more intensively. But there is another basis of personal liability of an officer, employee, or agent to the corporation that has not been mentioned. When an officer acts without authority, but in a way that makes the corporation liable, the officer is personally liable to the corporation for its loss due to the unauthorized act. Examples of this "liability over" by an agent to the corporation for the corporation's liability to an outsider include such disparate events as an accident caused by an employee's negligent driving of a delivery truck in the course of employment and making of a contract by a corporation's president without proper authority, but which nevertheless binds the corporation because making the contracts is within the president's inherent powers. In short, there is a specific legal requirement that those who act as agents for corporations observe the limitations on what they are authorized to do: the truck driver, to driving carefully; the president, to making authorized contracts.

(d) Criminal, administrative, and civil liabilities generally

In addition to personal liabilities resulting from specific requirements of corporation and agency law, many other kinds of laws impose specific requirements that can make you personally liable for what you do or fail to do while doing your corporate job. Like everyone else, you are subject individually to the general constraints and sanctions of criminal laws—federal, state, local, and sometimes foreign. You are also subject to a variety of special regulatory and administrative constraints depending upon the size and nature of your business. And some of these criminal and administrative laws provide that private civil actions can be brought against you individually.

Federal securities, antitrust, and tax laws have generated the most apprehension of personal liability among corporate officers and directors, with laws on bribery and political contributions recently joining this group. Chapters 7 and 9 detail some of the dangers of individual liability under securities and antitrust laws. Officers and directors are more vulnerable to these liabilities than are shareholders. However, a controlling shareholder is presumed liable for violations by the corporation of §§11 and 12 of the Securities Act of 1933 and of all violations by the corporation of the Securities Exchange Act of 1934, although this presumption can be rebutted by proof of individual innocence.

You will, of course, be individually liable to outsiders for your own contractual undertakings even though they are made to further the interests of your corporation. For example, a contract creditor of your corporation may insist—particularly if the creditor is sophisticated and your corporation is small—that you individually guarantee a corporate obligation, thereby eliminating the barriers of limited liability.

> ▪ **To avoid unintentionally assuming personal liability for your corporation's contracts, the contract should state that the corporation is the party and you should take care to sign in a way to make it clear that**

you are signing as an agent for the corporation and not as a party. The customary way to do this is:

Dighaldoe Corporation
By:_____
    Donald Digges, President

When it is intended that both you and the corporation are to be parties, the contract should specify your obligations and you should sign twice: once for the corporation as indicated above, and once for yourself.

You can also be individually liable to outsiders, along with your corporation, if you direct or participate in wrongful acts (torts), even though these acts are done on behalf of the corporation. Under this rule corporate officers have been held personally liable for unfair competition, fraud and misrepresentation, conversion of another's goods, and injury to another's land. However, if the tort requires knowledge (sometimes called "scienter") or bad intent (e.g., as with malicious prosecution), an officer lacking the required knowledge or intent may direct or participate in the tort for his corporation without personal liability. And officers and directors are generally not liable for the tort of inducing breach of contract if they advise, in a good faith exercise of their business judgment, that their corporation repudiate a contract.

Section 11.2 Disregard of Corporate Separateness

We are seeing that the limited liability granted by corporateness is modified by various kinds of individual liabilities. The preceding section, covering liabilities arising from specific legal requirements, deals with what happens when incorporation is defective—we find judges searching for ways to avoid having to impose personal liabilities. The defective incorporation problem is really part of a larger problem: when will the law refuse to go along with the efforts of persons seeking the benefits of corporateness? With defective incorporation, the legal rule seems to require personal liabilities (because there is no corporation), but the equities often speak for no liability. With abuse of corporate separateness, the roles of law and equity are reversed. Judges search for ways to impose personal liabilities, usually upon shareholders, for obligations that ostensibly are those of properly formed corporations. Examples are torts resulting from corporate employees or property, or contracts made in the corporate name.

Our discussion of the nature and separateness of corporations in Section 2.1(a) indicates that most of the practical interest about the existence or non-existence of a corporation as a separate legal entity arises from questions about when shareholders are to be held liable, or otherwise treated, as though the corporation does not exist. The process by which judges reach through the corporation to get at the persons behind it has, in the words of Judge Cardozo, been "enveloped in the mists of metaphor" (*Berkey* v. *Third Ave. Ry.,* 155 N.E. 58 (N.Y. 1926)); he was referring to phrases like "disregard of the corporation fiction" and "piercing the corporate veil" (the British are more likely to call it "lifting the corporate veil"). With a close corporation, the person behind the veil is an individual; with a subsidiary corporation, it is another corporation. Because this chapter is about individual liabilities, we are mainly interested in how this process affects shareholders of a close corporation, who are usually also its officers and directors.

In Europe there has been much concern about the legitimacy of a single individual doing business as a corporation. In Great Britain if the number of shareholders falls below a statutory minimum (two for private companies; seven for public companies) each shareholder who knows this fact is individually liable for all the corporation's debts. Until 1966, a French corporation owned by a single shareholder was automatically annulled; and in France and Germany individual liability may result if a single shareholder dominates a corporation's affairs. This concern has been much less evident in the United States. The Model Act (§§36, 53) and the Delaware Act (§§101(a), 141(b)) authorize corporations to have one incorporator and one director; New York authorizes a corporation with one shareholder to have one director (N.Y. Bus. Corp. L. §702(a)). With a one-person corporation it would seem difficult for that person to avoid "dominating" it.

Most of the law about abuse of corporate separateness comes from judicial decisions rather than from statutes. Factors which influence judges to disregard separateness include: failing to observe corporate formalities, resulting in operation of the corporation as an "agent or instrumentality" of the shareholder; failing to give the corporation sufficient resources to meet its obligations; causing third persons to think that they are getting the credit of the shareholders; and using the corporate form to avoid legal obligations. We will examine how these factors operate in cases involving tort and contract liability, and how corporate separateness may be disregarded in the public interest.

(a) Tort liability

Assume that S is the sole shareholder of C corporation and that T, a third person, is injured under circumstances that make C clearly liable to T, but that C's assets are insufficient to compensate T. If the law respects the separateness of S and C it will not let T recover anything from S. When will the law decline to respect this separateness and allow T to recover from S? We find our two largest states, California and New York, approaching this question quite differently.

In the leading California case, C corporation operated a public swimming pool; it had no assets and no insurance. S, an attorney, was an organizer, director and officer of C (which never actually issued any shares). T's daughter drowned in C's pool due to the alleged negligence of C. In holding that S could be personally liable to T for C's negligence, the most important factor influencing the court appears to have been "inadequate capitalization": people who organize a corporation without giving it enough assets to operate should pay its debts themselves (*Minton* v. *Cavamey,* 364 P.2d 473 (Cal. 1961)).

This question has been presented in New York most notably in cases where C is one of several corporations owned by S, each of which operates one or two taxicabs with minimum insurance. T is injured by a C taxicab and seeks recovery from S because C's assets and insurance do not cover T's damages. In deciding these cases the crucial factor in New York seems to be whether C can be regarded as S's "agent": whether S is really doing business in his individual capacity, with C acting as S's agent; or whether C is conducting its own business, with S merely exercising control of C through corporate channels. In a non-taxicab, parent-subsidiary case the court said that if S gives orders to C's officers who assemble directors' meetings to adopt these orders and communicate them to the operating people, S will escape liability (*Berkey* v. *Third Ave.* Ry., 155 N.E. 58 (N.Y. 1926)). The same result was reached in the leading taxicab case, where the complaint could be interpreted that S gave orders to himself or as president of C and where New York expressly rejected the California approach (*Walkovszky* v. *Carlton,* 223 N.E. 2d 6 (N.Y. 1966)). However, if S gives orders directly to C's operating people thereby short-circuiting C's corporate procedures, C becomes S's agent and S may be liable for C's torts (*Mangan* v. *Terminal Transp. System, Inc.,* 286 N.Y.S. 666 (1936); *Walkovszky* v. *Carlton,* 244 N.E. 2d 55 (1968), after T amended his complaint to allege that S was conducting a taxicab business in his "individual capacity as opposed to the corporate form").

Both the California and the New York approaches present difficulties: inadequate capitalization is vague; agency is formalistic. Most of the California cases have involved corporations with virtually no assets, leaving uncharted how much is "adequate." It appears that New York declined to adopt the California approach because its judges thought that, while they should decide whether C should be regarded as S's agent, it is for the legislature to say how much capital entitles C to be treated as a corporation. Judges in most other states probably still side with New York on this issue.

(b) Contract liability; subordination

Assume again that S is the sole shareholder of C corporation. T, a third person, makes a contract with C that C fails to perform, making C clearly liable to T. Again, if the law respects C's separateness, T will be unable to recover from S for C's default. As with torts, in deciding whether there are reasons for not respecting C's separateness, courts will consider whether C is really an agent or instrumentality of S and whether S has provided C with enough capital; and California courts, emphasizing capitalization, have taken more initiative in imposing individual contract liability than have New York and most other states.

There is an important factual difference in the position of T in contract and tort cases: when T contracts with C, T chooses to deal with C, but when T suffers a tort from C his relationship with C is thrust upon him. This difference has at least two consequences. It can be argued that capitalization should be less important with contract than with tort cases because T in a contract case can check up on C's capitalization. And a third factor in disregarding corporateness, in addition to agency and capitalization, is introduced: whether T has been led to believe that he is getting the credit of S as well as that of C. This factor was not mentioned in the torts discussion because there rarely can be this sort of misleading in a torts case.

S can, of course, incur direct personal liability to T if S induces T to make a contract with C by misrepresentation and if T suffers injury as a result. But then S's liability would not depend on a court disregarding the corporate separateness of C, because it would be an ordinary kind of personal liability of the sort we discuss above in Section 11.1(d). Now we are concerned with when S can incur personal contractual liability to T on a contract that purports to be only between T and C. It appears that in dealing with this question a court will consider, in addition to the factors of actual agency and adequate capitalization, whether in making the contract with C, T has been led to believe (not necessarily by S) that C is simply an alter ego of S, or that S will stand behind C's debts, or that some of S's assets belong to C. If T has been misled into thinking that he is getting the credit of S as well as of C, the court may give him what he thought he was getting.

> **■ For example, S, a shoe retailer, forms C corporation to lease a store from T, who thinks that he is "really" leasing to S. The assets of S and C are mingled. C sells no shoes and S pays the rent. In *Weisser* v. *Mursam Shoe Corp.*, 127 F.2d 344 (2d Cir. 1942), the court said S could be found personally liable on the lease, mainly on the basis of what it was reasonable for T to expect, although its decision was buttressed by S's intrusion in C's management and C's inadequate capitalization.**

Akin to a shareholder's individual liability for the corporation's contracts is the status of the shareholder's own debt claims against the corporation if it becomes insolvent. Will these claims be subordinated to claims of outside creditors? Suppose that S operates a plumbing business as an individual proprietorship with a capital investment of $50,000. Seeing trouble ahead, S incorporates the business as C corporation, taking $2,000 in shares and $48,000 in promissory notes. C becomes insolvent. In receivership or bankruptcy will S's notes share C's assets equally with C's outside creditors? In *Costello* v. *Fazio*, 256 F.2d 903 (9th Cir. 1958), from which this illustration is adapted, S's claims were subordinated.

But note that if the legal separateness of shareholder and corporation is observed, S will be treated the same as other creditors. In Great Britain the House of Lords stuck to this position in the landmark case of *Salomon* v. *Salomon & Co.*, [1897] A.C. 22; American judges appear to be less rigorous in observing separateness when they think it is being abused. The factors they consider in subordination cases resemble those used in individual liability cases: Is C a mere agent, instrumentality, or alter ego of S without "real" independent legal existence? Is C adequately capitalized to do its business? Is there deception of outsiders? The plumber's case has elements of each of these factors:

—C is formed not for business purposes of its own but for S's personal purpose to transform a proprietary interest into a debt interest in anticipation of insolvency.

—C is launched with only $2,000 capital to conduct a business that requires a capital of $50,000.

—Outside creditors can justifiably believe that they will not be competing with S for the assets of the business.

(c) Disregard of corporate separateness in the public interest

Thus far the victims of abuse of the corporate entity we have talked about have been individuals whom we have symbolized as T, a third party with a tort or contract claim against the corporation. When the corporate form is used to escape government regulation the victim is ordinarily not a specific individual but rather the public in general. In this kind of abuse judges have had little difficulty, even in Great Britain, in disregarding corporate separateness. The following statement summarizes this judicial attitude:

> [W]hen the notion of legal entity is used to defeat public convenience, justify wrong, protect fraud, or defend crime, the law will regard the corporation as an association of persons. U.S. v. Milwaukee Refrigerator Transit Co., 142 F. 247, 255 (E.D. Wis. 1905).

This kind of departure from the purity of corporateness covers a wide variety of situations where the operation of some law for the public good is in danger of being frustrated by interposition of a corporation. Examples include criminal laws, tax laws, securities regulations, labor relations, public utility rate regulations, and laws relating to public health and safety. And American courts have on occasion extended the doctrine that corporations cannot be used to defeat the public good to protect private parties against fraud or evasion of contract. Courts frequently have disregarded the separate entity of a corporation to which assets have been conveyed by an insolvent debtor. But except in unusual situations, the separate existence of a corporation will not be disregarded for the benefit of the corporation itself or its shareholders.

Section 11.3 Duties of Care and Loyalty

Thus far we have dealt with your individual liabilities to your corporation only to the extent they are expressed in statutes or arise from unauthorized acts purportedly done on your corporation's behalf. Now we need to consider a broad group of potential liabilities *to* your corporation arising from your duties of care and loyalty.

This section, while having some application to officers, employees, agents, and controlling shareholders, is mainly concerned with directors, since it's to them that the law entrusts the powers of corporate management. In the words of the Model Act:

> *All corporate powers shall be exercised by or under the authority of, and the business and affairs of a corporation shall be managed under the direction of, a board of directors, except as may be otherwise provided in this Act or in the articles of incorporation. ... A director shall perform his duties ... in good faith, in a manner he reasonably believes to be in the best interest of the corporation, and with such care as an ordinarily prudent person in like position would use under similar circumstances. (§35)*

In brief, a corporate director is supposed to exercise care of "an ordinarily prudent person" in his position and loyalty to "the best interests of the corporation" in making decisions for the corporation. Unlike a shareholder, a director may neither entrust his vote to someone else nor agree with someone else about how he will vote. Chapter 4 details some of the kinds of decisions directors are called upon to make. The goal of this section is to give meaning to these duties of care and loyalty in the contexts of actual business decisions. We first examine directors' duty of care and then several aspects of directors' duty of loyalty, including conflicts of interest, corporate opportunities, and executive compensation; we also look briefly at obligations of controlling shareholders. The section that follows examines obligations of insiders in buying and selling their corporation's shares.

(a) Duty of care

We start with what might be called the "malpractice" liability of corporate directors, arising when the corporation, like a doctor's patients, asserts it has been mismanaged due to the directors' lack of care, skill, or competence. The analogy breaks down, however, when we compare the standards for and the way they are applied to doctors and directors. Perhaps a closer and more useful parallel is maladministration of public office, sometimes called "misprison of office"; as with a corporation, and unlike the doctor-patient situation, the damage is done not to a specific individual but to an institution, which seems to make our person-oriented law more lenient.

A director's duty of care—like that of doctors, public officials, and other people—is a part of the broader law of negligence, which is built upon two concepts (though some claim they are parts of a single concept): reasonable prudence and causation. People are supposed to conduct themselves in the various situations in which they find themselves (including sitting on boards of directors) so that they do not create unreasonable risks of harm to others (including their corporations). But they are legally responsible for what happens to others only if they could have prevented what happens by acting with reasonable care (as an "ordinarily prudent" director)—i.e., only if their lack of care "caused" the others harm. Consider the following example where a court found lack of due care, but no causation:

> ▪ **D, a director of C corporation, formed to manufacture automobile and airplane starters, was a mere figurehead and did not participate in C's management. C failed because of conflicts among its operating people. Judge Learned Hand found that D had been negligent but refused to hold him liable, because it had not been shown that D, by doing his duty as a director could have prevented the collapse of C's business. Judge Hand said: "No man of sense would take the office if the law imposed upon them a guarantee of the general success of their companies as a penalty for any negligence." *Barnes v. Andrews, 298 F. 614 (S.D.N.Y. 1924)*.**

Thus our questions are: What is the standard of care for a corporate director (D)? And what kinds of harm to the corporation (C) are within the director's power to prevent by being careful?

The Model Act statement of D's standard for care— "such care as an ordinarily prudent person in a like position would use under similar circumstances" (§35)—is the usual formulation, although some statutes and decisions vary it by requiring the care that prudent persons would use "in their personal business affairs." This language was in the Pennsylvania corporation act prior to 1968 when it was removed because it was thought to mandate a standard that was exceptionally "stringent and harsh." See *Selheimer* v. *Manganese Corp. of America*, 224 A.2d 634 (Pa. 1966). Thus, it appears that the usual formula requires less care than D would use for himself.

D's standard of care must also be assessed in light of the so-called "business judgment" rule: courts will ordinarily refrain from interfering with a good faith exercise by D of business judgement, even when the results are disastrous for C. Judge Shientag of New York tried to reconcile due care and business judgment as follows:

> *When courts say that they will not interfere in matters of business judgment it is presupposed that judgment—reasonable diligence— has in fact been exercised. A director cannot close his eyes to what is going on around him in the conduct of the business of the corporation and have it said that he is exercising business judgment. Courts have properly decided to give directors wide latitude in the management of the affairs of a corporation provided always that judgement, and that means an honest unbiased judgment, reasonably is exercised by them.* Casey v. Woodruff, 49 N.Y.S. 2d 625, 643 (1944).

Largely as a consequence of this "wide latitude," in only a few cases have directors of industrial corporations been held liable for negligence alone without the added ingredient of conflict of interest.

Judicial notions of what harms to C are preventable by D have also contributed to the scarcity of successful duty of care suits. Here we see a difference between industrial and financial corporations. A judge is less likely to be convinced that D can prevent the consequences of incompetent management if C is an industrial concern than, if C is a financial institution, that D by proper oversight can prevent embezzlement or the making of illegal or unsafe loans. Many of the cases where D is held liable for negligence involve inadequate supervision of bank employees. In this area there has been in both federal and state courts a tendency, contrary to most other tendencies on D's duties, to treat reasonable supervision as requiring more attention than was held sufficient in earlier cases.

As corporations get bigger, directors become further removed from operating people. In a sense, D's restricted liability for his negligence is a realistic reflection of his restricted power in most corporations. We have seen in earlier chapters that in close corporations shareholders typically wield real power and that in publicly-held corporations power tends to pass to the officers through their control of the proxy machinery.

Suppose D quite regularly fails to attends C's board meetings. A decision is required on a matter clearly within the directors' province—say, settlement of a claim which C has against an outsider. In making a decision at a meeting from which D is absent the rest of the board acts on erroneous advice of C's lawyer to accept a less favorable settlement than it is entitled to. D's failure to attend the meeting will not be an excuse; nor would his age or ill health relieve him from liability, because it then may be D's duty to resign. In fact, D's almost complete abandonment of his duties appears to be negligence of a sort that cannot be saved by the business judgment rule—he is not exercising any judgment. But he can probably escape liability on the grounds ennunciated by Judge Hand in Barnes v. Andrews: his presence at the meeting would not have averted the erroneous legal advice. And here the business judgement rule does help him, because it is normal business practice to follow the advice of counsel on legal matters.

(b) Conflicts of interest

Much as directors' duty of care is derived from the law of torts pertaining to negligence, directors' duty of loyalty is derived from legal rules that cast certain people—such as trustees, agents, guardians, executors and administrators of estates, and government officials—in a special legal role known as "fiduciaries." A fiduciary is a person who stands in a relation of trust, confidence, and responsibility to others. Dictionaries sometimes use a corporate director or an agent of a principal as examples of fiduciaries. The existence of and respect for this relationship is fundamental to having a legal system at all: it gives people the confidence to entrust their wealth and well-being to other people who have undertaken not to act in their own interests when they are acting as fiduciaries. In the balance of this section we examine how the fiduciary principle is tested in several kinds of corporate transactional contexts, starting with conflicts of interest.

Contracts and other transactions between C corporation and D, its director, or between C and another corporation (Delta), of which D is a director or officer or in which D is financially interested, involve conflicts of interest for D because his loyalties are necessarily divided. How can D perform his duty as a C director to act in the best interests of C when the other party to the transaction is D himself or Delta, another corporation in which he is financially interested or to which he owes duties of loyalty? This is, of course, a very old problem.

> *No man can serve two masters: for either he will hate the one, and love the other; or else he will hold to the one, and despise the other. Ye cannot serve God and mammon.* Matthew 6: 24.

Justice Harlan Stone referred to this problem forcibly in 1934 in a much-quoted address at the University of Michigan, when he said:

> *I venture to assert that when the history of the financial era which has just drawn to a close comes to be written, most of the mistakes and major faults will be ascribed to failure to observe the fiduciary principle .... No thinking man can believe that an economy built on a business foundation can permanently endure without some loyalty to that principle. The separation of ownership from management, the development of the corporate structure so as to vest in*

small groups control over the resources of great numbers of small and uninformed investors, make imperative a fresh and active devotion to that principle if the modern world of business is to perform its proper function. 48 Harv. L. Rev. 1, 8 (1934)

Notwithstanding these calls to fiduciary faithfulness, the history of legal treatment in the United States of directors' conflicts of interest in the past century seems to read as a chronicle of growing laxity. One hundred years ago it was the general rule that any transaction between D and C was voidable at the option of C, and that any transaction between C and Delta (assuming D is a director of Delta) was voidable at the option of either corporation. The current general rule as expressed in the Model Act is that such a transaction will be enforced if it is approved by a vote of disinterested and informed fellow directors or of informed (but not necessarily disinterested) shareholders, or if it is fair and reasonable to C (§41). For a shareholder resolution ratifying an insider transaction, see Appendix D.5(e).

This apparently dramatic change warrants analysis. It has long been the rule, both in the United States and Great Britain, that a C-D (or C-Delta) transaction, if its terms are fair to C, can be ratified by C shareholders at a meeting where D votes as a shareholder; and where the terms are unfair or even fraudulent to C, shareholders of C (including D) can still ratify if they have full knowlege of the material facts. Thus, aside from tightening of disclosure requirements under modern proxy rules, the law remains essentially unchanged as to shareholder ratification. As to director approval and fairness, however, there have been substantial changes:

—In 1880 director approval and fairness were irrelevant because any C-D transaction remained voidable at C's option.

—By 1910 a C-D transaction that was fair could be made binding on C by approval of a disinterested, informed board; if a majority of directors were interested, the transaction remained voidable by C without regard to fairness.

—By 1960 no C-D transaction was automatically voidable, even if there was no disinterested majority, but courts would void a transaction they found to be unfair.

—Now under the Model Act a C-D transaction binds C, even if unfair, if it is approved by sufficient votes (not counting D's) of informed, disinterested directors (D may be counted in determining a quorum); and if it is fair it does not require such approval.

These changes in the law, shifting emphasis from the status of the parties (the C-D fiduciary relationship) to the particulars of the transaction (how other directors vote, whether they are interested, whether they are informed, and the fairness of the transaction itself) seem to reflect judicial recognition that business people expect many transactions involving self-dealing to be binding. (As we have seen, the law also reflects this expectation in permitting closely-held and even one person corporations). Thus, the problem has become more complex than it seemed in 1934 to Justice Stone: the fiduciary principle is the beginning rather than the end of distinguishing between permissible and impermissible self-dealing. This means that we need to look more closely at how courts handle conflict of interest cases.

While the Model Act makes disclosure to other directors, shareholder ratification, and fairness separate elements in determining enforceability, the cases frequently intermingle these factors. A finding that D has acted unfairly is often based on his failure to disclose all material facts. Failure to make sufficient disclosure to fellow directors or to shareholders is sometimes called "procedural" unfairness, as distinguished from "substantive" unfairness which goes to the effect of the transaction on C or its shareholders. If C is subject to SEC proxy regulations, the issue frequently becomes not whether shareholder ratification of a C-D transaction is effective but whether there was adequate disclosure of the conflicting interests as required under the proxy rules.

On the frequently determinative question of whether defenders or attackers of a transaction have the burden of showing fairness or unfairness, the cases are in disarray. The majority view seems to be that those trying to uphold a C-D or a C-Delta transaction have the burden of showing that it is fair to C. The wording of the Model Act, that no C-D transaction shall be voidable because of their relationship "if … the contract or transaction is fair and reasonable to the corporation," lends some support for arguing that it is fairness rather than unfairness that needs to be proved. However, some cases put the burden on the attacking party to prove unfairness, particularly when the attack is by a minority shareholder rather than by the corporation acting through its directors. The intermediate view on burden of proof puts the initial burden on the attacking party to produce some evidence of unfairness; then, if such evidence is produced the burden shifts to the party trying to justify the transaction.

A series of New York cases seem to evolve a somewhat different intermediate view on burden of proof by making a distinction between procedural and substantive fairness. If the attacking party can show that the other members of the C board in approving C's transaction with D made "a biased exercise of judgment" (say, because they did not have complete information) or were "placed in a position of divided loyalty" (as where a majority of the boards of two corporations dealing with one another are interlocking), the defender of the transaction has the burden of showing substantive fairness; but when D makes full disclosure and a disinterested board makes "an unprejudiced exercise of judgment," the attacker has the burden of showing that D disregarded his duties to C and that C has been injured.

▪ Under the Model Act fairness seems irrelevant in the latter circumstances: the board's approval by itself makes the transaction binding on C.

Compare *Globe Woolen Co.* v. *Utica Gas & Elec. Co.*, 121 N.E. 378 (N.Y. 1918) (common director, incomplete disclosure, and "startling" unfairness), and *Chelrob* v. *Barrett*, 57 N.E. 2d 825 (N.Y. 1944) (interlocking boards and divided loyalty), with *Everett* v. *Phillips*, 43 N.E. 2d 18 (N.Y. 1942) (full disclosure, common directors, and "unprejudiced exercise of judgment"). The New York view seems to represent a sensible accommodation between two sometimes divergent legal principles, against self-dealing by corporate directors and against judicial interference with informed business judgments by corporate boards.

(c) Corporate opportunities

In conflict of interest situations D's loyalty to C is strained because C and D are dealing with one another; there is danger that D will use his corporate position to lead C into a disadvantageous bargain. D's loyalty to C is also strained when, instead of dealing with C, D deals with property or with a third party (T) under circumstances where he may be intercepting something that should be C's. Instead of subjecting C to possible disadvantage, D competes with C for possible advantage. These situations are called "corporate opportunities" because they are opportunities that a loyal fiduciary would pass on to his corporation. However, by becoming a fiduciary D does not renounce all his self-interest. Thus, the central problem is to distinguish opportunities that are "corporate" from those that are fair game for D.

While we continue to identify the corporate insider as D, this loyalty situation often involves—in addition to directors—corporate officers, employees, and agents. A special category of corporate opportunities, transactions by D in C's shares, is deferred until the next section.

Perhaps the clearest application of the corporate opportunity doctrine— and one that resembles conflict of interest because no third party need be involved—is where D simply uses C's property, confidential data, or working time for D's own benefit, often to establish his own enterprise. One of our hypotheticals in Chapter 7 on raising money assumed that computer programmers employed by a corporation develop a business plan that they now want to exploit for themselves. We called the plan a corporate opportunity and suggested that for them to use it without an express release (see Appendix H.4(h)) from the corporation would be inviting trouble (see Section 7.2(a)(i)).

From this clear loyalty situation the doctrine has been extended to propositions made by T where C can be said to have an "expectancy" that it will have an opportunity to accept or reject T's proposal. C's expectancy may be of varying strengths. For example, if C has had a lease for several years on valuable property and, when it comes up for renewal, D renews the lease in his own name, C has had a very strong expectancy frustrated. *Meinhard* v. *Salmon*, 164 N.E. 545 (N.Y. 1928). C's expectancy weakens if C is merely negotiating for a lease or purchase; and it becomes even more attenuated if C has only expressed an interest in leasing or purchasing property and lacks the resources to do so. Another way of approaching the problem, which usually gives a more expansive meaning to corporate opportunities, is from the point of view of D's duties rather than C's expectancies. Then the question becomes, not whether C can show a property right, expectancy, or interest, but whether a loyal corporate fiduciary would refer the opportunity to C.

Judicial finding of corporate opportunity usually results in a "constructive trust" for the benefit of C being imposed on the property, contract, or profits secured by D through taking the opportunity, placing D under a duty to account to C for these benefits. The objective is to put C in the position it would be in if D had done his duty.

> ▪ **Note that there is some windfall to C because C gets the benefits of the deal without having taken the risks.**

Corporate opportunity is largely a judge-made rather than a statutory concept. To deal with the central problem of separating corporate and individual opportunities, we will try to extract from some of the decided cases factors to which judges seem to give weight.

Relationship of the opportunity to C's business.—Suppose that C is a paper company that regularly buys timberlands and D, a director, buys a tract of timberland from T for himself and re-sells it to C at its fair market value but at a profit to D. It is quite clear that D would be required to turn over his profit to C. *N.Y. Trust Co.* v. *American Realty Co.*, 155 N.E. 102 (N.Y. 1926).

> ▪ **Note that, unlike the conflict of interest cases, C is not trying to rescind. C wants to keep the land it bought from D, but at the price D paid for it.**

In contrast, if D learns of a chance to buy land that might have oil under it, he will be free to proceed without referring the opportunity to C. Between these extremes are more difficult cases. A Delaware court permitted D to retain patents useful in making aircraft, even though C was in this business, saying the patents were not "essential" to C's business and that C had no real interest or expectancy in the opportunity. *Johnston* v. *Greene*, 121 A.2d 919 (Del. 1956).

> ▪ **We will see, however, that there were other factors that helped the court find this to be an individual opportunity.**

But an earlier Delaware court did not permit D to retain a trademark and secret formula for a cola drink (Pepsi-Cola), when C operated a chain of candy stores that dispensed cola drinks saying that while C had "no existing property right" in Pepsi-Cola, it cannot be said "that it had no concern or expectancy in the opportunity." *Guth* v. *Loft*, 5 A.2d 503 (Del. 1939).

Relationship of the opportunity to D's responsibilities to C.—In the timberlands situation, if the land that D sells to C is a tract that he acquired before becoming an officer or director of C or that he inherits while an officer or director, there will be no corporate opportunity even if it is D's job to buy land for C: corporate opportunity relates to D's acquisition of the land, not to his sale of it to C.

> ▪ **There will, of course, be a possible conflict of interest problem in D's sale to C, but we are assuming that D sells to C at fair market value.**

And if D is an employee, not a director, with no responsibilities for buying land (say he works in the personnel department) who learns of a chance to buy timberland at a bargain, his fiduciary duty to refer the opportunity to C is less clear, even though the opportunity relates directly to C's business. Similar problems arise when corporate employees learn of their employer's plan to build a new plant and act before the corporation does in securing options on desirable land. While this sort of disloyalty seems grounds for dismissal, whether a judge would impose a constructive trust on D's options depends in part on where D stands in the corporate hierarchy: a constructive trust would more likely be imposed upon an officer or director than upon an hourly-paid production worker.

How the opportunity comes to D.—In the aircraft patent case the Delaware court considered it significant that T approached D in D's individual capacity and was unaware of his connection with C. Conversely, if D learns of an opportunity as a part of his work for C, judges are likely to call it corporate even though it is not directly related to D's job or to C's business.

> ▪ **If D, while on a mission to buy raw materials for C in a foreign country, learns of a chance to buy a plant, this may be a corporate opportunity even if the plant is only remotely related to C's present business. But if D, while vacationing, picks up the same information from someone unaware of his connection with C, this is probably an individual opportunity.**

And in the new plant situation, a judge will be tougher on a secretary or clerical worker who uses information learned in an office than on a production worker who uses information learned from the company grapevine. More loyalty is expected of some employees than others.

C's interest in the opportunity.—Recall that corporate superiors of the computer programmers involved in the hypothetical we used in Section 7.2 expressed lack of interest in a business opportunity, but we concluded that the disclaimer was not sufficiently authoritative to be relied upon.

> **▪ Also it is one thing for C to indicate lack of interest in pursuing a project now and another thing for C to say to D: you can have it. C may want to stockpile the project.**

Again disclosure becomes important. An uninformed, albeit authoritative, disclaimer of interest on behalf of C will not protect D. But even without an express disclaimer, if D can convince the court that C was not interested in the opportunity, he may escape a constructive trust. A Massachusetts court permitted D to retain a department store, purchased when D was an officer and director of C, that was competitive with one of C's stores, in part because of the "absence of any interest, express or implied, on the part of the company in the purchase of this store," although D was held liable for damages to C from operating a store in competition with C while employed by C. The court said: "In the acquisition of a store, as distinguished from its operation," D violated no duty to C. *Lincoln Store* v. *Grant,* 34 N.E. 2d 704 (Mass. 1941).

> **▪ D was free to exercise initiative, but not on C's time. This case nicely illustrates the difference between the "clear case" of using C's property, and what the court saw as C's lack of expectancy.**

C's ability to finance the opportunity.—D may seek to justify taking an opportunity by asserting that C lacks funds to finance it. In a federal decision rejecting this argument because D had not made a good faith effort to raise the necessary funds for C, Judge Swan said: "If directors are permitted to justify their conduct on such a theory, there will be a temptation to refrain from exerting their strongest efforts on behalf of the corporation since, if it does not meet the obligations, an opportunity of profit will be open to them personally." *Irving Trust Co.* v. *Deutsch,* 73 F.2d 121 (2d Cir. 1934). D is, of course, in a stronger position to make this argument if it is not D's responsibility to raise money for C.

In summary, an opportunity that is closely related to C's business and to D's job with C, or that comes to D because of his connection with C, is probably a corporate opportunity if C is ready, willing, and able to take it. But an opportunity that is unrelated to C's business or to D's job, or that comes to D in his individual capacity, or in which C lacks the interest or ability to exploit, is probably an individual opportunity. If these indicia are unclear—as where an opportunity is vaguely related to C's business; or D's job is a responsible one but not directly connected with the opportunity; or D learns about it in a casual social conversation, but while on a business trip for C; or C's interest or ability is in doubt—whether a judge will impose a constructive trust will depend on how he sees the rival claims of fiduciary duty and individual initiative. From the corporation's point of view all agents, high and low, should with singleminded, unswerving loyalty put the corporation first all of the time. But from the point of view of the individual, who is not *just* a corporate agent, it is important that the law allow him to preserve some measure of business autonomy and initiative. In balancing these "goods"—loyalty versus autonomy—judges are more likely to resort to common sense judgments of what seems to them to be fair in particular situations than they are to give paramountcy to either good.

(d) Executive compensation

D can avoid the strains on his loyalty that we have been discussing by refraining from dealing or competing with C in his individual capacity. But D cannot avoid dealing with C as an individual about his own compensation. And the earlier assumption that directors and senior officers serve without compensation, getting their rewards in dividends and capital appreciation, has disappeared for officers and is disappearing for directors (see the discussion of trends in directors' compensation in Section 4.4(d)). While C-D transactions about D's compensation can usually be arranged so that someone else appears to act for C, judges may look through these arrangements and find self-dealing. Also, grounds for attacking compensation arrangements include, in addition to self-dealing, the notions of "corporate waste" and "retroactivity". This subsection examines special characteristics of compensation in close corporations; the concepts of self-dealing, waste, and retroactivity; the many kinds of compensation used in publicly held corporations and how they have been influenced by tax laws; when courts are likely to intervene in compensation matters; and some ways of minimizing your compensation problems.

(i) Close corporations

While legal theory makes little distinction between executive compensation by close and public corporations, in practice quite different forces are at work. When ownership and management coincide, as usually happens in close corporations, for tax reasons compensation in the form of salaries frequently is in lieu of dividends and represents, not only the value of D's services on the labor market, but also an entreprenurial return on his capital investment. The tax rule that compensation, if reasonable, is deductible by C (while profits distributed as dividends are taxed to both C and D) has generated much litigation about whether salaries are reasonable. Similar issues about the reasonableness of salaries can arise between management and non-management owners of close corporations, usually accompanied by charges of self-dealing and bad faith.

(ii) Self-dealing, waste, and retroactivity

Self-dealing seems to be a necessary but not a sufficient condition for a finding of unreasonable compensation: absent self-dealing, judges tend to apply the "business judgement" rule and refrain from interfering with corporate decisions that compensations are reasonable; but self-dealing is seldom enough by itself to show unreasonableness. However, where there is self-dealing the burden of proof is usually on D to show that the compensation he fixed for himself is reasonable—a rule that is in line with the allocation of burden of proof in other C-D transactions.

The Model Act provides: "The board of directors shall have authority to fix the compensation of directors unless otherwise provided in the articles of incorporation" (§35). This provision, combined with §41 that makes C-D transactions enforceable if approved by a vote of disinterested directors (even if unfair), seems to say that a permissible way to avoid a charge of self-dealing in fixing compensation of executive-directors is for the directors to act seriatim (one after the other) upon one another's compensation.

> ▪ **This procedure, which resembles that used for replacing directors when there has been a transfer of control, was held unacceptable by a Wisconsin court on the theory that the directors were not really "disinterested" and were acting for their own rather than the corporation's benefit. *Stoiber* v. *Miller Brewing Co.,* 42 N.W. 2d 144 (Wis. 1950). This decision prompted a change in the Wisconsin corporation act authorizing a board "irrespective of any personal interest of any of its members ... to establish reasonable compensation of all directors for services to the corporation as directors, officers, or otherwise" (§180.31).**

The Model Act is silent on compensation for officers and employees.

If identity of parties on the two sides of a compensation arrangement can be avoided, the issue moves from "self-dealing" to "corporate waste" and "retroactivity." Waste involves comparison of compensation with value of services and seems to require a greater degree of disproportion than does the reasonableness test discussed above: something approaching a "gift" of corporate assets. But the courts talk about gifts not only in the sense of compensation which is much more than D deserves for what he has done for C but also in the sense of compensation which has not been contracted for in advance, invoking the dogma that corporations lack power to give retroactive compensation for services already performed. The equating of gratuity and retroactivity is seen in the following statement by a federal judge about bonuses:

> *As to bonuses, which are merely gratuitous payments, and as to similar retroactive increases in salary, it is Hornbook [black letter] law that, except when there has been an express or implied understanding that they may be granted if conditions warrant, there is no*

consideration for them, and their grant by directors alone will not sustain them against attack by stockholders. It is true that normally the stockholders may grant them or ratify their granting. Hurt v. Cotton States Fertilizer Co., 159 F.2d 52 (5th Cir. 1947).

As this statement indicates, shareholder approval is a powerful curative in compensation matters. Self-dealing, retroactivity, and waste, short of gross disproportion in value between compensation and services, all seem to yield to shareholder ratification.

(iii) Public corporations

The self-dealing problem will be eased for a publicly held corporation if a majority of its board is made up of outside directors. And, whether or not outsiders comprise a majority, they can be assigned to a compensation committee and the board can adopt a resolution giving it "all of the authority of the board of directors" (Model Act §42) in fixing compensation for senior officers. If the president wishes to have control of compensation for his subordinates, the committee's authority can be limited to the president's compensation. In Section 4.4(c) it was suggested that such a committee pass not only on salaries for top management but also on their bonuses, stock options, deferred compensation, and other special benefits. Other kinds of benefits, not usually confined to senior officers and thus not as subject to charges of self-dealing, include retirement, profit sharing, phantom stock, and insurance plans.

In this century executive compensation has gone through several phases. The first shift was the one already mentioned from compensation through proprietorship to compensation through salaries. Then in some corporations top echelon salaries came to be supplemented with bonuses based on annual profits. Perhaps the most notorious arrangement was the American Tobacco Company plan approved by its shareholders in 1912 which by 1930 was yielding George Washington Hill, president of American Tobacco, total annual compensation of over $1¼ million. Notwithstanding shareholder approval and absence of self-dealing or retroactivity—making it a pure waste problem—a plan which yielded bonuses of this magnitude was held by a United States Supreme Court generally sympathetic to business "to constitute misuse and waste of money of the corporation." *Rogers* v. *Hill,* 289 U.S. 582 (1933). Justice Butler quoted with approval the following statement by Judge Swan in his dissenting opinion below:

> *If a bonus payment has no relation to the services for which it is given, it is in reality a gift in part and the majority stockholders have no power to give away corporate property against the protest of the minority.* 60 F.2d 109, 113.

We will see this argument repeated about other kinds of compensation.

In its most recent phase, roughly since World War II, executive compensation has been geared to federal income taxes. Ways have been sought to provide benefits that are not immediately taxable. Stock option plans have waxed and waned in favor as their tax treatment has changed. Apart from taxes, the efficacy and even the legitimacy of stock options have been warmly debated along the following lines:

—Proponents see stock options as effective performance incentives which also provide a means of inducing younger professional managers, with scant accumulations of capital, to acquire proprietary interests in their corporations, without cost to their employers. And, perhaps most significantly, corporate employers offer options because their competitors for executive talent offer them.

—Opponents of stock options question their incentive value, because individual performances seldom determine market prices for corporate shares. They also question whether options retain executives, because optionees tend to sell their shares at first opportunity. They argue that options are not cost-free to other shareholders, because the bargain purchases they permit have a diluting effect like that of watered shares; and options can yield profits rivaling American Tobacco bonuses in their being disproportionate to the value of the services given for them.

Other largely tax motivated forms of compensation include retirement or pension plans and profit-sharing plans, which can "qualify" under the Internal Revenue Code if they are non-discriminatory—i.e., not tailored exclusively for the benefit of top officers and directors. Tax consequences of qualification include the following:

—contributions by the corporation are immediately deductible;
—the trust receiving the contributions is tax exempt and its investment income tax-free;
—distributions from the trust are taxable to employees when received by them, not when contributions are made to the trust by the corporation (usually employees will receive distributions after retirement when they are in lower tax brackets); and
—distributions to employees on account of death or termination of employment may receive favorable tax treatment.

Deferred compensation arrangements, under which an executive agrees that after retirement he will remain available for consultation and will not compete with the corporation, also have been used to reduce taxes by spreading income into retirement years. "Phantom stock" plans, where employees receive "units" which vary in value with dividends and market value of the employers' shares, provide a method of giving employees (including lower echelon people than would normally be granted stock options) rights that resemble stock options but do not require capital outlays nor entail market risks; tax liability for the employee is deferred until he receives the cash equivalent of his units. And other fringe benefits—like life, medical, and hospital insurance—have the advantage over salaries of not being taxable.

(iv) Judicial intervention

The business judgment rule has held down judicial intervention in compensation decisions. Litigation has been heaviest about stock option plans in Delaware, the law of which is fashioned to encourage both liberal plans and easy access to Delaware courts. Where attack on a plan has succeeded the plan has usually contained some feature inconsistent with the objective of retaining valued employees: such as option grants which became immediately exercisable or remained exercisable after termination of employment, thereby enabling an employee to take his profits and run.

> ▪ In response to attacks on stock option plans, provisions were put in the Model Act (§20) and the Delaware Act (§157) to the effect that in the absence of fraud, judgment of the directors as to the adequacy of the consideration received for stock options "shall be conclusive."

With other kinds of plans it seems to take an unusual case and a strong judge for shareholder approved plans not involving retroactivity to be invalidated. In addition to *Rogers* v. *Hills,* other cases where benefits were questioned or found to bear no relation to the value of services include:

—a pension plan adopted shortly before a corporation's president was to retire which gave him annual pension benefits of $54,000, more than eight times the next highest pension (*Fogelson* v. *American Woolen Co.,* 170 F.2d 660 (2d Cir. 1948) (Judge Swan again); and

—a phantom stock plan with units based on the market value of the corporation's shares, where the judge thought the plan was vulnerable to the disproportion argument used against stock options with the added weakness that holders of units took no risk (*Berkwitz* v. *Humphrey,* 163 F.Supp. 78 (N. Ohio 1958).

(v) Minimizing your compensation problems

To keep trouble over your compensation arrangements with your corporation at a minimum, the following precautions are suggested:

—Self-dealing: Avoid the appearance of self-dealing by having someone else, not your corporate subordinate, represent the corporation in transactions fixing your salary or granting you other benefits.

—Waste: Make clear that business judgment was exercised in fixing your benefits with attention to some rational basis for relating compensation to the value of your services, such as data on what other corporations competing for your services are paying their executives. Resist the use of maximums in benefit plans based on formulas, because inflation may make them inappropriate and seeking shareholder approval of increases may be embarrassing.

—Retroactivity: See that compensation arrangements are made or provided for in advance of performance of services. Bonuses can be based on profits, but the formula should be fixed before the beginning of the period.

—Your own voting: While you may vote as a shareholder upon matters in which you are interested, you should refrain from voting as a director upon such matters; but you can attend the board meeting and help make up a quorum.

—Shareholder approval: Insist that any compensation plan, above and beyond basic salaries and insurance coverage provided for salaried employees generally, from which officers and directors may benefit, be submitted to shareholders for their approval in advance of effectiveness (see Appendix D.5(a) and (b)). If your corporation is subject to SEC proxy rules, make sure that you fulfill all SEC disclosure requirements (see Section 3.2(b)).

—Compensation committee: If you have outside directors, use some or all of them on a compensation committee with power to act for or make recommendations to the board on compensation matters concerning the president, and perhaps other officers and directors (see Appendix F.5(a)).

—Litigation: If your compensation is attacked, you will usually want to try to keep the case out of the federal courts, since federal judges seem more likely to question the judgment of directors on compensation matters.

(e) Controlling shareholders

We have seen that as a shareholder you are under fewer constraints about how to use your corporate powers than you are as an officer or director. You are relatively free to vote your shares in your own interest, even on transactions between you and your corporation (including compensation matters), and you generally need not refer business opportunities to the corporation. Now we need to consider whether status as a *controlling* shareholder will increase your potential for personal liability. We have seen that publicly held corporations can be subjected to "working control" by considerably less than a majority of voting shares through the access of incumbent management to the proxy machinery. In Chapter 10 we learned of fiduciary limits on what you can do as a controlling shareholder in transferring your control to someone else. Now we assume that you retain control and are concerned about how you may incur individual liability by its exercise.

There seem to be two legal routes for imposing individual liability on a controlling shareholder (S) of a corporation (C): directly, for S's own acts as shareholder; indirectly, or "vicariously", for acts of directors of C whom S controls (S frequently being a holding company and C its subsidiary). Direct liability usually results from a finding that S has acted deceptively or unfairly in voting S's shares at a shareholders' meeting on a matter in which S has an interest adverse to that of C or its minority shareholders. Examples include approval of a recapitalization, merger, or sale of assets; ratification of voidable acts of directors, such as a transaction between a director and C; and amendment of the articles of incorporation: as when C shares are sold to the public on the representation that they will be listed on the New York Stock Exchange and S then, in order to sell more shares and still maintain his control position, uses his voting power for an amendment authorizing non-voting shares which will lead to de-listing. Direct liability has been imposed for manipulations, not involving voting or transfers of control of majority shares to the detriment of the minority (see *Jones* v. *H.F. Ahmanson & Co.*, introduced in Section 10.3 and further discussed below). Vicarious liability may be imposed on S—under such legal theories as principal-agent, joint tort feasor, and participation in breach of trust—if S's dominance of C's directors causes them to breach *their* fiduciary duties to C and all its shareholders.

The cases do not emphasize the distinction between S's direct and vicarious liabilities and much the same factors seem to operate as to both. Whether S acts directly or through C's directors, it appears that S's self-interest and detriment to minority shareholders are not sufficient reasons for making S liable unless they are accompanied by dishonesty (fraud or deception) or unfairness. While dishonesty can be quite objectively determined by asking whether S lied or misled, what is unfair is more subjective. We will try to give a flavor of what unfairness can mean by sketching three cases.

The text book case on fiduciary duties of controlling shareholders involves a World War II tobacco inventory owned by C, which had greatly appreciated in value. S acquired most of C's shares which were divided into two classes, A and B. Class A shares had superior dividend and liquidation rights, were convertible into B shares, and were callable by the C board at $60 per share plus accrued dividends. Class B shares were not callable. Without disclosing its intention to liquidate C by selling its tobacco inventory, S converted its Class A shares to Class B, caused the C board to call the outstanding Class A shares at $80.80 and then liquidated C realizing $240 per share. In holding that former Class A shareholders whose shares had been called could recover from S the difference between what they received for their shares and what they would have received if they had converted their shares to Class B shares, a federal court said that a "puppet-puppeteer relationship" existed between C directors and S and that the call was made at the direction of S in order to profit S, while it was the board's duty "to act disinterestedly ... and to make the call with due regard to its fiduciary obligations," and concluded:

> *it follows that the directors of Axton-Fisher [C], the instruments of Transamerica [S], have been derelict in that duty. Liability which flows from that dereliction must be imposed upon Transamerica which ... constituted the board of Axton-Fisher and controlled it.* Zahn v. Transamerica Corp., 162 F.2d 36 (3d Cir. 1947).

There is some unreality in the assumption that the board of a controlled corporation can "act disinterestedly." While the decision is in terms of fiduciary obligations of directors, its actual basis seems to be that S should be liable because it reaped an unfair profit at the expense of minority shareholders.

A more forthright expression of fairness as the basis of shareholder liability, without recourse to the fiduciary duties of directors, is found in the California case, mentioned in Section 10.3 as illustrating how control power can be turned to private gain. S, holding 85 percent of C's shares for which there was no market (because of book value of over $4,000 per share and lack of publicity), exchanged C shares for shares of a holding company at a high ratio (giving the holding company shares a book value of about $40 per share), created a market for the holding company shares, and excluded minority shareholders of C from exchanging their C shares. The court held that minority shareholders should "be placed in a position at least as favorable as that the majority created for themselves," justifying its decison as follows:

> *Thus defendants [S] chose a course of action in which they used their control of the Association [C] to obtain an advantage not made available to all stockholders. They did so without regard to the detriment to the minority stockholders and in the absense of any compelling business purpose. Such conduct is not consistent with their duty of good faith and inherent fairness to the minority stockholders. Chief Justice Traynor in* Jones v. H.F. Ahmanson & Co., 460 P.2d 464 (Cal. 1969).

A Delaware decision going the other way shows how considerations of fairness are likely to be limited by the business judgment rule. S, a parent corporation holding 97 percent of C's shares, used its control of C to declare dividends which depleted C's working capital available for investment in new enterprises which S allocated to itself or to other subsidiaries. The court held that the test was not one of "intrinsic fairness" shifting the burden to S to prove fairness, but rather one of business judgment, because there was no self-dealing, S having received nothing from C to the exclusion of minority shareholders; and, in matters of business judgment, "a court will not interfere ... unless there is a showing of gross and palpable overreaching," which was not made here. *Sinclair Oil Corp.* v. *Levien*, 280 A.2d 717 (Del. 1971).

In summary, where S is careful to follow legal procedures and to avoid giving C directors the appearance of "puppets", it generally takes—much as with executive compensation—both a strong case, involving deception or extreme unfairness which results in considerable detriment to minority shareholders, and a strong judge, like Chief Justice Traynor of California, before there will be judicial interference with "business judgments" about how control is to be exercised.

Section 11.4 Transactions in Your Corporation's Shares

Among your many potential personal liabilities as corporate officer or director, perhaps the least clearly defined and most rapidly developing is what may happen when you buy or sell your corporation's shares on your own behalf. It is almost inevitable that you will know more about your corporation than other people. Often the corporate interest dictates that what you know not be publicized: for example, if the information is a trade secret or would be useful to the corporation's competitors or damaging to its credit. Frequently the information is too uncertain or preliminary to be made public. And, even when data can be safely released, it is seldom possible for the dissemination of data to keep up with its accumulation.

This disparity in information about a corporation (C) between an insider (D) and an outsider (T) creates two kinds of potential liability for D when he deals with T in C shares: to T because of their unequal bargaining positions, and to C because D has preempted a corporate opportunity (arguably D should use information obtained through his position with C to buy or sell C's shares for C rather than for himself).

There would seem to be at least three ways that the law can react to what may be perceived as the injustices of "insider trading": non-interference; absolute prohibition; and selective prohibition. We have already discussed, in Section 7.3(e) among the consequences to you of your corporation going public, what might be called the limited absolute prohibition on insider trading in §16(b) of the Securities Exchange Act of 1934, which makes officers, directors, and 10 percent shareholders automatically liable to their corporations for their "short swing" profits from purchases and sales or sales and purchases of their corporations' shares taking place within six month periods. Now we need to look at broader questions of insider liability, both to investors and to the corporation and involving both publicly held and close corporations, for share transactions under judge-made rules and under SEC Rule 10b-5 issued under §10(b) of the 1934 Act. We find that the choice has been between non-interference and selective prohibition. Apart from §16(b), no rule, state or federal, has tried to impose an absolute ban on insider trading.

(a) Judge-made rules

Looking first at D's potential liabilities to T, we find that common law approaches to an insider's obligations to present and prospective investors in their corporations have followed three paths:

—a "majority rule" that D owes no special duties to T and may deal with him at arm's length,

—a "minority rule" that D has a fiduciary duty to disclose material facts to T, and

—a "special circumstances" rule that D may sometimes be under such a duty.

Supporters of the majority rule use the following arguments:

—The law should let T's losses fall where they may as it does in other situations where one party to a bargain is wiser, luckier, or better informed than the other.

—D owes his fiduciary duties to C not to T. The fiduciary relationship will cease to have meaning if the law tries to spread it to the unidentifiable mass of people with whom D may have share transactions.

—In a market economy information is a commodity that has value which the holder should be able to exploit on the market, both in order to create a more rational market and to provide incentives to D to undertake the responsibilities that yield him investment information.

—Since it is impossible to define material market information, acknowledgement of any liability of D to T will open the flood gates to law suits.

To these arguments, supporters of the minority rule make the following responses:

—Insiders' share transactions require more rigorous rules than other transactions because they are more susceptible to overreaching. Also the trend is to require disclosure of material facts in many other kinds of transactions.

—C is merely a symbol for its investors who are the real objects of D's fiduciary duties, as citizens are of the duties of public officers. The law recognizes that large classes of people can possess legal rights.

—If insiders' information is a commodity it belongs to C not to D. The market will work better if both buyers and sellers are informed. And less harmful ways can be found to give D incentives to accept responsibilities than permitting him to trade on inside information.

—Judges can sort out cases where nondisclosure is crucial and thus evolve tests for the materiality of information which will control case loads.

The special circumstances rule was devised by the federal courts as a middle position between the majority and minority rules. It is identified with a Supreme Court decision where D, who was director, chief executive, and 75 percent shareholder of C, bought T's shares without disclosing an imminent sale of C to the United States government being negotiated by D which made T's shares worth ten times the price D paid for them. *Strong* v. *Repide,* 213 U.S. 419 (1909). However, when the general federal common law was eliminated by the Supreme Court in *Erie R.R.* v. *Tompkins,* 304 U.S. 64 (1938), the special circumstances rule went with it.

State courts have taken differing approaches to this problem, as the following early 1930s cases from Massachusetts and Kansas show:

—D, president and director of C mining company, knowing about a theory of an experienced geologist that large copper deposits existed under C's property in northern Michigan, bought C shares on the Boston stock exchange from T, a member of that exchange. In refusing to rescind T's sale, the court emphasized that stock exchange transactions are "impersonal affairs" and distinguished *Strong* v. *Repide* because that case involved a face-to-face transaction. Chief Justice Rugg said:

Law in its sanctions is not coextensive with morality. It cannot undertake to put all parties to every contract on an equality as to knowledge, experience, skill and shrewdness. It cannot undertake to relieve against hard bargains made between competent parties without fraud. Goodwin v. Agassiz, 186 N.E. 659 (Mass. 1933).

—D, president and director of C, three days before C declared a dividend of $1 per share, purchased the C shares of T, a widow, for $1.25. When T asked D whether a dividend would be declared, the jury found that D correctly answered that he did not know. In permitting T to rescind her sale, the court held that D had a duty to disclose to T "all material facts," saying that without such a rule, "experience teaches such transactions too often result in gross fraud." *Hotchkiss* v. *Fischer,* 16 P.2d 531 (Kan. 1932).

As these cases suggest, courts are more likely to find a fiduciary relationship between D and T if they deal face-to-face than if they deal anonymously on a stock exchange. The state cases seem to exhibit a trend, probably aided by federal Rule 10b-5, away from the majority toward the minority rule.

There are relatively few cases dealing with D's duties to C in buying or selling C's shares, mainly because the question is unlikely to be raised where D is part of the control group of C. The following cases from Delaware and New York where the issue was raised both have unusual factors:

—D, who was not a director of C but was a "confidential secretary" to a C director and officer, made purchases of C shares for himself in advance of when he knew that C planned to make purchases. In imposing a constructive trust on D's profits, the court said that since he occupied a position of trust and confidence with C he could not use "for his own personal gain" information acquired "in the course of his employment." *Brophy* v. *Cities Service Co.,* 70 A.2d 5 (Del. 1940).

—C financed computer installations through sales and lease backs of computers which it was obligated to service. For such servicing it relied on IBM. When IBM sharply increased its service charges, C's earnings declined. Before this information was made public, D, C's president and director, sold his holdings of C shares and then repurchased them after the market price for C shares declined on announcement of C's reduced earnings, realizing a profit of $800,000. In a derivative suit by a minority shareholder to compel D to account to C for his profit, D argued that what he had done had not hurt C. The court rejected this argument. Chief Judge Fuld said in his opinion: "there can be no justification for permitting officers and directors ... to retain for themselves profits ... derived solely from exploiting information gained by virtue of their inside position as corporate officials." Furthermore, what D did may have injured C's reputation. *Diamond* v. *Oreamuno,* 248 N.E. 2d 910 (N.Y. 1969).

(b) Rule 10b-5

In order to reach insider trading covered by neither §16(b) nor the majority rule in the states, the SEC and the federal courts have created Rule 10b-5 which seems to constitute a new and stronger federal special circumstances rule that eliminates any distinctions between face-to-face and stock market transactions.

Section 10(b) of the 1934 Act makes it unlawful to use, in connection with the purchase or sale of any security, any manipulative or deceptive device or contrivance in contravention of such rules as the SEC may prescribe for the protection of investors. Under this authority the SEC issued Rule 10b-5, which became effective in 1943, making it unlawful (1) to employ any device to defraud, (2) to make any untrue statement of a material fact or *to omit to state a material fact,* or (3) to engage in any act which operates as a fraud, *in connection with the purchase or sale of any security.* Mainly on the basis of the emphasized words, there has been built a new specialized federal common law in the corporate area directed against fraud in securities transactions.

While we are discussing Rule 10b-5 as a part of "insider trading"—and most of the cases have involved liability on insiders for failure to make adequate disclosure—the words of the statute and the rule are not limited to insiders nor to non-disclosure of information. It is unlikely that in enacting §10(b) Congress intended to establish what has developed; it is particularly doubtful that it intended to authorize private suits for rule violations, as distinguished from SEC enforcement proceedings. In the words of Justice Rehnquist:

> *"When we deal with private actions under Rule 10b-5, we deal with a judicial oak which has grown from little more than a legislative acorn.* Blue Chip Stamps *v.* Manor Drug Stores, 421 U.S. 723 (1975).

Nevertheless, the courts have firmly established a right to private suits. We will consider a sampling of the principal cases in an effort to give meaning to the parts of the rule emphasized above that most significantly determine its limits: what are "material facts," and what is meant by "in connection with the purchase or sale" of securities?

(i) Nature of the information

The SEC has not provided a list of material facts that need to be disclosed in security trading comparable to the disclosures specified for public distributions of securities and for proxy solicitations. Materiality has come to be roughly translated as: likely to affect investment decisions to buy or sell. But it is not clear how far materiality depends on individual investor sophistication.

Early 10b-5 cases involved information the materiality of which was scarcely arguable. The first private case applying the rule involved a close corporation (C) making paper products which was equally owned by two families. One family (D) learned of an advantageous chance to sell the assets of C to National Gypsum Company and bought the shares of the other family (T) without disclosing the opportunity. The court required D to share with T D's profits from the sale to National Gypsum, assuming without discussion that the undisclosed information about the National Gypsum proposal "would materially affect the judgment of the other party to the transaction." *Kardon* v. *National Gypsum Co.*, 73 F.Supp. 798 (E.D. Pa. 1947).

Another early 10 b-5 case involved the tobacco inventory situation in *Zahn* v. *Transamerica Corp.*, which we discussed in Section 11.3(e) in connection with liabilities of controlling shareholders. In a class suit former shareholders (T) of Axton-Fisher (C) sought damages from Transamerica (D) for offering to buy T's C shares without disclosing the increased value of C's tobacco inventory or D's plans to liquidate C. In upholding the suit the court said that the omitted information "would have affected the judgment of the sellers." *Speed* v. *Transamerica Corp.*, 99 F.Supp. 808 (D. Del. 1951).

More recently, in the landmark *Texas Gulf Sulphur* (TGS) case, the undisclosed information was a fabulous copper and zinc discovery in Canada. Insiders who bought TGS shares between the discovery and its publication were required to turn their profits over to the corporation as a fund against which sellers of TGS shares during this period could assert claims. The corporation itself was held to have violated Rule 10 b-5 by issuing a misleading press release. In explaining what is meant by "material inside information" the court said that an insider is not foreclosed from investing in his own corporation "merely because he may be more familiar with company operations than are outside investors," nor is he obligated to confer upon outsiders "the benefit of his superior financial or other expert analysis by disclosing his educated guesses or predictions" if access to the "basic facts" is "enjoyed equally." But an insider is foreclosed where the undisclosed information is about "an extraordinary situation" that is "reasonably certain to have a substantial effect on the market price" if it is disclosed. When undisclosed facts relate to a particular event, materiality will depend "upon a balancing of both the indicated probability that the event will occur and the anticipated magnitude of the event." In other words, a discovery like TGS's which may be worth hundreds of millions of dollars requires less probability to become material than would a more modest discovery. And the importance attached to a fact by those who know about it will be a major factor in determining materiality. *SEC* v. *Texas Gulf Sulphur Co.*, 401 F.2d 833 (2d Cir. 1968), cert. denied, 394 U.S. 976 (1969).

From the cases it appears that when D buys or sells C shares on the strength of D's knowledge of an undisclosed *event*—such as a discovery, a business opportunity, an earnings statement, dividend action, merger plans, etc.—as distinguished from D's general knowledge about C, D is likely to be held to have traded upon material inside information in violation of Rule 10 b-5.

(ii) Nature of the transaction

Assuming that information is material, what "connection" need there be between D, the insider, and T, the outside investor, and between each of them and a purchase or sale of C's shares? Because in the early cases the connection between the parties was very close—usually D bought from T—the notion arose that there must be "privity" between them: i.e., they must be dealing with one another as buyers and sellers of C shares. However, it now seems clear that it is not necessary to match up D and T in a transaction involving the same shares. The fact that TGS insiders were buying before the information was made public was sufficient to make them liable to outsiders who were selling during the same period. In fact, defendants can be liable under 10 b-5 without themselves being buyers or sellers. TGS, the corporation, was in violation of the Rule for putting out information that misled investors even though it was not in the market itself. And defendants do not need to be connected with C as officers or directors: they can include brokers and others who pass along information and "tippees" who receive information. It is necessary, however, that the information *originate* with an insider.

In contrast with the looseness of 10 b-5 about who can be a defendant, the connection required for a plaintiff is considerably more rigorous. The law now appears to be that T must be a seller or buyer of C shares. In section 10.3(c) we discussed the transfer of control of Newport Steel as a breach of the controlling shareholder's fiduciary duties to minority shareholders. In an earlier case these minority shareholders were denied relief under 10 b-5 because they were neither sellers nor buyers. *Birnbaum* v. *Newport Steel Corp.,* 193 F.2d 461 (2d Cir. 1952).

This requirement that plaintiffs be sellers or buyers, which has become known as the "Birnbaum rule," was reaffirmed by the Supreme Court in *Blue Chip Stamps* v. *Manor Drug Stores,* 421 U.S. 723 (1975). There an antitrust decree required C to offer its shares to retailers who had used C's trading stamp services. T, an offeree who did not purchase C shares, sued C and its directors under 10 b-5 claiming that the prospectus offering C shares was materially misleading in being overly pessimistic (like the TGS press release) in order to discourage T from buying. In dismissing this suit Justice Rehnquist said that 10 b-5 suits are not available to potential purchasers who do not purchase because of misleading pessimism, to actual shareholders who decide not to sell because of misleading optimism, or to C's shareholders, creditors, and others who may be injured by nondisclosure of material facts. Notwithstanding the Blue Chip decision, it appears that 10 b-5 plaintiffs can include the corporation itself, when shares that it owns or issues are fraudulently sold by insiders, and shareholders whose interest in a corporation are changed by a merger or other recapitalization. And some commentators question whether Mr. Justice Rehnquist's statement, to the extent that it excludes from 10 b-5 protection actual shareholders fraudulently dissuaded from selling their shares, will be followed.

Section 11.5 Legal Actions Against You

Thus far in this chapter we have been detailing personal liabilities that may arise because you are a corporate officer, director, or shareholder. But I suspect that you may be less interested in these legal theories of liability than in what their consequences to you are likely to be. In the rest of the chapter our concern is with actual legal proceedings that may be brought or threatened to be brought against you individually because of your corporate connection. First we examine how you may defend against such proceedings, particularly shareholders' derivative suits. Then we look at the extent that your corporation can protect you against the results and expenses of these proceedings through indemnification and insurance.

(a) Defending legal actions

To transform a potential liability into a law suit somebody must take the initiative and somebody else must be willing to hear the case. Initiative can come from within or on behalf of the corporation or from outside. Frequently the initiator is a lawyer eager to earn a fee or make his name known by bringing suit. Sometimes it is a disgruntled minority shareholder, or a corporate creditor that sees you as the "deep pocket," or a government official "just doing his job." And it can be a fellow officer, director, or major shareholder with whom you have had a falling out. Often the person taking the initiative is acting on behalf of a larger class of persons.

The proceeding that is threatened or started may be a criminal prosecution, a civil law suit, an administrative proceeding, or an investigation. It may seek to subject you to a fine or imprisonment, a penalty, money damages, rescission of a contract of other transaction, an accounting of your profits, an injunction, an order to cease and desist, a direction to produce documents or books and records, or something else. Often its real objective is to induce you to pay something in settlement which will provide a source for a lawyer's fee. The usual sequence for defending these proceedings include hiring a lawyer; deciding whether to settle, fight all of the way, or fight part of the way; learning all you can about your opponent's case through investigation and discovery, and disclosing as little as possible about your own; making and responding to preliminary motions; and, eventually, if the case cannot be disposed of some other way, going to trial. We focus first on corporate and shareholder claims against you, which create special problems because of your dual roles.

(i) Corporate and shareholder claims

Your corporation (C) might bring an action against you for such relief as:

—Recovery of money damages because you have done such things as declared illegal dividends, acted for C without authority, not exercised due care in doing your job, or made profits from trading in C shares in violation of §16(b) or Rule 10 b-5.

—Rescission of a transaction, including compensation arrangements, between you and C.

—Imposition of a constructive trust on your profits from a corporate opportunity, including one involving your purchase or sale of C shares.

If you remain on good terms with your fellow officers and directors, as a practical matter they are not likely to cause C to sue you. And if you can secure director or shareholder ratification (see Appendix D.5(e)) of what you have done you will have gone a long way in defusing potential claims against you. However, as we learned in Chapter 2, under some circumstances a minority shareholder can force C to sue you through a "derivative suit." We suggest you now re-examine Section 2.4, which sets out how these suits work and also describes suits that a shareholder can bring against you on his own behalf and as "class actions" for himself and other shareholders "similarly situated." In Section 2.4 we used the following illustrations of these shareholder suits arising within but not on behalf of C:

—Individual suit: a shareholder of a close corporation might seek to enjoin other shareholders from reducing his participation in C by issuing C shares to their wives.

—Class suit: a preferred shareholder might seek on behalf of himself and other preferred shareholders a court order that C directors observe their rights set out in C's articles of incorporation.

An initial problem in defending a derivative suit is your choice of a lawyer. Can you use the lawyer who regularly represents C, on behalf of which you are being sued? As suggested in Section 2.4(a), the trend is to require that C and you be separately represented, although this question is still uncertain enough to make it worth trying to have only one lawyer or law firm. However, the lawyer himself will have an ethical problem in representing possibly adverse interests. The Code of Professional Responsibility of the American Bar Association provides as follows:

A lawyer employed or retained by a corporation ... owes his allegiance to the entity and not to a stockholder, director, [or] officer .... Occasionally a lawyer for an entity is requested by a stockholder, director, [or] officer ... to represent him in an individual capacity; in such case the lawyer may serve the individual only if the lawyer is convinced that differing interests are not present. EC 5-18.

If C's lawyer is convinced that the claims against you are groundless, it would seem that he can undertake your defense without violation of this provision: he can argue that he is acting in C's interest in seeking your vindication. And if he is neither employed nor retained by C, even though he is C's "regular" lawyer it would seem that he can represent you in a particular case—with C being represented by another lawyer if the court insists—and still continue to represent C in other matters.

Since a derivative suit against you can be embarrassing and time-consuming for you, C, and its other managers, defense lawyers look for ways to dispose of the suit in its early stages. Some examples:

—Dismissal on jurisdictional grounds: Since C must be a party, suit can only be brought where both you and C can be served. If suit is brought against you in a federal court on a non-federal cause of action—i.e., if federal jurisdiction must be based on "diversity of citizenship"—you will be able to have the case dismissed for lack of federal jurisdiction if the plaintiff is a citizen of the same state as you or C. (A corporation is a citizen both of the state where it is incorporated and the state where it has its principal place of business.)

—Attacking plaintiff's eligibility to sue: If plaintiff participated in your alleged wrong or was not a shareholder when it happened he will lack standing to sue you.

▪ **This may be a temporary victory because a persistent lawyer can usually find a plaintiff not subject to these disabilities.**

Also Federal Rule 23.1 and most state rules require that the plaintiff must show he made efforts to have the directors and, if necessary, the shareholders, bring the action. The cases, both federal and state, are in disagreement as to whether shareholders can ratify acts claimed to be fraudulent and whether, if they cannot, plaintiffs must show that they have made demand on the shareholders. Some cases excuse such demand when shareholders are numerous and widely dispersed.

—Dismissal under a statute of limitations: There are time limits on bringing "stale" claims that may provide you a quick way out.

—Dismissal on the merits: If you have a strong legal or factual defense (say, if your action allegedly injurious to C was done in compliance with a lawful order of a governmental agency), a motion to dismiss or for summary judgment may be the move to make. However, judges are slow to grant these motions before plaintiff has had a chance to develop the facts through discovery.

You can expect extensive pre-trial efforts from the plaintiff's side to try to turn up evidence to support his allegations (and perhaps uncover the grounds for some new ones) under the regular deposition and discovery provisions of federal and state procedures and under corporation act provisions that permit shareholders to inspect documents and records of the corporation. You can also expect the plaintiff to object to your counsel if he also represents the corporation. And, as we will see, if C demands that plaintiff post security for costs, the plaintiff probably will ask C for its shareholder list to enable him to try to recruit more shareholders to join the suit as plaintiffs, and so fulfill the statutory requirement.

It is difficult to generalize about the trial of a law suit since what happens depends so much on the specifics of your particular case and the abilities, methods, and personalities of the judge, the lawyers, and sometimes the jurors. But most derivative suits do not go the full route but rather end with settlement or voluntary dismissal. Rules 23 and 23.1 of the Federal Rules of Civil Procedure provide that class actions and shareholders' derivative suits "shall not be dismissed or compromised without approval of the court." They also say that notice of the proposed dismissal or compromise must be given to class members or shareholders in such manner as the court directs. In contrast, the Model Act provision on derivative suits does not require court approval of dismissals or compromises (§49).

Unlike the procedure in Great Britain, in the United States the "costs" awarded to a successful litigant normally do not include reimbursement of attorney's fees. There are departures from this norm in shareholders' derivative suits. A shareholder who succeeds in obtaining money or property for C through a derivative suit is entitled to be reimbursed out of the proceeds for reasonable attorney's fees and other expenses; and he is entitled to such reimbursement from C even though it doesn't produce a fund as long as it results in some benefit to C. Example: It achieves cancellation of a burdensome contract. In the other direction, when the shareholder is unsuccessful the Model Act provides that the court upon "a finding that the action was brought without reasonable cause, may require the plaintiffs to pay to the parties named as defendants [C and you] the reasonable expenses, including fees of attorneys, incurred by them in defense of such action," and in cases where the plaintiffs hold less than five percent of the shares, (unless the shares have a market value of more than $25,000), C may require plaintiffs to give security for such expenses incurred by C and you (§49).

This provision is supposed to discourage derivative suits. However, if C asks for security, as we noted above plaintiff may counter by asking for a shareholder list so he may circularize other shareholders to get enough plaintiffs to satisfy the 5 percent-$25,000 requirement. Since this move may publicize inflammatory charges that are better kept unpublicized, you may decide against asking for security for costs.

(ii) Claims by outsiders

In addition to claims against you from within C, an even larger number can be asserted from outside C by individuals and classes of individuals, other corporations, and government agencies. Your obligation to pay for C shares can be enforced either by C or its creditors. If C has not been validly incorporated, its contract or tort creditors may sue you. You may be sued by third persons with whom you have purported to deal for C but without power to bind C. You may be prosecuted for criminal law violations or have civil or investigation proceedings brought against you by administrative or other governmental agencies—especially under federal securities, antitrust, and tax laws. Outsiders may sue you in contract if you bind yourself along with C and in tort if you join C in a wrongful act. Outsiders may sue you on ostensibly corporate tort or contract obligations by claiming that you have abused the privilege of doing business in the corporate form by doing such things as operating C as your agent or failing to give it sufficient capital. Government agencies may also try to reach through C and get at you individually. And investors who have bought or sold C shares may sue you for failing to make sufficient disclosure of inside information.

If the legal proceeding against you by an outsider arises from your job and if your colleagues are convinced that you acted in the best interests of C they will ordinarily agree to having C's lawyer take over your defense. Whether you will want to retain your own lawyer will depend on your estimate of the ability of C's lawyer and on whether possible disparity of interests between you and C may affect his motivation to give you an all-out defense. For example, C's lawyer will be more strongly motivated to vindicate you (and C) of an antitrust accusation than he will be to protect your profits from trading in C shares from an attack under §16(b) or Rule 10 b-5. We next explore how your interests and C's are brought together if C is obliged to indemnify you when you are sued because of your connection with C.

(b) Indemnification and liability insurance

(i) Indemnification: in general

We first introduce "indemnification"—reimbursement to you by C for individual liabilities and expenses arising from your corporate position—in Section 1.5(c), which suggests that you put specific grants of indemnification powers in C's articles of incorporation (see Appendix A.9). This topic has been steadily growing in importance since about 1940. In response to proliferation of potential personal liabilities, private and governmental, to which you can be exposed, and to development of class and derivative suits as vehicles for asserting these liabilities, state corporation acts have expanded the powers of C to protect you from the consequences of this exposure.

Common law doctrines of indemnification of agents by their principals (see Section 5.2(b)(iii)) called for reimbursement to an agent who suffered loss while litigating with third parties on his principal's behalf. But judges balked at extending this agency protection to a suit brought by or for a corporation charging an officer or director with malfeasance in office, although occasionally vindicated officials have recovered their defense expenses, and there was some indication in the 1940s and 1950s that reimbursement in derivative suits could be authorized by charter, by-law, or contract provisions. In any event, in the 1960s indemnification became largely statutory with changes in the New York (§§721-27) and Delaware (§145) corporation acts and with adoption by the Model Act (§5) of the Delaware provisions almost word-for-word. While earlier statutes usually chose between two different theoretical approaches—grants of power to C to indemnify you and grants of rights to you to be indemnified, with partiality to the former approach—modern statutes combine these approaches, making some indemnification permissive and some mandatory.

Indemnification statutes are complicated because they involve so many factual variables. For example:

—Proceedings against you can be by third parties or by the corporation.

—They can be threatened, started but not finished, or carried to completion.

—They can be successfully defended (on the merits or otherwise), settled, or lost.

—You may be seeking reimbursement of expenses, an amount paid in settlement, or a judgment, fine, or penalty.

—A settlement may be with or without court approval.

—You may have acted in the corporation's, your own, or someone else's interest, and with or without reasonable cause to believe that what you did was unlawful.

—You may or may not have been adjudged liable for negligence or misconduct.

—Indemnification may be with or without court approval.

—Indemnification may be with or without authorization by directors, shareholders, or independent legal counsel; and directors may or may not be disinterested.

(ii) Indemnification: Delaware-Model Act

The Delaware-Model Act provisions can be stated as follows:

(a) Permissive indemnity in third party actions, whether or not successfully defended, for expenses, judgments, fines, and settlements: C may indemnify you when you were or are a party or are threatened to be made a party to a threatened, pending, or completed civil, criminal, administrative, or investigative action (other than an action by or for C) because you are or were a director, officer, employee or agent of C, against your expenses (including attorney's fees) and payments for judgments, fines, and settlements, provided that you have met the following standard of conduct:

> You must have acted in good faith and in a manner that you reasonably believed to be in or not opposed to the best interests of C, and, as to a criminal action, with reasonable cause to believe your conduct was not unlawful. Termination of an action by judgment, order, settlement, conviction, or upon plea of nolo contendere shall not, of itself, create a presumption about how you acted.

(b) Permissive indemnity in corporate actions, whether or not successfully defended, for expenses only: C may indemnify you when you were or are a party or are threatened to be made a party to a threatened, pending, or completed action by or in the right of C to procure a judgment in its favor because you are or were a director, officer, employee, or agent of C, against your expenses (including attorneys' fees) in connection with the defense or settlement of such action, provided that you have met the following standard of conduct:

> You must have acted in good faith and in a manner that you reasonably believed to be in or not opposed to the best interests of C.

But no indemnification shall be made without court approval where you have been adjudged liable for negligence or misconduct in performance of your duty to C.

(c) Mandatory indemnity for expenses in successfully defended third party or corporate actions: To the extent that you are successful, on the merits or otherwise, in defense of an action referred to in (a) or (b), you shall be indemnified against your expenses (including attorneys' fees).

(d) Authorization of indemnification upon determination concerning standard of conduct: Unless ordered by a court, indemnification under (a) or (b) shall be made by C only as authorized in the specific case upon a determination that your indemnification is proper in the circumstances because you have met the standard of conduct set forth in (a) or (b). Such determination shall be made (1) by the board of directors by a majority vote of a quorum consisting of disinterested directors, or (2) absent a disinterested quorum or if a disinterested quorum so directs, by independent legal counsel in a written opinion, or (3) by the shareholders.

(e) Advance of expenses: Your expenses (including attorneys' fees) incurred in defending a civil or criminal action may be paid by C in advance of the action's final disposition as authorized in the manner provided in (d) if you undertake to repay the advance unless it shall ultimately be determined that you are entitled to be indemnified by C.

(f) Non-exclusivity and continuance of statutory rights: Statutory indemnification is not exclusive of your other rights under any by-law, agreement, vote of shareholders, or disinterested directors, or otherwise, both as to your acts in your official capacity or in another capacity while holding such office; and your statutory indemnification rights shall continue when you have ceased to be a director, officer, employee, or agent and shall inure the benefit of your executors and administrators.

(g) Liability insurance: C may purchase and maintain insurance for you against any liability asserted against you and incurred by you in your capacity as a director, officer, employee, or agent of C or arising out of your status as such, whether or not C would have the power to indemnify you against such liability under the provisions described above.

(iii) Indemnification: New York

Indemnification in New York is somewhat less permissive than under the Delaware-Model Act provisons. The major differences relate to the greater court supervision required in New York of settlements of actions against you by or for your corporation. In addition to requiring judicial approval of settlement of corporate actions, and providing that such approval can limit indemnification in connection with the settlement, New York prohibits indemnification not only of amounts paid by you to C in settlement of C's claims against you (as do Delaware and the Model Act), but also of amounts paid in defending a threatened action or a pending action which is settled without court approval (which Delaware and the Model Act do not do). The court supervision mandated in New York is aimed at preventing you and the plaintiff from agreeing to a settlement in which you make a small, unindemnifiable payment to C and a large, indemnifiable payment to plaintiff's lawyer. Other less permissive features of the New York indemnity statute include the following:

—Indemnification payments not made by court orders or with shareholder approval (see Appendix D.5(f)-(h)) must be reported to shareholders

—For indemnification of officers and directors the statutory provisions are exclusive and can not be varied or supplemented by charter, by-law, resolution, agreement, or otherwise.

(iv) Liability insurance

The Delaware-Model Act provision on liability insurance seems to say that C can insure you against any liability asserted against you and incurred by you by reason of your corporate office whether or not C would have the power to indemnify you against such liability. Does this mean that all of your problems detailed in this chapter can be solved with an insurance policy?

The typical officer and director liability policy comes in two parts: to reimburse C for its indemnification payments to you, and to reimburse you directly for certain indemnifiable and perhaps unindemnifiable losses. Generally insurers issue policies only through C, with C paying 90 percent and you ten percent of the premium. Policies typically cover situations where you have been negligent but exclude your acts of deliberate dishonesty. The status of fines, punitive damages, liabilities imposed without determination of fault, and litigation expenses—as distinguished from straight judgments and settlements—is frequently unclear. Can insurance against losses from intentional misconduct, which seems permissible under the Delaware-Model Act language, withstand a public policy attack? If C is not permitted to buy such insurance, can you buy it yourself and have C increase your compensation to cover the cost of your premiums? The SEC takes a somewhat ambivalent position; it maintains that indemnification of liability for 1933 Act misrepresentations or omissions in a registration statement is against public policy, but permits C to purchase insurance covering both C and its directors against such liability.

The economic effect of insider liability insurance is to spread the costs of insiders' liabilities among insurance buyers over time.

> ■ **New York codifies this idea and attempts to head off contrary policy declarations by the SEC or federal courts by providing: "This section is the public policy of this state to spread the risk of corporate management, notwithstanding any other general or special law of this state or of any other jurisdiction including the federal government" (§727 (e)).**

It has been estimated that total premium cost has been running at least 1 ½ to 2 times the total amounts paid out to settle liability claims, which indicates that for a corporation the cost of insuring liabilities is probably substantially higher than the cost of indemnifying these liabilities itself. Thus, from C's point of view it perhaps should, on the basis of direct cost, consider being a "self-insurer" for its indemnification liabilities. But direct cost to C is not the only consideration. Insurance coverage may enable you to do a better job for C as an officer or director by contributing to your peace of mind and by giving you broader protection than may be possible under your state's indemnification statute.

CHECKLIST OF POINTS TO WATCH OUT FOR
CONCERNING YOUR INDIVIDUAL LIABILITIES

(References after headings are to Sections of Chapter 11.)

1. Liabilities expressly imposed by your state's corporation act (Section 11.1(a))

For what are you accountable as shareholder, director, or officer?

As a shareholder you are accountable for paying for your shares in money, other property, or services already performed: a promise to pay money or to perform future services will not do. In New York the ten largest shareholders of close corporations are liable for wage claims.

As a director you are accountable for corporate assets illegally distributed to shareholders with your vote or assent, whether by dividend, share purchase, or otherwise. However, you can require other directors voting for or assenting to the illegal distribution, and shareholders knowingly receiving it, to share your liability. And in approving a distribution you may rely on the corporation's financial statements.

As an officer or agent you are accountable for 10% of the value of shares of a shareholder to whom you illegally deny access to the corporation's books and records. Denial is justified as to shareholders who have previously sold shareholder lists or improperly used corporate information, or who do not now have a "proper purpose." Securing a shareholder list for a proxy contest or a shareholder suit is a proper purpose.

2. Shareholder liabilities resulting from defective incorporation (Section 11.1(b))

When may shareholders lose the corporate shield?

While judges often overlook omission of formal steps in the incorporation process (for example, some states require filing of duplicate articles in the county of your corporation's principal office), especially if articles are filed with the Secretary of State, logically a defective corporation (like a defective marriage) is no corporation at all, leaving shareholders without the "corporate shield", and thus liable as partners for obligations of the enterprise.

The Model Act seems to make filing of articles with the Secretary of State crucial: If they are filed, only the State can question corporate existence (§56); but all who "assume to act for a corporation without authority to do so" become individually liable for obligations "arising as a result thereof" (§146).

As suggested in Chapter 1, your best defense against defective incorporation is a lawyer who does not make mistakes.

3. Liabilities from unauthorized acts for a corporation (Section 11.1(c)

To whom may officers and agents be liable when they act for a corporation without authority?

Officers and agents who exceed their corporate authority are liable to third persons who deal with them in good faith unless their corporation chooses to ratify the transaction. Officers and agents who do not disclose that they are acting for someone else are liable to third persons, whether or not they are authorized, but authorized officers and agents are entitled to be made whole by the corporation. Those who act for a corporation before it is formed may be liable to those with whom they deal.

If a corporation is liable because of unauthorized acts of its officers or agents, they in turn are liable to the corporation. Examples: a corporate employee negligently injures someone while working for the corporation; a corporate president makes an unauthorized contract with someone that binds the corporation because it is within a president's inherent power.

4. Criminal, administrative, and civil liabilities (Section 11.1(d))

When may you be individually liable for authorized acts for your corporation?

The limited liability provided by incorporation shields you from the corporation's debts and the torts or crimes of your colleagues, but it does not shield you from illegal acts that you yourself may commit while you are doing your job. Officers, directors, and sometimes shareholders may be individually charged with criminal, administrative, and civil violations of the law—for example, violations of federal securities and antitrust laws—and they will be liable for their own contracts and torts: in none of these situations is it a defense that they were acting to further the corporation's interests. The indemnification and insurance protections discussed in Point 13 have been a response to these potential liabilities incurred "by reason of" being a corporate officer or director (see Appendix A.9).

5. Preserving the corporate fiction (Section 11.2)

How can you guard against a court refusing to recognize the difference between a shareholder and a corporation?

A public corporation and its subsidiaries, or a dominant shareholder and a close corporation, may be treated by judges as single legal entities—i.e., the corporate fiction may be disregarded—on a variety of grounds: actual operation of the disregarded corporation as an agent or instrumentality of its shareholder; creation of the appearance that the shareholder is really the one with whom the outsiders are dealing; failure to provide the corporation adequate capital; or using it to escape government regulation or taxes. New York and most other states make preservation of the corporate fiction turn on whether the corporation operates as the shareholder's agent; California is more concerned with the adequacy of capital provided the corporation by the shareholder (a question that New York judges do not consider a proper judicial concern).

When a corporation is disregarded, as when it is fatally defective (see Point 2), shareholders become directly liable for its tort, contract, and other obligations. They are treated as though the corporation does not exist. Since with close corporations shareholders are usually also officers and directors, loss of the corporate shield is an important source of individual liability for corporate officers and directors.

Precautions for avoiding having a corporation disregarded: Keep it legally independent by making sure that it holds meetings, keeps books and records, and has its own bank accounts, and that its own structure is not ignored in receiving instructions from the shareholders. Don't create the impression that people are "really" dealing with the shareholders. Give it enough capital to cover its regular operations, and avoid financing operations by borrowing from shareholders (which is likely to be treated as equity by the IRS and subordinated in bankruptcy to claims of other creditors). And give the corporation a credible "business purpose" other than to escape being regulated or taxed.

6. Corporate director's duty of care (Section 11.3(a))

How can you avoid charges of being a careless director?

The law says that a director should do his job with the care that "an ordinarily prudent person would use under similar circumstances" (Model Act §35). But directors who do not meet this standard are not thereby liable for harm to their corporations that they could not prevent. And directors who make honest but faulty "business judgments" are not liable for the results, although they must exercise "reasonable diligence," which means that they must at least attend meetings. Directors of financial institutions are more likely than other directors to be held liable for inadequate oversight of subordinates.

Precaution: Do not accept directorships, particularly of banks, unless you plan to attend most meetings and to take your duties seriously. Being a director "in name only" has some of the dangers of endorsing other people's promissory notes.

7. Conflicts of interest (Section 11.3(b)

How can a corporate director identify and handle conflict-of-interest situations?

Your business sense will usually tell you when your interests and your corporation's conflict in a particular transaction. Putting yourself in the corporation's position, would you want someone in your position making decisions for it, or would you ask such a person to disqualify himself?

Having identified a conflict-of-interest situation, what do you do about it? As a minimum you do not vote as a director on the transaction and you disclose to your fellow directors your own financial interest in it. As a further precaution, shareholders may ratify the transaction after you have disclosed to them your interest in it. For a shareholder resolution to this effect, see Appendix D.5(e). While you may decide not to participate in the shareholder vote for other than legal reasons, your interest does not legally inhibit you from voting as a shareholder.

Under the Model Act (§41) a contract or transaction in which a director is financially interested does not need either director or shareholder approval if it is "fair and reasonable to the corporation." It may, however, be unwise to rely on this provision. It is not the law in all states, and your own judgment of what is fair and reasonable may not prevail. And in some states, neither director nor shareholder approval will make legal a transaction found to be unfair to the corporation. It would seem, therefore, that if you think the transaction is unfair to the corporation your options are to resign as a director, abandon the transaction, or go forward with it only after disclosing to other directors and shareholders all of the information you would want if you were in their shoes, including your own reasons for thinking the transaction unfair to the corporation.

8. Corporate opportunities (Section 11.3(c))

How do corporate directors, officers, employees, and agents distinguish business opportunities that should go first to the corporation from those that they can seize for themselves?

The central issue is whether your loyalty to the corporation requires that you give it a chance to exploit the opportunity.

Questions to ask yourself in finding an answer: Is the opportunity related to the corporation's business? Is it related to your corporate position? Do you know about it because of that position? Would you be expected to report it to the corporation? Is the corporation interested in it? Is the corporation able to exploit it? Is this ability dependent on you? If the number of "yes" answers to these questions is large enough to make you think that it would be unfair to the other people interested in the corporation for you to take this opportunity for yourself, you probably should give the corporation first crack at it.

A judicial finding that you have intercepted a corporate opportunity usually means that you turn over any profits that you make from it to the corporation. While this may seem like a mild penalty, it does mean that you enter a bargain on which you may lose but on which you can not gain.

9. Executive compensation (Section 11.3(d))

How may corporate officers and directors guard against challenges to the compensation and benefits they receive from the corporation?

Successful challenges to executive compensation are rare, but even unsuccessful ones are sufficiently troublesome to justify efforts to prevent their emergence. Legal attacks usually feature claims that compensation is determined or benefits granted by the recipients themselves (self-dealing), that the compensation or benefits are unrelated to the value of the executive's services (waste of the corporation's assets), or that they are gifts because the services have already been performed (retroactivity).

These claims suggest the following precautions: Be sure that someone else equal or superior to you in the corporate hierarchy acts for the corporation. Make clear that your compensation or benefits are the result of business judgment, taking into account the competitive market for your services. Be sure that the action granting your compensation is taken before the beginning of the period of service. If possible, use outside directors as a compensation committee to act for or make recommendations to the board. Refrain from voting as a director on your own compensation or benefits and obtain shareholder approval of benefit plans.

Interposition of an independent compensation committee and having board action ratified by the shareholders are particularly effective counters to claims of self-dealing and waste.

10. Controlling shareholders (Section 11.3(e))

What restraints should controlling shareholders observe?

Ordinarily shareholders may vote their shares as they please. However, if they turn corporate directors into puppets, or deceive their fellow shareholders, or use their control unfairly to inflict serious harm on the corporation or other shareholders, they may find themselves being sued for misusing their control power. The best defense against such a charge is to provide the judge with a basis for finding that the controlling shareholders were simply exercising business judgment.

11. Transactions in your corporation's shares (Section 11.4))

How do insiders determine when they can buy or sell their corporation shares?

If a corporation has assets exceeding $1 million and 500 or more shareholders, its officers, directors, and 10% shareholders are liable to the corporation under §16(b) for any profits from purchases and sales or sales and purchases of their corporation's securities occurring within a six-month period.

In contrast, Rule 10 b-5, outlawing deceptive practices in buying and selling securities, applies whatever the corporation's size or share distribution. The test is whether insiders or their "tippees" have bought or sold their corporation's securities on the basis of material inside information. It is permissible for insiders to base investment decisions on their familiarity with their corporation's operations or on superior financial or other expert analysis, but it is not permissible to buy or sell because of knowledge of specific extraordinary situations or events which are almost certain to affect the market. Examples: discoveries, disasters, business opportunities, earning statements, dividend changes, share splits, merger plans.

The constraints of Rule 10 b-5 are, of course, removed when the material inside information, good or bad, is made public and it has had a reasonable time to circulate. But when the corporate interest demands that information *not* be made public, insiders have no choice but to refrain from buying or selling their corporation's shares.

12. Defending legal actions against you (Section 11.5(a))

How should you respond when sued because of your corporate position?

Your initial response will be to hire a lawyer and with his help decide whether you want to try to settle or to fight. If you are sued in a derivative suit on behalf of the corporation, you may not be able to use the lawyer who represents the corporation. But if the claim against you is by an outsider, there will ordinarily be no difficulty in having the corporation's lawyer represent you.

Your lawyer will look for procedural grounds to have the suit dismissed at an early stage. If it is a derivative suit, he may also suggest that you make it more expensive for the shareholder suing you by requiring him to post security for your costs. If the early settlement or dismissal efforts do not succeed, you will become involved in the protracted pre-trial discovery period when each side tries to find out as much as possible about the other side's case. Chances are high that the claim will be settled before it comes to trial.

13. Indemnification and liability insurance (Section 11.5(b))

How can the corporation help protect those who are sued because of their corporate positions?

Most modern corporation acts provide for mandatory indemnification of your expenses, including attorney's fees, if you successfully defend suits brought against you, whether or not on behalf of the corporation, by reason of the fact of your being a corporate director, officer, employee, or agent. However, for suits that are not successfully defended—i.e., which end in settlement or a judgment against you—internal corporate action is needed to authorize indemnification. For suggested steps to provide such corporate action, see articles in Appendix A.9, by-laws in Appendix B.5, and shareholder resolutions in Appendix D.5(f)-(h).

The Model Act (§5(e)) permits advances to you by the corporation for litigation expenses upon your undertaking to repay them if it is ultimately determined that you are not entitled to indemnification.

In most states the corporation can supplement indemnification by insuring you against any liability, except for deliberate dishonesty, asserted against you because of your corporate position. Premiums are ordinarily paid 90% by the corporation and 10% by the individual. High premium costs compared with amounts paid to settle claims suggest that a corporation can save money by being a self-insurer as to such risks. However, self-insurance might be confined to the same limits as indemnification, and thus fail to add any protection not already provided by indemnification.

12

Problems of Your Allegiances: To Corporation, Society, and Self

CONTENTS

407

12

Problems of Your Allegiances: To Corporation, Society, and Self

Chapters 1 to 8 sketch how your corporation is structured and functions and how it pumps money in and out. Chapters 9 to 11 examine special problems when your corporation succeeds and changes hands and some of your own individual liabilities. This concluding chapter looks more broadly at interaction of your multiple and sometimes competing allegiances—i.e., your legal, political, social, and ethical obligations of loyalty—to your corporation, to the society of which you are part, and to your own moral autonomy and integrity.

Chapter 11 concerns itself with your legal duty of loyalty to your corporation and the strains put upon it when you deal for yourself with your corporation or you receive business opportunities that arguably belong to your corporation. These problems involve interaction of corporate and individual interest: your prudence as an officer or director interacting with your prudence as self-interested economic person.

> ▪ While we are concerned with conflicts of interest in Chapter 11, personal and corporate interests can, of course, interact positively as well as negatively—as when a corporate officer works hard for his corporation to promote his own career.

We now assume that you are able to sort out your own business interest from that of your corporation, and we turn to more complex problems regarding not interest but allegiance: interaction of legal and ethical claims made on you by your corporate and societal positions and by your own conscience.

409

▪ **Again, while most problems arise from conflicting allegiances, allegiances can also reinforce one another. Being a good officer or director can help make you a good citizen and person, and vice versa.**

Chapter 11 emphasizes the distinction between you as a part of your corporation and you as a separate legal person but does not try to analyse your responses to the claims of multiple allegiances.

As our concluding inquiry we examine how you respond when you are expected to be, simultaneously, a faithful and effective manager of your corporation, a good citizen, and a moral person before the tribunal of your own conscience.

▪ **Recall that Sir Thomas More got into trouble with Henry VIII because he withheld his moral approval of Henry's divorce while remaining steadfast in his loyalty to his king as a subject.**

In this chapter we will look first at how corporate and societal interests interact at the corporate and governmental level and then at how corporate allegiance interacts with individual conscience.

▪ **To provide a factual context for thinking about how interests and allegiances affect the decision-making of corporate officers and directors, a hypothetical illustration is woven into this chapter. Assume that Adam is a vice president and a director of Eden Corporation who wants to stay loyal to his corporation, his society, and his self. Among those reporting to him are Edward, an engineer, and Lawrence, a lawyer, both of whom he respects for their professional abilities and honesty. They come to him separately with the following concerns:**

Edward tells Adam he is convinced that an important Eden product may be unsafe, and presents some impressive but inconclusive data to support his conviction. Safety of the product is not Edward's assigned responsibility. It has been declared safe by those in Eden who are assigned this responsibility after testing procedures which follow government regulations. Edward urges that the product be withdrawn from the market until it can be retested, which would take several months.

Lawrence tells Adam he is convinced that a form contract, approved several years ago by Eden's board of directors for use in purchasing materials for its operations, is so one-sided in Eden's favor that it is unconscionable, citing court decisions refusing to enforce similar but not identical contracts. Lawrence urges that the Eden contract be revised to make it less one-sided, even though in the existing market those who sell to Eden under the contract do not have enough economic power to insist that Eden change it.

What should Adam do?

Section 12.1 Interaction of Corporate and Societal Interests

We have learned that corporations exist, at least in theory, as governmental constructs in legally organized societies. They appear and disappear by operation of law. While what they do frequently transcends the boundaries of governments to which they owe their existence, they ordinarily function within and alongside other social structures; and the people who make up a corporation—incorporators, shareholders, directors, officers, employees, and agents—also belong to other groupings, such as families, communities, and nation-states (and, sometimes, religions, ethnic groups, and social classes). In this section we look for points where faithfulness to corporation interacts with broader societal responsibilities. We start by examining the history and nature of the relationship between corporations and the public interest. Then we look at how the factual power of corporations exercised by their managers is made legitimate and accountable. And finally we investigate the claim that private corporations and public governments are tending to converge.

(a) Corporations and the public interest

Until well into the 19th century corporations were closely tied to the public interest by the assumption that to receive and retain a corporate charter a group of people must be promoting the public good (the common wealth). Early business corporations were chartered by English kings to advance English trade and colonization abroad and, later, to provide internal public services such as transportation by canal, turnpike, and rail.

Vestiges of this older "public interest" thinking can be found in modern cases where our state courts debate whether non-profit corporations can be formed for "anti-social" purposes. For example, New York has held that a charter cannot be denied to an organization formed to promote racial separation (*Association for the Preservation of Freedom of Choice* v. *Shapiro*, 174 N.E. 2d 487 (N.Y. 1961)), while Ohio has upheld denial of a charter to the Greater Cincinnati Gay Society (*Grant* v. *Brown*, 313 N.E. 2d 847 (Ohio 1974)). Both cases arose under statutes, which have become general, providing for incorporation for any "lawful" purpose; and, the Ohio court notwithstanding, little connection remains between granting of corporate charters and promotion of the public interest.

Divergence of private and public interest seems to have accompanied industrialization and ascendancy of private enterprise. Limitations on what a corporation can do, originally conceived as limits of royal grants imposed for reasons of state, came to be seen as contractual limitations agreed to for the protection of investors—so they could know how their money was being used. But when state corporation acts began to permit corporate charters with no effective boundaries, even contractual limitations disappeared and corporations became free, like other "private" persons, to do as they please within the confines of general laws.

By the late 19th century the notion became firmly established, both in England and the United States, that business corporations do not operate for the public good but rather for the private profit of shareholders. It can still be said that the basic legal duty of corporate officers and directors is to generate profits for distribution or growth. However, the 20th century has seen considerable flexibility develop in application of this legal and ethical norm, and in recent years an extensive literature has emerged concerning "corporate responsibility" for social problems. This change in attitude is illustrated by comparison of two classic cases, one from the late teens and the other from the early fifties:

—In 1916 the Dodge brothers, who later started their own automobile company but who were then large shareholders in Ford Motor Company, sought to force Henry Ford to distribute accumulated Ford profits as dividends. Henry Ford resisted because he believed that the bulk of Ford profits should be used to increase production and lower prices, thereby making Ford automobiles available to more people. While the Michigan Supreme Court refused to enjoin his expansion plans, it did order distribution of substantial dividends, saying: "it is not within the lawful powers of a board of directors to shape and conduct the affairs of a corporation for the merely incidental benefit of shareholders and for the primary purpose of benefiting others." *Dodge* v. *Ford Motor Co.*, 170 N.W. 668 (Mich. 1919).

—In 1951 a New Jersey corporation, A.P. Smith Manufacturing Company, gave $1500 to Princeton University. When the gift was questioned by a shareholder, the corporation sought and obtained a declaratory judgment that the gift was lawful. The New Jersey Supreme Court kept its decision within the traditional rule that corporate expenditures should "benefit" the corporation, but gave the rule a liberal interpretation to permit a gift "voluntarily made in the reasonable belief that it would aid the public welfare and advance the interests of the plaintiff as a private corporation and as a part of the community in which it operates." *A.P. Smith Mfg. Co.* v. *Barlow*, 98 A.2d 581 (N.J. 1953), appeal dismissed, 346 U.S. 861 (1953).

The legality of charitable contributions by corporations was reinforced between 1930 and 1960 by federal income tax cases permitting corporations to take charitable deductions and by decisions, state and federal, treating charitable contributions by public utilities as allowable expenses for rate-making purposes.

It can now be said that corporate giving "for the public welfare or for charitable, scientific or educational purposes" (Model Act §4(o)) has become not only permitted but expected. Going beyond donations into operations (as did the Ford case), a new ethic has developed that corporations, particularly big corporations, should be good citizens and assume responsibilities for operating in the public interest. Employment opportunities for minorities, protection of the environment, conservation of energy, reversal of urban decay by plant and office location: these are some of the areas where corporate managers are being asked to make operational decisions which take into account factors other than pure profit-maximization.

While we seem to have reached the point that it is accepted that shareholders are not the only constituency for whom corporations are managed, the limits of managers' legal and ethical obligations to these other constituencies—employees, customers and suppliers, consumers, communities, regions, the nation, the world—remain ill-defined. Since corporations as we know them cannot survive without some return for investors, it appears that the first duty of managers of private corporations will continue to be to operate at a profit. But this duty does not dictate that profits be maximized. As to individual decisions made for corporations that are operating at an over-all profit, managers seem to feel increasingly free to decide that the most profitable alternative is not always the best one. This freedom expands with the size, stability, and resources of the enterprise. And, of course, not all public-interest decisions are made from ethical choice. A growing array of laws—against false weights and measures, child labor, sweat shops, shoddy goods, monopolies and restraints of trade, deceptive sales practices, pollution, discriminatory hiring, etc.—in the name of public interest impose legal constraints on business decision-making that work against profit maximization.

▪ **In responding to Edward and Lawrence about the product claimed to be unsafe and the contract claimed to be unconscionable, how far should Adam let corporate interest yield to public interest (which, of course, favors safe products and fair contracts)? If profit maximization were his only yardstick, Adam would do nothing to disturb either the product or the contract. But a possibly unsafe product raises countervailing considerations, dictated not only by possible long-term corporate interests but also by Eden's social responsibilities, that are not raised by a possibly unconscionable contract. Consumers, lacking their own testing facilities, are virtually defenseless against unsafe products and have no choice but to trust Eden to make them safe. In contrast, Eden's suppliers know that their contracts are arm's length bargains that they can choose to forego; and Adam's corporate duty to make the best deals he can for Eden survives any qualms of individual consciences about the fairness of the deals to the other parties. While a judge may someday find the Eden contract unconscionable, Adam**

should not now prejudge Eden and refuse to give it the benefit of legal doubt. But doubts as to a product's safety are not bloodlessly legal: they should be resolved in favor of the people likely to be hurt.

(b) Making corporate power legitimate and accountable

In the preceding subsection we viewed the interplay of corporate and societal allegiances largely from within the corporation. We asked: To what extent can and should corporate managers use public interest as a yardstick in making business decisions? Now we need to look at this decision-making power more from the outside, from a societal point of view, and to ask: How can this power be reconciled with the rule of law—i.e., how can it be made legitimate and accountable?

(i) Legitimacy

It is crucial to survival of democratic society that those who exercise power over other people do so legitimately: according to legally enacted rules. It is crucial that there be clearly perceived and accepted differences between organized business and organized crime. The very substantial powers of corporate officers and directors are made legitimate by following the legal procedures detailed in the early chapters of this book. While the niceties of calls, notices, proxy statements, quorums, resolutions, and voting often are seen as legalistic trivia by busy executives, they ignore these procedures at the peril of casting doubt on the legitimacy of corporate actions. Rules simply as rules have ethical weight, as we recognize in our constitution by the central place we give to the principle of "due process of law." When a significant body of the legal rules of a society are ignored or meaningless, that society is in danger of being ruled by naked power.

The problem of legitimacy of corporate power is more complex and deep-seated than a question of following rules. When a corporation becomes widely held and its shares actively traded, its shareholders cease to know or care how it is managed so long as prospects for dividends or capital gains remain acceptable; when prospects become unacceptable, shareholders sell their shares (vote with their feet, by leaving). When they vote at meetings most shareholders support management. As we have seen, control of the proxy machinery puts almost unrestrained governmental power in the hands of incumbent officers and directors, who select their successors not unlike a private club. While the SEC has sought to improve the fairness of proxy voting by the disclosures required in proxy statements, these documents are actually read by few shareholders. It is, therefore, difficult to legitimatize corporate government by invoking an elective mandate. And it is doubtful whether efforts to promote "corporate democracy" will amount to much.

In recent years major attacks on the legitimacy of corporate managements have not involved how they are elected and stay in power but rather how they exercise their power. It appears that some corporate managers have put their corporate allegiance ahead of societal interests to the extent of engaging in conduct on behalf of their corporations ranging from clearly criminal acts to disregard of administrative rulings. This conduct has included bribery of government officials, domestic and foreign; commercial bribery of purchasing agents of other corporations; illegal political contributions; rigging of bids and other kinds of non-competitive pricing; and incomplete compliance with laws concerning employment opportunities, environmental protection, distribution of energy, product safety, consumer credit, employee safety and pensions, and payment of taxes, federal, state, and local. The number and complexity of these constraints on doing business and the expenses involved in compliance has made compliance unattractive, especially when corporate managers suspect it will entail competitive disadvantages.

Possible corrective measures include fewer rules, their more vigorous enforcement, and formulation of ethical codes for self-regulation—all steps which might encourage a more positive, less cynical attitude by business managers toward the public interest. While ethical codes by themselves do not, of course, assure ethical conduct, they help to blunt the argument that unethical conduct is acceptable, and even necessary, because "good guys finish last." The corporate manager who wants to be ethical needs some assurance that his competitors are playing by the same rules.

> ▪ Note that Eden's product and its contract are both "within the law" in the senses that prescribed procedures were followed in adopting them and that neither of them has been officially declared illegal.

(ii) Accountability

Closely linked with making corporate power legitimate is the problem of making it accountable. Much of the public suspicion about the power of corporations derives from a feeling that no one who is not on their payrolls knows whether what they are doing is legal or in the public interest. Americans have learned that high government officials can make costly mistakes and, perhaps even more ominously, can consider themselves "above" the law. People wonder whether officials of large corporations may not be making similar mistakes that threaten our safety and may not be considering themselves "beyond" much of the law. This feeling grows as corporations become multinational and as their power begins to dwarf some of the governments under which they operate. But what is meant when it is urged that corporations should be accountable: accountable to whom and for what; and how is accountability to be enforced?

If corporations are purely private aggregations of wealth, put together to yield profits, presumably it is enough if a corporation's officers and directors account to those who have made or are considering making investments in its securities. Such accounting, which is the goal of federal securities laws, is generally confined to reporting material events (dividend action, management changes, acquisitions, and other happenings that might influence investment decisions) and financial data as reflected in balance sheets, income statements, and cash flow records. Financial statements are ordinarily certified by independent auditors, but their audits do not assure disclosure of illegal or dangerous or immoral activities.

Is it enough that corporations provide financial and investment information for actual or potential investors, or should there also be an accounting— sometimes called a "social audit"—to employees, consumers, and communities that feel the consequences of corporate decisions? But what kind of information should be included in such broader, beyond-profits accounting? And how can it be made meaningful without revelations that will burden the corporation with competitive disadvantages? Most publicly held corporations do present what might be called "social audits without auditors" in their annual reports to shareholders and their presidents' reports at annual meetings. And the proxy rules require full disclosures in proxy statements about matters being submitted to shareholder vote (see Section 3.2(b)).

While the accounting required of most corporations is now largely limited to investment, financial, and proxy data mandated by federal securities regulations, on specific issues there are other ways that corporations can be called to account. These include law suits, requests for action by the many government agencies with regulatory functions, and use of the proxy machinery through shareholder proposals. In fact, managers of our larger corporations may feel that they are the most "accountable" people on the American scene. Section 2.4 shows that shareholder derivative suits can function as an extra conscience that prods officers and directors to do the right thing for their corporations. Similarly, class suits on behalf of shareholders, employees, consumers, and those affected by environmental impacts, can compel justifications of corporate decisions; and suits by individuals and regulatory agencies may be brought under many statutes, such as the securities, labor, antitrust, and employment opportunity laws. Under SEC rules in effect since 1973, a shareholder may put a proposal in the management proxy statement—and thereby usually cause management to explain why it is opposed to the proposal—even if the proposal promotes "general economic, political, racial, religious, social, or similar causes" if the subject of the proposal is "significantly related" to the corporation's business and is "within its control" (Rule 14 a-8(c)).

▪ **The 1973 amendment to the rule on shareholder proposals was preceded by a lengthy effort to require Dow Chemical Company to submit to its shareholders a proposal concerning its sale of napalm for use on human beings.** *Medical Committee for Human Rights* v. *SEC,* **432 F.2d 659 (D.C. Cir. 1970), vacated and dismissed as moot, 404 U.S. 403 (1972).**

Other proposals to increase corporate accountability include the following:

—Audit committees: Greater use of audit committees composed of outside directors is being encouraged. It is hoped that these committees will provide independent but authoritative groups within corporations to whom comptrollers, internal auditors, legal counsel, and others can report matters that they might be reluctant to report to officers and inside directors.

—Outside auditors: A proposal is being considered by the accounting profession that outside auditors take on a responsibility to make public serious irregularities within a corporation that they discover. It seems unlikely, however, that the large accounting firms will want to assume the role of public inspectors.

—Federal incorporation: Influential public interest advocates are urging legislation to require federal incorporation of very large corporations, on the grounds that only the federal government is powerful enough to make these corporations, many of which have world-wide operations, effectively accountable to the public and national interest. (A step towards making corporate accountability more world-wide has been taken in federal legislation outlawing certain corrupt practices in foreign countries by American corporations.)

▪ **In our hypothetical about Eden corporation, Edward, the engineer, and Lawrence, the lawyer, are questioning decisions by "legitimate" authority within the corporation, and one of Adam's problems is whether to rock the boat by reopening these decisions. But if the facts and the law are, respectively, as Edward and Lawrence claim, the legitimacy of the product and purchase contract come into question. The issue for Adam then becomes: how can this legitimacy be determined if he does *not* rock his corporate boat? And this gets into accountability. Edward and Lawrence may go out of channels to press accountability in shareholder suits, shareholder proxy proposals, or appeals to a government agency; but if they do, as the discussion in Section 12.2(a) below shows, Eden can probably fire them. Since Adam values their services, this may be a factor in persuading him to rock the boat to the extent of reporting their con-**

clusions to Eden's president and of recommending that at least the product safety claim be reported to the board.

(c) Convergence of corporations and government

As corporations grow and become more socially accountable, they come to resemble arms of the national government. And if private interest and public interest are perceived as essentially the same (what is good for General Motors is good for the United States, and vice versa), the divided loyalty problem that is the subject of this section fades away—to be replaced, however, with a more disturbing question of whether a society can remain free and open if corporations and government join forces. In this subsection we briefly examine how corporations and government are seen to be coming together and some of the consequences of this process.

(i) Forces for convergence

For a while it appeared that the activism of the late 1960s and early 1970s, much of it directed at large corporations, was going to transform them into arenas for political struggles. Confrontations at shareholders' meetings, harassment of campus recruiters, picketing and boycotts, and bombings and burnings were some of the more forceful manifestations of this phenomenon. Efforts to promote shareholder concern about the moral consequences of corporate policies—particularly as to shares held by church groups, universities, and foundations—were the quieter and perhaps more lasting part of this activism. These experiences seem to have made corporate managers more sensitive to political issues and more sophisticated in handling them. While substantive social and moral questions raised by activists—relative lack of human concern of some weapons, dealings with racist regimes abroad, misuse of the environment, underrepresentaion of blacks and women on corporate boards, etc.—have not disappeared, they have lost some of their urgency. Problems of world-wide shortages of physical resources and resulting economic dislocations are not chargeable to or remediable by individual corporations, no matter how powerful.

The intractability of these problems is likely to contribute to a long-term trend, more basic than shorter-term waves of activism and a quietism, for economic and political power to converge. As problems become more complex and inter-connected, the apparent need for central planning grows. Government and industry have long operated in partnership to produce and maintain military capability. Space and ocean exploration, energy, communications, transportation, health care, agriculture, and utilization of government-owned lands (one third of our land area) are other projects that intermingle public and private interests. Proliferation of information and development of new methods for its generation, storage, retrieval, and utilization open wider vistas for planning and put higher premiums on fusion of economic and political power and institutions.

(ii) Consequences of convergence

On the corporate side the process of becoming less private is being accompanied by shrinkage of the population of medium-sized businesses. If such concerns succeed, they are likely to be acquired by larger corporations; if they do not succeed, they are likely to be dismantled or fragmented. We seem to be working towards a relatively small number of very large corporations and a large number of quite small ones. And differences in structure and functioning between the two types are likely to sharpen: small corporations will become even more like chartered partnerships with shareholders in operational control; while shareholders of large corporations will continue to wield little governmental power.

On the government side, convergence of corporations and governments is changing the nature of law and the operation of governments. As large corporations become less private, the role of private law (contracts, torts, property, agency, trusts, etc.) diminishes and is displaced by public law, especially administrative law.

> ▪ **Comparison of current law school course offerings with those of 20 or 30 years ago reveals the shrinkage of private law in relation to public law. And even where the course names remain unchanged (e.g., torts, property, and corporations), their content has become less private.**

A consequence of the ascendency of administrative law is that traditional separation of powers among legislature, judiciary, and executive has weakened, with administrators, operating under broad "enabling acts," combining the functions of making, interpreting, and enforcing important segments of the law. And much of law itself is changing from being normative (a statement of what should and should not be done) to being instrumental (a statement of "guidelines" as to how objectives are to be achieved). As law becomes instrumental rather than normative, obeying the law ceases to have value for its own sake: questions of what is right and wrong turn into questions of what is expedient and inexpedient.

Experience indicates that government administrators come to work with rather than against corporations they are empowered to regulate and that individuals move easily back and forth between corporations and government agencies. Agency and corporation work together to develop "plans" with the help of data cooperatively generated. Confrontations in court happen only as a last resort when, in the jockeying for advantage, the agency or the corporation pushes the other too far. And in many administrative controversies the party on the "other side" turns out to be another agency.

For democratic institutions to survive the convergence of corporations and government and the ascendancy of administrative, instrumental law, there will need to be people, in corporations and government, with strong individual consciences and motivations to further the public interest.

> **▪ The Eden situation illustrates the areas where corporations and government have and have not converged. In guaranteeing product safety, corporations have assumed governmental functions: the general welfare of consumers rather than profits for Eden is the objective. For consumers, Eden has become its brothers' keeper. But it is not yet its brothers' keeper as to its suppliers. Here the relationship continues to be economic. Perhaps Eden has pushed its economic advantage so far that a court will refuse to enforce the contracts it has made, but it will not yet do so on the grounds that Eden is responsible for the welfare of those with whom it deals.**

Section 12.2 Interaction of Corporate Allegiance and Individual Conscience

In the preceding section we examined claims of corporate and societal interests from the institutional points of view of corporations and governments. Now, in this concluding section, we examine these and some more personal claims from the point of view of individual corporate managers and employees. We start by recognizing that individuals who manage and work for corporations may find that their corporate allegiance is at variance with their societal allegiances. We close by recognizing that corporate allegiance may also impinge, in other even more subtle ways, upon individuals' feelings of integrity and autonomy.

(a) Balancing corporate allegiance against societal allegiance

How to resolve conflict between commands of an authority we have undertaken to obey and those of some "higher" authority has perplexed philosophers, religious writers, judges, soldiers, and ordinary citizens for thousands of years. An early version of this conflict is Abraham's dilemma whether to obey the law against murder and his feelings as a father or what he takes to be the voice of God telling him to sacrifice his son, Isaac (Genesis 22:1-18). More recently the trials of German and Japanese leaders after World War II posed on a grand scale the problem of whether we sometimes have a duty to disobey "lawful" commands of an authority to which we have pledged allegiance. On a more modest scale Ralph Nader posed this dilemma to corporate employees when he urged them to become "whistle blowers" by reporting to an outside organization policies or practices of their corporations which they consider illegal, hazardous, or unconscionable.

> ▪ **For a perceptive analysis of this appeal and related problems, on which some of the following discussion draws, see Blumberg, "Corporate Responsibility and the Employee's Duty of Loyalty and Obedience: A Preliminary Inquiry," 24 *Okla. L. Rev.* 279 (1971), reprinted in P. Blumberg, *Corporate Responsibility in a Changing Society* (Boston University School of Law, 1972) 101-36.**

Using the Nader appeal for whistle blowers to weigh the allegiances of individuals to their corporations against their allegiances as citizens to society, we consider: duties flowing from corporate allegiance; how such duties are likely to be enforced in public interest situations; and how a corporate officer or director should proceed if he disapproves of what his corporation is doing.

(i) Duties of corporate allegiance

Allegiance that directors, officers, and employees owe to their corporations can be particularized as duties of obedience, loyalty, and confidentiality. Some of these duties are discussed in Chapter 11 as bases for potential individual liability. While our present concern goes beyond legal liability to ethical obligation, we can start with consideration of those duties, owed by any agent (A) to his principal (P), described in the Restatement of the Law of Agency (to which section numbers mentioned below refer).

—Obedience: A has a duty to obey reasonable directions of P, but business or professional ethics may be considered in determining whether directions are reasonable; and A is relieved of his duty to obey or act for P if performance involves acts that are criminal, illegal, tortious, unethical, or contrary to public policy (§§383, 384, 411). However, freedom to disobey a direction does not mean that A may disclose it, even after his agency has ended.

—Loyalty: In matters connected with his agency, A has a duty to act solely for P's benefit and to refrain from acting for other persons whose interests conflict with P's; but, outside his agency, A may act in good faith in ways that may injure P's business: an insurance company employee may advocate legislation that will require changes in his employer's policies (§§387, 394).

—Confidentiality: A has a duty not to use or to communicate information acquired in his agency to P's injury nor to A's advantage, unless the information is a matter of general knowledge; but if the information reveals that P is committing or is about to commit a crime, A may disclose it (§395). Thus, while disobedience may be based on consequences short of criminality, disclosure must be based on crime or its prospect.

▪ This rule derives from a citizen's responsibility to report crimes. Failure to report a felony constituted a common law misdemeanor called "misprison of felony"; this offense became almost obsolete, but it has started to be enforced again in recent years.

(ii) Impact of public interest

The Restatement rules seem to limit the whistle blowing freedom of corporate employees to crimes. However, it is doubtful that these rules will be rigorously applied where disclosure is made to protect the public interest. The rules are aimed at unfair competitive tactics by employees for their own economic advantage rather than at disclosures made in the public interest and without malice, which are likely to work to the economic disadvantage of the employees. A 1967 English case supports a public interest defense by an employee sued for damages by his former employer for making unrewarded, non-malicious disclosures to a newspaper of information received in confidence about the employer's business practices. *Initial Services, Ltd.* v. *Putterill*, [1967] 3 W.L.R. 1032, 84 L.Q. Rev. 8 (1968).

Employee rights in this area are likely to be tested in cases involving powers of employers to discharge employees making disclosures. Unlike government employees, employees of private corporations cannot invoke freedom of speech rights based on the first amendment, because these rights are only protected against governmental interference. Absent some contractual restraint, the law has long been that private employees may be discharged at the will of their employers. It is possible, however, that employees of large corporations may develop some citizens' rights that will protect them not only from damage suits but also from discharge as punishment for disclosures made in the public interest.

While such a rule has the appearance of fairness it would entail dangers for all organizations and the people connected with them. Traditional concepts of loyalty are likely to be eroded, and the confidentiality of trade secrets and other data of organizations (including personal information about other people connected with the organizations) will be in jeopardy if individual employees are encouraged to decide for themselves when the public interest requires that private information be made public.

▪ Under the traditional concepts of employee rights and duties, neither the engineer nor the lawyer could take his disagreement with Eden management outside of the corporation without risk of being fired and even of being sued for an injunction and damages.

(iii) The disapproving officer or director

How should you proceed as a corporate officer or director if your corporation is doing or is about to do something that you consider legally or morally wrong? It would seem that you should first try to persuade your colleagues to change their plans. If this effort fails and if you are convinced that the action amounts to a crime, you will need to resign if you do not want to be chargeable as a party to the crime. If the action would be a felony (i.e., a crime punishable by a year or more in prison) you are also under a duty to report it to law enforcement officers, although it is unlikely that you will be prosecuted for misprison of felony if you do not make such a report.

If the action is not criminal, your alternatives are to go along with the majority or to resign quietly. There may be situations where the corporation's interests arguably require that it break a contract, commit a tort, violate a regulation, or strike an unconscionable bargain; or, on a more public scale, its interests may dictate that it take action that does harm to the environment, energy resources, the national or world economy, or human rights. In deciding whether you will oppose such actions and perhaps even resign if you cannot stop them, you should keep in mind that your fiduciary position as a corporate officer or director may require that you do some anti-social things for the corporation that you would not do for yourself. Thus, in balancing your corporate and societal allegiances you will need to take care that you are not asking that your corporation sacrifice interests which may be essential to its survival in order to ease your own conscience.

> ▪ **This constraint, which applies to how Adam and Lawrence treat Eden's possibly unconscionable purchase contracts, is not, of course, peculiar to corporate managers. Anyone in a fiduciary position—lawyer, trustee, guardian, etc.—is under a duty to put the interests of those for whom he is acting ahead of the rest of the world. Because there are others whose job it is to see that justice is done, and because the lawyer defending a client accused of a crime is the only one acting solely in his client's interest, the lawyer may not allow his own love of justice to cause him to shrink from using any legal means to defend his client—even though he would choose not to use these means on his own behalf.**

(b) Balancing corporate allegiance against allegiance to self

The preceding subsection matches, at the level of corporations and governments, corporate allegiance against allegiance to society. Now corporate allegiance is matched, at the level of individual officers and directors, against their allegiance to themselves. Allegiance to self is illusive, both because self itself is illusive and because allegiance to self is easily confused with other allegiances. Some of this confusion can be confined if we acknowledge that allegiance to self can be neither chosen nor renounced the way that group allegiance and fiduciary duties can be assumed and resigned from. Self is the unique and paradoxical part of our existence from which there is no escape and about which we have the most ethical freedom: self is a cage that we fashion for ourselves. While we cannot choose to be someone else, we can choose whether or not we will be ethical persons. Most of this concluding subsection is addressed to this paradox—the life sentences we each have of living with ourselves, mitigated by the choices we have about what sort of persons we will be—as it applies to the parts of our lives that we choose to spend as corporate officers and directors.

While corporate managers are faced with many kinds of ethical choices that help define the kinds of persons that they are, perhaps most pervasive are choices whether to act fairly in particular situations, many of which have been discussed in this book. Fairness choices also seem appropriate for singling out from other ethical choices because they tend to fall in a gray area between right and wrong. While taking unfair advantage is not commendable, it less clearly marks one as a bad person than does murder, theft, or deceit. Thus we start by asking how does one go about being a fair person and how does being a corporate manager affect this effort. Then we broaden our inquiry to ask how our autonomy as ethical persons may be diminished by role-playing and by not doing things for their own sake.

An objective of this concluding subsection is to make the point that those who serve as corporate officers and directors need to be aware and concerned, not only with reference to the corporate structures, functions, and problems that this book has been detailing, but also with reference to how they see themselves in the midst of all of this corporate machinery.

(i) Being a fair person

Unfairness is more easily described than fairness; and it is more easily approached from the point of view of the victim than from that of the actor. It can be called being treated as a thing to be manipulated rather than as a person with ends of his own—i.e., in a way that the actor would resent being treated himself. We recognize intuitively, emotionally, and intensely when we are being treated unfairly. Justice Oliver Wendell Holmes was fond of saying that even a dog knows the difference between being kicked and tripped over. We willingly wait our turns when everyone is doing so on some rational basis (such as first come, first served), but we become resentful when someone pushes in ahead of us. Significantly, we are less resentful when someone pushes into the line behind us.

While detection of unfairness by its victims comes easily, it is harder for an actor to sense when he is being unfair to others. He may feel that he has good reasons for what he is doing (he may push ahead because he is in a hurry); and he may not realize how his conduct seems to others (he may be the product of a culture that does not bother with queues). Some of these difficulties can be overcome if he adopts principles or rules about fairness in advance, because it is easier to acknowledge the claims of fairness if one does not know what his particular situation will be. As Harvard philosopher John Rawls argues: a rational person would not agree to supremacy of a particular race or sex in advance of finding out what his or her own race and sex happen to be.* Similarly, if A and B want to divide a pie evenly, they should let A do the cutting and then B have the first choice of pieces; A will cut as evenly as he can because he does not know which piece B will choose, and any unevenness may be used against him.

Unfortunately, most of us do not work out principles of fairness in advance. And by the time we start to think about being fair we frequently have acquired needs and interests that seem to make being fair in particular situations a luxury we cannot afford. About the best we can do is to remember the Golden Rule and try to reverse roles with the other people involved and ask ourselves: would we like to be treated this way? Even though role reversal does not come easily in the heat of pursuing our own goals, if we want to be fair persons we need to find some way to make ourselves think about how we would receive what we are dishing out.

Being corporate officers and directors creates special problems in being fair persons because now we must weigh the cost of being fair against the needs of our corporations to survive by operating profitably. Neil Chamberlain points up the conflict between individual ethics and the needs that dictate institutional conduct as follows:

> But there is a profound difference between the ethical standards of governing personal conduct and the organizational imperatives governing institutional conduct. Whatever the legal fiction which regards the corporation as a person, it is no more a person than is the Catholic Church or Harvard University . ... Even the Catholic Church has found it necessary to substitute for the Christian creed of self-sacrifice the institutional imperative of a continuing mission, regulating its conduct by quite different standards than those it preaches . ... Hence the Inquisition . ... But hence, too, its survival.**

It appears that when one acts for a corporation he is obligated to press its legal advantages and to resolve doubts in its favor unless some benefit results to the corporation by being gracious on its behalf. In other words, you are foreclosed

---

*John Rawls, *A Theory of Justice* (Cambridge, MA: Harvard University Press, 1971), p. 12.
**Neil W. Chamberlain, *The Limits of Corporate Responsibility,* (New York: Basic Books, Inc., 1973), p. 205

from being fair to outsiders, just for the sake of being fair and when a cost of being fair will fall on your corporation. However, as earlier chapters in this book indicate, legal rules governing conduct by and for corporations are increasingly including the notion of fairness in determining legal obligations (rules concerning additional issues of shares, adequate capitalization, de facto mergers, and unconscionable contracts are a few examples). While you may not be free to follow the dictates of your own conscience, as such, in making corporate decisons, the promptings of your conscience may be relevant in determining what you may and may not do on behalf of your corporation under the law. And, of course, when you are acting on your own behalf, as you are in many fairness situations (conflicts of interest, corporate opportunities, and transactions in the corporation's shares are examples), you not only are free from any fiduciary obligations to refrain from imposing your conscience on your corporation, but you may also be under a positive legal duty to act fairly. In summary: being a corporate manager limits your freedom to act fairly when you are acting for your corporation, but it is not a general license to act unfairly; and you are still faced with choosing the kind of person you want to be.

> ▪ **The above discussion supports our earlier suggestion that Adam should not urge that Eden give up the advantages of its one-sided contracts just for the sake of being fair.**

(ii) Being an automous person

The above discussion casts doubt on whether corporations and other group-persons can be ethical persons in light of their "organizational imperatives" to survive. It also casts doubt on whether individuals should ever allow their consciences to be taken over by institutions or causes. The history, particularly in this century, of giving group-persons—such as nation-states and political parties and movements—ethical personality has been largely tragic: decent people have been led to do indecent acts on behalf of institutions and causes that have betrayed them. And it is individuals who suffer when institutions and causes go astray. Of course, good institutions and causes may inspire apathetic people to be more decent and less inhumane than they otherwise might be. But, either way, ethical responsibility seems to be a matter of individual choice rather than administrative decision. In the corporate context, the consequences of individual ethical responsibility would seem to be that when you serve a corporation—as manager, employee, or legal counsel—you must work out for yourself a "sticking point" beyond which you will not go in allegiance to your corporation's organizational imperatives of survival and profits. If you want to be a law-abiding person, the law helps you set some minimum requirements. If you want to be an ethical person, you may not be satisfied with what the law requires.

A factor in arriving at your sticking point will be how deeply you are convinced that your corporation *should* survive and thrive.

In preserving your individual ethical autonomy it is also essential that you sort out the difference between the role you play in your corporation and your real self. Like other roles—citizen, parent, soldier, judge, priest—the corporate role of officer or director can impose deep and intense commitment, and all other allegiances may grow pale when you are throwing yourself into your corporate role. A judge deciding a case or a soldier carrying out a mission may feel that he has become almost an automaton (a "small movable fort" in Thoreau's phrase) obligated to set aside all considerations extraneous to his "office." And it is easy to slip from playing a role into being it: to see our roles as part of our identities, without which we would become different persons. Disorientation suffered when people retire or when their children grow up are examples of feeling diminished by loss of role. This confusion of the value and importance of role and self can work both ways: exalted roles lead to high self-esteem and demeaning roles to self-degradation. Perhaps most dangerously, the blurring of difference between role and self can make us unaware of our freedom to do what is legal and ethical. A soldier ordered to shoot an unarmed civilian may feel that he has no choice; and a corporate executive caught in a situation where bribery of government officials, or kickbacks, or bid-rigging appears to him to be the way of doing business may feel similarly powerless to say "no."

> ▪ **Adam is put in a bind something like this by Edward's assertion that an important product of Eden is unsafe. Those in authority have decided differently, and both Adam and Edward may hazard their positions in Eden if they question that decision after the product is on the market. Note that I made Adam a vice president, not the president.**

It may be easier to refuse to do what we know is wrong (and even illegal) if more of what we do is done for its own sake rather than as a means to some other end. When we do not value what we are doing for the joy or satisfaction or opportunity for expressing ourselves that it itself provides but only instrumentally for some other good that we think it will accomplish—say, a paycheck, or prestige, or power—our attitudes about what we do change. It is easier to act unfairly, or to cut legal and ethical corners, if we think what we are doing "does not matter." And if we evaluate what we are doing, not from our own point of view, but from the point of view of how much permanent, useful impact it will have on the external world, we are probably justified in thinking that it will not matter.

As people play games for fun as well as for physical fitness, people manage corporations for other objectives than money, prestige, and power. But it is generally harder to do things for their own sake as a corporate manager than it is in more self-directed occupations, particularly if you find yourself one or more rungs from the top of your corporate ladder. A possible strategy is to find other means than your corporate function for expressing yourself. Kafka worked by day as a lawyer for a Prague insurance company and did most of his writing at night; he died shortly before his 41st birthday. His unhappy vision of life has been ascribed in part to what he saw as the deadening monotony of his job. While this experience probably enriched what he wrote, it points up the danger for many of us in building a wall between what we do for money and what we do for its own sake. If our work becomes drudgery, few of us have the genius or patience or time to develop alternative avenues of self-expression.

If we are diligent and fortunate, however, I am convinced that we can remain faithful to our allegiances to corporation, society, and self by the ways that we serve our corporations; we can find in what we do for our corporations work that serves the public interest, that allows us to be ethical persons who are more than mere role-players, and that calls upon us to express ourselves in decisions made and tasks done with the parental love and care that we invest when we value what we are doing for its own sake.

CHECKLIST OF POINTS TO WATCH OUT FOR CONCERNING YOUR ALLEGIANCES

(References after headings are to Sections of Chapter 12.)

1. Corporations and the public interest (Section 12.1(a))

When may a corporate officer or director decide, in the public interest, to sacrifice a chance to maximize profits?

While corporations, particularly big ones, are now expected to operate in the public interest, they must make profits to survive. Individual decisions for a generally profitable enterprise may be based on factors other than immediate profit. And in some areas, including product safety, where the public is protected weakly or not at all by market forces, corporations have a positive legal duty to use funds than otherwise would be profit to do things to protect the public. However, in the area of buying and selling, corporate officers and directors are generally supposed to obtain the best bargains they can for their corporations; and, if they are very successful, these bargains may be one-sided.

2. Making corporate power legitimate and accountable (Section 12.1(b))

How can corporate power be reconciled with the rule of law?

Self-interest does not justify illegal acts: there is a difference between business and organized crime. While officers and directors should usually give their corporations the benefits of legal doubts, they should not create doubts where they do not exist. And there has been pressure for more effective ways of checking on what corporations are doing, including wider use of director audit committees, wider responsibilities of outside auditors, and increased federal intervention: procedures which provide more systematic checks than the shareholder suits or proxy proposals that happen to surface.

3. Convergence of corporation and government (Section 12.1 (c))

Which decisions of corporate officers and directors have become governmental and which remain business decisions?

Decisions like product safety have become governmental, because they are reached as the result of a joint effort with regulatory agencies to negotiate out how much protection the general welfare will receive at the expense of profits. Governmental functions are turned over to corporations. But buying and selling decisions generally remain in the private sector and have kept more of their separateness from government.

4. Balancing corporate and societal allegiances (Section 12.2(a))

When may employees "blow the whistle" on their corporation?

Employees may disobey their employers, without legal liability but with no assurance of keeping their jobs, where obedience would be illegal, unethical, or against public policy. But the right to disobey does not carry the right to disclose information gained from their employment, unless a crime is involved.

If officers, directors, employees, or agents disapprove of corporate action which is not criminal, their alternatives are to go along or to resign quietly. And remember that fiduciaries are under a duty to do things for those they represent that they would not do for themselves.

5. Balancing corporate allegiances against allegiances to self (Section 12.2(b))

How far can we go as officers, directors, employees, and agents in being persons who are fair and autonomous?

All of us are free to be fair when we are not acting as fiduciaries for the corporation, and we are required to be fair when acting for the corporation in situations where the law requires that the corporation itself be fair. But in other situations, we are not free to be fair at the corporation's expense. There are, of course, many situations where it is to the corporation's advantage to be fair.

Remaining autonomous persons requires a "sticking point" in our corporate loyalty where we are prepared to resign rather than do what is repugnant to us. And keeping our autonomy requires that we keep separate our selves and our corporate roles, so there is someone there to say "no." We are more likely to keep our autonomy if, instead of doing our corporate jobs for the money, prestige, or power they bring us, we do them for their own sake and for the opportunities they give us to express ourselves.

APPENDIX
OF
MODEL DOCUMENTS,
AGREEMENTS, AND FORMS

Table of Contents of Appendix

APPENDIX

OF

MODEL DOCUMENTS, AGREEMENTS, AND FORMS

(Section references (§) are to the Model Act)

A. Articles of Incorporation

35 Sample Provisions

A.1 The Corporation's name, duration, and purposes (§54(a)—(c))*

A.1 (a) Name:

The name of the corporation is DIGHALDOE CORPORATION.

> ▪ **The name must contain the word "corporation," "company," "incorporated," or "limited," or an abbreviation of one of such words (§8).**

A.1 (b) Duration:

The duration of the corporation is perpetual.

A.1 (c) Purposes:

The purposes for which the corporation is organized are:

(1) To transact any or all lawful business for which corporations may be incorporated under the laws of the State of _____, including, without limitation, the business of extracting, transporting, processing, and selling coal;

(2) To manufacture, buy, sell, and deal in goods, wares, merchandise, and personal property of every kind;

(3) To the same extent as natural persons could do, to acquire, construct, maintain, develop, improve, rent, use, mortgage, and dispose of real property and interests therein;

(4) To act as agent or representative, in any capacity, and to perform services for others;

(5) To acquire, develop, improve, use, grant, and receive licenses in respect of, and mortage, dispose of, and deal in letters patent of the United States and of any other country, patent rights, licenses and privileges, inventions, trade secrets, improvements and processes, copyrights, trademarks, and trade names;

---

*Section references (§) are to the Model Act.

(6) To acquire, own, and dispose of rights, privileges, permits, and franchises convenient for any of the purposes of its business;

(7) To acquire, own, pledge, dispose of, and deal in shares, rights, bonds, debentures, notes, trust receipts, and other securities, obligations, choses in action, and evidences of indebtedness or interest which are issued or created by any corporations, associations, partnerships, firms, trusts, estates, or persons, public or private, or by the government of the United States, or by any foreign government, or by any state, territory, province, municipality, county, or other political subdivision, or by any governmental agency, domestic or foreign, and as owner thereof to possess and exercise all the rights, powers, and privileges of ownership, including the right to execute consents and to vote thereon and to do any and all acts necessary or advisable for the preservation, protection, improvement, and enhancement of value thereof;

(8) To aid in any manner any corporation, association, partnership, firm, trust, estate, or person, any of whose securities, evidences of indebtedness, obligations, or shares are held by the corporation directly or indirectly, or in which or in the welfare of which, the corporation shall have any interest, and to guarantee securities, evidences of indebtedness and obligations of other corporations, associations, partnerships, firms, trusts, estates, and persons;

(9) To acquire, and pay for in cash, shares, bonds, or other securities of the corporation or otherwise, the goodwill, rights, assets, and property, and to undertake and assume the whole or any part of the obligations or liabilities of any corporation, association, partnership, firm, trust, estate, or person;

(10) To enter into, make, and perform contracts of every kind;

(11) To borrow money and personal property, and, from time to time without limit as to amount, to issue, accept, endorse, and execute promissory notes, drafts, checks, bills of exchange, warrants, bonds, debentures, and other negotiable and non-negotiable instruments and evidences of indebtedness, and to secure the payment of any thereof and of the interest thereon by mortgage upon or by pledge, conveyance, or assignment in trust of the whole or of any part of the property of the corporation, whether at the time owned or thereafter acquired, and to sell, pledge, or otherwise dispose of such bonds or other obligations of the corporation for its corporate purposes;

(12) To lend any of its funds or property, either with or without security;

(13) To acquire, hold, and dispose of its own shares and securities and rights thereto;

(14) To carry out all or any part of the foregoing purposes as principal or as agent, or in conjunction with any other corporation, association, partnership, firm, trust, estate, or person, or as a partner or as member of a partnership, syndicate, or joint venture or otherwise, in any part of the world and to the same extent and as fully as natural persons might or could do;

(15) To do all things necessary and incidental to the attainment of the above stated purposes; and

(16) To have and to exercise all the powers now or hereafter conferred by the laws of State of _____ upon corporations formed under the laws of such State.

Purposes specified in the foregoing clauses are not, except as otherwise expressed, limited or restricted by reference to, or inference from the terms of any other clause in these articles of incorporation, and purposes specified in each of the foregoing clauses are to be regarded as independent purposes. Such purposes are to be construed also as powers, but such enumeration of specific powers does not limit or restrict the powers of the corporation now or hereafter granted to it by law. Only the business for which a corporation may be formed under the laws of the State of _____ may be conducted by the corporation.

A.2 Authorized shares and par values (§54(d))

A.2 (a) One class of common shares:

The aggregate number of shares which the corporation has authority to issue is 5,000, and the par value of such shares is $10 per share, amounting in the aggregate to $50,000.

A.2 (b) Two classes of common shares, one non-voting and one voting:

The aggregate numbers of shares of all classes which the corporation has authority to issue is 5,000, and the par value of such shares is $10 per share, amounting in the aggregate to $50,000. Two thousand of such shares are Class A non-voting shares and 3,000 are Class B voting shares. Class A and Class B shares have identical rights, without regard to class, except that Class A shares do not entitle holders thereof to vote on any matter unless specifically required by law.

A.2 (c) Two classes of shares, one preferred and one common:

The aggregate number of shares of all classes which the corporation has authority to issue is 5,000; of which 2,000 shares of the par value of $100 per share, amounting in the aggregate to $200,000, are preferred shares, and 3,000 shares of the par value of $10 per share, amounting in the aggregate to $30,000, are common shares.

A.3 Classes of shares: designations, preferences, limitations, and relative rights (§54(e))

A.3 (a) Designations:

The preferred shares are designated "8% Cumulative Preferred Shares" (hereinafter called "Preferred Shares") and the common shares are designated "Common Shares."

A.3 (b) Dividends:

Holders of Preferred Shares are entitled to receive, when and as declared by the board of directors out of funds legally available therefor, cumulative preferential dividends in the cash rate of, but not exceeding, 8% of the par value per annum, payable quarterly on the first days of March, June, September, and December of each year. Dividends on the first issue of Preferred Shares commence to accrue and be cumulative, whether or not declared, from and after the date of issue thereof. Dividends on Preferred Shares subsequently issued commence to accrue and be cumulative, whether or not declared, from and after the date when the rights of the holders of such subsequently issued shares in respect of unpaid dividends are the same as the rights of the holders of the then outstanding shares. So long as any Preferred Shares remain outstanding, no dividend shall be paid upon or declared or set apart for Common Shares, nor any Common Shares purchased, retired, or otherwise acquired by the corporation, unless all dividends on outstanding Preferred Shares for all past quarterly dividend periods are paid or declared and set apart for payment, but without interest, and the full dividends thereon for the then current quarterly dividend period are concurrently paid or declared and set apart for payment. After past and current dividends on the Preferred Shares are paid or declared and set apart for payment, dividends may be declared and paid on the Common Shares when and as determined by the board of directors out of any funds legally available for dividends.

A.3 (c) Redemption:

The corporation at the option of the board of directors may redeem all or any outstanding Preferred Shares upon notice given as hereinafter provided, by paying therefor in cash the sum of $100 per share plus an amount in cash equal to accrued and unpaid dividends thereon to the date fixed for redemption. If less than all outstanding Preferred Shares are to be redeemed, shares to be redeemed shall be selected pro rata or by lot or by such other equitable method as the board of directors may determine. Notice of redemption of Preferred Shares shall be mailed, postage prepaid, to holders of record thereof at their respective addresses then appearing on the books of the corporation, not less than 15 nor more than 60 days prior to the redemption date. If such notice is duly given, and if on or before the redemption date funds necessary for the redemption are set aside by the corporation in trust for holders of Preferred Shares to be redeemed so as to be and continue available therefor, then, from and after giving of such notice and setting aside of such funds, notwithstanding that any certificates for Preferred Shares to be redeemed are not surrendered for cancellation, shares represented thereby are no longer deemed outstanding, and holders of certificates therefor have with respect to such shares no rights in or with respect to the corporation except the right to receive the redemption price thereof and accrued and unpaid dividends thereon to the redemption date, without interest, upon surrender of their certificates. The term "an amount in cash equal to accrued and unpaid dividends" with respect to any Preferred Share means an amount computed at the rate of 8% per annum on the par value of such share for the period from the date upon which dividends thereon commenced to accrue and be cumulative to the date as of which accrued and unpaid dividends are being determined, less the amount of all dividends theretofore paid on such share.

A.3 (d) Liquidation:

Upon voluntary or involuntary liquidation, dissolution, or winding up of the affairs of the corporation, holders of Preferred Shares are entitled to receive $100 in cash for each share, plus an amount in cash equal to accrued and unpaid dividends thereon to the date of such payment, before any distribution of assets of the corporation is made to holders of Common Shares. After such payment is made in full to holders of outstanding Preferred Shares or funds necessary for such payment are set aside in trust for such holders so as to be and continue available therefor, such holders are entitled to no further participation in distribution of assets of the corporation, and remaining assets shall be divided and distributed among holders of Common Shares then outstanding according to their respective shares. If assets are insufficient to permit such payment to holders of Preferred Shares, the entire assets shall be distributed ratably among such holders. A consolidation or merger of the corporation, a sale or transfer of all or substantially all of its assets as an entirety, or any purchase or redemption of shares of the corporation of any class, is not a "liquidation, dissolution, or winding up of the affairs of the corporation" within the meaning of this paragraph.

A.3 (e) Election of directors:

If on the date fixed by the by-laws for the holding of the annual meeting of shareholders any dividend accrued on Preferred Shares for any past quarterly dividend payment is not declared and paid, then at such annual meeting holders of Preferred Shares voting as a separate class shall be entitled to elect a majority of the directors and the balance of the directors shall be elected by holders of Common Shares voting as a separate class. Directors so elected hold office until the next annual meeting of shareholders and until election of their successors.

A.3 (f) Voting power:

Except as expressly required by law and as herein provided, holders of Preferred Shares have no voting power nor are they entitled to notice of meetings of shareholders, all rights to vote and all voting power being vested exclusively in holders of Common Shares.

A.4 Issuance of preferred shares in series (§54(f))

(Alternative to A.2 and A.3)

A.4 (a) Authorized shares and par value:

The aggregate number of shares of all classes which the corporation has authority to issue is 5,000 shares of which 2,000 shares of the par value of $100 each, amounting in the aggregate to $200,000, are preferred shares and 3,000 shares of the par value of $10 each, amounting in the aggregate to $30,000, are common shares.

A.4 (b) Authority of board of directors concerning series of preferred shares:

The preferred shares may be issued from time to time in one or more series. The designations, preferences, and other rights and limitations or restrictions of preferred shares of each series are such as may be fixed by the board of directors (and authority so to do is hereby expressly granted) and stated in a resolution or resolutions adopted by the board of directors providing for the initial issue of preferred shares of such series. The resolution or resolutions shall fix as to shares of such series (a) dividend rights of holders, (b) terms on which shares may be redeemed if such shares are to be redeemable, (c) rights of holders upon dissolution or any distribution of assets, (d) terms or amount of the sinking fund, if any, to be provided for the purchase or redemption of shares, (e) terms upon which shares may be converted into or exchanged for shares of any other class or classes or of any one or more series of preferred shares if the shares are to be convertible or exchangeable, (f) voting rights, if any, of the shares, and (g) such other designations, preferences, and relative, participating, optional or other special rights, and qualifications, limitations or restrictions of the shares desired to be so fixed.

A.4 (c) Voting power:

Except as otherwise provided in the resolution or resolutions of the board of directors providing for the initial issue of shares of a particular series or as expressly required by law, holders of preferred shares of a series are entitled to one vote for each such share, to be voted share for share with holders of common shares without distinction as to class, and are not entitled to vote separately as a class or series of a class. The number of authorized preferred shares may be increased or decreased from time to time by the affirmative vote of the holders of a majority of the shares of the corporation entitled to vote, and holders of preferred shares are not entitled to vote separately as a class or series of a class on any such increase or decrease.

A.4 (d) Relative rights and preferences within and between series:

All shares of any one series of preferred shares are identical with each other in all respects except that shares of a series issued at different times may differ as to the dates from which dividends thereon shall accumulate, and all series of preferred shares rank equally and are identical in all respects except as variations in the relative rights and preferences as between series are fixed and determined in the respective resolutions of the board of directors providing for the initial issue thereof.

A.4 (e) Dividends:

Subject to the prior and superior rights of preferred shares as set forth in any resolution or resolutions of the board of directors providing for the initial issue of a particular series of preferred shares, such dividends (payable in cash, shares, or otherwise) as may be determined by the board of directors may be declared and paid on common shares from time to time out of funds legally available therefor, including the depletion reserves of the corporation, and preferred shares are not entitled to participate in any such dividend.

A.5 Preemptive rights (§§54(g), 26, 26A)

A.5 (a) Denial thereof:

No holder of shares of the corporation is entitled as a matter of right, preemptive or otherwise, to subscribe for or to purchase any part of any shares of the corporation, now or hereafter authorized to be issued, or shares thereof held in the treasury of the corporation or securities convertible into shares, whether issued for cash or other consideration or by way of dividend or otherwise.

A.5 (b) Unrestricted grant thereof:

Except as otherwise expressly required by law, shareholders of the corporation have a preemptive right to acquire unissued or treasury shares or securities convertible into such shares or carrying a right to subscribe to or acquire such shares.

A.5 (c) Restricted grant thereof:

Except as otherwise provided in these articles or as expressly required by law, shareholders of the corporation have a preemptive right to acquire unissued or treasury shares or securities convertible into such shares or carrying a right to subscribe to or acquire such shares. Such preemptive right is subject to the following restrictions:

—Shares issued with shareholder approval to directors, officers, or employees: No preemptive right exists to acquire any shares issued to directors, officers, or employees pursuant to approval by affirmative vote of the holders of a majority of the shares entitled to vote thereon or when authorized by and consistent with a plan theretofore approved by such a vote of shareholders.

—Shares not sold for cash: No preemptive right exists to acquire any shares sold otherwise than for cash.

—Preferred shareholders: Holders of shares of any class that is preferred or limited as to dividends or assets are not entitled to any preemptive right.

—Common shareholders as to preferred shares: Holders of common shares are not entitled to any preemptive right to shares of any class that is preferred or limited as to dividends or assets or to any obligations, unless convertible into common shares or carrying a right to subscribe to or acquire common shares.

—Non-voting common shareholders as to voting common shares: Holders of common shares without voting power have no preemptive right to common shares with voting power.

—Restrictions imposed by board of directors: The preemptive right is limited to an opportunity to acquire shares or other securities under such terms and conditions as the board of directors may fix for the purpose providing fair and reasonable opportunity for the exercise of such right.

A.6 Provisions for regulating internal affairs of the corporation (§54(h))
(Intended mainly for close corporations)

A.6 (a) Number of directors (§36):

The number of directors of the corporation is three (3) who are to be elected annually. The number of directors may be increased or decreased from time to time by amendment to the articles of incorporation or by resolution duly adopted by the shareholders, but no decrease shall have the effect of shortening the term of any incumbent directors.

A.6 (b) Cumulative voting for election of directors (§33):

At each election for directors by the shareholders every shareholder entitled to vote at such election has the right to vote, in person or by proxy, the number of shares owned by him for as many persons as there are directors to be elected and for whose election he has a right to vote, or to cumulate his vote by giving one candidate as many votes as the number of such directors multiplied by the number of his shares shall equal, or by distributing such votes on the same principle among any number of such candidates.

A.6 (c) Greater than majority quorum of and action by shareholders (§§32,143):

Ninety percent (90%) of the shares entitled to vote, represented in person or by proxy, constitute a quorum at a meeting of shareholders. If a quorum is present, the affirmative vote of ninety percent (90%) of the shares represented at the meeting and entitled to vote on the subject matter is the act of the shareholders.

A.6 (d) Greater than majority quorum of and action by directors (§40):

Three-fourths of the number of directors stated in the articles of incorporation or fixed by resolution duly adopted by the shareholders constitute a quorum for transaction of business. The act of three-fourths of the directors present at a meeting at which a quorum is present is the act of the board of directors.

A.6 (e) Transfers of shares and options for their purchase:

Shares of the corporation are not transferable, other than by will or by operation of the laws of descent and distribution, unless they are first offered by the holder for sale to the corporation, and, if such shares are not purchased by the corporation, such shares are then offered for sale to other shareholders on a pro rata basis; and the corporation and other shareholders have respectively, first and second options to purchase such shares at fair market value.

A.6 (f) Options for purchase of shares upon holder's death or cessation of employment:

The corporation and other shareholders on a pro rata basis have, respectively, first and second options to purchase shares at fair market value of a shareholder who dies or who ceases to be an employee of the corporation.

A.6 (g) Determination of fair market value of optioned shares:

Fair market value of shares subject to options to purchase by the corporation or by other shareholders is the higher of a price offered for such shares by another bona fide prospective purchaser and the value of such shares fixed by agreement of shareholders within the prior 12 months; if no such value has been fixed by agreement of shareholders a value shall at the request of the seller or the option holder, be fixed by an appraiser agreed to by the seller and the option holder or, if they cannot agree, by an appraiser appointed by the American Arbitration Association.

A.7 Office and agent; initial directors; incorporators (§54 (i)-(k))

A.7 (a) Office and agent:

The address of the corporation's initial registered office is _____, and the name of its initial registered agent at such address is _____.

A.7 (b) Initial directors:

The number of directors constituting the initial board of directors is three (3), and the names and addresses of the persons who are to serve as directors until the first annual meeting of shareholders or until their successors be elected and qualify are: _____, _____; _____, _____; and _____, _____.

A.7 (c) Incorporators:

The names and addresses of each incorporator are: _____, _____; _____, _____; and _____, _____.

A.8 Express powers of the board of directors (§§27,78,4(h), 70,45(b), 42):

In furtherance and not in limitation of powers conferred by statute, the board of directors is expressly authorized:

(1) Subject to by-laws adopted by the shareholders, to make, alter, or repeal the by-laws of the corporation;

(2) To authorize and cause to be executed mortgages and liens, with or without limit as to amount, upon the real and personal property of the corporation;

(3) To authorize the guaranty by the corporation of securities, evidences of indebtedness, and obligations of other persons, corporations, and business entities;

(4) To set apart out of any of the funds of the corporation available for dividends a reserve or reserves for any proper purpose and to abolish any such reserve;

(5) To declare and pay dividends in cash out of the depletion reserves of the corporation, but each such dividend shall be identified as a distribution of such reserves and the amount per share paid from such reserves shall be disclosed to the shareholders receiving the same concurrently with the distribution thereof;

(6) By resolution adopted by a majority of the full board of directors, to designate from among its members an executive committee and one or more other committees (with such name or names as may be stated in the by-laws or as may be determined from time to time by resolution adopted by the board of directors) each of which committees, to the extent provided in such resolution or in the articles of incorporation or the by-laws of the corporation, having all the authority of the board of directors, except that no such committee shall have authority denied to it by statute.

▪ **The Model Act provides:**

no such committee shall have authority to (i) declare dividends or distributions, (ii) approve of or recommend to shareholders actions or proposals required by this Act to be approved by shareholders, (iii) designate candidates for the office of director, for purposes of proxy solicitation or otherwise, or fill vacancies on the board of directors or any committee thereof, (iv) amend the by-laws, (v) approve a plan of merger not requiring shareholder approval, (vi) reduce earned or capital surplus, (vii) authorize or approve the reacquisition of shares unless pursuant to a general formula or method specified by the board of directors, or (viii) authorize or approve the issuance or sale of, or any contract to issue or sell, shares or designate the terms of a series of a class of shares, provided that the board of directors, having acted regarding general authorization for the issuance or sale of shares, or any contract therefor, and in the case of a series, the designation thereof, may, pursuant to a general formula or method specified by the board by resolution or by adoption of a stock option or other plan, authorize a committee to fix the terms of any contract for the sale of the shares and to fix the terms upon which such shares may be issued or sold, including, without limitation, the price, the dividend rate, provisions for redemption, sinking fund, conversion, voting or preferential rights, and provisions for other features of a class of shares, or a series of a class of shares, with full power in such committee to adopt any final resolution setting forth all of the terms thereof and to authorize the statement of the terms of a series for filing with the Secretary of State under this Act. (§42)

A.9 Indemnification of Directors, Officers, Employees, and Agents (§5):

Any person who was or is a party or is threatened to be made a party to any threatened, pending, or completed action, suit, or proceeding, whether civil, criminal, administrative, or investigative, by reason of the fact that he, or a person of whom he is a legal representative, is or was a director, officer, employee, or agent of the corporation, or is or was serving at the request of the corporation as a director, officer, employee, or agent of another corporation, partnership, joint venture, trust, or other enterprise shall be indemnified by the corporation, to the fullest extent legally permissible under the laws of the State of _____, against all expenses (including attorneys' fees), judgements, fines, and amounts paid in settlement actually and reasonably incurred by him in connection therewith. Such right of indemnification is a contract right which may be enforced in any manner desired by such person and is not exclusive of any other right which he may have or hereafter acquire. The board of directors may adopt by-laws from time to time with respect to indemnification to provide at all times the fullest indemnification by the corporation permitted under the laws of the State of _____ and may cause the corporation to purchase and maintain insurance on behalf of any person who is or was a director, officer, employee, or agent of the corporation, or is or was serving at the request of the corporation as a director, officer, employee, or agent of another corporation, partnership, joint venture, trust, or other enterprise, against any liability asserted against him and incurred by him in any such capacity or arising out of his status as such, whether or not the corporation would have the power to indemnify him.

A.10 Right to amend articles of incorporation (§58):

The corporation reserves the right to amend, alter, change, or repeal any provision contained in these articles of incorporation, in the manner now or hereafter prescribed by statute, and all rights conferred upon shareholders herein are granted subject to this reservation.

A.11 Reservation to shareholders of power to change by-laws (§27):

Power to alter, amend, or repeal the by-laws or to adopt new by-laws is reserved to the shareholders.

A.12 Multiple classes of shares, without destroying Subchapter S eligibility (for use in states where cumulative voting is not available):

The aggregate number of shares of all classes which the corporation has authority to issue is 3,000, and the par value of such shares is $10 per share, amounting in the aggregate to $30,000. One thousand of such shares are Class A Common Shares, 1,000 are Class B Common Shares, and 1,000 are Class C Common Shares. The shares of all classes are identical in every respect, except that each class, voting as a class, has the right to elect members of the board of directors in the same proportion which the number of shares in that class bears to the total number of shares of all classes then outstanding.

B. By-Laws

50 Sample Provisions

B.1 Offices (§§12,13)

B.1 (a) Principal office:

The principal office of the corporation in the State of _____ is located in the City of _____, County of _____. The corporation may have such other offices, within or without the State of _____, as the board of directors may designate or as the business of the corporation may from time to time require.

B.1 (b) Registered office (§§12,13):

The registered office of the corporation, required by the laws of the State of _____ to be maintained in such state may be, but need not be, the same as its principal office in such state, and the address of the registered office may be changed by resolution duly adopted by the board of directors and by following the procedure set forth in the laws of the State of _____.

B.2 Shareholder meetings (§§28, 29, 144, 32)

B.2 (a) Place (§28):

Meetings of shareholders shall be held at the principal office of the corporation in the State of _____ unless another place, within or without such State, is determined by the directors and stated in the notice of meeting or in a duly executed waiver thereof.

B.2 (b) Holding annual meetings (§28):

Annual meetings of shareholders shall be held at 2:00 p.m. on the third Wednesday in October each year (or, if this day is a legal holiday on the next day thereafter that is not a legal holiday) for the purpose of electing directors and for transaction of such other business as may be brought before the meeting.

459

B.2 (c) Calling special meetings (§28):

Special meetings of shareholders, for any purpose or purposes, unless otherwise prescribed by statute, may be called by the president or by the board of directors, and shall be called by the president at the request of the holders of not less than one-tenth of all outstanding shares of the corporation entitled to vote at the meeting. In calling a special meeting the president or the board of directors shall specify in the call the place, day, hour, and purpose or purposes of the meeting, and no unspecified matters shall be considered at the meeting or any adjournment thereof.

B.2 (d) Notices of meetings (§§29, 144):

Written notices stating the place, day, and hour of each annual meeting and the place, day, hour, and purpose or purposes of each special meeting shall, unless otherwise prescribed by statute, be delivered not less than ten nor more than fifty days before the meeting, either personally or by mail, by or at the direction of the president, the secretary, or the officer or other person calling the meeting, to each shareholder of record entitled to vote at the meeting. Notices are deemed delivered when deposited, postage prepaid, in the United States mail, addressed to shareholders at addresses appearing on the stock transfer books of the corporation. Any shareholder may waive notice of any meeting.

B.2 (e) Quorum of and action by shareholders (§32):

If a quorum of shareholders, as provided by statute or in the articles of incorporation, is present, the affirmative vote of the majority [or of, say, "ninety percent (90%)," if greater than majority action is desired] of the shares represented at the meeting and entitled to vote, on the subject matter is the act of the shareholders. If a quorum of shareholders is not present, a majority [or a higher percentage if desired] of the shares represented at the meeting may adjourn the meeting from time to time without further notice. At such adjourned meeting at which a quorum is present, any business may be transacted which might have been transacted at the meeting as originally noticed. Shareholders present at a duly organized meeting may continue to transact business until adjournment, notwithstanding withdrawal of enough shareholders to leave less than a quorum.

B.3 Board of directors (§§35, 36, 38, 43, 144, 40, 42, 44)

B.3 (a) General powers (§35):

All corporate powers are exercised by or under authority of, and the business and affairs of the corporation are managed under the direction of, the corporation's board of directors, except as is otherwise provided by statute or in the articles of incorporation.

B.3 (b) Tenure of directors (§36):

Directors hold office for the terms for which they are elected and until their successors are elected and qualified.

B.3 (c) Qualifications (unrestricted) (§35):

Directors need not be residents of the State of _____ nor shareholders of the corporation.

B.3 (d) Qualifications (shareholders) (§35):

Directors need not be residents of the State of _____ but shall be shareholders of the corporation.

B.3 (e) Number of directors, fixed by by-laws and changed by amendment thereto (§36):

The number of directors of the corporation is _____.

B.3 (f) Number of directors, fixed by by-laws and changed by director resolution (§36):

The number of directors of the corporation is _____, and, from time to time, by vote of not less than a majority [or of a higher proportion if desired] of directors then in office, the board of directors may increase or decrease the number of directors, but no decrease shall have the effect of shortening the term of any incumbent director.

B.3 (g) Number of directors, fixed and changed by shareholder resolution (§36):

The number of directors of the corporation is the number fixed by a resolution duly adopted by the shareholders; such number may be increased or decreased from time to time by a similar resolution, but no decrease shall have the effect of shortening the term of any incumbent director.

B.3 (h) Resignations:

Directors may resign their offices at any time by delivering written resignations to the corporation; acceptance of a resignation, unless required by its terms, is not necessary to make it effective.

B.3 (i) Filling vacancies (§38):

A vacancy occurring in the board of directors, whether caused by death, resignation, removal, increase in the number of directors, or otherwise, may be filled by the affirmative vote of a majority of the remaining directors though less than a quorum of the board of directors.

B.3 (j) Holding regular meetings (§43):

A regular meeting of the board of directors shall be held without other notice than this by-law immediately after, and at the same place as, the annual meeting of shareholders, for election of corporate officers and transaction of other business. The board of directors may provide by resolution the time and place, either within or without the State of _____, for holding of additional regular meetings without other notice than such resolution.

B.3 (k) Calling special meetings (§43):

Special meetings of the board of directors may be called by or at the request of the president or any two directors to be held at a time and place, either within or without the State of _____, designated in the call.

B.3 (l) Notice of meetings (§§43, 144):

The secretary shall give notice of the place, day, and hour of special meetings of the board of directors or any committee designated thereby by mailing such notice at least three days, or by personally delivering, telegraphing, or telephoning the same at least one day before the meeting to each director or committee member at his business address. Any director or committee member may waive notice of any meeting. Attendance of a director or committee member at a meeting constitutes waiver of notice of such meeting, except when he attends a meeting for the express purpose of objecting to the transaction of any business because the meeting is not lawfully called or convened. Neither the business to be transacted at, nor the purpose of, any regular or special meeting need be specified in the call or the notice or the waiver of notice of such meeting. No notice of any adjourned meeting need be given.

B.3 (m) Quorum of and action by directors (§40):

If a quorum of the board of directors, as provided by statute or in the articles of incorporation, is present at a meeting, the act of the majority [or of, say, "three-fourths," if greater than majority action is desired] of directors present at the meeting is the act of the board of directors. If a quorum of directors is not present, a majority [or a higher proportion if desired] of directors present may adjourn the meeting from time to time without further notice.

B.3 (n) Compensation of directors (§35):

By resolution duly adopted by the board of directors, provision may be made that directors be reimbursed for their expenses of attending meetings, and that they be paid fixed sums for attendance at each meeting or stated annual compensation for serving as directors, or both; and such payments shall not preclude directors from serving the corporation in other capacities and receiving compensation therefor.

B.3 (o) Committees of and created by the board of directors (§42):

By resolution duly adopted by a majority [or of a higher proportion if desired] of the full board of directors, the board may designate from among its members such committees as it may determine and assign duties and grant powers thereto, except as otherwise provided by statute or in the articles of incorporation, and establish, or authorize establishment of, procedures for holding regular and special meetings thereof. Such committees may include: an executive committee, which may, between meetings of the board and while the board is not in session, be granted the powers and authorized to exercise the duties of the board in the management of the corporation's business; an audit committee, which may be authorized to supervise the work of the corporation's auditors, internal and external, and report thereon to the board; a compensation committee, which may be directed to make recommendations to the board concerning compensation of the corporation's directors, officers, and employees; a finance committee, which may be directed to make recommendations to the board concerning raising funds for the corporation's business. Such committees may be granted such other and different powers and duties as the board may determine. By resolution duly adopted, the board may create from among the corporation's directors, officers, employees, and agents other committees, and assign such duties and grant such powers thereto as the board may determine, except as otherwise provided by statute or in the articles of incorporation or in these by-laws.

B.3 (p) Action by directors or committees without a meeting (permitted) (§44):

Any action required to be or which may be taken by the board of directors or by a committee created thereby may be taken without a meeting if a consent in writing, setting forth the action so taken, is signed by all of the directors or committee members. Such consent has the same effect as a unanimous vote.

B.3 (q) Action by directors or committee without a meeting (not permitted) (§44):

Any action required to be or which may be taken by the board of directors or by a committee created thereby may be taken only at a meeting of the board or committee which is lawfully called and convened.

B.4 Officers (§§50, 51, 23)

B.4 (a) General provisions (§50):

Officers of the corporation elected by the board of directors are a president (who shall be chosen from the board of directors), at the discretion of the board one or more vice presidents with such titles and duties as the board may determine, a secretary, and a treasurer. Other officers, assistant officers, and agents may be elected or appointed by the board of directors, or chosen in such other manner as the board of directors may determine, or, in the absence of such determination, may be appointed by the president or his delegate. Any two or more offices may be held by the same person, except the offices of president and secretary.

B.4 (b) Election and tenure of office (§50):

Officers elected by the board of directors are elected annually by the board at its first meeting held after the annual meeting of shareholders. If election of officers is not held at such meeting, election is to be held as soon thereafter as conveniently may be. Officers hold office until their successors are elected and have qualified or until their death, resignation, removal, or disqualification.

B.4 (c) Removal of officers and agents (§51):

Any officer or agent of the corporation may be removed by the board of directors, and any officer or agent appointed by the president or his delegate may be removed by the president, whenever in the judgment of the board or the president, as the case may be, the best interests of the corporation will be served thereby, but removal is without prejudice to the contract rights, if any, of the person removed. Election or appointment of an officer or agent does not itself create contract rights.

B.4 (d) Filling vacancies:

A vacancy in any office because of death, resignation, removal, disqualification, or otherwise, may be filled by, or as determined by, the board of directors for the unexpired portion of the term.

B.4 (e) President:

The president is the principal executive and administrative officer of the corporation and, subject to direction of the board of directors, supervises and controls its business and affairs. Duties and powers of the president include appointment of such officers, other than those elected or appointed by the board of directors, and appointment and delegation of power to appoint such employees and agents, as in the president's judgment are necessary or proper for transaction of the business of the corporation; determination of the duties and powers of those so appointed; and, subject to approval of the board of directors, determination of their compensation. The president presides, when present, at meetings of shareholders and the board of directors.

> ▪ **If it is desired to have the separate office of chairman of the board, the president would preside at meetings only in the absence of the chairman of the board, and the latter might be named principal executive officer of the corporation in place of the president and given some of the president's appointing powers.**

The president signs, with the secretary or an assistant secretary, certificates of shares of the corporation [§23], and deeds, mortgages, bonds, contracts, and other instruments which the board of directors has authorized to be executed, except when signing and execution thereof is expressly delegated by the board of directors or the president to some other officer or agent of the corporation or shall be required by law to be otherwise signed or executed. The president has the duties and powers as are duly assigned to the president by the board of directors. The president reports annually, or more frequently as the board of directors may specify, to the board concerning the operations and financial condition of the corporation.

B.4 (f) Vice presidents:

Upon absence, death, disability, or refusal to act of the president, the vice president (or, if there are several vice presidents, the vice presidents in the order designated upon their election, or, in absence of such designation, then in the order of their election) performs the duties and has the powers of, and is subject to the restrictions upon, the president. Duties and powers of a vice president include signing, with the secretary or an assistant secretary, certificates of shares of the corporation

[§23], and such other duties and powers as are duly assigned to such vice president by the board of directors, the president, or a designated vice president.

B.4 (g) Secretary:

The secretary records proceedings of meetings of the shareholders, the board of directors, and, to the extent the board of determines, committees of and created by the board of directors, in one or more books kept for that purpose; sees that notices are given pursuant to these by-laws, resolutions of the board of directors, or as required by law; is custodian of corporate records and of the corporate seal; affixes the seal to and countersigns documents execution of which on behalf of the corporation is duly authorized; keeps or causes to be kept a record of the post office addresses of the corporation's shareholders; signs, with the president or a vice president, certificates of shares of the corporation [§23] issuance of which is authorized by the board of directors; has general charge of the share transfer books of the corporation; maintains a record of those authorized to act for the corporation in transactions with other persons; and has the duties and powers incident to the office of secretary and such other duties and powers as are duly assigned to the secretary by the board of directors, the president, or a designated vice president.

B.4 (h) Treasurer:

The treasurer is custodian of and receives, disburses, and administers the funds and securities of the corporation under the direction of the board of directors, the president, or a designated vice president; and has the duties and powers incident to the office of treasurer and such other duties and powers as are duly assigned to the treasurer by the board of directors, the president, or a designated vice president.

B.4 (i) Assistant secretaries and assistant treasurers:

Assistant secretaries, when authorized by the board of directors, sign, with the president or a vice president, certificates of shares of the corporation [§23] issuance of which is authorized by the board of directors. Assistant secretaries and assistant treasurers have such duties and powers as are duly assigned to them by the secretary or treasurer, respectively, or by the board of directors, the president, or a designated vice president.

B.4 (j) Compensation:

The compensation of corporate officers elected or appointed by the board of directors is determined by the board of directors. The compensation of other officers appointed by the president or his delegate is determined by the president, subject to approval of the board of directors.

B.5 Authorizations to act for the corporation in transactions with others:

The board of directors authorizes officers, employees, and agents of the corporation to act for the corporation in transactions with other persons which are necessary and proper to the business of the corporation, including, without limitation, making contracts, acquiring and selling property, borrowing and lending money, issuing evidences of indebtedness, maintaining bank accounts, and settling claims by and against the corporation. Such authorizations may be confined to specific instances or continuing. They may grant authority to individuals by name or to the holders of specified offices or positions. Grantees of authority may be authorized not only to act for the corporation themselves, but also to delegate authority to act to other officers, agents, and employees, and to grant authority to such other officers, agents, and employees to further delegate authority to act to still other officers, agents, and employees. The secretary maintains records of such authorizations.

B.6 Indemnification of directors, officers, employees, and agents (§5):

This by-law exercises the power granted by the articles of incorporation authorizing adoption from time to time of by-laws which provide the fullest indemnification by the corporation permitted under the laws of the State of _____ against expenses (including attorney's fees) judgments, fines, and amounts paid in settlement incurred in a legal proceeding by a person by reason of the fact that he, or a person of whom he is a legal representative, is or was a director, officer, employee, or agent of the corporation or of another enterprise at the request of the corporation.

B.7 Certificates representing shares and transfers of shares (§§23,30)

B.7 (a) Share certificates (§23):

Certificates representing the number of shares owned are issued to shareholders in such form not inconsistent with the articles of incorporation as is approved by the board of directors. Such certificates, consecutively numbered or otherwise identified, are signed by the president or a vice president and by the secretary or an assistant secretary and sealed with the seal of the corporation or a facsimile thereof. Such signatures may be facsimiles if the certificate is manually signed on behalf of a transfer agent or registrar other than the corporation itself or an employee of the corporation, and a certificate signed by a person who has ceased to be an officer may be issued by the corporation with the same effect as if that person were an officer at the date of its issue.

B.7 (b) Share transfers:

Transfers of shares are made only on the books of the corporation by holders of record or their legal representatives who have furnished proper evidence of authority to transfer, or by their attorneys by powers of attorney duly executed and filed with the secretary, and on surrender of certificates for such shares, properly assigned.

B.7 (c) Lost, destroyed, mutilated, or stolen certificates:

New certificates are not issued until the former certificate or certificates for a like number of shares are surrendered and cancelled, except that in cases of lost, destroyed, mutilated, or stolen certificates new certificates may be issued upon such terms and upon such provision for indemnity to the corporation as the board of directors may prescribe.

B.7 (d) Rules on issue, transfer, and registration of shares:

The board of directors may make such rules and regulations as it deems expedient concerning issue, transfer, and registration of certificates representing shares of the corporation, including designation of transfer agents and registrars for such shares.

B.7 (e) Closing of transfer books and fixing record dates (§30):

For the purpose of determining shareholders entitled to notice of and to vote at a meeting, or entitled to receive payment of a dividend, or to make a determination of shareholders for any other proper purpose, the board of directors may close the transfer books of the corporation for not more than fifty days and, in case of a meeting of shareholders, not less than ten days immediately preceding the meeting. In lieu of closing the transfer books, the board of directors may fix a record date for such determination of shareholders not more than fifty days and, in case of a meeting of shareholders, not less than ten days before the date on which action is to be taken. If transfer books are not closed and a record date is not fixed, the record date for such determination is deemed to be the date of mailing of notice of a meeting or the date of adoption by the board of directors of a resolution declaring a dividend or taking other action requiring a determination of shareholders.

B.8 Dividends (§45):

The board of directors may, from time to time, declare and the corporation may pay dividends on its outstanding shares in the manner and upon the terms and conditions provided by law and the articles of incorporation.

B.9 Corporate seal (§4(c)):

The seal of the corporation is in such form as may be adopted by the board of directors. It is to be circular in shape and to bear the name of the corporation, the state of incorporation, and the words "Corporate Seal." It may also bear the year of incorporation of the corporation.

B.10 Waiver of notice (§144):

Whenever notice is required to be given as provided by law, the articles of incorporation, or these by-laws, a waiver thereof in writing signed by the person or persons entitled to such notice, whether before or after the time stated therein, is deemed equivalent to the giving of such notice.

B.11 Fiscal year:

The fiscal year of the corporation begins on the first day of July in each calendar year and ends on the last day of June in the next following calendar year.

B.12 Amendments (§27):

Power to alter, amend, or repeal these by-laws or to adopt new by-laws, subject to repeal or change by action of the shareholders, is vested in the board of directors unless otherwise provided by the articles of incorporation.

B.13 Emergency by-laws (§27A):

B.13 (a) When emergency by-laws are in effect:

The special emergency by-laws adopted by this section are operative during an emergency in the conduct of the business of the corporation resulting from an attack on the United States or a nuclear or atomic disaster, notwithstanding any different provision in the corporation act of the State of _____, the articles of incorporation, or other parts of these by-laws. To the extent not inconsistent with these emergency by-laws other parts of these by-laws remain in effect during an emergency and upon its termination these emergency by-laws cease to be operative.

B.13 (b) What emergency by-laws provide:

During any such emergency the business of the corporation may be conducted as set forth below:

Call and notice: A meeting of the board of directors may be called by any officer or director of the corporation who may give notice of the time and place of meeting to such directors as it is feasible to reach by any available means of communication at such time in advance of the meeting as circumstances permit in the judgment of the person calling the meeting.

Quorum: At any such meeting of the board of directors, a quorum is _____ [here insert the particular provisions desired, which may be "the director or directors in attendance at the meeting"].

Who are deemed directors: To the extent required to provide a quorum at a meeting of the board of directors the following are deemed directors for such meeting:

(i) Officers or other persons designated on a list approved by the board of directors before the emergency, in the order of such priority, subject to such conditions, and for such period of time (not longer than is reasonably necessary after termination of the emergency) as provided in the resolution approving the list;

(ii) in absence of such a resolution, officers of the corporation who are present in order of rank and within the same rank in order of seniority.

Lines of succession and location of offices: The board of directors, either before or during any such emergency, may

(i) provide, and from time to time modify, lines of succession in the event that during the emergency any or all of the officers or agents of the corporation are for any reason rendered incapable of discharging their duties;

(ii) effective in the emergency, change the head office or designate several alternative head or regional offices, or authorize the officers so to do.

B.13 (c) Limitation of liability:

No director, officer, employee, or agent acting in accordance with these emergency by-laws is liable except for willful misconduct.

B.13 (d) Amendment of emergency by-laws:

These emergency by-laws are subject to repeal or change by action of the board of directors or the shareholders, except that the above provisions on limitation of liability are not subject to repeal or change with regard to action taken prior to such repeal or change. Amendment of these emergency by-laws may make further or different provisions that are practical or necessary for circumstances of the emergency.

B.14 Provisions intended mainly for close corporations

(The following clauses requiring greater than majority quorums and votes and restricting share transfers, suggested for the articles of incorporation at A.6 above, may be used in the by-laws where it is desired that they be more easily changed:

—Greater than majority quorum of and action by shareholders;
—Greater than majority quorum of and action by directors;
—Transfers of shares and options for their purchase;
—Options for purchase of shares upon holder's death or cessation of employment;
—Determination of fair value of optioned shares.)

C. Other Start-Up Documents and Forms

Nine Items for Name, Meetings, and Share Certificates

C.1 Reserving a corporate name (§9)

C.1 (a) Application for reservation of name for 120 days:

To the Secretary of State of the State of _____:

Pursuant to the provisions of the corporation act of the State of _____, the undersigned, being a person intending to organize a corporation in this State, hereby applies for reservation for a period of 120 days of the exclusive right to use the following corporate name: DIGHALDOE CORPORATION.

Dated _____

<u>Lawrence Lawyer</u>
<u>(address)</u>

▪ **The Secretary of State then issues a certificate of reservation good for 120 days from the date thereof. Applications for reservation of names may be made not only by persons intending to organize new corporations but also by existing domestic or qualified foreign corporations intending to change their names and by unqualified foreign corporations intending to qualify.**

C.1 (b) Notice of transfer of reservation of name:

To the Secretary of State of the State of _____:

Pursuant to the provisions of the corporation act of the State of _____, you are hereby notified that the undersigned has transferred to Donald Digges, Howard Hall, and Desmond Doe, whose addresses are _____, _____, and _____, the corporate name of DIGHALDOE CORPORATION, which was reserved in your office for the exclusive use of the undersigned for a period of 120 days thereafter.

Dated _____

Lawrence Lawyer
(address)

▪ **The Secretary of State then issues a certificate of transfer of reserved corporate name which shows the date of the original reservation and the names and addresses of the transferees.**

C.2 Initial meetings

▪ **The Model Act makes it unnecessary for incorporators to meet because authority to adopt by-laws is given to directors (§27) and initial directors are required to be named in the articles of incorporation (§54(j)). In contrast, the Delaware Act makes naming of directors in the articles optional and provides that if they are not so named powers of incorporators, including power to adopt by-laws, continue until directors are elected by incorporators or shareholders (§§102(6), 107). Thus, the suggested minutes of a meeting of incorporators are intended for states with provisions like Delaware's, and the suggested minutes of a first meeting of the board of directors would omit reference to filing of the articles of incorporation and adoption of by-laws if these steps have already been taken by the incorporators.**

C.2 (a) Minutes of meeting of incorporators:

A meeting of the incorporators of Dighaldoe Corporation was held at (place), on (date), at (time), pursuant to waiver of notice signed by all of the incorporators. There were present Donald Digges, Howard Hall, and Desmond Doe, being all of the incorporators. Upon motion duly made, seconded, and unanimously carried, Mr. Digges was chosen chairman and Mr. Hall was chosen secretary of the meeting. The waiver of notice of the meeting signed by all of the incorporators was presented and the secretary was instructed to file it with the minutes of the meeting.

The chairman reported that the articles of incorporation of the corporation had been filed in the office of the Secretary of State of the State of _____ on _____.

▪ **If other filing of the articles or certificate of incorporation is required, such as with the clerk or recorder of the county of the corporation's registered office, here also recite the place and date thereof.**

The secretary was instructed to place in the minute book a copy of the articles of incorporation certified by him or by the Secretary of State of the State of _____.

Adoption of by-laws:

The chairman presented proposed by-laws of the corporation. On motion duly made, seconded, and unanimously carried, the following resolution was adopted:

Resolved that the by-laws presented to this meeting be and the same hereby are adopted as the by-laws of this corporation, and the secretary is instructed to certify such by-laws and place them in the minute book.

Election of board of directors:

The chairman stated that the next business before the meeting was the election of three directors to serve until the next annual meeting of shareholders and until their successors are elected and qualified. Donald Digges, Howard Hall, and Desmond Doe were nominated for election as directors. There being no other nominations, on motion duly made, seconded, and unanimously carried, such nominees were elected as directors for such terms.

There being no further business, on motion duly made, seconded, and unanimously carried, the meeting was adjourned.

_____
Secretary

Approved:

_____
Chairman

C.2 (b) Minutes of first meeting of board of directors:

The first meeting of the board of directors of Dighaldoe Corporation was held at (place), on (date), at (time), pursuant to a waiver of notice signed by all of the directors. There were present Donald Digges, Howard Hall, and Desmond Doe, being all of the directors. Lawrence Lawyer was also present by invitation. Upon motion duly made, seconded, and unanimously carried, Mr. Digges was chosen temporary chairman and Mr. Lawyer was chosen temporary secretary of the meeting. The waiver of notice of the meeting signed by all of the directors was presented and the secretary was instructed to file it with the minutes of the meeting.

The chairman reported that the articles of incorporation of the corporation had been filed in the office of the Secretary of State of the State of _____ on _____.

▪ If other filing of the articles or certificate of incorporation is required, such as with the clerk or recorder of the county of the corporation's registered office, here also recite the place and date thereof.

Adoption of by-laws:

The chairman presented proposed by-laws of the corporation. On motion duly made, seconded, and unanimously carried, the following resolution was adopted:

Resolved that the by-laws presented to this meeting be and the same hereby are adopted as the by-laws of this corporation, and the secretary is instructed to certify such by-laws and place them in the minute book.

Election of officers:

The following persons were nominated to be officers of the corporation to serve until the first meeting of the board of directors after the next annual meeting of shareholders and until their successors are elected and qualified:

president	—	Donald Digges
vice president	—	Howard Hall
treasurer	—	Desmond Doe
secretary	—	Lawrence Lawyer

There being no other nominations, on motion duly made, seconded, and unanimously carried the nominees were elected to such offices for the terms indicated.

Adoption of form of certificate representing shares:

The secretary presented a form of certificate representing shares of the corporation. On motion duly made, seconded, and unanimously carried, the following resolution was adopted:

Resolved that the form of certificate representing shares of the corporation presented to this meeting be and the same hereby is approved and adopted, and the secretary is instructed to place a specimen thereof in the minute book.

Adoption of corporate seal:

The secretary presented a form of seal for the corporation. On motion duly made, seconded, and unanimously carried, the following resolution was adopted:

[impression
of seal]

Resolved that the seal an impression of which is hereto affixed be and the same hereby is adopted as the seal of the corporation.

Regular meetings of the board of directors:

On motion duly made, seconded, and unanimously carried, the following resolution was adopted:

Resolved that regular meetings of this board of directors be held without further notice at the corporation's principal office at _____ on the third Wednesdays in each month at 2:00 p.m., except in October when such meetings are to be held as provided in the by-laws immediately after and at the same place as the annual meeting of shareholders; provided, however, that any such meeting other than the October meeting may be held at such other places and times as this board of directors may from time to time designate.

Authorization to open and operate bank account:

On motion duly made, seconded, and unanimously carried, the following resolution was adopted:

Resolved that the president and treasurer be and they hereby are authorized to establish a bank account at _____ (name of bank), to deposit therein funds of the corporation and to draw upon such funds, and to authorize other officers, employees, and agents of the corporation to make such deposits and to draw upon such funds subject to such limitations as such officers may designate.

Qualification of the corporation in other states:

On motion duly made, seconded, and unanimously carried, the following resolution was adopted:

Resolved that the officers of the corporation be and they hereby are authorized to qualify the corporation as a foreign corporation authorized to conduct business in the States of _____ and _____, and in connection therewith to designate such offices and to appoint such agents, and to take all other action necessary and proper to secure such qualification.

Purchases of shares for money or other property:

The chairman reported that the corporation had received offers to purchase for money or other property a total of 2000 shares of the $10 par value common shares of the corporation as follows:

> Donald Digges, 200 shares, to be paid for at $100 per share ($20,000) in money;
>
> Howard Hall, 800 shares, to be paid for at $100 per share ($80,000) in tangible property in the form of five trucks for hauling coal having a fair market value of $80,000; and
>
> Desmond Doe, 1000 shares, to be paid for at $100 per share ($100,000) in money.

On motion duly made, seconded, and unanimously carried the offers of Donald Digges and Desmond Doe to purchase 200 and 1000 shares, respectively, for money were accepted and the officers of the corporation were authorized and directed to cause to be issued to them, in the indicated amounts, fully paid and non-assessable shares of the $10 par value, common shares of the corporation upon receipt of the agreed price therefor.

On motion duly made, seconded, and carried with Howard Hall not participating in the vote, the following resolution was adopted:

> Resolved that the offer of Howard Hall to purchase 800 shares of the $10 par value common shares of the corporation for the consideration of tangible property in the form of five trucks for transporting coal having a fair market value of $80,000 be and the same hereby is accepted.
>
> Further resolved that in the judgment of this board of directors said trucks are necessary to the business of the corporation and are of a value to the corporation of $80,000 and should be entered at such amount upon the books of the corporation.
>
> Further resolved that the officers of the corporation are authorized and directed to cause to be issued to Howard Hall 800 fully paid and non-assessable shares of the $10 par value common shares of the corporation upon receipt of the agreed consideration therefor.

Appointment of independent public accountants:

On motion duly made, seconded, and unanimously carried, the following resolution was adopted:

> Resolved that _____ be and the same hereby are appointed, subject to ratification by the shareholders, to serve as independent public accountants for the corporation for the current fiscal year and until their successors are appointed.

There being no further business, on motion duly made, seconded, and unanimously carried, the meeting was adjourned.

Secretary _____

Approved:

_____

Chairman

C.2 (c) Shareholder resolution ratifying acceptance of property for shares:

Resolved that the judgment of the board of directors concerning the consideration paid by Howard Hall to the corporation for its shares of tangible property in the form of five trucks for transporting coal that said trucks are necessary to the business of the corporation and are of a value to the corporation of $80,000, be and the same hereby is ratified and affirmed.

C.2 (d) Resolutions of board of directors authorizing issuance of shares for services:

The chairman reported that the corporation had received offers to purchase a total of 1000 shares of the $10 par value common shares of the corporation as follows:

Donald Digges, 800 shares, to be paid for at $100 per share ($80,000) in services actually performed for the corporation in getting its mining operations started having a fair value of $80,000; and Howard Hall, 200 shares, to be paid for at $100 per share ($20,000) in services actually performed for the corporation in getting its trucking operations started having a fair value of $20,000.

On motion duly made, seconded, and carried with Donald Digges not participating in the vote, the following resolution was adopted:

Resolved that the offer of Donald Digges to purchase 800 shares of the $10 par value common shares of the corporation for the consideration of services actually performed for the corporation in getting its mining operations started having a fair value of $80,000 be and the same hereby is accepted.

Further resolved that in the judgment of the board of directors such services were actually performed, were necessary to the business of the corporation, and were of a value to the corporation of $80,000 and should be entered at such amount upon the books of the corporation.

Further resolved that the officers of the corporation are authorized and directed to cause to be issued to Donald Digges 800 fully paid and non-assessable shares of the $10 par value common shares of the corporation.

On motion duly made, seconded, and carried with Howard Hall not participating in the vote, the following resolution was adopted:

Resolved that the offer of Howard Hall to purchase 200 shares of the $10 par value common shares of the corporation for the consideration of services actually performed for the corporation in getting its trucking operations started having a fair value of $20,000 be and the same hereby is accepted.

Further resolved that in the judgment of the board of directors such services were actually performed, were necessary to the business of the corporation, and were of a value to the corporation of $20,000 and should be entered at such amount upon the books of the corporation.

Further resolved that the officers of the corporation are authorized and directed to cause to be issued to Howard Hall 200 fully paid and non-assessable shares of the $10 par value common shares of the corporation.

C.2 (e) Shareholder resolution ratifying acceptance of services for shares:

Resolved that the judgment of the board of directors, concerning the consideration paid by Donald Digges and Howard Hall to the corporation for its shares of services performed in getting its mining and trucking operations started, that such services were actually performed; were necessary to the business of the corporation, and were of value to the corporation of $80,000 and $20,000, respectively, be and the same hereby is ratified and affirmed.

C.3 Certificate representing common shares (§23)

C.3 (a) Front side:

Number _____ _____ shares

Incorporated under the laws of the State of _____

DIGHALDOE CORPORATION
Common Shares

This certifies that (shareholder's name) is the owner of (number of shares) fully paid and non-assessable shares of the common shares of the par value of $10 each of Dighaldoe Corporation, transferable on the books of the corporation by the holder hereof in person or by authorized attorney upon surrender of this certificate properly endorsed. This certificate and the shares represented hereby are issued by the corporation and accepted by the holder subject to all the provisions of the articles of incorporation and by-laws of the corporation as from time to time amended, to all of which the holder by acceptance hereof assents.

Dated _____

_____   [Corporate
Secretary (or   _____
Assistant Secretary)   Seal]   President (or
                                                                  Vice President)

C.3 (b) Reverse side:

Dighaldoe Corporation will furnish to any shareholder upon request and without charge a full statement of the designations, preferences, limitations, and relative rights of the shares of each class authorized to be issued.

      For value received, _____ (I or we) hereby sell, assign, and transfer unto _____

_____(name and address of assignee)_____(number of shares) of the shares represented by the within certificate, and do hereby irrevocably constitute and appoint _____

attorney, to transfer said shares on the books of the corporation with full power of substitution in the premises.

Dated _____

                                        _____

Notice: The signature of this assignment must correspond with the name or names written upon the face of the certificate in every particular, without alteration or enlargement, or any change whatever.

D. Shareholder Materials

23 Items, Including
Meeting Documents and Resolutions About
Shareholders, Directors, and Officers

D.1 Basic annual meeting documents

▪ Material in brackets is generally not needed by close corporations not subject to federal proxy regulations.

D.1 (a) Notice (§29):

DIGHALDOE CORPORATION
Notice of Annual Meeting of Shareholders
October _____

Notice is hereby given that the annual meeting of shareholders of Dighaldoe Corporation will be held at (place) on Wednesday, October _____, at 2:00 p.m., for the following purposes:

to elect directors:

to ratify appointment of independent public accountants;

[to act upon a shareholder proposal concerning _____;]

and to transact such other business as may come before the meeting or any adjournment or adjournments thereof.

By order of the board of directors,
Lawrence Lawyer
Secretary

(place) _____

(date) _____

[To enable you to be represented if you do not expect to attend the meeting, or if you expect to attend but desire to vote by proxy, please sign and date the enclosed proxy and return it promptly in the enclosed envelope which requires no postage if mailed in the United States.]

483

D.1 (b) Proxy (§33):

DIGHALDOE CORPORATION
Proxy for Annual Meeting of Shareholders
October _____

[This proxy is solicited on behalf of the Management of Dighaldoe Corporation (to be printed in bold-face type).]

The signer hereby appoints Donald Digges and Lawrence Lawyer and each of them, with power of substitution, the proxies of the signer to vote at the annual meeting of shareholders of Dighaldoe Corporation to be held at __(place)__ , on Wednesday, October _____, at 2:00 p.m., and at any adjournments thereof, the shares the signer would be entitled to vote, if personally present, upon the election of directors and other matters legally coming before the meeting, including those listed in the notice of the meeting [and listed below and more fully set forth in the proxy statement dated _____].

[1. Authorizing proxies to vote for director-nominees named in the proxy statement. The directors favor FOR.
□ FOR   □ AGAINST.

2. Ratification of appointment of _____ as independent public accountants. The directors favor FOR.
□ FOR   □ AGAINST.

3. A shareholder proposal concerning _____. The directors favor AGAINST. □ FOR   □ AGAINST]

[Unless otherwise marked, this proxy will be voted FOR items 1 and 2 and AGAINST item 3 (to be printed in bold-face type).]

Dated _____

_____

_____

_____

[If executed by a corporation, an authorized officer should sign. Executors, administrators, and trustees should so indicate when signing.]

[Please mark your proxy, date and sign it, and return it promptly in the accompanying envelope which requires no postage if mailed in the United States.]

D.1 (c) Minutes:

DIGHALDOE CORPORATION
Minutes of Annual Meeting of Shareholders
October _____

Pursuant to notice duly given, the annual meeting of shareholders of Dighaldoe Corporation was held at the principal office of the corporation at _____ on Wednesday, October _____, at 2:00 p.m.

The meeting was called to order by Donald Digges, president, who presided as chairman of the meeting. Lawrence Lawyer, secretary, recorded the proceedings as secretary of the meeting. At the request of the chairman, the secretary stated that notice of the meeting had been given in accordance with the by-laws to each shareholder of record at the close of business on _____, being the date fixed by the board of directors for determining shareholders entitled to notice of and to vote at the meeting [, and submitted his affidavit of mailing of such notice]. The secretary was instructed to file [his affidavit and] a copy of the notice of the meeting with the minutes of the meeting.

[_____ and _____, inspectors of election appointed by the board of directors, were present and took their oath, which is annexed to these minutes.]

> ▪ **Functions of inspectors of election, who are usually employees of the bank that serves as transfer agent, may be performed by the secretary of a close corporation. For a suggested director resolution appointing inspectors, see F.3(d).**

The secretary reported that [he had been advised by the inspectors or election that], of the _____ shares of the corporation entitled to vote at the meeting, holders of _____ shares were present in person or represented by proxy.

> ▪ **While Dighaldoe is still owned by its original shareholders, attendance at the meeting can be reported less impersonally, say as follows: "The secretary reported that, of the 3,000 shares of the corporation entitled to vote at the meeting, Donald Digges and Howard Hall, each holding 1,000 shares, were present in person, and Desmond Doe, holding 1,000 shares, was present by proxy."**

Election of directors:

The chairman called for nominations for directors. The following nominations were made: Donald Digges, Howard Hall, and Desmond Doe.

A share vote was taken. The secretary reported that [he was advised by the inspectors of election that] the result of the vote was as follows: Donald Digges, 3,000 votes; Howard Hall, 3,000 votes; and Desmond Doe, 3,000 votes.

> ▪ **The above statement is compatible with either seat-by-seat or cumulative voting. In the former case, where each shareholder has votes for each seat to be filled equal to his shares, each of the shareholders in our Dighaldoe hypothetical would vote for himself and his two colleagues. In the latter case, where each shareholder has votes equal to his shares times the number of seats to be filled which may be distributed among nominees as he pleases, while shareholders can (and usually do in a public corporation) vote the same way as with seat-by-seat voting, in a close corporation it is prudent for each shareholder to cast all of his votes for himself.**

The chairman declared that Donald Digges, Howard Hall, and Desmond Doe had been duly elected directors of the corporation to serve until the next annual meeting of shareholders and until their successors are elected and qualified.

Ratification of appointment of independent public accountants:

The chairman reported that the board of directors has appointed, subject to ratification by the shareholders, _____ to serve as independent public accountants for the corporation for the current fiscal year and until their successors are appointed. [The chairman also stated that if such ratification is rejected, or if the named firm declines or becomes unable to act, or if their employment is discontinued, the board of directors will appoint other independent public accountants whose continued employment after the next annual meeting of shareholders shall be subject to ratification by the shareholders.]

On motion duly made and seconded, the following resolution was proposed:

> Resolved that the appointment by the board of directors of _____ to serve as independent public accountants for the corporation for the current fiscal year and until their successors are appointed be and the same hereby is ratified.

> ▪ **It is appropriate for shareholders to "authorize" action yet to be taken, to "approve" action that is taken but not yet effective, and to "ratify" and "affirm" action that is already effective.**

A share vote was taken. The secretary reported that [he was advised by the inspectors of election that] the vote on the above resolution was _____ shares for [and _____ shares against]. The chairman declared the above resolution duly adopted.

[A shareholder proposal concerning _____ *:*
The chairman reported that a shareholder had notified the management of the corporation of his intention to present a proposal for action at the meeting concerning _____, and that the management had set forth in its proxy statement the proposal, a statement of the proponent in support thereof, and a statement of reasons of the board of directors for opposing it.

On motion duly made and seconded, the following resolution was proposed:

Resolved that _____.

After discussion a share vote was taken. The secretary reported that he was advised by the inspectors of election that the vote on the above resolution was _____ shares for and _____ shares against. The chairman declared the above resolution duly defeated.]

[Report of inspectors of election:
The chairman directed that the report of the inspectors of election concerning the foregoing be annexed to the minutes of the meeting.]

[President's report, discussion, and questions:
The president reported on the business and affairs of the corporation. There followed a period of discussion during which questions of shareholders were answered by the president and by other directors and officers.]

There being no further business, on motion duly made, seconded, and carried, the meeting was adjourned.

_____
Secretary

Approved:

_____
Chairman

D.2 Formal meeting documents, not needed for close corporations

D.2 (a) Affidavit of mailing of notice (§29):

DIGHALDOE CORPORATION
Affidavit of Mailing of Notice of Shareholder Meeting

State of _____ ⎫
County of _____ ⎬ SS

Lawrence Lawyer, being duly sworn, deposes and says that on _____, as secretary of Dighaldoe Corporation, he caused notice of a meeting of shareholders of Dighaldoe Corporation to be held on _____ to be mailed to each shareholder of record entitled to vote at such meeting by depositing such notice in the United States mail addressed to the shareholder at the shareholder's address as it appears on the books of the corporation, with postage thereon prepaid.

_____

Sworn to before me
this ____ day of _____, 19____

_____
Notary public

D.2 (b) Oath of inspectors of election:

DIGHALDOE CORPORATION
Oath of Inspectors of Election at Shareholders Meeting

State of _____ }
                                    } SS
County of _____   }

Each of the undersigned, being duly sworn, deposes and says that he will faithfully execute with strict impartiality and according to the best of his ability the duties of inspector of election at the meeting of shareholders of Dighaldoe Corporation to be held at (place), on (date), at (time), and at any adjournments thereof.

_____

_____

Severally sworn to before me
this ____ day of _____, 19____

_____
Notary public

D.2 (c) Report of inspectors of election:

DIGHALDOE CORPORATION
Report of Inspectors of Election

We, the undersigned inspectors of election, appointed at the meeting of shareholders of Dighaldoe Corporation held at (place), on (date), at (time), do hereby certify:

That the meeting was so held and, of the _____ shares of the corporation entitled to vote at the meeting, holders of _____ shares were present in person or represented by proxy.

That the result of the vote taken for election of three directors was Donald Digges, 3,000 votes; Howard Hall, 3,000 votes; and Desmond Doe, 3,000 votes.

That the result of the vote taken on a resolution to ratify appointment of independent public accountants was _____ shares for and _____ shares against.

That the result of the vote taken on a resolution to adopt a shareholder proposal concerning _____ was _____ shares for and _____ shares against.

In witness whereof, we have signed this certificate on (date)

_____

_____

State of _____ } SS
County of _____

On this ____ day of _____, 19____, before me personally came _____ and _____, to me known and known to me to be the individuals described in and who executed the foregoing certificate, and they severally acknowledged to me that they executed the same.

_____
Notary Public

D.2 (d) Ballot for election of directors:

DIGHALDOE CORPORATION
Ballot for Meeting of Shareholders, (date)

Instructions: Not more than three names may be voted for. Cross out names not voted for. Names of other nominees may be inserted in blank spaces.

Donald Digges, Howard Hall, Desmond Doe,

_____, _____, _____.

The undersigned hereby votes for the election of the above named persons as directors of Dighaldoe Corporation the number of shares stated below.

As shareholder, ("all" or a specified number) of the shares registered in my name on the record date.

(signature of shareholder)

As proxies, _____ shares, for which authorizations to so vote are filed with the inspectors of election.

(signature of proxies)

_____

D.2 (e) Ballot on resolution:

DIGHALDOE CORPORATION
Ballot for Meeting of Shareholders, (date)

Resolved that (set forth resolution).

The undersigned hereby votes for and against the above resolution the number of shares of Dighaldoe Corporation stated below.

As shareholder, of the shares registered in my name on the record date, _____ shares □ FOR;

_____ shares □ AGAINST.

(Insert the word "all" or a specified number.)

(signature of shareholder)

As proxies, under authorization to so vote filed with the inspectors of election, _____ shares □ FOR;

_____ shares □ AGAINST.

(signature of proxies)

_____

D.3 Resolutions concerning shareholders

**D.3 (a) Authorizing distributions to shareholders
      from capital surplus (§46):**

 ▪ **Not needed if articles of incorporation contain provision at E.1 (d)**

Resolved that the board of directors of Dighaldoe Corporation be and it hereby is authorized from time to time to distribute to its shareholders out of capital surplus of the corporation a portion of its assets, in cash or property, provided that no such distribution shall be made at a time when the corporation is insolvent or when such distribution would render the corporation insolvent, nor unless all cumulative dividends accrued on all preferred or special classes of shares entitled to preferential dividends shall have been fully paid, nor if such distribution would reduce the remaining net assets of the corporation below the aggregate preferential amount payable in the event of involuntary liquidation to the holders of shares having preferential rights to the assets of the corporation in the event of liquidation.

**D.3 (b) Authorizing purchase of corporation's own shares
      from capital surplus (§6):**

Resolved that the board of directors of Dighaldoe Corporation be and it hereby is authorized from time to time to cause the corporation to purchase its own shares to the extent of unreserved and unrestricted surplus, earned or capital, available therefor, provided that no such purchase shall be made at a time when the corporation is insolvent or when such purchase would make it insolvent.

D.4 Resolutions concerning board of directors

D.4 (a) Fixing number of directors (§36):

Resolved that, pursuant to powers granted to the shareholders in the articles of incorporation and by-laws, the number of directors of Dighaldoe Corporation be and the same hereby is fixed at three (3), who are to be elected annually.

Further resolved that such number may be increased or decreased from time to time by resolution of the shareholders, but no decrease may shorten the terms of an incumbent director.

D.4 (b) Increasing number of directors and filling vacancies (§§36, 38):

Resolved that the number of directors of Dighaldoe Corporation be and the same hereby is increased from three (3) to five (5).

Further resolved that _____ and _____ be and the same hereby are elected directors of Dighaldoe Corporation to serve until the next annual meeting of shareholders and until their successors are elected and qualified.

D.4 (c) Decreasing number of directors (§36):

Resolved that the number of directors of Dighaldoe Corporation be and the same hereby is decreased from five (5) to three (3) effective at this [or "the next" if the resolution is adopted between annual meetings] annual meeting of shareholders.

D.4 (d) Removing directors and decreasing number of directors (§§39, 36):

Resolved that _____ and _____ be and the same hereby are removed as directors of Dighaldoe Corporation effective immediately.

> ▪ Removal requires action at a meeting of shareholders "called expressly for that purpose." Model Act §39

Further resolved that the number of directors of Dighaldoe Corporation be and the same hereby is decreased from five (5) to three (3).

D.4 (e) Removing directors and filling vacancies (§§39, 38)

Resolved that _____ and _____ be and the same hereby are removed as directors of Dighaldoe Corporation effective immediately.

Further resolved that _____ and _____ be and the same hereby are elected directors of Dighaldoe Corporation to serve until the next annual meeting of shareholders and until their successors are elected and qualified.

D.5 Resolutions concerning benefits for individual directors, officers, employees, and agents

(For the director resolutions that usually precede these resolutions, see F.6.)

D.5 (a) Compensation (§35):

Resolved that the action of the board of directors of Dighaldoe Corporation on _____ fixing the compensation for the fiscal year ending June 30, 19___, of directors, and of officers and employees of the corporation earning more than $_____ per year, be and the same hereby is ratified and affirmed.

D.5 (b) Employee benefit plans:

> ▪ **Includes bonuses, stock options, deferred compensation, and other special benefits of executives, as well as retirement, profit sharing, phantom stock, and insurance plans not usually confined to senior executives.**

Resolved that the _____Plan that was on _____ formulated by the board of directors of Dighaldoe Corporation and recommended for adoption by its shareholders be and the same hereby is adopted effective _____.

D.5 (c) Loans to employees, including directors (§47):

Resolved that the action of the board of directors of Dighaldoe Corporation on _____determining that for the corporation to lend money to or to use its credit to assist _____, an employee [and director] of the corporation, may benefit the corporation, and authorizing the president to cause the corporation to make such loan or to extend such assistance in an amount not to exceed $_____, and for a term not to exceed _____, and subject to such other terms and conditions as the president may determine, be and the same hereby is ratified and affirmed.

D.5 (d) Loans to non-employee directors (§47):

> ▪ **Model Act §47 requires "authorization in the particular case by its shareholders."**

Resolved that the president of Dighaldoe Corporation be and he hereby is authorized to cause the corporation to lend money to or to use its credit to assist _____, a director who is not an employee of the corporation, in an amount not to exceed $_____ , and for a term not to exceed _____. and subject to such other terms and conditions as the president may determine.

D.5 (e) Insider transaction authorized, approved, or ratified by shareholders:

Resolved that, the relationship to or interest in of _____, a director [officer, employee, agent] of Dighaldoe Corporation, a transaction concerning _____ between the corporation and said _____ or an entity in which he is financially interested having been disclosed or being known to shareholders entitled to vote, such transaction be and the same hereby is authorized [approved, ratified].

> ▪ **"Authorized" is appropriate for a future transaction; "approved," for one entered into but not yet effective; "ratified," for one that has already taken effect.**

D.5 (f) Indemnification for an action or suit not by or for the corporation (§5(a)):

Resolved that the action of the board of directors of Dighaldoe Corporation on _____ determining that expenses and other obligations legally indemnifiable by the corporation totalling $_____ were actually and reasonably incurred by _____ in connection with his involvement, by reason of his service to the corporation, in an action or suit not by or in the right of the corporation, and that said _____ acted in good faith and in a manner he reasonably believed to be in or not opposed to the best interests of the corporation [and had no reasonable cause to believe his conduct was unlawful], be and the same hereby is ratified and affirmed.

> ▪ **The final bracketed clause is appropriate for a criminal action or proceeding.**

D.5 (g) Indemnification for an action or suit by or for the corporation, with no adjudication of liability (§5(b)):

Resolved that the action of the board of directors of Dighaldoe Corporation on _____ determining that expenses legally indemnifiable by the corporation totalling $_____ were actually and reasonably incurred by _____ in connection with his involvement, by reason of his service to the corporation, in an action or suit by or in the right of the corporation, that said _____ acted in good faith and in a manner he reasonably believed to be in or not opposed to the best interests of the corporation, and that said _____ has not been adjudged to be liable for negligence or misconduct in the performance of his duty to the corporation, be and the same hereby is ratified and affirmed.

D.5 (h) Indemnification for an action or suit by or for the corporation, with court determination of indemnity despite adjudication of liability (§5(b)).

Resolved that the action of the board of directors of Dighaldoe Corporation on _____ determining that expenses legally indemnifiable by the corporation totalling $_____ were actually and reasonably incurred by _____ in connection with his involvement, by reason of his service to the corporation, in an action or suit by or in the right of the corporation, that said _____ acted in good faith and in a manner he reasonably believed to be in or not opposed to the best interests of the corporation, and that, despite an adjudication that said _____ is liable for negligence or misconduct in the performance of his duty to the corporation, the court in which such action or suit was brought has determined upon application that in view of all of the circumstances of the case said _____ is fairly and reasonably entitled to idemnity for expenses in said amount of $_____, be and the same hereby is ratified and affirmed.

E. Documents to Accomplish Basic Corporate Changes

26 Sample Documents Needed for Going Public, Merger, and Dissolution

E.1 Going public: board of directors resolutions proposing amendments to articles of incorporation

• Model Act procedure for amending articles of incorporation is for the board of directors to adopt a resolution setting forth the proposed amendment and directing that it be submitted to shareholder vote (§59); if approved, articles of amendment are delivered to the Secretary of State (§§61-62). By-law changes are made by the board unless reserved to shareholders in the articles of incorporation (§27) and need not be delivered to the Secretary of State. Below are set forth suggested documents for use by Dighaldoe Corporation in preparation for offering its securities to the public as described in Section 7.3 of the text. References in brackets are to relevant parts of Sections A and B of this appendix.

E.1 (a) To change authorized shares and par value and to effect a share split (§59):

Resolved that it is proposed that Article ____ of the articles of incorporation of Dighaldoe Corporation on authorized shares and par value [A.2(a)] be amended to provide that the aggregate number of shares which the corporation has authority to issue be increased from 5,000 to 150,000 shares, that the par value of such shares be decreased from $10 to $1 per share, amounting in the aggregate to $150,000, and that each $10 par value share be changed into ten $1 par value shares; and it is directed that such proposed amendment be submitted to a vote at a meeting of shareholders on _____.

E.1 (b) To deny shareholders' preemptive rights (§§59, 26 or 26A):

Resolved that it is proposed that Article ____ of the articles of incor-

495

poration of Dighaldoe Corporation on shareholders' preemptive rights [A.5(b)] be amended to provide that no holder of shares of the corporation is entitled as a matter of right, preemptive or otherwise, to subscribe for or to purchase any part of any shares of the corporation, now or hereafter authorized to be issued, or shares held in the treasury of the corporation or securities convertible into shares, whether issued for cash or other consideration, or by way of dividend or otherwise [A.5(a)]; and it is directed that such proposed amendment be submitted to a vote at a meeting of shareholders on _____.

E.1 (c) To fix number of directors by by-laws (§§59, 36):

Resolved that it is proposed that Article _____ of the articles of incorporation of Dighaldoe Corporation on number of directors [A.6(a)] be amended to provide that the number of directors shall be fixed by, or in the manner provided in, the by-laws and may be increased or decreased from time to time by amendment to, or in the manner provided in the by-laws, but no increase shall have the effect of shortening the term of any incumbent director; and it is directed that such proposed amendment be submitted to a vote at a meeting of shareholders on _____.

E.1 (d) To empower board of directors to make distributions from capital surplus (§46):

Resolved that it is proposed that Article _____ of the articles of incorporation of Dighaldoe Corporation on express powers of the board of directors [A.8] be amended to provide that the board of directors of the corporation may, from time to time, distribute to its shareholders out of capital surplus of the corporation a portion of its assets, in cash or property, provided that no such distribution shall be made at a time when the corporation is insolvent or when such distribution would render the corporation insolvent, nor unless all cumulative dividends accrued on all preferred or special classes of shares entitled to preferential dividends shall have been fully paid, nor if such distribution would reduce the remaining net assets of the corporation below the aggregate preferential amount payable in event of involuntary liquidation to the holders of shares having preferential rights to the assets of the corporation in the event of liquidation.

E.1 (e) To permit purchase of corporation's own shares from capital surplus (§6):

Resolved that it is proposed that Article _____ of the articles of incorporation of Dighaldoe Corporation on express powers of the board of directors [A.8] be amended to provide that the board of directors may, from time to time, cause the corporation to purchase its own shares to the extent of unreserved and unrestricted surplus, earned or capital, available therefor, provided that no such purchase shall be made at a time when the corporation is insolvent or when such purchase would make it insolvent.

E.1 (f) To eliminate reservation to shareholders of power to change by-laws (§§59, 27):

Resolved that it is proposed that Article ____ of the articles of incorporation of Dighaldoe Corporation on reservation to shareholders of power to change by-laws [A.11] be eliminated; and it is directed that such proposed amendment be submitted to a vote at a meeting of shareholders on _____.

E.1 (g) To eliminate other provisions unsuitable for a public corporation (§§59, 33, 32, 143, 40):

Resolved that it is proposed that the following provisions in the below listed Articles of the articles of incorporation of Dighaldoe Corporation be eliminated:

on cumulative voting for election of directors [A.6(b)] in Article ____;

on greater than majority quorum of and action by shareholders and directors [A.6(c) and (d)] in Articles _____;

on transfers of shares and options for their purchase [A.6(e)], options for purchase of shares upon holder's death or cessation of employment [A.6(f)], and determination of fair value of optioned shares [A.6(g)] in Articles _____; and

on multiple classes of shares without destroying Subchapter S eligibility [A.12] in Article ____;

and it is directed that such proposed amendments be submitted to a vote at a meeting of shareholders on _____.

E.2 Going public: shareholder approval and filing of amendments to articles of incorporation

E.2 (a) Shareholder resolution adopting amendments to articles of incorporation (§§59, 60):

▪ **Model Act §60 requires voting by classes on amendments such as those proposed above when there are several classes of shares.**

Resolved that the following amendments to the articles of incorporation of Dighaldoe Corporation proposed by its board of directors on _____ be and the same hereby are adopted and the proper officers of the corporation are directed to execute and deliver to the Secretary of State of the State of _____ articles of amendment in accordance with such amendments:

(Insert amendments)

E.2 (b) Articles of amendment (§61):

Articles of Amendment
to the
Articles of Incorporation
of
DIGHALDOE CORPORATION

Pursuant to the provisions of the corporation act of the State of _____, the undersigned corporation adopts the following articles of amendment to its articles of incorporation:

1. The name of the corporation is DIGHALDOE CORPORATION.

2. The following amendments of the articles of incorporation were adopted by the shareholders of the corporation on _____ in the manner prescribed by the corporation act of the State of _____:

(Insert amendments)

3. The number of shares outstanding at the time of such adoption was 3,000 shares; and the number of shares entitled to vote thereon was 3,000 shares.

4. The number of shares voted for such amendments was 3,000; and the number of shares voted against such amendment was 0.

5. The manner in which any exchange, reclassification, or cancellation of issued shares provided for in the amendment shall be effected is as follows: each of the 3,000 issued $10 par value shares, being changed by the amendment into ten $1 par value shares, shall be exchanged for $1 par value shares on such basis.

6. The manner in which such amendments effect a change in the amount of stated capital, and the amount of stated capital as changed by such amendment are as follows: stated capital remains unchanged at $30,000, since 3,000 $10 par value shares are changed into 30,000 $1

par value shares; authorized capital increases from $50,000 to $150,000.

Dated _____

Dighaldoe Corporation

By _____

President (or Vice President)

and _____

Secretary (or Assistant
                Secretary)

State of _____ ⎫
                                   ⎬ SS
County of _____ ⎭

   I, _____ , a notary public, do hereby certify that on this _____ day of _____, 19___, personally appeared before me _____, who, being by me first duly sworn, declared that he is the _____ of Dighaldoe Corporation, that he signed the foregoing document as _____ of the corporation, and that the statements therein are true.

Notarial
Seal   _____
                 Notary Public

▪ **Verification in this form is to be made by one of the officers signing the document.**

E.3 Going public: board of directors resolutions amending by-laws

▪ **Of course, if the articles contain the provision in A.11 reserving to shareholders power to change the by-laws, these resolutions must be adopted by the shareholders.**

E.3 (a) On quorum of and action by shareholders (§§27, 32):

Resolved that Article ____, Section ____, of the by-laws of Dighaldoe Corporation on quorum of and action by shareholders [B.2(a)] be and the same hereby is amended to read as follows:

  If a quorum of shareholders as provided by statute or in the articles of incorporation is present, the affirmative vote of a majority is the act of the shareholders. If a quorum of shareholders is not present, a majority of the shares represented at the meeting may adjourn the meeting from time to time without further notice.

E.3 (b) On number of directors (§§27, 36):

Resolved that Article ____, Section ____, of the by-laws of Dighaldoe Corporation on number of directors [B.3(a)] be and the same hereby is amended to read as follows:

The number of directors of the corporation is _____.

E.3 (c) On quorum of and action by directors (§§27, 40):

Resolved that Article ____, Section ____, of the by-laws of Dighaldoe Corporation on quorum of and action by directors [B.3(m)] be and the same hereby is amended to read as follows:

A majority of the number of directors fixed by these by-laws constitute a quorum for the transaction of business. The act of a majority of the directors present at a meeting at which a quorum is present is the act of the board of directors. If a quorum of directors is not present, a majority of the directors present may adjourn the meeting from time to time without further notice.

E.3 (d) To eliminate other provisions unsuitable for a public corporation (§§27, 32, 40):

Resolved that the following provisions in the below listed Articles and Sections of the by-laws of Dighaldoe Corporation intended mainly for close corporations [B.14] be and the same hereby are eliminated:

On greater than majority quorum of and acts by shareholders and directors in Article(s) ____, Section(s) ____; and on transfers of shares and options for their purchase, options for purchase of shares upon holder's death or cessation of employment, and determination of fair value of optioned shares in Article(s) ____, Section(s) ____.

E.4 Merger or Consolidation (§§71—77):

▪ **Model Act procedure to merge or consolidate two domestic corporations is for the board of directors of each corporation to adopt a resolution approving a plan of merger or consolidation (§72) and a resolution directing that the plan be submitted to shareholder vote (§73). Upon shareholder approval, articles of merger or consolidation are delivered to the Secretary of State (§74). Below are set forth suggested resolutions for Dighaldoe directors and shareholders (similar resolutions would be needed for Pigmy directors and shareholders), plus articles of merger, that might be used to effect a merger of Pigmy Coal Company into Dighaldoe Corporation in the situation assumed in Section 10.1 of the text, with the further assumption that the merger was done before 90% of the Pigmy shares were acquired by Dighaldoe. Material in brackets shows alternative**

wording appropriate for consolidation (when, instead of one corporation merging into another, two existing corporations consolidate to form a new corporation).

E.4 (a) Board of directors resolution approving plan of merger or consolidation (§§71, 72):

Resolved that the following Plan of Merger [Consolidation] be and the same hereby is approved by this board of directors of Dighaldoe Corporation:

1. The names of the corporations proposing to merge [consolidate] are Dighaldoe Corporation and Pigmy Coal Company, and the name of the [new] corporation into which they propose to merge [consolidate] is Dighaldoe Corporation [_____], which is hereinafter designated as the surviving [new] corporation.

2. The terms and conditions of the proposed merger [consolidation] are that the surviving [new] corporation will acquire all of the assets and will assume all of the liabilities of the merging [consolidating] corporations with the exception of the following:

(Set forth any exceptions)

3. The manner and basis of converting the shares of each corporation into shares of the surviving [new] are that each share of Dighaldoe Corporation will entitle the holder to continue to hold [receive] one share of the surviving corporation, and each share of Pigmy Coal Company will entitle the holder thereof to receive ten shares of the surviving [new] corporation.

4. No changes in the articles of incorporation of the surviving corporation are to be effected by the merger. (Set forth the articles of incorporation of the new corporation.)

E.4 (b) Board of directors resolution directing submission of plan of merger or consolidation to shareholders (§73):

Resolved that it is directed that the Plan of Merger [Consolidation] approved this date by this board of directors be submitted to a vote at a meeting of shareholders on _____.

E.4 (c) Shareholder resolution approving plan of merger or consolidation (§73):

Resolved that the following Plan of Merger [Consolidation], approved by the board of directors of Dighaldoe Corporation on _____, be and the same hereby is approved by the shareholders of such corporation and its proper officers are directed to execute, together with the proper officers of Pigmy Coal Company, and deliver to the Secretary of

State of the State of _____ articles of merger [consolidation] in accordance with such Plan:
(Set forth the Plan)

E.4 (d) Articles of merger or consolidation (§74):

Articles of Merger [Consolidation]
of Domestic Corporations
into
DIGHALDOE CORPORATION [_____]

Pursuant to the provisions of the corporation act of the State of _____, the undersigned corporations adopt the following articles of merger [consolidation] for the purpose of merging [consolidating] them into one of such corporations [a new corporation]:

1. The following Plan of Merger [Consolidation] was approved by the shareholders of each of the undersigned corporations in the manner prescribed by the corporation act of the State of _____:

(Set forth the Plan)

2. As to each of the undersigned corporations, the number of shares outstanding and entitled to vote on such Plan are as follows: Dighaldoe Corporation, 100,000 shares; Pigmy Coal Company, 1,000 shares.

3. As to each of the undersigned corporations, the number of shares voted for and against such Plan, respectively, are as follows: Dighaldoe Corporation, _____ shares for and _____ shares against; Pigmy Coal Company, _____ shares for and _____ shares against.

Dated _____

Dighaldoe Corporation
By _____
President (or Vice President)
and _____
Secretary (or Assistant
Secretary)

(Add verification by a signing officer as suggested at E.2 (b).)

Pigmy Coal Company
By _____
President (or Vice President)
and _____
Secretary (or Assistant
Secretary)

(Add verification by a signing officer as suggested at E.2 (b).)

▪ **Under the Model Act, if Pigmy is incorporated in a different state than Dighaldoe, each corporation must comply with the laws of the state of its incorporation; and if the surviving or new corporation is to be governed by the laws of a state other than Dighaldoe's state of incorporation, it must comply with provisions on foreign corporations in Dighaldoe's state of incorporation if it is to transact business in that state (§77).**

E.5 Merger of subsidiary corporation (short merger) (§75)

▪ **The Model Act permits a parent corporation owning at least 90% of the shares of a subsidiary to merge the subsidiary into the parent through a procedure, called a "short merger", which omits shareholder action altogether (although each shareholder of the subsidiary is to be mailed a copy of the plan of merger) and confines director action and execution of the articles of merger to the parent (§75). Below are short merger documents that would be appropriate if Dighaldoe had acquired 90% or more of the shares of Pigmy.**

E.5 (a) Board of directors resolution approving plan of merger of subsidiary corporation (§75):

Resolved that the following Plan of Merger of a Subsidiary Corporation be and the same hereby is approved by this board of directors of Dighaldoe Corporation:

1. The name of the subsidiary corporation is Pigmy Coal Company and the name of the corporation owning at least ninety per cent of its shares is Dighaldoe Corporation, which is hereinafter designated as the surviving corporation.

2. The manner and basis of converting the shares of the subsidiary corporation into shares of the surviving corporation are that each share of the subsidiary corporation will entitle the holder thereof to receive ten shares of the surviving corporation.

Further resolved that it is directed that a copy of such Plan of Merger of a Subsidiary Corporation be mailed to each shareholder of record of the subsidiary corporation.

E.5 (b) Articles of merger of subsidiary corporation (§75):

Articles of Merger
of Domestic Subsidiary Corporation
into
Domestic Parent Corporation

Pursuant to the provisions of the corporation act of the State of _____, the undersigned corporation adopts the following articles of merger for the purpose of merging a subsidiary corporation into the undersigned as the surviving corporation:

1. The following Plan of Merger of a Subsidiary Corporation was approved by the board of directors of the undersigned, as the surviving corporation, in the manner prescribed by the corporation act of the State of _____:

(Set forth the Plan)

2. The number of outstanding shares of the subsidiary corporation, Pigmy Coal Company, is 1,000 and the number of such shares owned by the surviving corporation is _____.

3. A copy of the Plan of Merger of a Subsidiary Corporation set forth in paragraph 1 was mailed on _____ to each shareholder of the subsidiary corporation of record on _____.

Dated _____

Dighaldoe Corporation
By _____
(President or Vice President)
and _____
Secretary (or Assistant
Secretary)

(Add verification by a signing officer as suggested at E.2 (b).)

■ **The above procedure may be followed even if the subsidiary is a foreign corporation. Where the subsidiary is a domestic corporation and the parent a foreign corporation, articles of merger should recite, in addition to recitals on share ownership and mailing of the plan, that laws of the state of the parent's incorporation permit the merger, that the plan was adopted as prescribed by such laws, and that the foreign corporation agrees to comply with provisions on transacting business in the state as a foreign corporation.**

E.6 Disposition of assets other than in the regular course of business (§79)

■ **Model Act procedure for a corporation to sell, lease, exchange, or otherwise dispose of all or substantially all of its assets, with or without good will, not in the regular course of its business, is for the board of directors to adopt a resolution recommending such disposition and directing a shareholder vote thereon (§79). Since the legal status of the corporation remains unchanged, the Secretary of State need not be informed.**

E.6 (a) Board of directors resolution recommending disposition (§79):

Resolved that the disposition, not in the usual and regular course of its business, of all, or substantially all, the property and assets, [not] including the good will, of Dighaldoe Corporation to _____, upon such terms and conditions and for such consideration as the shareholders may fix, or may authorize the board of directors to fix, be and the same hereby is recommended; and it is directed that such proposed disposition be submitted to a vote at a meeting of shareholders on _____.

E.6 (b) Shareholder resolution authorizing disposition (§79):

Resolved that the disposition, not in the usual and regular course of its business, of all, or substantially all, the property and assets, [not] including the good will, of Dighaldoe Corporation to _____ be and the same hereby is authorized.

Further resolved that the board of directors be and it hereby is authorized to fix the terms and conditions of such disposition and the consideration to be received by the corporation therefor, which may consist in whole or in part of cash or other property, including shares, obligations, or other securities of any other corporation, domestic or foreign.

E.6 (c) Board of directors resolution fixing terms and conditions of and consideration for disposition (§79):

Resolved that, pursuant to a resolution adopted by the shareholders of Dighaldoe Corporation on _____ authorizing the disposition, not in the usual and regular course of its business, of all, or substantially all, the property and assets, [not] including the good will, of the corporation to _____, and authorizing the board of directors to fix the terms and conditions of such disposition and the consideration to be received by the corporation therefor, the president of Dighaldoe Corporation be and he hereby is authorized to cause such disposition to be made upon the following terms and conditions and for the following consideration to be received by the corporation therefor:

(Set forth terms and conditions, and consideration)

E.7 Dissolution of a corporation (§§82-96)

> ▪ While the Model Act provides for voluntary dissolution by incorporators (§82) and by written consent of all shareholders (§83), and for involuntary dissolution by decree of court (§§94-96), the usual route is voluntary dissolution by act of the corporation (§84) for which suggested documents are set forth below.

E.7 (a) Board of directors resolution recommending dissolution (§84):

Resolved that dissolution of Dighaldoe Corporation be and it hereby is recommended; and it is directed that the question of such dissolution be submitted to a vote at a meeting of shareholders on _____.

E.7 (b) Shareholder resolution to dissolve (§84):

Resolved that Dighaldoe Corporation be dissolved by act of the corporation and that the officers of the corporation be and they hereby are authorized to execute and deliver to the Secretary of State of the State of _____ a statement of intent to dissolve the corporation by act of the corporation.

E.7 (c) Statement of intent to dissolve (§84):

State of Intent to Dissolve
DIGHALDOE CORPORATION
By Act of the Corporation

To the Secretary of State of the State of _____:

Pursuant to the provisions of the corporation act of the State of _____, the undersigned corporation submits the following statement of intent to dissolve the corporation by act of the corporation:

1. The name of the corporation is Dighaldoe Corporation.

2. The names and respective addresses of its officers are: Donald Digges, president, _____; Howard Hall, vice president, _____; Lawrence Lawyer, secretary, _____; and Desmond Doe, treasurer _____.

3. The names and respective addresses of its directors are: Donald Digges, _____; Howard Hall, _____; and Desmond Doe, _____.

4. The following resolution to dissolve the corporation was adopted by the shareholders of the corporation on _____:

(Set forth resolution)

5. The number of shares outstanding and entitled to vote at the time of adoption of such resolution was _____.

6. The numbers of shares voted for and against such resolution, respectively, were _____ and _____.

Dated _____

Dighaldoe Corporation

By _____

President (or Vice President)

and _____

Secretary (or Assistant

Secretary)

(Add verification by a signing officer as suggested at E.2 (b).)

▪ The Secretary of State files the statement of intent to dissolve if it conforms to law and if all fees and franchise taxes are paid (§85). Except as necessary for winding up, the corporation ceases to carry on its business, but its corporate existence continues (§86). It mails notice of dissolution to known creditors and proceeds to liquidate its business and affairs (§87) until it is ready to execute articles of dissolution (§92).

E.7 (d) Articles of dissolution (§92):

Articles of Dissolution

of

DIGHALDOE CORPORATION

Pursuant to the provisions of the corporation act of the State of _____ , the undersigned corporation adopts the following articles of dissolution for the purpose of dissolving the corporation:

1. The name of the corporation is Dighaldoe Corporation.

2. A statement of intent to dissolve the corporation was filed by the Secretary of State of the State of _____ pursuant to the provisions of the corporation act of the State of _____.

3. All debts, obligations, and liabilities of the corporation have been paid and discharged, or adequate provision has been made therefor.

4. All the remaining property and assets of the corporation have been distributed among its shareholders in accordance with their respective rights and interests.

5. There are no suits pending against the corporation in any court in respect of which adequate provision has not been made for the

satisfaction of any judgment, order, or decree which may be entered against it.

Dated _____

Dighaldoe Corporation

By _____

President (or Vice President)

and _____

Secretary (or Assistant
                    Secretary)

(Add verification by a signing officer as suggested at E.2 (b).)

▪ **The Secretary of State files the articles of dissolution, if they conform to law and if all fees and franchise taxes are paid, and issues a certificate of dissolution, which terminates the existence of the corporation "except for the purpose of suits, other proceedings and appropriate corporate action by shareholders, directors, and officers" as provided in the corporation act of the state (§93).**

F. Board of Directors Resolutions

41 Sample Resolutions About Shares and Shareholders, Directors and Officers

F.1 Shares and their issuance

F.1 (a) Calling for payment on subscriptions for original issues (§17):

Resolved that all outstanding subscriptions for common shares of Dighaldoe Corporation be and the same hereby are called for payment in full on or before _____ [in installments, as follows: _____].

Further resolved that in case of default in any such payments the president be and he hereby is authorized to cause the corporation to proceed to collect the amount due in the same manner as any other debt due the corporation.

F.1 (b) Authorizing additional issue and fixing consideration therefor (§18):

Resolved that the president be and he hereby is authorized to cause Dighaldoe Corporation to issue _____ common shares of its authorized but unissued [treasury] shares.

Further resolved that the consideration for which such shares may be issued be and the same hereby is fixed at $_____ per share payable in money.

> ■ For director and shareholder resolutions concerning exercise of judgment as to value of consideration for shares in the form of property or services, see C.2 (b)-(e).

F.1 (c) Creating and issuing rights to purchase (§20):

Resolved that rights, evidenced as set forth below, entitling holders thereof to purchase, upon the terms, within the time or times, and at the price or prices set forth below, an aggregate of not more than _____ shares of the common shares of Dighaldoe Corporation be and the same hereby are created:

(Set forth the manner of evidencing such rights, their terms, and when and at what prices they may be exercised.)

Further resolved that in the judgment of this board of directors the consideration received for such rights is adequate.

Further resolved that the president be and he hereby is authorized to cause the corporation to issue such rights to the following persons in the amounts indicated:

(Set forth recipients of rights and the number of shares each is authorized to purchase.)

Further resolved that the president be and he hereby is authorized to cause the corporation to issue or to transfer shares to holders of such rights upon proper exercise thereof.

> ▪ If rights are to be issued to directors, officers, or employees of the corporation or of a subsidiary, and not to shareholders generally, such issuance requires shareholder as well as director approval (§20). For a shareholder resolution approving a stock option plan for employees, see D.5 (b); and for a director resolution formulating such a plan, see F.7 (b).

F.1 (d) Allocating consideration received for no par shares to capital surplus (§21):

Resolved that, of the consideration of $ _____ per share received for the issuance by Dighaldoe Corporation of _____ common shares without par value on _____, the portion of $ _____ per share be and the same hereby is allocated to capital surplus.

> ▪ Such director action is not needed for shares with a par value, since consideration received therefor is stated capital to the extent of par and any excess is capital surplus. In contrast, all consideration received for no par shares is stated capital unless the directors, within 60 days after issuance, allocate a portion to capital surplus; and, with shares having a preference upon liquidation, only consideration in excess of the preference may be so allocated (§21).

F.1 (e) Authorizing purchase of fractional shares (§24):

Resolved that the president be and he hereby is authorized to cause Dighaldoe Corporation to pay in cash the fair value of fractions of a share in the corporation to those entitled to receive such fractions, such value to be determined as of the time when those entitled to receive such fractions are determined.

▪ **As noted in the text at §2.2 (b), fractional share interests may result from share dividends or from structural changes, such as splits, recapitalizations, or mergers. To avoid the inconvenience of fractional share certificates, the corporation may buy up fractional interests, as provided above, or issue scrip therefor, as provided below. Still another alternative is for the corporation to "arrange for the disposition of fractional interests by those entitled thereto" (§24).**

F.1 (f) Issuing scrip for fractional shares (§24):

Resolved that the president be and he hereby is authorized to cause Dighaldoe Corporation to issue scrip for fractions of a share in the corporation in registered or in bearer form which shall entitle the holder to receive a certificate for a full share of the corporation upon surrender of scrip aggregating a full share.

Further resolved that such scrip shall become void if not exchanged for certificates representing full shares before _____.

[Alternative: Further resolved that such scrip is subject to the condition that the shares for which it is exchangeable may be sold by the corporation and the proceeds thereof distributed to the holders of the scrip.]

F.1 (g) Fixing terms and conditions for exercise of shareholders' preemptive right (§26A):

Resolved that, for the purpose of providing a fair and reasonable opportunity for the exercise of the preemptive right of shareholders of Dighaldoe Corporation to acquire unissued or treasury shares of the corporation, as provided in its articles of incorporation [A.5 (o)], the following terms and conditions be and the same hereby are fixed for the exercise of such right in connection with _____ shares of the corporation sale of which by the corporation was authorized on

_____.

(Set forth terms and conditions, such as: "To exercise such right shareholders shall pay to the corporation the consideration of $_____ per share payable in money on or before _____.")

F.1 (h) Establishing and regulating a series of preferred shares (§54(f)):

Resolved that, pursuant to authority granted to this board of directors in the articles of incorporation [A.4] of Dighaldoe Corporation, 1,000 of the 2,000 preferred shares authorized to be issued by the articles of incorporation [A.4 (a)] be and the same hereby are designated Series A preferred shares.

Further resolved that the preferences and other rights and limitations or restrictions of Series A preferred shares be and the same hereby are fixed as follows:

(Set forth, as provided in A.4 (b), dividend rights of holders, terms on which shares are to be redeemable, rights of holders upon dissolution or distribution of assets, terms or amount of any sinking fund for redemption of shares, terms for any conversion rights into other series or classes, voting rights, if any, and any other preferences, rights, limitations, or restrictions of Series A preferred shares desired to be fixed. Since A.4 (c) of the articles would give Series A preferred shares equal voting rights with common shares unless this resolution provides otherwise, the following limitation should be used if it is desired to limit voting to common shares: "Except as expressly required by law, holders of Series A preferred shares are not entitled to vote at nor to receive notice of meetings of shareholders.")

Further resolved that the following variations in the relative rights and preferences as between Series A and other series of preferred shares of the corporation be and the same hereby are fixed and determined:

(Set forth any variations between series as to dividends, voting, liquidation, redemption, conversion, etc. Under A.4 (d) of the suggested articles, all series rank equally except as variations are fixed and determined by the board when it provides for the initial issue of shares in series.)

F.2 Holding meetings of shareholders

F.2 (a) Determining place of meeting (§28):

Resolved that, pursuant to authority granted to this board of directors in the by-laws [B.2 (a)] of Dighaldoe Corporation, _____ be and it hereby is determined to be the place of the meeting of shareholders of the corporation to be held on _____, at _____, and it is directed that such place be stated in the notice of meeting.

F.2 (b) Calling special meeting (§28):

Resolved that, pursuant to authority granted to this board of directors in the by-laws [B.2 (c)] of Dighaldoe Corporation, a special meeting of shareholders of the corporation be and the same hereby is called to be held at _____, on _____, at _____, for the following purpose or purposes:

(Set forth purpose or purposes. Under the suggested by-law provision at B.2 (c) special meetings may also be called by the president, either upon his own initiative or at the request of one-tenth of the voting shares.)

F.2 (c) Approving meeting documents (§29):

Resolved that the notice of meeting [D.1 (a)], form of proxy [D.1 (b)], and proxy statement for the annual [special] meeting of shareholders of Dighaldoe Corporation to be held on _____ presented to this meeting be and the same hereby are approved and the secretary is directed to cause such documents to be delivered to each shareholder of record entitled to vote at such meeting.

> ▪ This resolution is the basis for the statement in the suggested form of notice at D.1 (a) that it is given by the secretary "By order of the board of directors."

F.2 (d) Appointing inspectors of election:

Resolved that _____ and _____ be and the same hereby are appointed inspectors of election to serve at the meeting of shareholders of Dighaldoe Corporation to be held on _____.

> ▪ As noted in connection with suggested minutes of annual meeting of shareholders at D.1 (c), functions of inspectors of election may be performed by the secretary of a close corporation, in which case a director resolution would not be needed.

F.3 Record dates, dividends, distributions, and share repurchases

F.3 (a) Fixing record date (§30):

Resolved that, for the purpose of determining shareholders of Dighaldoe Corporation entitled to _____, the close of business on _____ be and the same hereby is fixed as the record date for such determination.

> ▪ This resolution may be used for situations where it is necessary to fix a shareholder list, such as meetings, dividends, rights offerings, etc. As indicated in the following dividend and distribution resolutions, a record date is often fixed in the resolution creating the shareholder right.

F.3 (b) Declaring dividend out of earned surplus (§§45, 2 (l)):

Resolved that a dividend of $_____ per share be and the same hereby is declared, payable on _____ to shareholders of record of Dighaldoe Corporation at the close of business on _____ out of the unreserved and unrestricted earned surplus of the corporation.

▪ **While articles of incorporation usually entitle preferred shareholders to fixed dividends, to become payable such dividends, like those on common shares, must be duly declared by the board of directors out of funds legally available therefor.**

F.3 (c) Declaring nimble dividend out of current earnings (§45 (a)):

Resolved that a dividend of $_____ per share be and the same hereby is declared, payable on _____ to shareholders of record of Dighaldoe Corporation at the close of business on _____ out of the unreserved and unrestricted net earnings of the corporation of the current fiscal year and the next preceding fiscal year taken as a single period.

▪ **Nimble dividends require express statutory authorization.**

F.3 (d) Declaring dividend out of depletion reserves by corporation exploiting natural resources (§45 (b)):

Resolved that a dividend of $_____ per share be and the same hereby is declared payable on _____ to shareholders of record of Dighaldoe Corporation at the close of business on _____ out of the depletion reserves of the corporation and it is directed that such dividend be identified as a distribution of such reserves and the amount per share paid from such reserves be disclosed to the shareholders receiving the same concurrently with the distribution thereof.

▪ **Dividends out of depletion reserves may be declared by corporations exploiting natural resources if their articles of incorporation so provide (§45 (b)). Such a provision is suggested for Dighaldoe Corporation at A.8.**

F.3 (e) Declaring dividend in corporation's own treasury shares (§§45 (c), 2 (h)):

Resolved that a dividend of _____ shares per share be and the same hereby is declared payable on _____ to shareholders of record of Dighaldoe Corporation at the close of business on _____ in the corporation's own treasury shares.

F.3 (f) Declaring dividend in corporation's own authorized but unissued shares out of surplus (§45 (d)):

Resolved that a dividend of _____ shares per share be and the same hereby is declared payable on _____ to shareholders of record of Dighaldoe Corporation at the close of business on _____ in the corporation's own authorized but unissued shares out of the unreserved and unrestricted surplus of the corporation.

Further resolved that $ _____, being the aggregate par value of the shares to be issued as a dividend, be and the same hereby is transferred from surplus to stated capital on the books of the corporation.

> ▪ If shares to be issued as a dividend are without par value, the board of directors adopts an additional resolution fixing their stated value; aggregate stated value of shares being issued is then transferred to stated capital, and shareholders are advised of the amount per share so tranferred (§45 (d) (2)).

F.3 (g) Making distribution from capital surplus (§46):

Resolved that, pursuant to authority granted to this board of directors in the articles of incorporation [by the shareholders] of Dighaldoe Corporation, the president be and he hereby is authorized to cause $_____ per share to be distributed to shareholders of record at the close of business on _____ out of the capital surplus of the corporation, and it is directed that such distribution, when made, be identified as a distribution from capital surplus and the amount per share disclosed to the shareholders receiving the same concurrently with the distribution thereof.

> ▪ For the enabling provision for such a distribution in the articles of incorporation, see E.1 (d); for authorization by shareholders, see D.3 (a). The Model Act recognizes either method of authorization (§46 (b)).

F.3 (h) Authorizing purchase of corporation's own shares (§6):

Resolved that the president of Dighaldoe Corporation be and he hereby is authorized to cause the corporation to purchase from time to time the corporation's own shares in an aggregate amount not exceeding _____ shares for a total consideration not exceeding $_____ to the extent of unreserved and unrestricted [earned] surplus available therefor.

> ▪ The board has statutory power to authorize purchases using earned surplus; but purchases using capital surplus may be made (as with distributions from capital surplus) only if the articles of incorporation so permit or if shareholders so authorize (§6). For such permission in the articles of incorporation, see E.1 (c); for such shareholder authorization, see D.3 (b).

F.4 Directors and officers

F.4 (a) Making nominations for election of directors by shareholders (§36):

Resolved that the following persons be and the same hereby are designated as nominees of this board of directors at the election of directors of Dighaldoe Corporation to be held at the annual meeting of shareholders on October _____:

(Set forth names of nominees.)

Further resolved that the secretary be and he hereby is directed to solicit proxies from shareholders for election of such nominees at such meeting.

> ▪ The Model Act, while specifying that "shareholders shall elect directors" (§36), is silent on how nominees are chosen. In close corporations nominations are usually made at the shareholders' meeting; in public corporations, where most voting is by proxy, management nominees are designated in advance by the incumbent board by a resolution such as that suggested above.

F.4 (b) Filling vacancies in a board of directors (§38):

Resolved that _____ and _____ be and the same hereby are elected directors of Dighaldoe Corporation to serve until the next annual meeting of shareholders and until their successors are elected and qualified.

> ▪ While shareholders elect directors at annual meetings and can do so at special meetings to fill vacancies, as when they have increased the number of directors (see D.4 (b)) or removed an incumbent director (see D.4 (e)), ordinarily vacancies are filled between annual meetings by the directors.

F.4 (c) Electing or appointing officers, assistant officers, and agents (§50):

Resolved that _____ be and he hereby is elected [appointed] to the office [position] of _____ of Dighaldoe Corporation to serve until the first meeting of the board of directors after the next annual meeting of shareholders and until his successor is elected [appointed] and qualified.

> ▪ For election of officers in the minutes of the first meeting of a board of directors, see C.2 (b). Officers required to be elected by the board are a president, one or more vice presidents as may be prescribed by the by-laws, a secretary, and a treasurer (§50). Under by-laws suggested for Dighaldoe Corporation at B.4 (a), other officers, assistant

officers, and agents are elected or appointed by, or chosen as determined by, the board, or are appointed by the president or his delegate.

F.4 (d) Determining procedures for choosing officers, assistant officers, and agents not elected or appointed by board of directors:

Resolved that the following procedure be and the same hereby is determined for filling the below named offices and positions in Dighaldoe Corporation which are not filled by election or appointment by this board of directors:

(Set forth procedure, such as appointment by the president or his delegate or by a committee of the board, and name the offices and positions covered. These are likely to be assistant officers and senior agents, since officers are usually elected or appointed by the board, and appointments of subordinate agents are usually left to the president or his delegate.)

F.4 (e) Removing officers and agents (§51):

Resolved that, _____ being a duly chosen officer [agent] of Dighaldoe Corporation with the title of _____ and this board of directors having determined that in its judgment the best interests of the corporation will be served by his removal from such office [position], said _____ be and he hereby is so removed effectively immediately.

> **▪ Removal is without prejudice to contract rights, if any, of the removee; but election or appointment does not of itself create such rights (§51). To fill a vacancy created by removal (or by death, resignation, disqualification, or otherwise), a resolution in the form of F.4 (c) or the procedure set forth under F.4 (d) or appointment by the president or his delegate would be used, the choice depending on how the office or position is filled.**

F.4 (f) Creating the office of chairman of the board:

Resolved that Article _____, Section _____ of the by-laws of Dighaldoe Corporation on officers [B.4] be and the same hereby is amended as follows: before the provisions on the duties of the president [B.4 (e)], add "Chairman of the board: The chairman of the board presides, when present, at meetings of shareholders and the board of directors"; and at the beginning of the third sentence in the provisions on the duties of the president, add "In the absence of the chairman of the board,".

▪ **This amendment leaves unchanged the president's position as principal executive and administrative officer of the corporation.**

F.5 Committees

▪ **For by-law provisions on committees of and created by the board of directors, see B.3 (o).**

F.5 (a) Determining committees of the board of directors (§42):

Resolved that the committees of this board of directors of Dighaldoe Corporation, to be designated from among its members by resolution adopted by a majority of the full board of directors, be and the same hereby are determined to be as stated below and that such committees be and the same hereby are, except as otherwise provided by statute or in the articles of incorporation or by-laws of the corporation, assigned duties and granted powers as follows:

—an executive committee of _____ directors, which is assigned the duties and granted the powers of the board of directors in management of the corporation's business between meetings of the board and while it is not in session;

—an audit committee of _____ directors, which is directed to supervise the work of the corporation's auditors, internal and external, and to report thereon to the board;

—a compensation committee of _____ directors, which is directed to make recommendations to the board concerning compensation of the corporation's directors, officers, and employees; and

—a finance committee of _____ directors, which is directed to make recommendations to the board concerning raising funds for the corporation's business.

▪ **Section 42 of the Model Act lists matters which may not be delegated to committees: declaring dividends; recommending acts requiring shareholder approval; designating director candidates and filling vacancies on the board and committees thereof; amending by-laws; approving a merger not requiring shareholder approval; reducing earned or capital surplus; authorizing reacqusition of shares, unless pursuant to a general formula or method specified by the board; authorizing issuance or sale of shares or designating the terms of a series, provided that the board, having granted a general authorization for issuance or sale of shares, may, pursuant to a general formula or method specified by the board by resolution or by**

adoption of a stock option or other plan, authorize a committee to fix the terms of issue or sale of shares.

Section 42 also provides that, for a director who is not a member of a specific committee, neither the designation of the committee, delegation to it of authority, nor action by it pursuant to such authority, shall alone constitute compliance "with his responsibility to act in good faith, in a manner he reasonably believes to be in the best interests of the corporation, and with such care as an ordinarily prudent person in a like position would use in similar circumstances." In short, directors do not escape personal liabilities discussed in Chapter 11 of the text by delegating board functions to committees.

F.5 (b) Designating directors to serve on a committee (§42):

Resolved that _____, _____, and _____, directors of Dighaldoe Corporation, be and the same hereby are designated members and _____ is designated chairman of the _____ committee, with the duties assigned and powers granted to such committee by the resolution of this board [F.5 (a)] adopted on _____, to serve, while remaining directors, until the first meeting of the board of directors after the next annual meeting of shareholders and until their successors are designated and qualified.

▪ Since this resolution must be adopted "by a majority of the full board of directors" (§47), if a corporation has five directors of which three are a quorum, affirmative votes of two directors at a meeting at which three are present, although ordinarily the act of the board, would be insufficient.

F.5 (c) Creating a committee not confined to directors:

Resolved that, pursuant to authority granted to this board of directors by the by-laws [B.3 (o)] of Dighaldoe Corporation, a _____ committee of _____ members be and the same hereby is created from among the corporation's directors, officers, employees, and agents and is, except as otherwise provided by statute or in the articles of incorporation or by-laws of the corporation, assigned duties and granted powers as follows:

(Set forth duties and powers.)

Further resolved that _____, _____, and _____, directors, officers, employees, or agents of Dighaldoe Corporation, be and the same hereby are designated members and _____ is designated chairman of the _____ committee, to serve at the pleasure of the board of directors.

F.5 (d) Authorizing committees to establish meeting procedures:

Resolved that committees of and created by this board of directors of Dighaldoe Corporation be and the same hereby are authorized to provide by resolution the time and place, either within or without the State of _____, for holding regular meetings, which may be so held without further notice, and, subject to the by-laws [B.3 (l)], the manner of calling and giving notice of special meetings, and rules as to quorums of and action by such committees.

F.5 (e) Removing a committee member:

Resolved that _____, being a duly designated member of the _____ committee, a committee of or created by this board of directors of Dighaldoe Corporation, and this board of directors having determined that in its judgment the best interest of the corporation will be served by his removal from such committee, said _____be and he hereby is removed effective immediately.

F.5 (f) Filling a committee vacancy:

Resolved that, to fill a vacancy on the _____ committee, a committee of [created by] this board of directors of Dighaldoe Corporation, _____ be and he hereby is designated a member of such committee to serve the unexpired term of his predecessor thereon.

> ▪ **If there is no predecessor, as would be the case if a vacancy results, not from removal, death, resignation, or disqualification, but from increasing the size of the committee, the last clause should read either "to serve, while remaining a director, until the first meeting of the board of directors after the next annual meeting of shareholders and until his successor is designated and qualified" or "to serve at the pleasure of the board of directors," depending on whether a committee of directors is involved, which must be reconstituted annually with each new board of directors (as suggested in F.5 (b), or one not limited to directors, whose members are given an indefinite tenure at the pleasure of the board (as suggested in F.5 (c)).**

F.6 Benefits

> ▪ **Resolutions suggested below are counterparts, at the director level, of shareholder resolutions suggested at D.5.**

F.6 (a) Compensation (§35):

Resolved that [, having received the recommendations thereon of the compensation committee,] amounts of compensation for the fiscal year ending June 30, 19_____, of its officers and employees earning more than $_____ per year be and the same hereby are fixed as follows [, subject to ratification by shareholders of the corporation]:

> (Set forth names, titles, and amounts. The first statement in brackets is more appropriate for public corporations; the second, for close corporations.)

F.6 (b) Employee benefit plans:

Resolved that the _____ Plan set forth below be and the same hereby is formulated by this board of directors of Dighaldoe Corporation and recommended for adoption by its shareholders at a meeting to be held on _____:

> (Set forth plan: bonus, stock option, deferred compensation, retirement, profit sharing, phantom stock, insurance, etc.)

F.6 (c) Loans to employees, including directors (§47):

Resolved that for Dighaldoe Corporation to lend money to or to use its credit to assist _____, an employee [and director] of the corporation, be and the same hereby is determined to be an action that may benefit the corporation.

Further resolved that the president be and he hereby is authorized to cause the corporation to make such loan or to extend such assitance in an amount not to exceed $_____ and for a term not to exceed _____, and subject to such other terms and conditions as the president may determine [, subject to ratification of such authorization by shareholders of the corporation].

> ■ While Model Act §47 does not require that shareholders ratify loans or assistance to employees where the board "decides that such loan or assistance may benefit the corporation," it is usually prudent to have them do so, particularly where the borrower is a director. And where the borrower is a non-employee director, the situation covered in the next resolution, Model Act §47 forbids the corporation to lend or assist "without authorization in the particular case by its shareholders."

F.6 (d) Loans to non-employee directors (§47):

Resolved that authorization by shareholders of Dighaldoe Corporation to its president to cause the corporation to lend money to or to use its credit to assist _____, a director who is not an employee of the corporation, in an amount not to exceed $_____ and for a term not to exceed $_____, and subject to such other terms and conditions as the president may determine, be and the same hereby is recommended to shareholders for consideration at their meeting to be held on _____.

F.6 (e) Insider transaction authorized, approved, or ratified by directors (§41):

Resolved that, the relationship of _____, a director [officer, employee, agent] of Dighaldoe Corporation, to or his interest in a transaction concerning _____ between the corporation and himself or an entity in which he is financially interested having been disclosed or being known to this board of directors, such transaction be and the same hereby is authorized [approved, ratified].

> ▪ This resolution must be adopted "by a vote or consent sufficient for the purpose without counting the votes or consents of such interested directors" (§41 (a)), but interested directors may be counted in determining the presence of a quorum. It is appropriate that a transaction be "authorized" when it is still in the future; "approved" when it has been entered into but is not yet effective; and "ratified" when it has already taken effect.

F.6 (f) Insider transaction; recommending authorization, approval, or ratification thereof by shareholders (§41):

Resolved that, subject to the relationship of _____, a director [officer, employee, agent] of Dighaldoe Corporation, to or his interest in a transaction concerning _____ between the corporation and himself or an entity in which he is financially interested being disclosed or known to the shareholders entitled to vote, authorization [approval, ratification] by shareholders of such transaction be and the same hereby is recommended to shareholders for consideration at their meeting to be held on _____.

> ▪ Shareholder action is appropriate when there are too few disinterested directors for the directors to act. Note that, as with loans to non-employee directors, the board simply recommends that shareholders consider the matter rather than that they take action already formulated by the board, as with employee benefit plans.

F.6 (g) Indemnification for an action or suit not by or for the corporation (§5 (a)):

Resolved that the following be and the same hereby is determined: that expenses and other obligations legally indemnifiable by Dighaldoe Corporation totalling $_____ were actually and reasonably incurred by _____ in connection with his involvement, by reason of his service to the corporation, in an action or suit not by or in the right of the corporation; and that said _____ acted in good faith and in a manner he reasonably believed to be in or not opposed to the best interests of the corporation [and had no reasonable cause to believe that his conduct was unlawful].

■ **The final bracketed clause is appropriate for a criminal action or proceeding.**

F.6 (h) Indemnification for an action or suit by or for the corporation, with no adjudication of liability (§5 (b)):

Resolved that the following be and the same hereby is determined: that expenses legally indemnifiable by Dighaldoe Corporation totalling $_____ were actually and reasonably incurred by _____ in connection with his involvement, by reason of his service to the corporation, in an action or suit by or in the right of the corporation; that said _____ acted in good faith and in a manner he reasonably believed to be in or not opposed to the best interests of the corporation; and that said _____ has not been adjudged liable for negligence or misconduct in the performance of his duty to the corporation.

■ **Note that, for actions or suits by or for the corporation, only expenses (including attorneys' fees) are indemnifiable; whereas, for other actions or suits, indemnifiable items include, in addition to expenses, "judgments, fines, and amounts paid in settlement" (§5 (a)).**

F.6 (i) Indemnification for an action or suit by or for the corporation, with court determination of indemnity despite adjudication of liability (§5 (b)):

Resolved that the following be and the same hereby is determined: that expenses legally indemnifiable by Dighaldoe Corporation totalling $_____ were actually and reasonably incurred by _____ in connection with his involvement, by reason of his service to the corporation, in an action or suit by or in the right of the corporation; that said _____ acted in good faith and in a manner he reasonably believed to be in or not opposed to the best interests of the corporation; and that, despite an adjudication that said _____ is liable for negligence or misconduct in the performance of his duty to the corporation, the court in which such action or suit was brought has determined upon application that in view of all of the circumstances of the case said _____ is fairly and reasonably entitled to indemnity for expenses in said amount of $_____.

G. Authorizations to Act for the Corporation

28 Director Resolutions and Officer Delegations of Authority

▪ Model resolutions and delegations suggested below implement discussion in Section 5.3 of the text on deciding and keeping track of who acts for the corporation in its most common transactions with outsiders: purchasing and selling particular property, purchasing for operations, hiring, banking, borrowing, and building. As indicated in the text, authorizations are of two types: one-shot and continuing. With both, power is handed down from the board to the president, from him to his subordinates, and from them to their subordinates. Exercise of powers to delegate authority granted by board resolutions may appropriately take the form of memoranda from the president or other person making the delegation to the corporate secretary, the officer normally responsible for keeping track of who can legally act for the corporation. As noted in Section 5.3 (b) of the text, the secretary may want to combine data in his corporation's articles, by-laws, resolutions, delegations, and appointments to provide a convenient source of information about who is authorized to do what on behalf of the corporation.

G.1 Purchasing and selling particular property

G.1 (a) Resolution granting authority to purchase or sell a particular property:

Resolved that the president be and he hereby is authorized to purchase [sell] and to delegate, subject to such limitations as he may determine, to other officers, employees, and agents of Dighaldoe Corporation authority to purchase [sell] on behalf of the corporation for a price not exceeding [less than] $_____ and upon such other terms and conditions as the president may determine the following item of real [personal] property:

(Set forth a description of the property.)

525

Further resolved that the president be and he hereby is authorized to delegate, subject to such limitations as he may determine, to other officers and employees of the corporation authority to sub-delegate such authority to employees and agents of the corporation to purchase [sell] on behalf of the corporation such item of property subject to such limitations as may be determined by the president and by the other officer or employee making the sub-delegation of authority.

G.1 (b) Delegation of authority to purchase or sell a particular property:

Pursuant to the board of directors resolution adopted on _____ authorizing the president to delegate to other officers, employees, and agents of the corporation authority to act for the corporation within a designated price limit and upon such other terms and conditions as the president may determine in connection with the purchase [sale] of property described therein, the president hereby delegates to the below designated persons authority, limited as stated below, to so act for the corporation within the following terms and conditions:

(Set forth titles or names of delegates. As to each, state any limitations on his authority to purchase or sell, such as by time or geography. Also set forth any additional terms and conditions of the purchase or sale, such as method of payment or security arrangements. As suggested in the text at §5.3 (b), use of titles rather than names reduces need for new delegations when people change jobs.)

G.1 (c) Delegation of authority to sub-delegate authority to purchase or sell a particular property:

Pursuant to the board of directors resolution adopted on _____ authorizing the president to delegate to other officers and employees authority to sub-delegate authority to act for the corporation within a designated price limit and upon such other terms and conditions as the president may determine in connection with the purchase [sale] of property described therein, the president hereby delegates to the below designated persons authority, limited as stated below, to so sub-delegate to employees and agents of the corporation authority, limited as stated below and in such sub-delegations, to so act for the corporation within the following terms and conditions:

(Set forth titles or names of delegates. As to each, state any limitations on his authority to sub-delegate, such as by the kinds of employees and agents who may be chosen as sub-delegates;

and any limitations on the authority to purchase or sell that can be sub-delegated by him. Also set forth any additional terms and conditions of the purchase or sale.)

G.1 (d) Sub-delegation of authority to purchase or sell a particular property:

Pursuant to the resolution of the board of directors adopted _____ and the memorandum of the president dated _____ authorizing the undersigned, within designated limitations, to sub-delegate to other employees and agents of the corporation authority to act for the corporation within a designated price limit and upon such other terms and conditions as the president may determine in connection with the purchase [sale] of property described in such resolution, the undersigned hereby sub-delegates to the below designated persons authority, limited as stated below and in such memorandum of the president, to so act for the corporation:

(Set forth titles or names of sub-delegates. As to each, state any further limitations on his authority determined by the officer or employee making the sub-delegation.)

G.2 Purchasing equipment, materials, and supplies for regular operations

G.2 (a) Resolution granting authority to purchase:

Resolved that the president be and he hereby is authorized to purchase and to delegate, subject to such limitations as he may determine, to other officers, employees, and agents of Dighaldoe Corporation authority to purchase on behalf of the corporation equipment, materials, and supplies needed for regular operation of the corporation's business.

Further resolved that the president be and he here is authorized to delegate, subject to such limitations as he may determine, to other officers and employees of the corporation authority to sub-delegate to employees and agents of the corporation authority to purchase on behalf of the corporation specified kinds of equipment, materials, and supplies needed for regular operation of the corporation's business, for such dollar amounts per transaction and per time period, for such time periods, for such facilities and in such geographical areas, through such transactions, from such sellers, and subject to such other limitations as may be determined by the president or by the other officer or employee making the sub-delegation of authority.

G.2 (b) Delegation of authority to purchase:

Pursuant to the board of directors resolution adopted on _____, the president hereby delegates to the below designated persons authority to purchase on behalf of the corporation the below specified equipment, materials, or supplies needed for regular operation of the corporation's business subject to limitations stated opposite their titles or names:

> (Set forth titles or names of delegates. As to each, specify what he is authorized to purchase; and state any limitations on this authority, such as by dollars, time periods, geography, transactions, and sellers.)

G.2 (c) Delegation of authority to sub-delegate authority to purchase:

Pursuant to the board of directors resolution adopted on _____, the president hereby delegates to the below designated persons authority, limited as stated below, to sub-delegate to employees and agents of the corporation authority, limited as stated below and in such sub-delegations, to purchase on behalf of the corporation specified kinds of equipment, materials, and supplies needed for regular operation of the corporation's business:

> (Set forth titles or names of delegates. As to each, state any limitations on his authority to sub-delegate, such as by kinds of items to be purchased and by kinds of employees and agents who may be chosen as sub-delegates; and any limitations on the authority to purchase that can be sub-delegated by him, as suggested in the second paragraph of the resolution.)

G.2 (d) Sub-delegation of authority to purchase:

Pursuant to the board of directors resolution adopted on _____, and the memorandum of the president dated _____, the undersigned hereby sub-delegates to the below designated persons authority to purchase on behalf of the corporation the below specified kinds of equipment, materials, or supplies needed for regular operation of the corporation's business subject to limitations stated opposite their titles or names and in such memorandum of the president:

> (Set forth titles or names of sub-delegates. As to each, specify what he is authorized to purchase; and state any further limitations on his authority determined by the officer or employee making the sub-delegation.)

G.3 Hiring employees

G.3 (a) Resolution granting authority to hire a particular person:

Resolved that the president be and he hereby is authorized to hire on behalf of Dighaldoe Corporation (employee) as (title) at a salary not exceeding $_____ per year for a term not exceeding _____ years.

> ▪ **Employment contracts for terms exceeding five years are exceptional. There will seldom be need for delegation or sub-delegation of authority to hire a particular person.**

G.3 (b) Resolution granting authority to hire for regular operations:

Resolved that, subject to such limitations as to compensation as the compensation committee may determine, the president be and he hereby is authorized to hire and to delegate, subject to such limitations as he may determine, to other officers, employees, and agents of Dighaldoe Corporation authority to hire on behalf of the corporation employees needed for regular operation of the corporation's business.

Further resolved that the president be and he hereby is authorized to delegate, subject to such limitations as he may determine, to other officers and employees of the corporation authority to sub-delegate to employees and agents of the corporation authority to hire on behalf of the corporation specified categories of employees needed for regular operation of the corporation's business, for such compensation and terms of employment, to serve at such facilities or in such geographical areas, through such kinds of transactions, and subject to such other limitations as may be determined by the president or by the other officer or employee making the sub-delegation of authority.

G.3 (c) Delegation of authority to hire for regular operations:

Pursuant to the board of directors resolution adopted on _____, the president hereby delegates to the below designated persons authority to hire on behalf of the corporation the below specified categories of employees needed for regular operation of the corporation's business subject to limitations stated opposite their titles or names:

(Set forth titles or names of delegates. As to each, specify categories of employees he is authorized to hire; and state any limitations on this authority, such as by compensation, terms of employment, geography, and transactions.)

G.3 (d) Delegation of authority to sub-delegate authority to hire for regular operations:

Pursuant to the board of directors resolution adopted on _____, the president hereby delegates to the below designated persons authority, limited as stated below, to sub-delegate to employees and agents of the corporation authority, limited as stated below and in such sub-delegations, to hire on behalf of the corporation specified categories of employees needed for regular operation of the corporation's business:

(Set forth titles or names of delegates. As to each, state any limitations on his authority to sub-delegate, such as by categories of jobs to be filled, and by kinds of employees and agents who may be chosen as sub-delegates; and any limitations on the authority to hire that can be sub-delegated by him, as suggested in the second paragraph of the resolution.)

G.3 (e) Sub-delegation of authority to hire for regular operations:

Pursuant to the board of directors resolution adopted on _____, and the memorandum of the president dated _____, the undersigned hereby sub-delegates to the below designated persons authority to hire on behalf of the corporation the below specified categories of employees needed for regular operation of the corporation's business subject to limitations stated opposite their titles or names and in such memorandum of the president:

(Set forth titles or names of sub-delegates. As to each, specify categories of employees he is authorized to hire; and state any further limitations on his authority determined by the officer or employee making the sub-delegation.)

G.4 Bank accounts: opening, deposits, withdrawals

G.4 (a) Resolution authorizing opening an account:

Resolved that the president and treasurer be and they hereby are authorized to open an account on behalf of Dighaldoe Corporation, to be designated its _____ Account, with (name of bank) at (location of bank).

G.4 (b) Resolution granting authority to deposit, without specifying source of deposits:

Resolved that the president and treasurer be and each of them hereby is authorized to deposit and to delegate, subject to such limitations as the delegating officer may determine, to other officers, employees, and agents of Dighaldoe Corporation authority to deposit on behalf of the corporation funds of the corporation in its _____ Account with _____.

**G.4 (c) Delegation of authority to deposit funds
where board has not specified source:**

Pursuant to the board of directors resolution adopted on _____,
the undersigned hereby delegates to the below designated persons authority to deposit on behalf of the corporation funds of the corporation
from the below specified sources in its _____ Account with
_____, subject to limitations stated opposite their titles or names:
(Set forth titles or names of delegates. As to each, make any
desired specification of the source of funds authorized to be deposited; and state any limitations on this authority, such as by
dollar amount or time.)

**G.4 (d) Resolution granting authority to deposit funds
from a designated source:**

Resolved that the president and treasurer be and each of them hereby is
authorized to deposit and to delegate, subject to such limitations as the
delegating officer may determine, to other officers, employees, and
agents of Dighaldoe Corporation authority to deposit on behalf of the
corporation in its _____ Account with _____ transfer checks
drawn on its _____ Account with _____.

**G.4 (e) Delegation of authority to deposit funds
where board has designated source:**

Pursuant to the board of directors resolution adopted on _____,
the undersigned hereby delegates to the below designated persons authority to deposit on behalf of the corporation in its _____ Account
with _____ transfer checks drawn on its _____ Account
with _____, subject to limitations stated opposite their titles or
names:
(Set forth titles or names of delegates. As to each, state any
limitations on his authority.)

**G.4 (f) Resolution granting authority for
single signature withdrawals:**

Resolved that the president and the treasurer be and each of them
hereby is authorized to withdraw and to delegate, subject to such limitations as the delegating officer may determine, to other officers, employees, and agents of Dighaldoe Corporation authority to withdraw on
behalf of the corporation funds of the corporation from its _____
Account with _____.

G.4 (g) Delegation of authority to make single signature withdrawals:

Pursuant to the board of directors resolution adopted on _____, the undersigned hereby delegates to the below designated persons authority to withdraw on behalf of the corporation funds of the corporation from its _____ Account with _____, subject to limitations stated opposite their titles or names:

> (Set forth titles or names of delegates. As to each, state any limitations on his authority, by dollar amounts per withdrawal or within stated time periods, by purposes or payees of withdrawals, or otherwise.)

G.4 (h) Resolution granting authority for dual signature withdrawals:

Resolved that the treasurer and the comptroller be and they hereby are authorized to withdraw and each of them hereby is authorized to delegate, subject to such limitations as the delegating officer may determine, to other officers, employees, and agents of Dighaldoe Corporation authority to withdraw on behalf of the corporation funds of the corporation from its _____ Account with _____, provided that each check, draft, or other withdrawal order shall be signed on behalf of the corporation by two authorized signers, one of whom shall be the treasurer or a signer authorized by him and one of whom shall be the comptroller or a signer authorized by him.

G.4 (i) Delegation of authority to make dual signature withdrawals:

Pursuant to the board of directors resolution adopted _____, the undersigned hereby delegates to the below designated persons authority, when acting with another similarly authorized person other than the undersigned or a delegate thereof, to withdraw on behalf of the corporation funds of the corporation from its _____ Account with _____, subject to limitations stated opposite their titles or names:

> (Set forth titles or names of delegates. As to each, state any limitations on his authority.)

G.5 Borrowing

G.5 (a) Resolution granting authority to borrow:

Resolved that, subject to such limitations as the finance committee may determine, the president be and he hereby is authorized to borrow and to delegate, subject to such limitations as he may determine, to other officers, employees, and agents of Dighaldoe Corporation authority to borrow on behalf of the corporation funds needed for regular operation of the corporation's business, provided that the total outstanding debt incurred by the corporation under authority of this resolution shall not at any time exceed $_____.

G.5 (b) Delegation of authority to borrow:

Pursuant to the board of directors resolution adopted on _____ and subject to the limitations therein, the president hereby delegates to the below designated persons authority to borrow on behalf of the corporation funds needed for regular operation of the corporation's business subject to limitations stated opposite their titles or names:

(Set forth titles or names of delegates. As to each state any limitations as to amounts borrowed, per loan or within stated time periods, terms of loans, types of lenders, types of transactions, or otherwise.)

G.6 Project to build and equip a new facility

▪ These authorizations might be preceded by authorizations to borrow, as in G.5, and to purchase land, as in G.1. And, when the new facility is ready to operate, they might be followed by new sets of authorizations to purchase, hire, and bank, as in G.2, G.3, and G.4, respectively.

G.6 (a) Resolution authorizing project to build and equip a new facility:

Resolved that the president be and he hereby is authorized to cause Dighaldoe Corporation to take action necessary to build and equip at _____ upon land owned [leased, to be acquired] by the corporation, at a total cost for the project herein authorized (to be known as the _____ Project) not exceeding $_____, a facility for the following purposes:

(Briefly describe purpose of new facility.)

Further resolved that, in carrying out the _____ Project, the president be and he hereby is authorized to delegate, subject to such limitations as he may determine, to other officers, employees, and agents of the corporation authority to act on behalf of the corporation in purchasing equipment, materials, and supplies and in contracting for services needed for such project.

Further resolved that, in carrying out the _____ Project, the president be and he hereby is authorized to delegate, subject to such limitations as he may determine, to other officers, employees, and agents of the corporation authority to sub-delegate to employees and agents of the corporation authority to act on behalf of the corporation in purchasing specified kinds of equipment, materials, and supplies and in contracting for specified kinds of services needed for such project, for such dollar amounts per transaction and per time periods, for such time periods, in such geographical areas, through such transactions, from such sellers or contractors, and subject to such other limitations as may be determined by the president or by the other officer or employee making the sub-delegation of authority.

G.6 (b) Delegation of authority to purchase or contract for a project:

Pursuant to the board of directors resolution adopted on _____ authorizing the _____ Project, the president hereby delegates to the below designated persons authority, to act on behalf of the corporation in purchasing the below specified kinds of equipment, materials, and supplies and in contracting for the below specified kinds of services needed for such project, subject to the limitations stated opposite their titles or names:

> (Set forth titles or names of delegates. As to each specify what he is authorized to purchase or contract for; and state any limitations on this authority, such as by dollar amounts, time periods, geographical areas, kinds of transactions, and sellers or contractors.)

G.6 (c) Delegation of authority to sub-delegate authority to purchase or contract for a project:

Pursuant to the board of directors resolution adopted on _____ authorizing the _____ Project, the president hereby delegates to the below designated persons authority, limited as stated below, to sub-delegate to employees and agents of the corporation authority, limited as stated below and in such sub-delegations, to act on behalf of the corporation in purchasing specified kinds of equipment, materials and supplies and in contracting for specified kinds of services needed for such project:

> (Set forth titles or names of delegates. As to each, state any limitations on his authority to sub-delegate, such as by kinds of equipment, materials, supplies, and services, and by kinds of employees and agents who may be chosen as sub-delegates; and any limitations on the authority to purchase or contract that can be sub-delegated by him, as suggested in the third paragraph of the resolution.)

G.6 (d) Sub-delegation of authority to purchase or contract for a project:

Pursuant to the board of directors resolution adopted on _____ authorizing the _____ Project, and the memorandum of the president dated _____, the undersigned hereby sub-delegates to the below designated persons authority to act on behalf of the corporation in purchasing the below specified kinds of equipment, materials, and supplies and in contracting for the below specified kinds of services needed for such project, subject to limitations stated opposite their names and in such memorandum of the president:

(Set forth titles or names of sub-delegates. As to each specify what he is authorized to purchase or contract for; and state any further limitations on this authority determined by the officer, employee, or agent making the sub-delegation.)

H. Agreements:

22 Sample Agreements with Insiders and Outsiders

H.1 Getting a corporation started

H.1 (a) Forming, naming, financing, and operating a new corporation:

This agreement is made on _____ among Donald Digges, Howard Hall, and Desmond Doe concerning their formation and operation of a corporation to engage in the coal mining business.

The parties hereby agree as follows:

1. They shall cause to be formed in the State of _____ a corporation with the name Dighaldoe Corporation with perpetual duration for the purposes of transacting all lawful business for which corporations may be incorporated under the laws of such state, including the business of extracting, transporting, processing, and selling coal.

2. They shall cause their attorney, Lawrence Lawyer, to file on their behalf with the Secretary of State of the State of _____ an application for reservation of the name Dighaldoe Corporation for 120 days and shall instruct Lawyer to ascertain the availability of such name.

3. The corporation shall have one class of common shares the initial issue of which shall be equally divided among the parties and which shall be paid for as follows: Donald Digges shall provide $20,000 in cash and services in getting mining operations started worth $80,000; Howard Hall shall provide trucks for transporting coal worth $80,000 and services in getting trucking operations started worth $20,000; and Desmond Doe shall provide $100,000 in cash.

4. The corporation shall be qualified to do business in the following states: _____, _____, and _____.

5. The corporation shall elect to be a Subchapter S corporation; and, to the extent possible, its shares shall be qualified as §1244 shares.

537

6. Unless otherwise agreed by the parties, the board of directors shall consist of three members. The parties shall vote their shares so that each of them, or a person nominated by a party, is a director. It is the intention of the parties that Donald Digges and Howard Hall shall be president and vice president, respectively, that Lawrence Lawyer be secretary, and that Desmond Doe or a person designated by him be treasurer.

7. No major business decisions shall be made for the corporation without the concurrence of all parties. If they can not agree on such a decision, a majority of them may request that it be submitted to an arbitrator agreed to by all parties; or, if they cannot so agree, to an arbitrator appointed by the American Arbitration Association. The decision of an arbitrator shall be binding on all parties.

H.1 (b) Clearing a proposed corporate name:

▪ **The text, at Section 1.3 (b), supposes that Digges, Hall, and Doe discover that one John Dighaldo had been doing business as Dighaldo Mining Company but is willing to relinquish his rights for $500.**

This assignment and agreement is made on _____ between John Dighaldo (Dighaldo) and Lawrence Lawyer (Lawyer).

For consideration of $500 paid by Lawyer to Dighaldo, receipt of which Dighaldo hereby acknowledges, Dighaldo hereby does the following:

1. Transfers and assigns to Lawyer and his assigns all of Dighaldo's right, title, and interest in and to all of the good will connected with the business name "Dighaldo Mining Company" and any registrations thereof, state, federal, or foreign;

2. Covenants and agrees that Dighaldo will not use the names or words "Dighaldo," "John Dighaldo," "Dighaldo Mining Company," or any other name, word, phrase, or mark confusingly similar thereto, in connection with the business of extracting, transporting, processing, or selling coal or products derived therefrom, or in connection with any other business if such use is likely to cause confusion with coal business using such or similar names or words;

3. Consents and agrees to use by Lawyer and his assigns of the name "Dighaldoe Corporation" and the word "Dighaldoe" in connection with any lawful business; and

4. Covenants and agrees that he will not interfere with such use

and that he will execute any documents and take any further action requested by Lawyer or his assigns, at the expense thereof, that may be reasonably necessary to assure thereto the quiet enjoyment of the rights of Lawyer and his assigns in and to such use.

H.2 Among all of the shareholders of a close corporation

H.2 (a) Restricting transfers of shares:

> ▪ **For suggested articles of incorporation on transfers of shares, options for their purchase, and valuing optioned shares, see A.6 (e)-(g).**

This agreement is made on _____ among Dighaldoe Corporation (the corporation) and Donald Digges, Howard Hall, and Desmond Doe (the shareholders), who own all of the shares of the corporation.

For the welfare of the corporation and the best interests of the shareholders, the corporation and the shareholders, for themselves and for their successors and transferees, including executors, administrators, trustees, guardians, and other fiduciaries, hereby agree that transfers of shares of the corporation will be subject to the following restrictions:

1. If a shareholder desires to transfer his shares during his lifetime, or if he dies or ceases to be an employee of the corporation, his shares shall first be offered for sale to the corporation at fair market value, determined as provided in paragraph 2 hereof. If the offer is not accepted by the corporation within 30 days after its receipt, shares covered thereby shall be offered on a pro rata basis to other shareholders, who shall have 30 days in which to accept the offer. If such an offer is not accepted by an offeree within 30 days after its receipt, shares covered thereby shall be offered on a pro rata basis to other offerees, who shall have 30 days in which to accept the offer.

2. Fair market value of the corporation's shares is the higher of a price offered for such shares by another bona fide prospective purchaser and the value of such shares determined as follows:

Share value as of the date of this agreement is fixed at $_____ per share. Share value shall be redetermined by the shareholders at the end of each fiscal year of the corporation. If the shareholders are unable or fail to agree on a new value within one month after the end of a fiscal year, then share value shall be fixed by an appraiser agreed to by the shareholders or, if they cannot agree, by an appraiser appointed by the American Arbitration Association.

H.2 (b) Limiting right to compete:

This agreement is made on _____ among Dighaldoe Corporation (the corporation) and Donald Digges, Howard Hall, and Desmond Doe (the shareholders), who hold all of the shares of the corporation.

Each shareholder hereby agrees that, while he remains a holder, beneficial owner, or in control of any shares of the corporation, he will not, without the express agreement of the corporation and the other shareholders, engage or accept employment or any financial interest, direct or indirect, in a business that is the same as or similar to that then conducted by the corporation, or in any manner compete with the corporation.

H.2 (c) Preserving Subchapter S election:

This agreement is made on _____ among Dighaldoe Corporation (the corporation) and Donald Digges, Howard Hall, and Desmond Doe (the shareholders), who hold all of the shares of the corporation.

It being the desire of the corporation and the shareholders that the corporation make a Subchapter S election under the United States Internal Revenue Code, and that the corporation should terminate and revoke such election only in accordance with a determination of holders of a majority of the outstanding shares of the corporation; therefore, in order to prevent termination of such election by transfer of shares to more than fifteen shareholders or to an unqualified or unconsenting shareholder, the corporation and the shareholders, for themselves and for their successors and transferees, including executors, administrators, trustees, guardians, and other fiduciaries, hereby agree as follows, and the shareholders further agree that they will vote their shares, execute the necessary documents, and otherwise exert their best efforts at all times to accomplish the following objectives:

1. If holders of a majority of the outstanding shares of the corporation determine to terminate or revoke a Subchapter S election, the corporation will make such election by timely filing of appropriate documents. Each shareholder will give written consent thereto and will take such other action necessary or advisable to effect such determination, and each shareholder hereby appoints the secretary of the corporation his attorney-in-fact to execute such documents or to take any other action which a shareholder is unable or otherwise fails to take.

2. No shareholder will sell, assign, or transfer any of his shares in the corporation to any person or in any manner which would cause a Subchapter S election to terminated or revoked without the prior con-

sent by vote or in writing of the holders of a majority in interest of all of the outstanding shares of the corporation.

3. No shareholder will sell, assign, or transfer any of his shares in the corporation to any person unless such person (and, if under applicable law shares to be so sold, assigned, or transferred will be community property of husband and wife, or income therefrom will be community income, unless the spouse of the transferee) first becomes a party to this agreement and evidences his consent to and approval of its terms by execution of this agreement.

H.2 (d) Buy-sell agreement:

This agreement is made on _____ among Donald Digges, Howard Hall, and Desmond Doe, who hold all of the shares of Dighaldoe Corporation (the corporation).

The parties hereby agree as follows:

A party to this agreement may at any time give written notice to one or more other parties stating the sum of money per share of the corporation which he is willing either to pay for the shares of such other parties or to accept for his own shares if such other party or parties elects or elect to buy them. A party receiving such notice shall within 90 days elect either to sell his shares or to buy the shares of the party giving the notice and shall notify the party giving the notice of his election. If a party receiving such notice fails to make such election within 90 days, then the party giving notice may elect whether he will sell his own shares to or buy the shares of the party failing to make such election. When a determination to buy and sell has been made as provided above, then the party selling shall assign his shares to the party buying upon payment by the party buying of the stated price, and the party selling shall thereupon resign from any position held by him in the corporation as director, officer, employee or otherwise.

▪ **The purpose of a buy-sell agreement, in contrast with that of a transfer restricting agreement such as H.2 (a) to keep a corporation close, is to provide a way out of a corporation, less drastic than outside arbitration or dissolution, when shareholders find themselves at an impasse. Of course, for the buy-sell procedure to get under way, one of the deadlocked shareholders must be able to arrive at a price which is so fair that he would be willing to be on either side of the deal. Thus, a shareholder who simply wants to sell out would probably proceed under H.2 (a), which falls back on arbitration as a last resort, since under the buy-sell procedure he will not know in advance whether he will end up a buyer or a seller.**

H.2 (e) Dissolution (§83):

This agreement is made on _____ among Donald Digges, Howard Hall, and Desmond Doe, who hold all of the shares of Dighaldoe Corporation (the corporation).

The parties hereby agree as follows:

If holders of a majority of the outstanding shares of the corporation determine that the corporation should be dissolved and if they are unable to agree with the minority upon a price at which shares of the minority will be sold to the majority or at which shares of the majority will be sold to the minority, or to agree upon an appraiser to fix such a price, then each party will execute a written consent that the corporation be voluntarily dissolved, which consent is to be in such form that under the laws of the State of _____ officers of the corporation may execute and deliver to the Secretary of State of the State of _____ a statement of intent to dissolve the corporation.

H.3 To create a voting trust (§34)

This agreement to create, as authorized by the laws of the State of _____, a voting trust for shares of Dighaldoe Corporation (the corporation), a corporation of that state having its principal office at _____, is made on _____ among those shareholders of the corporation (the shareholders) who become parties to this agreement by signing it and _____, _____, and _____, the trustees of such trust (the trustees).

The parties hereby agree as follows:

1. By signing this agreement or its counterpart, shareholders assign the number of shares of the corporation set opposite their names, and any additional shares, now owned or subsequently acquired by them, to the trustees. Shareholders shall deposit with the trustees certificates, properly assigned to the trustees, representing such shares and shall receive in exchange voting trust certificates. Such deposited shares shall be transferred on the books of the corporation to the names of the trustees, who are authorized to cause to be made such transfers and any further transfers thereof which may become necessary through change of trustees as provided below. While this agreement is in force the trustees hold legal title to deposited shares and may exercise rights thereof, including the right to vote such shares in person or by proxy. However, holders of voting trust certificates are entitled to receive payments of all dividends on deposited shares other than pro rata distribu-

tions of additional shares of the corporation by way of share dividends or partial distributions, which shares shall be issued in the names of the trustees as additional deposits hereunder and the trustees shall issue additional voting trust certificates therefor.

2. The voting trust certificates to be issued to shareholders by the trustees in exchange for shares deposited hereunder shall be in substantially the following form:

DIGHALDOE CORPORATION

Certificate
No. _____ Voting Trust Certificate _____ shares
This certifies that _____ has deposited _____ shares of the above corporation with _____, _____, and _____, trustees under a voting trust agreement dated _____ among certain shareholders of the corporation and the trustees. This certificate and the interest it represents is transferrable on the books of the trustees upon its presentation and surrender. The holder of this certificate takes it subject to all the terms and conditions of the voting trust agreement and becomes a party thereto and is entitled to the benefits thereof.

In witness whereof, the trustees have caused this certificate to be signed this ____ day of _____, 19____.

_____

_____

_____

Trustees

3. Except as this agreement otherwise provides, the trustees shall cause dividends declared by the corporation upon deposited shares to be distributed pro rata among the shareholders in proportion to the shares represented by their voting trust certificates.

4. This voting trust agreement shall be in force during the following period:

(Set forth the period. Under Model Act §34, it may not exceed ten years.)

5. While this agreement is in force the shareholders may not sell, transfer, or otherwise dispose of their deposited shares, but may sell, transfer, or otherwise dispose of their voting trust certificates. Upon presentation and surrender of a voting trust certificate that has been sold or transferred, the trustee shall issue to its purchaser or transferee a new certificate in the above form.

6. If the corporation is dissolved or liquidated while this agreement is in force, the trustees shall cause any liquidating dividends to be

distributed pro rata among the shareholders in proportion to the shares represented by their voting trust certificates.

7. If the corporation participates in a merger or consolidation while this agreement is in force, this agreement shall terminate upon the effective date of the merger or consolidation unless the trustees give notice not less than 30 days after such effective date to holders of voting trust certificates of the election of the trustees to continue this agreement for its full term and to substitute where appropriate shares issued to the trustees as a result of the merger or consolidation for deposited shares.

8. Upon termination of this agreement, certificates representing deposited shares, or shares substituted therefor, shall be delivered by the trustee to holders of voting trust certificates in proportion to their respective holdings upon presentation and surrender of their voting trust certificates.

9. This agreement shall not deprive the trustees, as individuals, of the privileges of the shareholders to deposit shares under this agreement; to sell, transfer, or otherwise dispose of their voting trust certificates; and to purchase or otherwise acquire additional voting trust certificates and shares of the corporation.

10. The shareholders shall reimburse and hold the trustees harmless for their expenses and disbursements reasonably incurred in connection with litigation concerning this agreement or the corporation to which the trustees are necessary parties. The shareholders shall compensate the trustees for their services as trustees as follows:

> (Set forth compensate arrangement, if any. If none, substitute for the last sentence: "The trustees shall not be entitled to any compensation for their services as trustees.")

11. A vacancy among the trustees created by the death, disability, or resignation of a trustee, shall be filled by majority vote of the remaining trustees (or by appointment by a single remaining trustee), at a meeting duly called by a trustee, of which notice shall be given to remaining trustees. If a majority is unable to agree on a replacement, the vacancy shall be filled by a plurality vote of holders of voting trust certificates, with each holder having one vote for each deposited share, at a meeting called by the remaining trustees or by a shareholder, of which ten days written notice shall be given to all holders of voting trust certificates.

12. In voting at shareholders meetings of the corporation, the trustees shall exercise their best judgment but shall not be responsible

for errors of law or for anything done or omitted under this agreement except for their own individual malfeasance.

13. The trustees may receive deposits of additional certificates representing fully paid shares of the corporation upon the terms and conditions of this agreement and shall issue and deliver voting trust certificates therefor in the above form entitling holders to all rights above specified.

14. The trustees by signing this agreement, or a counter part hereof, accept the trust herein created.

In witness whereof the parties hereto have hereunder set their hands as of the date first above written.

Shareholders	Address	Number of shares deposited
_____	_____	_____
_____	_____	_____
_____	_____	_____
		Trustees: _____
		_____
		_____

H.4 Between a corporation and its employees

This agreement is made on _____ between Dighaldoe Corporation (the corporation) and _____ (the employee).

The parties hereby agree that the terms and conditions of employment by the corporation of the employee include the following:

▪ **Terms are set forth in H.4(a)-(h).**

H.4 (a) Fixing term of employment and compensation:

1. The corporation shall employ the employee in an executive capacity for a term of ____ years, beginning on _____ and ending at the close of business on _____. During such period of employment the employee shall devote his entire working time and best efforts to the business and affairs of the corporation, and he shall perform such duties and have such titles and authority as may be assigned from time to time by the board of directors, the president, and other officers of the corporation.

2. Compensation paid by the corporation to the employee shall be $_____ per year payable in equal monthly installments. Such compensation may be increased by the board of directors upon recom-

mendation of the president and the compensation committee. If shareholders of the corporation elect the employee to be a director, he will serve as such during the period of this agreement without additional compensation.

> ▪ Employment agreements for fixed terms and salaries are ordinarily available only to employees with strong bargaining positions. Most corporate employees not covered by collective bargaining agreements serve at the pleasure of the corporation. And when a term is fixed, it is generally considered that a board of directors or a president should not tie up for more than, say, five years the power of their successors to make their own selections of employees.

H.4 (b) Providing for profit sharing by employee:

While the employee remains an employee of the corporation, the corporation shall pay to him each year, in addition to other compensation, an amount equal to _____ percent of the net earnings of the corporation before taxes determined in accordance with generally accepted accounting practice applied by the corporation's independent public accountants. Such determination shall be made within 60 days and such payment shall be made within 90 days after the end of each fiscal year.

H.4 (c) Providing for payment of deferred compensation upon retirement, death, or discharge without cause:

1. Commencing at the employee's retirement from employment by the corporation, the corporation will pay to him deferred compensation for services prior to retirement in the amount of $_____ (or a pro rata portion thereof if a portion of a year is involved) for each period of 12 consecutive months of employment under this agreement, payable in 120 consecutive equal monthly installments. If the employee dies before receiving all of such installments, the balance unpaid at his death shall be paid to his executor or administrator or to such person or persons as may be designated to receive such payments in his will.

2. If the employee voluntarily severs his employment by the corporation before retirement, or if the corporation discharges him without his consent but with proper cause, no deferred compensation shall be paid under this agreement and this agreement shall be considered terminated.

3. If the corporation discharges the employee before retirement without his consent and without proper cause, or if the employee dies while employed by the corporation, this agreement shall remain in full

force and effect and the corporation shall pay deferred compensation hereunder commencing when the employee is discharged or dies. Such deferred compensation may be paid, at the discretion of the corporation, in a lump sum or in 120 consecutive equal monthly installments; in the case of the employee's death, such payments shall be made to his executor or administrator or to such person or persons as may be designated to receive such payments in his will.

H.4 (d) Preserving employee's rights in event of merger, consolidation, or sale of assets:

The corporation will not merge or consolidate with or sell all or substantially all of its assets to another corporation unless such other corporation assumes the obligations of the corporation to the employee.

H.4 (e) Restricting an employee's other business affiliations:

Employee shall not, without the express approval of the board of directors of the corporation, make any other business affiliations during his employment by the corporation, nor, during such employment and for _____ years thereafter, engage in or accept any financial interest, direct or indirect, in a business similar to that of the corporation, or in any manner compete with the corporation.

H.4 (f) Requiring employee to be available for consulation after retirement:

Commencing at employee's retirement from employment by the corporation and continuing for _____ years thereafter, the employee will, when called upon by the corporation and to the extent that employee's health permits, render such consulting services for the corporation as its board of directors or officers may request for such periods and at such rates of compensation as may be agreed upon by the parties.

H.4 (g) Protection of the corporation's industrial property:

1. The employee will assign to the corporation all inventions, discoveries, and trade secrets discovered or developed by him in the course of his employment by the corporation and will refrain from disclosing the same, in patent applications or otherwise, without the express approval of the board of directors of the corporation.

2. The employee will not, during his employment by the corporation or thereafter, make or participate in the making by others of any business use not solely in the interest of the corporation of any trademark, brand name, or trade name of the corporation.

H.4 (h) Release by corporation of inventions, discoveries, and trade secrets:

The corporation hereby releases to the employee all of its right, title, and interest in and to the below described invention, discovery, or trade secret discovered or developed by the employee in the course of his employment by the corporation, and agrees to refrain from disclosing the same and from interfering with any use thereof by the employee or by his successors and assigns:

(Set forth a description of the invention, discovery, or trade secret being released. With trade secrets, care should be exercised to preserve their confidentiality. A release of this sort would be appropriate for the hypothetical computer programmers, suggested at Section 7.2 (a) of the text, who want to exploit on their own a business plan developed for but rejected by a former employer.)

H.5 With outsiders

H.5 (a) For confidential treatment of the corporation's trade secrets:

This agreement is made on _____ between Dighaldoe Corporation (Dighaldoe) and _____.

The parties hereby agree that, in consideration of Dighaldoe doing business with _____ and in the course of such business making known to said _____ certain trade secrets, said _____ shall keep confidential all such trade secrets of Dighaldoe, including without limitation information about its technical processes, operating methods, suppliers, customers, sales, and profits, and shall refrain from using or disclosing any trade secret of Dighaldoe for any purpose.

H.5 (b) Guarantee by a shareholder of corporation's obligations:

This agreement is made on _____ between Desmond Doe (Doe), a shareholder of Dighaldoe Corporation (Dighaldoe), and _____.

The parties hereby agree that, in consideration of _____ doing business with and extending credit to Dighaldoe, Doe guarantees performance by Dighaldoe of its obligations to _____.

H.6 In connection with raising and distributing funds

H.6 (a) For sale and purchase of shares, with promise to provide assurance of investment intent:

This agreement is made on _____ between Dighaldoe Corporation (the corporation) and _____ (the investor).

The parties hereby agree as follows:

The corporation shall sell and the investor shall purchase, at the price of $_____ per share, _____ shares of the authorized but unissued common shares of the corporation. The closing therefor shall take place at _____ on _____. Prior to the closing the investor shall provide to the corporation satisfactory assurance that such purchase is for investment and not for resale.

H.6 (b) Assurance of investment intent (investment letter):

Dighaldoe Corporation _____(date)_____
(address)
Dear Sirs:

By agreement dated _____ I have contracted to purchase from you _____ of your common shares for $_____ per share. Your obligation to issue these shares to me is subject to your receipt from me of satisfactory assurance that my purchase is for investment and not for resale. This letter is intended to provide this assurance.

I recognize that the shares I am to acquire would be subject to a registration statement under the Securities Act of 1933 unless an exemption is applicable to the transaction and that my investment representation to you will be relied upon by you as the basis for such an exemption. And I understand that my representation to you about my intention in acquiring your shares means that I have a bona fide present intention to so acquire and hold the shares and that any change of intention will be the result of an unanticipated and substantial change in circumstances occurring after the acquisition.

With the foregoing in mind, I hereby represent to and assure you that it is my intention to acquire and to hold for investment and not for resale or distribution all of the _____ shares which I have contracted to purchase, and that I have no present intention of selling or of otherwise disposing of any of such shares; and I hereby agree that I will not make any disposition of any such shares which will involve you in a violation of the Securities Act of 1933.

During the course of our negotiations you have caused to be furnished me such financial and other information about your corporation and its business as I have considered desirable to enable me to decide upon my proposed investment in your shares.

Very truly yours,

(investor)

H.6 (c) Escrowing shares:

This agreement is made on _____ between _____ (the shareholder), a shareholder of Dighaldoe Corporation (the corporation), and _____ (the escrowee).

The parties hereby agree as follows:

The shareholder hereby appoints the escrowee his escrow agent for _____ shares of the corporation, which are this date delivered by the shareholder to the escrowee in negotiable form; and, from this date until _____, the shareholder irrevocably grants to the escrowee the following powers:

(Set forth the powers of the escrow agent. As indicated in the text, escrow arrangements can be used where it is desired that transfers of shares be placed under independent control for various reasons. These include protection of exemptions from SEC registration (Section 7.2 (b)), and protection of the acquiring corporation from unknown liabilities of the acquired corporation in a shares-for-shares acquisition (Section 10.1 (b)). Shares may also be escrowed to facilitate their delivery on the closing date of a share purchase agreement, such as suggested at H.6 (a) above.)

H.6 (d) Installment repurchase of shares:

▪ The following is suggested to implement the hypothetical transaction, posed at Section 8.1 (b) of the text, of Dighaldoe Corporation purchasing the shares of one of its major shareholders, Desmond Doe, and agreeing to pay for them in ten annual installments.

This agreement is made on _____ between Dighaldoe Corporation (the corporation) and Desmond Doe (the shareholder), a shareholder thereof.

The parties hereby agree as follows:

1. The shareholder shall sell and the corporation shall purchase for $400 per share the 1,000 shares in the corporation held by Doe. The corporation shall pay the $400,000 purchase price in ten annual installments of $40,000 each as provided below.

2. Upon execution of this agreement the shareholder shall assign such 1,000 shares to the corporation and the corporation shall pay to the shareholder the first installment of $40,000. The remaining nine $40,000 installments, together with interest on the unpaid balances of the corporation's obligations under this agreement at the rate of ___% per annum, shall be paid by the corporation to the shareholder on the successive anniversaries of this agreement.

Index